Readings in International Economics

THE SERIES OF REPUBLISHED ARTICLES ON ECONOMICS

Volume XI

Selection Committee for This Volume

RICHARD E. CAVES

HARRY G. JOHNSON

The participation of the American Economic Association in the presentation of this series consists in the appointment of a committee to determine the subjects of the volumes and of special committees to select the articles for each volume.

READINGS IN INTERNATIONAL ECONOMICS

Selected by a Committee of

THE AMERICAN ECONOMIC ASSOCIATION

London
GEORGE ALLEN AND UNWIN LTD

695,384

Preface

THIS COLLECTION constitutes one of the "second generation" of volumes of reprinted articles prepared under the auspices of the American Economic Association. A backward glance at its predecessor, *Readings in the Theory of International Trade*, issued in 1949 under the editorship of Howard S. Ellis and Lloyd A. Metzler,[1] reveals at least two major differences between the two collections. First, both in their editorial introduction and in their selection of articles for inclusion, Ellis and Metzler saw fit to emphasize the incorporation into the theory of international trade of advances that had occurred in general economic theory during the preceding two decades or so. The articles selected for the present volume convey the impression that theoretical work in international economics no longer comprises a lagging sector. Second, the editors of *Readings in the Theory of International Trade* felt compelled to eschew, sadly but firmly, the inclusion of quantitative empirical work, for fear that it would prove too perishable to warrant enshrining in an archive that aspired to lasting interest. The views of international economists have probably altered on this point in the intervening years, during which several important pieces of empirical work have provided powerful stimuli for further research, both theoretical and empirical, as well as treasured issues for classroom discussion. Therefore, empirical studies have been included, and their presence is recognized implicitly by a title for the book which abandons reference to "theory."

Although chosen in the same general way as the contents of other volumes in this series, our selections were influenced by some special principles adopted by the editors. We began by consulting a number of recognized experts in the field of international economics, including those working in the English language but located outside of the United States. Because the principal use of the American Economic Association's volumes has clearly been as a teaching resource in graduate and advanced undergraduate courses, we also collected reading lists for many such courses and tabulated the frequencies with which individual articles appeared thereon. These preferences of leading international economists, expressed directly and through their trading lists, provided the starting point for our own selection process.

The potentially vexing question of how many topics or themes to include proved relatively simple in practice because of the similar balance of content and emphasis found in the basic courses in international

---

[1] Philadelphia: Blakiston Company, 1949, London: Allen and Unwin 1950.

economics now given at most leading universities. Although tastes varied with respect to the order in which topics were taken up, we detected a professional consensus on their relative importance that could govern the space given to different aspects of international economics in this volume. The hard choices concerned the inclusion or exclusion of topics that are important but not central. We felt it desirable to insure relatively complete coverage of selected major topics at the cost of excluding shorter sections or individual articles on minor ones, in order to improve the book's usefulness as collateral course reading, as well as to avoid devoting space to topics of current interest but uncertain permanence.

In choosing individual contributions a number of principles were given some weight. Our strongest preference was for articles that have made clear presentations of original and important ideas and stimulated further thought and research, and seem likely to retain this seminal role in the future. In some cases, however, we passed over an article of greater originality in favor of a subsequent one possessing superior clarity or pedagogical effectiveness. We slightly favored articles which originally appeared in the less widely available journals; on the other hand, we have not penalized the authors of works reprinted in their own collected writings. In general, survey articles have not been considered for inclusion unless this could be justified by original contributions embedded in them. Finally, we did not restrict our attention solely to articles originally appearing in the English language, although in fact no foreign-language works survived the screening process.

Surveys of the literature of international economics have been exceptionally numerous in the past decade, and we shall not undertake to provide another. Nonetheless, some brief comments about the sections of this book may serve both to relate their contents to the major developments in the field and also to call attention to a number of important articles necessarily excluded from a volume of limited size. Because, with but one exception, the items in this book have appeared since the publication of *Readings in the Theory of International Trade* in 1949, these comments relate largely to work done in the last decade and a half.

The great bulk of research in the static "pure" or real theory of international trade has come to center upon simple general-equilibrium models, especially the so-called two-by-two-by-two version of the Heckscher-Ohlin model (two countries, goods, and factors of production). The contributions included in the first section of the volume, "Theory of Comparative Advantage," lie almost entirely within the framework of this highly popular model and, taken as a group, seem to "close" it by covering all functional relations needed to make it determinate. Concentration upon this relatively homogeneous group of contributions has, however, forced the exclusion of some other lines of development, such as extensions of the model to an indefinite number of entities,[2] the employment of the tools of linear programming,[3] and the introduction of location-theory considerations. Useful innovations in geometrical technique[4] have had to be omitted, as has one aspect of the Heckscher-Ohlin model itself, the effect of the variation of factor supplies in response to changes in their real wages.[5]

Because the relation between trade and factor movements can be easily and clearly established in the Heckscher-Ohlin model, research on international factor movements has become closely integrated with other aspects of international economics. In the section on "International Factor Movements," this integration is shown in the contribution by Mundell. The classic literature on the "transfer problem" of adjustments in response to exogenous changes in international capital flows is represented by the essays of Samuelson and Johnson; they are included here rather than in sections on monetary processes of adjustment because they continue the classical emphasis upon the equilibrating role of changes in the terms of trade. It has not been possible to include parallel contributions on adjustments associated with international migration.[6] MacDougall's essay on foreign investment not only points out the special characteristics of this form of international factor movement but also raises important normative issues about international factor flows.[7]

Recent work in the normative theory of international trade has been somewhat more diverse than that on the analytical or positive side, but two main lines of development are apparent. First, formal concepts and criteria of welfare economics have been used to evaluate alternative trade policies with greater sophistication than was evident in classic discussions

---

[2] E.g., Paul A. Samuelson, "Prices of Factors and Goods in General Equilibrium," *Review of Economic Studies*, Vol. XXI, No. 1 (1953–54), pp. 1–20.

[3] E.g., T. M. Whitin, "Classical Theory, Graham's Theory, and Linear Programming in International Trade," *Quarterly Journal of Economics*, Vol. LXVII (November, 1953), pp. 520–44; L. W. McKenzie, "Specialization and Efficiency in World Production," *Review of Economic Studies*, Vol. XXI, No. 3 (1953–54), pp. 165–80.

[4] E.g., R. C. O. Matthews, "Reciprocal Demand and Increasing Returns," *Review of Economic Studies*, Vol. XVII (February, 1950), pp. 149–58; and K. M. Savosnick, "The Box Diagram and the Production Possibility Curve," *Ekonomisk Tidskrift*, Vol. LX (September, 1958), pp. 183–97.

[5] Murray C. Kemp and Ronald W. Jones, "Variable Labor Supply and the Theory of International Trade," *Journal of Political Economy*, Vol. LXX (February, 1962), pp. 30–36.

[6] Cf. W. M. Corden, "The Economic Limits to Population Increase," *Economic Record*, Vol. XXXI (November, 1955), pp. 242–60.

[7] The normative issues raised in MacDougall's paper have since been studied in a general-equilibrium framework, specifically a variant of the Heckscher-Ohlin model with one factor internationally mobile. See Murray C. Kemp, "Foreign Investment and the National Advantage," *Economic Record*, Vol. XXXVIII (March, 1962), pp. 56–62; and Ronald W. Jones, "International Capital Movements and the Theory of Tariffs and Trade," *Quarterly Journal of Economics*, Vol. LXXXI (February, 1967), pp. 1–38.

of the "gains from trade." Of this work we have included the article by
Baldwin; a number of recent contributions must regretfully be omitted on
the ground that their interest may lie more in welfare economics than in
international economics per se.[8] The second major line of development in
the normative theory of international trade has been the so-called "theory
of the second best," an outgrowth largely of international economics that
seems destined for great importance in the rest of the discipline as well.
We have included the classic contributions of Haberler and Fleming and
the synthesis by Bhagwati and Ramaswami, omitting several interesting
specific treatments of this general normative problem.[9] Other lines of
development of the normative theory have also had to be excluded, such
as extensions of the theory of the "optimum tariff"[10] and analyses of
efficient protection undertaken for non-economic reasons.[11] A special
branch of the normative theory of international trade is the theory of
customs unions, represented here only by Lipsey's essay but the subject of
a large and fast-growing literature. Just as the theory of customs unions
explores the effects of tariffs in a setting of several countries, another recent development which might be called the "theory of tariff structure"
explores the measurement of the incidence of tariffs when they are levied
on multiple products that function as both inputs and outputs. It is represented by Balassa's essay in the concluding section of this volume.

As we proceed to the section on "Trade, Growth, and Development,"
the diversity of recent research and writing forces considerable guess
work about what contributions will prove to possess long-run value. A
rough distinction can be made between work on "growth" and work on
"development," the latter incorporating assumptions thought to be
specifically appropriate to the economies of the presently underdeveloped
countries. In the former category, Johnson's essay provides a framework
that many writers have subsequently employed or extended.[12] Omitted
were examples of a model including two regions in an essential way, such

---

[8] E.g., Harry G. Johnson, "The Cost of Protection and the Scientific Tariff,"
Journal of Political Economy, Vol. LXVIII (August, 1960), pp. 327–45; Paul A.
Samuelson, "The Gains from International Trade Once Again," *Economic Journal,*
Vol. LXXII (December, 1962), pp. 820–29; M. C. Kemp, "The Gains from Inter-
national Trade," *Economic Journal,* Vol. LXXII (December, 1962), pp. 803–19.

[9] E.g., E. E. Hagen, "An Economic Justification of Protectionism," *Quarterly
Journal of Economics,* Vol. LXXII (November, 1958), pp. 496–514.

[10] E.g., Harry G. Johnson, "Optimum Tariffs and Retaliation," *Review of Economic
Studies,* Vol. XXI, No. 1 (1953–54), pp. 142–53.

[11] E.g., Harry G. Johnson, "An Economic Theory of Protectionism, Tariff Bargaining, and the Formation of Customs Unions," *Journal of Political Economy,* Vol.
LXXIII (June, 1965), pp. 254–83.

[12] E.g., V. K. Ramaswami, "The Effects of Accumulation on the Terms of Trade,"
Economic Journal, Vol. LXX (September, 1960), pp. 514–18.

as those by Johnson, Oniki, Uzawa, and Bensusan-Butt.[13] In the latter category, the essays by Singer and Myint provide examples of models or hypotheses about international trade in the context of underdevelopment. We have had to omit a number of other lines of analysis dealing with trade and economic development, such as the controversy over the gains from trade in primary products[14] and the discussion of the "balanced growth" prescription[15] for allocating resources in a developing economy, since these discussions emphasize institutional issues concerning the characteristics of and appropriate domestic policies for such economies, rather than analytical issues concerned with international trade.

The fifth section of this collection turns to developments in the monetary aspects of trade theory, particularly the analysis of the balance of payments and exchange stability. The main development in this area during the past two decades has been the attempt to incorporate the Keynesian theory of income adjustments into the analysis of the effects of exchange-rate variations, and four of the five essays in the section deal with this problem. Although later work has modified its results somewhat, the paper by Harberger still provides a valuable statement of the income relations involved and their effect on stability conditions. The paper by Alexander set off an extended controversy over the relative usefulness of "absorption" and "elasticity" concepts in the practical analysis of the effects of devaluation on the trade balance and the relative completeness of the two approaches in providing an integrated account of all of the underlying adjustments. Rather than include the papers which carried this controversy forward,[16] we have chosen two which appear to have gone some distance toward settling it by showing the essential role of both income and price effects. Tsiang's paper does this in the framework of a formal model, Johnson's in the spirit of providing guidance in the operational analysis of the effects of devaluation.

Of other issues relating to the exchange market, the proposal of exchange-rate flexibility has received much attention in recent years, and

[13] E.g., Harry G. Johnson, "Economic Expansion and International Trade," *Manchester School of Economic and Social Studies*, Vol. XXIII (May, 1956), pp. 95–113; H. Oniki and H. Uzawa, "Patterns of Trade and Investment in a Dynamic Model of International Trade," *Review of Economic Studies*, Vol. XXXII (January, 1945), pp. 15–38; D. M. Bensusan-Butt, "A Model of Trade and Accumulation," *American Economic Review*, Vol. LXIV (September, 1954), pp. 511–29.

[14] E.g., Raul Prebisch, "Commercial Policy in the Underdeveloped Countries," *American Economic Review*, Vol. XLIV (May, 1959), pp. 251–73.

[15] E.g., J. Sheahan, "International Specialization and the Concept of Balanced Growth," *Quarterly Journal of Economics*, Vol. LXXII (May, 1958), pp. 183–97.

[16] E.g., Fritz Machlup, "Relative Prices and Aggregate Spending in the Analysis of Devaluation," *American Economic Review*, Vol. XLV (June, 1955), pp. 255–78; Machlup, "The Terms-of-Trade Effect of Devaluation upon Real Income and the Balance of Trade," *Kyklos*, Vol. IX (1956), pp. 417–52; and S. S. Alexander, "Effects of a Devaluation: A Simplified Synthesis of Elasticities and Absorption Approaches," *American Economic Review*, Vol. XLIX (March, 1959), pp. 22–42.

Friedman's paper is included as a forthright statement of the case for flexible rates. The discussion of exchange flexibility has spawned several other significant papers that had to be omitted, among them the analysis by Laursen and Metzler of the extent to which flexible rates can insulate domestic income from exogenous changes in the trade balance[17] and Mundell's formulation of the debate in terms of optimum currency areas.[18] Another topic that might have been included is the analysis of exchange-market stability, which has been pushed more into line with the analysis of market stability in general economic theory.[19]

Moving beyond research on the balance of payments and exchange stability, narrowly conceived, we encounter during the last two decades a large amount of theoretical work inspired more or less by issues of public policy and tied to the contemporary terms in which those issues were conceived. Dollar shortage, dollar glut, the revival of international capital markets, and the problem of international liquidity have all led to significant new theoretical work aimed at identifying the essential elements of the policy problem involved or testing hypothetical solutions. The dilemma for the compilers of this volume was, of course, to decide which of the resulting works are likely to remain stimulating and relevant in years to come, when the issues that gave rise to them may disappear or alter beyond recognition. It has seemed to us that the most important and enduring thread running through these policy issues is the problem, delineated and emphasized by Meade and Tinbergen, of attaining consistency between international and domestic policy and employing available policy instruments to attain multiple objectives. The essay by Hicks on productivity growth and the balance of payments was among the most fruitful contributions to the literature of the "dollar shortage." Swan's paper is concerned with the relation of payments equilibrium to employment equilibrium and the effects of policies upon these two objectives. The contributions by Metzler and Mundell[20] examine similar issues but consider explicitly the effect of international capital movements.

Regrettably, our approach to selecting contributions in the field of international monetary and financial policy leaves the current controversy over international monetary institutions without direct representation,

---

[17] E.g., S. Laursen and L. A. Metzler, "Flexible Exchange Rates and the Theory of Employment," *Review of Economics and Statistics,* Vol. XXXII (November, 1950), pp. 281–99.

[18] E.g., R. A. Mundell, "A Theory of Optimum Currency Areas," *American Economic Review,* Vol. LI (September, 1961), pp. 657–65.

[19] E.g., R. W. Jones, "Stability Conditions in International Trade: A General Equilibrium Analysis," *International Economic Review,* Vol. II (May, 1961), pp. 199–209.

[20] Also see R. A. Mundell, "The Monetary Dynamics of International Adjustment under Fixed and Flexible Exchange Rates," *Quarterly Journal of Economics,* Vol. LXXIV (May, 1960), pp. 227–57.

although this discussion has induced some basic theoretical work.[21] As a partial excuse for omitting it, we note that several compendia and surveys have already consolidated research addressed to the problem.[22]

Quantitative empirical work in international economics has suffered, at least relative to some other branches of economics, both from a lack of operational predictions drawn from trade theory and a lack of data relevant for testing those predictions that can be developed. Consequently, much of the quantitative research has pursued empirical regularities that do not directly test any hypotheses drawn from the main body of theory concerning international trade and payments, however interesting and useful they may be on other grounds. Because of the primarily theoretical orientation of this and other volumes in the series, we have felt constrained to slant our selections toward empirical papers closely connected to the main body of trade theory. Leontief's first study of factor proportions and United States trade was, therefore, an easy choice; although Leontief's later work[23] somewhat modified his initial results, the irritant value of his first findings would by itself warrant their inclusion. MacDougall's 1951 paper testing the classical theory of comparative costs possesses a somewhat similar status and was thus chosen over later investigations of the same type.[24] Orcutt's discussion of the measurement of price elasticities in international trade here represents an extensive empirical literature motivated by theoretical findings about the importance of critical values of price-elasticities of demand in determining the stability of the exchange market and the effectiveness of devaluation in improving a nation's trade balance. Finally, Balassa's essay both represents the recent upsurge of interest in the problem of establishing the true protective incidence of tariffs and includes a set of empirical measurements.

This volume follows the practice of others that have recently appeared in the series of omitting a bibliography, on the ground that the American Economic Association's *Index of Economic Journals* definitively performs this function. The *Index* does not include articles in languages other than

[21] Cf. P. B. Kenen, "International Liquidity and the Balance of Payments of a Reserve-Currency Country," *Quarterly Journal of Economics*, Vol. LXXIV (November, 1960), pp. 572–86.

[22] H. G. Grubel, ed., *World Monetary Reform: Plans and Issues* (Stanford: Stanford University Press, 1962); Fritz Machlup and Burton Malkiel, *Plans for Reform of the International Monetary System*, Special Papers in International Economics, No. 3 (Princeton, N.J.: International Finance Section, 1964).

[23] W. W. Leontief, "Factor Proportions and the Structure of American Trade: Further Theoretical and Empirical Analysis," *Review of Economics and Statistics*, Vol. XXXVIII (November, 1956), pp. 386–407.

[24] Bela Balassa, "An Empirical Demonstration of Classical Comparative Cost Theory," *Review of Economics and Statistics*, Vol. XLV (August, 1963), pp. 231–38; R. M. Stern, "British and American Productivity and Comparative Costs in International Trade," *Oxford Economic Papers*, Vol. XIV (October, 1962), pp. 275–96.

English, however, nor does it fulfill the need that some users may feel for
a selective bibliography. Bibliographies which some users may find more
suitable for these reasons can be found in the numerous surveys recently
produced or the whole or parts of the field of international economics,
such as those of Bhagwati, Caves, Chenery, Chipman, Corden, Haberler,
and Mundell.[25]

In preparing the volume for publication, we have allowed the authors
to make minor corrections and clarifications of their original texts. We
have also considered it desirable to abridge certain articles and to
eliminate repetitious summaries and illustrations of limited contemporary
interest.

We offer the usual acknowledgments to the original publishers of the
articles and papers for permission to include them in this volume. We
should also like to express our gratitude to the colleagues who assisted us
in the selection process described above and to the authors for their
cooperation in furnishing offprints and accepting editorial suggestions.
Finally, we should like to thank Judith Kidd for the care with which she
has kept track of the manuscripts and correspondence and seen the
volume to the press.

Harvard University   RICHARD E. CAVES
London School of Economics   HARRY G. JOHNSON
   and University of Chicago

---

[25] J. Bhagwati, "The Pure Theory of International Trade: A Survey," *Economic Journal*, Vol. LXXIV (March, 1964), pp. 1–84; R. E. Caves, *Trade and Economic Structure* (Cambridge, Mass.: Harvard University Press, 1960); H. B. Chenery, "Comparative Advantage and Development Policy," *American Economic Review*, Vol. LI (March, 1961), pp. 18–51; J. S. Chipman, "A Survey of the Theory of International Trade," *Econometrica*, Vol. XXXIII (July, 1965), pp. 477–519, Vol. XXXIII (October, 1965), pp. 685–760, Vol. XXXIV (January, 1960), pp. 18–76; W. M. Corden, *Recent Developments in the Theory of International Trade*, Special Papers in International Economics, No. 7 (Princeton: International Finance Section, 1965); G. Haberler, *A Survey of International Trade Theory*, Special Papers in International Economics, No. 1 (rev. ed.; Princeton: International Finance Section, 1961); R. A. Mundell, "The Pure Theory of International Trade," *American Economic Review*, Vol. L (March, 1960), pp. 67–110.

Table of Contents

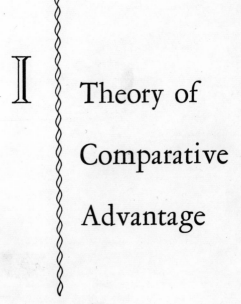

I | Theory of Comparative Advantage

1. Factor Proportions and

Comparative Advantage[*]

By ROMNEY ROBINSON[†]

THIS PAPER SEEKS to examine and to criticize the factor proportions account of comparative advantage. By "comparative advantage" is meant the array of forces which explain export-import patterns under free trade conditions. The problem concerns, not the *gains* from trade, but the *nature* of such trade. The "factor proportions account," originated by Eli Heckscher[1] and developed by Bertil Ohlin,[2] finds this nature to reside in the relative endowments of primary factors of production possessed by different countries.

I shall try to argue that this factor proportions account of trade considered in terms of production functions, taste functions and the like, rests on a tenuous base. Its assumptions are too demanding to be likely to fit any real-life circumstances. In consequence, and particularly where the factor "capital" is involved, its account of the nature of comparative advantage and of international trade is seriously misleading.

I. LEONTIEF'S U.S. CAPITAL-LABOR INPUT RATIOS

According to the Heckscher-Ohlin account, particular goods require for economical production comparatively large amounts of particular factors. Such goods will therefore be cheap in countries well endowed with the needed factor; if a factor is in short supply, goods associated therewith will be expensive in that country by comparison with other

---

[*] *Quarterly Journal of Economics*, Vol. LXX, No. 2 (May, 1956), pp. 169–92. This paper was written whilst the author was a faculty member of the Massachusetts Institute of Technology. Its development was greatly benefited by the criticisms of Gottfried Haberler, Ronald Jones, Charles P. Kindleberger, Svend Laursen, Paul A. Samuelson, and T. M. Whitin.

[†] University of Toronto.

[1] See "The Effect of Foreign Trade on the Distribution of Income," *Ekonomisk Tidskrift*, XXI (1919), 497–512, reprinted in translation in *Readings in the Theory of International Trade* (Philadelphia: Blakiston, 1949), pp. 272–300.

[2] See *Interregional and International Trade* (Cambridge: Harvard University Press, 1933). An abbreviated account is found in P. T. Ellsworth's *International Economics* (1st ed.; New York: Macmillan, 1938), chaps. V and VI. Although refinements of analysis since its publication now raise occasional problems as to meaning, this remains an excellent short statement of factor proportions theory.

parts of the world. Differing factor endowments, by having influenced the pre-trade commodity price relationships, will determine the composition of exports and imports. Certain qualifications to this basic hypothesis are made. Differing national tastes, too, may influence the price pattern, perhaps even to the point of reversing the trade flow indicated by factor supplies. External economies may form a basis for trade even in circumstances of identical factor supplies. But in general these are considered minor qualifications. Relative factor endowments are the major determinants.

Since by common consent the United States has more capital per worker than any other nation, there is the strongest of presumptions, according to the theory, that its comparative advantage position will lie in capital-demanding (capital-intensive) goods. But Professor Wassily W. Leontief's recently-published figures show the opposite.[3] Derived from his input-output studies, they show U.S. exports to be less capital-intensive than U.S. "imports."[4]

Leontief evidently does not wish to upset existing theory. On the contrary, the hypothesis he offers to explain these figures would sustain the factor proportions account. The United States, so he argues, is really a capital-poor, labor-abundant country—not in terms of total available workers, but in terms of "labor efficiency units." Leontief hazards the guess that on the average three such units are vested in the average American worker for each single unit in a foreign worker. The total labor supply, reckoned in such efficiency units, is three times that which a count of heads would indicate.

This is a very different matter from the frequently heard statement that the American worker is more productive than his foreign counterpart because he is equipped with more capital. Leontief considers him more productive when working with the *same* amount as a foreign worker—three times as productive. (With more capital, his relative productivity would be still higher.) This is a much stronger statement, although it is a necessary one if the theory is to be rescued with this particular lifeline. If the U.S. worker is more productive *only* in circumstances of more capital, then the orthodox factor proportions trade outcome is to be expected,[5] not that contained within the Leontief figures.

Published criticisms have not shown enthusiasm for this explanation.

---

[3] "Domestic Production and Foreign Trade; the American Capital Position, Re-Examined," read at the American Philosophical Society, Philadelphia, April 24, 1953, and published in the Society's *Proceedings,* Vol. XCVII, pp. 332–49.

[4] The necessity of using U.S. input-output data forced Leontief to measure, not the actual capital-labor ratio involved in foreign production of goods imported by the United States, but the ratio in U.S. industries producing goods competitive with these imports. Ellsworth's criticism of this procedure is reviewed in Section III of this paper.

[5] For similar reasons, as Leontief notes, it is difficult to appeal to "entrepreneurship" as an explanation for the alleged superiority of U.S. labor, since we need an element that will raise the productivity of labor but *not* that of capital, if the data are

Boris C. Swerling[6] has instead questioned the validity of the two capital-labor ratios themselves. He points out that careful scrutiny of the 1947 data on which they were based shows the aggregate figures to be heavily influenced by the capital-labor positions of a very few industries with significant export or import positions. In particular, the agriculture and fisheries industry weighs heavily on the import side, and it is not beyond question that it ought to occupy any such position.[7]

Yet Swerling's conclusions give little comfort to the orthodox position. In general, it is his observation that as between exports and imports, *no* significant difference between capital-labor ratios seems to exist. Any such result would be less paradoxical; but it would be almost as damning to the factor proportions hypothesis (at least in so far as interpretations of this hypothesis run in terms of relative quantities of capital and labor).

The views of two other Leontief critics, P. T. Ellsworth[8] and Stefan Valavanis-Vail,[9] will be considered later in this paper. Valavanis-Vail, it may be noted, offers a hypothesis similar to that of this paper: that factor proportions may have no great part to play in determining the proportions of goods produced or of goods exported. But his discussion does not refer to the Heckscher-Ohlin doctrine; and his reasoning seems in part based on an assumption regarding differing tastes fully recognized by that doctrine. In other respects, his conclusions seem quite contrary to those indicated in this paper.

II. TAUTOLOGY IN THE FACTOR PROPORTIONS ACCOUNT

Leontief's figures, according to Ellsworth, "subvert common sense."[10] But the essential conclusion of the theory—that under free competitive

---

to be reconciled with factor proportions theory. Leontief, in short, himself demolishes the most appealing arguments that might be cited in support of his own hypothesis.

P. T. Ellsworth, in a comment discussed later in this paper, "The Structure of American Trade: A New View Re-Examined," *Review of Economics and Statistics,* Vol. XXXVI (Aug., 1954), pp. 279–85, may possibly disagree, since his comments in Section III seem in part to indicate that superior productivity resulting solely from entrepreneurship and more capital may account for the data. But I find his discussion difficult to fit into the formal structure of the factor proportions theory which it is his intention to defend. Leontief's reasoning on these points seems clear and adequate.

[6] "Capital Shortage and Labor Surplus in the United States?" *Review of Economics and Statistics,* Vol. XXXVI (Aug., 1954), pp. 286–89.

[7] This industry makes by far the single most important contribution on the *import* side, and it has the highest of all the capital-labor ratios. But Swerling notes that in 1947 it ranked in absolute terms on the *export* side. The fact that 1947 was a year of extremely high export surplus for the United States explains this anomaly. Leontief assumed a *balanced* trade reduction—the consequences of a $1 million reduction in exports matched by an *equal* increase in import substitutes. Agricultural imports, though absolutely smaller (dollar-wise) than agricultural exports, bulked sufficiently large in the total of imports to acquire a percentage value exceeding the percentage value of agricultural exports in total exports.

[8] "The Structure of American Trade: A New View Re-Examined," *op. cit.*

[9] "Leontief's Scarce Factor Paradox," *Journal of Political Economy,* Vol. LXII (Dec., 1954), pp. 523–28.

[10] "The Structure of American Trade," *op. cit.,* p. 279.

conditions, each country will tend to export those commodities requiring large quantities of productive factors which it possesses in relative excess—has no status as a universal truth. It is simply derived from a particular set of assumptions. What Ellsworth must mean is that these assumptions fit the facts of life so well as to leave virtually no doubt of their appropriateness.

The problem of suitable assumptions will be uppermost throughout this paper. But before a detailed examination, it may be appropriate to consider another sense in which the factor proportions account can be regarded as "common sense." Common sense may degenerate into mere tautology; and the theory in question is not without such tendencies.

The difficulty concerns the use and meaning of the terms "factor of production" and "production function." The distinction between them is not always well defined. Differing climates may be considered as giving rise to different production functions. Or climate may be considered a factor of production, by giving the production function a climate dimension. Ricardo's labor-cost production functions, differing as between countries, illustrate the point. He assumed the following relationships between labor input and cloth output:

Portugal:	$C = 1/90\ L$
England:	$C = 1/100\ L$

These are not necessarily different production functions. The two countries may be regarded as sharing a common production function, $C = f(L, W)$, with W signifying weather or climate, or whatever aspect of "the peculiar powers bestowed by nature" (Ricardo's phrase) is considered relevant.[11] The two countries share the same function, but operate in different regions thereof, each defined by a particular W-axis point. No matter how unlike the productive environments of two countries happen to be, they can be considered as sharing a common production function if that function is given a sufficiently large number of dimensions. The concept of "factor" must then, of course, bear a heavier burden; and it may become more difficult to compare factor supplies so as to speak meaningfully of "relative endowments."

Ohlin assumes, for each commodity, a common production function: "The physical conditions of production . . . are everywhere the same."[12] Such treatment seems necessary for a factor proportions theory. To be sure, in models which demand that all supply phenomena be subsumed either under production functions or under factor availability, it means

---

[11] Ricardo was not concerned with the problem of the nature of comparative advantage at all. He was preoccupied with a related but none the less quite different question, that of the gains from trade. His numerical examples afforded a convenient way of expressing the obvious fact that nations *are* different in their productive performance. This conceptual device for summing up these differences was quite good enough for his purpose.

[12] *Op. cit.,* p. 14. Ellsworth's brief comment on this assumption is interesting. *International Economics, op. cit.,* p. 91 note 1.

that there is nothing left on the supply side but factor proportions to account for price differences. Yet if different production functions were admitted, then the theory, confronted with evidence of trade contrary to that indicated by factor supplies, could always take refuge in the plea: "different production functions." But that would reduce it to a banality. *Any* pattern of trade could be explained in such terms. Comparative advantage theory, to be of the slightest analytic value, would then require an explanation of when and how production functions come to differ.

The problem is to stop the theory from degenerating into a surface explanation, capable of explaining anything *ex post* and nothing *ex ante*.[13] Leontief's suggestion, advanced to explain his own figures, illustrates the point. His "labor efficiency unit" explanation is presumably intended to fit within the framework of existing factor proportions theory. But if this theory can be maintained by applying a coefficient to the total of one or more factor supplies, squeezing or stretching that supply to appropriate size, it becomes a façade of a theory and no more. Superficially, this may perhaps maintain the assumption of uniform production functions; but it might just as well be considered an introduction of differing production functions. The Heckscher-Ohlin account is important, and different from earlier work, I would take it, because it seeks to explain the nature of comparative advantage; and this would be an admission of failure, an admission that the explanation lies elsewhere. Whether or not Leontief's figures subvert common sense, as Ellsworth holds, his hypothesis subverts the theory.

It is clear that factor proportion models can be constructed which are not tautologies, of which it may be said: this is what the theory means. Yet the problem remains of associating particular concepts with particular aspects of reality; the task is still to seize on those aspects of "the real world" of major importance in explaining the nature of export-import positions. More incisive meanings for "factor" and "production function" would be extremely helpful (and might also settle some disputes over "productivity" and the like). In any event, if we agree with Hicks that "the place of economic theory is to be the servant of applied economics,"[14] perhaps it is not unreasonable to express dissatisfaction with a theory so prolific with after-the-event wisdom, and yet so inscrutable toward underdeveloped countries, anxious to learn something of what their future export-import pattern will or should be.

III. THE MEANING OF "FACTOR INTENSIVE"

This section will be concerned with the assumption that particular goods require relatively large quantities of particular factors for their

---

[13] Samuelson makes this point also in "International Trade and the Equalisation of Factor Prices," *Economic Journal,* Vol. LVIII (June, 1948), p. 182. Thus his ironic example: "The tropics grow tropical fruits because of the relative abundance there of tropical conditions."

[14] *Value & Capital* (2d ed.; Oxford: Clarendon, 1936), Preface, p. vi.

production, or that such quantities are needed for "efficient" production of the goods in question. This amounts to an assumption that production functions have particular and special shapes.

The efficient factor mix for producing a given quantity of any good (in the particular sense of the least-cost mix) can, of course, be determined once the price ratio of factors is known. But the problem here is to define "capital-intensive" (i.e., requiring relatively large amounts of capital) and "labor-intensive" commodities *no matter what* this price ratio may be.[15] The fixed factor proportions case meets this requirement (if proportions vary from one commodity to another), since the factor mix is uniquely determined as a matter of definition.

FIGURE Ia   FIGURE Ib

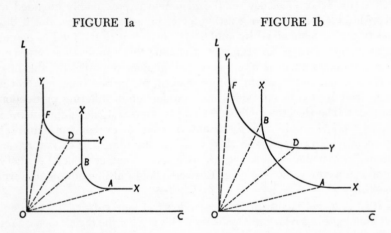

The fixed proportions case can be "softened," and an unequivocal classification by factor intensiveness retained in such a case as that of Figure Ia. This refers to a two-factor production function, quantities of capital and labor inputs being plotted on the axes. Illustrated are equal-product curves "typical" for commodity X and for commodity Y, superimposed on one another.[16] Factor substitution is possible for both commodities (e.g., for Y it is possible to vary the capital-labor mix within limits indicated by OD and OF). But "economical" input ratios (those within which the marginal product of both factors is positive) are separate and distinct. Relative to Y, commodity X is capital-intensive.

Isoquants that satisfy the essential requirement of Heckscher-Ohlin analysis can be obtained in a further "softened" case. In Figure Ib, eco-

---

[15] The part which factor price relationships have to play in the factor proportions account is solely that of reflecting Ohlin's four "fundamental" realities: factor quantities, conditions of factor ownership, production functions, and tastes. From these four elements alone, according to the theory, comparative advantage positions emerge.

[16] These isoquant diagrams assume constant returns to scale in production, so that any single isoquant can be taken as typical of all isoquants for the good in question.

nomical input ratios for the two commodities overlap. But *for any given factor price ratio common to producers of both commodities,* X's capital-labor input ratio, in a competitive equilibrium, will always exceed that of Y. In this sense, X can still be considered the capital-intensive good, even though, if the softening is carried far enough for the isoquant to reach the L-axis before becoming vertical, X *could* be produced by labor alone. This is the definition of factor intensity which Samuelson has used:[17] X is capital-intensive relative to Y when, for each and any factor price ratio, X's equilibrium capital-labor ratio[18] exceeds Y's. The fixed proportions case and those of Figures Ia and Ib are all particular instances of the class thus defined.

FIGURE II

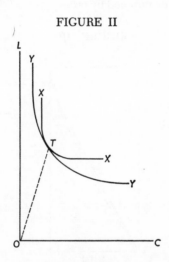

The significant aspect of this discussion is that there exist particular pairs of isoquants wherein the Samuelson definition cannot be used and which do *not* meet Heckscher-Ohlin requirements, those of Figure II for example. Given such a pair, there is a particular labor-capital price ratio at which the equilibrium factor mix would be the same for both goods. These isoquants are tangential at point *T;* when the factor price ratio equals the common isoquant slope at *T,* the labor-capital input mix *for both* will be indicated by the slope of *OT.* Given a slightly higher price ratio, Y would be the relatively capital-intensive good; given a slightly lower one, X would be.

If Figure II isoquants happen to prevail, the factor proportions argument becomes very difficult to follow, since an unequivocal classification

---

[17] *Ibid.,* note, p. 165.

[18] The ratios referred to are, of course, those which would prevail in a competitive equilibrium, wherein producers seek to operate at least cost for the output produced, as a necessary ingredient in profit-maximization.

of goods by factor intensity is impossible. A brief excursion into box-diagrams (considered more fully in Section IV) should be sufficient to amplify this point. If a single country is assumed to possess given totals of capital and labor, then a Stolper-Samuelson box-diagram[19] can be employed, as in Figure III. Along the sides of the rectangle are measured total available factor quantities; within the box are plotted production functions in isoquant form, with X's function starting at the southwest corner and Y's at the northeast. Within the box will lie a "contract curve" or "efficient factor allocation curve," the locus of tangency points between X-isoquants and Y-isoquants. The equilibrium position will lie upon this curve (provided competition functions as theory expects it to do), its precise position being determined by tastes.

FIGURE IIIa   FIGURE IIIb   FIGURE IIIc

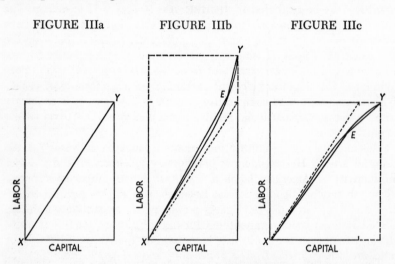

If isoquants *do* satisfy the Samuelson definition, and if X and Y occupy the relative intensity positions indicated by Figure I, this guarantees: (1) that the "factor allocation curve" will always lie *below* the southwest-to-northeast diagonal, regardless of what factor endowments may be; (2) hence that if any two countries both possess the same production functions, X will in both be the capital-intensive good and Y the labor-intensive one; (3) provisionally assuming "identical tastes" (a matter to be discussed in the next section) trade must go just as the factor proportions account indicates. The country possessing the relatively larger amount of capital will export the capital-intensive good.

The presence of Figure II isoquants may disrupt this pattern of ideas. A country which happens to have a total endowment of capital

[19] See Wolfgang F. Stolper and Paul A. Samuelson, "Protection & Real Wages," *Review of Economic Studies,* Vol. IX (Nov., 1941), pp. 58–73, reprinted in *Readings in the Theory of International Trade, op. cit.*

and labor in the proportions indicated by the slope of OT in Figure II will then have as its factor allocation curve the diagonal line; it will operate under constant opportunity cost conditions; and no classification of goods by factor intensity will be possible since the capital-labor input mix will be the same for both. If a country's total factor endowment ratio exceeds that indicated by OT, the factor allocation curve will lie below the diagonal, and X will be considered the capital-intensive good therein. If E is the equilibrium point, factor mixes will be indicated by XE and YE of Figure IIIb. But another country, with total factors in a ratio *below OT*, will have its allocation curve *above* the diagonal (Figure IIIc) and Y will be the capital-intensive good therein.

This does not mean, of course, that gainful trade between the two countries may be restricted by the presence of Figure II isoquants. The essential criterion for such trade is always this alone: that there be a pre-trade inequality in the commodity price ratio p_X/p_Y as between the two countries. Figure II isoquants mean simply that relative factor endowments can no longer stand out from the whole general equilibrium complex as *the* significant element (assuming some uniformity of tastes) in explaining trade and comparative advantage positions. It is no longer possible to associate particular relative factor endowments with particular commodities.

This analysis can be utilized to evaluate Ellsworth's criticism[20] of the Leontief article. He considers it unnecessary to appeal to the superior productivity of American labor to vindicate factor proportions theory. Ellsworth singles out for criticism Leontief's use of U.S. production figures on the import side—i.e., figures pertaining to production within the United States of goods competitive with and substituting for U.S. imports. His argument runs thus: (1) it is inappropriate to take the capital-labor ratio *prevailing in the United States* for "import" production; (2) the appropriate figure would be the *foreign* capital-labor ratio for actual production of such U.S. imports; and (3) if available, this figure would probably reveal a substantially lower capital-labor ratio—i.e., much greater labor intensity.

Even if inappropriate, the U.S. ratio cannot be forgotten. Why is it higher for "imports" than for exports? If I understand him correctly, Ellsworth considers it the probable result of a departure from the competitive equilibrium. It is the result of a lavish (and presumably uneconomic) use of capital, in order to offset the competition of foreign labor; it is a phenomenon that would probably vanish with the removal of tariff protection.

But this argument seems to rest either on the assumption of different production functions or else the assumption of Figure II type isoquants. Neither assumption can be reconciled with the factor proportions account

---

[20] *Op. cit.*

which Ellsworth seeks to defend. Suppose that unequivocal definitions of factor intensities are possible (i.e., they meet Samuelson's definition, being of the Figure I type) and that the same basic production functions apply both in the United States and abroad. Then if the capital-labor ratio in the United States for import-type goods exceeds that for export-type goods, in the face of the given U.S. factor price ratio, then by definition, these import-type goods are capital-intensive. And Ellsworth's contention is that they are not.[21] This holds whether these import-type goods enjoy protection in the United States or not, unless producers are so heedless of the dictates of profit-maximization that they refuse to minimize production costs.

IV. TRANSFORMATION CURVES AND COMMUNITY TASTES

Just as the factor proportions account assumes that production functions have particular shapes, so it assumes that taste functions have a particular shape. The restriction imposed on the taste side is perhaps even more demanding. The principal concern of this section will be to show that trade may very well controvert the theory even though community tastes as between two countries are identical.[22] It will assume that production functions are such as to permit commodities to be classified according to factor intensity.

This section will assume fixed factor proportions. A hurried defense of this assumption is perhaps needed. It is analytically and geometrically convenient; and as Section V will try to show, it is possible to pass from this to softened cases (using this term as in Section III) with little disturbance to the conclusions reached.

Moreover, a case not so far removed from right-angled isoquants seems well suited to the factor proportions account of trade. This is the "limited softening" case, that of Figure Ia isoquants. In addition to simplifying the meaning of "capital-intensive" and "labor-intensive," such isoquants are convenient for illustrating the Heckscher-Ohlin account of the gains from trade. These gains are said to arise out of differences in marginal rates of factor substitution as between countries in the pre-trade situation. In Country 1, in isolation, the marginal physical product (MPP) of factor C in its various occupations may be particularly low, by comparison with Country 2. Using his own country's equilibrium values as criterion, a citizen of Country 2 might therefore regard factor C as "underemployed" —in the sense of low MPP's—in Country 1. And he would be correct in

---

[21] Speaking of U.S. imports, Ellsworth says: "We import them because they can be produced cheaper abroad, and this is so for two reasons: labor is relatively abundant and cheap there, and such goods as we import *can be produced most economically by technical methods which require relatively large amounts of labor.* "The Structure of American Trade," *op. cit.*, p. 280. Italics mine.

[22] The circumstances under which it is meaningful to speak of "identical community tastes" will be discussed later in this section.

that an intercountry exchange wherein Country 1 gave up some part of her C in exchange for another factor (a once-and-for-all exchange) would be mutually advantageous in terms of total output. The *MPP* of C would rise, and so would that of the factor given in exchange. If factor immobility makes this exchange impossible, a transfer of C into particular occupations and a continuing exchange of goods will accomplish (partly or fully) the same end.

The property of Figure Ia isoquants is that they show wide variations in marginal factor substitution rates within a very limited change in the input ratio. Hence they admit more readily the possibility of very low *MPP*'s for particular factors, in given circumstances of factor endowments. The gain from raising *MPP*'s is more clearly evident. If technical conditions permit ready substitution of one factor for another over a wide range, trading gains are less likely to be impressive. There may then be no shortage of any *particular* factor, even when the *general* factor shortage is acute. In the extreme case wherein the factor substitution ratio between C and L is constant, regardless of product or the ratio of factor input (isoquants are straight lines), C and L are effectively one and the same factor,[23] and the matter of their relative supplies is unimportant. If the factor proportions account is valid, the profitability of trade is most easily seen when a country in isolation, producing the output it considers optimal, is at or near the vertical or horizontal region of isoquants—i.e., it is feeling the pinch of a shortage of particular factors.

The fixed proportions case simply converts instances of "underemployment" (low *MPP*'s) into those of "unemployment" (zero *MPP*'s).[24] But it may be well to repeat that conclusions reached in this case may be transferred to cases that have been softened to admit as much variation in factor proportions as one pleases.

In any box-diagram such as those of Figure III, any two adjacent sides of the box measure total factor quantities available. A change in factor endowment changes the dimensions of the box. In Figure IV, the flat rectangle BY_1AX indicates a box-diagram and a particular circumstance of factor endowment. An increase in the labor endowment and a decrease in the capital endowment would change the shape of the box: the corner Y_1 would move to some position such as Y_2. Further increases in labor

---

[23] Factor units can always be defined in such a way as to make the value of this *MRS* unitary. If the *MRS* figure is constant in any one occupation (isoquants are linear) but varies from one product to another, then each product will tend to be produced by a single factor, unless the demand is sufficiently great that a second factor must be called into service from another occupation. The resulting transformation curve will be similar to those of Figure V (Section IV) even though, substitutionwise, this case is at the opposite extreme from that illustrated by Figure V.

[24] Ohlin's reference to "goods which *require* large proportions of certain factors" (*op. cit.*, p. 12) quoted by Ellsworth, might well be interpreted as a fixed-coefficient reference right from the start. But as Ellsworth says, Ohlin refers in a preceding paragraph to alternative methods of production.

and decreases in capital would move the corner to such positions as Y_3 and Y_4.

Figure IV, then, represents four different productive situations, each defined by a particular circumstance of factor endowment. The four boxes are superimposed, with the X-corner common to all four.

It is assumed that factor proportions are fixed, hence that isoquants are right angles. X is taken as the capital-intensive commodity, with a required capital-labor mix of 4 to 1. The corners of the X-isoquants will accordingly lie along the line XY_1 in the first situation, or along as much of this line as is relevant in each of the other three.[25] Y is the labor-intensive good, with required capital-labor proportions of 1 to 4. Corners

FIGURE IV

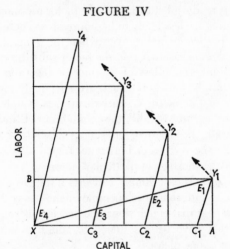

of Y-isoquants lie along Y_1C_1 in situation 1. Since the Y-corner of the box shifts with any shift in factor endowments, so does the YC line; appropriate YC lines are shown for the other three situations.

It is well known that in such fixed input circumstances there is only one point (one combination of X and Y quantities) at which both factors can be fully employed—at the intersection of XY_1 and the relevant YC line. In situation 1, this intersection, E_1, is right at one corner: factor proportions are so well suited for X-production that in isolation Y can be produced only at the cost of some capital unemployment. By situation 4, matters have been pushed to the reverse point where X-production is impossible without unemployment of labor. (If the term "unemployment" is particularly associated with a situation of deficiency of aggregate demand, perhaps "redundancy" would be preferable here. In the situation

[25] For simplicity, the right-angled isoquants themselves are not shown on this diagram.

being discussed, however, one factor may exist to unemployable excess because of deficiency of demand for a *particular* product.)

Assuming constant returns to scale, it is a simple matter to develop the transformation or production-possibility curves associated with these situations. They appear as in Figure V, with number-subscripts indicating the factor endowment situation pertinent to each of the four curves. The kink in curves 2 and 3 indicates the full-employment point.

With "country" substituted for "situation," the consequences of trade under conditions of differing factor endowments can be examined. Only the possible outcomes as between Countries 2 and 3 will be considered.

FIGURE V

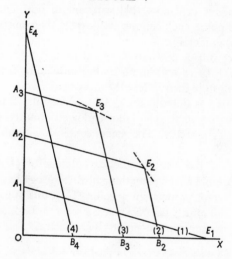

This range of outcomes takes account of all results to be had by including Countries 1 and 4, the more extreme instances of disproportionate factor endowments.

The trade outcome depends upon the nature of each country's *pre-trade* equilibrium position:

(*a*) If equilibrium is at *E*, as it will be if "community indifference curves" in the *E*-region have a slope intermediate between slopes of *AE* and *EB* (between ¼ and 4, sign neglected), both factors will be fully employed, and the *X-Y* price ratio will be dictated by the slope of the indifference curve at *E*.

(*b*) If equilibrium is elsewhere along *AE*,[26] the *X-Y* price ratio will be ¼, capital will be a free factor, and the simple labor theory of value will prevail.

---

[26] The extreme cases of a pre-trade equilibrium on one axis or the other are here ignored.

(*c*) If equilibrium is elsewhere along *EB*, the *X-Y* price ratio will be 4, labor will be a free factor, and the "simple capital theory of value" will prevail.

Now the consequences of trade indicated by factor proportions theory emerge most clearly if *either* country (or both) has a pre-trade equilibrium *away from* its full-employment point, *E*. For then it can always be said that if trade occurs at all, the country initially away from *E* (one or both) will through trade be brought to its full-employment point, and there will be greater specialization upon the export commodity.[27] This is not true if trade occurs with both countries initially at their respective *E*-points; such trade involves no reallocation of factors at all.

It does not follow, of course, that with one or both countries initially away from the *E*-point, each country will export the commodity indicated by its factor endowment. For:

(*a*) If both countries are initially on their *AE* sections (or both on their *EB* sections), there will be no trade. Both suffer from an excess of the same factor, despite their different endowments.

(*b*) If Country 3 is initially along *AE* and Country 2 is at *E* or along *EB*, trade will be perverse. The labor-endowed country will export the capital-intensive commodity. The same conclusion holds if Country 2 is initially along *EB*.

It can be argued that the unorthodox outcome of (*b*) results simply from different national tastes, something always recognized as a legitimate exception in the factor proportions account.[28] Yet this outcome may occur in a situation of "identical" tastes. The case wherein both countries are initially at their full-employment points will illustrate the point. Suppose

---

[27] There are in all nine combinations of pre-trade equilibria, of which eight place one country or both away from the full-employment *E*-point. Details of the analysis needed to reach the conclusions of this section have been omitted, as they involve only the familiar offer-curve treatment.

The situations here examined correspond to those of Valavanis-Vail, *op. cit.*, Section VI, wherein he argues that no inference as to production is to be derived from the fact of relative factor proportions. I find his argument somewhat difficult to follow because (1) he does not indicate the pre-trade equilibria of his two countries, (2) the second of the two numerical examples cited on p. 527 in illustration is typographically in error, placing both countries production-wise off their transformation curves, (3) the first such example seems to be a zero-gain case, and hence hardly appropriate to illustrate the normal consequences of trade. Unless I am mistaken, this case is compatible only with a before-*and*-after price ratio of ½ in both countries, or what in this paper would be considered a no-trade-opportunities case. It is not entirely clear to me that the use of Marshallian supply-and-demand curves is appropriate here. In any event, I trust I am not unfair to Valavanis-Vail in saying that in so far as his argument here is correct, a defender of factor proportions would consider it an instance of differing tastes, hence an already-recognized exception.

[28] Ellsworth (*International Economics*, 1st ed., p. 95) uses the term "relative differences in factor equipment" to point up the fact that where a country has a strong taste for the products made by its abundant factor, it may have no "exportable excess" of that factor, even though the absolute supply is large. ("Relative" is perhaps misleading, since we are already speaking of one country's factor supply by comparison with another's; but the meaning seems perfectly clear.)

pre-trade commodity price ratios to be such as indicated by the two broken lines of Figure V. Then the trade pattern will be unorthodox.

If one were to draw a single indifference curve (of normal curvature) passing through both E_3 and E_2, assuming this to be the relevant taste curve for both countries, then, of course (since the equilibrium price ratio must match the slope of the indifference curve), the unorthodox result illustrated would be impossible. But it would be quite improper, through a development of this approach, to conclude that if tastes are the same in the two countries and if indifference curves have their normal convexity, the unorthodox result is impossible.

Orthodoxy *will* hold if indifference curves have the property which in a production function diagram would be termed linear homogeneity or constant returns to scale—i.e., if any one indifference curve is typical of them all and can be used to develop the entire taste diagram, or in other words if all income elasticities of demand have unitary value. If this assumption about curve shapes is lacking, and if the two countries have differing per capita levels of real income,[29] no guarantee of the orthodox result exists.

For simplicity in illustrating this point, suppose the case to concern trade between two individuals, not countries. Suppose that Citizen 2, possessing exactly the same taste map as Citizen 3, enjoys a much higher level of real income. His Figure V transformation curve will accordingly be pushed much farther out, and E_2 will lie much farther to the northeast than its illustrated position. Unless his marginal taste-pattern remains unchanged throughout the range of real income increase (unless his income elasticity is unitary) there is no reason why his marginal rate of substitution should not shift sufficiently in favor of X to produce an indifference curve touching E_3 that is steeper than the curve touching E_2.

The same conclusion holds in the two-country case, although the fact of community indifference curves complicates the analysis somewhat. Such community curves may be close to a fiction, but they are much too convenient a fiction to expect them to be left unused. Yet if used, their attributes must be respected. The basis for the community function is the individual function. If it is said that two countries "have identical tastes," this must mean that the tastes of their individual citizens are in some sense identical. Suppose that one single indifference map indicates the taste-patterns of each and every citizen in both Countries 2 and 3. Only in the special unit-income-elastic case can it be said that the "community indifference map" of Country 2 must be the same as that of Country 3. This is perhaps most clearly seen by assuming, not two separate countries, but a single country which is shifted from situation 2 to situation 3. It is suddenly endowed with more capital, and certain citizens selected at random are (instantly and painlessly) removed. The identical taste-functions of those remaining persist unchanged. Since the object is to raise the

---

[29] If the two countries share a common indifference map, real income comparisons are simple.

per capita income level (and for a minimum of complications) let it be assumed furthermore that the entire stock of capital is owned by those remaining individuals who also possess the labor supplied. Unless income elasticities are unitary, the "community indifference map" must be disturbed. A new level of real income has been reached, and if the attraction of X at this new level is sufficiently great, the commodity price ratio may shift in the manner illustrated by the broken lines of Figure V.[30]

The moral of the foregoing is not simply that it makes little or no sense to talk about "identical tastes" as between two countries. A more meaningful conclusion is that a capital-endowed country may choose to import the capital-intensive commodity if it has reached a level of real income at which its income elasticity of demand with respect to such goods is high, and the labor-endowed country may concur if its income level disposes it, at the margin, more toward the labor-intensive commodity. Empiricism of even more than usual casualness suggests that this may be the attitude of U.S. buyers; some part of the Leontief phenomenon may perhaps be explainable in such terms.

To summarize the fixed proportions case: international trade appears as the indirect export of a factor existing in relative excess and hence unemployed. (In the softened case, next considered, "unemployment" reduces to "underemployment.") But profitable trade can occur with little or no factor reallocation, as where both countries are initially at their respective E-points. It is not necessarily true that the export good (through the factor proportions it requires) can be identified with the factor existing in relative excess; the flow of goods may well be unorthodox. If so, this is not necessarily a matter of "different tastes." This outcome may arise in a situation wherein each and every citizen in both countries has exactly the same taste function. If, however, this taste function is unit-income-elastic throughout (mathematically, if it is a homothetic function) the orthodox result is assured.

There does not seem much evidence to indicate that unit income elasticities are typically the order of the day. Matters would be simpler if human behavior were sufficiently co-operative to warrant using this assumption.[31] All-round unitary income elasticities make an easy job of aggregating individual tastes into a community taste function, for example.[32]

---

[30] Perhaps the community function idea here becomes so untrustworthy that it might better be discarded. But its Cheshire-Cat grin will persist even after it has vanished: one aspect of this function will continue in the form of the equilibrium price ratio, the community's marginal rate of substitution between commodities.

[31] For a discussion of comparable use of this type of function by Viner and others in different circumstances, see Paul A. Samuelson, "The Transfer Problem and Transport Costs," *Economic Journal,* Vol. LXII (June, 1952), pp. 295–98 and Vol. LXIV (June, 1954), p. 280.

[32] I am assuming throughout that it is meaningful to speak of such a community taste function. There is a parallel between this aggregation problem and that involving

It should be noted that the fixed proportions case is not an appropriate one to use, if the argument of one of Leontief's critics is valid. Stefan Valavanis-Vail argues that "fixed coefficients of production are generally incompatible with international trade."[33] Valavanis-Vail appraises this assumption because of its use in the Leontief input-output model. The export and import figures were obtained as a by-product of input-output work (although they do not seem to depend too critically on the fixed coefficient assumption).

Valavanis-Vail's assertion is a strong one if it means that a world characterized by fixed coefficients would ordinarily be one in which foreign trade would be impossible or unprofitable. His supporting argument is in brief as follows: In a static, two-country, two-factor, two-commodity model, the following four assumptions are inconsistent: (1) fixed production coefficients, (2) full employment of both factors in both countries before and after trade, (3) a gain resulting from international trade, and (4) a reduction in the world output of one commodity after trade. Such a situation is indeed impossible, as Valavanis-Vail's argument shows. But surely the culprit is assumption (4), not (1). In such a static model, it is not true that (following trade) "in general, the world output of some commodities will increase and that of others will decrease,"[34] unless the latter are inferior goods. Even in this case, some difficulty will be experienced in manipulating the usual transformation-curve-plus-offer-curve model (one also associated with the name of Leontief[35]) to produce a post-trade output decrease. In the rigid fixed proportions case, the attempt in a condition of full employment to decrease or increase output of any product, anywhere, will result in unemployment. But (in the static model) it is not clear that price changes resulting from the opening-up of trade will encourage any such attempt.

V. VARIABLE PROPORTIONS; FACTOR PRICE RELATIONSHIPS

Figure VI repeats Figure IV, save that the fixed factor proportions assumption has been dropped, and for simplicity extreme situations 1 and 4 have been omitted. In this "softened" case, it is possible to vary the proportions of inputs for commodity X between limits indicated by XL_L and

the Keynesian consumption function. If each and every community member possesses the same *linear* consumption function, aggregation into a community function is simple; the result is a blow-up of the individual function. Otherwise, a community function can be developed only by imposing special restrictions. Aggregation is likewise simple if the individual taste function is *linear homogeneous* (constant returns, unit-income-elastic, or more properly, homothetic); otherwise it demands similar restrictions.

[33] *Op. cit.*, Section II, p. 524.

[34] *Op. cit.*, Section IV, p. 524.

[35] W. Leontief, "The Use of Indifference Curves in the Analysis of Foreign Trade," *Quarterly Journal of Economics*, Vol. XLVII (May, 1933), pp. 493–503, reprinted in *Readings in the Theory of International Trade, op. cit.*

XL_C. Similar variation for Y is possible within the range of YC_C and YC_L. (As to each XL or YC, the letter-subscript indicates the factor whose marginal product has just reached zero thereon. Number-subscripts with YC's indicate the "country" or "situation" involved.) Within these "ridge lines," the marginal product of both factors is identifiable and positive.

Instead of a single full-employment point, there is now a diamond-shaped full-employment area with corners at P and Q in situation 3, R and S in situation 2. The broken lines PQ and RS indicate loci of

FIGURE VI

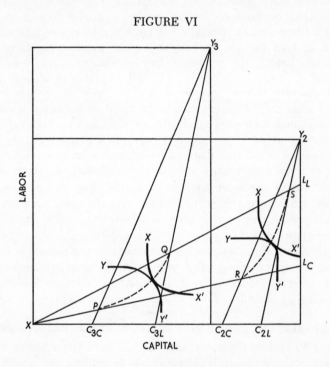

tangency points between isoquants, or "efficient allocation of factors" lines. If substitution opportunities were to be increased (i.e., still more softening introduced by spreading the two ridge lines farther apart), the full-employment area would grow and the exterior one-factor-unemployed area would shrink.

The transformation curve diagram (not illustrated) would undergo like changes. Just as the box-diagram now possesses a curved full-employment line (whose length is governed by the degree of factor substitution admitted) instead of a single full-employment point, so there will be a curved full-employment region of the transformation curve (i.e., the sharp kink of Figure V will have been rounded off). But the extremes of each transformation curve will still be linear (unless the full-employment area of Figure VI is so large as to extend to both axes), and slopes of these linear extremities will be common to both countries, as before.[36]

This softened case seems to involve only minor amendment to the conclusions of Section IV. The pre-trade case will now be one of "under-employment" rather than perhaps being one of actual unemployment. And if trade occurs, there will always be some movement of factors from one occupation to another, to remove this underemployment. But this shift cannot go so far as to move either country's post-trade production point to the linear section of its transformation curve. And the wider the range of substitution opportunities (the longer the curved section of this trans-formation curve) the more unlikely it is that trade will produce a dra-matic increase in real incomes. It is of course just as possible as before for trade to be "perverse."

The softened case, however, makes it possible to consider factor price relationships. Along PQ or RS, the ratio of factor prices will (in equi-librium) be indicated by the common slopes of the equal-product curves. Moving from P to Q (or from R to S), i.e., from one zero-MPP ridge line to the other, the ratio p_C/p_L steadily rises, starting from zero at P to reach infinity at Q.

Samuelson has shown [37] that under conditions of common production functions and constant returns to scale, there is a tight relationship be-tween factor prices and commodity prices that is common to both coun-tries. If trade is orthodox, with capital-rich Country 2 exporting capital-intensive commodity X, then the pre-trade factor price relationship must have been:

$$(P_C/P_L)_2 < (P_C/P_L)_3.$$

In the unorthodox case, this relation must be reversed, since it is not true after provision is made for demand elements that capital is Country 2's abundant factor.

Figure VII shows this relation between commodity and factor prices graphically. Operational limits for the commodity price relationship, P_X/P_Y (plotted horizontally), are dictated by the linear segments of the

[36] These slopes will not be the same as in Figure V, wherein they were governed by the relationship between fixed proportions. They will now be governed by the relation between the slopes of ridge lines.

[37] See Paul A. Samuelson, "International Trade and the Equalisation of Factor Prices," *Economic Journal*, Vol. LVIII (June, 1948), pp. 163–84; "International Factor-Price Equalisation Once Again," *Economic Journal*, Vol. LIX (June, 1949), pp. 181–97; "Prices of Factors and Goods in General Equilibrium," *Review of Economic Studies*, Vol. XXI, pp. 1–20. Samuelson's treatment assumes also that commodities are separable by factor intensity in the manner discussed in Section III. As Mr. Ronald Jones first pointed out to me, with Figure II isoquants trade will not necessarily equalize factor prices. By visualizing or drawing in the X-isoquants for Figures IIIb and IIIc, it is evident that no such post-trade factor price equality would be possible as between two such countries.

transformation curve[38]; within them the factor price ratio runs its full range.

If this functional relationship—expressed, say, by *AA*—is common to both countries, then (assuming perfect competition, as throughout this paper) it would be impossible to have a pre-trade factor price relationship out of harmony with the commodity price relationship. But were they to differ, strange results might occur. Suppose that *AA* reflects the factor-commodity price relation for Country 2, and *BB* that for Country 3. Let the pre-trade commodity price ratio in Country 2 be measured by *OF*, in Country 3 by *OH*. That is, before trade, the capital-intensive good is

FIGURE VII

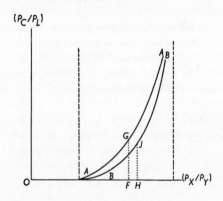

relatively cheap in the capital-rich country, a situation producing an orthodox trade flow. But it is also a situation wherein the ratio $(P_C/P_L)_3$ is less than $(P_C/P_L)_2$. Before trade begins, it is capital, not labor, that is the relatively cheap factor in the capital-poor country.

Given common production functions, this situation cannot occur under the constant returns assumption—i.e., if for each commodity any isoquant is a radial blow-up or contraction of any other isoquant. But this is a fairly demanding assumption.[39]

The debate over the appropriateness of the constant returns or linear homogeneous production function is an old one, and no attempt will be made to pursue it here, save to note that the production functions here employed are as thoroughly integrated as it is possible for them to be. They are vertically integrated; all of the various stages of production of

---

[38] As already noted, the limits of the transformation curves, when linear, have slopes which are the same for both countries. As in Section IV, the extreme case of an equilibrium (consumption-wise) on either axis is disregarded.

[39] It must, of course, be noted that the theory takes account of increasing returns as a source of profitable international exchanges. But perhaps it is not unfair to say that the phenomenon of other-than-constant returns is cited only as an alternative to differing factor proportions as a basis for trade; its consequences are not worked into the fabric of the factor proportions analysis.

X or of Y are lumped together, with no special attention paid to the fact that expanded production may bring about a different arrangement of stages, in which case constant returns are not necessarily the order of the day. It is not the expansion of production brought about by international trade that is considered here; what is involved is the before-trade situation, and the assumption that if one takes any given capital-labor ratio, the opportunities of substitution between capital and labor (the slopes of each succeeding isoquant) do not change in the slightest, no matter what the level of output may be.

The production function is integrated also as to firms operating at the same stage of production. Here the constant returns assumption is almost an analytic necessity, whatever its appropriateness, for the problems of aggregating the output of individual firms may otherwise be considerable. To say that this may be a necessary assumption for the maintenance of competitive conditions is perhaps not the most satisfactory of replies.

It is worth noting that the assumption regarding production functions is exactly the same as that implicitly employed with respect to tastes. The unitary-income-elastic indifference function has the property of a linear homogeneous function.[40] In a restricted sense, it can be said that such analysis is antimarginal in character. It is not necessary to pay special attention to what is happening at the margin in spending or in production, for what is happening there is no different from what has always happened there. Performance at the margin is simply a microcosm of performance of the whole.

It should not be surprising if the theory withstands complaints against such restrictive assumptions as these. Of the general equilibrium elements which go to make up export-import patterns (according to this model), factor supplies alone are empirically determinable. We can acquire only fragmentary information as to tastes or production functions. So long as it can be said that factor supplies tend to influence or to govern the trade pattern, the theory retains a strong appeal, and the fact that its assumptions, taken as a whole, are so very demanding may well be ignored.

But there remains for consideration the most exacting assumption of all. This is the assumption that factor supplies are fixed in total amount and perfectly price inelastic in supply. Since any theory concerned with the nature of comparative advantage would seem properly to be a "long-run" theory, a fixed-supply assumption seems curiously out of place. The consequences of relaxing it may be much more sweeping than anything in the preceding sections.

---

[40] Properly speaking, of course, the taste function need not be *linear*, since the problem of utility quantification is in no way involved. But in view of the production function assumption, this seems a convenient way of putting the matter.

2. Tariffs, the Terms of Trade, and the Distribution of National Income[*]

By LLOYD A. METZLER[†]

I

THE CLASSICAL CONCEPT of the gains from international trade was essentially a concept of increased productivity. The gains from trade, in the classical view, consisted of an increased output of all goods and services, made possible through specialization and exchange. In other words, the classical "law of comparative advantage" demonstrated that, with a given amount of productive resources in every country, it was possible, by an interchange of goods, for all countries to consume more of all commodities. In addition to its description of the potential gains from trade, the classical theory, from the time of John Stuart Mill, also gave an excellent account of how these gains are actually divided among different countries. Stated more broadly, the theory of reciprocal demand, which was added to the classical doctrine by Mill, indicated how international exchange affects the distribution of world income among countries.[1] With its strong emphasis upon productivity and upon the division of the gains from trade between different countries, however, the classical doctrine, as well as the subsequent theoretical work of neoclassical economists, seriously neglected the closely related problem of how international trade affects the division of income within each country among the various factors of production.[2] The classical theory and its neoclassical refinements could show well enough how a country, considered as a unit, tends to benefit from specialization and trade; but these doctrines had very little to say

[*] *Journal of Political Economy*, Vol. LVII, No. 1 (February, 1949), pp. 1–29.

[†] University of Chicago.

[1] J. S. Mill, *Essays on Some Unsettled Questions of Political Economy* (1844), Essay I.

[2] In view of the fact that the marginal-productivity theory of distribution did not appear until late in the nineteenth century and in view, further, of the generally recognized opinion that even the present theory of distribution has many deficiencies, it is perhaps not surprising that the influence of international trade upon the distribution of income was inadequately discussed by the classical economists. But, even with due allowances for the backward state of distribution theory, the lag in the development of this aspect of international trade was surprisingly long.

about how the gains of real income within each country are divided among labor, capital, and land.[3]

The division of the gains from trade among the different factors of production or, what amounts to substantially the same thing, the influence of international trade upon the distribution of national income is a subject which has received an adequate theoretical treatment only in comparatively recent times. The pioneer works in this branch of international economics were, of course, the studies which E. F. Heckscher[4] and B. Ohlin[5] made during the years between the two world wars. It is a curious fact that, just as the classical discussion of the terms of trade had neglected or left unsolved the related problem of the distribution of income, so the more recent contributions to the study of income distribution have neglected the complications arising out of changes in the terms of trade. Indeed, at the very beginning of his article Heckscher asserted that a discussion of the gains from trade has no relevance to the problem of income distribution. "No attention is paid," he said, "to the advantages one particular country may achieve, by means of protection, in altering the relation between supply and demand of a certain commodity and thereby wholly or partly letting the 'foreigner pay the duty'; since this problem has been discussed so widely, and since it is not relevant in the present connection, it seems unnecessary to discuss it here."[6] In the historical development of the theory of international trade, questions of income distribution have thus been rather sharply separated from questions of productivity and of gains or losses to a country as a whole.

In view of this distinct cleavage in the purely theoretical aspects of international trade, it is not surprising that the practical application of economic theory to the particular problem of tariffs has suffered from a similar lack of integration. On the one hand, the concept of reciprocal demand has been employed to demonstrate how tariffs may improve a country's terms of trade—i.e., reduce the prices it pays for its imports relative to the prices it receives for its exports—but little attempt has been made to employ this same concept in showing how the resulting increase of real income is divided among the different factors of production.

---

[3] Although the question of income distribution arose early in the nineteenth century in the English controversy over the Corn Laws, the results of the controversy in this respect were inconclusive and had no permanent influence on the theory of international trade. Cf., however, C. F. Bastable, *The Theory of International Trade* (London: Macmillan & Co., Ltd., 1903), chap. vi.

[4] "Utrikhandelns verkan på inkomstfördelningen" ["The Influence of Foreign Trade on the Distribution of Income"], *Ekonomisk Tidskrift* (1919), Part II, 1–32. Subsequent references to this paper have been taken from a translation into English prepared by Professor and Mrs. Svend Laursen.

[5] *Interregional and International Trade* (Cambridge, Mass., 1933), chap. ii and *passim*.

[6] Heckscher, *op. cit.*, p. 2.

Indeed, there has at times been a tendency in the classical theory to deny that tariffs exert any influence at all upon the distribution of national income.[7] On the other hand, when a theory of the influence of international trade upon the distribution of income was finally developed, this theory was based in part, as the preceding quotation from Heckscher demonstrates, upon the assumption that the influence of tariffs upon the terms of trade can be neglected. But, despite this historical separation of two important aspects of tariff theory, it is easily shown that changes in a country's terms of trade are closely related in a number of ways to changes in the distribution of its national income. It is the purpose of the present paper to show some of the relations between these two distinct and heretofore largely independent branches of tariff theory. Since Heckscher's work is basic to the later studies of tariffs and income distribution, it seems advisable to present a brief summary of his principal conclusions.

Heckscher began his discussion, as did the classical economists, with the assertion that trade between countries depends upon the law of comparative advantage, i.e., upon the fact that the ratio of the cost of production of two commodities is different in one country from the corresponding cost ratio in another. Unlike the classical economists, however, Heckscher placed great emphasis upon the way in which the supplies of various factors of production affect comparative costs. He argued, in particular, that comparative costs in one country differ from those in another primarily because the relative degree of scarcity of some factors of production differs between countries and because different commodities require varying proportions of the factors of production.[8] Suppose, for example, that one country, Alpha, has a large amount of land per worker as compared with another country, Beta. The ratio of rent to wage rates will then be lower in Alpha than in Beta, since land in the former country will be used to the point where its marginal product is relatively small. Consider, now, the comparative costs in the two countries of producing two products, wheat and textiles. Since wheat requires a larger amount of land per worker than textiles do, the money cost of producing a unit of wheat, relative to the cost of producing a unit of textiles, will be lower in Alpha than in Beta. In other words, Alpha will have a comparative advantage in wheat, the product requiring relatively large amounts of its

---

[7] The following statement by Taussig illustrates the point: "The general proposition that a high rate of wages is a result of high productiveness of industry is simple and undeniable. . . . Beyond doubt there remain questions which are more difficult. Just how and through what channel or mechanism does high productivity lead to the high wages? And what determines the share of the total product, be that great or small, which shall go to the laborer, the employer, the owner of capital, the owner of land? But these questions, the most important and perhaps the most complex in the field of economics, *lie quite outside the tariff controversy . . .*" (quoted from *Free Trade, the Tariff, and Reciprocity* [New York, 1920], p. 54). Italics added.

[8] Heckscher, *op. cit.*, p. 6.

abundant factor, while Beta will have a comparative advantage in textiles.

It is a simple step from these basic propositions concerning comparative advantage to the final conclusions of Heckscher with respect to the distribution of income. Suppose that Alpha and Beta are initially isolated and self-sufficient but that trade is finally opened up between the two countries. Alpha, the low-rent country, will then export wheat and Beta, where rents are comparatively high and wages low, will export textiles. This exchange of goods has a definite and predictable influence upon the demand for land and labor in the two countries. In each country the demand for factors of production is increased in the export industry and reduced in the industry competing with imports; but, as Heckscher pointed out, the proportions in which the factors of production are required in the export industry are not exactly the same as the proportions in which they are released by the industry competing with imports. In the present illustration the expansion of the wheat industry in Alpha requires, at prevailing wages and rents, a small number of workers per acre of land, while the contraction of the textile industry, under the pressure of competition from abroad, releases a relatively large number of workers and only a small amount of land. The shift of resources from textiles to wheat thus increases the relative scarcity of land in Alpha, the country which initially had a comparatively large supply of that factor. Wages per unit of labor accordingly fall in Alpha, relative to rent per unit of land. In other words, the shift in production which was brought about by international trade has given land, the relatively abundant factor in Alpha, a larger share of the total product. An analogous argument could easily be presented—and, indeed, has been presented both by Heckscher and, later, by Ohlin—to show that in Beta, where land is relatively scarce and labor abundant, international trade increases wage rates relative to rents. The central feature of the Heckscher-Ohlin analysis is thus the proposition that international trade, by increasing the demand for each country's abundant factors, tends to equalize the relative returns to the factors of production in different countries.[9]

---

[9] Whether international trade achieves a *complete* or only a *partial* equalization of relative and absolute factor returns in different countries has been a controversial issue. Heckscher, working with a simple model in which the coefficients of production were fixed, argued that the equalization would be complete in both an absolute and a relative sense. Thus, on p. 15 of the article previously cited, he said: "With fixed supplies of the factors of production and the same technique of production in all countries, we have seen that the final effect of international trade, with unimportant reservations, is the equalization of the *relative* prices of the factors of production. We must next inquire whether the equalization will be *absolute* as well as *relative, i.e.,* whether rent, wages and interest for the same qualities of the factors of production will amount to the same real return in all countries. This proposition has not thus far been demonstrated, but it is an inescapable consequence of trade." If the coefficients of production were variable, on the other hand, Heckscher believed that substitutions

With this brief introduction, we may now examine the relation of the Heckscher-Ohlin theory to the tariff problem. In view of the tendency of international trade to equalize relative factor returns among different countries, it might seem that the owners of a factor of production which is relatively scarce in a given country would have a strong interest in restricting international trade; for by so doing they could preserve the relative scarcity which might otherwise be threatened by competition from abroad. In a country with an abundant supply of land and a limited supply of labor, for example, the working class might well benefit by tarriffs on manufactured goods. Superficially at least, the Heckscher-Ohlin analysis lends support to the pauper-labor argument for tariffs.

Against this view, it may be objected that the conclusions with regard to the influence of trade upon the distribution of national income take account only of the *relative* position of a particular factor of production and make no allowance for the fact that the *absolute* return of the scarce factor may deteriorate even when its relative position improves. Tariffs interfere with the allocation of resources, and, if the real income of an entire nation is thus reduced by protective duties, it may be small compensation to the scarce factor that it now obtains a larger share of the reduced total. Fifty per cent of a national income of 75 is clearly worse than 40 per cent of a national income of 100.[10] But this possibility of a divergence in the movements of *real* and *relative* returns need not detain us further; for Stolper and Samuelson, in a study which forms a sequel to the works of Heckscher and Ohlin, have shown that the real return and the relative return of a particular factor of production are likely to move in the same direction.[11] In other words, if a tariff increases the share of the national income accruing to the working class, it will also improve the workers' standard of living, and conversely. According to the Stolper-Samuelson argument, a country with a comparatively small labor supply could thus increase its real wage rate by means of protection, even though national income as a whole were thereby diminished. To

of one factor for another would lead to different techniques of production and hence to differences in relative and absolute factor returns between countries (*ibid.*, p. 16). It was this latter conclusion, rather than the former one, which was subsequently adopted and elaborated by Ohlin and which became more or less the generally accepted view (*op. cit.*, pp. 37–39). Samuelson, however, in a recent study prepared independently of Heckscher's work, has shown that the equalization of relative and absolute returns may be complete even when account is taken of factor substitutions. In other words, Heckscher's first conclusion—i.e., the conclusion that equalization is *complete*—is applicable even to the case of variable coefficients of production (P. A. Samuelson, "International Trade and the Equalisation of Factor Prices," *Economic Journal*, Vol. LVIII [June, 1948], pp. 163–84). This suggests that the theory of international trade might have been advanced considerably, in the English-speaking world at any rate, by an earlier translation of Heckscher's pioneer article.

10 Unless conspicuous consumption and social standing are more important than the absolute standard of living.

11 W. F. Stolper and P. A. Samuelson, "Protection and Real Wages," *Review of Economic Studies*, Vol. IX (1941), pp. 58–73.

use a common expression, the workers would get not merely a larger share of a smaller pie but a share which was larger, in absolute magnitude, than their previous smaller share of a larger pie. The detrimental effects of the tariff would be shifted entirely upon the country's "abundant" factors of production.

These results follow directly from two assumptions. The first is that a tariff causes factors of production to be shifted from export industries to industries competing with imports. If labor, as before, is taken to be the country's relatively scarce and high-cost factor of production, it follows from the Heckscher-Ohlin conclusions that the export industries will be those requiring a comparatively small amount of labor in relation to other factors, while the industries competing with imports will require a large proportion of labor to other factors. In the absence of changes in factor prices, the shift of resources brought about by a tariff accordingly leads to a scarcity of labor and an excess supply of land and other factors. Wage rates rise relative to rents, and in all industries a substitution of land for labor occurs. This brings us to the second fundamental assumption, namely, that the marginal physical productivity of a given factor in any industry depends exclusively upon the proportion of that factor to the other factors of production. More explicitly, it is assumed that the marginal product of a factor declines as the ratio of that factor to others in a particular industry is increased. Stolper and Samuelson show that, when wages rise relative to rents, the resulting substitution of land for labor causes the ratio of labor to land to decline in all industries. To put the matter another way, the surplus of land and scarcity of labor arising from the shift of resources from exports to industries competing with imports can be eliminated only if there is a reduction, in all industries, in the ratio of labor to land. But if this occurs, then, according to our second assumption, the marginal product of labor must have increased in all industries, compared with the former position of equilibrium. If competitive conditions prevail or if the degree of monopoly is about the same in one industry as in another, it follows that the real wage rate must have increased, regardless of whether this real return is measured in export goods or in the commodities of the industries competing with imports.

Although this conclusion concerning the influence of tariffs upon real wages represented a definite improvement in the theory of tariffs, a number of questions still remained unanswered. Like the earlier works on the subject, the later study by Stolper and Samuelson made no allowance for changes in the terms of trade. The rigid separation between the classical theory of the gains from trade and the modern theory of the distribution of income has thus continued to exist even in the most recent contribution to the subject. This naturally raises the question of whether modifications in the existing theory of tariffs are required if changes in the terms of trade and in the distribution of income are considered simultaneously. The classical theory of the gains from trade demonstrated that, under certain conditions of international demand, a country could increase the external purchasing power of its exports by means of tariffs on imports and that, if this favorable movement in its terms of trade were sufficiently large, the real income of the country imposing the tariff might be increased despite the unfavorable effects of the tariff upon the allocation of resources. Now, since Stolper and Samuelson assumed that a country's external terms of trade were unaffected by a tariff, they were actually considering the least favorable case possible with respect to the real income of the country imposing the duty; the tariff, in the Stolper-Samuelson argument, interfered with the allocation of resources without bringing about any offsetting favorable movement in the terms of trade. Real income of the country as a whole was therefore unambiguously reduced by the import duty.

Let us consider, for a moment, a more favorable case. Suppose that a particular country's exports and imports are important influences on world markets and that a tariff reduces the external prices of imports, relative to the prices of exports, to such an extent that real income for the country as a whole is clearly increased. How does this alter the conclusions summarized above concerning real and relative wage rates? Assuming, as before, that the country has a scarcity of labor and therefore imports commodities requiring a large amount of labor, it might appear at first glance that the tariff would increase real wages, perhaps to a considerable extent; for, if the real as well as the relative returns of labor are increased by a tariff even when the duty reduces real income of the country as a whole (the Stolper-Samuelson case), it might seem that the rise in real wages would be even greater if real income as a whole were increased. To return to our previous analogy, it would surely seem better for labor to receive a larger share of an increasing pie than to receive a larger share of a diminishing pie. Although this argument seems plausible, it is actually misleading, for the improvement in terms of trade affects not only real income as a whole but also the degree of scarcity of the so-called "scarce" factors. Paradoxical as it may seem, when changes in the terms of trade are taken into consideration, tariffs or other impediments to imports do not always preserve or increase the scarcity of the scarce factors of production. Under some conditions of international demand the industries competing with imports and the scarce factors of production, which are usually required in large amounts in such industries, may benefit from free trade and suffer from protection.

The precise conditions of international demand required to bring about such an unexpected result are described in Section II. The argument is presented by means of the familiar Mill-Marshall schedules of reciprocal demand.[12]

---

[12] The reader will recognize that in adopting this method I have not added anything essentially new to the well-known classical technique. My purpose, rather, is

II

Whether a tariff injures or benefits a country's scarce factors of production depends largely upon how it affects the output of exports and of commodities competing with imports. If output expands in the industries competing with imports and contracts in the export industries, the increased demand for scarce factors of production in the expanding industries will normally exceed the supplies made available in the contracting export industries; and, as Stolper and Samuelson have shown, the real returns as well as the relative shares of the scarce factors in the national income will thus be increased. In a large part of the nontechnical literature dealing with tariffs, and even in some of the technical literature, a shift of this sort is normally taken for granted; indeed, it is frequently regarded almost as a truism that tariffs injure export industries and benefit industries competing with imports. Nevertheless, when both primary and secondary price changes are taken into consideration, this is by no means a self-evident proposition. To be sure, the tariff itself is the cause of a direct increase in the domestic prices of imports over and above world prices, and this constitutes an immediate benefit to the industries competing with imports. But, on the other hand, the tariff is also the cause of a series of events which tend to reduce the world prices of the country's imports relative to the prices of its exports—i.e., to improve the terms of trade—and this secondary reduction of world prices of imports relative to exports may more than offset the initial primary increase.

Now it is reasonable to suppose that resources will not be permanently shifted from the export industries to the industries competing with imports unless the net effect of all primary and secondary price changes is an increase in the domestic prices of imports (including tariffs) relative to the domestic prices of exports. Whether a tariff increases or reduces the real and relative returns of the scarce factors, therefore, depends upon the magnitude of the favorable movement in the terms of trade, compared with the size of the tariff. If the former is greater than the latter, the final effect of the tariff will be a reduction of the domestic prices of imports relative to the prices of exports, and resources will accordingly be shifted from industries competing with imports to the export industries. In other words, the industries producing commodities for export will expand, after tariffs are imposed, while industries competing with imports will contract, an outcome diametrically opposite to the usual expectation. Suppose, for example, that the ratio of the world prices of a country's imports to the world prices of its exports is initially

---

to apply this technique to a problem which was seldom discussed and never strongly emphasized in the classical literature. In doing this, I have made particular use of the classical theory in the form in which it was expounded by A. P. Lerner ("The Symmetry between Import and Export Taxes," *Economica*, Vol. III [new ser., 1936], pp. 308–13).

taken to be 1:1. Suppose, now, that a tariff of 50 per cent ad valorem is placed upon all imports and that, as a result of the ensuing reduced demand for imports, the ratio, in world prices exclusive of tariffs, of import prices to export prices falls to 1:2. The domestic price ratio, which differs from the world price ratio by the amount of the tariff, will then be 1.5:2, compared with 1:1 before the tariff was imposed. The tariff has thus reduced the domestic prices of imports relative to the prices of exports, and a transfer of resources from the "protected" industries to the export industries may accordingly be anticipated. Under these circumstances the effects of the tariff upon the distribution of income are ex-

FIGURE 1

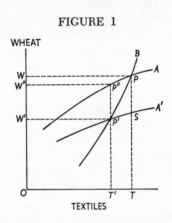

actly opposite to the conclusions reached by Stolper and Samuelson; the scarce factor of production, i.e., the factor relatively most important in the industries competing with imports, suffers both a relative decline in its share of the national income and an absolute decline in its real return. The most important factor of production in the export industries, on the other hand, enjoys both a relative and an absolute increase of income.

The magnitude of the favorable movement of the terms of trade which occurs when tariffs are imposed obviously depends upon conditions of international demands in a way that has been familiar to all economists at least since the time of Mill. It is therefore appropriate to state the argument in terms of the Mill-Marshall equations of reciprocal demand. As before, I shall assume that there are two countries—Alpha and Beta—producing two commodities—wheat and textiles—and that, for the reasons discussed above, Alpha has a comparative advantage in the production of wheat, while Beta has an advantage in textiles. In Figure 1, the curves *A* and *B* represent the reciprocal demand schedules of the two countries, Alpha and Beta, for imported textiles and wheat, respectively, under conditions of free trade.[13] Equilibrium is established at the point P, which implies that Alpha imports an amount OT of textiles in exchange for OW of wheat. Suppose, now, that Alpha imposes an ad valorem duty of 50 per cent upon imported textiles. If we neglect for a moment the effects of the spending of the proceeds of the tariff by the government of Alpha, it is clear that the initial effect of the tariff is to reduce the demand schedule facing the exporters of textiles in Beta from A to A'. In other words, textile importers in Alpha will now be willing to give to the exporters in Beta only TS units of wheat for OT of textiles; a money value equal to the additional amount, SP, which citizens of Alpha formerly gave to Beta, now goes to the Alpha government as a duty. This means that SP is 50 per cent of TS or that TS is two-thirds of TP, and similarly for any other point, such as P', on the new demand schedule.

After the tariff has been imposed, the new equilibrium in terms of quantities actually traded is at P', at which point OW' units of wheat are exported by Alpha and OT' units of textiles are imported. Unless B is a straight line from the origin, which implies that the demand in Beta for the exports of Alpha is infinitely elastic, it is obvious from Figure 1 that the tariff will improve the terms of trade of Alpha. The fraction OT'/OW' is clearly larger than OT/OW, which means that Alpha obtains more units of textiles for a given amount of wheat than was true under free trade. Or, to put the matter another way, the world price of textiles, exclusive of the tariff, has fallen, relative to the world price of wheat. The bargaining position of Alpha, the country imposing the tariff, is thus improved. Such an improvement in Alpha's terms of trade is, of course, completely explained by the classical theory of international trade and would not need to be considered further except for its influence upon the distribution of income. In order to see how the tariff has affected the distribution of income in Alpha, we must look at domestic prices rather than at world prices. This means that the tariff must be added to the world price of textiles. Measured in terms of their export commodity, the total outlay of the residents of Alpha for imported textiles, including their outlay for the tariff, is not OW', in Figure 1, but OW'', an amount 50 per cent greater than OW'. In other words, in terms of value actually expended, the residents of Alpha are giving up the equivalent of OW'' units of wheat for OT' units of textiles; the domestic ratio of exchange is therefore given by the fraction OT'/OW''. Now, since OT'/OW'' is less than OT/OW in Figure 1, it is obvious that, with

---

[13] In all the figures the reciprocal demand schedules are assumed to depend not only upon conditions of demand but also upon conditions of production. The elasticity of a given reciprocal demand schedule is thus a combined result of substitutions on the part of consumers and shifts of resources on the part of producers (see W. W. Leontief, "The Use of Indifference Curves in the Analysis of Foreign Trade," *Quarterly Journal of Economics*, Vol. XLVII [1933], pp. 493–503).

the schedules of reciprocal demand there assumed, the tariff has caused
the domestic price of textiles in Alpha to rise, relative to the price of
wheat; land and labor are therefore shifted from wheat to textile production; and the relative share of labor in the national income, as well as
the real wage rate, is increased.

It is easily shown that this conclusion is valid for reciprocal demand
schedules other than those depicted in Figure 1, as long as the demand
of Beta for the products of Alpha is elastic. The foregoing argument
may therefore be generalized as follows: If the world demand for a
country's exports is elastic and if we neglect the effects of government
expenditures on the demand for imports, (1) a tariff always increases

FIGURE 2

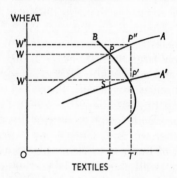

WHEAT

TEXTILES

the domestic prices of imports relative to the prices of exports; (2) the
improvement in the terms of trade is not sufficient, in this case, to offset
the tariff itself; (3) the protected industries become more profitable,
relative to the export industries; (4) resources are shifted from the
latter to the former; and (5) the real returns to the country's scarce
factors of production, as well as these factors' share in the national income, are increased. The Stolper-Samuelson conclusion is thus valid,
even when changes in the terms of trade are taken into account, as long
as the demand for exports is elastic.

When the demand for exports is inelastic, the conclusions of the last
paragraph must be reversed. This situation is depicted in Figure 2, where
the demand of Beta for the product of Alpha is assumed to be inelastic
at the equilibrium point, P. In other words, in the neighborhood of P
the residents of Beta are willing to give up decreasing amounts of textiles
in exchange for an increasing amount of wheat. The notation is the
same as in Figure 1. The original equilibrium is at P; but, after the
tariff is imposed, the point of balanced trade moves to P', at which point
Alpha gives up OW' units of wheat in exchange for OT' units of textiles.
As before, the terms of trade move in favor of Alpha. Indeed, in the
present example a greater amount of textiles is obtained for a smaller

amount of wheat, and the favorable movement in the terms of trade of Alpha is now so great that the domestic price of textiles, including the tariff, is lower, relative to the price of wheat, than it was before the tariff was imposed. This is shown in Figure 2 by the fact that OT''/OW'' is greater than OT/OW.

When the demand for a country's exports is inelastic, the foregoing argument shows that a tariff, far from protecting the industries competing with imports, may actually make these industries worse off than under free trade. In Figure 2, for example, the tariff on textile imports into Alpha reduces the domestic price of textiles, relative to the price of wheat, and leads to a shift of resources in Alpha from the textile industry to the wheat industry. This result is, of course, well known from the classical and neoclassical theories of international trade; but, so far as I am aware, its implications for the distribution of income have never been fully discussed. Figure 2 implies that, when the demand for a country's exports is inelastic, the scarce factors of production—those required in comparatively large amounts in the import industries—actually suffer both a relative and an absolute decline in income when tariffs are increased. Although it seems paradoxical, the scarce factors of production and the industries competing with imports, under the conditions of Figure 2, actually achieve economic gains from free trade and suffer losses from protection. In other words, if labor is the scarce factor of production and the standard of living is therefore high, a country is not likely to be able, by means of tariffs, to protect its workers from the competition of "cheap foreign labor" unless the demand for its exports is elastic. Some of the implications of this conclusion for producers of primary products who are attempting to industrialize by means of tariffs are discussed in Section III.

Nothing has been said, as yet, about how the government which imposes import duties disposes of the resultant revenue. In this respect the preceding discussion of Figures 1 and 2 is deficient, for the manner in which the government revenues are spent will obviously influence the reciprocal demand schedule of the country introducing the tariffs. If the customs revenues are used in part to purchase imported goods, for example, the reciprocal demand schedule of Alpha will not fall from A to A' but will lie somewhere between these two curves. In the classical discussion of this question two limiting examples were usually considered: the customs revenues were assumed to be spent either entirely upon the export goods of the taxing country or entirely upon imports.[14] The reader will no doubt have recognized that Figures 1 and 2 belong to the first of these alternatives. No part of the tariff proceeds, in these two illustrations, is spent on imported goods; for, if it were, the reciprocal

---

[14] See, e.g., A. Marshall, *Money, Credit, and Commerce* (London: Macmillan & Co., Ltd., 1929), pp. 344–48.

demand schedule would not fall, as assumed in the figures, by the full amount of the tariff. Moreover, it is easy to see that both diagrams implicitly assume the full proceeds of the tariffs to be spent on goods formerly exported from Alpha. Thus at the new equilibrium point, P', Alpha exports OW' of wheat to T. The equilibrium point, P', however, is stated in world prices, and this equilibrium corresponds to a domestic ratio of exchange in Alpha, including tariffs, of OT' units of textiles for OW''' units of wheat. In other words, at the new domestic price ratio, exporters in Alpha offer OW''' units of wheat, an amount which exceeds the purchases of wheat in Beta by $W'W'''$. The supply of wheat is thus not equal to the demand unless this excess supply is purchased by the government of Alpha. But the excess supply of wheat, $W'W'''$, is simply the amount of duties collected by the government of Alpha, measured in the export product of that country. Figures 1 and 2 are thus implicitly based upon the assumption that the tariff-imposing country uses the entire proceeds of the tariff to purchase goods from its own exporters.

Such an assumption is clearly unrealistic. It would be more reasonable to suppose that the purchasing power acquired through customs duties is divided in some manner between the purchase of domestic goods and the purchase of imports. Before considering this intermediate case, however, it may be useful, following the Marshallian tradition, to go from the one extreme, at which customs revenues are used entirely in the purchase of the tariff-imposing country's export product, to the other extreme, at which the customs revenues are devoted entirely to the purchase of imports. This second extreme case is represented by Figure 3. As in the earlier diagrams, equilibrium is initially at P, with Alpha giving up OW units of wheat in exchange for OT units of textiles. A tariff of 50 per cent is imposed upon textile imports into Alpha, but, unlike the earlier examples, the government collecting the duties is now assumed to spend the entire proceeds upon imported textiles. The additional demand for imports by the government accordingly prevents the demand schedule of Alpha for the products of Beta from falling as far as it otherwise would have fallen. In Figure 3 the new demand schedule, including government demand for imports, is given by the line A'', whereas the private demand alone has fallen, as before, to the line A'.

The relations between the three demand schedules—A, A', and A''—may be illustrated by considering the point P'' on the old schedule, A. This point indicates that, before the tariff was imposed, the traders in Alpha would have been willing to give up OW' units of wheat for OT'' units of textiles. When the new tariff becomes effective, the private traders' demand schedule drops, as before, from A to A'. The vertical distance between A and A' thus indicates the amount of the tariff, measured in wheat, corresponding to any given level of textile imports. In Figure 3, for example, the distance SP'' is 50 per cent of $T''S$. Suppose, for purposes of illustration, that the world rate of exchange between

FIGURE 3

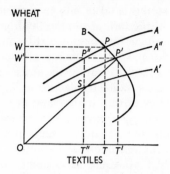

wheat and textiles, exclusive of any tariffs, were given by the slope of
the line OSP' drawn through the origin of Figure 3. Consumers and
traders in Alpha would then purchase OT'' units of textiles, for which
they would pay $T''S$ units of wheat to B and an additional SP'' units of
wheat to their own customs officials. But the government of Alpha is
assumed, in the present example, to spend the entire tariff revenues on
imported commodities, and this means that the amount SP'' must be
exchanged for textiles at the world price ratio. At this given ratio, the
government collecting the duties would accordingly acquire an amount
of textiles equal to $P''P'$ in exchange for customs revenues which, measured in wheat, amount to SP''. The final effect of the tariff on the demand
schedule of Alpha, including the government demand for imports as
well as the private demand, is thus found to be a horizontal shift in
the entire schedule, the relative extent of the shift being exactly equal to
the rate of the tariff. The distance $P''P'$, in Figure 3, for example, is
50 per cent of the distance $W'P'$. The new demand schedule, A'', might
have been derived by more direct methods, but the preceding argument,
I believe, shows more clearly than most others why A'' must lie between
A and A'.[15]

With these preliminary remarks we may now return to the effects
of the tariff on prices at home and abroad. As in the earlier examples,
the tariff improves the terms of trade of the country imposing it, which
means that the price of Alpha's imports, exclusive of the tariff, declines
relative to the price of that country's exports. This is shown in Figure 3
by the fact that Alpha now imports a larger amount of textiles (OT')
in exchange for a smaller amount of wheat (OW'). These terms of trade,
however, are measured in foreign prices, and, as before, it is the domestic price ratio rather than the foreign price ratio which governs
the distribution of income in the taxing country. The domestic price of

---

[15] If the demand of Alpha for the product of Beta is inelastic, A' will actually lie
above the curve A; i.e., under these circumstances a tariff will *increase* the demand of
Alpha for the products of Beta.

textiles in Alpha is higher than the foreign price by exactly the amount of the tariff; and, when this is taken into account, it is clear from Figure 3 that the final effect of the tariff, including both primary and secondary effects, is to raise the domestic price of textiles relative to the price of wheat. In other words, under the conditions assumed in Figure 3, the direct influence of the tariff in raising the price of textiles in Alpha is more important than is its indirect influence in improving that country's terms of trade. As far as private traders and consumers are concerned, the domestic rate of exchange is given, as in the earlier examples, by the point P''. The private traders obtain OT'' units of textiles in exchange for OW' units of wheat. The remaining $T''T'$ units of textiles are, in effect, paid to the government of Alpha as customs duties. Now, since the demand schedule A'' was derived from the schedule A by a horizontal shift, it is apparent from the diagram that the point P'' on the old schedule must lie to the left of the original equilibrium point P. And, as in Figure 1, unless the demand schedule of Alpha has an infinite elasticity, the point P'' represents for that country a higher domestic price of textiles relative to the price of wheat than does the point P.

When the proceeds of a tariff are spent entirely on imports, as in Figure 3, it is evident that the domestic price of imports rises, in the country imposing the tariff, relative to the domestic price of exports, even though the foreign demand for the exported commodity is inelastic. The tariff accordingly leads, as in the earlier example depicted by Figure 1, to a shift of resources from the export industry, wheat, to textiles, the industry competing with imports. Both the real income and the relative share in the national income of the scarce factor, labor, are thereby increased in the manner envisaged by Stolper and Samuelson. In other words, when customs duties are employed entirely in the purchase of imports, no modifications are required in the Stolper-Samuelson conclusion that tariffs benefit the factors of production which are required in relatively large amounts in the industries competing with imports. And this is true regardless of the size of the elasticity of demand for a country's exports. If the foreign demand is extremely inelastic, the improvement in terms of trade will, of course, prevent import prices in the high-tariff country from rising by a large amount and will thereby mitigate to some extent the influence of the tariff on the distribution of income. But in any event the direction, if not the size, of the change in income distribution will be substantially as envisaged in the earlier work on the subject.

We have now illustrated the effects of a tariff with two extreme examples. In the first, the customs duties were assumed to be spent entirely upon the export goods of the taxing country, while in the second the duties were spent entirely in the purchase of imports. It remains only to consider the intermediate and more realistic case in which expenditure of the tariff revenues is divided in some manner between export goods and imports. Before presenting a geometric illustration of this inter-mediate case, however, a few general statements are needed concerning the relations between tax revenues and governmental expenditures.

The fiscal systems of most modern states are so complex that it is vir-tually impossible to associate any particular expenditure with a given type of revenue. What sense does it make, under such conditions, to assert that the proceeds of a tariff are spent in a certain manner on home goods and imports? How can any particular expenditure or group of ex-penditures be identified as a direct consequence of tariff revenues? Some economists have gone so far as to say that the problem is an impossible one and that the circular flow of income through the government accounts can-not be traced in such an exact manner. Although there is considerable sub-stance to this argument, it seems to me that the conclusion to which it leads is nevertheless unduly pessimistic. Even without attempting to find a di-rect link between every individual expenditure and every item of revenue, it may yet be possible to say that expenditures as a whole, including private expenditures as well as public, have been affected in a certain way by an increase or a decrease of tariffs. For most purposes, including the present one, it is probably best to regard government expenditures as fixed and largely independent of the particular type of taxation employed to collect revenues. If the over-all budgetary deficit or surplus is like-wise the result of an independent decision, tariffs can then be envisaged as replacing or supplementing other forms of taxation. In other words, an increase in government revenues from customs duties can be associ-ated directly with a decrease in some other form of taxation or can be considered as making unnecessary an increase in some other form of taxation. When viewed in this way, the problem of tracing the effects of tariffs on the circular flow of income is largely shifted from the gov-ernmental to the private sphere of the economy. The question now is not how the tariff affects *government* expenditures on export and import goods but how the change in taxation affects *private* expenditures. The increase in customs revenues means that other forms of taxation, such as income taxes, for example, can be correspondingly reduced; and the added income thereby made available to the private sector of the economy will normally be spent in a certain way on imports and domestic goods. Suppose, for example, that income-earners, on the average, spend about 20 per cent of their incomes on imported goods, including raw materials and semifinished goods as well as finished goods. A reduction of income taxes, made possible by increased customs duties, will then lead to an increase in expenditures on imports equal to roughly two-tenths of the customs duties. Although there is no immediate connection between the customs revenues themselves and the added expenditures on imports, we can nevertheless say that the latter were indirectly the result of the former. More generally, if the marginal propensity to import of the private sector of the economy is k, we can carry out our examination of the effects of the tariff *as though* a fraction k of all customs revenue was actually spent on imported goods; the remaining part of the remitted taxes, or a fraction $1 - k$ of customs duties, can then be regarded as spent, directly or indirectly, on the purchase of export goods.[16] The size of k will, of course, vary with the nature of the taxation system, but this is a refinement which cannot be discussed here.

With these ideas in mind, consider, now, the situation in Figure 4. As in the earlier diagrams, foreign trade is initially in equilibrium at the

FIGURE 4

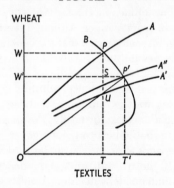

point P, with Alpha exporting OW units of wheat and importing OT units of textiles; and once again this equilibrium is disturbed by a 50 per cent tariff on textile imports. Unlike the previous illustration, however, the proceeds of the tariff are now assumed to be divided in the proportions k and $1 - k$ between the purchase of imports and exports, respectively. It makes no fundamental difference in the geometric argument whether these proportions are determined directly by government purchases or indirectly through the reduction of other taxes.[17] Figure 4 has been drawn with such values for k, the marginal propensity of Alpha to import, and η, the price elasticity of demand for Alpha's exports that the favorable movement in that country's terms of trade exactly offsets

---

[16] The argument at this point is distinctly classical in that added income is assumed to be entirely spent, directly or indirectly, in the purchase either of home goods or of imports. There is, of course, no logical reason why a propensity to save could not be introduced along with the two propensities to spend; but this would raise a number of vexatious questions concerning the effects of tariffs upon employment which could not possibly be given adequate treatment within the limits of the present study.

[17] This statement is an approximation which is strictly accurate only when the size of the tariff is small. If the tariff is substantial, the shift in demand will not be the same when the government spends the customs revenues as when they are spent by private traders. The difference is attributable to the fact that private traders pay duties on their added purchases from abroad, whereas the government does not. But this is a matter of detail which does not affect the substance of the argument, and it may accordingly be left over to a later paper.

the direct effect of the tariff itself, leaving the domestic price ratio of the two commodities unchanged. But, before discussing the relation between the marginal propensity to import and the price elasticity which is necessary to bring about this result, a word should be said about the three reciprocal demand schedules A, A' and A''. The line A', as in Figure 3, represents the private demand for imports after the tariff is imposed, without making any allowance for the expenditure, direct or indirect, of the customs revenues. Thus the distance UP is 50 per cent of TU, etc. Now consider a world rate of exchange of the two commodities, exclusive of the tariff, represented by the slope of the diagonal OP'. Neglecting the effects of spending the duties, private traders and consumers in Alpha, at this rate of exchange, would import OT of textiles and would export TU of wheat. The tariff received by the government, expressed in the exports of the taxing country, would then be UP. This amount would be returned to the residents of Alpha in the form of reduced taxes, and part of the income so received would be used to augment the demand for imports. In the diagram the assumption is made that a proportion equal to US/UP of this added income is spent on imports; in other words, $k = US/UP$. At the given foreign price ratio, importers in Alpha would thus obtain an additional amount of textiles equal to SP', or TT', which means that expenditure of the tariff revenues would have the effect of shifting the point U on the line A' over to the point P' on line A''.[18] A similar construction could be developed for any other point on A'.

After the tariff becomes effective, the new demand schedule of Alpha facing the exporters of Beta, including indirect as well as direct effects on the tariff, is, of course, the line A''. The demand schedule of Beta for the products of Alpha has not been altered, and the point of equilibrium between the two countries, in terms of quantities actually imported and exported, accordingly shifts from P to P' in Figure 4. Where Alpha formerly exported OW units of wheat and imported OT of textiles, she now exports a smaller quantity of wheat (OW') in exchange for a larger quantity of textiles (OT'). The gain to the taxing country, regarded as a unit, is obvious; the foreign price of textiles has fallen, relative to the foreign price of wheat, and this favorable movement in Alpha's terms of trade is so great that the country obtains more textiles than before in exchange for a smaller amount of wheat. And yet, if we look at the domestic price ratio in Alpha, including the tariff, we find that this ratio is exactly the same as before the tariff became effective. To put the matter another way, the direct effect of the customs duty in raising the price of textiles in Alpha, relative to the price of wheat, is exactly offset by its indirect effect through the change of world prices. The new foreign price ratio—i.e., the ratio exclusive of the tariff—is shown in Figure

---

[18] This statement again ignores the fact that the private traders pay duties on their added imports as well as on their original imports. If the tariff is small, however, these "duties on duties" will be insignificant compared with the duties on total imports.

4 by the line OP'. The domestic price ratio in Alpha, which differs from the foreign ratio only by the tariff, will therefore be given by the slope of a line through the origin (not shown in the diagram) whose vertical distance from the OT axis is 50 per cent above the vertical distance of a corresponding point on OP'. Since OP' cuts the schedule, A', at U, a point which is directly below P, and since the original schedule A is 50 per cent above A', it follows that the new domestic price ratio in Alpha is represented by the original equilibrium point, P. In other words, the relative prices actually paid and received by consumers and producers of the two goods in Alpha are unaltered by the tariff.

Under these circumstances it may, at first, seem paradoxical that the country imposing the tariff should alter the physical quantity of its exports and imports at all. Relative domestic prices remaining unchanged, producers of both textiles and wheat in Alpha presumably continue to produce the same quantities of the two commodities as before. No shift in resources between the two industries takes place, and the distribution of income earned in production is therefore the same as before the tariff was imposed. How does it happen, then, that Alpha exports a smaller amount of wheat than in the original equilibrium and imports a larger amount of textiles? The answer to this question is to be found in the effects of the customs duties upon the circular flow of income. Since the revenues received from the tariff enable the government of Alpha to reduce other taxes without disturbing its expenditures upon goods and services, income available to the factors of production increases, even though total output remains unchanged. And, according to our original assumption, a fraction k of this increased income is devoted to imports, while $1 - k$ is spent on goods produced by the export trades. Thus both the rise in imports (TT') and the fall in exports ($W'W$) are indirect consequences of added purchases in Alpha from the proceeds of the customs duties themselves. Indirectly, the customs proceeds are used both to purchase goods which would otherwise have been available for export and to increase the volume of imports. Here is perhaps the clearest case imaginable in which, to use a familiar expression from innumerable tariff controversies, "the foreigner pays the tax."

In Figure 4 the reciprocal demand schedules of both countries and the marginal propensity of Alpha to import have been drawn in such a way that a tariff on imports leaves all domestic price ratios in the taxing country unaltered. We must now see whether this result can be generalized. In other words, instead of considering a given tariff rate of 50 per cent, we shall consider a general rate, τ, and, instead of assuming a particular set of reciprocal demand schedules and a given marginal propensity to import, we shall assume a general set of demand schedules and a general propensity to import. We may then inquire what relations must exist between all these functions in order that a tariff shall leave the taxing country's domestic price ratios unchanged. It turns out that the answer to this question depends upon only two functions, the price elasticity of demand for imports abroad, i.e., the price elasticity in Beta, and the marginal propensity of the taxing country, Alpha, to import. The symbol, η, will be used to indicate the elasticity of demand for imports in Beta, while k, as before, will be used to indicate the marginal propensity of Alpha to import. The precise relation between η and k which is required to bring about the situation depicted in Figure 4 was first derived more than a decade ago by Lerner; but, since Lerner's work was presented in a somewhat different context, it seems desirable to give a slightly modified version here.[19]

If relative prices in the taxing country are unaffected by the tariff, this means, as noted before, that the primary influence of the duty in raising the domestic price of imports in Alpha is exactly offset by its secondary influence upon world prices or upon the terms of trade. Suppose that this is actually true. In other words, suppose that the decline in the world price of textiles, relative to the world price of wheat, is just sufficient to offset the tariff in Alpha. We now wish to know what conditions of demand and supply must prevail in order that this new world price ratio shall be an equilibrium ratio. In view of the fact that the reciprocal demand schedules represent both a demand for one commodity and a supply of another, it will be sufficient to consider either the supply and demand for textiles or the supply and demand for wheat. Equilibrium in the one market implies equilibrium in the other, and it is therefore unnecessary to consider both. As a practical matter it is perhaps easiest to consider the supply and demand for textiles.

Since the domestic price ratio in Alpha remains unchanged, that country's demand for textile imports is influenced only by the expenditure of the tariff proceeds. With a tariff rate of τ, customs duties as a percentage of the value of private imports will likewise be τ. By assumption, a proportion, k, of these duties is spent on imports. The relative increase in the demand for imports in Alpha will therefore be $k\tau$. The question now is whether and under what circumstances this increased demand in Alpha will be matched by an equivalent increase in supply from Beta. The demand in Beta for the exports of Alpha is assumed to be inelastic; and, when the world price of textiles declines, as it does when the tariff is imposed, Beta therefore offers an increased amount of textiles in exchange for a reduced quantity of wheat. Using the notation of Figure 4, the relative increase in the supply of textile exports from Beta is TT'/OT. This, in turn, is approximately equal to $-\beta(W'W/OW)$, where β is the elasticity of the reciprocal demand schedule, B. But $W'W/OW$ represents the additional wheat consumption in Alpha, relative to the previous level of exports, and this additional expenditure arises entirely from the proceeds of the tariff. An amount $k\tau$ was spent

[19] Lerner, *op. cit.*, pp. 310–11.

on imports, and the remainder, or $(1-k)\tau$, is accordingly spent on wheat formerly exported. The quantity $W'W/OW$ is thus equal to $(1-k)\tau$, and the additional supply of textile exports from Beta may be expressed thus: $-\beta(1-k)\tau$. If this additional supply is to equal the additional demand, we must have[20]

$$k\tau = -(1-k)\,\tau\beta, \tag{1}$$

or, dividing both sides by τ,

$$k = -(1-k)\beta. \tag{2}$$

This is one way of expressing the condition that must be met if a tariff is to leave the taxing country's internal prices unaltered. The term β, however, represents the elasticity of the reciprocal demand schedule B, and it is frequently more useful to express the results, as Lerner has done, in terms of the elasticity of the ordinary money demand schedule. If η represents this latter elasticity, it is well known that, subject to certain supply limitations, $\beta = 1 - 1/\eta$.[21] Substituting this value of β in equation (2), we have

$$k = -(1-k)\left(1 - \frac{1}{\eta}\right), \tag{3}$$

and, after simplifying, this becomes

$$\eta = 1 - k. \tag{4}$$

In words, this says that, if a tariff is to leave domestic price ratios and the distribution of income within the taxing country unaltered, the foreign elasticity of demand for that country's exports must be equal to the difference between unity and the marginal propensity to import of the country imposing the tariff. If a country has a marginal propensity to import of 0.25, for example, a tariff imposed by that country will not leave domestic price ratios unchanged unless the foreign elasticity of demand for its exports is 0.75. If the foreign elasticity is smaller than this, the tariff will cause the domestic prices of imports to fall relative to the domestic prices of exports. On the other hand, if the foreign elasticity is larger than 0.75, the tariff will increase domestic import prices relative to export prices.

The practical consequences of these results will be discussed in Section III; but before proceeding further it seems desirable to summarize the

---

[20] The expression $(1-k)\tau\beta$ is positive because, with an inelastic demand for imports in Beta, β is negative.

[21] Let t equal the quantity of textiles that Beta is willing to export, and let w represent that country's demand for imported wheat. The elasticity, β, of the reciprocal demand schedule is then $dt/dw \cdot w/t$. But the quantity t, from one point of view, is simply the total outlay of Beta for imports, w. In money terms, in other words, $t = pw$, where p is the import price of wheat. β may therefore be written $\beta = d(pw)/dw \cdot w/pw$. Upon simplifying and carrying out the indicated differentiation, this becomes $\beta = 1 + dp/dw\,(w/p) = 1 - 1/\eta$, the elasticity, η, being defined now in the Marshallian sense.

main argument of the present section. The conclusions are intimately related to the proposition developed by Stolper and Samuelson that any event, other than a change in technology, which leads to a shift in resources from one industry to another will increase both the real income and the relative share in total income of the factor required in relatively large amounts in the expanding industry. A corollary of this, of course, is the proposition that the factor of production required in relatively large amounts in the contracting industry will find both its real return and its relative share of the total income reduced. The problem of how a tariff influences the distribution of income is, therefore, largely resolved into a discussion of the effects of the tariff in shifting resources from one industry to another. The shift in resources, in turn, depends upon how the tariff affects domestic prices; for it may be taken for granted that, if resources shift at all, they will move into industries the products of which have enjoyed relative price increases. The present section has therefore been devoted largely to a discussion of the influence of customs duties on domestic prices of both exports and imports.

We have found that a tariff has two effects, which influence relative domestic prices in opposite directions. On the one hand, the tariff itself represents a direct increase in import prices, and, on the other hand, the resulting reduction in the demand for imports depresses the foreign prices of these goods relative to corresponding prices for export goods. The net effect upon relative prices at home thus depends upon which of these forces is the stronger. By following a technique originally expounded by Lerner, we have shown that a tariff will not increase the relative domestic price of imports unless η, the foreign elasticity of demand for the country's exports, is greater than $1 - k$, where k is the marginal propensity to import.

Although the final conclusions with respect to prices have been presented in four diagrams, the first three are really special cases of the fourth. In Figures 1 and 2, the proceeds of the tariff were assumed to be spent entirely on export goods, and the marginal propensity to import was thus implicitly set at zero. Since the expression $1 - k$ then had a value of unity, it was found that the tariff would not increase the relative domestic price of imports unless the foreign elasticity of demand for the country's exports was greater than unity. In Figure 3, on the other hand, the proceeds of the tariff were assumed to be spent entirely upon imports, and this was equivalent to assuming a marginal propensity to import of unity. The value of $1 - k$ for the special case represented by Figure 3 was thus zero; and we found that a tariff always increased the relative domestic price of imports, no matter how small the foreign elasticity of demand for the country's exports. Now, since $1 - k$ is in all circumstances less than unity, it is clear that, if the foreign demand for a country's exports is elastic with respect to prices, a tariff will always increase domestic import prices relative to export prices. In all such cases the shift of resources will be toward industries competing with imports and away from the export industries. The factors of production used in relatively large amounts in the protected industries will consequently gain, both absolutely and relatively, while the factors used in large amounts in the export trades will lose. All this is completely in accord with the Heckscher-Ohlin conclusions as well as with the work of Stopler and Samuelson. It is only when the foreign demand for a country's exports is inelastic that the earlier works on the subject require modification. When the foreign demand is sufficiently inelastic, a tariff, far from protecting industries competing with imports at the expense of the export trades, may actually benefit the latter at the expense of the former. If this happens, resources tend to be shifted from the "protected" industries to the export industries, and the factors of production which are used in relatively large amounts in the export industries enjoy both a relative and an absolute increase in real income.

III

The aspect of tariff theory which the preceding discussion outlines most sharply is the potential or actual conflict of interests that may arise between a country's relatively scarce factors of production and the remainder of the economy. The classical dictum that real wages and the returns to other factors of production depend upon productivity remains true in a general way, of course; but the preceding argument shows that this dictum cannot be applied to the particular problem of tariffs without numerous reservations and exceptions. It cannot be asserted, for instance, that tariffs necessarily reduce productivity and thereby lower the real incomes of all factors of production. In the first place—and this is an argument of which the classical economists were fully aware— tariffs, under favorable circumstances, may improve a country's terms of trade so much that real income for the country as a whole is thereby increased. But this is a familiar argument to which the present paper has made no particular contribution. The point to be emphasized is a second reservation, namely, that the returns to each of the factors of production do not necessarily move in the same direction as general productivity or real income of the economy as a whole. In other words, regardless of whether a high-tariff policy increases or diminishes real income for a country as a whole, such a policy is likely to affect some factors of production favorably and others adversely. This point of view, in fact, might be stated even more strongly: the real income of a country's scarce factors of production is not likely to be increased by a tariff unless world demand is such that the tariff clearly diminishes the country's total income; and, conversely, the scarce factors are not likely to be injured by a tariff unless the tariff benefits the rest of the economy.

To clarify these propositions, consider a country having a comparative scarcity of labor and importing commodities with a high labor content. Stolper and Samuelson have shown that, *if the terms of trade are not affected,* a tariff in such a country will probably increase both the real wage rate and the proportion of the national income accruing to the working class. Now, if the terms of trade remain unchanged, this means that the tariff, while disrupting the allocation of resources and thereby tending to reduce real income for the country as a whole, has not succeeded in bringing to the economy the benefits of a more favorable bargaining position in world markets. In other words, when the terms of trade remain unaltered, a tariff causes an unambiguous reduction in a country's real income as a whole. But this is precisely the condition, according to the Stolper-Samuelson argument, when a tariff increases the absolute and relative return to labor, the country's scarce factor of production. If I may return to an earlier metaphor, the scarce factor of production receives a larger piece of a smaller pie. But what if the size of the pie is increased by the tariff? How does labor fare under these circumstances? An increase in real income for the economy as a whole is, of course, possible, provided that the tariff causes a sufficient improvement in the terms of trade to offset its interference with the allocation of resources. A substantial improvement in the terms of trade could take place, however, only if the foreign demand for the country's exports was inelastic; and in this event, as we have seen, there is a strong probability that the tariff, far from protecting the industries competing with imports, would actually injure these industries and lead to a transfer of resources from them to the export industries. This shift in resources would reduce the degree of scarcity of labor and thereby lead to a reduction in both its relative and its absolute return.

The conflict of interests which the preceding summary emphasizes is in sharp contrast to the doctrine of a harmony of interests which occupied such a prominent place in the work of many nineteenth-century liberal economists. The preceding argument has shown that, with respect to problems of commercial policy, the economic interests of such broad groups as manual workers, landlords, and capitalists are not likely to coincide. A policy of reducing tariffs may therefore be the source of widespread political cleavages, quite apart from the pressure which is inevitably exerted by the industries immediately affected. This, of course, is no argument against reducing trade barriers. Rather, it is simply an indication that the political conflicts inherent in tariff reduction may have a much broader base than would be supposed from concentrating one's attention upon the protected industries alone.

The fact that the influence of tariffs on the distribution of income can be a matter of considerable economic and political significance is demonstrated, I believe, by a well-known report on the tariff in Australia, which was published in 1929.[22] This report, prepared by a committee of Australian economists at the request of the Australian prime minister, pre-

---

[22] *The Australian Tariff: An Economic Enquiry* (Melbourne, Australia, 1929).

sented both the terms-of-trade argument and the distribution-of-income argument in favor of the Australian tariffs. The Australian economy is characterized by an abundant supply of land, relative to the supply of labor and capital; and Australia, therefore, has a comparative advantage in agriculture, particularly in wheat and wool. The committee argued that if tariffs were reduced, Australian manufacturing would be retarded and resources would be diverted from manufacturing to agriculture. But, since the world demand for agricultural products, especially the demand for wheat, is decidedly inelastic, it was felt that an increase in Australian wheat exports would lead to a substantial reduction in world wheat prices. In short, the eventual effect of the tariff reduction would be a considerable deterioration in the Australian terms of trade.[23] Much more important than the deterioration in terms of trade, however, was the effect which the committee expected a tariff reduction to have upon the distribution of income. In general, the labor component of most manufactured products is considerably greater than the labor component of agriculture. A shift of resources from manufacturing to agriculture would therefore lessen the relative scarcity of labor, thus reducing real wages and increasing rents. It was this adverse effect upon the distribution of income which the committee of Australian economists regarded as the principal deterrent to a general tariff reduction.[24]

What can be said about the Australian point of view in the light of the discussion in Section II? In the abstract a good case can be made both for the terms-of-trade argument and for the distribution-of-income argument in favor of tariffs. *But this is true only when each argument is considered separately.* When the two are presented together, the validity of one of the two arguments becomes doubtful. It may well be true that the world demand for Australian wheat is inelastic, as the committee implies, and that a tariff reduction might therefore lead to serious deterioration of Australia's terms of trade. But if this is actually the case, then it is unlikely, as we have seen in Section II, that a tariff reduction would lead to a shift of resources from manufacturing to agriculture. When the Australian economy finally became adjusted to the tariff reduction, domestic prices of manufactured goods might actually be higher relative to agricultural prices than before the tariff was reduced. And, if this should happen, the reduction of tariffs would be the cause of a shift of resources *into* the protected industries, with a concomitant increase in the proportion of the national income accruing to workers. Paradoxical as it seems, the Australian manufacturing industries might be better "protected" and receive more encouragement under free trade than under a system of protective tariffs.[25]

---

[23] *Ibid.*, p. 80.

[24] *Ibid.*, Part VII.

[25] This statement, as well as subsequent remarks concerning the foreign trade of the Latin-American countries and the United States, requires one modification. The theoretical treatment in Sec. II was based upon the assumption that the protective

This idea is not new. Quite the contrary, it is implicit in much of the nineteenth-century work on the theory of reciprocal demand. Nevertheless, it is an idea which would no doubt be received with great incredulity, not to say outright disbelief, by the average Australian businessman. How, he might ask, could he possibly benefit from a reduction of the tariff on his own manufactures? To some extent his disbelief is probably a result of an instinctive and well-founded distrust of what the economist calls the "process of adjustment"; for, if Australia should attempt, after a substantial unilateral reduction of tariffs, to maintain her exchange at the old rates relative to other currencies, a new equilibrium in her balance of payment could be achieved only by a reduction in real income or by a general deflation of prices and costs. The businessman is rightfully suspicious of both of these "processes of adjustment." If Australia were willing to alter the foreign value of her currency, on the other hand, the adjustment to the new situation might be achieved in a less painful manner. Even in this event, however, it seems doubtful whether producers in the protected industries would concede that a reduction in tariffs would benefit them; for most of them would probably be unwilling to carry through the argument to its logical conclusion. Of course, if a typical producer were asked whether he would prefer a 50 per cent tariff with the pound sterling selling for 1.25 Australian pounds or no tariff with the pound sterling selling for 2.50 Australian pounds, he would probably immediately see the advantage to himself of the latter arrangement. And, if the demand for Australia's exports is really inelastic, this is precisely the sort of choice with which the producer is confronted; for, as we have seen, when the foreign demand is inelastic, there is a strong probability that the indirect effects of the tariff on the terms of trade will more than offset the direct effects on domestic prices. Nevertheless, if tariffs were actually reduced in Australia and if the Australian pound began to depreciate as a consequence, it seems highly probable that many businessmen would complain of their losses from the tariff reduction without associating the tariff in any direct way with their gains from the depreciation of their currency.

This tendency to look only at immediate effects and to ignore secondary consequences is well illustrated by Australia's tariff experience after the first World War, recounted by A. H. Tocker in the *Economic Journal.*[26]

---

duty was a general duty applicable to all or virtually all types of import. If this is not true, the final results will obviously differ somewhat from those presented in Sec. II. It is intuitively evident, for example, that a tariff on a particular commodity constituting a small part of total imports will increase the domestic price of that commodity relative to the prices of exports, even though the foreign demand for the country's exports is quite inelastic; for in this case the adjustment of the terms of trade will occur largely through price changes among the duty-free imports. Whether the presence of nontaxed imports requires a substantial revision of the conclusions of Sec. II depends upon the ratio of duty-free imports to total imports. But this is a question which I shall discuss in a later paper.

[26] "The Monetary Standards of New Zealand and Australia," *Economic Journal,* Vol. XXXIV (1924), pp. 556–75.

Under the pressure of a balance-of-payments deficit, Australian tariffs were substantially increased in 1921. The higher customs duties, together with Australian borrowing in London and a generally improved world economic situation, brought about a marked improvement in the balance of payments; and the Australian banks began to accumulate sterling balances in London. At that time Australia was on a sort of informal sterling-exchange standard, but with no legal commitment to maintain a fixed rate of exchange between the Australian pound and the pound sterling. The accumulation of sterling balances by the Australian banks in 1922 finally induced the banks to sell these balances at a discount, whereas in 1921 a slight premium on pounds sterling had prevailed. The decline in the Australian price of sterling was clearly a result, to some extent at least, of the higher tariffs; but, despite this obvious connection, there were complaints, according to Tocker, that the banks were deliberately pursuing an independent foreign-exchange policy that was detrimental to Australian business interests. "The Australian," said Tocker, "who recently complained that the banks were using their big balances in London to nullify the effects of the tariff, and to attack the protected Australian industries, voiced an economic truth more profound than he knew, and one quite beyond the power of bankers to control."[27]

Although it was a comparatively small incident, the Australian experience illustrates a rather widespread tendency on the part of businessmen to take account only of the immediate or direct effects of tariffs and to ignore their secondary or indirect repercussions upon exchange rates and relative costs. This attitude largely explains, in my opinion, why protective tariffs frequently are strongly supported by the industries directly affected, even though it is widely recognized, at the same time, that the demand for a country's exports is quite unresponsive to changes in price. With their constant and unremitting attention required in the solution of immediate and pressing problems of production and sales, few businessmen have either the time or the inclination to trace the final consequences of tariffs through all their various ramifications; and the price that is paid for this "direct" approach is an exaggerated idea of the effectiveness of tariffs in protecting home industries.

The tendency to exaggerate the effectiveness of tariffs in raising or maintaining the incomes of a country's scarce factors of production is by no means limited to Australia. Quite the contrary, it is a tendency which is perhaps even more pronounced in other countries, particularly

---

[27] *Ibid.*, p. 571. In citing these Australian experiences, I have no intention of casting a reflection upon the intelligence of any particular group. The so-called "direct" approach to international economics and the neglect of secondary repercussions are perhaps even more common in the United States. A typical example is the belief that in normal times export surpluses are desirable, while foreign loans are undesirable. This point of view is encountered with regrettable frequency in the halls of Congress as well as among Americans of other walks of life.

in Latin America. Like Australia, the Latin-American countries have a comparative advantage in the production of foodstuffs and raw materials. Their leading exports include such products of agriculture and the extractive industries as coffee, crude petroleum, copper, sugar, cotton, nitrates, wheat, and meat.[28] Most of these exports are commodities for which the world demand is decidedly inelastic; and, since the Latin-American countries in many instances provide a substantial proportion of the world's supply of such goods, it seems likely that the external demand for their exports as a whole may be quite inelastic even over considerable periods of time. The Latin-American foreign trade, which consists largely of exporting primary products, for which the world demand is inelastic, in exchange for manufactured goods, thus has marked similarities to the Australian foreign trade. And, like the Australians, the Latin-Americans are dissatisfied with the distribution of national income which this type of trade engenders. Indeed, the problem of income distribution is probably a much more pressing one in many parts of Latin America than it is in Australia, for the Latin-American people as a whole have not benefited, as have the Australians, from the scarcity of labor in relation to natural resources. In other words, the Latin-American problem is not simply a problem of maintaining the standard of living in the face of a growing population but rather a problem of raising the standard of living as a whole.

Although Latin America's comparative advantage up to the present time has clearly been in the agricultural and extractive industries, the region as a whole has nevertheless had many areas of subsistence farming; in which the productivity of workers was extremely low; and one of the important economic purposes of the present move toward industrial development is to provide alternative and more useful employment for these low-productivity workers. Whether the current programs of industrialization will attain the various economic, political, and social goals which have been set for them is a question which cannot be discussed here. My purpose in mentioning the Latin-American programs is simply to indicate their relation to the tariff problems analyzed in this paper. To a very considerable extent the governments of South and Central America have sought to encourage domestic manufacturing by means of tariffs upon the importation of competing products; and, in view of what has been said above, it seems probable that this particular part of the program may contain a basic inconsistency.[29] If the demand for Latin America's exports as a whole is actually inelastic—and

---

[28] For an excellent summary of the pattern of Latin-American trade see R. F. Behrendt, *Inter-American Economic Relations* (New York: Committee on International Policy, 1948), pp. 1–33.

[29] The extent to which the Latin-American programs of industrial development depend upon tariff protection is indicated by a survey made by the United Nations (see United Nations, Department of Economic Affairs, *Economic Development in Selected Countries* [Lake Success, 1947], pp. 1–150).

there is little reason to doubt this—the preceding discussion suggests strongly that tariffs may accomplish little either in protecting Latin-American manufacturing or in increasing the share of the workers in national income.

This does not mean, of course, that the tariffs entail no economic benefits to the countries imposing them, but the benefits may be quite different from those originally contemplated. With the low price elasticity of demand for their products, the countries of Latin America are in a particularly good position to employ tariffs as a means of achieving more favorable terms of trade. A favorable movement in the Latin-American terms of trade, however, means an increase in the prices received for exports relative to the prices paid for imports; and, to the extent that such a shift occurs, part or all of the protection intended for domestic manufacturing is wiped out. In other words, since tariffs do not alter the basic techniques of production, any benefits which they confer upon one industry or one segment of the population are likely to be at the expense of another industry or another segment of the population. The Latin-American tariffs cannot, at the same time, benefit industry at the expense of agriculture and benefit agriculture at the expense of industry; and, although these tariffs are imposed upon manufactured goods, it is possible that, in the end, world conditions of demand may be such that the tariffs actually injure the industries which they are intended to protect. In the language of the foregoing discussion, the favorable movement in the terms of trade may more than offset the initial effects of the tariff in raising domestic prices of manufactured goods. And, even if the conditions of demand are not so extreme, it remains true, in any event, that the degree of protection afforded by Latin-American tariffs is much smaller than appears at first glance to be the case.

It should perhaps be emphasized that these remarks are by no means intended to imply that industrialization is a bad policy for Latin America. This broader problem, involving as it does sociological and political as well as extremely complex economic questions, is entirely beyond the scope of the present paper. My purpose here is simply to indicate one of the limitations to a policy of industrialization by means of protective tariffs.

The foregoing remarks concerning the influence of tariffs on the industrial development of agricultural countries bear a close resemblance to a proposition stated more than a century ago by Friedrich List. Although List thought that protective duties on manufactures are a useful means of promoting industrial growth, it was by no means his view that such duties are appropriate under all circumstances and at all stages of economic development. He divided the economic growth of a country into four periods, and it was in only two of these periods that he regarded protective duties as beneficial to manufactures. "In the first period, agriculture is encouraged by the importation of manufactured articles; in the second, manufactures begin to increase at home, whilst the importation of foreign manufactures to some extent continues; in the third, home manufactures mainly supply domestic consumption and the internal markets; finally, in the fourth, we see the exportation upon a large scale of manufactured products, and the importation of raw materials and agricultural products."[30] It was in the second and third of these periods that List thought protective duties would be effective in raising the level of industrial activity. With regard to countries in the first and fourth stages of development, free trade was preferred to protection. In other words, free trade was thought to be better than protection both for an undeveloped country specializing in agriculture and raw materials, and for a highly developed industrial nation. For the latter, tariffs on manufactures were considered unnecessary, since the industrial country had already achieved a strong competitive position in the world's markets for manufactured goods.[31] For the former, i.e., for the completely undeveloped country, List thought that tariffs were likely to defeat their purpose.[32] It is in this respect that his conclusions are similar to those given in the present paper, for it has been argued above that, in countries whose exports consist largely of primary products, tariffs will probably afford little, if any, encouragement to manufacturing.

The comparison must not be carried too far. Although List concluded, as I have above, that a policy of protection is a questionable method of increasing manufacturing output in an undeveloped country, his reasons for holding this view were not exactly the same as my own. According to List, a prosperous and powerful industrial nation must possess a well-developed commercial system in addition to its factories. And in the early stages of economic development List believed that free trade rather than protection would promote this prerequisite to industrialization. Commercial enterprises would be encouraged because free trade would increase the volume of commercial transactions. In this manner an undeveloped country, according to List, would achieve a certain degree of economic and cultural sophistication more quickly under free trade than under protection. But, once this position was reached and the country was ready to begin the development of manufacturing, List believed that further economic progress would be promoted by protective tariffs.[33]

It is somewhat ironical that, by employing the classical method of comparative statics, I have reached a conclusion which, in one respect

---

[30] Friedrich List, *National System of Political Economy*, trans. G. A. Matile (Philadelphia, 1846).

[31] *Ibid.*, chap. iv.

[32] "The economical education of a country of inferior intelligence and culture, of one thinly populated, relatively to the extent and fertility of its territory, is effected most certainly by free trade, with more advanced, richer, and more industrious nations. Every commercial restriction in such a country aiming at the increase of manufacturers, is premature, and will prove detrimental, not only to civilization in general, but the progress of the nation in particular . . ." (*ibid.*, pp. 78–79).

[33] *Ibid.*, pp. 181–82.

at least, is in agreement with one of the most anticlassical economists of
the nineteenth century. List's approach to the problem was highly dependent upon a dynamic theory of economic development and involved,
in addition, a liberal admixture of political considerations. My own
approach, by contrast, has been static in character and limited exclusively
to economic arguments. But both the dynamic and the static approaches
have led, in one respect, to the same conclusion. It is a moot question
whether List, in advocating free trade for backward countries, could
have had in mind some of the arguments advanced in the present paper
concerning the elasticity of demand for raw materials and agricultural
commodities. In view of his aversion to classical economics, however,
such a possibility seems rather remote.

The arguments in favor of free trade for undeveloped countries,
whether stated in List's terms or in the terms of the present paper, might
be called "infant-country" arguments for free trade, just as the arguments for protection of undeveloped industries have generally been
called "infant-industry" arguments for protection. And just as the latter,
in practical application, frequently raise difficult questions concerning
exactly what constitutes an infant industry, so the former also raise questions as to what constitutes an infant country. In discussing the tariff
history of the United States, for example, List assumed that by the early
decades of the nineteenth century the United States had passed beyond
the primitive and undeveloped stage in which free trade would have
been beneficial. He believed, in other words, that tariffs were helpful
in promoting manufacturing in the United States throughout the early
part of the nineteenth century.[34] In order to substantiate or refute this
assertion from List's point of view, it would be necessary to make a detailed factual study of the state of American agriculture and commerce at
the time. But if the question is approached from the point of view of the
present paper, there is at least one circumstance which suggests that the
actual degree of protection to American manufacturing may have been
considerably less than intended and considerably less important in American economic development than List supposed. Throughout the first
half of the nineteenth century the United States was in a position, as
far as foreign trade was concerned, quite like the position of Australia
and the Latin-American countries today. She was predominantly an exporter of raw materials and agricultural products and an importer of
manufactured goods. Thus, in the period from 1820 until the outbreak
of the Civil War, American exports of raw materials and unprocessed
foodstuffs accounted for more than two-thirds of the total value of exports.[35] Moreover—and this is perhaps even more important—approxi-

[34] *Ibid.*, chap. ix.

[35] These and subsequent figures on United States foreign trade have been computed from data in United States Department of Commerce, *Statistical Abstract of the
United States.*

mately three-fourths of these exports of primary products consisted of raw cotton, of which the United States at the time was by far the most important source of world supply. In view of the dominant position of the United States in the world cotton market and in view, further, of the dominance of cotton and other primary products in American exports as a whole, there is a strong probability that the demand for American exports during the first half of the nineteenth century was inelastic with respect to price. If this conjecture is correct, it follows from the analysis above that, considering both the primary and the secondary effects of the tariffs on domestic prices, the policy of protection to manufactures must have had a relatively small effect upon the rate of industrial growth in the period before the Civil War. Indeed, the net effect of protection during this priod may even have been slightly adverse to manufacturing as a whole.[36]

The conjecture that early American tariff policy probably exerted a comparatively minor influence upon the growth of domestic manufactures is in substantial agreement with the well-known conclusion which Taussig reached by a somewhat different method. After a detailed study of a number of protected industries, including the textile and iron and steel industries, Taussig concluded that their rate of expansion had not been substantially affected by the ebb and flow of protective measures. Thus, in discussing the period before 1860, he said in his *Tariff History of the United States:*

. . . In the main, the changes in duties have had much less effect upon the protected industries than is generally supposed. Their growth has been steady and continuous, and seems to have been little stimulated by the high duties of 1842, and little checked by the more moderate duties of 1846 and 1857.[37]

In his *International Trade,* published thirty years later, Taussig recognized the special nature of United States exports during the first half of the nineteenth century—i.e., the high proportion of raw materials and agricultural products for which the world's demand was comparatively rigid—but there is no evidence that this feature of American trade had anything to do with his original conclusion concerning the effects of protective duties.[38] His views regarding the early tariffs were largely derived from empirical observation, and, when he later studied the history of protected industries during the years 1860–1930, he modified his earlier opinions somewhat.[39] In particular, he cautiously advanced the

[36] This statement, like others in the present section, must be interpreted in a long-run sense. There is no intention to deny that during the period of adjustment a tariff on a particular product may afford the protected industry a substantial measure of protection.

[37] F. W. Taussig, *The Tariff History of the United States* (4th ed.; New York, 1898), p. 152.

[38] F. W. Taussig, *International Trade* (New York, 1928), p. 148.

[39] See F. W. Taussig, *Some Aspects of the Tariff Question* (3d enl. ed.; Cambridge, Mass., 1931), *passim.*

view that the protective system may have contributed to the development of American manufactures.

At first glance, this later conclusion of Taussig's seems to contradict the argument of the present paper that exporters of raw materials and other primary products are not likely to find a general tariff system, short of completely prohibitive duties, an effective means of promoting industrial development. A further examination of the statistics of United States exports, however, resolves at least a part of this apparent conflict. Although foodstuffs and raw materials, particularly raw cotton, continued throughout the nineteenth century to be important United States exports, these products, with the passing of the years, nevertheless became considerably less significant, relative to total exports. At the close of the nineteenth century, for example, exports of primary products accounted for less than half of total exports, compared with a proportion of two-thirds in 1830. The decline in the relative importance of primary exports was, of course, accompanied by a corresponding increase in the importance of manufactured exports. Thus, during the second half of the nineteenth century, American exports were not dominated by primary products to the extent that had been true earlier. Increasingly the United States was becoming an exporter of a wide variety of manufactures as well as the staple raw materials and foodstuffs. It follows that, with regard to the second half of the nineteenth century at any rate, there is no conflict between the results of this paper and Taussig's conclusion that the tariff system provided a limited stimulus to manufactures; for the United States after the Civil War was rapidly developing beyond the simple stage of an agricultural exporter.[40] The character of American exports was changing sufficiently to reduce some of the earlier rigidity of foreign demand and, accordingly, to make tariffs more effective in increasing the domestic prices of the protected products.

IV

In concluding this paper, a word should be said about the relation of the arguments presented here to the earlier work of Heckscher and Ohlin. As noted in Section I, the well-known view of both Heckscher and Ohlin is that international trade tends to equalize the relative returns to different factors of production among the trading countries. In other words, it is their view that trade increases the relative demand, and therefore the relative return, of the factor of production which is comparatively most abundant and comparatively cheapest in a particular country. In this manner wages tend to be raised relative to the returns to other factors of production, in countries which have a large population in relation to their other resources. Superficially it might seem that

---

[40] A further factor in the increasing effectiveness of tariffs in protecting domestic industries was the lower proportion of dutiable imports to total imports.

any measure, such as a tariff reduction, which reduces the impediments to international trade, would have these same effects. In a country with a large supply of land, for example, it might be expected, following the Heckscher-Ohlin argument, that a tariff reduction would increase rents and lower wages. But we have found in Section II that, if the demand for a country's exports is inelastic, this result does not necessarily follow. Under some conditions with respect to international demand a reduction of tariffs may *increase* the demand for a country's scarce factors and *reduce* the demand for its abundant factors. How can this conclusion be reconciled with the view of Heckscher and Ohlin that international trade always increases the demand for a country's abundant factors?

Despite superficial differences, the conclusions reached in this paper are essentially consistent with those of Heckscher and Ohlin. The contradictory appearance of the conclusions is attributable entirely to a difference in the point of comparison. When Heckscher and Ohlin say that international trade increases the demand for a country's scarce factors, they mean that the demand is increased *compared with the demand in a state of complete isolation*. In other words, they are comparing free trade or restricted trade with a state of affairs in which there is no trade at all; and this is by no means the same as comparing trade under one tariff system with trade under smaller tariffs. The argument presented in Section II, that an increase in customs duties may reduce the demand for a country's scarce factors of production, was limited in its application to tariff changes within a range for which the foreign demand for the country's exports had a certain degree of inelasticity. In other words, the argument was valid only for movements along a limited part of the foreign reciprocal demand schedule. Now, in order to make the present analysis comparable to that of Heckscher and Ohlin, we should have to consider an increase in tariffs so large that all imports were eliminated. In short, all tariffs on all commodities would have to be completely prohibitive. From the nature of the reciprocal demand schedules, however, it is apparent that if tariffs were gradually increased to a level where they threatened to cut off all trade, the point of equilibrium would sooner or later move to a position where the foreign demand for the tariff-imposing country's exports was elastic. Thereafter, any further increases in tariffs would increase the demand for the country's scarce factors and reduce the demand for its abundant factors, in the manner envisaged by Heckscher and Ohlin. When the present technique is applied to changes in foreign trade as great as those envisaged by Heckscher and Ohlin, my conclusions are thus in agreement with theirs. An appearance of conflict arises only when one attempts to apply to the entire reciprocal demand schedule an argument which is applicable only to a segment of that schedule.

3. International Factor-Price Equalisation Once Again*

By PAUL A. SAMUELSON†

1. INTRODUCTION

MY RECENT PAPER[1] attempting to show that free commodity trade will, under certain specified conditions, inevitably lead to complete factor-price equalisation appears to be in need of further amplification. I propose therefore (1) to restate the principal theorem, (2) to expand upon its intuitive demonstration, (3) to settle the matter definitively by a brief but rigorous mathematical demonstration, (4) to make a few extensions to the case of many commodities and factors, and finally (5) to comment briefly upon some realistic qualifications to its simplified assumptions.

I cannot pretend to present a balanced appraisal of the bearing of this analysis upon interpreting the actual world, because my own mind is not made up on this question: on the one hand, I think it would be folly to come to any startling conclusions on the basis of so simplified a model and such abstract reasoning; but on the other hand, strong simple cases often point the way to an element of truth present in a complex situation. Still, at the least, we ought to be clear in our deductive reasoning; and the elucidation of this side of the problem plus the qualifying discussion may contribute towards an ultimate appraisal of the theorem's realism and relevance.

2. STATEMENT OF THE THEOREM

My hypotheses are as follows:

1. There are but two countries, America and Europe.
2. They produce but two commodities, food and clothing.

* *Economic Journal*, Vol. LIX, No. 234 (June, 1949), pp. 181–97.

† Massachusetts Institute of Technology.

[1] "International Trade and the Equalisation of Factor Prices," *Economic Journal*, Vol. LVIII (June, 1948), pp. 163–84. I learn from Professor Lionel Robbins that A. P. Lerner, while a student at L.S.E., dealt with this problem. I have had a chance to look over Lerner's mimeographed report, dated December 1933, and it is a masterly, definitive treatment of the question, difficulties and all.

3. Each commodity is produced with two factors of production, land and labour. The production functions of each commodity show "constant returns to scale," in the sense that changing all inputs in the same proportion changes output in that same proportion, leaving all "productivities" essentially unchanged. In short, all production functions are mathematically "homogeneous of the first order" and subject to Euler's theorem.
4. The law of diminishing marginal productivity holds: as any one input is increased relative to other inputs, its marginal productivity diminishes.
5. The commodities differ in their "labour and land intensities." Thus, food is relatively "land using" or "land-intensive," while clothing is relatively "labour-intensive." This means that whatever the prevailing ratio of wages to rents, the optimal proportion of labour to land is greater in clothing than in food.
6. Land and labour are assumed to be qualitatively identical inputs in the two countries and the technological production functions are assumed to be the same in the two countries.
7. All commodities move perfectly freely in international trade, without encountering tariffs or transport costs, and with competition effectively equalising the market price-ratio of food and clothing. No factors of production can move between the countries.
8. Something is being produced in both countries of both commodities with both factors of production. Each country may have moved in the direction of specialising on the commodity for which it has a comparative advantage, but it has not moved so far as to be specialising completely on one commodity.[2]

All of this constitutes the hypothesis of the theorem. The conclusion states:

Under these conditions, real factor prices must be exactly the same in both countries (and indeed the proportion of inputs used in food production in America must equal that in Europe, and similarly for clothing production).

Our problem is from now on a purely logical one. Is "If H, then inevitably C" a correct statement? The issue is not whether C (factor-price equalisation) will actually hold; nor even whether H (the hypothesis) is a valid empirical generalisation. It is whether C can fail to be true when H is assumed true. Being a logical question, it admits of only one answer: either the theorem is true or it is false.

One may wonder why such a definite problem could have given rise to misunderstanding. The answer perhaps lies in the fact that even so simple a set-up as this one involves more than a dozen economic variables: at least four inputs for each country, four marginal productivities for each country (marginal productivity of American labour in food, of American land in food . . .), two outputs for each country, the prices of

---

[2] Actually we may admit the limiting case of "incipient specialisation," where nothing is being produced of one of the commodities, but where it is a matter of indifference whether an infinitesimal amount is or is not being produced, so that price and marginal costs are equal.

the two commodities, the price in each country of the two inputs, the proportions of the inputs in different lines of production, and so forth. It is not always easy for the intellect to move purposefully in a hyperspace of many dimensions.

And the problem is made worse by the fact, insufficiently realised, that constant returns to scale is a very serious limitation on the production functions. As soon as one knows a single "curve" on such a surface, all other magnitudes are frozen into exact quantitative shapes and cannot be chosen at will. Thus, if one knows the returns of total product to labour working on one acre of land, then one already knows everything: the marginal productivity schedule of land, all the iso-product curves, the marginal-rate-of substitution schedules, etc. This means one must use a carefully graduated ruler in drawing the different economic functions, making sure that they are numerically consistent in addition to their having plausible qualitative shapes.

3. INTUITIVE PROOF

In each country there is assumed to be given totals of labour and land. If all resources are devoted to clothing, we get a certain maximum amount of clothing. If all are devoted to food production, we get a certain maximum amount of food. But what will happen if we are willing to devote only part of all land and part of total labour to the production of food, the rest being used in clothing production? Obviously, then we are in effect sacrificing some food in order to get some clothing. The iron law of scarcity tells us that we cannot have all we want of both goods, but must ultimately give up something of one good in getting some of another.

In short there is a best "production-possibility," or "transformation" curve showing us the maximum obtainable amount of one commodity for each amount of the other. Such a production-possibility schedule was drawn up for each country in Figure 1 of my earlier article. And in each case it was made to be a curve *convex* from above, so that the more you want of any good the greater is the cost, at the margin, in terms of the other good. This convexity property is very important and is related to the law of diminishing marginal productivity. Few readers had any qualms about accepting convexity, but perhaps some did not realise its far-reaching implications in showing why the factor-price equalisation theorem had to be true. I propose, therefore, to show why the production-possibility curve must obviously be convex (looked at from above).[3]

To show that convexity, or increasing relative marginal costs must hold, it is sufficient for the present purpose to show that concavity, or decreasing marginal costs, involves an impossible contradiction. Now at

---

[3] I am indebted for this line of reasoning to my colleague at M.I.T., Professor Robert L. Bishop, who for some years has been using it on beginning students in economics, with no noticeable disastrous effects. This proof is suggestive only, but it could easily be made rigorous.

the very worst, it is easily shown we can move along a straight-line opportunity cost line between the two axes. For suppose we agree to give up half of the maximum obtainable amount of food. How much clothing can we be sure of getting? If we send out the crudest type of order: "Half of all labour and half of all land is to be shifted to clothing production," we will (because of the assumption of constant returns to scale) *exactly halve* food production; and we will acquire *exactly half* of the maximum amount of clothing produceable with all resources. Therefore, we end up at a point, *R*, exactly half-way between the limiting points A and Z. Similarly, if we decide to give up 10, 20, 30 or 90% of the maximum amount of food produceable, we can give out crude orders to transfer exactly 10, 20,

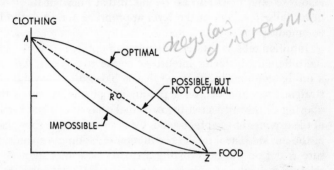

30 or 90% of *both* inputs from food to clothing. Because of constant returns to scale, it follows that we can be sure of getting 90, 80, 70 or 10% of maximum clothing.

In short, by giving such crude down-the-line orders that transfer both resources *always in the same proportion,* we can at worst travel along a straight line between the two limiting intercepts. Any concave curve would necessarily lie inside such a constant-cost straight line and can therefore be ruled out: hence decreasing (marginal, opportunity) costs are incompatible with the assumption of constant returns to scale.

But of course we can usually do even better than the straight-line case. A neophyte bureaucrat might be satisfied to give crude down-the-line orders, but there exist more efficient ways of giving up food for clothing. This is where social-economist (or "welfare economist") can supplement the talents of the mere technician who knows how best to use inputs in the production of any one good and nothing else. There are an infinity of ways of giving up, say, 50% of food: we may simply give up labour, or simply give up land, or give up constant percentages of labour and land, or still other proportions. But there will be only one best way to do so, only one best combination of labour and land that is to be transferred. Best in what sense? Best in the sense of getting for us the maximum obtainable amount of clothing, compatible with our pre-assigned decision to sacrifice a given amount of food.

Intuition tells us that, qualitatively, we should transfer a larger proportion of labour than of land to clothing production. This is because
clothing is the labour-intensive commodity, by our original hypothesis.
This means that the proportion of labour to land is actually declining in
the food line as its production declines. What about the proportion of
labour to land in clothing production? At first we were able to be generous
in sparing labour, which after all was not "too well adapted" for food
production. But now, when we come to give up still more food, there is
less labour left in food production relative to land; hence, we cannot con-
trive to be quite so generous in transferring further labour to clothing
production. As we expand clothing production further, the proportion of
labour to land must also be falling in that line; but the labour-land ratio
never falls to as low as the level appropriate for food, the land-intensive
commodity.[4]

Intuition tells us that by following an optimal pattern which recognises
the difference in factor intensities of the two goods, we can end up on
a production possibility curve that is bloated out beyond a constant-cost
straight line: in short, on a production possibility curve that is convex,
obeying the law of increasing marginal costs of one good as it is expanded
at the expense of the other good. Or to put the same thing in the language
of the market-place: as the production of clothing expands, upward pressure is put on the price of the factor it uses most intensively, on wages
relative to land rent. An increase in the ratio of wages to rent must in
a competitive market press up the price of the labour-intensive commodity relative to the land-intensive commodity.

This one-directional relationship between relative factor prices and
relative commodity prices is an absolute necessity, and it is vital for the
recognition of the truth in the main theorem. Let me elaborate therefore
upon the market mechanism bringing it about. Under perfect competition,
everywhere within a domestic market there will be set up a uniform
ratio of wages to rents. In the food industry, there will be one, and only
one, optimal proportion of labour to land; any attempt to combine productive factors in proportions that deviate from the optimum will be
penalised by losses, and there will be set up a process of corrective adaptation. The same competitive forces will force an adaptation of the input
proportion in clothing production, with equilibrium being attained only
when the input proportions are such as to equate exactly the ratio of the
physical marginal productivities of the factors (the "marginal rate of

---

[4] Some readers may find it paradoxical that—with a fixed ratio of total labour to
total land—we nevertheless lower the ratio of labour to land *in both industries* as a
result of producing more of the labour-intensive good and less of the other. Such
readers find it hard to believe that men's wages and women's wages can both go up at
the same time that average wages are going down. They forget that there is an
inevitable shift in the industries' weights used to compute the average-factor ratio.
Really to understand all this the reader must be referred to the Edgeworth box-
diagram depicted in W. F. Stolper and P. A. Samuelson, "Protection and Real Wages,"
Review of Economic Studies, Vol. IX (1941), pp. 58–73.

substitution" of labour for land in clothing production) to the ratio of factor prices prevailing in the market. The price mechanism has an unconscious wisdom. As if led by an invisible hand, it causes the economic system to move out to the optimal production-possibility curve. Through the intermediary of a common market factor-price ratio, the marginal rates of substitution of the factors become the same in both industries. And it is this marginal condition which intuition (as well as geometry and mathematics) tells us prescribes the optimal allocation of resources so as to yield maximum output. Not only does expanding clothing production result in the earlier described qualitative pattern of dilution of the ratio of labour to land in both occupations; more than that, a price system is one way of achieving the exactly optimal quantitative degree of change in proportions.

I have established unequivocally the following facts:

Within any country: (a) *a high ratio of wages to rents will cause a definite decrease in the proportion of labour to land in both industries;* (b) *to each determinate state of factor proportion in the two industries there will correspond one, and only one, commodity price ratio and a unique configuration of wages and rent; and finally,* (c) *that the change in factor proportions incident to an increase in wages/rents must be followed by a one-directional increase in clothing prices relative to food prices.*

An acute reader may try to run ahead of the argument and may be tempted to assert: "But all this holds for one country, as of a given total factor endowment. Your established chain of causation is only from factor prices (and factor proportions) to commodity prices. Are you entitled to reverse the causation and to argue that the same commodity-price ratio must—even in countries of quite different total factor endowments—lead back to a common unique factor-price ratio, a common unique way of combining the inputs in the food and clothing industries, and a common set of absolute factor prices and marginal productivities?"

My answer is yes. This line of reasoning is absolutely rigorous. It is only proportions that matter, not scale. In such a perfectly competitive market each small association of factors (or firm, if one prefers that word) feels free to hire as many or as few extra factors as it likes. It neither knows nor cares anything about the totals for society. It is like a group of molecules in a perfect gas which is everywhere in thermal equilibrium. The molecules in any one small region behave in the same way regardless of the size of the room around them. A sample observed in the middle of a huge spherical room would act in the same way as a similar sample observed within a small rectangular room. Similarly, if we observe the behaviour of a representative firm[5] in one country it will be exactly the same

---

[5] The representative firm concept is in the case of homogeneous production functions not subject to the usual difficulties associated with the Marshallian concept; in this case, it should be added, the "scale" of the firm is indeterminate and, fortunately, irrelevant.

in all essentials as a representative firm taken from some other country—
regardless of the difference in total factor amounts and relative industrial
concentration—provided only that factor-price ratios are really the same
in the two markets.

All this follows from the italicised conclusion reached just above, especially from (*c*) taken in conjunction with (*a*) and (*b*).

This really completes the intuitive demonstration of the theorem. The
same international commodity-price ratio, must—so long as both commodities are being produced and priced at marginal costs—enable us to
infer backwards a unique factor-price ratio, a unique set of factor proportions, and even a unique set of absolute wages and rents.

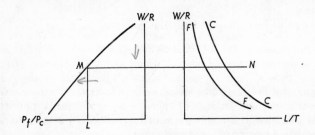

All this is summarised in the accompanying chart. On the right-hand
side I have simply duplicated Figure 2 of my earlier paper. On the left-
hand side I have added a chart showing the one-directional relation of
commodity prices to factor prices.[6] As wages fall relative to rents the
price of food is shown to rise relative to clothing in a monotonic fashion.
The accompanying chart applies to either country and—so long as neither

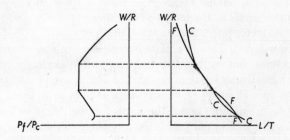

---

[6] The left-hand curve is drawn in a qualitatively correct fashion. Actually its exact
quantitative shape is determined by the two right-hand curves; but the chart is *not*
exact in its quantitative details.

We may easily illustrate the importance of point (5) of our hypothesis, which
insists on differences in factor intensities. Consider the depicted pathological case
which does not meet the requirements of our hypothesis, and in which factor intensities are for a range identical, and in still other regions food becomes the labour-
intensive good. The resulting pattern of commodity prices does *not* necessarily result
in factor-price equalisation. Cf. p. 175, n. 1 of my earlier article.

country is specialising completely—its validity is independent of their differing factor endowments. It follows that when we specify a common price ratio (say at L), we can move backward unambiguously (from M to N, etc.) to a common factor-price ratio and to a common factor proportion set-up in the two countries.

4. MATHEMATICAL PROOF

Now that the theorem has been demonstrated by common-sense reasoning, let me confirm it by more rigorous mathematical proof. The condition of equilibrium can be written in a variety of ways, and can be framed so as to involve more than a dozen equations. For example, let me call America's four marginal physical productivities—of labour in food, of land in food, of labour in clothing, of land in clothing—a, b, c and d. I use Greek letters—α, β, γ, δ—to designate the corresponding marginal productivities in Europe. Then we can end up with a number of equilibrium expressions of the form

$$\frac{a}{b} = \frac{c}{d}, \frac{a}{\beta} = \frac{\gamma}{\delta}, \frac{a}{c} = \frac{\alpha}{\gamma}, \ldots \text{ etc.}$$

A number of economists have tortured themselves trying to manipulate these expressions so as to result in $a = \alpha$, etc., or at least in $a/b = \alpha/\beta$, etc. No proof of this kind is possible. The essential thing is that these numerous marginal productivities are by no means independent. Because proportions rather than scale are important, knowledge of the behaviour of the marginal productivity of labour tells us exactly what to expect of the marginal-productivity schedule of land. This is because increasing the amount of labour with land held constant is equivalent to reducing land with labour held constant.[7]

Mathematically, instead of writing food production, F, as any joint function of labour devoted to it, L_f, and of land, T_f, we can write it as

$$F = F(L_f, T_f) = T_f f\left(\frac{L_f}{T_f}\right) \tag{1}$$

where the function f can be thought of as the returns of food on one unit of land, and where the number of units of land enters as a scale factor. The form of this function is the same for both countries; and there is, of

[7] J. B. Clark recognised in his *Distribution of Wealth* that the "upper triangle" of his labour-marginal-productivity diagram must correspond to the "rectangle" of his other-factors diagram. But his draughtsman did *not* draw the curve accordingly! This is a mistake that Philip Wicksteed in his *Co-ordination of the Laws of Distribution* (London School of Economics Reprint) could not have made. Clark, a believer in Providence, was unaware of the blessing—in the form of Euler's theorem on homogeneous functions—that made his theory possible. Wicksteed, a man of the cloth, appreciated and interpreted the generosity of Nature. Cf. also F. H. Knight, *Risk, Uncertainty and Profit*, ch. IV, for a partial treatment of these reciprocal relations. G. J. Stigler, *Production and Distribution Theories: the Formative Period*, gives a valuable treatment of Wicksteed's theory as exposited by Flux and others.

course, a similar type of function holding for cloth production, C, in terms of L_c and T_c namely

$$C = C\ (L_c, T_c) = T_c\ c\!\left(\frac{L_c}{T_c}\right) \tag{2}$$

It is easy to show mathematically, by simple partial differentiation of (1), the following relations among marginal physical productivities

$$\text{M.P.P. labour in food} = \frac{\partial F}{\partial L_f} = f'\left(\frac{L_f}{T_f}\right)$$

where f' represents the derivative of f and depicts the schedule of marginal product of labour (working on one unit of land). This must be a declining schedule according to our hypothesis of diminishing returns, so that we must have

$$f''\left(\frac{L_f}{T_f}\right) < 0.$$

By direct differentiation of (1), or by use of Euler's theorem, or by use of the fact that the marginal product of land can also be identified as a rent residual, we easily find that

$$\text{M.P.P. land in food} = \frac{\partial F}{\partial T_f} = f\left(\frac{L_f}{T_f}\right) - \frac{L_f}{T_f} f'\left(\frac{L_f}{T_f}\right) = g\left(\frac{L_f}{T_f}\right)$$

where g is the name for the rent residual. It is easy to show that

$$g'\left(\frac{L_f}{T_f}\right) = -\frac{L_f}{T_f} f''\left(\frac{L_f}{T_f}\right).$$

By similar reasoning, we may write the marginal productivity of land in clothing production in its proper relation to that of labour

$$\text{M.P.P. labour in clothing} = \frac{\partial C}{\partial L_c} = c'\left(\frac{L_c}{T_c}\right)$$

$$\text{M.P.P. land in clothing} = \frac{\partial C}{\partial T_c} = c\left(\frac{L_c}{T_c}\right) - \frac{L_c}{T_c} c'\left(\frac{L_c}{T_c}\right) = h\left(\frac{L_c}{T_c}\right)$$

$$h'\left(\frac{L_c}{T_c}\right) = -\frac{L_c}{T_c} c''\left(\frac{L_c}{T_c}\right).$$

The art of analysis in these problems is to select out the essential variables so as to reduce our equilibrium equations to the simplest form. Without specifying which country we are talking about, we certainly can infer from the fact that something of both goods is being produced with both factors the following conditions:

Real wages (or labour marginal "value" productivities) must be the same in food and clothing production when expressed in terms of a common *measure*, such as clothing; the same is true of real rents (or land marginal "value" productivities). Or

(food price) (M.P.P. labour in food)

= (clothing price) (M.P.P. labour in clothing)

(food price) (M.P.P. land in food)
$$= \text{(clothing price)} \ \text{(M.P.P. land in clothing)}$$
which can be written in terms of previous notation[8] as

$$\left(\frac{P_f}{P_c}\right) f'\left(\frac{L_f}{T_f}\right) - c'\left(\frac{L_c}{T_c}\right) = 0$$

$$\left(\frac{P_f}{P_c}\right)\left[f\left(\frac{L_f}{T_f}\right) - \frac{L_f}{T_f} f'\left(\frac{L_f}{T_f}\right) \right] - \left[c\left(\frac{L_c}{T_c}\right) - \frac{L_c}{T_c} c'\left(\frac{L_c}{T_c}\right) \right] = 0.$$

Now these are two equations in the three variables

$$\frac{L_f}{T_f}, \frac{L_c}{T_c}, \text{ and } \frac{P_f}{P_c}.$$

If we take the latter price ratio as given to us by international-demand conditions, we are left with *two* equations to determine the *two* unknown factor proportions. This is a solvent situation, and we should normally expect the result to be determinate.

But a purist might still have doubts: "How do you know that these two equations or schedules might not twist around and intersect in multiple equilibria?" Fortunately, the answer is simple and definite. On our hypothesis, any equilibrium configuration turns out to be absolutely unique. We may leave to a technical footnote the detailed mathematical proof of this fact.[9]

5. MULTIPLE COMMODITIES AND FACTORS

Adding a third or further commodities does not alter our analysis much. If anything, it increases the likelihood of complete factor-price

---

[8] In terms of our earlier $a, b, \ldots, \alpha, \beta \ldots$, these equations are of the form
$$\frac{P_f}{P_c} a = c, \frac{P_f}{P_c} b = d, \text{ etc.}$$

[9] The Implicit Function Theorem tells us that two suitably continuous equations of the form $W_1(y_1, y_2) = 0 = W_2(y_1, y_2)$, possessing a solution (y_1^0, y_2^0), cannot have any other solution provided

$$\Delta = \begin{vmatrix} \dfrac{\partial W_1}{\partial y_1} & \dfrac{\partial W_1}{\partial y_2} \\ \dfrac{\partial W_2}{\partial y_1} & \dfrac{\partial W_2}{\partial y_2} \end{vmatrix} \neq 0$$

In this case, where $y_1 = L_f/T_f$, etc., it is easy to show that

$$\Delta = \begin{vmatrix} \dfrac{P_f}{P_c} f'' & -c'' \\ -\dfrac{P_f}{P_c}\dfrac{L_f}{T_f} f'' + \dfrac{L_c}{T_c} c'' \end{vmatrix} = \frac{P_f}{P_c} f'' c'' \left[\frac{L_c}{T_c} - \frac{L_f}{T_f} \right]$$

By hypothesis of diminishing returns f'' and c'' are negative, and the term in brackets (representing the respective labour intensities in food and clothing) cannot be equal to zero. Hence, the equilibrium is unique. As developed earlier, if the factor intensities become equal, or reverse themselves, the one-to-one relation between commodity and factor prices *must* be ruptured.

equalisation. For all that we require is that at least *two* commodities are simultaneously being produced in both countries and then our previous conclusion follows. If we add a third commodity which is very much like either of our present commodities, we are not changing the situation materially. But if we add new commodities which are more extreme in their labour-land intensities, then we greatly increase the chance that two regions with very different factor endowments can still come into complete factor-price equalisation. A "queer" region is not penalised for being queer if there is queer work that needs doing.

I do not wish at this time to go into the technical mathematics of the n commodity, and r factor case. But it can be said that: (1) so long as the two regions are sufficiently close together in factor proportions, (2) so long as the goods differ in factor intensities, and (3) so long as the number of goods, n, is greater than the number of factors, r, we can hope to experience complete factor-price equalisation. On the other hand, if complete specialisation takes place it will do so for a whole collection of goods, the dividing line between exports and imports being a variable one depending upon reciprocal international demand (acting on factor prices) as in the classical theory of comparative advantage with multiple commodities.[10]

When we add a third productive factor and retain but two commodities, then the whole presumption towards factor-price equalisation disappears. Suppose American labour and American land have more capital to work with than does European labour and land. It is then quite possible that the marginal physical productivities of labour and land might be double that of Europe in both commodities. Obviously, commodity-price *ratios* would still be equal, production of both commodities will be taking place, but nonetheless absolute factor prices (or relative for that matter) need not be moved towards equality. This is our general expectation wherever the number of factors exceeds the number of commodities.

6. THE CONDITIONS OF COMPLETE SPECIALISATION

If complete specialisation takes place in one country, then our hypothesis is not fulfilled and the conclusion does not follow. How important is this empirically, and when can we expect complete specialisation to take

---

[10] The real wage of every resource must be the same in every place that it is used, when expressed in a common denominator. This gives us $r(n-1)$ independent equations involving the $(n-1)$ commodity-price ratios and the $n(r-1)$ factor proportions. If $n = r$, we have a determinate system once the goods price ratios are given. If $n > r$, we have the same result, but now the international price ratios cannot be presented arbitrarily as there are constant-cost paths on the production-possibility locus, with one blade of Marshall's scissors doing most of the cutting, so to speak. If $n < r$, it is quite possible for free commodity trade to exist alongside continuing factor-price differentials. It is never enough simply to count equations and unknowns. In addition we must make sure that there are not multiple solutions: that factor intensities in the different commodities and the laws of returns are such as to lead to a one-to-one relationship between commodity prices and factor prices.

place? As discussed earlier, the answer depends upon how disparate are the initial factor endowments of the two regions—how disparate in comparison with the differences in factor intensities of the two commodities.[11]

Unless the two commodities differ extraordinarily in factor intensities, the production-possibility curve will be by no means so convex as it is usually drawn in the neo-classical literature of international trade, where it usually resembles a quarter circle whose slope ranges the spectrum from zero to infinity. It should rather have the crescent-like shape of the new moon. Opportunity costs tend to be more nearly constant than I had previously realised. This is a step in the direction of the older classical theory of comparative advantage. But with this important difference: the same causes that tend to produce *constant* costs also tend to produce *uniform* cost ratios between nations, which is not at all in the spirit of classical theory. (Undoubtedly much of the specialisation observed in the real world is due to something different from all this, namely decreasing-cost indivisibilities, tempered and counteracted by the existence of localised resources specifically adapted to particular lines of production.)

A parable may serve the double purpose of showing the range of factor endowment incompatible with complete specialisation and of removing any lingering element of paradox surrounding the view that commodity mobility may be a perfect substitute for factor mobility.

Let us suppose that in the beginning all factors were perfectly mobile, and nationalism had not yet reared its ugly head. Spatial transport costs being of no importance, there would be one world price of food and clothing, one real wage, one real rent, and the world's land and labour would be divided between food and clothing production in a determinate way, with uniform proportions of labour to land being used everywhere in clothing production, and with a much smaller—but uniform—proportion of labour to land being used in production of food.

Now suppose that an angel came down from heaven and notified some fraction of all the labour and land units producing clothing that they were to be called Americans, the rest to be called Europeans; and some different fraction of the food industry that henceforth they were to carry American passports. Obviously, just giving people and areas national labels does not alter anything: it does not change commodity or factor prices or production patterns.

But now turn a recording geographer loose, and what will he report? Two countries with quite different factor proportions, but with identical real wages and rents and identical modes of commodity production (but with different relative importances of food and clothing industries). Depending upon whether the angel makes up America by concentrating primarily on clothing units or on food units, the geographer will report a very high or a very low ratio of labour to land in the newly synthesised

---

[11] The reader may be referred to the earlier paper's discussion of Figures 1 and 2, with respect to "step-like formations" and overlap.

"country." But this he will never find: that the ratio of labour to land should ever exceed the proportions characteristic of the most labour-intensive industry (clothing) or ever fall short of the proportions of the least labour-intensive industry. Both countries *must* have factor proportions intermediate between the proportions in the two industries.

The angel can create a country with proportions *not* intermediate between the factor intensities of food and clothing. But he cannot do so by following the above-described procedure, which was calculated to leave prices and production unchanged. If he wrests some labour in food production away from the land it has been working with, "sending" this labour to Europe and keeping it from working with the American land, then a substantive change in production and prices will have been introduced. Unless there are abnormal repercussions on the pattern of effective demand, we can expect one or both of the countries to specialise completely and real wages to fall in Europe relative to America in one or both commodities, with European real rents behaving in an opposite fashion. The extension of this parable to the many-commodities case may be left to the interested reader.

7. SOME QUALIFICATIONS

A number of qualifications to this theoretical argument are in order. In the first place, goods do not move without transport costs, and to the extent that commodity prices are not equalised it of course follows that factor prices will not tend to be fully equalised. Also, as I indicated in my earlier article, there are many reasons to doubt the usefulness of assuming identical production functions and categories of inputs in the two countries; and consequently, it is dangerous to draw sweeping practical conclusions concerning factor-price equalisation.

What about the propriety of assuming constant returns to scale? In justice to Ohlin, it should be pointed out that he, more than almost any other writer, has followed up the lead of Adam Smith and made *increasing returns* an important cause for trade. It is true that increasing returns *may* at the same time create difficulties for the survival of perfect competition, difficulties which cannot always be sidestepped by pretending that the increasing returns are due primarily to *external* rather than internal economies. But these difficulties do not give us the right to deny or neglect the importance of scale factors.[12] Where scale is important it is

---

[12] Statical increasing returns is related to, but analytically distinct from, these irreversible cost economies induced by expansion and experimentation and which provide the justification for "infant industry" protection. Statical increasing returns might justify permanent judicious protection but not protection all around, since our purpose in bringing about large-scale production is to achieve profitable trade and consumption.

One other point needs stressing. For very small outputs, increasing returns to scale may take place without affecting the above analysis provided that total demand is large enough to carry production into the realm of constant returns to scale. Increasing the "extent of the market" not only increases specialisation, it also increases the possibility of viable pure competition.

obviously possible for real wages to differ greatly between large free-trade areas and small ones, even with the same relative endowments of productive factors. And while it may have been rash of me to draw a moral concerning the worth of emigration from Europe out of an abstract simplified model, I must still record the view that the more realistic deviations from constant returns to scale and the actual production functions encountered in practice are likely to reinforce rather than oppose the view that high standards of life are possible in densely populated areas such as the island of Manhattan or the United Kingdom.

There is no iron-clad a priori necessity for the law of diminishing marginal productivity to be valid for either or both commodities.[13] In such cases the usual marginal conditions of equilibrium are replaced by inequalities, and we have a boundary maximum in which we go the limit and use zero of one of the inputs in one industry. If it still could be shown that one commodity is always more labour intensive than the other, then the main theorem would probably still be true. But it is precisely in these pathological cases that factor intensities may become alike or reverse themselves, giving rise to the difficulties discussed in my earlier footnote 6.

In conclusion, some of these qualifications help us to reconcile results of abstract analysis with the obvious facts of life concerning the extreme diversity of productivity and factor prices in different regions of the world. Men receive lower wages in some countries than in others for a variety of reasons: because they are different by birth or training; because their effective know-how is limited and the manner of their being combined with other productive factors is not optimal; because they are confined to areas too small to develop the full economies of scale; because some goods and materials cannot be brought to them freely from other parts of the world, as a result of natural or man-made obstacles; and finally because the technological diversity of commodities with respect to factor intensities is not so great in comparison with the diversity of regional factor endowments to emancipate labourers from the penalty of being confined to regions lacking in natural resources. In the face of these hard facts it would be rash to consider the existing distribution of population to be optimal in any sense, or to regard free trade as a panacea for the present geographical inequalities.

---

[13] A "Pythagorean" production function of the form $F = \sqrt{L^2 + T^2}$ is an example of such a homogeneous function with increasing marginal productivity. So long as neither factor is to have a negative marginal productivity, *average* product must not be rising; but this is quite another thing. Surprisingly enough, the production possibility curve may still be convex with increasing marginal productivity. I have been asked whether any essential difference would be introduced by the assumption that one of the commodities, such as clothing, uses no land at all, or negligible land. Diminishing returns would still affect food as more of the transferable factor is added to the now specific factor of land; but no essential modifications in our conclusions are introduced.

4. Factor Endowment and Relative Commodity Prices[*][1]

By T. M. RYBCZYNSKI[†]

1. The purpose of this paper is to investigate the effect of an increase in the quantity of a factor of production upon production, consumption and the terms of trade. Although in the model used here the quantity of only one factor is varied, the analysis can easily be extended to variations in the quantities of two factors—the variations in these factors being proportionate or disproportionate.

2. We assume a closed economy with only two factors of production, X and Y, which are perfectly divisible, perfectly mobile, and in some degree substitutable. There are but two industries and each of them is subject to a linear homogeneous production function. They are producing two commodities L and K. The "factor intensity" of each industry is different. By this we mean that technical conditions of production are such that the ratio (marginal physical product of X)/(marginal physical product of Y) is always equalised as between the two industries by using a higher ratio of X/Y in one of the industries (the X-intensive industry) and a lower ratio of X/Y in the other (the Y-intensive industry).

3. We shall use the box diagram as employed by Stolper and Samuelson[2] to depict production conditions. Thus in Figure 1 the box $ABCD$ depicts an economy with AB of Factor X and AD of Factor Y. Isoquants for the commodity L are shown by the family of curves convex to the origin A; similarly isoquants for the commodity K are shown by the family of curves convex to the origin C.

If we make commodity K X-intensive and commodity L Y-intensive, the contract curve AC must be convex to D. Equilibrium must lie some-

[*] *Economica*, Vol. XXII, No. 84 (November, 1955), pp. 336–41. The first diagram has been redrawn to meet a criticism by E. J. Mishan ("Factor Endowment and Relative Commodity Prices: A Comment," *Economica*, Vol. XXIII, No. 88 [November, 1956], pp. 352–59).

[†] Lazard Bros., London.

[1] I wish to express my thanks to Dr. H. Makower for valuable suggestions regarding the exposition of this paper.

[2] See W. F. Stolper and P. A. Samuelson, "Protection and Real Wages," reprinted in *Readings in the Theory of International Trade*, pp. 347 *et seq.* Allen and Unwin 1950.

where on this curve. The position on the curve is determined by the condition that the substitution rate between L and K in production (as indicated by the isoquants) must be equal to the substitution rate in consumption (as indicated by the consumer preference system).

4. Suppose this condition is fulfilled at the point S. An increase in the quantity of Factor X may be shown by extending BA to BA'. The new production box is now $A'BCD'$. The horizontal extension of the box leaves the family of the isoquants originating from C unaffected; the family of

FIGURE 1

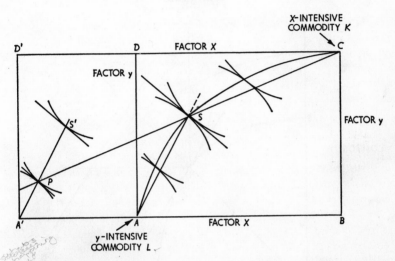

isoquants originating previously from A must now be shifted to the new origin A'. As the production functions of both commodities are homogeneous and of the first degree, the line AS intersects all members of the family of L-isoquants at points where their slopes are the same as at the point S; similarly CS intersects all members of the family of K-isoquants at points where these curves have this same slope. Therefore, when the line $A'S'$ is drawn parallel to AS it must cut the family of isoquants originating from A' at points where these curves all have the same slope as the curves at S.

Let the line CS be prolonged to cut $A'S'$ at P. Point P must be on the new "contract" curve because the slopes of the two isoquants passing through that point are by the above reasoning equal, both being the same as the slope of the tangent at S. If the same rates of substitution in production were to remain after Factor X had been increased by AA', P would be the new point of equilibrium.

5. Because of the property of linearity of the two production functions, the amount of a commodity produced may be measured by the distance

along any given radial from the origin. Thus since the length $A'P$ is necessarily shorter than AS, production of the Y-intensive commodity must be less at P than at S. The fact that CP is longer than CS shows on the other hand that production on the X-intensive commodity is expanded. This proves *that the maintenance of the same rates of substitution in production after the quantity of one factor has increased must lead to an absolute expansion in production of the commodity using relatively much of that factor, and to an absolute curtailment of production of the commodity using relatively little of the same factor.*

FIGURE 2

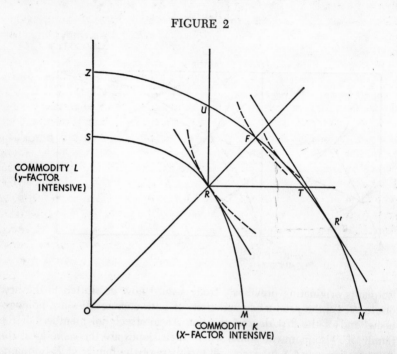

COMMODITY L
(y-FACTOR
INTENSIVE)

COMMODITY K
(X-FACTOR INTENSIVE)

6. The above proposition may now be carried over into a diagram showing "production possibility" curves. Thus in Figure 2 the horizontal and vertical co-ordinates measure quantities of commodities K and L respectively. With the given initial quantities of X and Y, the boundary of possible L, K, combinations, or the "production possibility" curve, is SM. The concavity of this curve to the origin connotes conditions of increasing rate of substitution on the production side.

7. The original position of equilibrium is defined by the equality of substitution rates in consumption and production and is represented graphically by the point of tangency between the "production possibility" curve and an indifference curve (point R in Figure 2). To find the new point of production and consumption equilibrium when the quan-

tity of Factor X is increased, it is necessary to discover the new point of tangency between the new "production possibility" curve and (another) indifference curve. This requires the derivation of the new "production possibility" curve and its analysis in relation to the indifference curve system. Each will be examined below.

8. Now in virtue of our proposition that the maintenance of the same substitution rate in production, after Factor X has increased, requires an absolute increase in the output of the X-intensive commodity, and an absolute reduction in the output of the Y-intensive commodity, it follows that the slope found at R on the production curve SM (Figure 2) must, on the production curve ZN, lie below RT where less of L is produced. We shall suppose that it lies at R'.

9. So much for the shape of the new "production possibility" curve. What is its relationship to the system of indifference curves? We assume the absence of any inferior good. This means that as income increases more of both commodities must be consumed. This in turn implies that for any indifference curve above that passing through R, the slope prevailing at R must be found on a sector of the higher indifference curve which lies within the quadrant URT. Let the indifference curve passing through F have at that point the same slope as at R where F is the point of intersection between OR prolonged and ZN. Then since the new "production possibility" curve above R' is flatter than at R and the indifference curve through F has the same slope as at R, it follows that the indifference curve passing through F must cut the new "production possibility" curve from above at that point. But it also follows that, since below F the indifference curves become flatter, there must be a point of tangency between a (higher) indifference curve and the "production possibility" curve below F, but above R'. At such a point the slope of the "production possibility" curve and indifference curve must be flatter than at R. This implies that the terms of trade of the X-intensive commodity have worsened as against the Y-intensive commodity, and proves the proposition that the terms of trade of the commodity using relatively much of the factor whose quantity has increased must deteriorate.

10. No reference has been made so far to the conditions of demand. The fact that the point F was assumed to fall on the straight line OR was equivalent to the assumption that the Marginal Propensity to Consume is equal to the Average Propensity to Consume (the latter falling over the whole range of the change in the position of equilibrium). The implications arising from the possibility of the former being different from the latter must now be examined.

When the Marginal Propensity to Consume the X-intensive good exceeds the Average Propensity to Consume, the income consumption curve will cut the new "production possibility" curve somewhere between T and

F. Since it has been proved that the new point of equilibrium must always be below the point where an indifference curve with the same slope as at *R* (i.e. defined by the income consumption curve) intersects the new "production possibility" curve, it follows that the more the Marginal Propensity to Consume favours the commodity using relatively much of the factor whose quantity has been increased, the smaller is the worsening of the terms of trade of that commodity.

The reverse holds equally true: when the Marginal Propensity to Consume the good which uses a relatively low proportion of the increased factor exceeds the Average Propensity to Consume, an indifference curve with the same slope as at *R* will cut the new "production possibility" curve somewhere between *U* and *F*, signifying that the terms of trade have turned more against the commodity using relatively much of the increased factor. The greater is the difference between the Marginal and the Average Propensity to Consume, the greater will be the deterioration in the terms of trade for the commodity using relatively much of the increased factor.

11. Our conclusion is that an increase in the quantity of one factor will always lead to a worsening in the terms of trade, or the relative price, of the commodity using relatively much of that factor. The Marginal Propensity to Consume influences the degree of deterioration, but it can never reverse its direction.

12. Despite the change of the relative prices of the two commodities the patterns of production and consumption may remain unaltered, or change in favour of one good or the other. By the unchanged pattern of production and consumption we mean that the quantity of both products has increased proportionately; a shift in the direction of one commodity signifies a greater than proportionate increase in production and consumption of that good combined with a less than proportionate rise of the other. The new equilibrium is determined again by the difference between the Marginal and the Average Propensity to Consume on the one hand and the shift of the production possibility curve; the latter in turn is determined by the proportion in which one factor has been increased and the technical production functions of the two commodities.

The unequivocal generalisation possible regarding the new production and consumption patterns is that they will change in the direction of the good using relatively much of the factor increased (i.e. the quantity of that good produced and consumed will increase more while that of the other will rise less than proportionately) if the Marginal Propensity to Consume the product using relatively much of the factor increased remains equal to, or is greater than, the Average Propensity to Consume. When the Marginal Propensity to Consume is less than the Average then the new production and consumption patterns may still change in favour of the commodity using much of the factor increased, or may remain unchanged or move in the direction of the other good; the ultimate outcome depends, in this case, on the numerical values assigned to the factors mentioned; it is possible, however, to offer tentative conclusions that the small excess of the Marginal over the Average Propensity to Consume in the direction of the good using little of the factor increased is still likely to shift the production and consumption patterns in favour of the other commodity; a moderate excess is likely to leave the production and consumption patterns unchanged, while a large difference may be expected to alter both production and consumption in favour of that good. All this is but a corollary of our previous proof.

13. If it is now assumed that the commodity using relatively much of the factor, the quantity of which had been increased, is an item of export, this means that external terms of trade will deteriorate; conversely, should the commodity be an import, the terms of trade must improve.

5. Factor Endowments, International Trade, and Factor Prices*

By HARRY G. JOHNSON[†]

IN THE PAST FEW YEARS, there has been a revival of interest in the Heckscher-Ohlin model of international trade, and a closer scrutiny of two propositions associated with its analysis of the principle of comparative costs.[1] The first is that the cause of international trade is to be found largely in differences between the factor-endowments of different countries; the second that the effect of international trade is to tend to equalize factor prices as between countries, thus serving to some extent as a substitute for mobility of factors. The result, very briefly, has been to show that neither proposition is generally true, the validity of both depending on certain factual assumptions about either the nature of technology or the range of variation of factor endowments which are additional to, and much more restrictive than, the assumptions of the Heckscher-Ohlin model itself.

My purpose here is to survey the related problems of the relation between factor-endowment and international trade and the effect of trade on relative factor prices, with the aim of clarifying the nature and simplifying the explanation of some of the results of recent theoretical research. The main instrument employed to this end is a diagrammatic representa-

* *The Manchester School of Economic and Social Studies*, Vol. XXV, No. 3 (September, 1957), pp. 270–83. Also published in H. G. Johnson, *International Trade and Economic Growth: Studies in Pure Theory* (Cambridge: Harvard University Press, 1961), pp. 17–30.

† The London School of Economics and the University of Chicago.

[1] See in particular: Abba P. Lerner, "Factor Prices and International Trade," *Economica*, N.S., Vol. XIX, No. 1 (February, 1952), pp. 1–15; I. F. Pearce, "A Note on Mr. Lerner's Paper," *loc. cit.*, pp. 16–18; S. F. James and I. F. Pearce, "The Factor Price Equalisation Myth," *Review of Economic Studies*, Vol. XIX(2), No. 49 (1951–52), pp. 111–20; Romney Robinson, "Factor Proportions and Comparative Advantage: Part I," *Quarterly Journal of Economics*, Vol. LXX, No. 2 (May, 1956), pp. 169–92; R. W. Jones, "Factor Proportions and the Heckscher-Ohlin Theorem," *Review of Economic Studies*, Vol. XXIV(1), No. 63 (1956–7), pp. 1–10; also Lionel McKenzie, "Equality of Factor Prices in World Trade," *Econometrica*, Vol. 23, No. 3 (July, 1955), pp. 239–57, which handles the same problems by linear programming methods.

tion of the technological side of the economy, developed from one originated by P. A. Samuelson and recently elaborated by R. F. Harrod.[2]

In common with other models of international trade, it is assumed, on
the consumption side, that tastes and the distribution of the means of
satisfying wants (property ownership, or claims on the social dividend)
are given; and that, on the production side, technology and the supply of
factors of production in each country are given (the latter implying that
factors are immobile between countries). Production functions and factors
are assumed to be identical in all countries; the outputs of goods are assumed to depend only on inputs of factors into the production processes
for those goods, and factors are assumed to be indifferent between uses.
Further, production is assumed to be subject to constant returns to scale,
so that the marginal productivities of factors depend only on the ratios in
which they are used. Finally, perfect competition and the absence of trade
barriers (tariffs and transport costs) are assumed. The argument is simplified still further by assuming, initially, the existence of only two countries, I and II, two goods, X and Y, and two factors of production, labour
and capital,[3] the available quantities of the factors being given independently of their prices.

The given technical possibilities of production, summarized in the production functions, imply a definite relationship between the optimum capital : labour ratios in the two industries, relative factor prices, and relative
costs of production of commodities. This relationship is represented in
Figure 1. For any given relative price of labour in terms of capital (such
as w_i) there will be an optimum ratio of capital to labour in the production of each good ($r_{x.e}$ in X and $r_{y.e}$ in Y) which equates marginal productivities to factor prices, and a relative cost of X in terms of Y (c_I)
which embodies the ratio of their costs of production at the given factor
prices with the associated capital : labour ratios.

An increase in the relative price of labour above the given level will
make it profitable to substitute capital for labour in both industries, thus
raising the optimum capital : labour ratio in both;[4] it will also increase the
relative cost of the labour-intensive good (X in the neighbourhood of w_I),

---

[2] P. A. Samuelson, "International Factor-Price Equalisation Once Again," *Eco-
nomic Journal*, Vol. LIX, No. 234 (June, 1949), pp. 181–97, especially p. 188; R. F.
Harrod, "Factor Price Relations Under Free Trade," *Economic Journal*, Vol. LXVIII,
No. 270 (June, 1958), pp. 245–55.

[3] The simplicity of these assumptions is a virtue rather than a defect, in an
argument whose purpose is to show how little can be said.

[4] The shapes of the curves relating optimal capital : labour ratios to the relative
price of labour assume increasing difficulty in substituting capital for labour as the
capital-output ratio rises, and continuous substitutability of labour for capital in
response to changing relative factor prices. On linear programming assumptions the
curves would be step functions, the steps representing discontinuous changes in capital
intensity. At their left extremities, the curves will cut the Ow axis if labour can
entirely replace capital in production, and the Or axis if it cannot.

FIGURE 1

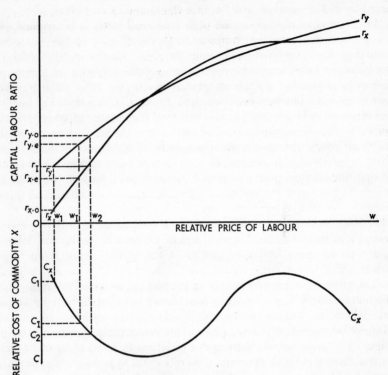

since its costs will be raised more than those of the capital-intensive good
by the increase in the relative price of labour.[5] Further increases in the
relative price of labour will continue to raise the optimum capital : labour
ratio in both industries; but either one of two possibilities may be the
effect on the relative cost ratio, depending on the relative ease of substituting capital for labour in the two lines of production. The first, and
simpler, occurs when one commodity remains labour-intensive and the
other capital-intensive, whatever the relative factor price. In this case, one
commodity can be definitely identified as labour-intensive and the other
as capital-intensive; and the relative cost of the labour-intensive good will
continue to rise as the relative price of labour rises, so that the latter can
be deduced from the former. The second occurs when, owing to greater
facility in substituting capital for labour in the initially labour-intensive

---

[5] If the capital : labour ratios in the two industries remained constant as the relative
price of labour was increased, the relative cost of the labour-intensive good would
obviously increase; and the effect on relative costs of the substitution of capital for
labour in both industries induced by the increase in the relative price of labour can
be neglected, since in the neighbourhood of the minimum cost point substitution of
one factor for the other does not alter cost.

good, the difference in capital-intensity between the two goods narrows and eventually reverses itself, so that the labour-intensive good becomes capital-intensive and *vice versa;* such a reversal of factor-intensities may occur more than once (as illustrated in Figure 1), as variation in relative factor prices induces variation in the capital-intensity of production of both goods. In this case, a commodity can only be identified as labour-intensive or capital-intensive with reference to a range of relative factor-prices or (what is the same thing) a range of capital-intensities; and the relative cost of a commodity will alternately rise and fall as the relative price of labour rises, as that commodity varies from being labour-intensive to being capital-intensive. Consequently more than one factor price ratio may correspond to a given commodity cost ratio, and the factor price ratio cannot be deduced from the commodity cost ratio alone. The distinction between the two cases, which turns on the facts of technology, is fundamental to what follows.

The analysis so far has been concerned with the relationships implicit in the given technological possibilities of production. But only a limited range of the techniques available can actually be used efficiently by a particular economy with a given factor endowment; and the possible range of relative factor prices and relative commodity costs is correspondingly limited. The factor endowment of the economy sets an overall capital : labour ratio, to which the capital : labour ratios in the two industries, weighted by the proportions of the total labour force employed, must average out. At the extremes, the economy's resources may be used entirely in the capital-intensive industry or entirely in the labour-intensive industry; and the relative prices of factors, and the relative costs of commodities, must lie within the limits set by these two extremes.[6]

The restrictions imposed by the factor endowment on the techniques the economy can employ and on the possible variation of factor prices and relative costs of production are illustrated in Figure 1, where r_I represents the economy's overall capital : labour ratio. If all resources are used in the production of Y, the relative price of labour will be w_1, if all are used in the production of X the relative labour price will be w_2; the corresponding relative costs of commodity X are c_1 and c_2. As w rises from w_1 to w_2, the capital : labour ratio in Y rises from r_I to $r_{y.o}$ and the ratio in X from $r_{x.o}$ to r_I; the increases in these ratios are reconciled with the constancy of the overall capital : labour ratio by a shifting of resources from production of Y to production of X, which frees the capital required for the increases in the ratios. It can easily be shown that, for any relative factor price, the proportions of the total labour supply employed in one

---

[6] At the extremes, the country is completely specialized on one or other commodity; in a closed economy, there would therefore be no exchange ratio between commodities, though the non-produced one might have a "virtual" price (equal to or less than its cost of production); in an open economy, the price of the non-produced good would be an international one (equal to or less than the domestic cost of production).

of the industries is equal to the ratio of the difference between the other industry's capital : labour ratio and the overall ratio, to the difference between the capital : labour ratios in the two industries; thus, for example, the proportion of the labour force employed in producing X at the relative labour price w_I is $(r_{y.e} - r_I)/(r_{y.e} - r_{x.e})$.

As can readily be seen from the diagram, the range of variation of relative factor prices and commodity costs possible in the economy depends broadly on two technological factors: the spread between the optimum capital : labour ratios in the two industries (reflected in the vertical distance between the r_y and r_x curves), and the difficulty of substituting capital for labour (reflected in the gentleness of the slopes of the two curves). The greater the difference between optimum factor-intensities and the greater the difficulty of substituting capital for labour, the greater the range of variation of factor prices and commodity costs possible between the extremes of specialization on one or other product. If, on the other hand, capital : labour ratios were the same in the two industries or factors were perfect substitutes, there would be no possibility of variation of relative factor prices and commodity costs.

Before proceeding, it may be as well to notice that the assumption that the quantities of factors available are fixed, can be relaxed without trouble. Dependence of factor supplies on their relative prices can be readily introduced by making the overall capital : labour ratio depend on the relative price of labour; in the normal case the curve representing the relationship will be downward-sloping, reflecting the reduction in the supply of capital and increase in the supply of labour as the price of the former falls relatively to the latter. The effect (in the normal case) would be to restrict the range of possible variation more than would otherwise be the case; in the extreme case of perfect elasticity of factor supply, only one relative factor price ratio and commodity cost ratio would be possible.

Within the range of variation permitted by technology and factor endowment, the factor price and commodity cost ratios will be determined by the forces of demand. For a closed economy, this determination is most readily conceived as follows: to any given relative price of labour will correspond a certain pattern of production, a certain distribution of income, and a certain price ratio between the commodities at which the recipients of the income will be just willing to consume the quantities of both goods produced at the given price of labour. As the relative price of labour rises and resources are shifted out of producing the capital-intensive commodity into producing the labour-intensive commodity, the equilibrium demand price of the latter is very likely to fall,[7] while its

---

[7] The exceptional case is that in which the reduction in the supply of the capital-intensive good is offset by a reduction in demand because the owners of labour have a stronger preference for the labour-intensive good than the owners of capital. It makes no fundamental difference to the analysis unless the effect is so strong that the equilibrium demand price of the labour-intensive good rises more rapidly than its cost of production, a possibility of instability which will be ignored here.

relative cost is rising. The equilibrium levels of commodity prices (costs) and factor prices will be determined by the condition that the relative costs of production should be just equal to the relative prices at which the outputs of the two commodities will be absorbed.[8]

The next stage of the argument is to introduce the possibility of international trade and examine its effects. This is done in Figure 2, which

^a FIGURE 2

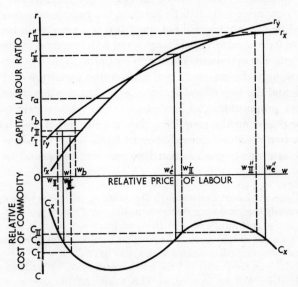

reproduces Figure 1 with the deletion of certain parts of it no longer necessary to the argument. In the diagram, the country previously analysed ("country I") is represented by its factor endowment ratio r_I, and its closed-economy equilibrium factor price and comparative cost ratios w_I and c_I. The possibility of trade is introduced *via* another country ("country II") similarly represented on the diagram by its factor price and cost ratios w_{II} and c_{II}, with a different closed-economy equilibrium comparative cost ratio. It is assumed in all cases that country II is endowed with a higher ratio of capital to labour than country I.

So long as the closed-economy equilibrium comparative cost ratios of the two countries are different, international trade will be profitable, and each country will export the good in which it has a comparative cost advantage (as measured by equilibrium commodity price ratios in the absence of trade). In the assumed absence of trade barriers, the effect of

---

[8] The determination of full general equilibrium could be represented by drawing in the bottom half of Figure 1 a curve expressing the equilibrium price of X as a function of the relative price of labour (and, implicitly, of the factor endowment), whose intersection with the relative cost curve would determine the equilibrium of the system.

trade will be to equate the price ratios in the two economies at a level (c_e in the diagram) somewhere between the two closed-economy comparative cost ratios, this level being determined by the demand and supply conditions in the two countries taken together.

At the new international price ratio, both countries may continue to produce both commodities, or one may specialize completely in the production of the commodity in which it has the comparative advantage, or both may specialize. Which will be the case is governed by two principles —that the new price ratio will lie between the two closed-economy price ratios, and that a country will not specialize at a price ratio between the extremes of its comparative cost range—and is determined by the relations between four cost ratios—the maximum cost ratio in the country with the lower maximum, the minimum cost ratio in the country with the higher minimum, and the two closed-economy equilibrium price ratios. The following four propositions can be deduced from the two principles stated above; for diagrammatic simplicity, they are illustrated only for cases in which the two countries' capital : output ratios lie in the same range, so that there is a one-to-one relation between cost ratios and factor price ratios.

(i) If the minimum cost ratio in the country with the higher minimum exceeds the maximum cost ratio in the other country, so that the comparative cost ranges of the two countries do not overlap, one country at least must specialize completely. This would be the case if country II's endowment ratio coincided with r_a in Figure 2.

(ii) If the cost ratio ranges of the two countries overlap, at least one of the countries will not specialize. This would be the case if country II's endowment ratio were either r_b or r_{II} in Figure 2.

(iii) If one country's cost ratio range includes the other's closed-economy equilibrium price ratio, the former country will not specialize. For example, if country II's endowment ratio were r_b and its closed-economy equilibrium labour price w_b, the labour price ratio corresponding to the new price must fall between w_b and w_I, so that country I would produce both goods.

(iv) If each country's closed-economy equilibrium price ratio falls within the other's cost ratio range, neither will specialize completely. For example, with country II's endowment ratio r_{II} and closed-economy equilibrium labour price w_{II}, the labour price ratio corresponding to the new equilibrium price must fall between w_I and w_{II}, in which range both countries would produce both goods.

In the explanation of the causes of international trade presented above, comparative advantage was measured by equilibrium prices in the absence of trade. Such an explanation, amounting to the statement that those goods are traded which it is profitable to trade, is little more than a tautology. The next problem requiring analysis, and the one which the apparatus built up earlier in this chapter is designed to elucidate, is the relation between comparative advantage so defined and differences in factor supplies. Closely related to this problem is the problem of the effect of international trade on the prices of factors, which can be dealt with by modifications of the same argument.

To begin with, it is necessary to notice a difficulty: relative scarcity or abundance of a factor may be defined in either of two ways—relative cheapness, a matter of price, and relatively high endowment ratio, a matter of physical quantity. These two definitions may not be synonymous, and it is necessary to investigate the relationship of differences in factor supplies on both definitions to differences in comparative advantage.

The investigation is most conveniently divided into two parts, corresponding to the two cases distinguished in the discussion of the technological data above.

The first case is that in which there is no reversal of the factor-intensities of commodities in the range of capital : labour ratios between the endowment ratios of the two countries. This situation (exemplified by the combination of r_I with r_a, r_b, or r_{II} in Figure 2) may be the consequence either of technological conditions which exclude the possibility of such a reversal, or (as in the diagram) of sufficiently similar endowment ratios in the two countries. In this case, owing to the one-to-one relation between comparative cost and factor price ratios, a relatively lower commodity price in one country necessarily implies a relatively lower price there of the factor used relatively intensively in the production of that commodity. Hence comparative advantage is necessarily associated with factor abundance, and disadvantage with factor scarcity, when abundance and scarcity are defined in terms of cheapness or dearness of the factor concerned in one country as compared with the other.

But scarcity and abundance in this sense are not necessarily the same as scarcity and abundance as measured by factor endowment ratios, since factor prices depend on demand as well as on supply, and the influence of demand may outweigh the influence of supply.

Thus a country with relatively abundant labour, judged by its endowment ratio, may be a country with a relatively high price of labour, and hence export the capital-intensive commodity. This possibility is illustrated in Figure 2 by the combination of $r_I c_I$ with $r_{II} c_{II}$: country I is at a comparative disadvantage in the production of X, the labour-intensive commodity ($c_I > c_{II}$), labour being more expensive there than in country II ($w_I > w_{II}$); but this is quite consistent with country I having a relatively more abundant endowment of labour, and less abundant endowment of capital, than country II ($r_{II} > r_I$).

For this possibility to occur, two conditions must be fulfilled. The first is that each country's comparative cost range must overlap the other's closed-economy equilibrium price ratio, which entails (proposition (iv) above) that international trade will lead neither country to specialize completely. The second, and more important, is that each country must have a strong preference for the good which uses intensively the factor with which the country is relatively abundantly endowed.[9]

The effect of trade on relative factor prices in this case is a comparatively simple matter: owing to the one-to-one relationship between commodity cost ratios and relative labour prices, the equalization of commodity prices through trade will tend to equalize relative factor prices.[10] If both countries continue to produce both goods under international trade, equalization will necessarily be complete. (In the case shown in Figure 2, the relative price of labour in both countries will be w_e, the price corresponding to the common commodity price ratio c_e).[11]

The second case is that in which the endowment ratios of the two countries are separated by one or more reversals of factor-intensities in the production of the goods. In this case, there is no possibility of the country with the higher capital : labour endowment ratio having a lower relative price of labour, since by assumption the ranges of relative factor prices possible in the two countries do not overlap: factor scarcity and abundance can therefore be measured indifferently by endowment ratios or relative factor prices. But because of the intervening factor-intensity reversal(s) and the associated reversal(s) of direction of the effect of a relative factor price change on the commodity cost ratio, it is not possible to relate comparative cost advantage in the production of a particular good to relative abundance (in either sense) of the factor utilized relatively intensively in producing that good—or even, in some cases, to identify goods as relatively labour- or capital-intensive in the world as a whole. The commodity in which the labour-abundant country has a comparative advantage may be either labour-intensive or capital-intensive in that country, and either capital-intensive or labour-intensive in the capital-abundant country. And since the effect of trade is to raise the relative price of the commodity in which the country has a comparative advantage, and therefore the relative price of the factor used relatively more in the production of that commodity, its effect on relative factor prices may be to move them in the same direction in the two countries, towards each other, or away from each other. Moreover, in equilibrium

---

[9] Using the ratio measure of the proportions of labour employed in the two industries referred to above, it can easily be shown that at the pre-trade country I price of labour country II would have a smaller proportion of its labour force engaged in the production of the labour-intensive good than country I; at the lower pre-trade country II price of labour, the proportion must be still smaller. At the common price-ratio established by trade, country II must devote a larger proportion of its resources to the capital-intensive industry than will country I.

[10] Since production functions are identical in the two countries, equalization of relative factor prices also means equalization of absolute factor prices (marginal productivities).

[11] If the equilibrium price ratio lies outside a country's range of commodity cost ratios, its relative factor price will be that corresponding to the cost ratio in the range nearest to the equilibrium price ratio.

both countries may continue to produce both goods, even though factor prices are different in the two countries.

Two sub-cases may be distinguished for analysis of the effect of trade on factor prices, according to whether the factor-endowment ratios of the two countries are separated by an odd or an even number of reversals of factor-intensities.

If the number of reversals is odd, a commodity which is labour-intensive in one country will be capital-intensive in the other, so that the export commodities of the two countries must have the same relative factor-intensity in the country of origin, being either both capital-intensive or both labour-intensive. The effect of trade will be to move factor prices in the same direction in both countries, and the difference between them may either narrow or widen according to circumstances. If the relatively labour-abundant country has a comparative advantage in its labour-intensive commodity, trade will raise the price of labour in both countries; conversely, if its comparative advantage lies in its capital-intensive commodity, trade will lower the price of labour in both countries. The latter case is illustrated by the combination $r_I c_I, r_{II} c_{II}$ in Figure 2, where country I, the relatively labour-abundant country, has a comparative advantage in its capital-intensive commodity Y: the effect of trade is to lower the relative price of labour in both countries, from w_I to w_e in country I and from w''_{II} to w'_e in country II. In the particular case shown, both countries continue to produce both commodities, though their relative factor prices are different.

If the number of intervening reversals of factor-intensities is even, a commodity is either labour-intensive or capital-intensive in both countries. The effect of trade is therefore to move factor prices in the two countries in opposite directions; but the movement may be convergent or divergent. If the labour-abundant country has a comparative advantage in the production of the labour-intensive commodity, factor prices in the two countries will move towards each other; if it has a comparative advantage in the production of its capital-intensive commodity, factor prices will move away from each other. This latter case is illustrated by the combination $r_I c_I, r''_{II} c_{II}$ in Figure 2, where country I has a comparative advantage in its capital-intensive commodity Y and the effect of the equalization of commodity prices through trade is to lower the relative price of labour in country I from w_I to w_e and raise it in country II from w_{II} to w_e. In the case shown, both countries continue to produce both goods though with different relative factor prices.

The conclusions to be drawn from the foregoing analysis with respect to the influence of differences in factor supplies on the pattern of international trade, and of trade on relative factor prices, may now be summarized and illustrated by reference to the three cases shown in Figure 2. First, it is not necessarily true that a country will export the commodity which uses relatively intensively the factor with which the country is relatively heavily endowed; in all three cases shown, the country endowed with the lower[12] ratio of capital to labour exports the capital-intensive good. Second, it is not necessarily true that a country will export the commodity which uses relatively more of the factor which would be relatively cheaper in the absence of trade. This proposition will be valid only if, as a consequence either of the nature of the available technology or of the endowment of countries with factors in not too dissimilar proportions, the relative factor-intensities of goods do not reverse themselves as the capital : labour ratio varies between the endowment ratios of the two countries—the condition required to exclude the possibility of such cases like r_I, r_{II} and r_I, r_{II}'' in Figure 2. Thirdly, the proposition that trade will tend to equalize relative factor prices, and will in fact do so if both countries continue to produce both goods, is valid only on the same condition; otherwise, trade may have any effect on factor prices, and production of both goods in both countries is consistent with widely different factor prices.[13] Consequently, it is only on the assumption that this condition is fulfilled that it can be maintained that trade is a partial or complete substitute for factor mobility, and free trade a substitute for removal of restrictions on factor movements. Thus the conclusions of the Heckscher-Ohlin model depend not only on the assumption of competition, absence of trade barriers, constant returns to scale, and so forth, but also on an empirical assumption about the nature of technology or the degree of variation in the factor endowments of countries.

In conclusion, something must be said about the extension of the technique of analysis beyond the simple two-country, two-commodity, two-factor case.

Analysis of cases involving more than two countries requires merely the representation of the additional countries by their endowment ratios

---

[12] A corollary of this result is that the so-called "Leontief scarce-factor paradox"—that the U.S.A. is a labour-abundant, capital-scarce country, deduced from the statistical finding that U.S. exports are more labour-intensive and less capital-intensive than U.S. import-competing products—rests on a theoretically invalid assumption since the nature of a country's factor endowment, relative to that of the rest of the world, cannot be inferred from the relative factor-intensities of exports and import substitutes in its domestic production. See W. Leontief, "Domestic Production and Foreign Trade; The American Capital Position Re-Examined," *Proceedings* of the American Philosophical Society, Vol. 97 (September, 1953), reprinted in *Economia Internazionale*, Vol. VII (1954); *ibid.*, "Factor Proportions and the Structure of American Trade: Further Theoretical and Empirical Analysis," *Review of Economics and Statistics*, Vol. XXXVIII, No. 4 (November, 1956), pp. 386–407. To the list of critics in Footnote 2 of the latter should be added Jones, *loc. cit.* The theoretical analysis is not, of course, the only questionable feature of Leontief's argument.

[13] Compare P. A. Samuelson, "International Trade and the Equalisation of Factor Prices," *Economic Journal*, Vol. LVIII, No. 230 (June, 1948), pp. 163–84, and *ibid.*, "International Factor Price Equalisation Once Again," *loc. cit.*, Vol. LIX, No. 234 (June, 1949), pp. 181–97. The condition required for equalization, that factor-intensities do not reverse between the endowment ratios, is assumed implicitly in the first of these articles, and stated explicitly in the second. See James and Pearce, *loc. cit.*

and pre-trade comparative cost ratios. Similarly, additional goods can be represented by additional curves showing the relation between the optimal capital : labour ratios used in their production and the relative factor price. Little can be said about the effect of allowing for a number of countries, since this depends on the dispersion of their endowment ratios. The effect of allowing for a number of commodities, however, is to strengthen the proposition that a country will tend to export those goods which use relatively most of the factor which would be relatively cheaper in the absence of trade, and that trade will tend to equalize factor prices. The reason for this is that the more goods there are, the more likely it will be that two can be found whose relative factor intensities do not reverse at a capital : labour ratio between the endowment ratios of the two countries.

The relatively labour-intensive commodity of such a pair must be cheaper in the country with the relatively lower price of labour, and conversely, in the pre-trade situation; and the effect of trade in establishing a common price-ratio between the pair must therefore be to raise the price of labour in the labour-abundant country and reduce it in the capital-abundant country. If both goods continue to be produced in both countries, factor prices must be equalized completely.

While the technique can be easily adapted to handle more countries and more commodities, it cannot easily be extended to allow for a larger number of factors of production, since each additional factor introduces an additional factor price and endowment ratio. Two points can, however, be made with respect to the conditions under which countries will necessarily export the commodities intensive in their relatively cheap factors, and trade will tend to equalize factor prices. The first is that, unless the number of goods is at least equal to the number of factors, no relationship between commodity prices and factor prices such as that assumed in Figure 1 will exist, so that it will not be possible to establish conditions on which factor prices are in a one-to-one relationship with commodity prices. The second is that, once the number of factors (and goods) exceeds two, the conditions required for the one-to-one relationship to hold cannot be stated in any economically meaningful way, because the concept of "factor-intensity" loses its simplicity.

6. Distribution, Demand, and Equilibrium in International Trade: A Diagrammatic Analysis *

By PETER B. KENEN [†]

SOME TWENTY YEARS AGO, Professors Leontief and Lerner brought the community indifference map into common use in international trade theory.[1] Since then, however, economists have repeatedly observed that the community indifference map is an unsatisfactory tool of analysis because it is unstable. Whenever international prices change, each country's product-mix will change and its income distribution will be altered. In consequence, community indifference curves will change shape and position.[2]

Yet most treatises and texts on international trade still employ the community indifference map to depict equilibrium in the two-country, two-commodity case.[3] Though faulty, it has proved too convenient to be quickly discarded. It is nevertheless possible to adduce most of the important propositions in international trade theory without employing community indifference curves. In another article, I have reproduced the major welfare propositions of trade theory using a device which fixes the (ordinal) utility of all but one of the persons within a country and assigns the gains from trade or from optimal protection to the remaining

---

* *Kyklos,* Vol. XII (fasc. 4, 1959), pp. 629–38.

† Columbia University.

[1] Wassily W. Leontief, "The Use of Indifference Curves in the Analysis of Foreign Trade," *Quarterly Journal of Economics,* May, 1933, reprinted in *Readings in the Theory of International Trade* (Philadelphia, 1949); Abba P. Lerner, "The Diagrammatical Representation of Demand Conditions in International Trade," *Economica,* August, 1934, reprinted in his *Essays in Economic Analysis* (New York, 1953).

[2] See, e.g., Tibor De Scitovszky, "A Reconsideration of the Theory of Tariffs," *Review of Economic Studies,* Summer, 1942, reprinted in *Readings, loc. cit.;* and Paul A. Samuelson, "Social Indifference Curves," *Quarterly Journal of Economics,* February, 1956.

[3] See, e.g., James E. Meade, *A Geometry of International Trade* (London, 1952); Donald B. Marsh, *World Trade and Investment* (New York, 1951); and Charles P. Kindleberger, *International Economics* (Homewood, 1958).

person.[4] Here, I set out a second diagrammatic method which takes explicit account of variations in the distribution of income and traces their impact upon the pattern of international trade.

I

We shall deal with two commodities, cloth and steel, and two factors of production, labor and capital. We assume throughout that pure competition prevails in all markets, that the supplies of labor and capital are fixed and fully employed, and that production functions are linear and homogeneous. We assume at the outset that all workers have equal incomes and identical indifference maps and that all capitalists have equal incomes and identical indifference maps.

We begin our argument with the production transformation curve BLA in the northwest quadrant of Figure 1. That schedule describes the combinations of cloth and steel that can be produced and the ratio of steel to cloth prices at which each combination will be forthcoming. If, for example, the ratio of steel to cloth prices equals the slope of the line CLD and, therefore, the slope of BLA at L, LM ($= OH$) units of steel and LH ($= OM$) units of cloth will be produced. The national income measured in units of steel will be OC:

National income = Steel output × Price of steel
+ Cloth output × Price of cloth
= OH × Price of steel + HL × Price of cloth.

Hence:

$$\frac{\text{National income}}{\text{Price of steel}} = OH + HL \times \frac{\text{Price of cloth}}{\text{Price of steel}}.$$
$$= OH + HC = OC.$$

We next consider the rectangle $OEFG$ in the southwest quadrant of Figure 1. That construction is the Stolper-Samuelson box.[5] It describes the supplies of capital (OG or EF) and of labor (OE or FG) available for the production of steel and cloth and the ways in which they may be combined. If OW units of capital and WJ ($= GK$) units of labor are used to produce steel, WG ($= JK$) units of capital and KF units of labor are available to produce cloth. The steel output corresponding to this combination of inputs is that associated with the steel isoquant a_s, defined relative to the axes OE and OG, passing through J. The cloth output corresponding to this combination of inputs is that associated with the cloth isoquant a_c, defined relative to the axes FG and FE, passing through

---

[4] "On the Geometry of Welfare Economics," *Quarterly Journal of Economics*, August, 1957.

[5] Wolfgang Stolper and Paul A. Samuelson, "Protection and Real Wages," *Review of Economic Studies*, November, 1941, reprinted in *Readings, loc. cit.*

J. As these isoquants are tangent at *J*, the combination of inputs just described is "efficient"; steel output cannot be increased (decreased) without decreasing (increasing) cloth output.

The point *J*, therefore, is the counterpart of some point on the production transformation curve *BLA*. To locate its counterpart we first observe that steel production at *F* corresponds to steel production at *B* (*OB* units), for at *F* all of the labor and capital available are employed in the steel industry making steel output a maximum and cloth output zero. We next observe that a movement along *FIO* from *F* toward *O* reduces steel output in proportion to the distance travelled from *F*, for our production functions evince constant returns to scale. If, then, the distance *OF* denotes a steel output of *OB* units, the distance *OI* denotes a steel output of *OH*, for *OFB* and *OIH* are similar triangles. Now the isoquant a_s passes through *I* and *J*. At *J*, therefore, steel output is *OH* units. At *J*, furthermore, cloth output is at a maximum given steel output. Hence production at *J* implies a cloth output of *HL* units, the largest compatible with a steel output of *OH*, and corresponds to production at *L* on *BLA*.

Now let us recall that production at *J* implies a unique ratio of wage rates to rates of return on capital; the ratio of wage rates to the return on capital must equal the slope of a_c at *J*. If, then, we construct at *F* the line *FN* having a slope equal to that of a_c at *J*, we may measure the wage bill (the total of labor income) in units of capital. It is *GN*. Concomitantly, the national income measured in units of capital is *ON*, leaving *OG* as the share of capitalists in the national income. This proposition can be quickly proved:

$$\text{National income} = \text{Labor force} \times \text{Wage rate}$$
$$+ \text{Capital stock} \times \text{Return on capital}$$
$$= FG \times \text{Wage rate} + OG \times \text{Return on capital}.$$

Hence:

$$\frac{\text{National income}}{\text{Return on capital}} = FG \times \frac{\text{Wage rate}}{\text{Return on capital}} + OG$$
$$= GN + OG = ON.$$

Suppose, now, that the international rate of exchange of steel for cloth (the system of international prices) *were* given by the slope of *CLD*. Then *OH* of steel and *OM* of cloth *would be* produced in the country we are examining and the national income of that country measured in units of steel would be *OC*. The ratio of wage rates to the return on capital would equal the slope of *FN*, the wage bill in units of capital would be *GN*, the income of capitalists *OG*, and the national income *ON*.

Let us mark off on the abscissa of our diagram a distance *OC'* equal to *OC*, drop perpendiculars from *C'* and from *N* through *P*, and draw the diagonal *OP*. As *OGQ* and *ONP* are similar triangles, *OG/ON* =

GQ/NP. $GQ(= OR)$ is therefore the income of capitalists measured in units of steel and RC' is the income of labor. We now construct the indifference map of the capitalists relative to the axes OC' and OS and the capitalists' budget restraint RS. The latter is, of course, a line of identical slope to that of CLD. The capitalists' equilibrium position is the point T, where an indifference curve Ω_c is tangent to RS. The capitalists will consume VT $(= OU)$ units of cloth and UT $(= OV)$ units of steel.

Extending the lines QR and UT until they meet in O', we draw the workers' indifference map relative to the axes $O'R'$ and $O'S'$ and their budget restraint $R'S'$. The workers' equilibrium position is at T, where the indifference curve Ω_L is tangent to $R'S'$. The workers will consume $V'T'$ $(= O'U')$ units of cloth and $U'T'$ $(= O'V')$ units of steel.

Clearly, the aggregate consumption of cloth is $OU + O'U'$ or OY $(= ZX)$. In that case, however, aggregate consumption of steel, $OV + O'V'$, must equal XY $(= OZ)$. This may be easily demonstrated:

Labor income   = Workers' steel consumption × Price of steel
             + Workers' cloth consumption × Price of cloth
             = $O'V'$ × Price of steel + $O'U'$ × Price of cloth.

And:

Capitalists' income = Capitalists' steel consumption × Price of steel
             + Capitalists' cloth consumption × Price of cloth
             = OV × Price of steel + OU × Price of cloth.

But:

National income   = Labor income + Capitalists' income
             = $(O'V' + OV)$ × Price of steel
             + $(O'U' + OU)$ × Price of cloth.

Hence:

$$\frac{\text{National income}}{\text{Price of steel}} = (O'V' + OV) + XZ \times \frac{\text{Price of cloth}}{\text{Price of steel}}$$

$$CO = (O'V' + OV) + CZ$$
$$CO - CZ = O'V' + OV) = ZO.$$

Our country, then, produces at L and trades at X; it imports MY units of cloth and exports HZ units of steel.

II

Our diagram may be used to illustrate a number of important propositions in the theory of international trade.

First, it indicates that factor proportions do not measure factor scarcity. The capital-to-labor ratio, OG/OE, may be smaller than in other countries, yet cloth—the imported commodity—uses capital less intensively than steel; $JK/KF < OW/WJ$. The "scarce factor" explana-

FIGURE 1

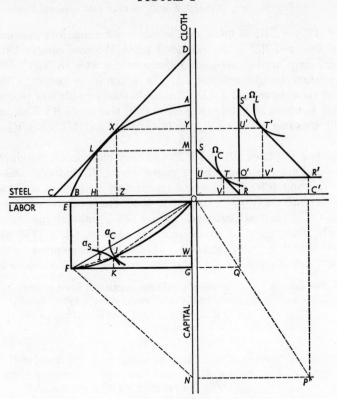

FIGURE 2

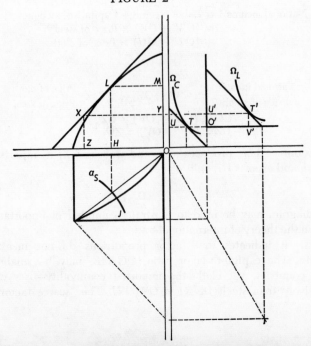

FIGURE 3

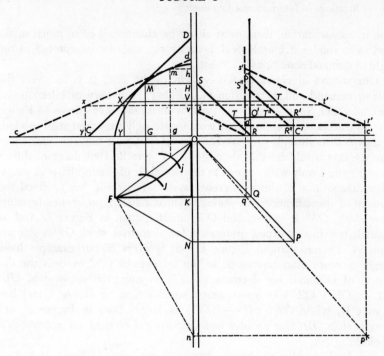

FIGURE 4

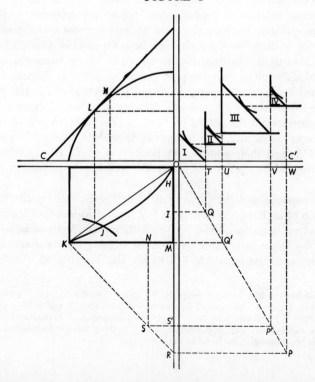

tion of specialization, then, must either be abandoned or so much modified as to render it tautological. Scarcity can only be interpreted in the
light of demand conditions.[6]

Our second objective is closely akin to the first. It is to stress the
role of demand and distribution in ordering the pattern of international
specialization. Suppose that the systems of indifference curves in Figure
1 were transposed; suppose that workers strongly preferred steel to cloth
and capitalists strongly preferred cloth to steel. Under these circumstances
our solution would be that described in Figure 2. That diagram differs
from Figure 1 only with respect to the character of the indifference maps.
The transposition of the indifference systems, however, has reversed the
pattern of specialization. As workers evince a strong preference for steel
over cloth, $O'V'$ is longer, and $O'U'$ shorter, than in Figure 1. And as
capitalists evince a strong preference for cloth over steel, OV is shorter,
and OU longer, than in Figure 1. But workers in our example have
larger incomes than capitalists, so the increase of $O'V'$ exceeds the decrease of OV, and the decrease of $O'U'$ swamps the increase of OU.
OY ($= OU + O'U'$) is consequently smaller than in Figure 1 and less
than OM, while OZ ($= OV + O'V'$) is larger than in Figure 1 and
greater than OH. Our country now imports ZH of steel and exports MY
of cloth.

Our final exercise involves a change in the terms of trade. It is generally supposed that an improvement in the terms of trade (an increase
of export prices relative to import prices) augments economic welfare.
It is of course possible to prove that such an improvement *makes possible*
an increase of welfare, for the losers can be compensated. Our diagram,
however, allows us to illustrate circumstances in which improved terms
of trade seriously injure one group in the community. In Figure 3 we
have assumed trade to take place at X and production at M; HV units
of cloth are exported and GY units of steel are imported. To production
at M there corresponds the point J on $FJjO$ and the ratio KN/FK of wage
rates to returns on capital. The income of capitalists expressed in units
of steel is OR, and their equilibrium position is at T. The incomes of
workers expressed in steel is RC' ($= R'O'$), and their equilibrium position is at T'.

We now suppose that the price of steel decreases, causing the international ratio of exchange to shift from CD to cd. Cloth output increases
and steel output decreases, bringing production from M to m and from
J to j. At j, the factor price ratio favors labor, causing labor's share of the
national income to rise from KN/ON to Kn/On. Marking off a distance

---

[6] This point has recently been made by R. W. Jones ("Factor Proportions and the
Heckscher-Ohlin Theorem," *Review of Economic Studies,* 1956/57, pp. 1–10), and by
Kelvin Lancaster ("Protection and Real Wages: A Restatement," *Economic Journal,*
June 1957, pp. 200–210). The implications of this analysis for the Leontief scarce-
factor paradox are thoroughly explored in those articles.

$c'O$ equal to cO on the abscissa of our diagram and dropping perpendiculars from c' and n we produce the point p and the diagonal Op in place of OP. Note that the angle pOn is smaller than the angle PON. This can be established using our national income identities:

$$On \times \text{Return on capital} = Oc' \times \text{Price of steel}.$$

Hence:

$$Oc'/On \; (= np/On) = \frac{\text{Return on capital}}{\text{Price of steel}}.$$

But the ratio return on capital/price of steel is the marginal product of capital in steel production which has declined with the change in production from J to j. The ratio np/On, therefore, must be smaller than the ratio NP/ON, and the angle pOn must be smaller than the angle PON.

As a result of the change in international prices, production and factor returns, the income of capitalists expressed in steel is reduced from OR to Or. At the same time, the budget line has diminished in slope to reflect the change in commodity prices. The equilibrium position for capitalists is consequently removed from T to some such point as t, a distinctly inferior position.

But the income of labor expressed in steel has risen from RC' to rc', and the axes for labor's indifference map—$O'R'$ and $O'S'$—have been replaced by $o'r'$ and $o's'$. Labor's equilibrium position is therefore changed from T' to t'. Aggregate demand for cloth decreases from $OV \; (= YX)$ to $Ov \; (= yx)$, increasing exports of cloth to vh and imports of steel to gy.

Labor has clearly gained by the change in the terms of trade. This may be confirmed by transferring the initial budget line, $R'S'$ to the new axes $o'r'$ and $o's'$. The initial equilibrium position of labor, T'', on that budget line, $R''S''$, obviously falls on a lower indifference curve than the new equilibrium position, t', on the budget line $r's'$.

III

At the beginning of this discussion we assumed "that all workers have equal incomes and identical indifference maps and that all capitalists have equal incomes and identical indifference maps." We can now relax that assumption. Let us suppose that OI capitalists in Figure 4 have one set of indifference maps and IM have a different set, and that KN of the labor force have one set of indifference maps and NM another. Beginning with production at L and J and with a ratio of factor returns equal to MR/KM, we may divide the national income measured in units of capital into four parts: OI, IM, MS' and $S'R$. That MS' and $S'R$ stand in the same relation to MR as do KN and NM to KM can easily be established, for KSN and SRS' are similar triangles. We may then proceed as in Figure 1. Dropping perpendiculars from OR to the diagonal OP we locate the points Q, Q', and P', mark off the incomes of each group of persons on the axis OC', and construct the indifference maps

pertaining to each group. The first group of capitalists, *OI*, receives an
income equal to *OT* units of steel and operates on the indifference map I.
The second group of capitalists, *IM*, receives an income equal to *TU* units
of steel and operates on the indifference map II. The first group of workers, *KN*, receives an income equal to *UV* units of steel and operates on
the indifference map III. And the second group of workers receives an income equal to *VW* units of steel and operates on the indifference map IV.
The position of each indifference map depends, of course, upon the
equilibrium position of the preceding group. Adding up the cloth consumption of our four groups, we secure the trading point *X*.

The procedure just described might be extended to treat differences
in income among persons. If, for instance, the stock of capital *OI* were
divided among three persons, one of them owning *OH* units, the others
sharing *HI* equally, we could treat *OH* and *HI* as separate groups. We
should, in fact, have to do so. Though the indifference maps of the three
persons are identical (they all belong to the group *OI*), the person owning *OH* units might purchase steel and cloth in different proportions
than the persons sharing *HI* units. The three persons owning *OI* units of
capital could be treated as a single group for purposes of demand analysis
only if their individual indifference maps evinced unit elasticity of demand for cloth and steel.

Finally, the diagram used in this discussion can also be employed to
construct an offer curve. Were we to alter slightly the international ratio
of exchange, *CLD*, in Figure 1 we would generate a new production
point, *L*, and a new trading point, *X*. Repeating this process, we would
eventually secure a schedule showing the amounts of cloth and steel
that would be traded at various sets of prices. This schedule *is* an offer curve.

II | International Factor Movements

7. International Trade and

Factor Mobility *

By ROBERT A. MUNDELL[†‡]

COMMODITY MOVEMENTS ARE at least to some extent a substitute for factor movements. The absence of trade impediments implies *commodity*-price equalization and, even when factors are immobile, a tendency toward *factor*-price equalization. It is equally true that perfect mobility of factors results in *factor*-price equalization and, even when commodity movements cannot take place, in a tendency toward *commodity*-price equalization.

There are two extreme cases between which are to be found the conditions in the real world: there may be perfect factor mobility but no trade, or factor immobility with unrestricted trade. The classical economists generally chose the special case where factors of production were internationally immobile.

This paper will describe some of the effects of relaxing the latter assumption, allowing not only commodity movements but also some degree of factor mobility. Specifically it will show that an increase in trade impediments stimulates factor movements and that an increase in restrictions to factor movements stimulates trade.[1] It will also make more specific an old argument for protection.

I. TRADE IMPEDIMENTS STIMULATE FACTOR MOVEMENTS

Under certain rigorous assumptions the substitution of commodity for factor movements will be complete. In a two-country two-commodity two-factor model, commodity-price equalization is sufficient to ensure factor-price equalization and factor-price equalization is sufficient to ensure commodity-price equalization if: (*a*) production functions are homoge-

---

* *American Economic Review*, Vol. XLVII, No. 3 (June, 1957), pp. 321–35.

† The University of Chicago.

‡ The author has benefited considerably from the suggestions and criticisms of M. Corden, M. Friedman, A. Harberger, H. G. Johnson, R. Lipsey, J. E. Meade, S. A. Ozga, and T. Rybczynski. Any mistakes that remain are his responsibility.

[1] This proposition is implied in Bertil Ohlin, *Interregional and International Trade* (Cambridge, 1933), ch. 9; Carl Iversen, *Aspects of the Theory of International Capital Movements* (London, 1935), ch. 2; and J. E. Meade, *Trade and Welfare* (London, 1955), ch. 21, 22.

neous of the first degree (i.e., if marginal productivities, relatively and absolutely, depend only on the proportions in which factors are combined) and are identical in both countries; (*b*) one commodity requires a greater proportion of one factor than the other commodity at any factor prices at all points on any production function; and (*c*) factor endowments are such as to exclude specialization.[2]

These assumptions are not always satisfied in the real world, so a model employing them is somewhat limited. But they do isolate some important influences determining the pattern of international trade and for present purposes will be adhered to. It will become clear later that relaxing them does not seriously affect the conclusions of the paper.

First we shall show that an increase in trade impediments encourages factor movements, and to do this we shall make some rather drastic assumptions regarding mobility. Assume two countries, A and B, two commodities, cotton and steel, and two factors, labor and capital.[3] Country A is well endowed with labor but poorly endowed with capital relative to country B; cotton is labor-intensive relative to steel. For expositional convenience we shall use commodity indifference curves.

For the moment we shall assume that country B is the rest of the world and that country A is so small in relation to B that its production conditions and factor endowments can have no effect on prices in B.[4]

Let us begin with a situation where factors are immobile between A and B but where impediments to trade are absent. This results in commodity- and factor-price equalization. Country A exports its labor-intensive product, cotton, in exchange for steel. Equilibrium is represented in Figure 1: *TT* is A's transformation function (production-possibility curve), production is at *P* and consumption is at *S*. Country A is exporting *PR* of cotton and importing *RS* of steel. Her income in terms of steel or cotton is *OY*.

Suppose now that some exogenous factor removes all impediments to the movement of capital. Clearly since the marginal product of capital is the same in both A and B no capital movement will take place and equilibrium will remain where it is. But now assume that A imposes a tariff on steel and for simplicity make it prohibitive.[5] Initially the

---

[2] For the necessity of these assumptions and a fairly complete list of references to the literature on factor-price equalization see P. A. Samuelson, "Prices of Factors and Goods in General Equilibrium," *Rev. Econ. Stud.*, Vol. XXI, No. 1 (1953–54), pp. 1–21.

[3] Capital is here considered a physical, homogeneous factor which does not create any balance-of-payments problems when it moves internationally. It is further assumed that capitalists qua consuming units do not move with their capital, so national taste patterns are unaltered.

[4] It will become evident in Section II that the terms of trade and factor prices do not change even if A is fairly large.

[5] Actually, under the assumed conditions any tariff is prohibitive, as will eventually become clear.

FIGURE 1

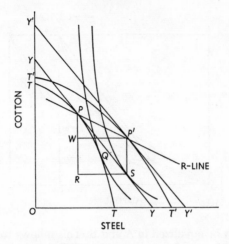

price of steel will rise relative to the price of cotton in A and both production and consumption will move to Q, the autarky (economic self-
sufficiency) point. Factors will move out of the cotton into the steel
industry; but since cotton is labor-intensive and steel is capital-intensive, at constant factor prices the production shift creates an excess
supply of labor and an excess demand for capital. Consequently the
marginal product of labor must fall and the marginal product of capital
must rise. This is the familiar Stolper-Samuelson tariff argument.[6]

But since capital is mobile, its higher marginal product in A induces
a capital movement into A from B, changing factor endowments so as
to make A more capital-abundant. With more capital A's transformation curve expands until a new equilibrium is reached.

Some help in determining where this new equilibrium will be is provided by the box diagram in Figure 2. Country A initially has OC of
capital and OL of labor; OO' is the efficiency locus along which marginal
products of labor and capital are equalized in steel and cotton. Equilibrium is initially at P which corresponds to P on the production block in
Figure 1. Factor proportions in steel and cotton are given by the slopes
of OP and $O'P$ respectively.

After the tariff is imposed production moves along the efficiency locus
to Q, corresponding to the autarky point Q in Figure 1. The slopes of
OQ and $O'Q$ indicate that the ratios of labor to capital in both cotton
and steel have risen—i.e., the marginal product of capital has risen and
the marginal product of labor has fallen. Capital flows in and the cotton
origin O' shifts to the right.

With perfect mobility of capital the marginal products of both labor

---

[6] Cf. W. F. Stolper and P. A. Samuelson, "Protection and Real Wages," *Rev. Econ.
Stud.*, Vol. IX (Nov., 1941), pp. 58–73.

FIGURE 2

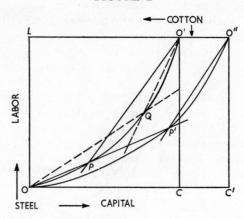

and capital must be equalized in A and B. This follows from the assumption that the production functions are linear, homogeneous and identical in both countries. Since marginal products in the rest of the world can be considered constant, the returns to factors in A will not change. Factor proportions in both steel and cotton in A then must be the same as before the tariff was imposed—so equilibrium must lie along OP-extended at the point where it is cut by a line $O''P'$ parallel to $O'P$, where O'' is the new cotton origin. But this is not yet sufficient to tell us exactly where OP-extended along the point P' will be.

Since marginal products in the new equilibrium are the same as before the tariff, commodity prices in A will not have changed; but if both incomes earned by domestic factors and commodity prices are unchanged, consumption will remain at S (in Figure 1). Production however must be greater than S because interest payments must be made to country B equal in value to the marginal product of the capital inflow. In Figure 1, then, production equilibrium must be at some point above or to the northeast of S.

To find the exact point we must show the effects of a change in capital endowments on the production block. Because steel is capital-intensive we should expect the production block after the capital movement has taken place to be biased in favor of steel at any given price ratio; that this is so has been recently proved by Rybczynski.[7]

---

[7] T. M. Rybczynski, "Factor Endowment and Relative Commodity Prices," *Economica*, Vol. XXII (Nov., 1955), pp. 336–41. The proof can be easily demonstrated in Figure 2. At unchanged prices equilibrium must lie along OP-extended. With the larger endowment of capital, $O''P'$ must be shorter than OP. Since these lines have the same slope and constant returns to scale apply, output of cotton at P' must be less than at P. A paper by R. Jones written at the Massachusetts Institute of Technology in the spring of 1955 contained a similar proof.

Since the same price ratio as at P will prevail, the locus of all tangents to larger and larger production blocks based on larger and larger endowments of capital must have a negative slope. Such a line, which I shall call the R-line, is drawn in Figure 1.

Capital will flow in until its marginal product is equalized in A and B, which will be at the point where A can produce enough steel and cotton for consumption equilibrium at S without trade, and at the same time make the required interest payment abroad. This point is clearly reached at P' directly above S. At any point along the R-line to the northwest of P', country A would have to import steel in order to consume at S—i.e., demand conditions in A cannot be satisfied to the northwest of P'. At P' demand conditions in A are satisfied and the interest payment can be made abroad at the same price ratio as before the tariff was levied. Thus the capital movement need not continue past this point, although any point to the southeast of P' would be consistent with equilibrium.

Production takes place in A at P', consumption is at S and the transfer of interest payments is the excess of production over consumption in A, SP' of cotton.[8] The value of A's production has increased from OY to OY' in terms of steel, but YY' (which equals in value SP' of cotton) must be transferred abroad, so income is unchanged.

We initially assumed a prohibitive tariff; in fact even the smallest tariff is prohibitive in this model. A small tariff would not prohibit trade immediately: because of the price change some capital would move in and some trade would take place. But as long as trade continues there must be a difference in prices in A and B equal to the ad valorem rate of tariff—hence a difference in marginal products—so capital imports must continue. Marginal products and prices can only be equalized in A and B when A's imports cease.

The tariff is now no longer necessary! Since marginal products and prices are again equalized the tariff can be removed without reversing the capital movement. The tariff has eliminated trade, but after the capital movement there is no longer any need for trade.

This is not really such a surprising result when we refer back to the assumptions. Before the tariff was imposed we assumed both unimpeded trade and perfect capital mobility. We have then two assumptions each of which is sufficient for the equalization of commodity and factor prices. The effect of the tariff is simply to eliminate one of these assumptions—unimpeded trade; the other is still operative.

---

[8] SP' must equal in value the marginal product of the capital inflow at constant prices. In Figure 1, PP' is the change in output associated with the increase in capital; steel output increases by RS but cotton output decreases by PW. The marginal product of the capital inflow is the value of RS minus the value of PW which, in terms of cotton, is $P'S$.

However, one qualification must be made. If impediments to trade exist in both countries (tariffs in both countries or transport costs on both goods) and it is assumed that capital-owners do not move with their capital, the interest payments on foreign-owned capital will be subject to these impediments; this will prevent complete equalization of factor and commodity prices. (This question could have been avoided had we allowed the capitalist to consume his returns in the country where his capital was invested.) The proposition that capital mobility is a perfect substitute for trade still stands, however, if one is willing to accept the qualification as an imperfection to capital mobility.

II. EFFECT OF RELATIVE SIZES OF THE TWO COUNTRIES

The previous section assumed that country A was very small in relation to country B. It turns out however, that the relative sizes of the two countries make no difference in the model, provided that complete specialization does not result.

Suppose as before that country A is exporting cotton in exchange for steel. There are no impediments to trade and capital is mobile. But we no longer assume that A is small relative to B. Now A imposes a tariff on steel raising the internal price of steel in relation to cotton, shifting resources out of cotton into steel, raising the marginal product of capital and lowering the marginal product of labor. A's demand for imports and her supply of exports fall. This decline in demand for B's steel exports and supply of B's cotton imports raises the price of cotton relative to steel in B; labor and capital in B shift out of steel into cotton raising the marginal product of labor and lowering the marginal product of capital in B. Relative factor returns in A and B move in opposite directions, so the price changes in A which stimulate a capital movement are reinforced by the price changes in B. The marginal product of capital rises in A and falls in B; capital moves from B to A, contracting B's and expanding A's production block.

The assumption that capital is perfectly mobile means that factor and commodity prices must be equalized after the tariff. It is necessary now to show that they also will be unchanged. The price of cotton relative to steel is determined by world demand and supply curves. To prove that prices remain unchanged it is sufficient to show that these demand and supply curves are unchanged—or, that at the pretariff price ratio demand equals supply after the capital movement has taken place. But we know that at the old price ratio marginal products, hence incomes, are unchanged—thus demand is unchanged. All that remains then is to show that at constant prices production changes in one country cancel out production changes in the other country.

This proposition can be proved in the following way: If commodity and factor prices are to be unchanged after the capital movement has taken place then factor proportions in each industry must be the same as before; then the increment to the capital stock used in A will, at constant prices, increase the output of steel and decrease the output of cotton in A, and the decrement to the capital stock in B will decrease the output of steel and increase the output of cotton in B. But the increase in A's capital is equal to the decrease in B's capital, and since production expands at constant prices and with the same factor proportions in each country, the increase in resources used in producing steel in A must be exactly equal to the decrease in resources devoted to the production of steel in B. Similarly, the decrease in resources used in producing cotton in A is the same as the increase in resources devoted to cotton production in B. Then, since production functions are linear and homogeneous, the equal changes in resources applied to each industry (in opposite directions) imply equal changes in output. Therefore, the increase in steel output in A is equal to the decrease in steel output in B, and the decrease in cotton output in A is equal to the increase in cotton output in B—i.e., world production is not changed, at constant prices, by a movement of capital from one country to another. In the world we are considering it makes no difference in which country a commodity is produced if commodity prices are equalized.

This proposition can perhaps be made clearer by a geometrical proof. In Figure 3a, T_aT_a is A's transformation curve before the tariff, and $T_a'T_a'$ is the transformation curve after the tariff has been imposed and the capital movement has taken place. At constant prices equilibrium moves along A's R-line from P_a to P_a' increasing the output of steel by RP_a' and decreasing the output of cotton by RP_a. Similarly, in Figure 3b, T_bT_b is country B's transformation curve before the capital movement and $T_b'T_b'$ is the transformation curve after capital has left B. At constant prices production in B moves along B's R-line to P_b', steel production decreasing by SP_b and cotton production increasing by SP_b'.

To demonstrate the proposition that world supply curves are unchanged it is necessary to prove that RP_a' equals SP_b and that RP_a equals SP_b'. The proof is given in Figure 4. OL_a and OC_a are, respectively, A's initial endowments of labor and capital; OL_b and OC_b are the endowments of B. OO_a and OO_b are the efficiency loci of A and B with production taking place along these loci at P_a and P_b, corresponding to the same letters in Figures 3a and 3b.

Now when A imposes a tariff on steel suppose that C_bC_b' of capital leaves B, shifting B's cotton origin from O_b to O_b'. At constant prices labor-capital ratios in each industry must be the same as before so equilibrium must move to P_b', corresponding to P_b' in Figure 3b. Since the capital outflow from B must equal the capital inflow to A, A's cotton origin must move to the right by just the same amount as B's cotton origin moves to the left—i.e., from O_a to O_a'; and A's production equilibrium at constant prices must move from P_a to P_a'. The proof that

FIGURE 3a   FIGURE 3b

Country A   Country B

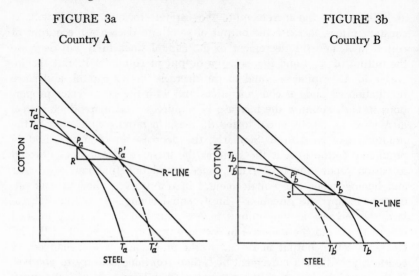

world supply is unchanged at constant prices is now obvious since JP_aP_a' and $KP_b'P_b$ are identical triangles. P_aP_a', representing the increase in steel output in A, equals P_bP_b', the decrease in steel output in B, and the decrease in cotton output in A, JP_a, equals the increase in cotton output in B, KP_b'.[9]

This relationship holds at all combinations of commodity and factor prices provided some of each good is produced in both countries. It means that world supply functions are independent of the distribution of factor endowments. More simply it means that it makes no difference to world supply where goods are produced if commodity and factor prices are equalized. Since world supply and demand functions are not changed by the capital movements, so that the new equilibrium must be established at the same prices as before, our earlier assumption that A is very small in relation to B is an unnecessary one.[10]

---

[9] The R-lines in Figures 3a and 3b must be parallel when output expands at the same price ratio in each country, and they must be straight since production changes are compensating.

[10] One qualification to the argument must be noted which is not necessary when the other country is very large. A condition for the marginal product of capital in A to rise as a result of the tariff is that the price of steel rise relative to the price of cotton. It is possible, if the foreign offer curve is very inelastic, that the improvement in A's terms of trade in raising the relative price of exports (cotton) will more than offset the effect of the tariff in raising the relative price of imports (steel). The condition that the "normal" case is satisfied requires that the sum of the foreign elasticity of demand and the domestic marginal propensity to import be greater than unity (the marginal propensity to import is relevant because the improvement in the terms of trade increases income). This is Metzler's qualification to the Stolper-Samuelson tariff argument. See Lloyd Metzler "Tariffs, the Terms of Trade and the Distribution of the National Income," *Jour. Pol. Econ.*, Vol. LVII (Feb., 1949), pp. 1–29. If this criterion is less than unity a tariff imposed by a labor-abundant country would stimulate for-

FIGURE 4

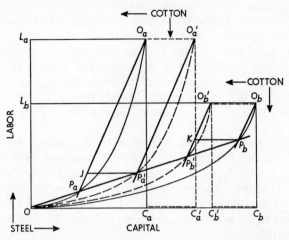

The general conclusion of Sections I and II is that tariffs will stimulate factor movements. Which factor moves depends, of course, on
which factor is more mobile. The assumption used here, that capital is
perfectly mobile and that labor is completely immobile is an extreme
one which would have to be relaxed before the argument could be
made useful. But a great deal can be learned qualitatively from extreme
cases and the rest of the paper will retain this assumption. When only
capital is mobile, a labor-abundant country can attract capital by tariffs
and a capital-abundant country can encourage foreign investment by
tariffs. The same is true for an export tax, since in this model the effect
of an export tax is the same as that of a tariff.

The analysis is not restricted to tariffs; it applies as well to changes
in transport costs. An increase of transport costs (of commodities) will
raise the real return of and thus attract the scarce factor, and lower
the real return and thus encourage the export of the abundant factor.
The effect of any trade impediment is to increase the scarcity of the
scarce factor and hence make more profitable an international redistribution of factors. Later we shall consider, under somewhat more realistic
assumptions than those used above, the applicability of this proposition
as an argument for protection.

III. INCREASED IMPEDIMENTS TO FACTOR MOVEMENTS STIMULATE TRADE

To show that an increase in impediments to factor movements stimulates trade we shall assume that some capital is foreign-owned and

eign investment rather than attract capital—a result, it should be noted, based on the
static assumptions of this model; if dynamic elements were involved the direction of
the capital movement would depend on whether the effects of the tariff on production
preceded or followed the effects on the terms of trade.

illustrate the effects on trade of taxing this capital. Strictly speaking this is not an impediment to a capital *movement;* but if it were assumed that a steady capital flow was taking place the tax on foreign-owned capital would operate as an impediment.

We shall use Figures 1 and 2. Begin with equilibrium initially at P' in Figure 1. No impediments to trade exist but since factor and commodity prices are already equalized no trade takes place. We assume that $O'O''$ of capital in Figure 2 is foreign-owned so a transfer equal in value to YY' in Figure 1 is made. Consumption equilibrium in A is at S.

If a tax is now levied on all foreign capital its net return will be decreased, and since factor prices must be equalized in A and B, all of it $(O'O'')$ must leave A. As capital leaves A, her production block contracts. At constant prices more cotton and less steel is produced. The price of steel relative to cotton tends to rise but, since there are no impediments to trade, is prevented from doing so by steel imports and cotton exports.

Since all foreign capital leaves A the final size of A's transformation function is TT, that consistent with domestically owned capital. Production equilibrium moves from P' to P, but consumption equilibrium remains at S because interest payments are no longer made abroad. PR is now exported in exchange of steel imports of RS. The effect of the tax has been to repatriate foreign capital and increase trade. By similar reasoning it could be shown that a subsidy will attract capital and decrease trade, although in the latter case the capital movement will only stop when factor prices change—i.e., specialization takes place.

In order to achieve efficiency in world production it is unnecessary that both commodities and factors move freely. As long as the production conditions are satisfied it is sufficient that *either* commodities *or* factors move freely. But if some restrictions, however small, exist to both commodity and factor movements, factor- and commodity-price equalization cannot take place (except in the trivial case where trade is unnecessary because prices are already equal). This principle applies only to those restrictions which are operative—obviously it does not apply to import tariffs on goods which are exported, transport costs for factors which are immobile anyway or quotas larger than those required for equalization to take place.

If it were not for the problem of transporting interest payments, referred to earlier, one mobile factor would be sufficient to ensure price equalization. When the labor-abundant country imposes the tariff, equalization will take place as long as the other country continues a free-trade policy and there are no transport costs involved. But if the capital-abundant country imposes a tariff, inducing the export of capital, prices cannot be equalized even if the labor-abundant country maintains free trade unless the transfer of goods constituting interest payments is also tariff-free.[11]

IV. AN ARGUMENT FOR PROTECTION

The proposition that an increase in trade impediments stimulates factor movements and an increase in impediments to factor movements stimulates trade has implications as an argument for protection. In order to examine these implications we shall relax some of the assumptions previously made—first, by introducing trade impediments, then decreasing the degree of factor mobility, and finally relaxing the assumption that constant returns to scale apply by taking account of external economies. We shall begin with a model similar with that of Section II except that we shall assume country A to be considerably smaller than country B.[12]

Take as a starting point the absence of trade impediments; trade is sufficient to ensure commodity- and factor-price equalization. Now suppose that, overnight, transport costs come into existence; this raises the price of importables relative to exportables, shifts resources into importables, raises the marginal product of the scarce factor and lowers that of the abundant factor in each country. Incomes of A-capitalists and B-workers increase while incomes of A-workers and B-capitalists decrease. These changes in factor returns create the incentive for a capital movement from B to A, a labor movement from A to B, or a combination of both movements. Where the final equilibrium will be depends on the degree of factor mobility. I shall assume that labor is immobile between countries but that capital is at least partially mobile.

If we assume that capital is perfectly mobile, but that capitalists do not move with their capital, the latter will move from B to A until the return from capital invested in A is the same as from that invested in B; but this implies that marginal physical products cannot be equalized since

---

[11] If trade were a perfect substitute for factor movements in the absence of trade impediments, a rough idea of the cost of trade impediments could be acquired by calculating the increase in world income which could take place if capital were redistributed from capital-rich to capital-poor countries until its marginal product throughout the world was equalized. Alternatively this could be considered the most of capital immobility. This statement would have to be qualified in the many-factor case.

[12] I make this assumption so that the change in the terms of trade resulting from A's tariff is small. In passing, however, it should be noted that the more mobile is capital, the smaller is the change in the terms of trade resulting from a tariff; this means that the optimum tariff will be smaller with, than without, capital mobility; and in the limiting case where capital is perfectly mobile, discussed in Sections I and II, the optimum tariff is zero.

Also, in what follows I neglect to discuss the tariff proceeds which are implicitly assumed to be redistributed in such a way as to leave A's indifference map unchanged. Alternatively, to abstract both from changes in the terms of trade and the tariff proceeds, it could be assumed that the tariff is prohibitive.

transport costs must be paid on the goods constituting interest payments.[13] The introduction of transport costs would, then, reduce world income even if capital were perfectly mobile unless capitalists are willing to consume their income in the country in which their capital is invested.

But we shall not assume that capital is perfectly mobile. Instead suppose that B-capitalists insist on receiving a higher return on any capital they invest in A than on that which they invest in B, perhaps because of political instability, patriotism, risk or economic uncertainty. Let us assume that B-capitalists require a 10 per cent higher return on capital invested in A than on that invested in B, but that if this interest differential rises above 10 per cent, capital is perfectly mobile. Suppose further that the return to capital in both countries before introducing transport costs was 12 per cent; and that the effect of introducing transport costs is to lower the marginal product of capital in B to 11 per cent and to raise it in A to 17 per cent. Since the interest differential is less than 10 per cent no capital movement will take place.

It is at this point that we shall consider the argument for a tariff in A. Let A impose a tariff, further increasing her relative scarcity of capital and B's relative scarcity of labor. Rates of return on capital change to, let us say, 25 per cent in A and 9 per cent in B, creating an interest differential of 16 per cent. Capital will now move from B to A until this differential is reduced to 10 per cent. Obviously the rates of return cannot return to the pretariff rates of 17 per cent for A and 11 per cent for B: first, because part of the tariff will be "used up" in bringing the marginal products of capital in A and B to the point where B has an incentive to export capital; and second, because transport costs must be paid on the interest returns.

If capital moves until the return in A falls to 20 per cent and in B rises to 10 per cent, what can be said about the economic effects of the tariff as far as country A is concerned?

First, A-capitalists are better off; the tariff increases and the capital inflow decreases capital scarcity, but the net effect is a higher return than before the tariff. Second, A-workers are worse off in spite of the fact that the total ratio of capital to labor in A has increased. Marginal products are determined not by the total ratio of capital to labor in a country, but by the ratio of capital to labor in each industry. The capital from B is largely absorbed by increasing the output of capital-intensive importables in A; it can never succeed in raising the capital-labor ratio in each

---

[13] However, interest rates must be the same! Since capital goods—call them machines—can move costlessly from one country to the other, the price of machines in money terms will be the same in both countries; and since machines will move to A until marginal products in money terms are equal, interest rates (the return to a machine as a proportion of the price of a machine) must be the same in both countries. The interest rate, of course, is not commensurable with the marginal product of capital unless the latter is defined as a proportion of the price of machines; in the new equilibrium the two are equal when the marginal product of capital is so defined.

industry to its pretariff level. Real wages must be lower than before the tariff.

Third, real national income in A is less than before the tariff; the tariff makes A's scarce factor relatively more scarce, and her abundant factor relatively more abundant, reducing her potential gains from international trade. Even under the most favorable assumptions, with capital perfectly mobile and capitalists moving with their capital, A's income would remain the same; it could not improve.

So far no valid tariff argument has been produced.[14] Capital can be attracted to a capital-scarce country by a tariff, but the capital movement can only alleviate some of the unfavorable effects of the tariff; it can not eliminate them.

The argument can be rescued if we assume the appropriate non-linearities of scale.[15] If external economies of scale[16] exist in the production of A-importables, the tariff will encourage more capital to enter than would otherwise be attracted since the marginal product of capital entering A will not fall as rapidly as it would fall in the absence of economies of scale. The new equilibrium will be established with a higher marginal product of labor, factor returns now being dependent not only on the proportions in which factors are combined, but also on the total output of importables. Real wages will be higher in A with than without economies of scale, though it is not certain that they will be higher than before the tariff; to demonstrate the latter it would have to be established that the economies of scale are sufficient to make up for the transport costs which

---

[14] It is true that B's national income has increased since the effect of A's tariff is to raise B-wages and stimulate capital investment in A, where B-capitalists receive a higher rate of return than at home; but it cannot be said that B-capitalists are better off since, *ex hypothesi*, they are indifferent between investment at home and an investment in A in which the rate of return is 10 per cent higher. In any case the purpose of policy makers in A is to raise A's not B's income.

[15] It may be possible to rescue the argument in other ways by assuming irrational, though possibly not implausible, behavior. For example, after B-capitalists have begun investing in A, they may acquire more confidence, and be willing to accept a smaller interest differential. In this case after the capital movement the marginal product of labor may be higher, and the marginal product of capital lower, than before the tariff, thereby increasing A's national income. Or, while some (relatively) capital-scarce countries may fear "exploitation" from foreign investment, others may view the increase in productive capacity resulting from it as desirable in itself (perhaps with the intent of future expropriation!)—in which case this factor would have to be balanced against the reduction in national income.

[16] It is sometimes overlooked that internal economies of scale do not constitute an argument for a tariff. An industry must not only be able to compete some years after the tariff; it must also earn a sufficient return to repay the economy for the loss of income resulting from the tariff in the period of the industry's infancy. The investment will then only be worthwhile if future output is sufficient to earn for the firm the current rate of interest on the capital involved. But when economies to scale are internal the investment will be profitable for private enterprise. Only when divergences between private and social costs due to *external* economies of scale are present is the case for government intervention valid.

E

must be paid on the interest returns. If they are sufficient, the tariff would be unequivocally beneficial.[17]

It is easy to see that economies of scale in importables or diseconomies of scale in exportables increase the likelihood that the net effect of the tariff in a labor-abundant country is favorable, and vice versa. To justify an argument for protection on the above grounds it would have to be established that capital-intensive industries are subject to external economies of scale and/or that labor-intensive industries are subject to external economies of scale; and these nonlinearities are of the required size.[18]

V. CONCLUDING REMARKS

Like all theory, the above analysis is remote from reality. The problems of many factors, goods and countries, monopolistic competition and differences in production functions have not been considered. In addition the model is nonmonetary and static. Still, these limitations do not interfere with the central theme, although any policy considerations would have to take them into account.

A number of questions present themselves. Did the growth of protection in the late nineteenth century in North America stimulate the large labor and capital inflows of that period (assuming land to have been the abundant factor)? Did the increased protection in Britain in this century stimulate capital export? Did the breakdown in international factor movements in the interwar period stimulate trade? And to what extent have the high tariff barriers between Canada and the United States contributed to the stimulus of American investment in Canada? It would be interesting to see what help this model offers in finding answers to these questions.

---

[17] But if the same nonlinearities of scale exist in B the argument is weakened; economies of scale in A-importables will cause the marginal product of capital to fall at a slower rate than in their absence, but in this case the marginal product of capital in B will rise at a much faster rate as capital is exported. Similar economies of scale in B, then, may cancel out the effect of economies in A in inducing a larger capital movement, although this effect could be neglected if B were the rest of the world and A a small country.

[18] A possible extension of the model to allow for many goods could be made as follows: All goods could be ordered in terms of their capital intensities—i.e., the ratios of capital to labor at any given price ratio. B would export those goods that are most capital-intensive and A those goods which are most labor-intensive. In the absence of trade impediments one of the intermediate commodities would be produced in common, establishing the ratio of factor returns in much the same way as goods produced in common establish the ratio of international values in a Graham model. Now the effect of a tariff in A (as of any impediment) is to increase the relative price of capital-intensive goods in A and to lower them in B thus raising in A and lowering in B the marginal product of capital. Now not one commodity but a whole series of commodities would be produced in common, A's exports comprising only the most labor-intensive and B's exports only the most capital-intensive goods. In A new capital-intensive industries, and in B new labor-intensive industries, would be created. If some capital were not allowed to move to A, the margin of comparative advantage would be extended to capital-intensive industries in A, thus increasing the number of goods produced in common in both countries.

8. The Transfer Problem & Transport Costs*

By PAUL A. SAMUELSON[†]

THE MORE THINGS CHANGE the more they are the same. After the First World War economists discussed the effects of a unilateral transfer—such as reparations—on the terms of trade. And in the 1950s, as the end of the Marshall Plan comes into sight, economists must once again consider an identical analytic problem—the possible effects of a cessation of unrequited imports on the terms of trade.[1]

It is perhaps fair to say that most economic theorists subscribe to the so-called "orthodox" doctrine: Any increase in unilateral payments will in probability shift the terms of trade against the paying country; any reduction in its unilateral payments will probably shift the terms of trade in its favor.

In the first part of this paper, I shall raise a few questions concerning the validity of the reasoning underlying this view; but in the end I shall not seriously impugn its substantive conclusions. My main purpose here is to treat the rather neglected analytic issues raised for international trade by transport costs, and to show that in their complete absence the orthodox view rests on shaky logical foundations. In the second part of the paper, I analyse in some detail the effects of impediments to trade on international equilibrium, thereby tending to restore some validity to the orthodox position.

PART I: THE TERMS OF TRADE WHEN IMPEDIMENTS ARE ABSENT[2]

A. Brief History of Doctrine

The debate between Keynes and Ohlin on the effects of transfer will be recalled. Keynes took the position that if a region like Europe made to

---

* Abridged from two articles which appeared in *Economic Journal*, Vol. LXII, No. 246 (June, 1952), pp. 278–304 and Vol. LXIV, No. 254 (June, 1954), pp. 264–89. These articles are reproduced in P. A. Samuelson, *Collected Scientific Papers*, Vol. II, Joseph E. Stiglitz (ed.) (Cambridge, Mass.: MIT Press, 1966), pp. 985–1037.

† Massachusetts Institute of Technology.

[1] A. C. Pigou, "Unrequited Imports," *Economic Journal*, Vol. LX (June, 1950), pp. 241–54. See also J. E. Meade, "A Geometrical Representation of Balance of Payments Policy," *Economica*, Vol. XVI (November, 1949), pp. 305–20.

[2] I am glad to acknowledge helpful comments from Professors R. L. Bishop, G. A. Elliott, C. P. Kindleberger, D. H. Robertson and Jacob Viner; and particularly from Professor G. Haberler, for whose 1936–37 Harvard seminar an earlier mathematical version of this paper was prepared.

a region like America a unilateral transfer (investment, reparations, gifts, etc.), then the terms-of-trade would have to shift against Europe; in addition to the "primary burden" on the paying country of the direct payment, there would in addition be a "secondary burden" as her export prices deteriorated relative to her import prices. Indeed, if the international demand curve of the receiving country were of elasticity of unity or less, there were fears that it would be quite impossible for the paying country to make the transfer—competition would tend to turn the terms of trade indefinitely against her. This analysis in terms of *price* elasticity was largely concurred in by Taussig, Viner, Pigou and others.

Ohlin and his followers adopted what they called the "modern view." This took into account income-effects and purchasing power passing between the two countries, and concluded that no change in the terms of trade was necessarily implied by a tribute or transfer. It was not always clear to the reader just what was meant by this somewhat mysterious flow of real purchasing power; and at times the "modern view" seemed to have about it strong overtones of Say's Law of Markets and conservation of purchasing power.[3] But abstracting from all dynamic business-cycle effects and from all problems of aggregate demand, we can interpret Ohlin as follows.

The Marshallian international-trade-offer curves of *both* countries are shifted in opposite directions, with this important result: the implied qualitative effect on the terms of trade does not depend upon the *price*-elasticity of one offer curve alone, or on the price-elasticities of the two curves; rather the more crucially important parameters are the *income*-elasticities or propensities in the two countries.[4]

As Viner's masterly survey makes clear, the above analytic formulation was acceptable to the holders of the orthodox view. By the 1930s the holders of this viewpoint had refined their analysis to take account of the mutual shifts of the offer curves. If some had previously thought that a deterioration of the terms of trade was inevitable, they dropped this view in favor of the more careful formulation: A deterioration of the terms of trade of the paying country is not inevitable, but *there is a strong presumption that the income elasticities of the different goods in the different*

---

[3] Examination of the historical literature soon suggested that the modern view had its classical precursors: Ricardo, Wheatley, Bastable and others, as against Thornton, Mill and others who favored the orthodox view. See J. Viner, *Studies in International Trade*, chap. 6, pp. 326–60, for historical discussion.

[4] See D. H. Robertson's essay, "The Transfer Problem," written in 1929, but first published in A. C. Pigou and D. H. Robertson, *Economic Essays and Addresses* (1931). Robertson pointed out Marshall's error in shifting but one of the curves, and on p. 180 says, "To speak geometrically, both curves must be shifted to a new common starting point . . . [and] it appears that, contrary to common opinion, the degree of change cannot be expressed in terms of the (price) elasticities of the original curves, though it can be expressed in terms of the utility and disutility schedules from which those curves are drawn up." Robertson acknowledges help from Pigou in arriving at this conclusion.

countries will be such as to create some deterioration in the terms of trade. At the same time holders of the modern view admitted that a change in the terms of trade might take place, but argued that it could be in either direction and that there was no presumption as to its direction. Thus, the area of disagreement was narrowed, but not to the vanishing point.

B. Graphical Analysis

The definitive analytic treatment of this problem was given by Pigou as far back as 1932.[5] His analysis rests upon a precise set of idealised assumptions, most of which I shall adhere to until contrary notice is given. It would be a great mistake, however, to try to interpret most of the writers as if they had these idealised conditions firmly in mind and as if they made rigorous deductions from them. An intuitionist like Keynes, for example, seems wrongly to have shifted the paying country's curve alone; but he may really have derived his belief about the terms of trade primarily from his notions about monetary effects of international trade on gold, employment and other aggregate magnitudes. In this paper I shall not go into the problems of the foreign-trade-multiplier and other issues of the modern theory of income determination. I shall confine myself to what may be called the pure theory or barter aspects of the problem, and shall ignore all problems concerned with absolute price levels and transitional gold flows.

Pigou reduces the transfer problem down to the Jevons–Walras–Edgeworth theory of barter of two goods between two individuals, whom I shall call Europe and America. Call the goods clothing and food, and for simplicity assume that the production of all goods is completely constant throughout our first analysis. If we like, we can think of Europe as producing little (or no) food and much clothing; of America as producing little (or no) clothing and much food. With most of the writers, I shamelessly assume collective indifference curves for Europe and also for America: if this simplification seems too much to swallow, the reader may imagine that he is dealing with the tastes between food and clothing of a representative citizen of each country, all other citizens being identical.[6]

---

[5] A. C. Pigou, "The Effects of Reparations on the Ratio of International Exchange," *Economic Journal,* Vol. XLII (1932), pp. 532–42. This is summarised in A. C. Pigou, *A Study in Public Finance,* 3rd ed. (1947), chap. XIX, and duplicates his 1950 article earlier cited. The latter contains a few obvious misprints which can be easily cleared up by referring to the older treatments or to Viner's excellent summary.

[6] Only in one special case can collective indifference curves validly summarise demand conditions for a country: only if all citizens have *identical* taste patterns *regardless* of income level will the ratio of the price of food to the price of clothing be a determinate function of total food and total clothing, *independently of their distribution.* Jacob L. Mosak's definitive study, *General-Equilibrium Theory in International Trade* (1944), pp. 56–63, 75–86, shows how the analysis can be completely freed from the assumption of collective indifference curves, and how the case of any number of people and commodities can be rigorously handled.

It will serve no useful purpose to follow Pigou's assumption that the two goods have independent utilities;[7] any indifference curves of normal concave curvature will do. In the beginning we assume that Europe and America trade under perfectly competitive conditions, with no transport costs or trade barriers. In the beginning there is no unilateral transfer either way.

Figure 1 is the familiar box-diagram that shows the final equilibrium. The base and altitude dimensions of the box are respectively the fixed world totals of clothing and food production. Any point in the box repre-

FIGURE 1

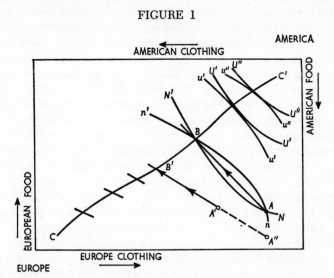

CC' is the contract curve where all trade must ultimately end. Reparation payments from *A* to *A'* shift the equilibrium from *B* to *B'*, and the crucial question is how the slope of mutual tangency flattens or steepens as we move down the contract curve.

sents four different magnitudes: referred to the lower south-western European corner of the box, a point represents European clothing and food; referred to the upper north-eastern American corner of the box, the same point represents American clothing and food. Initially, before trade we start off at the point marked *A*, where Europe is producing little food and America little clothing. After trade we end up at the equilibrium point *B*, where Europe is consuming more food than she produces, having exported her clothing surplus for America's food surplus. The arrow between the production point *A* and the equilibrium consumption point *B* repre-

---

[7] I shall later argue that Viner's demonstration, *Studies,* pp. 334–37, that tariff impediments predispose the terms of trade to be affected by transfer in the *unorthodox* way so as to *favor the paying country* is based upon the atypical peculiarity of the Pigou model of strict linearity and independence. The orthodox case is stronger than this model would suggest.

sents the amount of clothing traded for food; the arrow's slope represents Europe's terms of trade, the ratio of her clothing-export price to her food-import price.

The exact final equilibrium position is determined by the intersection at B of the two "offer" or "price-consumption" curves NN' and nn': at each point on a country's offer curve, the ruling price ratio of clothing to food is just equal (and tangent) to the country's marginal rate of substitution or indifference (as measured by the numerical slope of the indifference curve through that point).

To keep the diagram from becoming cluttered, I have not indicated the indifference curves in the neighborhoods of B and A, but the reader can supply them if he wishes. I have drawn in the important Edgeworth "contract curve" CC'. This is the locus with the following defined properties: (1) From any point *on* the contract curve, no mutually advantageous movements are possible; from any point *off* the contract curve, there always exist movements towards the contract curve which do benefit both countries. (2) Everywhere on the contract curve, the indifference curves of Europe (such as U' or U'') are tangent to the indifference curves of America (such as u' or u''). The common slopes of mutual tangency are drawn at various typical points along the contract curve. (3) No matter where we might place our initial starting point A, the final competitive equilibrium *must* be on the contract curve.

Now to introduce a unilateral payment from Europe to America into the picture. We shall see that it does not matter whether the payment is, in the first instance, expressed in terms of Europe's export good, clothing; or in terms of America's export good, food; or in terms of any combination of them; or, for that matter, in terms of some units of abstract purchasing power. In any case, the unilateral payment shifts the old initial point A to a new initial point A'. In Figure 1, I have adhered to the usual assumption of stating the payment in terms of the paying country's export good, in this case European clothing: so A' is due west of A by the amount of the payment.

From A' the reader can now draw two new offer curves,[8] which will have to intersect at a new equilibrium point on the contract curve, such as B' (which is recognisable by the fact that its slope of mutual tangency "points" directly at A').

The whole question of the effect of a transfer payment on the terms

---

[8] This shows the correctness of Robertson's criticism of Marshall for (1) not shifting both curves and (2) for arbitrarily shifting the one curve by the fixed amount of the reparation itself. See Robertson, *op. cit.*, p. 180, for the correct statement that both curves are probably shifted inward toward each other. This tends to be true so long as the payment is expressed in terms of the payer's export good and does not overshoot the contract curve. The box-diagram seems superior to Marshall's exchange diagrams for showing up such relations; but it is directly applicable only in the fixed-output case, whereas Marshall's exchange diagram also can handle the case of variable production.

of trade can now be simply restated: Does a downward movement along the contract curve from B to B' lead to a final slope of mutual tangency that is flatter or steeper? If the slope becomes flatter, Europe's unilateral payment causes its terms of trade to deteriorate as in the orthodox view; but if the slope remains the same or becomes steeper, the Ohlin view is vindicated. In this example, I have stacked the cards and drawn in the slopes along the contract curve so that below B there is an orthodox deterioration in Europe's terms of trade.[9]

Our geometrical construction shows us that under truly competitive conditions it does not qualitatively matter whether a reparation is made payable in one good rather than the other. For suppose the payment had been in terms of the receiving country's good and just large enough to take us from A to the point marked A'', which is on the extended line from A' to B'. Obviously such a food payment would end-up both countries in the same point B' as did the postulated clothing payment. In fact, any unilateral payment that involves enough of both goods to shift us from A to *any point on the line A' to A''* will represent an "equivalent payment" and will have exactly the same effects upon the terms of trade.[10]

---

[9] Taussig's concepts of gross barter terms of trade and net barter terms of trade are easily read off the diagram. The former is the slope of a line connecting A and B'; the latter is the slope of the trading line connecting A' and B'. The "secondary burden" on Europe is reflected by the fact that the new net-terms-of-trade arrow from A' to B' is flatter than a hypothetical arrow through A' drawn parallel to AB. See F. W. Taussig, *International Trade*, p. 113.

In the Taussig *Festschrift* volume, *Explorations in Economics* (1936), pp. 84–92, Professor Leontief out-moderned the moderns by presenting a case in which the terms of trade changed so much in favor of the *paying* country as to leave her actually better off after the unilateral payment. The secondary improvement in net terms of trade more than wiped out the primary transfer burden! Professor Leontief made sure that his example was consistent with concave indifference curves for both countries. However, it appears to me from a study of Figure 1 that, provided we rule out multiple intersections of the offer curves, the Leontief effect becomes impossible. See my *Foundations of Economic Analysis* (1947), p. 29, for a further comment on this point. M. Bronfenbrenner, "International Transfers and the Terms of Trade: An Extension of Pigou's Analysis," in *Studies in Mathematical Economics and Econometrics in Memory of Henry Schultz* (Chicago, Chicago Press, 1942), ed. O. Lange *et al.*, pp. 119–31, identifies the Leontief-effect with the "inferior-good" phenomenon; but I should rather relate it to multiple and unstable equilibria, which can certainly be illustrated with superior goods.

[10] One qualification must be made, if the amount of the reparation is specified to be greater than the amount initially possessed (or producible) by the paying country, then the new A' point will be *outside* the box. In this case it *may* happen that the two new offer curves never meet, making the reparation obligation an impossible one. See A. C. Pigou, *Public Finance* (1947), p. 176. It is true that the qualitative direction of shift in the terms of trade will be independent of the good in which the reparations are expressed. It is also true that any *ex post* burden of reparations and change in the terms of trade resulting from (1) reparations expressed in the payer's exports can be *exactly matched* by (2) some properly large reparation contract involving only its imports. But, as Professors Elliott, Viner and Baumol have rightly pointed out to me, before reparations are paid you will know only the *ex ante* price ratios and not the *ex post* price ratios. If *ex ante* 5 food = 1 clothing, it will definitely not be indifferent as to whether reparations are stipulated as 5 billion food, or 1 billion clothing, or as any

Why then after the Second World War was there felt to be special virtue in reparations in kind? Aside from transitional monetary effects, this would have seemed to involve a misapprehension of what it is about tied loans and payments in kind that minimises secondary burdens.[11] If the American Government takes German cameras and dumps them on competitive markets for what they will bring, the effect is no better than if Germany were forced to pay America so much American wheat. This is not to deny that payments in kind and tied loans may go smoothly and minimise transfer problems for a quite different reason from that included in our analysis: namely, when one country lends to another or gives to another, there may be a concomitant *shift* in the desires and needs of the countries (i.e., shifts in their indifference curves or more generally in the demand conditions underlying investment). Nineteenth-century harmonious international lending and borrowing may have been such a case.

But for our problem, the essential question boils down to this: As unilateral payments move the equilibrium along the contract curve, what is happening to the slope of mutual tangency?

C. The Crucial Marginal Income Propensities

What is it that determines whether the slopes are getting flatter or steeper as we move down the contract curve below *B*? The Pigou analysis, common-sense intuition[12] and Figure 2's magnification of the neighborhood around *B* all give the same answer. Whether the terms of trade will deteriorate in the orthodox manner or not depends upon *the relative strength of the European and American marginal-propensities-to-consume food and clothing*, and on no terms other than these income propensities.

Call the fraction of each extra dollar spent by Europe on food F_E, and on clothing C_E; call America's similar marginal propensities to consume F_A and C_A. Only the ratios C_E/F_E and C_A/F_A are of importance for the present argument; these ratios are easily compared between the two countries, independently of currency units, etc. Then Figure 2 will demonstrate the following important results:

If
$$\frac{C_E}{F_E} > \frac{C_A}{F_A}$$

---

weighted average in between. Until we know the qualitative and quantitative change in the *ex post* terms of trade, we cannot know which of these combinations would be most onerous.

[11] See Jacob Viner, "German Reparations Once More," *Foreign Affairs*, Vol. 21 (July, 1943), pp. 666–67 for an excellent statement on this issue.

[12] If £1 is taken from you and given to me and I choose to increase my consumption of precisely the same goods as those of which you are compelled to diminish yours, there is no Transfer Problem." (J. M. Keynes, "The German Transfer Problem," *Economic Journal*, Vol. XXXIX (1929), pp. 1–7, reprinted in *Readings in the Theory of International Trade* (1949), pp. 161–69; the quotation is from p. 163 of the *Readings*. See also Viner, *Studies*, p. 329, for a similar 1927 reference of H. K. Salvesen, and p. 354 for triangular expenditure diagrams.

FIGURE 2

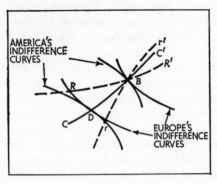

The income-consumption curves *RBR'* and *rBr'* are drawn by joining points on adjacent indifference curves that have the same slope as at *B*; they will always contain the contract curve *BD* between them. If *R* is above *r*, it follows that *D*'s slope is flatter than *B*'s.

the paying country's terms of trade (*i.e.*, Europe's) will deteriorate. This is because each dollar of income lost went relatively more largely for its own product than did each dollar of extra income received by the foreigner. If $C_E/F_E = C_A/F_A$ or $C_E/F_E < C_A/F_A$, then the terms of trade will remain the same or turn in favor of the paying country.[13]

How can we prove that the above income criterion is a valid criterion to indicate how the terms of trade will change? Figure 2 shows a magnification of the contract curve near the original equilibrium point *B*. It has drawn on it something that was left out of Figure 1—namely, the *income-consumption* or *Engel's* curves for each of the two individuals. These are the broken-line curves, which indicate *how people will expand their consumption of food and clothing as income increases but prices remain the*

---

[13] One should not confuse these marginal *income* propensities with income *elasticities*. Actually, in Figure 2, the marginal absolute changes in *physical* consumption were the true determinants; it so happens that with equal price ratios in America and Europe, we can convert the latter into marginal propensities expressed as fractions of extra dollars or pounds of income. When tariffs are in the picture, this will not be possible.

Let the European marginal physical propensity to consume $\partial(\text{clothing})/\partial(\text{income}) = C_E/P_C = c_E$, and similarly use small letters c_A, f_E, f_A to denote the other three physical propensities. Analysis like that of Mosak shows that in the "normal" or "stable case," the criterion is $(c_E f_A - c_A f_E)$; if no goods are "inferior," this can be written as $c_E/f_E - c_A/f_A$, which is P/P_F times our previous criterion. In the special case of two goods, no saving and no domestic goods, we can write the same marginal propensities $C_E + F_E = C_A + F_A = 1$. My colleague, Professor Robert L. Bishop, points out that $C_E - C_A$ or $F_A - F_E$ are then equivalent to my above criterion.

Note also, in this two-goods case we can write our criterion in the terms of import propensities alone, $\{(1 - F_E)/F_E\} - \{C_A/(1 - C_A)\}$, which is convertible into $1 - F_E - C_A$. This last form says that the orthodox deterioration of the terms of trade of the paying country will depend upon whether *the sum of the marginal propensities to import of the two countries in less than unity*. Professor Haberler has been using this criterion in his Harvard classes for some years; see also, J. E. Meade, *op. cit.*, pp. 307–8 and Figure 2.

same. Through each point there passes one such income-consumption line for each country. Geometrically we easily draw such a curve by joining together the points on the different indifference curves that have exactly the same slope—i.e., we hold relative prices constant as we vary income. Through the original equilibrium point B, BR represents Europe's income-consumption line, and Br represents America's.

Let D be any nearby point to B along the contract curve. Through D must pass two tangential indifference curves. It will be noted that as we pass south-east of D the slopes along Europe's indifference curves must be getting flatter, while the slopes of America's indifference curves must be getting steeper. This follows from the fact that the box-diagram turns America upside down and makes its indifference curves (which are really also convex to its origin) appear of the opposite curvature to Europe's. Similarly, as we pass north-west of D, the slopes of the two indifference curves move in *contrary* directions. It follows from this divergence that the two countries' income-consumption curves through a point like B must contain *inside* them the contract curve. For if D were completely above both income curves, its common slopes could not be equal to each other, but would instead have to be both greater and less than the slope at B, which is a contradiction to the tangency condition at D.

Thus in Figure 2 BD lies inside of BR and Br. It will be noted that by definition of an income-consumption curve, the point R must have the same indifference slope as B; and r, for America, must have the same slope as B. From the fact that R lies above and to the left of r, it then follows that we can infer that D must have a flatter slope than B, representing a deterioration of the terms of trade of clothing against food. Why? Because D lies over r, and hence in terms of the curvature of America's indifference curve it has a flatter slope than at r or B. And with D lying below R, the curvature of Europe's slope tells us that D must have a flatter slope than at R or B.

To sum up: the income-consumption curves through B contain the contract curve inside them; if the paying country's income curve below B lies above the receiving country's, then the slope at the intermediate contract curve point must represent a deterioration of the clothing-food price ratio; the relative slopes of the income curves are our sole criterion of price change.[14]

The common sense of this argument is easily explained. If and only if

---

[14] The reader can test his understanding of the geometrical argument by working through the details of the case where the two income-consumption curves coincide. The contract curve must then also coincide with them, and must then everywhere show *no* change in the terms of trade. *It will be noted that the present analysis nowhere makes any assumption about linearity or about smallness of the movement.* The only way that the above argument might fail and require qualification would be in the case where two countries' income-consumption curves were sufficiently twisty to give rise to more than one intersection after some finite movement; even in such a case, the criterion can be made rigorous.

a movement along one country's income curve causes it to give up the goods in exactly the same proportions as the other country takes them on will there be no change in the terms of trade. It will be noted that crucial slopes of the income curves depend only upon marginal physical income propensities to consume and not directly on the money income propensities expressed in terms of dollars or pounds. However, in the complete absence of impediments to trade, the price ratios will be the same for the two countries, and so we can convert the physical propensity criterion into an expenditure propensity criterion.[15]

D. Probability Evaluations

Our important criterion $C_E/F_E \gtreqless C_A/F_A$ has now been established.[16] It remains to assess the probabilities. Pigou is inclined to argue that there is a definite presumption in favor of the $>$ sign and the orthodox conclusion. Two separate elements seem to be involved in his argument: first, the assumption that the paying country, Germany in Pigou's example, is smaller in scale than is the receiving country, England, the rest of the non-German world in Pigou's example; second, the assumption that each country spends relatively more on its own products than does the other country spend on those products.

The first of these arguments, hinging as it does on absolute scale, would not necessarily become applicable to the example under consideration— payments between two large and almost equal regions, Europe and America. But aside from this, the argument seems to be logically invalid. Both Bronfenbrenner and Viner[17] have pointed out that mere differences in scale may affect the four terms in Pigou's criterion, but they do so in such a way as to affect the two ratios that must be compared in exactly the same way. We may put the matter most simply as follows: if very small relative to the receiving country, the paying country will "presumably" be spending the same smaller percentage of its income on its own product that the larger country is spending on those same products. Pigou's own mathematical analysis contains the antidote to his view that scale counts. For it shows that the whole problem can be handled by the slopes of the income-consumption curves of the *representative* citizens of the two countries. These are necessarily *independent of scale*, and would be numeri-

---

[15] One minor technical point should be noted. Figure 2 represents normal rather than inferior-good behaviour. No change in the argument is needed to handle the latter possibility; however, a change in algebraic sign of the criterion will result if but one of the countries has food as an inferior good.

[16] In Pigou's symbolism, this is $(\psi'/F') \gtreqless (\phi'/f')$. See *A Study in Public Finance*, p. 179, or Viner, *op. cit.*, p. 338. See also G. A. Elliott, "Transfer of Means-of-Payment and the Terms of Trade," *Canadian Journal of Economics and Political Science*, Vol. 2 (1936), pp. 481–92, for a valuable definitive treatment of all these issues.

[17] M. Bronfenbrenner, *op. cit.*, p. 125; J. Viner, *Studies*, p. 341.

cally equal to the slope of the aggregate income-consumption curves *whatever the number of identical people in each country.*

Nonetheless, one does feel that there is something plausible about the fact that Europeans spend relatively more on European goods than do Americans. This brings us to the second and more interesting strain in the Pigou argument.

To establish a definite presumption in favor of the > sign in the criterion, and therefore to lead to the orthodox conclusion, Pigou leans on the simple econometric fact that Europeans tend to spend more relatively on European products than Americans do; Americans likewise have a greater average propensity to consume American products than do Europeans.

There seems to be no good reason to question this fact. And yet it is well to realise that there is no theoretical necessity that this should be so. What makes it so is the fact that transport costs and tariffs are *not* zero. This means that European products are relatively cheaper in Europe than they are in America; and similarly for the relative cheapness of American products in America as compared to European products. Already in assessing the realistic probabilities, we seem to be departing from the strict assumption of the model—which assumed literally zero transport costs! Viner has called explicit attention to this inconsistency in the Pigou argument.

Let us accept the fact of transport costs and impediments to trade. It still requires some complex argument to deduce from this the orthodox presumption about the relative marginal propensities and the deterioration of the terms of trade. This will be demonstrated in Part II.

E. Summary of Failure of Orthodox Presumption in Absence of Transport Costs

The above sections have arrived at a far-reaching conclusion. If we rigidly adhere to the assumption of literally zero transport costs and admit no impediments to trade or imperfections of competition into our analysis, then the orthodox presumption that the terms of trade of the paying country will tend to deteriorate turns out to fall completely to the side. In every case where an orthodox presumption has been established, it turns out that somewhere in the chain of reasoning, consciously or unconsciously, impediments to trade have been brought into the picture.

Once we push the assumption of zero transport costs to its ultimate limit, there is absolutely no localisation of demand, and there can be no *a priori* correlation between regional patterns of production and tastes. This is the crucial point to be understood. We can number countries a, b, c, ... and goods 1, 2, 3, ... All permutations of marginal propensities are then equally admissible *a priori*, and when we come to compute a criterion of movements in the terms of trade this turns out to be a symmetric function with no basis for the presumption that it will be of one sign or another. In this limiting case of literally zero transport cost, it seems to me logically inescapable that the Ohlin or Modern View is correct in its agnosticism: there is no presumption that the terms of trade will deteriorate rather than favor the paying country.

Figures 1 and 2 illustrate this. As drawn, they seem to favor the orthodox view. But that is simply because, to be agreeable, I stacked the cards. What if the original A point had been on the other side of the contract curve, as would certainly have been possible before I labelled the axes? Then the behaviour of the slopes below B would have negated the orthodox view. Or suppose I had stipulated that America rather than Europe were the paying country. Then a careful examination of the diagram *above* B will show that I have stacked the cards against the orthodox view. The principle of sufficient reason—in its correct formulation, which out of ignorance deduces only ignorance—shows that until transport costs introduce asymmetry into the picture, no *a priori* presumptions are possible.

F. Variable Output and Multiple Commodities

My main task is done. But to underline this far-reaching conclusion in the zero-transport-cost case, let me briefly show that relaxing the assumptions that production is fixed and that there are only two goods will still not lead to the orthodox result. The box diagram of Figure 1 does not tell all the story once production becomes a variable. Each new pattern of output gives rise to new dimensions for the box. Nonetheless, students of the pure theory of international trade know that a determinate equilibrium can still be determined even when production is admitted as a variable.[18]

Graphical or mathematical analysis of the two-country two-good case, where production of the goods is variable along a given technological transformation curve, shows that our *exact same criterion* determines the qualitative direction in which the terms of trade must change as a result of transfer; so again no orthodox presumption is possible. I shall relegate to a footnote a statement of the mathematical system involved for any interested reader to check, and shall very briefly formulate in common-sense terms the reason for this surprisingly simple result.[19]

---

[18] Ricardian constant costs is one simple case. The next simplest case is one in which costs are variable and in which for each price ratio between the two goods, there is an optimal production pattern for each good, as determined by tangency conditions along a production-possibility or (opportunity-cost) production transformation curve. See G. Haberler, *Theory of International Trade;* W. Leontief, "The Use of Indifference Curves in the Analysis of Foreign Trade," *Quarterly Journal of Economics,* 1933, reprinted in *Readings in the Theory of International Trade* (1949). General equilibrium handles these and more general cases with complete rigor.

[19] Throughout, let capital letters stand for European variables and small letters for American; let X_1 and x_1 represent consumption of clothing and X_2 and x_2 consumption of food; let Y_1, y_1, Y_2, y_2 represent the corresponding production figures,

First suppose the equilibrium configuration of production and consumption has determined itself. Now introduce a unilateral payment of the usual type. Presumably everything will have to change, including of course production. But just suppose we were able to find *a* new equilibrium *without* any change in output; then since the equilibrium is assumed unique, that lucky guess of ours would correctly portray *the* new equilibrium. A little reflection tells us when we can hope to find a new equilibrium without any change in production: it is when the criterion worked out in the previous section is exactly zero, and it is only in this case. This can be verified by the box-diagram, which, so long as we are tentatively holding production constant, can be legitimately applied. This diagram has told us which is the one critical case where no change in price will be necessary. The case where $C_E/F_E = C_A/F_A$ is the razor's edge; in this case, existing production gets re-allocated between the countries without any relative price change; and without any relative price change, no change in production can take place.[20]

---

which are related in each country by transformation functions of the usual convex type, $Y_2 = T(Y_1)$ and $y_2 = t(y_1)$; let Ps stand for prices and let primes and double primes stand for differentiation; let the tastes for each country be given by indifference curves that are defined by the following marginal-rate-of-substitution functions for food and clothing $R = R(X_1,X_2)$ and $r = r(x,x_2)$; finally, let the algebraic payment or transfer paid by Europe to America in terms of clothing be B. Then the conditions of equilibrium determining all variables are given by

$$X_1 + x_1 = Y_1 + y_1, \; X_2 + x_2 = Y_2 + y_2, \; (X_2 - Y_2) = \frac{P_1}{P_2}(Y_1 - X_1) + B,$$

$$- T'(Y_1) = R(X_1,X_2) = \frac{P_1}{P_2} = \frac{p_1}{p_2} = r(x_1,x_2) = - t'(y_1).$$

This Leontief-type system becomes the Pigou–Jevons system if we make the Ys all constant, dropping the outside equations in the last line, and if we specialise R and r to be ratios of independent and linear marginal utilities. The criterion for the algebraic sign of the change in P_2/P_1 with respect to a change in B can be shown to be $(\partial R/\partial X_1)(\partial r/\partial x_2) - (\partial R/\partial X_2)(\partial r/\partial x_1)$, which is equivalent to our earlier criterion. (To introduce tariffs in the picture we must distinguish between the Ps and the ps; to introduce real transport cost, we must in addition modify the relations between the total Xs and Ys.)

[1966 Postscript: This section on variable production could have been handled by the "trade-indifference" contours of J. E. Meade, *Geometry of International Trade.* These are defined as loci of maximum satisfaction obtainable, with given domestic production-possibility frontier, from each (algebraic) configuration of trade $(X_1 - Y_1, X_2 - Y_2)$. If the indifference contours are regularly convex and the frontier regularly concave, Meade's contours come from subtracting corresponding (X_i, Y_i) points of equal slope. The Engel's curves of the resulting trade-indifference field have at every point a slope easily shown to be identical to that of the original indifference field; and hence our earlier criteria apply without modification.]

[20] Professor Viner has noted the singular case where the orthodox presumption breaks down regardless of income propensities. In the Ricardian case of constant cost, where one of the countries incompletely specialises and the price ratio is at its limiting comparative cost ratio, the transfer cannot affect the terms of trade. In this singular case of infinite elasticity of supply, we may think of our criterion as trying to indicate a change in the terms of trade but as having zero leverage in doing so. See Viner, *Studies,* p. 349.

We may relax the assumption that output depends on relative prices alone. Thus

From this reasoning it follows that the criterion of the fixed-production case still provides us with the watershed between the two possible directions of change in the terms of trade. Variability of production may affect the quantitative intensity of the change in export-import prices, but it cannot affect their qualitative direction.[21] Income propensities alone are relevant for the qualitative question.

Thus, we have seen that (1) whether production is constant, (2) whether costs are increasing or (3) whether costs are constant, there is the same absence of presumption concerning the effects of transfer on the terms of trade.

There remains the question of what happens to our results when we go beyond the two-goods case. Of course, when there are more than two goods the concept of the terms of trade becomes ambiguous. We could try to define some index number, but for the present purpose no such approximation is necessary; there is nothing that prevents us from considering the effects of a transfer payment on *all* price ratios of each possible pairings of the goods.

So long as transport costs are literally zero, there is again no localisation of demand and no *a priori* correlation between regional tastes and regional comparative advantages in production. We are again in a position of symmetrical ignorance: with transport costs literally zero, the orthodox presumption becomes completely untenable.

To my knowledge the only logically air-tight successful defense of the orthodox view is that given by Viner, in which he explicitly introduces into the problem transport costs great enough to make international trade prohibitive for some "domestic commodities."[22] Naturally a high percentage of our income is spent on such commodities. And from this fact it is often concluded that the orthodox presumption can be justified. Actually, Professor Viner has shown how all this can be made completely rigorous in a model. His model involves the reasonable assumption that outputs of a country's export and domestic goods are variable and substitutable and will be discussed in the sequel.

Nonetheless, I should like to report an illuminating experiment that definitely failed. Years ago, before Viner's masterpiece had appeared, I attempted to deduce the orthodox presumption by postulating, in addition

---

people in the receiving country may now feel rich enough to work fewer hours, while the payers work more hours. But when we permute the assumption concerning the labor intensity of the payer's export good, the symmetry of our ignorance seems to permit of no definite presumption.

[21] A similar statement can be made about the role of price elasticities of demand and of supply generally, although the literature abounds with contrary statements.

[22] *Studies,* pp. 348–49, seems the best reference for this; note the interesting use in 1937 of Hicks-like composite commodities. Viner and Bronfenbrenner also make frontal attacks on the effects of tariff duties. G. A. Elliott, "Protective Duties, Tributes, and Terms of Trade," *Journal of Political Economy,* Vol. XLV (1937), 804–7, showed that a prohibitive tariff can convert a traded commodity into a domestic one, and thereby increase the presumption that the terms of trade will move in the orthodox direction.

to the two freely traded international goods, the existence of domestic goods in one or both countries. But I assumed *production of each good to be absolutely constant and inelastic in supply*. Mathematical and logical analysis then showed that the orthodox presumption could not be maintained.[23]

In terms of graphs, a box-diagram like Figure 1 was still applicable to this case. But in drawing up each party's indifference curves, I had to hold constant the consumption of the domestic goods. Depending upon taste patterns of complementarity and competitiveness between the domestic and traded goods, the levels at which the domestic goods were held constant could cause shifts in the slope and appearance of the indifference curves, but need not affect their general curvature. Exactly the same reasoning of Figure 2 could be used to show that the same criterion $(C_E/F_E) - (C_A/F_A)$ would apply, provided these marginal propensities were calculated *ceteris paribus*, i.e., with domestic goods' production and consumption held constant.

This being so, I was in for a surprise. In trying to evaluate this criterion so as to arrive at the orthodox presumption, I soon found that the modern view continued to hold. In the absence of knowledge concerning the pattern of complementarity, and provided the traded goods were absolutely free of transport costs and non-localised in their demand, it was just as easy to imagine a world in which the paying country produced an export that would appreciate rather than depreciate in relative value. So long as our ignorance is thus symmetrical,[24] there is nothing to do but study the econometric facts of each situation and be prepared for a change in the terms of trade in either direction.

G. Conclusion to Part I

This completes what has been a fairly exhaustive analysis of the transfer problem. I have pursued the implication of literally zero transport costs to the bitter end, and have arrived at the conclusion that there is then no presumption in favor of the orthodox view that a transfer will tend to deteriorate the terms of trade of the paying country. This serves to clear the way for a later more detailed analysis of transport costs in the international trade mechanism, in the course of which the orthodox view will turn out to be partially vindicated.

PART II: ANALYSIS OF EFFECTS OF TRADE IMPEDIMENTS

A. Equilibrium Conditions

As in Part I, Europe and America consume clothing and food. Because Europe is relatively well endowed with clothing (or clothing-

---

[23] G. A. Elliott in the 1936 cited article had already arrived at this conclusion.

[24] Viner's successful vindication of the orthodox presumption was possible because of his (quite realistic) introduction of an element of asymmetry into the problem: his domestic good is made (infinitely) substitutable for the region's export good production and not at all substitutable for the import good production.

producing factors), she exports clothing for American food. The price ratio in Europe's markets of clothing to food represents her net terms of trade, and must in equilibrium equal Europe's indifference-ratio or relative marginal utilities of the goods. A similar equilibrium condition will hold for the price ratio in the American market and America's indifference ratio. If there are zero transport costs, these price ratios will be identical even though an ocean intervenes.

With no unilateral payments, trade must balance. For each country, value of imports = value of exports, expressed in common units. These units may be dollars, francs, ergs, food units or clothing units. There is no need to write a separate balance equation for each country, since the exports of Europe are the imports of America and vice versa.

Now we admit a unilateral payment from Europe to America. The common balance equation of the countries becomes

Value of American imports = Value of American exports + Value of unilateral payment

or

Value of Europe imports = Value of Europe exports — Value of unilateral payment.

Part I and Pigou's earlier discussion showed that it matters little for our model in what units the unilateral payment is prescribed. Readers seem to find it most natural to imagine that Europe's unilateral payment to America is initially prescribed in terms of Europe's own export good —clothing in my example. Let then the payment be K clothing units per unit of time. So long as clothing and food prices, P_c and P_f, are the same in both countries, we may rewrite the balance of payments

$$P_f \text{ (American Food Exports)} = P_c \text{ (European Clothing Exports)} - P_c K$$

or using Pigou's notation of X for the receiving country's export and Y for the paying country's export, we get

$$\frac{P_c}{P_f} = \frac{X}{Y - K} \tag{1}$$

as an expression for Europe's net terms of trade. (Without the K units of clothing payments, we would have Taussig's gross barter terms of trade; and if $K = 0$, the two concepts are identical.)

All this is familiar ground. If we write down our demand or marginal utility conditions, the full equilibrium conditions are summarised by

$$\left(\frac{\text{M.U. of Clothing}}{\text{M.U. of Food}} \right)_{\text{America}} = \frac{P_c}{P_f} = \frac{X}{Y - K} = \left(\frac{\text{M.U. of Clothing}}{\text{M.U. of food}} \right)_{\text{Europe}} \tag{2}$$

where the marginal utility or indifference ratios depend upon consumption in the respective countries—and hence, with production determined, on the export variables X and Y alone.[25]

The three equations of (2) are sufficient to determine the three unknowns: X, Y, P_c/P_f. If we change K—say from 0 to $+100$—new equilibrium values of the unknowns are determined. How the price ratio changes was shown to depend on the relative slopes of the Engel or income-consumption curves of the two countries (i.e., upon the derivatives of their relative-marginal-utility functions).

B. Explicit Introduction of Real Transport Costs

I now propose to come directly to grips with transport costs. The simplest assumption is the following: To carry each good across the ocean you must pay some of the good itself. Rather than set up elaborate models of a merchant marine, invisible items, etc., we can achieve our purpose by assuming that just as only a fraction of ice exported reaches its destination as unmelted ice, so will a_x and a_y be the fractions of exports X and Y that respectively reach the other country as imports. Of course, $a_x < 1$ and $a_y < 1$, except in the costless model, where they were each unity.

With transport costs in the picture, we must distinguish between price ratios in the two countries and also between the numerical exports of one country and the numerical imports of the other. America's clothing imports are now less than Europe's clothing exports Y, being instead $a_y Y$. Similarly, Europe's food imports are now $a_x X$ rather than X.

The balance of payments for either country can most simply be written using her *domestic* price ratios and her exports and imports. Thus, for America

$$\left(\frac{P_c}{P_f}\right)_A \quad \text{clothing imports} = \text{food exports}$$

all transfers being provisionally assumed away. Or

$$\left(\frac{P_c}{P_f}\right)_A = \frac{X}{a_y Y}$$

For Europe

$$\left(\frac{P_c}{P_f}\right)_E \quad \text{clothing exports} = \text{food imports}$$

---

[25] In *Public Finance*, p. 179, Pigou writes (2) in the form

$$\frac{\phi(Y)}{f(X)} = \frac{X}{Y-K} = \frac{\psi(Y)}{F(X)} .$$

Because he usually expresses Europe's payment in terms of the receiving country's good, he usually (see p. 176) writes instead of $X/(Y - K)$ the equivalent expression $(X + R)/Y$, where R is Europe's payment expressed in physical units of America's export product. I have set the number of representative individuals equal to one in each country and have omitted Pigou's m and n.

Or

$$\left(\frac{P_c}{P_f}\right)_E = \frac{a_x X}{Y}$$

These two relations enable us to deduce the discrepancy between the two price ratios that transport costs must create and maintain. So long as goods are flowing in both directions

$$\left(\frac{P_c}{P_f}\right)_E = a_x \frac{X}{Y} = a_x a_y \frac{X}{a_y Y} = a_x a_y \left(\frac{P_c}{P_f}\right)_A < \left(\frac{P_c}{P_f}\right)_A \qquad (3)$$

Interpretation: goods are relatively cheapest in their place of origin for two reasons—there is a transport cost saved on the export good and a transport cost paid on the import good. Thus, if clothing were to cost $\frac{1}{4}$ of itself to transport west and food to cost $\frac{1}{3}$ of itself to transport east, the European price ratios of clothing to food would be $\frac{2}{3}$ of $\frac{3}{4}$ or $\frac{6}{12}$ of the American price ratio. The reader can verify that the American price ratio of food to clothing will be cheaper than the European for the same reason and *by the same numerical factor* of $\frac{6}{12}$; *i.e.*, symmetrically with (3), we have

$$\left(\frac{P_f}{P_c}\right)_A = a_x a_y \left(\frac{P_f}{P_c}\right)_E < \left(\frac{P_f}{P_c}\right)_E$$

These fundamental price relations were derived from comparing balances of payments. A more fundamental derivation would be via arbitrage relations that maintain "purchasing-power parity" relations among transportable goods. One unit of cloth is worth $(P_f/P_c)_E$ units of food in Europe. By sending it abroad we can buy $a_y(P_f/P_c)_A$ units of food in America, of which $a_x a_y(P_f/P_c)_A$ can be brought back to Europe. This last expression must not exceed $(P_f/P_c)_E$, or arbitrage will set in, restoring the equality. Q.E.D. If transport costs are great enough to make all trade unprofitable, then the equality[26] of (3) is to be replaced by $(P_f/P_c)_A > a_x a_y(P_f/P_c)_E$ and $(P_c/P_f)_E > a_x a_y(P_c/P_f)_A$, with similar inequalities holding in terms of opposite directional transport costs.

How shall we measure *the* terms of trade between clothing and food? By Europe's price ratio, $(P_c/P_f)_E$? Or by America's $(P_c/P_f)_A$? So long as the spatial markets remain connected by trade, these measures differ only by an invariant scale factor, $a_x a_y$.[27] Therefore, transfer payments

---

[26] See P. A. Samuelson, "Spatial Price Equilibrium and Linear Programming," *A.E.R.*, Vol. XLII (June, 1952), pp. 283–303, for a discussion of some of these spatial price relations.

[27] If transport costs varied with volume of trade, the *a*'s would not be constants. Realistically, since there are joint costs of a round trip, a_x and a_y will tend to move in opposite directions, depending upon the strengths of demands for east and west transport.

and any other disturbance will affect either measure in the same direction and relative degree. So we can use either as our measure of the terms of trade. Or for that matter, we can define a more symmetrical in-between measure, $(P_c/P_f)_I = a_y(P_c/P_f)_A = (P_c/P_f)_E/a_x$. This intermediate measure, which differs only in scale from the local measures, will be found to be a convenient variable for later use.

Now to combine our elements into a determinate trade equilibrium taking account of transport costs. Assuming no transfer payments, for America

$$\left(\frac{\text{M.U. clothing consumed}}{\text{M.U. food consumed}}\right)_A = \left(\frac{P_c}{P_f}\right)_A = \frac{\text{Food exports}}{\text{Clothing imports}} = \frac{X}{a_y Y}$$

for Europe

$$\left(\frac{\text{M.U. clothing consumed}}{\text{M.U. food consumed}}\right)_E = \left(\frac{P_c}{P_f}\right)_E = \frac{\text{Food imports}}{\text{Clothing exports}} = \frac{a_x X}{Y}$$

where in every case, imports are derived by applying the transport-cost a coefficient to our old symbols for exports.

These equations can be conveniently combined

$$a_y \left(\frac{\text{M.U. clothing consumed}}{\text{M.U. food consumed}}\right)_A = \frac{X}{Y} =$$

$$\frac{1}{a_x} \left(\frac{\text{M.U. clothing consumed}}{\text{M.U. food consumed}}\right)_E = \left(\frac{P_c}{P_f}\right)_I = a_y \left(\frac{P_c}{P_f}\right)_A = \frac{1}{a_x} \left(\frac{P_c}{P_f}\right)_E$$

Note that the relative marginal utility expressions for each country are determinate functions of food and clothing consumed; call this function r (clothing, food) for America and R (clothing, food) for Europe, where these functions have the usual curvature properties of marginal rates of substitution. With America producing O clothing and $\bar{F}$ food, and Europe O food and $\bar{C}$ clothing, we can express these demand functions in terms of exports alone: namely, $r(a_y Y, \bar{F} - X)$ and $R(\bar{C} - Y, a_x X)$.

To take account of a transfer payment from Europe to America, recall that this is stipulated in terms of Europe's export good. But is it to be so much clothing *in Europe*, or does the stipulated amount refer to clothing *delivered* in America? With transport costs, there is a difference. It is of no consequence which convention we adopt: a smaller stipulated amount of delivered clothing will be identical in its effects to a large stipulated amount of clothing paid in Europe itself.

For convenience, I shall let the stipulated unilateral payment K stand for clothing payable in Europe to America. In Europe's balance of payments, K will be seen to be a direct subtraction from its clothing export credit items, Y—exactly as in the transport-free case.

Hence, we can write down our final equilibrium system, including all previous ones as special cases.[28]

$$a_y r(a_y Y, \bar{F} - X) = \frac{X}{Y - K} = \frac{1}{a_x} R(\bar{C} - Y, a_x X) =$$

$$\left(\frac{P_c}{P_f}\right)_I = a_y \left(\frac{P_c}{P_f}\right)_A = \frac{1}{a_x} \left(\frac{P_c}{P_f}\right)_E \qquad (4)$$

With the parameters a_x, a_y, $\bar{C}$, $\bar{F}$ specified, we can vary the payment K and determine the resulting shift in the terms of trade.

C. Equilibrium with Artificial Tariff Impediments

So far we have confined attention to "real" trade impediments that literally use up resources in transporting goods. The almost as important case of artificial impediments such a tariffs or quotas has certain analytic similarities. But there are important differences, which must not be glossed over, and which require separate analysis and conclusions.

For simplicity of exposition suppose that all Custom duties are levied in terms of the imported goods themselves: thus an importer who brings a unit of clothing into America from outside finds that the government leaves him with only $a_y < 1$ units of clothing after he has passed through Customs; similarly, a European importer of food is left with but a_x units of food after he has paid the duty on a unit of imports.

Now as far as arbitragers are concerned, they do not care whether the impediments to trade are "natural" or "contrived." Clearly purchasing power parity relations between the spatial prices will be exactly the same as in the case of real transport costs. *I.e.*, so long as duties are not prohibitively high and goods are actually flowing in both directions, equilibrium requires

$$\left(\frac{P_c}{P_f}\right)_E = a_y a_x \left(\frac{P_c}{P_f}\right)_A < a_y \left(\frac{P_c}{P_f}\right)_A = \left(\frac{P_c}{P_f}\right)_I < \left(\frac{P_c}{P_f}\right)_A \qquad (3)'$$

This is the exact equivalent of equation (3), which showed the degree to which a country's own export good is relatively cheap at its place of origin.

Tariffs affect our balance-of-payments expressions quite differently from real transport costs. No matter how Custom officials alter the price tags of goods, the physical imports of each country are still fully equal to the physical exports of the other country. Tariffs do not literally *use up* goods as do transport costs. Our convention that governments collect duties in kind brings into prominence the problem that always

---

[28] With $a_x = 1 = a_y$, we have the transport-free case; with $K = 0$, we have no transfer. In the case of independent utilities, this may be written in Pigou's notation as

$$\frac{a_y \phi(a_y Y)}{f(X)} = \frac{X}{X - K} = \frac{\psi(X)}{a_x F(a_x X)} \qquad (4)'$$

which differs from his original equations only because of the a_x and a_y coefficients.

vexes the theorist dealing with tariffs: What does the government do with the tariff receipts? The usual convention followed is the one that is most natural for me to adopt here: The government is assumed to distribute the receipts to the (representative) consumer in a *lump-sum* fashion so that each consumer can act as if the true price to him for any expansion of purchase is equal to the price quoted within his country's markets.[29]

The balance of payments of America, or for a typical American consumer, can be written in either of the following ways when transfer payments are zero

Imports valued just outside of America = Exports valued just outside of America

Imports valued inside America = Exports valued in America + Lump-sum tariff rebate

Applying similar reasoning to Europe, and using our symbols, we get

$$\left(\frac{P_c}{P_f}\right)_I Y = X \tag{5}$$

and

$$\left(\frac{P_c}{P_f}\right)_A Y = X + \left\{\left(\frac{P_c}{P_f}\right)_A - \left(\frac{P_c}{P_f}\right)_I\right\} Y$$

Similarly, for Europe

$$\left(\frac{P_f}{P_c}\right)_E X = Y + \left\{\left(\frac{P_f}{P_c}\right)_E - \left(\frac{P_f}{P_c}\right)_I\right\} X$$

where the terms involving brackets represent the lump-sum rebates of tariff receipts.

Of these relations, we need only (5). To take account of transfer payments expressed in terms of the export good of the paying country, the specified place of delivery is no longer of substance. In all of our balance-of-payments relations, the transfer of K units of clothing must be regarded as a subtraction from Europe's credit items of exports, and so we simply rewrite (5) in the more general form

$$\left(\frac{P_c}{P_f}\right)_I = \frac{X}{Y - K} \tag{5}'$$

---

[29] The case of quotas does not directly give us a_x and a_y coefficients, but for any degree of import limitation these can be defined implicitly as the ratio of the price the importer must pay to the higher price that competition produces internally. By auctioning the limited quotas, the government can collect the difference and give it to whomever it deems worthy. More often, the difference is pocketed by importers, and for simplicity their tastes and demands are assumed to be like that of the populace at large. The same assumption was implicitly made about the government's disposition of the transfer payment.

Recalling that the representative consumer in each country equates his indifference-ratio or relative marginal utility to the domestic price ratio he faces, we can combine this fact with $(3)'$ and $(5)'$ to get our final conditions of equilibrium under tariffs:

$$a_y r(Y, \bar{F} - X) = \frac{X}{Y - K} = \frac{1}{a_x} R(\bar{C} - Y, X) = \qquad (6)$$

$$\left(\frac{P_c}{P_f}\right)_I = a_y \left(\frac{P_c}{P_f}\right)_A = \frac{1}{a_x} \left(\frac{P_c}{P_f}\right)_E$$

This should be compared with (2), the Jevons-Pigou equilibrium condition with no trade impediments and with (4), the equilibrium conditions with real as distinct from artificial trade impediments. Note that the a_y and a_x factors appear in (6) outside the r and R indifference functions exactly as they do in (4). But they do not appear inside the indifference functions because there is no literal using up of goods in transport.

The substantive difference between equilibrium conditions under artificial and real impediments described above is ignored in the following type of arguments. To the view that if the foreigner passes restrictive tariffs we should do the same, the analogy is brought forward: "If Nature silted harbors abroad, would you think it necessary or desirable to ruin your own harbors?" For polemical purposes and with non-specialists, this is a suitable argument to use. But to a pedantical specialist, there is a difference between the kinds of trade obstructions that needs to be analysed at least once.

D. Graphic Solution of Tariff Case

Figure 3 is an exact replica of Figure 1 of Part I, but now the indifference curves have been made to be concentric circles in accordance with the special numerical assumption of independent linear marginal utilities.[30] In accordance with Pigou's classic treatment of the problem, the dimensions of the box diagram are equal to total world production of the respective goods; Europe's origin is the lower left-hand corner of the box; America's origin is the upper right-hand corner. To approximate Jevons more nearly, I have placed the initial endowment point at the south-east corner of the box, marked A: this represents zero food production for Europe and zero clothing production for America, an extreme but inessential assumption.

With no impediments to trade, the offer curves through A will intersect at the equilibrium point B. Both the net and gross barter terms of trade are measured by the numerical slope of a line adjoining A to B. At B both

---

[30] By changing commodity units, we could change the circles to ellipses. My choice of numerical coefficients is special in its symmetry between goods; also, it is an inessential coincidence that the world totals of production would, if given to either country, lead to its exact point of saturation.

FIGURE 3

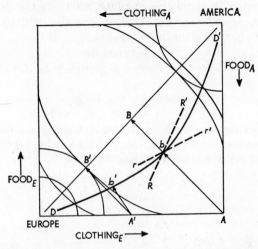

With zero transport costs, transfer leaves terms of trade AB unchanged at $A'B'$. With tariffs, transfer improves payer's terms, from Ab to $A'b'$: along DD', where domestic prices differ by duties, indifference slopes steepen from b to b' because Pigou model makes Engel's slopes RR' steeper than rr'.

countries' indifference curves are tangential, with their common tangent pointing at A; of course, B is on the contract curve of points of common tangency, which in this numerical case happens to be the straight-line diagonal joining the two origins.

A transfer payment of 100 clothing paid to America shifts the initial point from A to A'. New offer curves drawn through A' will intersect in a new equilibrium point, marked B'. With zero impediments, this new point must also be on the contract curve, where the nations' indifference curves are mutually tangential and pointing at the new initial point A'.

For this special numerical case, the income-consumption or Engel's curves through B happen for both countries to have the same slope.[31] It follows from Part I's demonstration that $A'B'$ must then be parallel to AB, so that the unilateral transfer payment causes no orthodox deterioration of the payer's net terms of trade, and no anti-orthodox improvement.

All the above duplicates the reasoning of Part I. To handle tariffs, we must recognise that the countries must end up—not with indifference-curve slopes equal as on the contract curve—but with Europe's final slope always in a constant ratio to America's. Why? To reflect the relative cheapness of each country's export good in its own market; *i.e.*, the slopes must differ by the constant factor, $a_x a_y < 1$.

---

[31] In the absence of transport costs and special information, Part I argued that we have no reason to presume either country's marginal income propensities will be dominant for either good.

The locus of points with indifference-curve slopes agreeing up to the specified numerical factor is given by DD'. All the final equilibria under tariffs must end up on this locus. Without transfer, the final equilibrium point is at b.[32] Graphically, this can be recognised by the fact that the intermediate slope at b, which is between the two countries' indifference slopes in the same degree as $(P_c/P_f)_I$ is intermediate between $(P_c/P_f)_A$ and $(P_c/P_f)_E$, points directly at b.

Just as transfer without tariffs moved us along the contract locus toward the payer's origin, so will transfer with tariffs move us along our new DD' locus from b to b', toward the payer's origin and away from the receiver's. The problem of what happens to the payer's net terms of trade can new be reworded in graphical terms:

As transfer moves us along this DD' locus of final equilibrium points under tariffs, what is happening to the indifference slopes of either (and both, since the prices are in constant ratio to each other) country? Are they becoming flatter, as in the orthodox view? Or steeper? Or remaining unchanged?

Readers of Part I will easily see that the reasoning applied there to Figure 2 can also be applied here. A comparison of the relative steepness of the two countries' income-consumption curves through any point on DD' tells us how the indifference-slopes are changing as we move along DD'.

To summarise:

The paying country's net terms of trade will, under tariffs, *improve* (*remain the same, deteriorate*), depending on whether its own product expands relative to the other product *more slowly* (*at the same rate, faster*) along its own income-consumption curve than it expands along the receiving country's income-consumption curve.[33]

On the Pigouian assumptions of Figure 1, a transfer had an antiorthodox effect on the terms of trade. The strict Pigou case of independent and linear marginal utilities is seen graphically to imply income-consumption curves that become steeper as the indifference curves become flatter! I.e., as a good becomes cheap, more of it is bought and its average propensity to consume increases; but its marginal income propensities—

---

[32] Geometrically, b could be defined by intersecting "offer curves," where the latter are newly defined so as to be generated—not by points on each country's indifference curves that are pointing directly at A—but by points that would be pointing at A after modification by the a_y and $1/a_x$ factors. After transfer shifts us from A to A', a similar argument can determine b'.

[33] The relevant criterion depends on relative *physical* marginal propensities—*i.e.*, upon the relative slopes of the Engel's curves in the Figures—and can be written as $c_A/f_A \gtreqless c_E/f_E$. Since the nations' price ratios differ, this is no longer equivalent to $C_A/F_A \gtreqless C_E/F_E$, the criterion previously defined in terms of nonphysical marginal income propensities. Paradoxically, the latter criterion will turn out to be the correct one when the trade impediments are real rather than artificial, as will be shown in Table I.

both physical and in terms of value—here move in the opposite direction. Thus, through b and b', Europe marginally contracts its purchase of America's product (relative to its own product) faster than America expands its purchase of its own product (relative to Europe's product). Note how Europe's Engel's curve RR' through b is in the Pigou model steeper than America's Engel's curve rr'. This causes the intermediate slope between the two indifference curves to steepen as transfer moves us down DD' from b to b'. (See Figure 2 of Part I for expansion of this argument.)

E. Orthodoxy Defended in the Tariff Case

Our analysis has no need for assumptions of independent or linear marginal utilities. And since they lead to bizarre results, the time has come to drop them. Viner and others have put forward an alternative convention. By use of the principle of sufficient reason or other argument, Viner assumes that the single best assumption in the presence of ignorance is the following: Average and marginal income propensities are equal, so that indifference curves should be drawn with income-consumption curves that fan out in straight-line spokes from the origin.

The assumption of this Basic Convention will restore the orthodox presumption in one of our three cases, namely in the present case of artificial tariff barriers. Figure 4 provides a graphical demonstration. Every American indifference curve is simply a radial blow-up of any other. The same is true of Europe. Assuming tastes to be the same, a

FIGURE 4

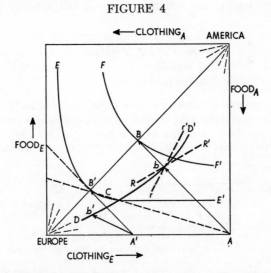

Basic convention implies Engel's curves are spokes out from origin, so tariffs produce orthodox deterioration. None the less, as Europe moves from B' to C, dearer imports cause relative expenditure on imports to rise; with "elasticity of substitution" less than one for both countries, terms of trade change in anti-orthodox fashion in real impediment cases.

fair assumption by our earlier arguments, we would still have no change in net terms of trade until we introduce trade impediments.

But tariffs cause the final equilibrium to shift—not from B to B' along the diagonal contract curve—but from b to b' along the DD' locus of final equilibria with proper spatial price relationships. Obviously, the tariff has made imports dear and shifted each country's physical consumption toward its own local goods. Europe's consumption is shifted south-eastward toward more clothing and less food; America's south-eastward toward more food and less clothing. We cannot tell whether a country spends a larger fraction of its income on imports or not. But that does not matter! We do know that in this case as a nation buys relatively more of its own good its income-consumption curve flattens out in an unambiguous manner. Hence, everywhere on the DD' locus, Europe's income-consumption slope is flatter than that of America: with $c_A/f_A < c_E/f_E$, we know that Europe's terms of trade must deteriorate in the orthodox fashion.[34]

F. Inconclusive Results in Case of Real Impediments

If we are willing to postulate the Basic Convention of unitary income elasticities (i.e., equal average and marginal propensities to consume), can we also re-establish the orthodox presumptions in the case of real transport costs? The answer is, Not necessarily. Our graphical analysis applied only to the tariff and zero-impediments. It fails to handle the real transport cost case, because then the final consumption equilibrium points for the two countries do *not* coincide, instead differing by a vector representing the amounts of the goods actually used up in transport.

As yet we have deduced no rigorous criterion to handle the real cost case. Such a criterion will be developed later by straightforward but tedious mathematical argument. For those uninterested in such derivations, I may briefly state the final result:

When there are real transport costs, the payer's terms of trade will improve, remain unchanged or deteriorate, depending upon whether the payer's marginal (income) propensity to consume its own product is less than, equal to or greater than the receiver's marginal (income) propensity to consume that same product.[35]

---

[34] Mathematically $r(Y,\bar{F} - X) = g[Y/(\bar{F} - X)]$, with $g > 0$, $g' < 0$; also $R(\bar{C} - Y, X) = G[(C-Y)/X]$, with $G > 0$, $G' < 0$. The criterion $c_A/f_A - c_E/f_E$ turns out to be $(\bar{F} - X)/Y - X/(\bar{C} - Y)$; because DD' lies eastward of the diagonal, this is seen to be algebraically negative.

[35] In symbols $C_A \gtrless C_E$ is our valid criterion for this case—or what is almost the same thing, $F_E \gtrless F_A$, or $C_A/F_V \gtrless C_E/F_E$. Note that the geometrical slopes of income-consumption curves are no longer relevant: such expressions as c_A/f_A and c_E/f_E must first be multiplied by $(P_c/P_f)_A$ and $(P_c/P_f)_E$ before they can be compared, and these last now differ by the factor $a_x a_y < 1$.

Now even with the assumption favorable to the orthodox view, namely Viner's Basic Convention, we *cannot* be sure how cheapening one's export good will affect its relative marginal (income) propensity to consume. Its physical output can be expected to decline relatively, but as argued in pp. 124–25 of Part I, no iron-clad presumptions are possible concerning *marginal propensities*.

Actually, our Basic Convention postulates unitary income elasticities, and therefore we can completely identify the marginal propensity to consume with the average propensity to consume. Casual econometricians, a class to which I belong, feel more confident in speculating about the latter than about the former. None the less, as the example of Figure 4 shows, relative expenditure on clothing may decline for Europe as it becomes cheaper. Europe's indifference curve EE' has been drawn with the usual shape and curvature: however, by measuring the relative lengths of the stretches on the budget line from each consumption point to the two axes, the reader may verify that for a considerable stretch eastward of the diagonal, the relative clothing price drops faster than its consumption expands. The crucial determinant of how relative expenditure changes can be shown to be the so-called "elasticity of substitution," whose magnitude permits of no uniform predictions.[36]

Unlike the case of tariffs, the case of real transport costs cannot therefore be definitely brought into the orthodox camp, even by means of the Basic Convention. As far as a pedantical economist can go seems to be the following:

Even with unitary income elasticities, real transport costs may cause average and marginal propensities to consume to decrease as a good becomes cheap, thereby reversing the orthodox effect on terms of trade.[37] Perhaps as transport costs become very great, thereby raising the costs of imports a great deal, there may be a presumption of ultimate extinction of consumption of the imported good permitting us to infer an ultimate move of marginal and average propensities to consume in the direction needed for the orthodox result.[38]

---

[36] Geometrically, the "elasticity of substitution" of Robinson–Hicks–Pigou may along an indifference curve be greater than, equal to or less than unity in magnitude. Nothing prevents Nature from presenting us with indifference curves that for stretches, and even everywhere, have elasticities of substitution less than unity. See R. G. D. Allen, *Mathmatical Analysis for Economists*, for discussion of the elasticity of substitution concepts and further references.

[37] Extreme transport costs and tariffs will almost certainly ultimately choke off imports by raising their prices beyond the point at which competing domestic supplies can fulfil the total domestic demand: when the markets have become split up and separated, the transfer will have to take place completely in terms of whichever good is specified in the payment contract. The result will be to shift the clothing-food terms of trade in opposite directions in the two countries, raising its price where one of the goods has become relatively scarce and lowering it where the good has become abundant. The orthodox view is not particularly realised in this extreme case of unconnected markets: indeed, with no sale of exports, the concept of a country's net terms of trade becomes vacuous.

[38] This presumption exists if the indifference curves are postulated to intersect the axes; if they become horizontal at interior saturation levels, the opposite presumption exists.

G. Fundamental Criteria for All Cases

In this section I present mathematical derivations of terms-of-trade criteria for all three cases: (*i*) zero impediments to trade, (*ii*) real cost impediments, and (*iii*) artificial impediments of tariffs or quotas.

Equations (4) define equilibrium in case (*ii*). Note that for $a_x = 1 = a_y$, (4) will also cover case (*i*). By differentiating the relation (4) with respect to the unilateral payment, K, we easily get three linear relations in the derivatives $d(P_c/P_f)_I/dK$, dX/dK, and dY/dK. Solving these, by determinants or otherwise, we can find the criterion that governs the algebraic sign of the derivative of the price ratio with respect to the indemnity.

We differentiate (4) totally with respect to K to yield equations that are linear in the three derivatives dY/dK, dX/dK, and most important for the present purpose, $d(P_c/P_f)_I/dK$:

$$a_y(a_y r_1)\frac{dY}{dK} - a_y r_2 \frac{dX}{dK} - 1\frac{d(P_c/P_f)_I}{dK} = 0$$

$$-\frac{1}{a_x}R_1\frac{dY}{dK} + \frac{1}{a_x}(a_x R_2)\frac{dX}{dK} - 1\frac{d(P_c/P_f)_I}{dK} = 0 \qquad (7)$$

$$+1\frac{dY}{dK} - \frac{1}{(P_c/P_f)_I}\frac{dX}{dK} - \frac{Y-K}{(P_c/P_f)_I}\frac{d(P_c/P_f)_I}{dX} = +1$$

where numerical subscripts on the r and R functions indicate partial derivatives with respect to the indicated argument, so that $r_1 = \partial r(c,f)/\partial c$, etc.

By means of determinants, or otherwise, we can solve these linear equations to determine what the change in the terms of trade depends on, namely

$$\frac{d(P_c/P_f)_I}{dK} = \frac{\begin{vmatrix} a_y(a_y r_1) & -a_y r_2 \\ -R_1/a_x & \frac{1}{a_x}(a_x R_2) \end{vmatrix}}{\Delta} = \frac{\left(-\dfrac{r_2}{r_1}\right) - a_x a_y \left(-\dfrac{R_2}{R_1}\right)}{a_x(-r_1)(-R_1)a_y^{-1}\Delta} \qquad (8)$$

where Δ is the determinant of all the left-hand coefficients of the linear equations (7), which can be shown to be positive as a condition for "stability" of our system. If neither good is an inferior good, every factor in the denominator of the last expression in (8) can be verified to be positive, and hence the numerator alone provides a rigorous criterion for the shift in the terms of trade. Since it is easy to show that the terms in parentheses in the numerator are the slopes of the income-consumption curves of the respective countries, namely c_A/f_A and c_E/f_E, we can rewrite our criterion in the form

$$\frac{d(P_c/P_f)_I}{dK} \underset{<}{\overset{>}{=}} 0, \text{ if } \frac{c_A}{f_A} \underset{<}{\overset{>}{=}} a_x a_y \frac{c_E}{f_E}$$

or

$$\left(\frac{P_c}{P_f}\right)_A \frac{c_A}{f_A} = \frac{C_A}{F_A} \gtrless \frac{C_E}{F_E} = \left(\frac{P_c}{P_f}\right)_E \frac{c_E}{f_E} = \left(\frac{P_c}{P_f}\right)_A a_x a_y \frac{c_E}{f_E}$$

Of course, if $a_x = 1 = a_y$ because there are zero impediments, then the physical marginal propensities, written in lower-case letters, will be proportional to the dimensionless marginal-income propensities, written in capital letters; and then either may be used as a criterion.

All our criteria are summed up in Table I. To handle the tariff case rigorously, the reader can supply for himself the differentiation of equations (6) with respect to K to get the linear equations in the derivatives. Because (6) differs from (4) only in the fact that the factor a_y no longer appears within r and a_x no longer within R, the new linear equations will differ from (8) only by the replacement of $(a_y r_1)$ and $(a_x R_2)$ by r_1 and R_2. Hence, for the artificial barrier case, our criterion becomes

$$\frac{d(P_c/P_f)_I}{dK} \gtrless 0 \text{ if } \frac{c_A}{f_A} \gtrless \frac{c_E}{f_E} \text{ or } a_x a_y \frac{C_A}{F_A} \gtrless \frac{C_E}{F_E}$$

Table I also relates Pigou's form of the criterion, based on independent utilities, to the different types of transport costs. Equation (4)′ of an earlier footnote showed how the Pigou analysis is modified by the appearance *inside* and *outside* of the r and R functions of the factors a_y and a_x. The reader can easily verify how the tariff-case version of these coefficients outside the functions leads to Table I's version of the Pigou criterion.

It will be noted that whether impediments are real or artificial, the Pigou criteria are modified so as to lead in the direction opposite to the orthodox presumption: *i.e.*, the a_x and a_y terms always appear as depressants on the right-hand side of the criteria. Clearly Professor Pigou intends the assumption of linearity of marginal utility to be only a local approximation. If we permit his coefficients ϕ', f', Ψ' and F' to be variables rather than constants, we can muster up some comfort for the orthodox view: Providing the rate of change of the rate of change of marginal utility (i.e., the *third* derivative of the utility function) is assumed to be sufficiently negative for all goods, then the depressing effects of the a_x and a_y coefficients may be more than offset by the change in the ϕ', f', Ψ' and F' coefficients, and the orthodox effect can result. Since rightly or wrongly, economists usually draw marginal utility curves that are concave from above, the orthodox case is not necessarily refuted by the assumption of independent utilities.[39]

---

[39] All this can be understood best in terms of a plotting of the indifference curves and their income-consumption curves. If each good becomes free at a finite level of consumption, the independent utility assumption does near the saturation levels lead to income or Engel curves that fan *in*ward, thereby negating the orthodox view (see Figure 3). But in between the zones of saturation, we can easily find examples of independent utilities where the Engel's curves fan out in a more realistic fashion. Note

TABLE I

Summary of Criteria for Paying Country's Terms-of-Trade Change

	Zero Trade Impediments	Real Transport Costs ($a_x < 1, a_y < 1$)	Tariff and Artificial Barriers ($a_x < 1, a_y < 1$)
Marginal income propensities to consume (dimensionless)	$C_A \gtrless C_E$ or $\dfrac{C_A}{F_A} \gtrless \dfrac{C_E}{F_E}$	$C_A \gtrless C_E$ or $\dfrac{C_A}{F_A} \gtrless \dfrac{C_E}{F_E}$	$a_x a_y \dfrac{C_A}{F_A} \gtrless \dfrac{C_E}{F_E}$
Physical marginal propensities or relative slopes of income-consumption curves	$\dfrac{c_A}{f_A} \gtrless \dfrac{c_E}{f_E}$	$\dfrac{c_A}{f_A} \gtrless a_x a_y \dfrac{c_E}{f_E}$	$\dfrac{c_A}{f_A} \gtrless \dfrac{c_E}{f_E}$
Pigou criterion	$\left|\dfrac{\psi'}{F'}\right| \gtrless \left|\dfrac{\phi'}{f'}\right|$	$\left|\dfrac{\psi'}{F'}\right| \gtrless (a_x a_y)^2 \left|\dfrac{\phi'}{f'}\right|$	$\left|\dfrac{\psi'}{F'}\right| \gtrless a_x a_y \left|\dfrac{\phi'}{f'}\right|$
Strict linear marginal utilities, identical tastes	No change in terms of trade	Anti-orthodox change in favor of payer	Anti-orthodox change in favor of payer
Basic convention of unitary income elasticities, ($MPC = APC$), identical tastes	No change in terms of trade	Either change depending on whether elasticity of substitution along an indifference curve is numerically greater than one (orthodox) or less than one (antiorthodox)	Orthodox change against payer
Export and import good with outputs variable ...	Same as above but with "less leverage."		
"Domestic" goods .	Orthodox view favored, provided domestic goods are "more competitive on the production side" with export goods than with import goods.		

H. Variability of Output

Dropping the assumption of fixed production of the two goods in both countries will not affect qualitatively our above analysis and conclusions, for reasons that were discussed in Part I. Even if food can be substituted for clothing along a familiar production-possibility sched-

---

that the independence assumption is incompatible with the Basic Convention of unitary income elasticities. If I were forced to accept one simple assumption, I should perhaps prefer the latter to the former.

ule. no change in production will take place unless our criterion dictates
a change in relative prices.[40] The only difference is this: If the criterion
does dictate a change in relative prices, the elasticity of response of outputs can be expected to moderate the quantitative degree of the resulting change in prices.

The late Frank D. Graham for thirty years insisted that "net elasticities" in international trade were greater than most writers thought.
Indeed, in Graham's view, they are infinite or almost so because of his
extreme constant-costs assumptions of the classical type.[41] I see no point
at this date in re-arguing whether both blades of the Marshallian scissors
do the cutting in such extreme cases. But on the substantive point of the
effect on elasticities of assuming many countries or many sources of
supply, I should put the matter this way: Introducing many alternative
supply sources exactly like what one already has seems to increase the
scale of all processes, and hence naturally leads to the same-sized disturbances having smaller price effects; but it is not clear to me why as
the world grows in scale, the size of the postulated disturbances should
not grow commensurately. Note, too, that introducing new supply sources
which produce at *different* constant-cost levels seems, in my view, to
work *against* the Graham thesis of almost infinitely elasticity. Similarly,
introducing many goods producible at constant costs will lessen the impact of one small micro-economic disturbance; but it is not at all clear
to me that the effect of, say, a post-war disturbance of macro-economic
type will be quantitatively different in its impact on an economy that

---

[40] To prove this rigorously, see Part I, Section F. The factors a_y and a_x must be
introduced into the systems shown there in an obvious way, and then the equation
must be differentiated to verify that our same criteria do apply. This involves about
ten equations in as many unknowns; by the following simple analysis, we can fortunately reduce the problem to a single derived equation in one unknown.

Let small letters stand for America, capitals for Europe, let p and $P = a_x a_y p$ be
short for $(P_c/P_f)_A$ and $(P_c/P_f)_E$. For each country, output will be determined so as
to yield, for each domestic price p or P, a maximum value of national product or
income expressed in, say, food-numeraire units; call these respectively $i(p)$ and $I(P)$,
where $i'(p) > 0, I'(P) > 0$.

The quantity of clothing supplied in each country will be given by positively inclined functions $s(p)$ and $S(P)$, and the demands for clothing will be given by
functions d and D; these depend upon clothing price (in food-numeraire units) and
upon each country's income (expressed in numeraire units) including algebraic
transfer payments of $+pa_y K$ for America and $-PK$ for Europe.

The equilibrium is defined by equality of the net demand of America for clothing
to the net supply of Europe's clothing that comes through to America after real
transport costs; or, recalling $P = a_x a_y p$, we have the single equilibrium equation

$$\{d(p, i(p) + pa_y K) - s(p)\} - a_y\{S(P) - D(P, I(P) - PK)\} = 0 = E(P, K)$$

This defines either unknown price in terms of the transfer K. Differentiating, we get

$$\frac{dP}{dK} = a_x a_y \frac{dp}{dK} = \left(p\frac{\partial d}{\partial i} - P\frac{\partial D}{\partial I}\right) \Big/ \Delta_1$$

where $\Delta_1 = -\partial E/\partial P > 0$ for a "stable" system, and where increases in the supply
slopes S' and s' cause the denominator to grow.

[41] See *Theory of International Values* (Princeton, 1948).

F

concentrates its consumption on a few goods producible at constant costs than on an economy that chooses to spend a very little on a great many such goods. Only if one brings in Chamberlinian phenomena of monopolistic competition do substantive effects arise, and then I suspect analysis of market imperfections due to product differentiation will show that this works against rather than for Graham's thesis of high elasticity.

I. Final Qualifications

The Pigou–Jevons two-good model in its slightly generalised form has been squeezed dry of its implications. Yet we are still a long way from the conditions of the real world, involving many goods and various types of market imperfections and trade impediments. With some diffidence, I venture a few tentative speculations as to what the effects of these complications are on the transfer problem.

Many goods with varying transport costs, a_x, a_y, a_z . . . can be first handled on the assumption of fixed outputs: Any criteria sufficient to hold all relative prices invariant under these conditions can apply to the case of varying outputs—since outputs will not in fact vary without relative prices varying. Expressing the indemnity or payment in terms of specified goods of one or both countries, we can ask the question: In addition to the "primary burden," what is the "secondary burden" on each country as measured by each country's price changes weighed by its *algebraic* imports.

Economic theory does not permit me to give an answer to this question. Even in the case where domestic goods are created in each economy by transport costs (which suggest that elasticity of substitution for the imported goods ultimately becomes elastic in the orthodox manner), it is not clear that the terms of trade, as defined in the previous paragraph or by comparing non-domestic import goods' prices with export prices, can be presumed to change in any one direction.[42]

Yet, as Part I indicated on p. 128, the Viner model of one or more domestic goods in each country which are perfect substitutes on the production side for export goods does provide us with one rigorous and impressive defense of the orthodox view. With export and domestic goods always having the same relative costs and prices, we may lump their expenditure together *à la* Hicks; then the Basic Convention will permit us to assume that less is spent marginally and on the average on input goods, so that our criterion leads to the orthodox presumption.

In a pure Ricardian constant-cost world, a country can usually be assumed to produce none of the goods it imports. Therefore, domestic goods must compete with export goods alone, as in the Viner case. Professor Haberler has asked me whether it would not be possible to find

---

[42] See Part I's discussion of the inconclusive case of fixed production with domestic goods.

models in which domestic goods were substitutable on the production side for imported goods, thus leading to anti-orthodox criteria. A number of such models are easily constructed.

Thus, suppose the same factors produced bricks in America as produced clothing; suppose, too, that the production-possibility schedule between food and clothing shows strongly increasing relative marginal costs, with the result that in equilibrium some clothing is produced as well as imported. Then for America bricks and clothing may be treated as a composite Hicksian commodity of high expenditure relative to food. Similarly, in Europe there will be low relative expenditure on its export goods relative to remaining goods. Assuming identical average and marginal propensities, we can deduce $C_A > C_E$ and an anti-orthodox improvement in the payer's net terms of trade.

The real world may be somewhere in between: domestic goods or goods whose transport costs are so heavy as to discourage their import relative to their home production may turn out to be substitutable on the production side with both *imports* and *exports*, being infinitely substitutable with neither. It then becomes a case of nice quantitative weighting, beyond the powers of casual econometricians and indeed under present conditions often beyond the powers of the most intensive statistical measurement and inference, to provide us with any final answers. On the whole, I—and I think Haberler—would be inclined to regard the relations between export and domestic goods as outweighing those between import and domestic goods, in accordance with the Viner hypothesis and the orthodox conclusion.

It is well to know just how strong or weak the orthodox view on the effects of transfer are. Findings of the present research on pure barter models are summarised in Table I.

9. The Transfer Problem and

Exchange Stability [*]

By HARRY G. JOHNSON [†] [1]

THE TRANSFER PROBLEM bulks large in the literature of international trade theory, both because international economic relations have abounded in transfer problems of various kinds and because the problem offers an attractive opportunity for the application of new theoretical techniques. My purpose here is not to survey the literature,[2] but to offer a straightforward and (it is hoped) simplified exposition of the theory of transfers in modern terms, based largely on recent literature but extending and unifying it in certain respects. In addition, it will be argued that transfer theory has a wider application than might appear at first sight and that, in particular, it can be applied directly to the problem of exchange stability.

In the context of modern international trade theory, the transfer problem can be posed in either of two ways—as a *real* problem or as a *monetary* problem. More precisely, it can be approached either on the classical assumption that the economic system works so as to maintain equality between income and expenditure at the level corresponding to full employment of resources in each country, or on the Keynesian assumption that the economy of each country is characterized by a perfectly elastic supply of labour and commodities at a fixed wage and price level,[3] so that output and income are determined by aggregate

[*] *Journal of Political Economy*, Vol. LXIV, No. 3 (June, 1956), pp. 212–25. Also published in *International Trade and Economic Growth: Studies in Pure Theory* (Cambridge: Harvard University Press, 1961), pp. 169–95. The latter version, reprinted here, extends the analysis to include the application of transfer theory to trade intervention. The argument has been revised to correct an error in the penultimate paragraph of Section I pointed out by Sir Donald MacDougall.

[†] London School of Economics and University of Chicago.

[1] This paper was drafted during my tenure of a visiting professorship at Northwestern University; it has benefited greatly, though perhaps insufficiently, from criticisms of colleagues there and elsewhere in the United States and the United Kingdom.

[2] For such surveys see Jacob Viner, *Studies in the Theory of International Trade* (New York, 1937), chap. vi; Paul A. Samuelson, "The Transfer Problem and Transport Costs." *Economic Journal*, Vol. LXII, No. 246 (June, 1952), pp. 278–304, and Vol. LXIV, No. 254 (June, 1954), pp. 264–89; and Gottfried Haberler, *A Survey of International Trade Theory* (Princeton, 1955).

[3] It is possible, but unnecessarily complicating, to assume a perfectly elastic supply of labour at a fixed money wage and an imperfectly elastic supply of output, as

effective demand. In this paper the problem will be discussed from both approaches.

On either set of assumptions, classical or Keynesian, the transfer problem can be separated into two problems for analysis. The first is whether the process by which the transfer is financed in the transferor country and disposed of in the transferee will affect each country's demand for imports (at unchanged prices) sufficiently to create the trade surplus and deficit necessary to effect the transfer. The financing and disposal of the transfer will tend to reduce the transferor's demand for goods and increase the transferee's demand for goods; both effects will tend to improve the balance of trade of the transferor and worsen that of the transferee, and the changes may fall short of, or exceed, the amount of the transfer. Unless the changes in trade balances are exactly equal to the amount of the transfer, there will remain a balance-of-payments disequilibrium which must be corrected by some adjustment mechanism. In the classical model the adjustment mechanism is assumed to be a change in the terms of trade of the countries, brought about by price deflation and inflation;[4] in the Keynesian model the adjustment mechanism may be assumed to be either deflation and inflation of effective demand or a terms-of-trade change brought about by devaluation. In either model an alternative method of adjustment would be the tightening and relaxation of trade restrictions.

The second part of the transfer problem is whether the adjustment mechanism will be effective in restoring equilibrium. This problem really raises two subsidiary questions, one of direction and one of magnitude of influence. Taking the classical mechanism of a change in the terms of trade as an example, there is, first, the question whether a small deterioration in a country's terms of trade will tend to improve or to worsen its trade balance—the stability problem. Second, on the assumption that the balance would be improved by a small deterioration in the terms of trade, there is the question whether the trade balance can be improved sufficiently by this means to achieve a surplus of a given size. The same two questions arise with respect to the Keynesian mechanism of demand deflation and inflation, and also with respect to the use of trade controls of various kinds. It is obvious that the second question is an empirical one on which theory can render little assistance, since it would always be possible to specify a surplus too large to be achieved by any method of adjustment. The question of direction of effect is, however, susceptible of theoretical analysis, and conditions for the mechanism to work in the right direction can be established.

To summarize, the transfer problem has two theoretical facets: whether

---

Keynes did in the *General Theory*. An analysis of this case may be found in James E. Meade, *The Balance of Payments* (London, 1951), and its *Mathematical Supplement*.

[4] Strictly speaking, what must change is the double-factoral rather than the commodity terms of trade, since with non-traded goods the commodity terms of trade can change in either direction as the price level changes.

the transfer will be undereffected or overeffected as a consequence of the process by which it is financed and disposed of (that is, the direction in which the adjustment mechanism will be required to operate) and whether the adjustment mechanism will operate in the direction of restoring equilibrium. This chapter is concerned mainly with the first of these problems, and the argument will assume that the adjustment mechanism will suffice. A large part of the answer to the second problem will, however, be provided by applying the results of the argument on the first problem to the general problem of exchange stability, and to the problem of the effect of various kinds of governmental intervention in trade on the trade balance.

The argument which follows makes the usual simplifying assumptions, namely, that the world consists of two countries, A and B, producing two commodities or commodity bundles, A-goods and B-goods, these being the commodities exported by A and B, respectively. It is assumed that A is the transferor and B the transferee.

1. THE CLASSICAL TRANSFER PROBLEM[5]

On classical assumptions, the question whether the transfer would be undereffected or overeffected at constant prices is extremely simple to deal with, since the assumption of automatic full employment implies that the transfer must be financed and disposed of in such a way as to reduce aggregate expenditure by the transferor and increase aggregate expenditure by the transferee by the amount of the transfer and thus rules out any multiplier effects. The transferor's balance of trade is improved both by the reduction in its expenditure on imports and by the increase in the transferee's demand for its exports. The total improvement, expressed as a proportion of the transfer, will be equal to the sum of the proportions of the expenditure changes in the two countries which fall on imports—more precisely, the sum of the proportions of the expenditure changes by which the receipts of the exporting country change. The transfer will be undereffected or overeffected, and the terms of trade will be required to change against, or in favour of, the transferor, according to whether the sum of these proportions is less or greater than unity. This general rule may be translated into several equivalent forms, by use of the fact that the proportion of the expenditure change which does not fall on imports must fall on exportable goods. The most convenient of these forms to work with is that the transfer will be undereffected or overeffected according to whether the sum of the proportions of expenditure change falling on the countries' export goods is greater or less than unity.

[5] This section reproduces, in a somewhat simpler form, the argument of my note, "The Transfer Problem: A Note on Criteria for Changes in the Terms of Trade," *Economica*, N.S., Vol. XXII, No. 86 (May, 1955), 113–21. That note and some of the additional argument of the present section owe much to Samuelson's two masterly *Economic Journal* articles cited in n. 2, and reprinted in this volume on pp. 115–47.

This rule, however, does not establish anything very interesting (beyond the demonstration that either result is possible), since nothing has been said about what determines the proportions of expenditure change. In general, these would depend on the nature of the transfer and the assumed conditions of international trade; as there is no reason for identifying the effects of the financing and disposal of a transfer with the effects of any other kind of economic change, nothing more can, in strictest generality, be said. Nevertheless, it is customary in the literature (and defensible in many cases) to identify the effects of the transfer on expenditure with those of an income tax and a subsidy. On this assumption the proportions of expenditure change can be related to the countries' marginal propensities to spend on exportables or importables, the precise relation depending on the assumed conditions of international trade. Three cases may be distinguished.

A. Free Trade, No Transport Costs

In this case all expenditure on imports constitutes receipts for the exporting country, and the proportions of expenditure change are equal to the marginal propensities to spend. The transfer criterion is therefore whether the sum of the marginal propensities to spend on exportables is greater or less than unity.

B. Tariffs, No Transport Costs

Tariffs introduce a difference between the price paid by residents of a country for imports and the receipts of the foreign exporters. In conformity with classical assumptions, the tariff proceeds cannot be allowed to disappear from circulation but must be assumed to be spent by someone. The simplest assumption is that they are redistributed as an income subsidy and spent like any other increment of income, in which case part of the initial change in expenditure on imports associated with the transfer will wind up as a change in expenditure on exportables (out of redistributed tax proceeds). Consequently, the proportions of expenditure change falling on exportables will be larger than the marginal propensities to spend on exportables, and the transfer criterion is accordingly whether the sum of the marginal propensities to spend on exportables is greater or less than a critical value which will be less than unity.[6]

---

[6] Let C and M be the marginal propensities to spend on exportables and imports and t be the proportion of the final price of imports taken in taxes. Then total expenditure at market prices will change by

$$1 + tM + (tM)^2 + \ldots = \frac{1}{1 - tM}$$

times the amount of the transfer, and the proportion of the transfer by which expenditure on exportables changes will be

$$\frac{C}{1 - tM} = \left(1 + \frac{tM}{1 - tM}\right)C.$$

C. Transport Costs, No Tariffs

In this case also there will be a difference between the price paid by residents for imports and the price received by the exporters, the difference representing the transport costs. To the extent that transport of exports utilizes the exported good, the transport costs will constitute receipts for the exporting country. In the extreme case where transport utilizes only the exported good, all expenditure on imports will be (direct, or indirect) receipts for the exporting country, the proportions of expenditure change will be equal to the marginal propensities to spend, and the transfer criterion will be the same as in the no-impediments case [(A) above]. But to the extent that transport utilizes the exportable good of the importing country, transport costs constitute an indirect demand for that good; consequently, the proportions of expenditure change falling on exportables will be larger than the (direct) marginal propensities to spend on exportables, and the critical value for the transfer criterion will be something less than unity, as in the previous case.[7]

The transfer criteria derived in the three cases just examined suggest a reference to a question which has concerned many writers on the transfer problem, namely, whether, even though the classical proposition that the terms of trade *must* turn against the transferring country is erroneous, there nonetheless remains a presumption in favour of this conclusion. Fundamentally, this is a meaningless question, since only ignorance can come from ignorance and no satisfactory basis exists for assessing the likely magnitudes of the marginal propensities to spend which enter into the criteria, short of measuring them in particular cases, when no question of presumption would arise.[8] An argument from "equal

---

Since the transfer will be undereffected or overeffected according to whether the sum of these proportions is greater or lss than unity, i.e. according to whether

$$\left(1 + \frac{t_a M_a}{1 - t_a M_a}\right) C_a + \left(1 + \frac{t_b M_b}{1 - t_b M_b}\right) C_b \gtrless 1,$$

the critical value of the transfer criterion will be

$$C_a + C_b = 1 - \frac{t_a M_a C_a}{1 - t_a M_a} - \frac{t_b M_b C_b}{1 - t_b M_b}.$$

The right-hand side of this expression must be less than unity, since t, M, and C are all positive fractions.

[7] Let k be the proportion of the price of imports representing transport cost incurred in the importer's exportable commodity; then the proportion of the transfer by which expenditure on exportables changes is $C + kM$, and the critical value of the transfer criterion is

$$1 - k_a M_a - k_b M_b,$$

which is less than unity.

[8] Statistical estimates of marginal propensities to import in the interwar period (1924–38) have produced results for some countries well above the average of ½ required by the criteria. For example, T. C. Chang (*Cyclical Movements in the Balance of Payments* [Cambridge, 1951], p. 37) found six agricultural countries with marginal propensities to import ranging from 0.52 to 0.73, though in all but one

ignorance" might, however, be drawn on the following lines: given only that the sum of the marginal propensities to spend on imports and exportables is unity, equal ignorance would suggest no presumption that the average marginal propensity to spend on exportables is either greater or less than ½. Thus in the no-impediments case there would be no presumption in favour of the classical conclusion; but there would be such a presumption in the cases of tariffs and of transport costs incurred in the exportable good of the importing country, since in these cases the transfer would be undereffected if the average marginal propensity to spend on exportables were exactly ½. In the latter case the presumption would be reinforced by the fact that, if these transport costs absorbed half the delivered price of imports on the average, the transfer would necessarily be undereffected for any positive values of the marginal propensities to spend on exportables.[9]

A less controversial, more "positive," approach to the classical presumption is to examine what it implies about the countries involved in the transfer. For this purpose it is convenient to use an alternative form of the transfer criterion, namely, that the transfer will be undereffected if the extra physical quantity of A-goods purchased (directly or indirectly) out of an increase in income in A is greater than it is in B;[10] that is, the transfer will be undereffected if the countries are biased (at the margin) toward the purchase of their exportables.

In the free-trade, no-transport-cost case the prices facing consumers are the same in both countries. Consequently, the classical presumption requires either that the countries differ in tastes and are biased toward consumption of their exportables or that, tastes being identical, the goods differ in degree of necessity and the country with the higher income per

case (Denmark, 0.54) the estimates are based on relatively short series. More recently J. J. Polak (*An International Economic System* [London, 1954], "Summary of Results," opposite p. 156) has obtained the following estimates: for the whole period, Denmark, 0.73; Norway, 0.67; for the 1920's Finland, 0.93; New Zealand, 0.65; Indonesia, 0.62; Union of South Africa, 0.57. While these estimates do not correspond very precisely with the theoretical concepts employed here (imports generally being valued c.i.f., which excludes tariffs but may include invisible receipts of the exporting country) and their application is complicated by the presence of many countries and many commodities, they are not inconsistent with the possibility that in some cases a transfer might be overeffected.

[9] On the assumption that $k_a + k_b = 1$, the criterion of n. 7 becomes $k_a C_a + k_b C_b$, which is necessarily less than $C_a + C_b$.

[10] One formulation of the rule developed in the first paragraph of this section is that the transfer will be undereffected or overeffected according to whether the proportion of expenditure change in the transferor which falls on exportables is greater or less than the proportion of expenditure change in the transferee which falls on the transferor's exportables. Since the latter deducts tariffs and transport costs from the delivered price and adds back in transport cost incurred in the exported good, which amounts to measurement at factor cost in the transferor, deflation by factor cost gives the criterion stated in the text. Further, it follows that, since the sum of the proportions of expenditure change measured in this way must equal unity for each country, the condition respecting A-goods, as stated previously, implies the reverse for B-goods.

F*

head produces the more "luxurious" good for export. In the case of tariffs and of transport costs the relative prices facing consumers differ, each commodity being relatively cheaper in the exporting than in the importing country. Consequently, if the economies were on identical consumption indifference curves before the transfer, each would have an *average* bias *in direct consumption* toward the purchase of its exportable commodity; and if *average* preferences are assumed to coincide with *marginal* preferences—which implies unitary income-elasticities of demand —*direct consumption* will display the marginal bias required by the classical presumption. To put the point the opposite way, so far as *direct* consumption is concerned, tastes must be biased toward imported goods or marginal preferences must be so biased either because marginal preferences behave contrarily to average preferences or because the country with the higher income per head produces the more necessary commodity, if the classical presumption is to be invalid. But *indirect consumption* must also be considered. In the case of tariffs without transport costs, indirect consumption out of tariff proceeds is assumed to behave in the same way as direct consumption, leaving the foregoing argument unaffected. In the case of transport costs and free trade, the bias toward direct consumption of exportables induced by the difference in prices is reinforced if transport costs are incurred entirely in the exportable good of the importing country and mitigated—perhaps outweighed—if transport costs are incurred entirely in the imported good. The effects of transport costs incurred in both goods are too complex to be analysed here, though analogy with the tariff case indicates that, in the case of identical pretransfer indifference curves and unitary income-elasticities, a necessary condition for invalidation of the classical presumption is that transport is more "import-intensive" than is marginal consumption expenditure in the importing country.

Before concluding this section, it is appropriate to consider briefly the effects of relaxing some of the simplifying assumptions. The possibility of varying home production of the imported good makes no difference, since this is conditional on the price ratio between the goods changing, which in turn depends on the criteria derived previously. The introduction of non-traded goods does alter the criteria, since changes in demand for such goods must be classed either as changes in (virtual) demand for exportables or as changes in (virtual) demand for imports, according to whether they are more substitutable in production and consumption for one or the other.[11] In both these cases, however, the direction of change of the commodity terms of trade is not uniquely determined by whether the transfer is undereffected or overeffected at constant prices. The introduction of more countries also alters the criterion, since the balances of

---

[11] If it can be assumed that non-traded goods are substitutes for exports, this strengthens the classical presumption that the terms of trade turn against the transferor; but contrary cases are conceivable (Samuelson, *loc. cit., Part II,* pp. 288–89).

payments of the two countries are no longer equal and opposite in sign. From the transferor's point of view, the transfer will be undereffected or overeffected (at pretransfer prices) according to whether the sum of the proportions of the transfer by which the transferor's expenditure on imports is reduced, and the transferee's expenditure *on the transferor's exports* (not on imports in general) is less or greater than unity. Again, the movement of the commodity terms of trade is not decided by whether the transfer is undereffected or overeffected.

II. THE KEYNESIAN TRANSFER PROBLEM[12]

For the analysis of the transfer problem in Keynesian terms, it is assumed that output in each country is in perfectly elastic supply at a fixed domestic-currency price level, so that output, income, and employment are determined by the aggregate demand for output. It is also assumed that each country fixes its exchange rate and level of interest rates by appropriate monetary action, though its policy in this respect may change in the event of a continuing balance-of-payments disequilibrium, and that, apart from accommodating financial transactions between monetary authorities, international capital movements are independent of the levels of national incomes.

These assumptions permit the derivation of multiplier equations relating changes in the national incomes of the countries and in the balance of payments between them to the various autonomous changes in demands for goods and transfers which may occur. The equations may be written as follows:

$$Y_a = I_a + c_a Y_a + M_b + m_b Y_b, \tag{1a}$$

$$Y_b = I_b + c_b Y_b + M_a + m_a Y_a, \tag{1b}$$

$$B_a = M_b + m_b Y_b - M_a - m_a Y_a - T, \tag{1c}$$

where Y_a, Y_b, and B_a are the total changes in the two countries' national incomes and in country A's balance of payments (all measured in international currency units); I_a and I_b are autonomous changes in the countries' demands for their own output; M_a and M_b are autonomous changes in their demands for each other's outputs; T is an autonomous change in capital movements from A to B; c_a and c_b are the marginal propensities to spend on the purchase of domestic output; and m_a and m_b are the marginal propensities to spend on imports. It is assumed in what follows that all marginal propensities, including the marginal propensities to save (represented below by s_a and s_b) are positive, an assumption which suffices to guarantee stability of the system. It should also be remarked that while the system is set up in the symbols of a simple Keynesian system (implying the absence of government, business, and transport sectors

[12] This section enlarges on my note, "The Reparations Problem: A Correction," *Economic Journal*, Vol. LXIII, No. 251 (September, 1953), pp. 724–25.

and the utilization of goods only for direct consumption), it can be extended simply by redefinition of symbols to represent aspects of more complicated economic systems, such as the presence of direct and indirect taxes (other than export duties, which would require modification of the balance-of-payments equation), the dependence of government and business expenditure on taxation and sales receipts, and the use of domestic and imported goods in the production process.[13]

The transfer problem in the Keynesian case differs from that in the classical (real) case in two respects. First, there is no reason to assume that the process of financing and disposal of the transfer leads to changes in aggregate expenditure in the two countries equal to the amount of the transfer—the funds may come out of dissaving or go into saving. Second, any changes in expenditure brought about by the financing and disposal of the transfer will have multiplier repercussions on the balance of trade between the countries. The problem in this case is therefore whether, when all multiplier effects have been taken into account, the changes in demands for goods which result from the financing and disposal of the transfer are less or more than sufficient to improve the transferor's balance of trade by the amount of the transfer—that is, whether the transferor's balance of payments worsens or improves as a consequence of the transfer.

To analyse this problem, it is necessary merely to substitute for the various autonomous changes in demands in the multiplier equations the proportions of the transfer by which the demands for domestic and foreign goods are reduced in the transferor and increased in the transferee. In doing so, however, it is most convenient to work with the changes in demand for imports and in saving associated with the transfer, using the property that the transfer must alter the demand for home goods, the demand for imports, or the accumulation of assets through saving. Representing the changes in demand for imports and in saving directly due to

---

[13] Let P represent the total change in sales proceeds at market prices, I and M autonomous changes in purchases of domestic and foreign output at these prices, h the proportion of a change in sales proceeds by which purchases of domestic output are further increased, and f the proportion by which purchases of foreign output are further increased. We may define h and f to include induced governmental expenditure from tax receipts, business expenditure from undistributd profits, and purchases of output for use in the production process, as well as final consumers' expenditure from disposable income. Then the multiplier equation for A, for example, may be written $P_a = I_a + h_a P_a + M_b + f_b P_b$. But since, for small changes, the change in national income at factor cost will be some given proportion of the change in sales proceeds, $Y = kP$, the multiplier equations based on sales proceeds may be rewritten in the standard form by defining

$$c = 1 - \frac{1-h}{k}, \quad m = \frac{f}{k},$$

and

$$s = \frac{1-h-f}{k}.$$

Consequently, it is unnecessary to assume, as is generally done, that imports are used only in final consumption, to avoid input-output complications.

the financing or disposal of the transfer, expressed as proportions of the amount transferred, by m' and s', respectively, the multiplier equations yield the following solutions for the resulting changes in incomes and country A's balance of payments:

$$Y_a = \frac{1}{s_a} (B_a + s'_a T), \tag{2a}$$

$$Y_b = -\frac{1}{s_b} (B_a + s'_b T), \tag{2b}$$

$$B_a = \left(m'_a + m'_b - \frac{m_a}{s_a} s'_a - \frac{m_b}{s_b} s'_b - 1 \right) \times \frac{s_a s_b}{\Delta} T, \tag{2c}$$

where $\Delta = s_a s_b + s_a m_b + s_b m_a$. From this it follows that the transfer will be undereffected or overeffected according to whether $m'_a + m'_b$ (the sum of the proportions of the transfer by which expenditure on imports is altered by the financing and disposal of the transfer) is less or greater than

$$\frac{m_a}{s_a} s'_a + \frac{m_b}{s_b} s'_b + 1$$

(1 plus the sum of the proportions of the transfer by which saving is altered—expenditure *not* changed—by the financing and disposal of the transfer, each weighted by the ratio of the marginal propensity to import to the marginal propensity to save in the country concerned).

The criterion just established, like that established earlier for the classical model, permits the transfer to be either undereffected or overeffected, according to the magnitudes of various parameters. This result is contrary to the findings of Metzler and Machlup,[14] whose analyses led to the conclusion that the transfer would necessarily be undereffected in the case under discussion (that is, on the assumption of positive marginal propensities to save in both countries).[15] This conclusion ran contrary to the findings of the classical analysis, a point of which Metzler, in particular, made much. However, the contradiction is attributable to the adoption of special assumptions, namely, that the financing and disposal of the transfer does not directly affect the demand for imports and that it changes the demand for domestic goods either by the amount of the

---

[14] Lloyd A. Metzler, "The Transfer Problem Reconsidered," *Journal of Political Economy*, Vol. L, No. 3 (June, 1942), pp. 397–414, reprinted in *Readings in the Theory of International Trade* (Philadelphia, 1949, London 1950); and Fritz Machlup, *International Trade and the National Income Multiplier* (Philadelphia, 1943), chap. ix.

[15] Metzler (*loc. cit., passim*) showed that the transfer would be overeffected if one country had a negative marginal propensity to save (in his analysis, a marginal propensity to invest higher than the marginal propensity to save)—a possibility allowed by the stability conditions—and if in that country the financing of the transfer altered demand for home output to the same extent. Machlup (*op. cit.*, 181) showed that the transfer would be exactly effected if the transferor had a zero marginal propensity to save.

transfer or not at all.[16] (In terms of the present system, the m'''s were assumed to be zero, and the s'''s to be either zero or unity,[17] which, with positive marginal propensities to save, insures that the transfer cannot be effected.) If, instead of these rather unrealistic assumptions, one version of the assumption of the classical analysis is chosen—that the transfer is accompanied by equal changes in expenditure in the two countries, divided in some way between domestic goods and imports—the criterion becomes the same as that for the classical case: the transfer will be undereffected or overeffected according to whether the sum of the proportions of the transfer by which import demands are changed is less or greater than unity. This is the assumption adopted by Meade.[18] One of its consequences is that the behaviour of incomes is determined by whether the transfer is undereffected or overeffected; it is obvious that this should be so, since the assumption reproduces the classical model, with the exception that switches of demand from one country's output to the other's influence outputs instead of prices.

The Meade-classical assumption, however, like the assumption of Machlup and Metzler, is only a special case. In general, there would seem to be less reason in a Keynesian model than in the classical model for identifying the direct effects of the transfer on demand with those of any other economic change. But if the usual assumption of the classical analysis is chosen—that the transfer affects demands in the same way as any other change in income—with the difference that it also affects saving (that is, $m' = m$ and $s' = s$), the transfer cannot be effected if the marginal propensities to save are positive,[19] since the equation for the change in the transferor's balance of payments reduces to

$$B_a = - \frac{s_a s_b}{\Delta} T. \tag{3}$$

---

[16] In the case of Metzler, this description refers to the mathematical analysis. Metzler's verbal argument identifies the effects of the transfer with those of other income changes—a case discussed in the next paragraph—rather than a change in demand for domestic output. As will be shown later, the two assumptions yield the same conclusions about the effects of the transfer on the balance of payments.

[17] Machlup (*op. cit.*, 183) allows s' in the receiving country to be positive but less than unity; he also discusses the possibility of the transfer affecting the demand for imports directly, without realizing that this might permit the transfer to be effected by the income-effects alone.

[18] *Op. cit., passim.*

[19] The results on this assumption are the same as on the Machlup-Metzler assumption, so far as the balance of payments is concerned, though the effects on income are different. This is not surprising, since the effects of the transfer in this case are the same as if the transfer financing led to an equal change in the demand for domestic output in each country, except that the first round of income change in each is wiped out. The conclusion that the transfer cannot be effected in this case can be generalized to any number of countries (see my article "A Simplification of Multi-country Multiplier Theory," *Canadian Journal of Economics and Political Science,* Vol. XXII, No. 2, [May, 1965], pp. 244–46).

The econometric model of the world economy constructed by H. Neisser and F. Modigliani (*National Incomes and International Trade* [Urbana, 1953]) can be

For this particular case, it is obviously unnecessary to investigate the influence of tariffs and transport costs, since the effects of the transfer on the balance of payments are unambiguous, while the "classical presumption" is a certainty. In the general case, analysis of these problems is possible, but too cumbersome to be worth pursuing here.

In concluding this section, it would be appropriate to comment on a paradox suggested to the writer by P. A. Samuelson, namely why, when the transfer is treated as an income change, the Keynesian analysis gives a definitely negative answer, whereas in the classical case the answer depends on the marginal propensities to buy foreign goods. To begin with, it may be pointed out that the transfer criterion for the Keynesian case can be made precisely the same as that for the classical case, by re-defining the "proportion of the transfer by which expenditure on imports changes" to allow for the indirect effect on import demand of the failure of the transfer to be fully reflected in a change in expenditure. This effect is represented in equation (2c) by the deduction from the direct effects of the transfer on import expenditure m' of the quantities $(m/s)s'$, which stand for the effects on import demand of the changes in income that would result from the missing changes in expenditure, if trade were kept balanced so that the closed-economy multipliers $(1/s)$ applied. If the terms $m' - (m/s)s'$ are taken as the proportions of the transfer by which expenditure on imports changes, then the Keynesian transfer criterion is the same as the classical, namely whether the sum of these proportions is greater or less than one. But where the transfer is treated as an income change, it so happens that the indirect effect exactly offsets the direct effect of the transfer on import demand, so that the total effect is zero.

There is in the Keynesian analysis, however, a more fruitful analogue to the "sum of the proportions of expenditure changes falling on imports" criterion of classical analysis, which runs in terms of the proportions in which changes in saving are divided between holdings of domestic and of foreign assets; and the definiteness of the Keynesian answer turns out to be a consequence of the assumption stated at the beginning of this section, that international capital movements are independent of the levels of national incomes, which implies that all changes in saving consequent on the transfer go into or come out of domestic assets. If this assumption is relaxed to permit changes in saving to be divided between domestic and foreign assets, as they would be on the other assumptions of the model, the balance of payments multiplier equations presented above become:

---

applied to throw some statistical light on the extent to which the transfer might be undereffected in practical cases. Their table 15 (p. 93), which calculates the effects of income changes on trade balances in 1928, allowing for all repercussions on national incomes, implies that a transfer between England and Germany would improve one country's trade balance and worsen the other's by about 32 per cent of the amount transferred, while a transfer between the United Kingdom and the United States would alter the former's trade balance by about 30 per cent, and the latter's by only about 11½ per cent, of the amount transferred.

$$B_a = M_b + (m_b + k_b s_b)Y_b - M_a - (m_a + k_a s_a)Y_a \qquad (1c)'$$
$$+ (k'_a s'_a + k'_b s'_b - 1)T,$$

$$B_a = (m'_a + m'_b - \frac{m_a}{s_a} s'_a - \frac{m_b}{s_b} s'_b - 1)(1 - k_a - k_b)$$

$$\times \frac{s_a s_b}{\Delta} T + (k'_a - k_a)s'_a T + (k'_b - k_b)s'_b T, \qquad (2c)'$$

$$B_a = (k_a + k_b - 1) \frac{s_a s_b}{\Delta} T, \qquad (3)'$$

where k represents the proportion of a change in saving which is devoted to the purchase of foreign assets [and, in $(3)'$, $k = k'$]. It follows from $(3)'$ that, if the transfer is treated as an income change, it will be under-effected or overeffected according as the sum of what may be described as "the marginal foreign investment ratios" is less or greater than unity; in other words, the transfer will be undereffected if there is a bias (at the margin) in each country towards investment in domestic assets—such as would result from additional ignorance and uncertainty about foreign conditions, or from exchange control, but not from difference in yields as such—and vice versa. In the more general case represented by $(2c)'$, if (as seems a reasonable simplification) the possibility of differences between the marginal foreign investment ratios applying to the initial and the induced effects of the transfer on savings is ignored, the transfer will be undereffected unless *either* the criterion discussed in earlier paragraphs is satisfied (for which a necessary but not sufficient condition is a marginal bias towards expenditure of transfer finance on foreign goods) *or* there is a marginal bias towards the purchase of foreign assets—but not if both occur together. More simply, unless there is some sort of marginal bias in the division of savings between domestic and foreign assets, no presumption is possible as to whether or not the transfer will be effected. Thus the division of savings between domestic and foreign assets plays a role in the Keynesian analysis analogous to that played by the division of expenditure between domestic and foreign goods in the classical analysis. This analogy will not, however, be pursued further here; nor will the remainder of the argument take account of the possibility that savings may be invested in foreign assets.

III. APPLICATIONS OF TRANSFER THEORY: THE EXCHANGE STABILITY PROBLEM

Transfer theory has generally been developed and applied in the analysis of such standard problems as reparations payments and international flows of long-term capital. It has, however, a far wider application in the field of balance-of-payments theory, since any actual balance-of-payments disequilibrium involves a transfer in some form from the surplus to the deficit country (or countries), and the problem of rectifying the disequilibrium can be framed as the problem of creating a transfer of equal amount in the opposite direction. Hence transfer theory can be applied to the analysis of methods for overcoming balance-of-payments disequilibria —whether automatic mechanisms of adjustment or planned governmental policies. For example, the analysis of the classical transfer problem shows that in a "full-employment" world the deficit country does not necessarily have to turn its terms of trade against itself to correct the deficit and that the deterioration of the terms of trade will be less (or the improvement greater), the more the deflation of expenditure in the deficit country and the inflation of expenditure in the surplus country fall on imports rather than on exportable goods. The Keynesian transfer analysis shows that (with positive marginal propensities to save in both countries) changes in income taxation sufficient to yield changes in budget surpluses or deficits (at the initial income levels) equal to the initial balance-of-payments deficit will not suffice to remedy the disequilibrium, though changes in government expenditures of this amount may do so.[20]

The examples just cited involve adjustment mechanisms directed in the first instance at aggregate incomes and expenditures; a more interesting application is to the effects of changes in relative price levels on the balance of payments. Such changes in relative prices may be brought about either by deflation or inflation of domestic currency prices at a fixed exchange rate or by alterations in the exchange rate with domestic currency prices remaining unchanged. The latter case is the one more usually treated in contemporary theoretical analysis. The problem is formulated *either* in terms of the effects of devaluation on the trade balance *or* in terms of the stability of the foreign exchange market, the formulation depending on whether or not it is assumed that the monetary authorities intervene in the market to peg the rate of exchange.[21] In either case the central theoretical problem concerns the conditions under which

---

[20] The Keynesian transfer analysis also shows that the gold-standard mechanism of adjustment (deflation and inflation of expenditure brought about by the effects of gold movements on interest rates) did not *necessarily* work by creating unemployment in the deficit country, as has often been alleged. This proposition requires a further assumption about the distribution of expenditure changes between importable and exportable goods.

[21] In the "classical" case, analysis of devaluation must also assume some policy or process whereby the altered relations between national income and expenditure in the two countries inherent in a change in the trade balance are effected. This introduces an important complication, since the total effect of a devaluation will depend on the effect of the assumed policy or process on the trade balance as well as on the effect of the relative price change; and the effect of the supporting policy may be so strong as to reverse the effect devaluation by itself would tend to have on the trade balance. For example, if devaluation by A increased the demand for A's goods at the expense of B's, and the sum of the marginal propensities to spend on imports exceeded unity, restoration of equilibrium between aggregate demand and supply for each country's goods would require inflation of expenditure in A and deflation of expenditure in B, which would more than offset the effect of A's devaluation and leave A's trade balance worse than before. This complication is ignored in the following argument, which is concerned chiefly with exchange stability.

a relative reduction in export prices would tend to improve a country's trade balance. This problem, which may be described generically as "the exchange stability problem," also arises as a phase of the transfer problem, as the latter has been posed in the introduction to this article.

The exchange stability problem can readily be formulated in terms of transfer theory, and the criteria which determine whether the transfer will be undereffected or overeffected can be transformed into criteria for exchange stability. For simplicity of exposition, it will be assumed (in addition to the assumptions of the preceding sections) that trade is initially balanced and that there are no barriers to trade.

A reduction in the price of A-exportables relative to B-exportables carries with it a transfer from A to B equal in amount, so far as A is concerned, to the increase in the cost of A's initial volume of imports and, so far as B is concerned, to the reduction in the cost of B's initial volume of imports. With initially balanced trade and a small price change, these two measures of the transfer will be approximately equal. The transfer is "financed" and "disposed of" through the effects of the relative price change, which will have income and substitution effects on the demands of the countries for their own and each other's goods. Alternatively, the price change will affect the two countries' aggregate expenditures and expenditures on imports, these expenditures being evaluated at the pretransfer prices because the effects of the price change on values are approximately subsumed in the transfer itself. For what follows, it is important to notice that if expenditure measured in exportables is constant in the face of an altered price of imports, expenditure measured at the initial price of imports alters by the amount of the change in the cost of imports, that is, by the amount of the transfer.[22]

The exchange stability problem is the problem whether the effects of the price change on expenditures will be sufficient to effect the transfer implicit in the price change itself. In the classical case the assumption that all income is spent insures that the transfer is accompanied by equal changes in the two countries' expenditures (valued at pretransfer prices). The transfer will be overeffected or undereffected and the exchange market stable or unstable[23] according to whether the sum of the proportions of

---

[22] Let $E = C + pM$ be aggregate expenditure, measured in exportables, where C and M are quantities of exportables and imports consumed, and p is the price of imports in terms of exports. Then the effect of a change in the price of imports (dp) is

$$dE = \frac{\delta C}{\delta p}\, dp + p\, \frac{\delta M}{\delta p}\, dp + M\, dp.$$

The first two terms on the right amount to the change in expenditure measured at the initial price of imports, the third is the change in the cost of the initial quantity of imports. These two changes will be equal in magnitude and opposite in sign if $dE = 0$.

[23] In a real model, the exchange rate has no independent existence; what is really under discussion is the stability or instability of the underlying real equilibrium of international trade.

the transfer by which the two countries' expenditures on imports change is greater or less than unity. These proportions are equal to the price elasticities of demand for imports of the countries,[24] so that the market is stable or not according to whether the sum of these elasticities is greater or less than unity.[25]

In the Keynesian case the transfer analogy leads to the conclusion that the exchange market will be stable or unstable according to whether the sum of the elasticities is greater or less than

$$1 + s_a' \frac{m_a}{s_a} + s_b' \frac{m_b}{s_b},$$

where m and s, as before, represent the marginal propensities to save and to import of the subscript country; s_a' represents the proportion of the transfer by which saving from the pretransfer level of income is reduced (expenditure at pretransfer prices not reduced) in A by the increase in the price of A's imports; and s_b' represents the proportion of the transfer by which saving from the pretransfer level of income is increased (expenditure at pretransfer prices not increased) in B by the decrease in the price of B's imports. Alternatively, the s''s represent the effect of a decrease in the price of imports on saving or an increase in the price of imports on expenditure, from the initial income, divided by the initial value of imports.[26]

It was in the latter version that the exchange stability criterion for the

---

[24] The change in expenditure on imports, valued at the pretransfer price, is

$$p \cdot \frac{\delta M}{\delta p} \cdot dp = \eta_m \left(- pM \frac{dp}{p} \right),$$

where

$$\eta_m \left(= - \frac{p}{M} \frac{\delta M}{\delta p} \right)$$

is the elasticity of demand for imports. Since the implicit transfer is $- pM(dp/p)$, the change in expenditure on imports expressed as a proportion of the transfer is η_m.

[25] This is, of course, the familiar Marshall-Lerner criterion. Since the elasticity of demand for importables consists of the sum of the marginal propensity to spend on importables and the "compensated" or "constant-utility" elasticity of demand, argument on the lines of the last part of the first section of this article shows that instability requires both a marginal bias toward the consumption of exportables and a low degree of substitutability between importable and exportable goods in consumption in the two countries. In the case in which both countries produce both goods, instability also requires a low degree of substitutability in production in the two countries.

It should be observed also that, though the argument of this section assumes the absence of trade impediments, the exchange stability criterion is unaltered by the introduction of tariffs or of transport costs incurred in the imported good, since the expenditure change in these cases depends only on the elasticity of final demand for imports.

[26] This follows from the fact that the contrasting signs of the savings changes, as defined, cancel the contrasting signs of the price changes and that the change in saving is equal and opposite to the change in expenditure.

Keynesian case was first published by Laursen and Metzler,[27] who saw correctly that any difference from the classical criterion hinged on the presence or absence of a terms-of-trade effect on aggregate expenditure and argued from the statistical evidence that (in the "short run" of the cycle) a rising proportion of real income is saved to the conclusion that an increase in the price of imports would increase expenditure, thus making the critical sum of the elasticities of import demand greater than unity. Their conclusion has recently been disputed by White,[28] on the grounds that time lags make the long-run behaviour of the savings ratio relevant and that in the long run the ratio is constant.

Prior to the publication of Laursen and Metzler's work, Harberger published an analysis of the problem,[29] in which the apparatus of formal value theory was employed to determine the effect of an increase in import prices on saving. Harberger assumed that saving, measured in exportable goods, is a function of real income only, changes in prices inducing no substitution between saving and consumption; that the marginal propensity to save for changes in real income due to changes in the terms of trade is the same as that for changes in output at constant prices; and that the effects of a change in the terms of trade on real income may be approximated by the change in the cost of the initial value of imports. On these assumptions each s' in the preceding formula becomes equal to the corresponding s, and the criterion of exchange stability becomes whether the sum of the elasticities of import demand is greater or less than 1 plus the sum of the marginal propensities to import.

All three of the assumptions by which Harberger derived this elegant result have recently been subjected to criticism. Day has argued that saving and imports may be substitutes, since imports may be consumers' durables yielding a flow of satisfaction comparable to the interest on

[27] S. Laursen and L. A. Metzler, "Flexible Exchange Rates and the Theory of Employment," *Review of Economics and Statistics*, Vol. XXXII, No. 4 (November, 1950), pp. 281–99.

[28] W. H. White, "The Employment-Insulating Advantages of Flexible Exchanges: A Comment on Professors Laursen and Metzler," *Review of Economics and Statistics*, Vol. XXXVI, No. 2 (May, 1954), pp. 225–28. I agree with the authors' "Reply" in the same issue; but the evidence for, and the theoretical explanations of, the constancy of the savings ratio in the long run are relevant to the present discussion of the exchange stability problem. In my review of Meade's *The Balance of Payments* ("The Taxonomic Approach to Economic Policy," *Economic Journal*, Vol. LXI, No. 244 (December, 1951), pp. 812–32) I derived a stability criterion identical with that of Metzler and Laursen and adopted their conclusion about the direction of the terms-of-trade effect; the argument of that review is therefore open to the same sort of criticism that White expressed.

[29] A. C. Harberger, "Currency Depreciation, Income, and the Balance of Trade," *Journal of Political Economy*, Vol. LVIII, No. 1 (February, 1950), pp. 47–60. Harberger erroneously attributed the difference between his results and those of earlier writers to the variability of production; in fact, this is merely a necessary condition, the fundamental explanation lying in the introduction of a non-zero effect of the terms of trade on saving.

saving.[30] Spraos has shown that, if this is so, the Harberger criterion over-estimates the critical value of the elasticities, though he is sceptical of the importance of such substitution.[31] Pearce has shown that Day over-looks the effects of a change in the price of imports on the real value of interest and that, when this is recognized, no presumption as to the direc-tion of substitution between imports and saving is possible.[32] Spraos has argued convincingly that the marginal propensity to save from a change in real income due to a change in import prices is likely to be substantially greater than the marginal propensity to save from a change in output at constant prices, thus making the Harberger criterion an underestimate. Both Spraos and Pearce have shown that Harberger's assumptions imply the presence of money illusion, since they ignore the effect of the increased price of imports in reducing the real value of saving.[33] Spraos attempted to correct for this by raising the approximation of the real income loss to allow for an estimate of the loss of real value of saved (unspent) income, but, as Pearce shows, this preserves elements of money illusion in the savings function by leaving money rather than real savings a function of real income and by ignoring the effect of the price change on the real value of accumulated saving and consequently on the incentive to save.

If substitution effects between imports and saving and the "Pigou effect" of import prices on saving are both ignored and if (following Spraos) it is assumed that saving is intended to be spent on imports and exportables in the same ratio as current consumption expenditure, the Harberger analysis can be reworked on the assumption that real, rather than money, saving is a function of real income, to yield this result:

$$s' = \frac{\bar{s}}{1 - \bar{s}} \, (\epsilon_s - 1), \qquad (4)$$

where $\bar{s}$ is the average propensity to save and ϵ_s is the income elasticity of demand for (real) saving.[34] This reworking reconciles the Harberger

[30] A. C. L. Day, "Relative Prices, Expenditure, and the Trade Balance: A Note," *Economica*, N.S., Vol. XXI No. 82 (May, 1954), pp. 64–69.

[31] J. Spraos, " 'Consumers' Behaviour and the Conditions for Exchange Stability," *Economica*, N.S., Vol. XXII, No. 86 (May, 1955), pp. 137–47.

[32] I. F. Pearce, "A Note on Mr. Spraos' Paper," *Econonica*, N.S., Vol. XXII, No. 86 (May, 1955), pp. 147–51.

[33] Harberger can be defended against this criticism by a careful reading of his argument. His "saving" is described as "hoarding" and is defined as the excess of income over expenditure; with initially balanced trade, current saving in this sense and presumably accumulated saving also are zero. On this reading (which would make all expenditure consumer expenditure) a positive marginal propensity to save ("hoard"), whether in money or in real terms, is sufficient to make the critical value of the stability criterion greater than the classical unity.

[34] Let the initial volume of domestic output be Y and the initial quantities of domestic and foreign output consumed be C and M, respectively, these quantities being measured in units such that the initial domestic prices are unity. On the

approach with that of Metzler and Laursen and confirms the latter in deducing the effect of devaluation on expenditure from the relation between the savings ratio and income. It assumes, however, that imports are demanded for consumption only. If some imports are required for investment and investment expenditure is fixed in real, rather than money, terms (an assumption supported by the assumption of fixed interest rates), a reduction in import prices affects money saving both by increasing consumers' real income and by reducing the cost of investment imports. The preceding result is then altered to

$$s' = m_c \frac{\bar{s}}{1-\bar{s}} (\epsilon_s - 1) + m_i, \qquad (5)$$

where m_c and m_i are the proportions of the initial volume of imports devoted to consumption and investment, respectively. This last result suggests that, though the Harberger-Metzler and Laursen finding that the critical value of the sum of the elasticities of import demand is greater than unity implies a questionable assumption about the behaviour of the savings ratio, it can be supported by the introduction of investment imports.

IV. APPLICATIONS OF TRANSFER THEORY: TRADE INTERVENTION

Another problem to which transfer theory can be applied, and which may also itself be part of the transfer problem as the latter has been formu-

---

assumptions stated previously, real income, Y_r, may be measured by output deflated by a price index, so that

$$Y_r = Y \div \frac{C + pM}{C + M},$$

where p represents the (real) price of imports, initially unity; and real saving, S_r, is a function of real income only and its money value (value in terms of domestic output) is

$$S = S_r \cdot \frac{C + pM}{C + M}.$$

Hence the change in money saving due to a reduction in the price of imports, expressed as a proportion of the initial value of imports, is

$$s' = -\frac{1}{M} \frac{\delta S}{\delta p} = \frac{1}{M} \left(\frac{YM}{C+M} \frac{\delta S_r}{\delta Y_r} - \frac{S_r M}{C+M} \right)$$

$$= \frac{S_r}{C+M} (\epsilon_s - 1)$$

$$= \frac{\bar{s}}{1-\bar{s}} (\epsilon_s - 1)$$

where

$$\bar{s} = \frac{S}{Y} = \frac{Y - C - M}{Y},$$

and

$$\epsilon_s = \frac{Y_r}{S_r} \frac{\delta S_r}{\delta Y_r}.$$

lated in the introduction to this article, is the problem of the conditions under which various types of governmental intervention in international trade will tend to improve the trade balance. Like the problem of relative price level changes discussed in the previous section, this problem appears in two versions: if the authorities are assumed to peg the exchange rate, the problem is the effect of intervention on the balance of trade; if the exchange rate is free, the problem is the direction in which the rate must move to preserve equilibrium.[35] But the central theoretical problem is the same in both cases.

Governmental intervention in international trade may take a wide variety of forms, ranging from the "classical" methods of import and export duties and export subsidies to more "modern" methods of export and import licensing, "directives," state trading, exchange control, and multiple exchange rates. For purposes of balance of payments theory, however, it is the objective rather than the form of intervention which matters;[36] and two types of intervention may be distinguished for analysis, according to whether intervention aims at improving the balance of payments by reducing expenditure on imports (through import-restriction) or by increasing export earnings. The latter comprises two sub-types, export-promotion to increase earnings by increasing the quantity of exports and export-restriction to increase earnings by increasing the unit value of exports; but since the conditions required for the one to succeed are clearly the conditions which will cause the other to fail, it is only necessary to consider one sub-type in detail. For contrast with the case of import-restriction, the case chosen for such analysis in this section is that of export-promotion.

Export promotion entails making the price of exportable goods to foreigners lower than their domestic value; the difference may be absorbed by the state (via an export subsidy, or a state trading or exchange authority loss) or it may be imposed on private citizens (via a lower profit margin on exports than on home market sales, or an excess of the price consumers would be willing to pay for the exportables they consume over the price charged to the home and foreign markets).[37] Similarly, import restriction entails making the domestic value of imports higher than the

---

[35] The qualifications stated in footnotes 21 and 23 above for the classical case, that rate-pegging must be supported by policies to effect the necessary alterations in the income-expenditure relations in the two countries, which policies complicate and may even reverse the results of other changes, and that the exchange rate has no independent existence, the analysis actually pertaining to the underlying real trade equilibrium, apply equally to the argument below.

[36] For an extensive and illuminating discussion of different forms of intervention and the economic problems of administration to which they give rise, see James E. Meade, *op. cit.*, Part V, chaps. XX and XXI.

[37] The former assumes that exportables are "directed" to the foreign market, the domestic price being allowed to ration out home market supplies; the latter assumes that the home market price is fixed at the same level as the export price, but domestic consumers are rationed in some more direct way.

price paid to foreigners, the difference either being absorbed by the
state (via an import duty, or a state trading or exchange authority profit)
or accruing to private citizens (via abnormal profits to licensed importers,
or an excess of the price consumers would be willing to pay over the price
they actually pay for the imports they consume).[38] Where the difference
between external price and internal value created by intervention is absorbed by the state, it will be assumed that the budgetary effect of intervention is offset by an opposite change in income taxation or government
expenditure. In the classical case this assumption is necessary to preserve
the equality of income and expenditure at the full employment level; in
the Keynesian case, it is necessary to isolate the effect of intervention per
se from the deflationary or inflationary effect of uncompensated increases
in taxes or subsidies.

Though the effects of export promotion and import restriction on the
balance of payments may each be formulated in terms of transfer theory,
the formulation required is different in the two cases. It is therefore convenient to treat the two separately.

A. Export Promotion

Export promotion by A entails a transfer from A to B equal to the
associated reduction in the cost of B's initial imports from A (the value
of A's initial exports to B). It is "financed" by the reduction in private income or government expenditure in A required to absorb this cost reduction, and "disposed of" through the income and substitution effects of the
reduction in the price charged to B for its imports. The problem of
whether export promotion will improve A's trade balance is therefore the
same as whether the effects of the financing and disposal of the transfer
on the two countries' aggregate expenditures and expenditures on imports
(measured at pretransfer prices) will suffice to effect the transfer.

In the classical case, the transfer is accompanied by equal changes in
expenditure (at pretransfer prices) in the two countries; and the transfer
will be overeffected or undereffected according as the sum of the proportions of the transfer by which the two countries' expenditures on imports
(at pretransfer prices) change is greater or less than unity. For A, where
domestic prices are unchanged, this proportion is given by the proportion
of the reduction in governmental expenditure which falls on imports, or
by the marginal propensity to spend on imports of the community, depending on how the transfer is financed; for B, the price of whose imports
is reduced, the proportion is equal to the price elasticity of demand for
imports (as in the case of exchange stability). Thus the transfer will be
effected, and export promotion succeed in improving the trade balance, if

---

[38] The former assumes rationing by price, the latter price control and some other
form of rationing. A third possibility, that the difference accrues to the foreign
exporters (which might happen, for example, if licences were granted to foreign
exporters rather than to domestic importers) is ignored in the following argument.

the elasticity of B's demand for imports is greater than one minus A's (governmental or private) marginal propensity to import, or, what is the same thing, A's (governmental or private) marginal propensity to spend on exportables. Conversely, export promotion would fail (and export restriction succeed) in improving the trade balance, if the elasticity of B's demand for imports were less than A's (governmental or private) marginal propensity to spend on exportables.

In the Keynesian case the critical value for the sum of the proportions of the transfer by which import demands are affected is not unity but

$$1 + \frac{m_a}{s_a} \, s'_a + \frac{m_b}{s_b} \, s'_b,$$

where the s''s represent, as before, the proportions by which the expenditure changes in the two countries fall short of the amount of the transfer. For B, where the transfer is received *via* a reduction in the price of imports, this proportion is determined by the reaction of savings to an improvement in the terms of trade, discussed in detail in the preceding section. For A, where relative prices are unchanged by export promotion, this proportion will be zero if the transfer is financed by a reduction in government expenditure, and equal to the marginal propensity to save if it is financed by increased income taxation—so that the term involving this proportion drops out in the former case, and reduces to the marginal propensity to import (which cancels out) in the latter case. In the former case, the transfer will be effected, and export-promotion successful, if the elasticity of B's demand for imports is greater than the proportion of the reduction of A's governmental expenditure falling on exportables, plus the product of the proportion of the transfer by which B's saving from the initial income level increases and the ratio of B's marginal propensity to import to its marginal propensity to save. In the latter case, the elasticity must exceed one plus the product of the ratios of saving change to transfer and marginal propensity to import to marginal propensity to save. It may be noted that if the defective Harberger approximation for the savings change ($s' = s$) is adopted, the criterion for the transfer to be effected becomes much simpler, since the term involving the change in B's saving reduces to B's marginal propensity to import, which can be cancelled against the income term in B's elasticity of import demand, making the requirement for success that B's "compensated" or "constant-utility" elasticity of demand for imports exceed the proportion of A's governmental expenditure reduction falling on exportables in the first case, and unity in the second case.[39]

---

[39] The analysis of the conditions required for export promotion to succeed also solves the problem, excluded in the previous footnote, of the requirements for import restriction to succeed when the difference between external price and internal value accrues to the foreigner, since that case amounts to export restriction by the foreigner and the conditions for success are the same as for export-promotion by the foreigner to succeed. Thus, in the classical case, A's balance of trade would be improved by such

B. Import Restriction

Import restriction by A may be conceived of as comprising two changes, each entailing a transfer. The first is the equivalent of export restriction by B, entailing a transfer from A to B equal to the increase in value of A's initial quantity of imports due to restriction, financed and disposed of via the increased price of A's imports; the second is the transfer back to A of an equal amount, financed in the same way by B as the first transfer was disposed of, and disposed of by A in the same way as any other transfer. The difference between the two transfers lies entirely in the difference in their effects on A's demand for imports, the first involving an increase in the price of A's imports and the second involving no price change; and the net effect will be favourable or not, according as the effect of the first transfer in reducing A's demand for imports is greater or less than the effect of the second transfer in increasing it.

In the classical case, the first transfer reduces A's demand for imports by a proportion of the transfer equal to A's elasticity of demand for imports, while the second transfer increases A's demand for imports by a proportion of the transfer equal to A's marginal propensity to spend on imports, or to the proportion of the increase in governmental expenditure falling on imports, depending on how the transfer is disposed of. Since the elasticity of demand for imports exceeds the marginal propensity to spend on imports by the "compensated" elasticity of demand, import restriction in this case must improve the balance of payments if the transfer is disposed of via an increase in private income. Only if A's elasticity of demand for imports is less than unity, and the transfer is disposed of via an increase in government expenditure which falls more heavily on imports than would an increase in private expenditure, is it possible for import restriction to worsen A's balance of payments in this case.

In the Keynesian case, the reduction in A's demand for imports due to the first transfer is governed by the difference between A's elasticity of demand for imports and the product of the ratio of A's marginal propensity to import to its marginal propensity to save and the proportion of the transfer by which A's saving is reduced as a result of the adverse terms of trade change. Similarly, the increase in A's demand for imports due to the second transfer is governed by the difference between the marginal propensity to spend on imports or the proportion of increased government expenditure falling on imports, and the product of the ratio of A's marginal propensity to import to its marginal propensity to save and the proportion of the transfer by which A's saving is increased as a result of its receipt. Where the second transfer is matched by an increase

---

import-restriction if the sum of A's elasticity of demand for imports and B's marginal propensity to spend on imports from A exceeded unity, i.e. if A's elasticity of demand for imports exceeded B's marginal propensity to spend in exportables. An analogous condition holds in the Keynesian case.

in government expenditure, so that there is no change in A's saving, the condition for import restriction to improve A's balance of trade is that A's elasticity of demand for imports exceed the sum of the proportion of the increase in government expenditure devoted to imports, and the product of the terms-of-trade effect on its saving and the ratio of its marginal propensity to import to its marginal propensity to save. Where the second transfer accrues as private income, the proportion of the transfer by which A's saving increases is equal to A's marginal propensity to save, so that the term containing this effect becomes equal to the marginal propensity to import and so reduces the influence of the second transfer on A's demand for imports to zero; in this case, the condition for import restriction to improve A's balance of trade is that A's elasticity of demand for imports exceed the product of the terms-of-trade effect on its saving and the ratio of its marginal propensity to import to its marginal propensity to save. If the Harberger approximation were valid, this latter condition would always be fulfilled, since the criterion would reduce to the marginal propensity to import.

10. The Benefits and Costs of Private Investment from Abroad: A Theoretical Approach[*]

By G. D. A. MACDOUGALL[†][1]

I

The benefits and costs of private investment from abroad are a matter of considerable importance for Australia. This paper suggests one possible method of analysing some general aspects of the problem. It is mainly theoretical and does not attempt to reach clear-cut practical conclusions. This would require much more factual analysis and consideration of many other aspects. Some of these were discussed by Professor Arndt in "Overseas Borrowing—the New Model" (*Economic Record*, August, 1957), an article which also deals with many of the points analysed below.

The analysis is for the most part static and thereby ignores certain dynamic considerations that may be important. It attempts to assess the difference made to the real income of Australia at a given moment of time by the presence of more or less foreign-owned private capital in the country, on the assumption that the economic forces involved have had time to work themselves out (the analysis is thus a long run one). For ease of exposition this is done by starting with a given situation and then considering the effects of an increase in the foreign-owned capital stock; the analysis could equally be applied to a reduction. The moment of time may be thought of as a number of years ahead, in which case we are considering the effects on Australian income at that time of a greater or smaller inflow of capital in the intervening period.

We shall consider only relatively small changes in the stock of foreign

[*] *Economic Record*, Special Issue, March, 1960. Also published in *Bulletin of the Oxford University Institute of Statistics*, Vol. 22, No. 3 (1960), pp. 189–211.

[†] Department of Economic Affairs, London.

[1] This article was written while the author was Visiting Professor of Economics and Finance at the Australian National University. I am grateful to several economists, including Professor T. W. Swan, Mr. H. P. Brown and Dr. W. E. G. Salter, for discussing these matters with me, and especially indebted to Dr. I. F. Pearce for his help.

capital. This simplifies the analysis and seems legitimate provided one is not looking too far ahead. For differences in capital inflow are then unlikely to make a large proportionate difference to the foreign capital stock or, *a fortiori,* to the total stock. It will be suggested later that, in real terms, the foreign private capital stock in Australia may have increased since the war by perhaps 6 per cent per annum on average. If this rate were increased or diminished by, say, one-half, it would make a difference of only around 15 per cent in the foreign capital stock in 5 years' time, and a much smaller percentage difference in the total stock—say 1½ per cent if we make a rough guess that the foreign-owned stock is of the order of one-tenth of the total;[2] certainly the great bulk of the capital is still owned by Australians.

We start with drastic assumptions. The main ones, which will be relaxed as the analysis proceeds, are:

1. The government maintains "full employment without over-employment" or, more generally, a constant degree of employment of Australian resources.
2. No taxation.
3. The size of the labour force is independent of the stock of foreign capital.
4. The stock of Australian-owned capital is independent of the stock of foreign capital.
5. No external economies.
6. Constant returns to scale.
7. Perfect competition.
8. More or less investment from abroad has no effect on the terms of trade.
9. It creates no difficulties for the balance of payments which can be adjusted smoothly, and without cost, as required.
10. The increase in foreign capital considered does not require changes in Australian policy that themselves may involve a loss to Australia.

II

The line *GK* in Diagram I relates the physical capital stock in Australia to the physical marginal product of capital, given the amount of other factors of production, which we shall call "labour." Initially, the capital stock is *AC,* of which *AB* is owned by Australians and *BC* by non-Australians (called "foreigners" hereafter). Since, on our assumptions, profits per unit of capital equal the marginal product of capital, total profits are

---

[2] This is only an illustrative order of magnitude based on various "back-of-the-envelope" calculations. For the sake of exposition it will be used on several occasions but the general arguments would be unaffected if the true figure were substantially higher, say one-fifth, and true *a fortiori* if it were less than one-tenth.

It is hard to say whether the ratio of the *flow* of new foreign investment to total new investment since the war has been greater than the ratio of the *stocks.* The ratio of the flows has been quite high in certain sectors such as manufacturing.

DIAGRAM I

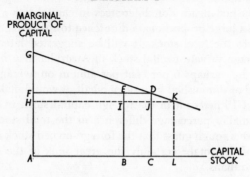

FEBA on Australian capital and *EDCB* on foreign capital. Output is *GDCA* so that labour gets *GDF*.[3]

Now suppose a small increase in foreign capital from *BC* to *BL*. Foreign profits become *IKLB*. The new foreign capital earns *JKLC* and the "old" foreign capital loses *EDJI* because the marginal product of capital, and hence the profit rate, have fallen. Total foreign profits are almost certain to rise on balance because, for reasons to be given shortly, the "elasticity of demand for foreign capital" (as we shall call the percentage increase in the stock of foreign capital associated with a 1 per cent fall in its marginal product) almost certainly exceeds unity.

Australian capitalists lose *FEIH*. Labour gains *FDKH*. Australia as a whole thus gains *EDKI*. Since *DKJ* is relatively small, Australia's gain is approximately *EDJI* which is the loss of income on the "old" foreign capital. Australia does not, as is sometimes thought, gain the whole of *FDJH*, i.e., the whole of the increase in real wages resulting from labour's higher marginal productivity, but only a proportion corresponding to the ratio of foreign to total capital; the great bulk of labour's gain is merely a redistribution from Australian capitalists.

(Here, incidentally, we have one argument for restriction of foreign investment by the investing countries—which we shall call "Britain." Assuming no risk differential, British investors, if left to their own devices, equate the returns on home and foreign investments. But, while the marginal *national* (British) product on investment in Britain equals the private return, it falls short of this on investment in Australia to the extent of the reduction in profits on existing British investments there—*EDJI* in the

---

[3] This assumes that labour could not produce any output in the absence of capital. If it could, such output should be added to the amounts shown for both total output (*GDCA*) and total real wages (*GDF*). Since the subsequent argument would be unaffected, we have retained our assumption for simplicity of exposition and to avoid the use of mathematics other than geometry. See also p. 177, n. 9, p. 179, n. 10 and p. 182, n. 12.

diagram.[4] This loss of profits goes to Australian labour whereas the corresponding loss when there is more investment in Britain goes to British labour. If there is a difference in risk on investments in the two places—in either direction—the conclusion is unaffected provided British investors correctly evaluate the difference.)

Australia's gain (and Britain's loss) from more foreign investment in Australia is, however, unlikely to be at all large on our present assumptions. If total capital is of the order of 10 times foreign capital, the "elasticity of demand" for foreign capital will be about 10 times that for total capital (i.e., 10 times the elasticity of the curve GK at D)[5]; and this latter elasticity is itself likely to be considerable because the substitutability of capital for labour is probably fairly high in Australia. The "elasticity of demand" for foreign capital is thus likely to be high, so that $EDJI$ will be small in relation to $JKLC$. In other words the great bulk of the extra output (approximately $JKLC$) will go to foreign capitalists; Australia's share will be small.

III

Now remove assumption (2) and allow for taxation. Suppose the rate of tax on foreign profits is t. This often approaches one-half where all profits are distributed and we shall, for simplicity, use this fraction as an illustrative order of magnitude, though it should be borne in mind that it is on the high side.[6] Australia now gains, in addition to $EDJI$, the tax on the net increase in foreign profits and this is likely to be a considerably more important gain. Put in another way, Australia now gains $t(JKLC)$ plus, it is true, only $(1-t)(EDJI)$ instead of $EDJI$, but this is a relatively small matter.

Taxation is not shown in the diagram to avoid complicating it. The case where the extra foreign capital is induced by lowering the tax rate will be considered in section XI; it is ruled out at present by assumption (10).

(We now have a much more important argument for restriction of investment by "Britain." Double taxation agreements are complicated things, but for our present purpose it is probably legitimate to assume that the British Treasury gets only the excess (if any) of the British rate of tax over

---

[4] If "Britain" is only one of a number of foreign countries with capital in Australia, and invests an additional CL there, the loss on her existing investments will, of course, be less than $EDJI$; part of Australia's gain will be at the expense of the other foreign countries.

[5] If a 1 per cent change in the marginal product of capital is associated with a change of x per cent in total capital, it will be associated with a change of $10x$ per cent in foreign capital if Australian-owned capital is constant.

[6] If there is a tax on profits of 7s. 6d. in the £ plus a withholding tax of 15 per cent on dividends, the total rate of tax will be 47 per cent. In fact, something approaching this rate seems to be fairly common although some foreign profits are charged substantially less for various reasons; and if profits are undistributed the rate is also, of course, lower.

the Australian rate, after the Australian Treasury has levied its tax in full. Now, if the British tax rate is the higher, British investors (ignoring differences in risk) equate the returns after the *British* rate of tax on investments in the two places, which means that they also equate the *gross* returns (before tax). But, while the marginal *national* (British) product is the gross return on investment in Britain (since Britain gets the tax), it is the net return, after Australian tax, on investment in Australia,[7] and this may be little more than half as great. If the Australian tax rate is the higher, the difference between the marginal national products equals tax at the British rate; the marginal national (British) product on investment in Australia may still be only about half that on investment in Britain.[8] These asides about "Britain" do not, of course, constitute a full analysis of the pros and cons of investment abroad from the point of view of investing countries.)

IV

Next remove assumption (3) and allow the size of the Australian labour force to be dependent on the amount of foreign capital. It is not unreasonable to suppose that immigration policy (and the supply of would-be immigrants) will be related in some way to the level of Australian incomes and these will be affected by the amount of foreign capital.

The gains from additional foreign capital so far described—there are more to come in later sections—will raise income per head if the labour force is not increased. It will thus be possible, if desired and if practicable, to increase population to some extent without reducing income per head below the "initial" level, by which we mean the level it would have attained in the absence of the extra foreign capital. (This could still, of course, be consistent with a rise in income per head over time.) It is impossible to say how immigration policy might in practice be related to levels of income and thus, indirectly, to foreign investment, but some highly simplified illustrations may be helpful.

Suppose that the extra foreign capital increased total capital by 1 per cent (which would mean a 10 per cent increase in foreign capital if this

---

[7] For simplicity of exposition we ignore here the reduction in profits on existing British investments in Australia discussed in the last section.

[8] Let r_a and r_b be the gross returns in Australia and Britain and t_a and t_b the rates of tax.
If $t_b > t_a$, British investors will make
$$r_b(1 - t_b) = r_a[1 - t_a - (t_b - t_a)] = r_a(1 - t_b)$$
i.e. $r_b = r_a = r$ (say).
The marginal national (British) product is r on investment in Britain but $r(1 - t_a)$ on investment in Australia, the ratio of the latter to the former being $(1 - t_a)$.
If $t_a > t_b$, British investors will make
$$r_b(1 - t_b) = r_a(1 - t_a).$$
The marginal national (British) product is then r_b on investment in Britain but $r_a(1 - t_a) = r_b(1 - t_b)$ on investment in Australia, the ratio being $(1 - t_b)$ which is still not much over one-half for many taxpayers.

were one-tenth of the total). If then the labour force were allowed to increase by 1 per cent there would, on our present assumptions, be an increase of 1 per cent in total output, total profits and total wages above the initial level; the wage rate would be reduced again to the initial level, the profit rate restored to the initial level. Assuming no taxation, and no change in the number of Australian capitalists, the average Australian worker (including the extra immigrants) and the average Australian capitalist would then be as well off as initially, i.e., as they would have been had there been no increase in foreign capital and no consequential increase in the labour force.

DIAGRAM II

The new position is shown in Diagram II. (This is the same as Diagram I apart from the addition of the lines *GN, DN, NK*.) *CL* is 1 per cent of *AC*. The 1 per cent addition to the labour force has shifted the line relating the marginal product of capital to the capital stock from *GK* to *GN*. Compared with the initial position, total output is up 1 per cent, from *GDCA* to *GNLA*; the wage bill is up 1 per cent, from *GDF* to *GNF*; total profits are up 1 per cent, from *FDCA* to *FNLA*.[9] Australian

---

[9] If labour could produce some output with no capital (see p. 174, n. 3), this output would be increased by 1 per cent as a result of the increase in labour. The wage bill and total output would still be up by 1 per cent.

It will be noticed that the new marginal product of capital curve goes through *G*, as the old one did. This obviously necessary for geometric reasons, if straight lines are used as in the diagram, to make the area under the curve increase by 1 per cent; and it can be shown mathematically that it is generally true, given our assumption of constant returns to scale. (With some production functions, the marginal product curve will be asymptotic to the vertical axis.)

profits are *FEBA,* the same as they were initially. Foreign profits are *ENLB,* higher than they were initially in proportion to the rise in foreign capital.

If we allow for taxation the outcome will depend on fiscal policy. Since we are merely giving an illustration let us make the simple, though admittedly unrealistic, assumption that only profits are taxed and that the resulting revenue is used wholly to finance social services for workers. Since tax revenue from profits (Australian and foreign) will be 1 per cent higher than it was initially, social services per worker will then be maintained at the initial level, as will profits after tax per Australian capitalist.

If the criterion for immigration were that it should vary with foreign investment in such a way that variations in the latter should not affect the standard of living of workers or the average income of Australian capitalists, it would then be possible, given our present assumptions, to increase the labour force (compared with what it would otherwise have been) in the same proportion as the higher foreign investment increased total capital, i.e., by 1 per cent in our example.

This would, however, reduce average income per head. Population would be up by 1 per cent (we assume that Australian capitalists are also workers and that the labour force is a constant fraction of the population). But total income accruing to Australia would be up by less than 1 per cent since total labour income would be up by 1 per cent while total Australian profits were constant. This would be true whether we assumed (*a*) no taxation or (*b*) taxation of profits to finance social services with the latter counted as part of labour income and profits reckoned after tax. More generally, Australian income per head would be down whatever the nature of fiscal policy (provided that, as we are at present assuming, the tax rate on foreign profits is unchanged) because output would be up by 1 per cent and foreign profits after tax by more than 1 per cent so that Australian income would rise by less than 1 per cent, i.e., by less than population was increased.

If the criterion for immigration were that variations in foreign investment should not affect total income per head (and it may be worth repeating that this would not preclude a rising income per head over time), it would not then be possible to increase population by as much as 1 per cent. But some smaller increase would be possible since, if there were none, income per head would be raised by the extra foreign capital.

Numerous other immigration policies are conceivable that would allow population to vary with investment from abroad. The policy actually chosen will depend on the relative importance attached to growth of population and of income per head; views on the distribution of income; fiscal policy; the supply of would-be immigrants; and so on. The question remains, however, whether more immigration resulting from more foreign capital would bring a gain of income to Australia *additional* to the gains already described in sections II and III.

While this is highly likely it is not absolutely certain. For, though the extra labour would raise output in Australia, it would also raise the marginal product of capital and so foreign profits after tax, and possibly by as much as, or more than, it raised output; there would then be no further increase in total Australian income (including the income of the extra immigrants) or even a reduction of earlier gains.

To illustrate the possibility, consider the case depicted in Diagram II. Compared with the position after the increase in foreign capital but before the increase in labour (with output $GKLA$), the increase in labour raises output by GNK but it also increases foreign profits, after tax, by $(1-t)ENKI$, and this could conceivably be as great as, or greater than, GNK.[10]

DIAGRAM III

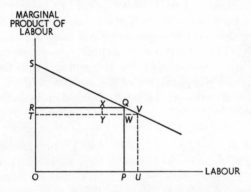

That an increase in Australian income is in fact very probable can conveniently be shown with the aid of a further diagram. The line SV in Diagram III shows the marginal product of *labour* corresponding to different amounts of labour, with the total capital stock fixed at the level reached *after* the increase in foreign capital. OP is the labour force initially. If it is now increased a little (by immigration) to OU, output goes up by $WVUP$ (ignoring the small triangle QVW). The wage bill goes up from $ROPO$ to $TVUO$, i.e., by $WVUP$ minus $RQWT$. Total profits go up by $RQWT$, Australian profits by $(1-c)RQWT$—shown as $RXYT$—and foreigners' profits by $c(RQWT)$—shown as $XQWY$—where c is the ratio of foreign to total capital. Foreigners' profits after tax go up by $c(1-t)(RQWT)$, i.e., by $(1-t)XQWY$. Total Australian income thus changes by $WVUP$ minus $(1-t)XQWY$, i.e., by $WVUP$ minus $c(1-t)RQWT$, so that it will increase if $WVUP/RQWT > c(1-t)$.

Now $WVUP/RQWT$ is the "elasticity of demand for labour" (as we

---

[10] If labour could produce some output with no capital, the increase in output would be greater than GNK, but it might still be less than $(1-t)ENKI$. (See also p. 177, n. 9).

shall call the elasticity of the amount of labour with respect to its marginal product, which equals the wage rate, i.e., of the line SV at Q).[11] If we call this elasticity e, the condition becomes $e > c(1 - t)$. Now e is likely to be considerable, because the substitutability of labour for capital is probably fairly high, and almost certainly greater than $c(1 - t)$, which is of the order of $\frac{1}{10} \times \frac{1}{2} = \frac{1}{20}$. (An elasticity as low as $\frac{1}{20}$ would mean that, to employ 1 per cent more workers—say 40,000—with a given capital stock, but allowing all the time necessary for long-run readjustments, the real wage rate would have to fall by nearly one-fifth.)

An increase in labour with capital constant is thus most likely to increase total Australian income. If extra immigration is allowed as a result of extra foreign investment it is thus most likely, on balance, to raise total Australian income beyond the level resulting from the gains described in sections II and III.

(It will be noticed that we have not relied in this section—as is sometimes done—on fixed technical coefficients, i.e., a fixed ratio of capital to labour, to show that more foreign capital will allow a larger labour force to be employed. The assumption of flexibility seems more realistic, especially as we are concerned with the long run and with the economy as a whole. The possible applicability of the analysis to "dual" economies in underdeveloped countries will be briefly touched on in section XII.)

V

Now remove assumption (4) that the stock of Australian-owned capital is independent of the amount of foreign capital. The higher the stock of foreign capital at some future date the higher must the inflow be between now and then and the higher is the stock likely to be at most intervening dates. The higher therefore is Australian income likely to be in most intervening years, for reasons given in previous sections, if Australian-owned capital is unaffected by the higher foreign investment.

This may suggest that Australian savings and investment are likely to be higher so that at the future date the stock of Australian-owned capital will in fact be higher. Such a conclusion, however, becomes considerably less certain when account is taken of such factors as the redistribution of income between capital and labour resulting from increased foreign investment and from any consequent increase in immigration; and it is hard to know how government fiscal, monetary and other policies will react to the changing circumstances—such reactions will be important. It is not inconceivable that Australian-owned capital will be lower at the future date than it would have been in the absence of the extra foreign capital. To take an extreme, and no doubt exaggerated, example, extra

---

[11] If L is the quantity of labour and M its marginal product,

$$\frac{WVUP}{RQWT} = -\frac{M \Delta L}{L \Delta M} \text{ approximately.}$$

investment from abroad might consist of purchases of existing Australian-owned assets, and the proceeds might be spent on extra foreign consumption goods, of a type not obtainable at home, whose importation was previously prohibited but is now allowed following the improvement in the balance of payments; the extra foreign-owned capital would then be fully offset by a reduction in Australian-owned capital.

The actual outcome is hard to predict. If, as is perhaps most likely, Australian-owned capital is increased, it can easily be seen, using the same type of diagrammatic analysis as before, that there will be a further increase in Australian income, over and above the increases described earlier, equal to the profits on the extra Australian capital plus the reduction in foreign profits, after tax, resulting from the lower profit rate. (The reduction in profits on the "old" Australian capital will be a gain to Australian labour.) If this higher income leads to more immigration there will be a still further increase in total Australian income for reasons given earlier.

If Australian capital is reduced, Australian income will be less than it would have been (i.e., the gain for other reasons will be diminished) by the profits on the Australian capital not created plus the increase in foreign profits, after tax, resulting from the higher profit rate; and if immigration is in consequence reduced there will be a further reduction in total Australian income.

If Australia is prodigal enough to allow the extra foreign capital to be fully offset by a reduction in Australian-owned capital (compared with what it would otherwise have been), then Australian income at the future date will, on our present assumptions, actually be lower than it would have been had the extra foreign capital not come in. For, assuming no change in immigration policy, total labour, total capital and total output will be the same as they would have been, but of this output foreigners will get an extra amount equal to the profits, after tax, on their extra capital; if, in the circumstances, immigration were reduced, there would be a further reduction in Australian income.

VI

Now remove assumption (5) and allow for possible external economies from extra foreign investment in Australia, i.e., economies external to the foreign firms investing the extra capital. If the value added to output by this capital exceeds the profits, before tax, earned on it the difference will be the value of such external economies. These will very probably bring a further gain to Australia.

We shall still assume that there are no external economies *of scale* resulting from the growth of the Australian economy generally; such economies will be considered in the next section. We shall be concerned at present only with external economies of foreign investment resulting from other factors such as (i) the breaking of bottlenecks (probably much less important now than it may have been in the early post-war years) and (*ii*) the introduction of "know-how" by foreign firms.

Such know-how is presumably becoming less important as Australian technical and administrative knowledge broadens. It is perhaps hardly worth mentioning that it can bring an additional gain to Australia only if it gets outside the foreign firms. This may happen where, for example, the latter train workers who are later employed by Australian firms or where the superior techniques they bring to the country are somehow passed on to locally-owned businesses which are both made aware of them and forced to adopt them if they are to survive foreign competition. If any gain accrues to Australia from this "know-how," it does not necessarily mean that it might not have been preferable to buy or hire it without importing the capital.

While these external economies seem likely to bring an extra gain to Australia, they might conceivably reduce the gains mentioned earlier. The extra gain (which may be negative) will be equal to (*a*) the resulting change in the wage bill plus (*b*) the resulting change in profits of Australian capitalists plus (*c*) the tax on the resulting change in profits on the "old" foreign capital. If the benefit of the external economies spreads to both capital and labour—and this seems *a priori* the most likely outcome—(*a*), (*b*) and (*c*) will all be positive and there must be a further gain to Australia. There must also be a further gain so long as labour benefits, even if capital loses; for, since the external economies will presumably increase output, labour's gain must exceed capital's loss, and only part of the latter is borne by Australia. There will still be a further gain even if labour does not benefit at all, provided there is no absolute reduction in the wage bill. But if there is an absolute reduction, Australia *may* lose.

Such a reduction might occur if, for example, the presence of extra foreign firms spread knowledge of production methods that enabled other firms to produce the same output with their existing capital but with less labour while the marginal product of labour at full employment was reduced. There would then, as a result of the external economies, be a higher total output in Australia but a lower wage bill. Profits would go up more than the wage bill fell. This would, however, presuppose an improvement in techniques rather heavily biased towards labour-saving as opposed to capital-saving.

The possibility is illustrated in Diagram IV[12] (p. 183). The external economies shift the marginal product of labour curve from the full to the dotted line. Output is up by $E - C - B$, which is positive. The wage bill is down by $A + B$. Profits are up by $E + A - C$.

Australia would, however, lose only if labour's loss was nearly as large as capital's gain. For she would get the great bulk of the latter, either in

---

[12] It is assumed that capital could produce no output if there were no labour. This is analogous to the assumption mentioned on p. 174, n. 3.

DIAGRAM IV

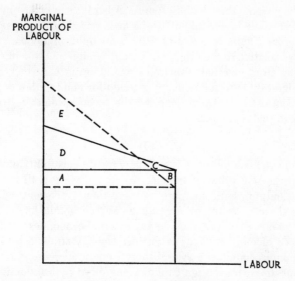

profits or in taxes, actually $1 - c(1 - t)$ of capital's gain where, as before, c is the ratio of foreign to total capital and t the rate of tax on profits. Taking c and t as of the order of $\frac{1}{10}$ and $\frac{1}{2}$, Australia would gain about $\frac{19}{20}$ of the increase in profits. She would thus lose only if labour's loss were more than about $\frac{19}{20}$ of capital's gain, i.e., only if the redistributive effect of the external economies were large compared with the gain in output.

Australia's loss could not, at worst, be more than about $\frac{1}{20}$ of labour's loss. While it cannot be proved that this would necessarily be small relative to the gains from foreign investment described above, it seems likely that it would be. It is hard to believe that an increase in foreign capital equal to, say, 1 per cent of total capital could change production methods sufficiently to redistribute more than say 1 per cent of the national income from labour to capital. But this would reduce Australian income by not more than about $\frac{1}{20}$ per cent, whereas it can be seen, by taking plausible figures, that the extra foreign capital might well increase Australian income by, say, $\frac{1}{2}$ per cent or more for reasons given in previous sections.[13]

In conclusion it seems likely that external economies (other than economies of scale) resulting from extra foreign capital will further increase Australian income. There is no obvious *a priori* reason why the econo-

---

[13] Of course, if the external economies benefited foreign more than Australian capitalists in relation to their respective capitals, Australia's loss could be greater; but this would be inconsistent with our present assumption of perfect competition which means that the profit rate is the same for Australian and foreign capital.

mies should be biased towards labour-saving rather than capital-saving; even if they were, they would reduce Australia's income only if they caused an absolute loss to labour, and a loss, moreover, that was nearly as large as capital's gain. Any loss to Australia would, in any case, probably not be large relative to the other gains from foreign investment.

Any gain from external economies would bring a further gain from extra immigration (given any likely criterion for immigration policy), and possibly from extra Australian capital; the reverse would be true of any loss from external economies.

VII

Now remove assumption (6) and allow for the possibility of economies of scale in the sense that, if labour and capital were both increased by 1 per cent, output would increase by more than 1 per cent, whether the extra capital were foreign or Australian. The economies of scale considered here do not, therefore, include any external economies resulting from the presence of more foreign, as distinct from Australian, capital; these latter economies could arise even if there were no increase in total capital or in labour, the extra foreign capital being offset by a reduction in Australian capital.

Economies of scale could be external to firms or internal; the latter type would be possible only under imperfect competition, about which more will be said in the next section. The economies could be biased in a labour-saving or in a capital-saving direction as in the case of the external economies described in the last section. They seem likely, however, to bring a further gain to Australia when foreign capital is increased. There could conceivably be a loss for reasons similar to those discussed in the last section, but this seems intuitively to be even more improbable, since a mere increase in scale seems less likely to cause drastic changes in methods of production than the presence of additional foreign capital, where the quantity of extra capital is the same in both cases.

Gains from economies of scale will, of course, allow further gains from extra immigration (and possibly from extra Australian capital), and conversely for losses.

VIII

So far we have assumed perfect competition. It might be argued that this was a reasonable assumption on the ground that, according to some post-war studies, it corresponds fairly closely to reality in the long run, or at least more closely than many pre-war theories implied. If, on the other hand, we remove assumption (7), and allow for imperfect competition, the analysis becomes much more complex and it is not easy to make useful generalisations about the modifications required in our previous analysis.

Assume first that the same "normal" rate of profits is earned everywhere. Wages plus "normal" profits will then exhaust the total output but the reward per unit of capital or labour will be the marginal *revenue* product,

which is the marginal *physical* product (assuming the firm expands) *less*
this product multiplied by the reciprocal of the elasticity of demand facing the firm (where this elasticity is defined so as to be positive).[14] The
ratio of the wage rate to the profit rate will still, however, equal the ratio
of the marginal *physical* products of labour and capital.

If, now, growth took place wholly through multiplication of identical
firms, and assuming no external economies, a given proportionate increase
in both capital and labour would result in the same proportionate increase in the number of firms and in total output. There would thus be
constant returns to scale for the economy as a whole. (The latent internal
economies of scale implicit in our assumptions—according to a well-known
theorem in the theory of the firm—would not be exploited.) It is intuitively
plausible that each factor would then receive its marginal (national)
physical product, even though it received less than what the marginal
physical product would have been had individual firms expanded; a proof
is given in the footnote.[15] On these assumptions, therefore, the preceding

---

[14] We assume a perfectly elastic supply of labour and of capital to the firm. Units
of each product are defined so as to make their prices unity. The demand curve for
each firm will be tangential to its average cost curve.

[15] Let the production function of each of n firms be $y = f(k, l)$, where y is output, k capital and l labour. Let Y, K, L be corresponding totals *for* the economy, π
the profit rate and w the wage rate. Suppose an increase in total capital sufficient
to allow for an extra firm producing the same output as each old one and for the
maintenance of the output of each old one. Part of the extra capital will go into the
new firm and part into the old firms to compensate for the labour withdrawn for
use in the new one.

The increase in total output is the output of the new firm which equals that of
each old one,

i.e. $$\Delta Y = y \qquad (1)$$
Rewards to the factors exhaust output in each firm,

i.e. $$y = k\pi + lw \qquad (2)$$
The increase in total capital is the capital in the new firm plus the increase in capital
in all the old ones,

i.e. $$\Delta K = (k + \Delta k) + n\Delta k \qquad (3)$$
There is no change in the output of the old firms,

i.e. $$\Delta k \frac{\partial y}{\partial k} + \Delta l \frac{\partial y}{\partial l} = 0 \qquad (4)$$
The ratio of the profit rate to the wage rate equals the ratio of the marginal physical
products of capital and labour (assuming firms were to expand),

i.e. $$\frac{\partial y/\partial k}{\partial y/\partial l} = \frac{\pi}{w} \qquad (5)$$
From (4) and (5), $$\pi\Delta k + w\Delta l = 0 \qquad (6)$$
From (1), (2) and (3), $$\frac{\Delta Y}{\Delta K} = \frac{k\pi + lw}{k + (n+1)\Delta k}$$
substituting from (6) $$\frac{\Delta Y}{\Delta K} = \pi \left[\frac{k\pi + lw}{k\pi - (n+1)w\Delta l} \right]$$
Now $-n\Delta l$ is the labour in the new firm (being the sum of the transfers from the
old firms) and therefore also the labour in each old firm in the new situation. In the
old situation their labour (l) was $-\Delta l$ greater. Therefore $-(n+1)\Delta l = l$.

Hence $$\frac{\Delta Y}{\Delta K} = \pi,$$
i.e., the profit rate equals the marginal national physical product of capital. Similarly for labour.

analysis applies. It would also seem to be a reasonable approximation even though firms are not identical, provided the new ones were representative.

If, at the other extreme, growth took place wholly within existing firms, each growing in the 'same proportion, the latent internal economies of scale would be exploited and capital and labour would get less than their marginal physical products. Extra foreign capital would then probably bring a gain to Australia as a result of the internal economies; for the profits it earned would be less than the extra output it created, the difference going to existing factors. This gain, however, is merely that resulting from economies of scale and already allowed for in the previous section.

On the above assumptions, therefore, imperfect competition does not seem to require much, if any, modification of our previous analysis. The assumptions are, of course, unrealistic. For example, in so far as the foreign capital creates new firms, these may, to get a foothold in the market, have to charge prices lower than those ruling for similar existing products that are in no way superior, simply because buyers are conservative in their habits. The new firms, if they used the same techniques, would then make a lower rate of profit than that earned elsewhere—there would no longer be the same "normal" rate everywhere—and there would be a gain to Australia additional to those already considered. The same might be true in so far as growth was within existing firms, for extra foreign capital would probably be concentrated on a small proportion of such firms, especially those in which foreign capital was already invested.

On the other hand, the growth of foreign firms might put them in a monopolistic position in which they could exploit Australian buyers, and this might involve a loss to Australia. (Foreign investment need not, of course, foster monopoly. On the contrary, it may break down local monopolies and, by accelerating the growth of the economy and so of the Australian market, widen the scope for competition by increasing the number of firms of reasonable size possible within existing industries.)

Endless further examples could be elaborated, but this would be pointless. The present method of analysis is admittedly unsatisfactory for dealing with imperfect competition and a better method might substantially modify our earlier results. On the other hand, we have seen that, on certain assumptions, the perfect competition analysis gives a reasonable first approximation, and that the removal of these assumptions leads to modifications that do not all work in the same direction and may partly cancel each other out.

IX

Now remove assumption (8) and allow for possible effects of investment from abroad on the terms of trade. We still assume in this section that the balance of payments can be adjusted smoothly as required, so that international reserves are held constant without economic or social cost by, among other things, variations in exchange rates or in Australia's cost level relative to cost levels abroad with fixed exchange rates.

Let us start by also assuming, as is quite common in the analysis of such problems, (*i*) that trade barriers are not raised and lowered to correct tendencies to international deficit and surplus respectively; (*ii*) that an improvement in the balance of payments requires a worsening in the terms of trade, and conversely. On these assumptions, which will be critically reviewed later, extra foreign investment may affect the terms of trade in three main ways.

First, the transfer of the profits abroad will tend to require a worsening in the terms of trade to generate the necessary surplus in the other items of the balance of payments.

Secondly, the terms of trade may be affected by the increase in output and income in Australia resulting from the extra foreign investment, and by any consequent changes abroad (output abroad might, for example, be less than it would otherwise have been because there is now less capital for investment there). The outcome will depend on such factors as the pattern of changes, at home and abroad, in supply of, and demand for, different types of goods (especially export-type, import-type and other). This raises very large questions that cannot be discussed here, but it seems that the terms of trade might tend to be either worsened or improved.

Thirdly, the movements of capital across the exchanges will affect the terms of trade. An inflow will tend to improve them, by creating a tendency to surplus in the balance of payments (which, on our present assumptions, has to be corrected), provided the capital does not reflect entirely additional imports of capital goods and remembering that the government is assumed to maintain a constant degree of employment (otherwise we should have to allow for the inflationary effects of complementary Australian investment and the like). Similarly, the terms of trade will tend to worsen if and when the foreign capital flows out again. (This may happen even with direct investment if, for example, depreciation allowances are repatriated or if foreign assets are sold to Australians.)

It is hard to say whether, on balance, these various forces will improve or worsen the terms of trade. Fortunately, however, this does not matter too much, since any change is unlikely to be very large—once more for three main reasons.

First, it is rather widely believed that the terms of trade are to all intents and purposes a *datum* for Australia. The supply of imports must certainly be highly elastic since imports are such a small fraction of consumption of similar goods abroad; and, while one cannot be so confident about the elasticity of demand for exports, this too seems likely to be high, in the long run we are here considering, especially when account is taken of competition between wool and synthetic fibres.

Secondly, even if the terms of trade are not a *datum*, deficits or surpluses may in practice be prevented, in part at least, by a raising or lowering of trade barriers which limits any worsening or improvement in the terms of trade.

Thirdly, even if trade barriers are not varied in this way, tendencies to imbalance may be largely corrected by other measures so that only small changes in the terms of trade are required. Dr. I. F. Pearce, in an interesting paper not yet published,[16] has argued that, assuming "full employment" is maintained at home and abroad, a country's balance of payments deficit, for example, can usually be removed in large part by (*i*) a cut in expenditure at home approximately equal to the deficit, together with a corresponding increase in other countries (which will be necessary to maintain full employment there as their surplus vanishes); (*ii*) a reduction, by exchange depreciation or otherwise, in the prices of non-traded goods at home relative to the prices of *both imports and exports*, and conversely abroad. These, in his view, are the important changes in relative prices necessary to restore balance. They will help to do so by stimulating production, and discouraging consumption, of both import-type and export-type goods at home, and conversely abroad. Any change in the ratio of import to export prices is, by contrast, likely to be relatively small. (He also reaches the somewhat surprising conclusion that any change in the terms of trade is equally likely to be in either direction; but whether this is a valid generalisation, and whether it applies to Australia, are questions that cannot be pursued here.)

For all these reasons any gain or loss through changes in the terms of trade resulting from extra investment from abroad seems unlikely to be large. If there is a loss it is most unlikely to offset the gains already mentioned (this could, I think, be shown by an analysis broadly similar to one developed in another context[17]); nor does it seem likely to be as important as the losses that could arise for reasons given in the next section.

X

We now remove assumption (9) and allow for the balance of payments problems that may arise if Australia runs into substantial deficit. If exchange rates are fixed, reserves inadequate, and emergency overseas borrowing impracticable or undesirable, there will probably have to be (*a*) deflationary measures that will interrupt growth and cause unemployment of resources—we are here removing assumption (1)—except in so far as the deficit can be removed by eliminating excess demand; and possibly (*b*) intensified import restrictions that may cause shortages, disrupt production and investment plans, create rigidities in the economy and involve more than optimum protection (this may also happen if tariffs are raised). If the currency is devalued there will be social problems and a weakening of trust in the Australian pound. Moreover, devaluation may not quickly remove the deficit because, though trade may be quite highly responsive to relative price changes in the long run, it is much less so in the short run; deflationary measures and restrictions may thus have to be main-

---

[16] "The Problem of the Balance of Payments," [subsequently published in *International Economic Review*, II (January, 1961), pp. 1–28].

[17] MacDougall, *The World Dollar Problem*, appendix XIIF.

tained for some time. Nor would freely fluctuating exchange rates solve the problem; and they have various disadvantages of their own.[18]

The question is whether extra investment from abroad might contribute to these troubles. The analysis required is quite different from that of possible effects on the terms of trade.

Let us assume for the moment that there are no large and rapid fluctuations in the flow of new investment. If then, with a given flow, the Australian balance of payments tends to improve over the years ahead with fixed exchange rates, an increase in foreign investment will not cause trouble by swelling the profits that have to be remitted across the exchanges, provided the increase is not too large. If, on the other hand, the balance tends to worsen with a given flow of investment, recurring crises will in any case be likely. Extra foreign investment would not necessarily then aggravate them; it might alleviate them. The higher payments of profits abroad might be offset, or more than offset, by the higher capital inflow and by favourable effects on the balance of payments resulting from the extra production; for this might be what is sometimes called "import-saving" or "export-creating."[19] Extra foreign investment might, however, aggravate the problem, especially if it were "import-creating" or "export-discouraging." There could then be more serious and more frequent crises and the resulting losses would have to be debited against the gains from extra foreign investment described earlier.

One convenient method of assessing the future trend of the balance of payments, given fixed exchange rates, is to consider first the likely course of the Australian price level relative to price levels abroad (i.e., the comparative rates of inflation, if any), and secondly any "structural" changes that might affect the balance of payments even if price levels at home and abroad moved in line. It is possible to be pessimistic or optimistic on both counts. No judgment is attempted here but, if one were only moderately optimistic, it would not seem that a continuation of something like the post-war rate of growth of private foreign investment in Australia during, say, the decade ahead would obviously cause trouble.

An uncritical interpretation of the crude figures may exaggerate the past rate of growth. They suggest that between mid-1947 and mid-1958 the value of direct foreign investments outstanding rose by an average of

---

[18] For a fuller discussion by the present author see, e.g., *op. cit.*, pp. 335–42, 383–87, and "Flexible Exchange Rates," *Westminster Bank Review*, August, 1954.

[19] The correct meaning of these much-abused terms varies with the context. Here we are really combining them and postulating that, apart from the capital inflow and the additional profits payable abroad, the extra investment is "balance-of-payments-improving," given fixed exchange rates. To determine whether this was likely, we should have to assess (*a*) any effects on Australia's price level relative to price levels abroad and (*b*) any "structural" effects on her trade (see next paragraph); these would comprise the effects of faster growth generally (whether financed by foreign or Australian capital) and of any special twist given by the foreign capital to the pattern of development. As is well-known, such an assessment is difficult, not least because the indirect effects can be so important.

15 per cent a year.[20] A more careful examination substantially alters the picture. First, the crude figures include undistributed profits of subsidiaries only since 1947; if those accumulated earlier were added, the rate of growth might be reduced to perhaps 13 per cent a year. Secondly, and much more important, it seems that a large part of the increase merely reflects the fall in the value of money (both between 1947 and 1958 and before 1947; for the fixed assets existing at mid-1947 were all installed before that date). A very rough (but complicated) calculation, based on a method used in another context,[21] suggests that the rate of increase of direct investments, in real terms, may have been only about 6 per cent per annum. While not much significance can be attached to this result, a check on its plausibility is that, in money terms, income on foreign investments in Australia (excluding public authority interest) rose from about 1.1 per cent to about 1.3 per cent of the gross national product during the same period.[22] This is not inconsistent with investments outstanding rising by 6 per cent a year in real terms and the real national product by, say, 4–5 per cent.

If, in future, foreign investments grew at 6 per cent per annum in real terms (one can admittedly make more startling extrapolations by taking U.S. and U.K. investments separately),[23] the growth of income on them would not obviously be embarrassingly rapid in relation to the growth of trade; for, with the real national product growing by, say, 5 per cent a year, trade may well tend to grow by, say, 4 per cent in real terms (there may be reasons why it will grow more slowly than the national product but the difference is unlikely to be very great). Since profits on foreign investments in Australia are still quite a small fraction of trade in goods and services, imports would not have to rise so very much more slowly than exports to cover the growing income payable abroad, even if we ignore the growing support to the balance of payments that would result from the rising inflow of new capital.[24]

If we now remove the assumption of no large fluctuations in this inflow, there is the possibility that these might help to cause crises, especially if a sharp reduction in the net inflow (allowing for withdrawals of foreign capital) coincided with a worsening in the balance of payments for other reasons. The higher the average flow over a period of years the more serious is this danger likely to be and this is a further cost of more rather than less investment from abroad. (The extra danger would, however, be diminished or removed if more investment resulted in an im-

---

[20] Including undistributed profits of subsidiaries since mid-1947. Calculated from tables 5, 6, 8, 9 of *Annual Bulletin of Oversea Investment, 1957–58*.

[21] MacDougall, *op. cit.*, pp. 534–35. There is no space to describe the calculations for Australia, and little need since the result is purely illustrative.

[22] Calculated from papers on *National Income and Expenditure;* adjusted for annual fluctuations. The figures are not quite comparable with those given earlier.

[23] See Arndt, *op. cit.*, p. 258.

[24] The relationships between growth of trade, foreign investment, and income on it could be further elaborated, but this seems unnecessary for our present purpose.

proved balance of payments, and a building up of reserves, either automatically or through deliberate policy.)

It is not obvious that the inflow of private capital will become a dangerously high fraction of the balance of payments in the foreseeable future. It has averaged only about 10 per cent of payments on current account in recent years (including undistributed profits),[25] and we have seen that it will not grow so very much faster than trade if the post-war trend continues. Nevertheless, the net inflow can contract sharply—it fell by over two-thirds between 1951–52 and 1952–53 and might even become negative—and a loss of even, say, 7–10 per cent in foreign exchange receipts can be embarrassing when reserves are low, especially if other receipts are falling at the same time.

Direct investment may be less dangerous in this respect than portfolio investment in Australian companies, since the latter is probably more volatile. (It also brings little, if any, know-how, one of the main gains from direct investment; and, though the rate of return on it may appear lower, this becomes less certain if allowance is made, as with direct investments, for the undistributed profits being set aside for the benefit of shareholders.)

XI

Finally let us remove assumption (10), that the increase in foreign capital considered does not require changes in Australian policy that themselves may involve a loss. The previous analysis would require no consequent modification if we were considering the effects of changing conditions abroad, say a fall in the rate of profit there that encouraged the flow of capital to Australia. But if, say, the government were considering whether to provide more information abroad about investment opportunities in Australia, the cost of so doing would have to be debited before striking a balance. Attempts to attract foreign capital by firmer guarantees on freedom to repatriate might increase the danger of future balance of payments difficulties. Higher protection, designed to encourage investment in Australia by foreign producers thereby prevented from exporting direct, might mean sacrificing some of the benefits of the international division of labour; there might also, of course, be further well-known benefits from higher protection, but some of these have already been allowed for in this paper.

Conversely, measures that might reduce capital inflow, such as insistence on a minimum Australian participation in the equity of subsidiaries of foreign firms or the outlawing of restrictions on exporting by such subsidiaries,[26] might bring other economic or political benefits.

The only case we shall consider in any detail is where investment from

---

[25] The balancing item is excluded; see R. J. Cameron, *Economic Record*, August, 1957, pp. 263–64.

[26] Cf. H. W. Arndt and D. R. Sherk, "Export Franchises of Australian Companies with Overseas Affiliations," *Economic Record*, August, 1959.

abroad is encouraged by a reduction in tax rates on foreign profits, whether or not this applies equally to domestic profits. (The analysis will, of course, apply in reverse to higher tax rates.) If rates are reduced, the gain from taxation will be smaller than that described in section III. There could even be a reduction in tax revenue from foreign profits.

It can easily be shown that this will be avoided if

$$\frac{\dfrac{1}{\eta_d} + \dfrac{1}{\eta_s}}{1 + \dfrac{1}{\eta_s}} \leqq t$$

where t is the tax rate as before and η_d and η_s the elasticities of demand[27] for, and supply of, foreign capital; they measure the relationship between changes in the *stock* of foreign capital in Australia and in the profit rate, before tax in the case of demand, after tax in that of supply. If we took the tax rate as one-half, this would reduce to

$$\eta_s \geqq \frac{1}{1 - \dfrac{2}{\eta_d}}.$$

If, for example, η_d were infinite, 10, 4 or 2, η_s would have to be not less than 1, 1¼, 2 or ∞. We have seen that η_d is probably high, so that a fall in tax revenue might be avoided if the elasticity of supply of foreign capital were not less than, say, some figure between 1 and 2.

It might be thought that this was highly probable since foreign capital in Australia is such a tiny fraction of foreign capital abroad. But the market is very imperfect; only a very small fraction of all foreign capitalists are interested in investment in Australia. An elasticity of supply of, for example, 1½ would mean that, if the rate of profit, after tax, on foreign capital were, say, 9 per cent rather than 8 per cent, this would in the long run make a difference of nearly one-fifth, or perhaps £250 million or more, in the amount of foreign capital in Australia. Whether this is likely it is very hard to say.

It certainly seems possible that, if investment from abroad were encouraged by tax remission, there would be no gain to Australia from increased tax revenue, at least if we confine our attention to the stage of the analysis reached in section III. The reduction in tax rates might still be worth while, for the other consequences might be favourable to Australian income on balance (and might possibly convert a tax loss into a tax gain). But it should be remembered that any gains from higher immigration, and possibly more Australian capital, would now be substantially smaller than in our previous analysis, because they there depended considerably on the rise in Australian income resulting from higher tax revenue from foreign profits.

[27] Defined so as to be positive.

XII

The main conclusions of this analysis are fairly straightforward and obvious. The most important direct gains to Australia from more rather than less private investment from abroad seem likely to come through higher tax revenue from foreign profits (at least if the higher investment is not induced by lower tax rates), through economies of scale and through external economies generally, especially where Australian-owned firms acquire "know-how" or are forced by foreign competition to adopt more efficient methods.

These gains may permit higher immigration, which will further increase Australian income, if immigration policies are related in some way to the standard of living. They may also lead to higher domestically financed investment, which will later increase Australian income still further, but this is problematical and depends considerably on government policy; if domestically financed investment were allowed to fall when more foreign capital came in, Australian income could actually be lower at some future date than it otherwise would have been.

The effects of extra foreign investment on the terms of trade, which might be favourable or unfavourable, are unlikely to be large. The effects on the balance of payments could be more important. They could be favourable, but the danger of future balance of payments crises might be increased; for there are inevitably fluctuations in the net inflow of private capital and part at least of the foreigners' profits have to be transferred across the exchanges.

These are some of the results obtained by applying rather conventional tools of economic analysis. The assumptions used are still highly simplified even after those listed at the beginning of the article have been removed. For example, allowance is made for only two factors of production. No distinction is made between fixed interest and equity investment. No explicit account is taken of government-owned capital or of government borrowing from abroad; throughout most of the paper these are implicitly assumed to be independent of changes in private investment from abroad. The analysis, as was emphasised at the outset, is mainly static. Even if it were made more dynamic it would still fail to take account of considerations not allowed for in most economic theories and about which the economic historian, for example, might have more useful things to say. Many aspects of the problem are left uncovered, such as the relative merits of government borrowing and private investment from abroad, and little is said about short-run implications. No attempt is made to assess the political costs and benefits.

The analysis will not apply to countries other than Australia without modification, but such modification may sometimes be possible. In many underdeveloped countries, for example, there may be heavy unemployment of labour, or under-employment where the marginal product is far less than the wage rate, and marginal product, of labour in the organised sector, or perhaps even zero. The foregoing analysis might then perhaps be adapted by considering the organised sector and assuming employment in it to be as great as was feasible at a given real wage rate; more investment from abroad would then make possible more "immigration" from the unorganised sector just as, in section IV, we allowed for the possibility that it might permit more immigration into Australia from overseas.

Despite its many limitations it is hoped that the analysis in this paper may be of some relevance, at least to Australia, and that it may provoke others to correct and improve it and to explore other aspects of the problem.

III Trade Policy and Welfare

11. The Symmetry between Import and Export Taxes[*]

By A. P. LERNER[†]

THIS NOTE DOES NOT arrive at any conclusions not previously obtained by Bastable, Marshall, and Pigou, but it shows the nature of the slip which led Edgeworth to conclusions contrary to theirs, and demonstrates the applicability of Marshall's "offer curve" apparatus to the elucidation of this problem.[1]

If there are two countries, e (England) and g (Germany), and two goods E and G which are produced by them respectively under condi-

[*] *Economica*, Vol. III, No. 11 (August, 1936), pp. 306–13 (revised).

[†] University of California, Berkeley.

[1] Edgeworth, in an article on "The Pure Theory of International Trade" (*Economic Journal*, 1894, p. 435), writes: "The want of symmetry between the effects of restriction, and in particular taxes, on exports and imports, is perhaps the conclusion which can be most peculiarly and exclusively attributed to the mathematical method. The truth does not seem to have been attained by the ordinary methods." The peculiar result is not due to the use of mathematical methods but to an error in their use committed by Edgeworth. He attributes to the manner in which a tax is collected effects which are really due to the form in which it is spent. This results from the ambiguity, in discussing barter conditions, of the phrase "a tax on exports." On page 624 of the same number of the *Economic Journal*, in a further article of the same series, Edgeworth points out that Bastable in his "International Trade" disagrees with this conclusion, but he fails to meet the point.

In the *Economic Journal*, 1897, p. 397, in a review of the second edition of Bastable's "International Trade," Edgeworth recants his general proposition about the asymmetry of import and export taxes, but maintains that it is still true in the case of taxes imposed *in kind*. He seems here to be aware that it is not really the form of imposition of the tax that matters but its expenditure by the government, for he is careful in his second line of defence to say "Let a tax be imposed . . . and *consumed by the Government, or at any rate not sold* . . ." (my italics). He refers also to some very obscure footnotes in his series of articles on "The Pure Theory of Taxation" in the *Economic Journal* of 1897, which he alleges to contain recantations of his error. Yet in the collected papers (Vol. II, p. 39), published in 1925, the sentence quoted at the head of this note is repeated without significant alteration, although a good deal of the argument which appeared originally to justify it is left out. The omission is pointed out in a footnote which declares the missing argument "to be true only of some import taxes *in kind*" (Edgeworth's italics).

The essence of the true theory is to be found in Marshall's *Money, Credit and Commerce*, pp. 181–82, and an admirable summary of the discussion is available in Pigou's *Public Finance*, pp. 198–200. One purpose of this note is to exonerate the "mathematical method" from Edgeworth's error—a task in which I am emboldened by my experience in having repeated this error in a Seminar at the London School of Economics.

tions of perfect competition and in the absence of transport costs, tariffs or capital movements between the countries, the equilibrium of international trade is depicted by Figure 1. Along the axes are measured quantities of the goods E and G. Any radiant from the origin (like OR) indicates a rate at which E can be exchanged for G (e.g., ON of E for NS of G). The curves e and g are the offer curves of the countries. They indicate the amount of trade the inhabitants of the country are willing to do with the other country at each rate of exchange or price. (E.g., at the price indicated by the radiant R, Germany wants to move from O to S, giving up NS of G for ON of E, while England wants to go as far as T, giving up OL of E for LT of G.) The supply of E for G is greater than the demand and the rate of exchange becomes less favourable for England; the radiant moves to the right to signify that a larger amount of E must be exchanged for each unit of G. The equilibrium position is reached when the radiant passes through the point where the offer curves cut. S coincides with T at P where OM of E is exchanged for MP of G, since both countries are willing to do just the same amount of trade. Supply is equal to demand.

The imposition of a tax, whether on imports or on exports, has the effect of making the price for traders in England different from that for traders in Germany, since some of the goods are intercepted at the customs house and appropriated by the tax collector. If the tax is on G and German traders give AC of G for OA of E (Figure 2), English traders receive only AB of G in exchange for the OA of E that they give up, BC being taken by the tax collector. The price to German traders is shown by the radiant Rg, while that to English traders is shown by Re.

These radiants form a *pencil*, the amplitude of which is a measure of the size of the tax, irrespective of whether E or G is the subject of the tax. The amplitude of the pencil must be measured not by the angle between the radiants but by drawing a perpendicular from any point on one of the radiants to the axis lying beyond the other radiant, and measuring the proportion of this perpendicular that lies within the pencil. The measure of the pencil is therefore CB/CA or BF/BH which are equal to each other—signifying the irrelevance for the measure whether E or G is taxed —since $CB/CA = CF/CO = BF/BH \ (= KC/KD)$. A pencil of the amplitude shown in Figure 2 indicates a 40 per cent. tax if imposed entirely on imports (G) or entirely on exports (E), or both an import and an export tax of such size that the sum of their effects is equal to a 40 per cent. tax.[2]

---

[2] E.g., two taxes of 20 percent. and 25 per cent. have a joint effect of 40 per cent. since if these percentages are subtracted consecutively from any item there will remain 60 per cent. of the original amount whatever the order in which this is done. In Figure 2 if T bisects CB, U bisects KB and S bisects KS. CT represents a 20% tax on G and TU a 25% tax on E. ($CK/DK = 40/100$, $TU/DS = CS/DS = 20/80 = 25\%$). Alternatively, the pencil may be considered as the sum of the two adjacent pencils which would be traversed by CT and TU respectively, remembering that in adding the measure of the pencils, they must be summed as consecutive percentage subtractions, so that 20 per cent. + 25 per cent. = 40 per cent,

Thus in place of the single price-radiant which was swung round to make supply equal to demand we have a pencil which must similarly be swung round to the equilibrium position, its amplitude being determined by the size of the tax or taxes and independent of whether they are imposed on imports or exports.

The point (*U* in Figure 2) where *Re* cuts the *e* curve shows the supply of *E* and the demand for *G* by English traders. The point (*C*) where *Rg* cuts the *g* curve shows the supply of *G* and the demand for *E* by German traders. It is at once clear that the supplies and demands thus given will never equal each other however much we swing the pencil round in either direction, since these points, lying on different radiants, can never coincide. We do not have enough information to enable us to find the equilibrium position. Let us arbitrarily draw a pencil such as is shown by *ORg* − *ORe* in Figure 2. If we draw a rightangle (*CTU*) parallel to and in the same sense as the axes, so that its upper extremity (*C*) lies at the point where the *g* curve is cut by *Rg* and its right hand extremity (*U*) lies at the point where the *e* curve is cut by *Re*, its vertical arm (*CT*) will measure the excess in the supply of *G* over its demand, while its horizontal arm (*TU*) will measure the excess of the supply of *E* over its demand.[3] But our rightangle, measured in this way, is nothing but the *absolute* measure of the amount of the taxes. Obviously our inability to find an equilibrium position where supply equals demand was due to our leaving out of account the demand by the government out of the proceeds of the tax.

We can now go ahead. Given the amplitude of the tax and the proportion in which the government (which here includes any beneficiaries from the taxation) consumes *E* and *G*, we find the equilibrium position by swinging the pencil round until the ratio between the length of the arms of the rightangle (*CT/TU*) corresponds to the ratio in which the government consumes *G* and *E*. Thus in Figure 2, the government demand for *CT* of *G* and *TU* of *E* meets the excess of supply by the traders, supply is equal to demand and we have the equilibrium. If the pencil were swung slightly towards the right, the rightangle would become flatter and wider, so that with the same government demand there would be an excess of the supply of *E* over the demand and an excess of the demand for *G* over its supply. This would make *E* cheaper relatively to *G* so that the pencil would swing back again towards the left to the equilibrium position.

In the limiting case where the government consumes only *E*, the rightangle reduces to a horizontal line which traverses the pencil and meets

[3] Some readers may find it more satisfactory to imagine *C* and *U* to be connected by a *rectangle*, with sides parallel to the axes (*CTUS* in Figure 2) of which the left side and the base constitute our rightangle. The excess of the supply of *G* over its demand is then measured by the *height* of the rectangle, while the excess of the supply of *E* over its demand is measured by the *width* of the rectangle. Similarly we may call *CT* the *height* of our rightangle and *TU* its *width*.

the offer curves. Where only G is consumed by the government it becomes a vertical line.

From this examination it becomes clear that whether the tax is collected in G or in E makes no difference since this plays no part in the determination of the equilibrium position. We can draw another right-angle which shows the tax in the form in which it is collected. This taxation rightangle, like the government consumption rightangle, must fit into the pencil, since the pencil measures the amplitude of the tax, but, unlike the consumption rightangle, it need not meet the offer curves in its extremities. That was necessary for the consumption rightangle only because the government expenditure had to raise the traders' demands to their supplies.

The taxation rightangle is transformed into a consumption rightangle by a movement of one of its arms along one of the radiants until it reaches the offer curve. Thus in Figure 2, if the tax had been raised entirely in G, the taxation rightangle would have had the limiting shape of the vertical line CB. The government would then exchange G for E with English traders, moving to right extremity of the rightangle along Re from B to U and the corner of the rightangle from B to T, the rightangle acquiring the shape CTU and becoming a consumption rightangle. If the tax had been collected entirely in E, the initial taxation rightangle would have been a horizontal line traversing the pencil and passing through U and T. The excess of E over UT would then be exchanged by the government for TC of G. Edgeworth's error may be considered as the failure to distinguish between these two rightangles.

One extremity of the taxation rightangle may be expected to touch an offer curve, otherwise it can be transformed into a consumption rightangle only by moving the arms along *both* radiants. This would mean that the government exchanges G for E as well as E for G—which is not impossible, since the prices at which it can do this are divergent so that a profit emerges, but such an excursion of the government into active participation in foreign trade is unnecessary, for these profits are just what would flow to it from the taxation on the trade when done by the traders.

The apparatus we have been developing enables us to see the final equilibrium position resulting from the imposition of a tax of given size, given the ratio of its consumption between E and G, without drawing any of the magnifications, projections or other distortions of the offer curves that Edgeworth found necessary and which led to his slip. All we need do is to fit a government consumption rightangle of the appropriate dimensions into the offer curves. Figures 3, 4, and 5 all show the two limiting cases of government consumption being restricted to E (C_1U_1) or to G (C_2U_2) and one intermediate case with some of both E and G being consumed (CTU). In Figure 3 both offer curves are elastic. In Figure 4 both are inelastic. In Figure 5 e is elastic while g is inelastic. This figure can be turned round to show the reverse case.

From a cursory study of these figures it appears that in all cases (*a*) English traders are better off (U_1 is further along *e* so that more *G* is bought and on better terms) while German traders are worse off the greater the ratio of government consumption of *E;* (*b*) English traders will be better off than in the absence of the tax (apart from any benefit they may derive from the government consumption) if the proportion of the tax (measured in *G*) that is spent on *E* is greater than the elasticity of the *g* curve over the relevant range;[4] and conversely that German traders will be better off than in the absence of the tax if the proportion of the tax (measured in *E*) that is spent on *G* is greater than the elasticity of the *e* curve. (*c*) In this latter case, the English nation, including those who enjoy the government expenditure, will be worse off than if there had been no tax, in the sense that the new position, including the government consumption, indicates more trade than England was willing to engage in and on inferior terms.

This can be seen in reverse in Figure 5, where the *g* curve is inelastic, if we assume that it is Germany instead of England that collects the tax. If the proportion of the tax that is spent on *E* is greater than the elasticity of the *g* curve, *U* (like U_1) will be at a point on the *e* curve *above* the intersection. This shows the German nation (including the consumers of the tax proceeds) engaging in more trade than the offer curve (*g*) indicates and on terms inferior to those that would rule in the absence of taxation as shown by a radiant through the point of intersection.

It is tempting to say that such a position must be considered inferior to the no-tax position because it is on a lower indifference curve as indicated by the offer curve. This raises many difficulties, but there is an unambiguous loss if both curves are inelastic, this as shown for the case of an English tax by a position being reached (C_2 in Figure 4) where England gives up more *E* and receives less *G* than in the absence of the tax.

So far we have spoken in barter terms, but to suppose that the tax is raised in money and the money then spent on the commodities hardly affects even the form of the argument. There is the same divergence be-

---

4 This can be demonstrated with the help of Figure 2. Suppose the *g* curve to turn down since it must be inelastic, otherwise it is impossible for the proportion of the tax spent on *E* (which <1 to be equal to the elasticity) and to pass through *C* and *U*. Draw a straight line through *C* and *U*, meeting the *G* axis in *M* and the *E* axis in *N*, and continue *UT* to meet *OG* in *L*. (This construction is not shown in the figure.) Then the elasticity of the offer curve (*cf.* Lerner, "Elasticity of Demand," *Review of Economic Studies,* Oct., 1933, p. 44 and p. 40, Figure 5) is $LO/MO = TB/CB$ which is the proportion of the tax, measured in *G* which is spent on *E*. In this case *U*, the English traders' equilibrium, will be at the point of intersection of the offer curves so that they do just the same trade as in the absence of the tax—the whole of the tax burden falls on the foreigner. If, however, the proportion of the tax spent on *E* were greater than this, the price of *E* would rise relatively to that of *G*, the pencil would swing round to the left, and *U* would move to a point on *e* further from the origin, indicating that the English traders buy more *G* and on better terms. The foreigner pays more than the whole of the tax.

tween the prices to the traders in the different countries, the same gap
between the radiants of the pencil, and it is filled in the same way by the
government demand. It enables us to consider the possibility of the
government taxing imports or exports but not spending the money at all.
In this case one must consider the rentier beneficiaries from the ensuing
deflation as being the recipients of the taxation proceeds, and it is the
form taken by their additional purchases that determines the effect of
the tax.

In inserting a rightangle to represent the government demand, we
have been assuming the proportions between government consumption
of *E* and *G* as given. It is obvious that this is not fixed but will depend
upon the relative prices of *E* and *G*. Closely bound up with this is the
implicit assumption that the shapes of the traders' offer curves (which
include the demand for imports) are independent of the taxation and
the expenditure by the government. Both of these complications can be
dealt with at the same time. The *e* curve can be stabilised by segregating
all the influences which might be considered to affect it and incorporating
them in the *government demand curve*. This is in accordance with our
procedure of including all demand by beneficiaries from government
expenditure in the government demand.

The government demand curve is the curve *SC* in Figure 6, which is
a kind of small replica of the *e* curve, something like the embryo orange
that one finds in a Jaffa. *US* is the size of the tax measured in *E*. At the
price *Rg*—which is the price at which the government can convert *E*
into *G*—it moves the top end of the rightangle from *S* to *C*. Instead of
inserting a rightangle we have to insert the wedge *CSU*, moving *U* down
the *e* curve, *SU* meanwhile contracting so as to measure the same size of
pencil, until the radiant (from the origin) passing through *S* meets the
government demand curve just at the point where it cuts the *g* curve.

This is not quite satisfactory in so far as it implies that the shape of
SC is independent of the size of the tax collected. An improvement on
this is to consider there to be a series of *SC* curves, more or less parallel
to each other and starting from different points on *US* and *US* continued. Each of these curves shows the government demand curve corresponding to the size of the tax, measured in *E*, as indicated by the
distance of the bottom of the curve from *U* along *US*. This series of curves
is then moved down in the same way until the curve which begins at
the point along *US* corresponding to the size of the tax is in a line with
the origin and with the point where it cuts the *g* curve. The line through
these points is *Rg* and this gives the equilibrium position as shown in
Figure 6, the government consuming *CT* of *G* and *TU* of *E*.

FIGURE 1

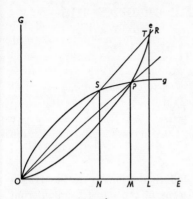

FIGURE 2

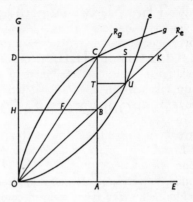

FIGURE 3

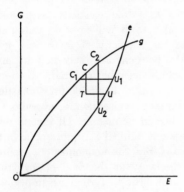

FIGURE 4

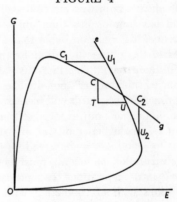

FIGURE 5

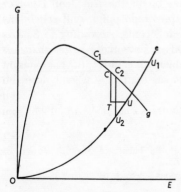

FIGURE 6

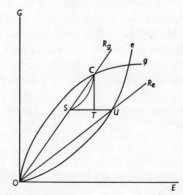

12. The New Welfare Economics and

Gains in International Trade*

By ROBERT E. BALDWIN†

I

UNDER THE NEW relatively value-free welfare economics of the Hicks-Kaldor-Scitovszky type, welfare comparisons of the gains from international trade with various degrees of restriction have been made in only a limited manner. Scitovszky, for example, states, ". . . that a suitable tariff always improves national welfare if the foreigners' reciprocal demand has unit or less than unit elasticity. If that elasticity is greater than one, it is only probable that a suitable tariff will improve national welfare; the probability diminishing as the elasticity of reciprocal demand increases."[1] The first case would be generally accepted as an increase in the society's potential real income over the free trade position because a suitable tariff will increase the quantities available for domestic consumption of both exports and imports and, consequently, everybody *could* be made better off for any distribution of income. Of course, in order to reach a complete welfare judgment, ethical assumptions about the distribution of income must be made. But the economist, by comparing income positions, can prepare the way for the final ethical assumptions without conflicting with a wide group of such assumptions that might be chosen.

The second part of Scitovszky's statement, as Little has pointed out, does not appear to be correct under his assumption of constant production.[2] An optimum tariff for the distribution of the fixed collection of goods produced which established the free trade point, will satisfy his double test for a potential increase in real income. According to Scitovszky, one collection of consumption goods is potentially better than another, if the people benefited by the change could fully compensate those prejudiced by it and still be better off than they were before the

* *Quarterly Journal of Economics*, Vol. LXVI, No. 1 (February, 1952), pp. 91–101.

† University of Wisconsin.

[1] Tibor de Scitovszky, "A Reconsideration of the Theory of Tariffs," *Review of Economic Studies*, Vol. IV (Summer, 1942), p. 97.

[2] I. M. D. Little, *A Critique of Welfare Economics* (Oxford, 1950), p. 236.

change; and also if the people who are harmed could not bribe those benefited without thereby losing more than they would if the change were put into effect. Now the optimum conditions of exchange for a trading nation require equality for each individual of the marginal rate of substitution between any two goods and the international marginal exchange ratio, i.e., the slope of the foreigners' reciprocal demand curve for these two commodities. Since these conditions are not fulfilled at the free trade point but are satisfied with an optimum tariff, it follows that the appropriate community indifference curves through the free trade and optimum tariff points cannot intersect between these two points. Hence the double bribe criteria will hold.

II

However, Samuelson recently has raised an objection to the manner in which Scitovszky judges two collections of commodities.[3] He suggests that an acceptable definition of an increase in potential real income necessitates a comparison among all the possible redistributions of income between two positions. A comparison with the two actually observed distributions of income will give false conclusions about the superiority of one income position over another on the basis of many ethical judgments about the distribution of income. According to his definition, we can say the bundle of goods under a suitable tariff represents a potential increase in real income over the free trade collection, only if everyone's position could be improved by redistributing the income under the tariff for any distribution of the free trade totals.

Samuelson's definition of a potential increase in real income and the difficulty involved with the double bribe criteria can be better understood with the concept of a utility-possibility function. A distinct advantage of this concept is that welfare analysis can be made without the use of indifference curves. First, some index of ordinal utility is assumed for each individual. The particular ordinal scale is not significant, since it is only the ordering relation which matters. For simplicity, assume there are only two individuals. With a fixed bundle of commodities, the maximum utility that one individual can reach (when the utility level of the other person is arbitrarily fixed) is found by distributing the goods in the optimum manner. The utility levels thus reached by each on the ordinal scales represent a point on the utility-possibility function. By taking all the different utility levels possible for the other individual and proceeding in the same way, the locus of all points on the utility-possibility function is found.[4] Samuelson calls this a utility-possibility function in

[3] Paul A. Samuelson, "Evaluation of Real National Income," *Oxford Economic Papers* (New Series), Vol. 2, No. 1 (January, 1950).

[4] The function can be plotted for the two individuals by measuring the ordinal utility of one individual along one axis and the other person's along the other axis. The curve will slope downward, provided there are not marked external economies of consumption.

the sense of a *point*, because it is formed from a fixed collection of goods. His definition of a potential real income increase requires the utility-possibility function derived from one collection of commodities to be entirely outside the function based on another collection. Only when there is more of one good and not less of any other can we be sure that the two utility functions do not cross. Scitovszky's criteria merely assure us that the utility-possibility functions do not cross between the two observed points on the functions. They may cross beyond these points.

III

If this stronger criterion of an increase in potential income is accepted, such an increase by a suitable tariff seems to be confined to the case of an inelastic foreign offer curve. Otherwise, the exchange process will diminish the quantity of the importable goods which the country consumes. However, this is not true if production is introduced into the problem.[5] It can be shown that a suitable tariff (combined with subsidies if necessary) or quota can lead to the consumption of a greater quantity of both exportable and importable goods than under free trade (with pure competition) as long as the foreigners' reciprocal demand curve is not infinitely elastic and production is carried on under increasing costs.[6]

Let *TN* in Figure 1 be the transformation curve of the country imposing the tariff. The curve is concave to the origin because of increasing costs. At first let us also assume a fixed supply of factors, indifferent between their use in producing commodities *A* and *B*. Under purely competitive conditions the country will produce at the point, *o*, where a price line, *oF*, is tangent to the transformation curve, and trade along this price line until it is tangent to a community indifference curve (not shown in the diagram) at *F*, offering *oD* of *B* for *DF* of *A*. The locus of all such points as *F* is *rsy*, which can be derived with all the possible prices from the appropriate community indifference curves. The only restrictions on the shape of the curve *rsy* are imposed by the concave transformation curve and the community indifference curves, each of which must be convex to the origin. Consider a price line steeper than the slope of *oF*. It will be tangent to the transformation curve to the right and below *o*. If the country offers commodity *B* for *A* at this price, this means that

---

[5] It has generally been the practice to assume constant production in studying the effects of tariffs on international trade. For example, see the early development of the reciprocal demand technique by F. Y. Edgeworth, in *Papers Relating to Political Economy* (London, 1925), vol. ii, Section IV, or later uses of the tool such as N. Kaldor, "A Note on Tariffs and the Terms of Trade," *Economica*, November, 1940. There are exceptions to this practice, however, such as P. A. Samuelson, "Welfare Economics and International Trade," *American Economic Review*, June, 1938, and J. De V. Graaf, "On Optimum Tariff Structure," *Review of Economic Studies*, Vol. XVII, No. 1 (1949–50).

[6] It is also assumed that the commodity transformation curve has a derivative at every point and the country produces some quantity of all the traded goods.

FIGURE 1

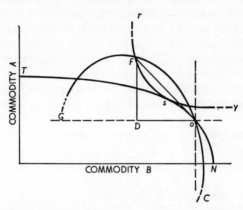

the point of tangency of this price line with a community indifference curve cannot be within the area enclosed by the line *oF*, extended until it crosses the *A* axis, and the transformation curve from *o* to *T*.

Assume that the slope of *oF* is the actual competitive free trade price. In other words, at the price represented by the slope of *oF*, foreigners will offer *DF* of *A* for *oD* of *B*. This is depicted by placing the origin of the foreigners' reciprocal demand curve, *CoFG*, at *o*.[7] This offer curve of foreigners shows the various amounts of the commodities which foreigners will trade at different prices, measured from a fixed origin, and shown in two quadrants. To the left and above the origin, they will offer commodity *A* for *B*, and to the right and below it, commodity *B* for *A*. The origin of the foreigners' offer curve can be placed at any point on this transformation curve with its *A* and *B* axes being kept parallel to those in Figure 1, since their offers are independent of where this country produces.

If the foreigners' offer curve is not infinitely elastic, the slope of this curve at the competitive exchange point, *F*, will not be as steep as the slope of the transformation curve at the competitive production point, *o*. With a concave transformation curve, it follows that at points on the curve to the left and above *o*, parts of the foreigners' offer curve drawn from these points will pass to the right and above *F*. Suitable tariff or quota policies will allow the country to reach these points where more of both commodities will be consumed.

Before giving an illustration of this, it should be pointed out that the maximum amount of commodity *A* that the country could attain for any given amount of *B* can be depicted by moving the origin of the foreigners' offer curve around this country's production curve, keeping

[7] For a more complete depiction of the free trade case, see my article, "Equilibrium in International Trade: A Diagrammatic Analysis," *Quarterly Journal of Economics*, November, 1948.

its axes parallel to those in Figure 2 (which is a redrawing of Figure 1). This will trace out an envelope curve, *uvw*. It can be proved that the foreigners' offer curve placed on the transformation curve in the manner described touches the envelope curve at the point where the slope of the transformation curve at the origin of the offer curve equals the slope of the offer curve.[8] For example, the offer curve with its origin at *H* touches the envelope at *K*, since the slope of the transformation curve at *H* equals the slope of the offer curve at *K*.

In the Figure, *H* is an example of a point on the production curve from which the foreigners' offer curve passes to the right and above

FIGURE 2

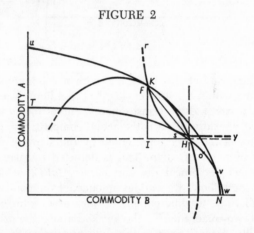

F. By imposing a tariff or quota, the nation can change its offers so that the international price becomes the slope of *HK* with *HI* of *B* being offered for *IK* of *A*. An appropriate distribution of the duty or redistribution of the traded goods will make a community indifference curve tangent to the foreigners' reciprocal demand curve at *K*. The domestic price will equal the marginal rate of substitution of the commodities, their marginal costs of production (the slope of the transformation curve at *H*), and their marginal exchange rate in international trade.

IV

However, even when one utility-possibility function, derived by redistributing a fixed collection of goods, lies entirely outside another utility-possibility function constructed from a different bundle of commodities, this is not entirely sufficient to indicate an increase in potential real income, as Samuelson has pointed out. Other totals of goods besides the two fixed collections compared might have been produced and traded. Consequently, to be general, the various production and trading possibilities must be admitted in the comparison. This results in wider possi-

---

[8] For this proof see my article, *ibid.*, p. 754.

bility-functions of the *situation* type in contrast to the above *point* kind. For example, under various tariffs or quotas the best combinations of the two commodities which this country could reach are those along the *uvw* curve in Figure 2. The utility-possibility function of the tariff situation should be built from all the commodity totals along this curve, redistributing each collection of goods in every possible manner. The utility-possibility function of this *situation* will be the envelope of the utility-possibility functions derived from each *point* on *uvw*.

What can be said about the free trade *situation* as compared with the tariff *situation?* If by free trade is meant that, while there are no government controls such as tariffs or quotas on international exchange, there may be controls on domestic production, we cannot be sure that the tariff situation is potentially better than the free trade one. For there is no reason why some or possibly all of the optimum totals that can be reached by a tariff cannot be reached by free international trade only. Specifically, from each point on the transformation curve (which could be reached and fixed by domestic lump-sum taxes) there will be an offer curve (built up by finding out how much would be traded at each price) for each distribution of the fixed collection, that will cut the envelope curve, *uvw*. For example, an offer curve from the point *H* on the transformation curve with a certain distribution of this fixed collection of goods could cross the envelope curve at *K*. Other equilibrium points on the envelope curve, *uvw*, could also be reached. Consequently, free international trade plus domestic lump-sum taxation, which can fix the production point, could be just as adequate as tariffs.

On the other hand, if there are no restrictions on the free trade of goods between the domestic and international sector, i.e., completely free trade, and the domestic and international prices are equal, the tariff situation will yield a potential increase in real income. The various collections will lie below the envelope curve, *uvw*, in Figure 2. In Figure 2 the point *F* is one such total of the two goods which could be reached. The locus of such points is found by taking the foreign offer at each price and measuring the offer from the point on the transformation curve in Figure 2 at which the price of the offer is equal to the slope of the transformation curve.[9] Since this curve will lie below *uvw*, the utility-possibility function of this situation will lie below that of the tariff situation.[10]

V

So far the analysis has been conducted on the assumption of fixed factors indifferent between their different uses. If this assumption is

---

[9] See my article, *ibid.*, p. 761.

[10] Of course at the point *v* in Figure 2, where the slope of the transformation curve equals the price at which foreigners would not be willing to trade, the utility-possibility functions of these various situations will touch.

dropped, everyone still could be made better off (in the sense of a *point* utility-possibility function) with a suitable tariff than under completely free trade. An additional optimum condition when this restrictive assumption is dropped will be that there exists a common rate of indifference, for all individuals supplying any factor for both uses, between the uses of that factor in producing the two goods. Furthermore, this rate must also be equal to the commodity transformation costs of the two goods. In the purely competitive, completely free trade case, this common ratio will be equal to the rate at which the commodities exchange for one another. Assume that *o* (Figure 1) is the free trade production point (ignoring the other parts of the transformation curve), *F* the totals obtained by production and trade, and the slope of *oF* the competitive price with all of the optimum conditions satisfied. Now if there exists increasing costs of commodity transformation with derivatives at every point, there must be points to the left and above *o* where each factor is still on the competitive level of indifference between the two uses. In other words, factors can be shifted from the production of commodity *A* without changing their total level of disutility. As has been pointed out before, more of both goods can be obtained than under free trade from some of the new production points above and to the left of the competitive one, *o*. This implies that through a shift in production from commodity *B* to commodity *A* effected by means of a suitable tariff and redistribution, everyone could be made better off than under free trade. The conclusions reached concerning the *situations* discussed also hold when this assumption is lifted.

The qualification of increasing costs also has been maintained in the foregoing discussion. If constant or decreasing costs exist throughout the entire transformation curve, the conclusions reached are somewhat modified. Under unrestricted free trade, the nation will specialize on one of the commodities in our example. This implies that a greater quantity of both commodities cannot be gained with a suitable tariff or quota for all potential trading prices. Hence, the utility-possibility functions for the three situations analyzed will touch at some points, but in no case will the function derived from the completely free trade situation be outside those of the other two situations. When there are constant or decreasing costs for only a part of the transformation range, the results previously reached hold as long as the curve has a derivative at every point and some of both goods are produced under trade.

VI

In recent years the importance of tariffs has faded somewhat with the emergence of various forms of bilateral agreement. A welfare discussion of international trade should consider this form of control also. In particular, the case of a country acting as a discriminating monopolist making maximum all-or-none offers will be examined. The various imposed offers will show the greatest quantity of exports other countries will exchange for a given amount of imports rather than not trade at all. This imposed foreigners' reciprocal demand curve will lie above their voluntary offer curve at every point except the origin, since for any given amount of exports it is possible to obtain a greater quantity of import by an all-or-none discrimination offer than by letting foreigners react merely to price. This implies not only that a suitable all-or-none offer could lead to a potential increase in real income for everyone in the country over a completely free trade or a tariff position under increasing, constant and decreasing costs, but that the utility-possibility function of the all-or-none *situation* is outside those functions in the cases of completely free trade, free international trade only, and suitable tariffs or quotas.

An unrealistic two-commodity world has been used in the preceding analysis. However, the introduction of many commodities does not alter the welfare conclusions with regard to the various cases. The main effect is to complicate through the substitution and complementary relationships movements in the terms of trade with a tariff. It may, for example, be necessary to use a combination of export and import taxes or subsidies to turn the terms of trade in a particular direction.

VII

The welfare conclusions for cases of completely free trade between the domestic and international sectors, free trade in the international sector only, suitable tariffs or quotas, and appropriate all-or-none offers can be summarized as follows. A suitable tariff or quota could make everyone in the imposing nation better off than any possible completely free trade collection of goods for any distribution of real income, except when the production possibilities do not have derivatives at every point or not all of the traded goods are produced by the country. However, the collection of commodities attained by an appropriate tariff or quota could also be reached by free international trade with domestic lump-sum taxes fixing production. This means that the tariff or quota *situation* and this limited kind of trading *situation* are indifferent, although both are potentially superior to the completely free trade *situation*. However, the discriminating *situation* is potentially superior to any of these three. It should also be pointed out for completeness that the *situation* of completely free trade is potentially better than one of no trade.[11] The other three *situations* discussed are also potentially superior to the *situation* of no trade.

It would be unwise indeed to carry the conclusions directly into the policy field. In the foregoing analysis foreigners were assumed to react passively to the trade controls of the imposing country. In general, of

---

[11] This was proved by Samuelson in "The Gains from International Trade," *Canadian Journal of Economics and Political Science*, Vol. V (May, 1939).

course, this is not true. Retaliations are the rule and not the exception these days, when countries use tariffs and bilateral agreements. The result might well be a position that is worse than the free trade one. In addition, it has been assumed that the controls discussed do not harm the efficiency of the imposing country. However, in practice such controls may prevent the attainment of some ideal position. We should really compare what Samuelson calls utility-feasibility functions.[12] These indicate the welfare positions which can actually be reached under various controls. For example, while the utility-possibility function of all-or-none discrimination lies outside that for unrestricted free trade, this is no guarantee that its utility-feasibility function does also. It is also difficult, for example, to believe that a tax fixing domestic production could actually be devised without infringing upon allocative efficiency.

Two other assumptions which have been made should also be kept in mind. One is that the utility of each individual is independent of the utility level of others. If this were dropped, we might get a case in which, although everyone obtained more of all goods than before, the utility level of everyone would not be higher than before. In other words, an increase of all goods would not be the same as an increase in utility. The other assumption is that of pure competition. If firms are already acting as monopolists, interference by the government may not produce any additional benefits in the form of increasing consumption of all goods.

Finally, the incomplete nature of this type of welfare analysis should always be remembered. It merely tries to go as far as possible without conflicting with a wide group of final ethical judgments. Not only are there some ethical assumptions with which our analysis might conflict, but the particular form of the policy decision to be taken, e.g., the exact all-or-none offer, requires value decisions concerning the distribution of income. Furthermore, Arrow has pointed out that, when there are more than two alternatives, a social welfare function cannot always be constructed which can be regarded as a true representation of individual preferences and still lead to a consistent social ordering of the alternatives.[13] Consequently, while this type of welfare analysis gives insight into general types of policy which have been argued in international trade in rarified theoretical terms, it does not contribute very much to the important questions that must be faced in a particular decision.

---

[12] Samuelson, "Evaluation of Real National Income," *op. cit.*, p. 18.

[13] K. J. Arrow, *Social Choice and Individual Values* (New York, 1951).

13. Some Problems in the Pure Theory of International Trade *

By GOTTFRIED HABERLER††

I

THE PRESENT ARTICLE discusses certain elaborations and applications of the now familiar and widely used presentation of the theory of comparative cost in terms of opportunity cost. It is largely an essay in welfare economics. I shall, however, not discuss the issue of real or labor cost versus opportunity cost, because it would not serve any useful purpose. For as Samuelson once said, "the doctrine of opportunity cost, properly stated, in no way contradicts the so-called pain cost theory of value. In fact, when stated with full qualifications, the doctrine of opportunity cost inevitably degenerates into the conditions of general equilibrium."[1] The issue seems to me no longer a live one, and its discussion can therefore be appropriately relegated to a footnote.[2]

---

* *Economic Journal,* Vol. LX, No. 238 (June, 1950), pp. 223–40.

† Harvard University.

‡ The author has elaborated the argument of the present paper in a reply to a critic: "Welfare and Freer Trade—A Rejoinder" (*The Economic Journal,* Vol. 61, No. 244 [December, 1951], pp. 777–84). The present reprint contains a few additional remarks in square brackets.

[1] "Welfare Economics and International Trade," *American Economic Review,* Vol. 28 (1938), p. 263.

[2] Ten years later Samuelson seems to have forgotten what he had written in 1938. In June, 1948, in the *Economic Journal* he said: "Professor Viner has steadfastly maintained the more general equilibrium approach of Walras, Pareto and Marshall against his opponents Knight, Haberler and Robbins. And one by one they have either had to maintain an empirically gratuitous position (that all factors must be perfectly inelastic in total supply and indifferent between different uses) or else have had to reformulate the opportunity cost doctrine so that it becomes not only a rather awkward mumbo-jumbo but loses all novelty and distinctiveness as well" (p. 182).

It could be easily shown that Böhm-Bawerk himself had already in 1894 (see his article "Der letzte Massstab des Güterwertes"—1894, Reprinted in *Gesammette Schriften von Böhn-Bawerk,* F. X. Weiss (ed.) (Vienna, 1924), especially pp. 428 *et seq.*) extensively, though perhaps not quite satisfactorily in all details, discussed the simplifying assumptions stated in parenthesis above which Samuelson chooses to call a "gratuitous position." These assumptions can, therefore, hardly be characterised as subsequent concessions grudgingly made "one by one."

Viner himself admits that the opportunity-cost approach (in the narrow, unqualified sense) is superior to the real-cost approach "in the case of land use" where "real costs are absent or unimportant" (*Studies,* p. 520). He speaks of a "genuine

II

As is usual in such discussions, I shall use a two-country, two-commodity approach. One country may stand for the rest of the world, and the external terms of trade will be assumed to be given. This does not mean that what will be said applies only to a country of so negligible a size in the world economy that it literally cannot by its action influence its terms of trade. It only means that the country is supposed to act competitively and that the possibilities of monopolistic doctoring of the terms of trade and oligopolistic or bilateralistic complications will not be discussed in the present paper. Dynamic aspects will also be ignored.

Let us now start with the familiar diagram (Figure 1) showing a production opportunity curve *AB*, which represents the maximum combinations of *A* and *B* that can be produced. The curve is drawn under the assumption of constant (inelastic) supply of factors of production and of perfect competition, in the factor and product markets.[3] The curve is drawn concave towards the origin signifying increasing opportunity cost of *A* in *B* and of *B* in *A*. Assume that in the absence of trade production takes place at point *P*, output (national income) being *Oa* of *A* and *Ob* of *B*. The tangent to the curve at *P* has then a double meaning: Its slope indicates (1) the exchange ratio between *A* and *B*, one unit of *A* being exchanged for two units of *B* (this is, of course, the reciprocal of the money price ratio and of the ratio of marginal money cost of *A* and *B*)

---

contribution" of the opportunity-cost technique "to the treatment of land-use costs." Surely, what holds of land also holds of other factors to some extent even of labor (*ibid.*, p. 525). He insists that "the opportunity-cost form of the income approach has no obvious advantage as compared to an outright income approach" (*ibid.*, p. 520).

Now I never regarded the opportunity-cost theory as anything but an "outright" income approach, in fact nothing but a somewhat simplified general equilibrium approach; and it does not require excessive generosity and tortuous interpretations to see that this is also the attitude of the other (including the original) propounders of the theory. Everybody seems to be agreed, in principle, on which factors have to be taken into consideration as determinants of income or, better, of economic welfare. But not being sufficiently skilful mathematicians, most of us resort to simplifications and allow for factors from which we abstract in our simplified models by means of somewhat vague verbal qualifications. Without pursuing this matter farther, I would still say that the simplifications made in the (unqualified) opportunity-cost approach are empirically much less absurd than those resorted to by any real-cost or pain-cost doctrine; the opportunity-cost approach is more fertile, because it can be readily extended into a general equilibrium system. It is therefore not surprising that the opportunity-cost approach has gained more and more popularity, and that it is used even by those who, in principle, attack it. (See, e.g., Samuelson in the very article from which the passage cited above is taken, and Stolper and Samuelson, "Protection and Real Wages," *Review of Economic Statistics*, 1941.)

[3] The assumption of inelastic factor supply is made for convenience, but is strictly speaking not necessary. How the production-opportunity curve is to be derived from the production functions of the two commodities is shown in W. F. Stolper and P. A. Samuelson, "Protection and Real Wages," *Review of Economic Statistics*, 1941, reprinted in *Readings in the Theory of International Trade*, Philadelphia, 1949. Stolper and Samuelson, too, assume inelastic factor supply. If they did not, they would need two additional dimensions, and their box diagrams would not work.

FIGURE 1

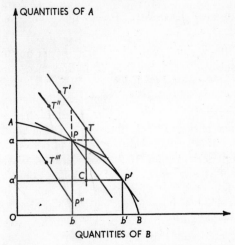

QUANTITIES OF B

and (2) the marginal transformation ratio: for one unit of A that is given up, two units of B can be produced.

It is very important to keep these two meanings apart, for only under special conditions will the two ratios be identical. These conditions are, roughly speaking, competition, indifference of factors with respect to the industry in which they are employed, and absence of external economies and diseconomies. If any one of these two conditions is not fulfilled, the exchange ratio (price ratio) and transformation ratio will diverge from one another and, as we shall see presently, very important welfare consequences flow from this divergence [or "distortions" as they are called in recent writings].

Assume now that trade is opened and the international-trade ratio is given by the slope of line *P'T*. That is to say, abroad one *B* buys about two *As*, while at home one *B* can be exchanged for only half an *A*. Our country will therefore specialise in *B*. Commodity *A*, which is cheap abroad, will be imported, while *B*, which is cheap at home, will be exported. The production point will travel from *P* to *P'*, where the marginal transformation ratio is equal to the new exchange ratio, and by trade the country will then move to, say, *T*, exporting *P'C* of *B* in exchange for *CT* of *A*.

How is the precise location of *T* on the line *TP'* determined? For our purposes it will be sufficient to answer: by demand conditions. Some writers prefer to say that the location of *T* is determined by the point of tangency of the trade line with an indifference curve. It must not be forgotten, however, that a shift in production will usually be accompanied by a redistribution of income. This precludes the uncritical application of community indifference curves, either as an explanatory device (we cannot say "the community" will choose the most preferred point on the trade line, because "the community" does not do any choosing except in a centrally planned economy) or as a criterion of welfare (we cannot simply say any point T on the trade line is "better" than P, on the ground that it obviously lies on a higher indifference curve). Things are not as simple as that. But we shall not pursue this matter any further, and the reader who wishes to think in terms of indifference curves may do so for the purposes of the present paper.[4]

But that point T is "superior," i.e., represents larger "national income" or "economic welfare" than point P, can be established without making use of indifference curves. If T is above and to the right of P, a larger quantity of A and B is available after trade than before, and it is natural to call this a superior position. If T were, as it may well be, above P but to the left of it, say at T', there would be consumed after trade more of A but less of B. In what sense, then, can T' be said to be a "better" position than P? I reject the anthropomorphic argument to the effect that the society could have chosen T, which is superior to P, and since it actually chose T', this, *a fortiori*, must be better than P. This argument is unsatisfactory, at least for an individualistically organised economy. In such an economy what is to be regarded as a better position, a larger national income or superior welfare position must be defined in terms of individual incomes or welfare positions. Modern welfare economics has, however, shown that in the following sense the situation after trade can be said to be better than before: if income were appropriately redistributed, every individual could be made better off than before.[5] It is not necessary that income will actually be redistributed so that everybody will in fact be better off; there will practically always be some individuals who are worse off than before. But it is sufficient that everybody *could* be better off. That is the definition of what is meant by saying that one situation is better and constitutes a larger national income than another.[6]

---

[4] T. de Scitovszky, in his article "A Reconsideration of the Theory of Tariffs" (*Review of Economic Studies*, 1942, reprinted in *Readings in the Theory of International Trade*) has made the only serious attempt, as far as I know, at constructing community indifference curves, taking into account changes in the income distribution. His solution of the problem is, however, not entirely satisfactory in my opinion.

[5] See especially Samuelson's formulation in "The Gains from International Trade" (*Canadian Journal of Economics and Political Science*, 1939, reprinted in *Readings in the Theory of International Trade*). ["Redistribution of income" must be broadly interpreted. It does not necessarily mean that the *actual* combination of goods produced and consumed under free trade can be so redistributed as to compensate all losers for their loss without taking away all the gains from the gainers. If gainers and losers have different tastes, compensation would require that the collection of goods be changed. That this change is in fact possible can be elegantly be demonstrated with the help of Samuelson's "utility possibility curves." (See R. E. Baldwin, "The New Welfare Economics and Gains in International Trade," *Quarterly Journal of Economics*, June, 1952; and Paul A. Samuelson, "The Gains from Trade Once More," *Economic Journal*, December, 1962.]

[6] It should be clearly realised that such a statement necessarily implies a value judgment on the part of the scientist, and in that sense is not entirely objective. But it seems to me that the formula in the text expresses clearly what we have in mind,

III

What we have stated above is an ideal case which underlies much of the free-trade reasoning. Everybody knows, of course, that it is an idealised case which is never completely realised in actual practice. There are many types of frictions and deviations from the ideal conditions ["distortions"] caused by monopolistic and oligopolistic imperfections of the market, external economies and diseconomies, price and wage rigidities, lack of information, irreversibilities of the various curves involved, etc. Each of these conditions *may* operate in such a way as to make certain deviations from the free-trade policy rational on purely economic grounds.[7] But these imperfections may just as well be such as to strengthen the economic case for free trade. A mere enumeration of possible imperfections and deviations from the ideal case does not prove more than the possibility that certain controls might be beneficial (provided of course that they are efficiently administered—which amounts to assuming quite a lot). On this practically all economists agree. In order to prove that the restriction of international trade (rather than the opposite) is justified, it is necessary to show that these imperfections are persistent (in other words that there is not even a tendency for the ideal situation to work itself out) and that they persistently operate in such a direction as to weaken (rather than to strengthen) the case for free trade.[8]

I shall now illustrate this by discussing with the aid of our diagrammatic apparatus a few cases of real and imaginary deviations from the ideal type.

---

when we say that trade (under certain assumptions) or something else, say technological advance (again under certain assumptions) increases national income and economic welfare. There are, of course, other alternative or supplementary valuations possible: for example, certain value postulates with respect to inequality of income distribution could be introduced. Moreover, it may be questioned whether a situation in which more goods are available for everybody is under all circumstances to be regarded as a better situation. But we need not go into these questions in the present paper. [Some critics have objected to the compensation criterion. It is not enough, they say, to show that every loser *could be* compensated for his loss. In order to demonstrate that one position is "better" than the other, it must be shown that the losers *actually* have been so compensated. Everybody is, of course, free to proclaim any value judgment he likes. But *actual* compensation as a criterion has implications which are hardly acceptable. Everybody prefers prosperity to depression despite the fact that there are always some deserving persons—the proverbial widows and orphans, pensioners, Oxford dons, etc.—who are worse off in prosperity than in depressions. Must we hold off our judgment that prosperity is better than depression until we have made sure that every deserving loser has been actually compensated?]

[7] The above list is not meant to be a complete catalogue of cases in which a certain amount of control can be justified. For example, protection for the purpose of improving the terms or for changing the income distribution will not be discussed in the present paper.

[8] Thomas Balogh does not betray any awareness of the complexity of these issues, and seems to believe that he has proved something by a loose and inexact enumeration of possible deviations from the competitive ideal. "The Concept of a Dollar Shortage," *The Manchester School,* May, 1949, p. 188.

It is often said that perfect mobility of factors within each country is a necessary condition for the ideal classical model. The old classical assumption of international immobility versus national mobility of labor[9] is undoubtedly responsible for this misconception.[10] It can be easily shown, however, that what really causes trouble and may make trade detrimental and justify protection is rigidity of factor prices, which may or may not be associated with immobility of factors.

If perfect mobility of factors between industries were required, the theory of comparative cost would indeed be useless. For it is obvious that land and other natural resources as well as man-made factors of production, such as fixed capital, are in fact immobile locally and occupationally. So is labor to a large degree, at least in the short run. In order to bring the basic principles out quite clearly, let us make the extreme assumption that there is no factor mobility whatsoever. (This assumption is, of course, even more unrealistic than the opposite extreme of perfect mobility. In any real economy there is a large amount of mobility, even if labor [were] occupationally almost entirely immobile, through the possibility of redirecting intermediate goods such as iron and steel and other materials and fuels, certain types of machinery, transportation services, etc., from one industry to the other.)

Under this highly unrealistic assumption the production opportunity or transformation curve shrinks to the broken line, aPb[11] (Figure 1). If all factors are in inelastic supply (implying that their prices are perfectly flexible), production will take place at point P. Assume that before trade the exchange ratio between A and B is the same as before, i.e., is given by the slope of the straight line drawn through P. (It is true we cannot now say that it is equal to the marginal rate of transformation, because there is none if there is a kink at P. But we need not discuss here how the exchange rate is determined. If we permit ourselves the use of community indifference curves, we would say that the slope of the indifference curve going through P determines the exchange ratio between A and B.)

Now assume foreign trade is opened at the rate shown by the trade line TP'. The production point will stay where it was, but the country will import a certain amount of A in exchange for B and move to, say, T''.

T'' is certainly inferior to T or T', and its superiority over P is not so

<hr/>

[9] Ohlin makes the same assumption as the early classical writers for his "region." His inter-regional trade is the same as classical international trade, for regions are characterised by internal-factor mobility. See his *Interregional and International Trade*.

[10] See, e.g., Thomas Balogh, *op. cit.* This paper is a convenient and inexhaustible store of fallacies and misconceptions in this field. He says "there must be free internal mobility of factors" (p. 188).

[11] It could be objected that in this case there is, by assumption, no transformation possible. This is quite true; still it is useful to regard the broken line, aPb, as a degenerate transformation curve.

obvious as that of T. Still it can be shown that with trade the country is better off than without in exactly the same sense as in the case of T': By redistributing income it would be possible to make everybody better off, although in fact the A-producers will be worse off and the B-producers better off than before.[12]

Now let us introduce in addition to immobility of the factors complete rigidity of factor prices. A-producers are, say, organised and their union does not permit any reduction of their members' real wage in the face of falling demand and a lower price of A. In that case, production of A will fall, and some (or all) A-producers will become unemployed. Production will fall to, say, P'', and the trading point may be T''', which is clearly inferior to P. Conversely, if by a tariff or some other protective device the *status quo ante* is restored, the result is a definite improvement. Protection thus may become highly beneficial.[13]

A number of questions remain to be answered. First, how is point P'' determined? Why is it not higher up or lower down? We may say that the extent to which production will fall depends on the shape of the marginal-cost curve. Production will fall to that point where marginal cost has fallen to the price level at which A is being imported. If the production function is homogeneous and all factor prices are rigid, constant costs will prevail and production of A will cease altogether. We need not, however, make such extreme assumptions. If the production function is not homogeneous or if some factor prices are not rigid (the price of land and of fixed capital equipment are likely to fall, in other words, these factors are likely to be in inelastic demand—barring dynamic complication, e.g., expectations that the price change will not last) or if inefficient workers will be dismissed first or if efficiency all around goes up, as is likely to be the case when unemployment rises—in all these cases marginal cost will fall when output is reduced, and P'' will not move all the way down.

A second question is whether T''' is necessarily inferior to P. The answer is no, not necessarily, not even if production of A ceases altogether. Suppose that the international terms of trade are extremely favorable, that is to say, that the trade line is very steep, for example, bT'' (not drawn in the diagram). Then it would be possible to reach T'' or a still

---

[12] The redistribution of income will, naturally, be much more drastic than in the case of mobility of factors. In fact, it may socially be intolerable.

On the other hand, it is perhaps worth pointing out that the distributional aspect may be absent: Suppose A and B are in joint supply (although without any possibility of changing their proportion). Then it would be impossible to distinguish between A- and B-producers.

In terms of indifference curves, it is clear that T'' is superior to P.

[13] If we make, however, the by no means unreasonable assumption that in the meantime wages of the B-producers have become rigid at the new real wage-level, a tariff will not carry us back from T''' to P. While production of A will expand, production of B will shrink, and we shall arrive at a point to the left and probably below P.

more favorable point beyond T'' on the line bT''. This is really obvious: If any commodity can be obtained from abroad almost without cost, it would be better to discontinue production altogether, even though it involves a lot of unemployment.[14]

What we have proved is the *possibility* of an unfavorable outcome, not its necessity. This possibility is, naturally, the greater the lower the production point (i.e., the greater unemployment) and the less favorable (i.e., the less steep) the trade line.

A third question concerns the implied change from the assumption of inelastic to that of perfectly elastic factor supply. For absolute rigidity of factor prices is equivalent to perfect elasticity of factor supply, while previously we assumed (for simplicity) inelastic factor supply.

Two kinds of supply curves of labor must be carefully distinguished: (*a*) The supply curve of the individual worker reflecting his subjective preferences for work (or income) as against leisure, and the market supply obtained by adding all individual supply curves; (*b*) the market supply curve as determined by union policy (or minimum-wage legislation or some other collective regulation). I suggest that failure to distinguish between these two meanings of labor supply has confused the discussion about voluntary versus involuntary unemployment. What is really meant by involuntary unemployment is an excess of supply in sense (*a*) over actual demand, more people wishing to work at the current wage than can be employed. This is quite compatible with supply in sense (*b*) being equal to demand.[15]

There would be complications from the point of view of the welfare interpretation, if contrary to our assumption the supply curve in the

---

[14] Of course, under the extreme assumption made with respect to complete factor immobility, it would be still better to let production of A continue *and* to import additional amounts. But that would require either flexibility of wage-rates of A-workers or an arrangement by which some of the gains made by B-producers through cheap imports of A can be transferred to the A-producers so as to maintain their real wage.

[15] We may put the distinction in the following way: from the point of view of the preference of the individual workers, that is to say, from the welfare standpoint, unemployment is involuntary; but from the point of view of the union it is voluntary, because the union voluntarily withholds labor supply at a lower wage. This does, however, not necessarily mean that the unions act against the wish of their members, not even of their unemployed members.

I think that our construction is in accord with, in fact gives life to, Prof. T. Haavelmo's forbiddingly abstract scheme: "The Notion of Involuntary Economic Decisions" (*Econometrica*, Vol. 18, No. 1 [January, 1950], pp. 1 *et seq.*). Haavelmo is troubled, as any theorist who values precision and clarity may well be, by the problem of how to interpret and to reconcile with accepted theoretical notions the concept of "involuntary" decisions and "involuntary" unemployment. He reaches the sensible conclusion that "the concept of involuntary decisions is related to the comparison of alternative economic systems, and not to the decisions within a given system" (*loc. cit.*, p. 2).

Applied to our case we would have to say, that in a system not characterised by wage rigidities employment would be larger, and the difference in the amount of unemployment between the two systems is "involuntary unemployment."

sense (*a*), i.e., the subjective, individual supply curve of labor, were not inelastic. Although it is impossibly unrealistic, let us assume that labor supply in that sense is entirely elastic. (Assume, for example, that people have income from other sources and don't care for work below a certain wage-level.) In that case the resulting unemployment would have to be called voluntary. Point T''' need then not be called inferior to P. If namely, economic welfare is then defined not only in terms of products A and B, but also interpreted to make allowance for "irksomeness" of labor, the reduction in commodity supply implied by T''' as compared with P would be offset by more leisure.[16]

IV

We have proved for the extreme case of factor immobility and factor-price rigidity that trade may be very detrimental. It should be observed that no adverse multiplier effects depending upon a temporary excess of imports over exports are involved. The balance of payments is in equilibrium all the time. The detrimental effect of trade, the failure to reach an optimum, is entirely due to the fact that a static optimum condition is not fulfilled: the equality between the price ratio and the marginal substitution ratio is not preserved.[17] The exchange ratio (reciprocal of money–price ratio) is given by the slope of $P''T'''$, while the ratio of marginal transformation is given by the slope of Pb (as was explained above, aPb can be regarded as a degenerate transformation curve). Thus, because the price mechanism does not function properly, the price line cuts the transformation curve instead of being tangential to it.[18]

It will be instructive to apply now the argument to a less extreme case in which only some, not all, factors are immobile and only some factor prices are rigid.

In Figure 2, we compare three cases, T, T' and T''. We have two transformation curves. The outer one APB is drawn under the assumption that most factors can be shifted and that the price system functions competitively. It thus portrays the "ideal" case. If P is the situation before trade, the country moves by production from P to p, and from there by trade to T.

---

[16] It is a terminological question whether in this case we should distinguish between national income and economic welfare, the former being defined in terms of products only, while the latter makes also allowance for disutility of labor and similar factors. It may be also observed that the case takes on another complexion, if labor supply becomes very elastic (as is likely to be the case) at a very low wage-level. It then would sound rather artificial, if not callous, to say that those workers who do not care for work at a very low wage "don't care" for work and "prefer leisure." But we cannot pursue this matter at this point.

[17] This is an optimum condition, because we assumed, for simplicity, the terms of trade as given. If that assumption were dropped we would have to substitute for the international price ratio what might be called the "marginal terms of trade."

[18] We may also say the ratio of private marginal cost, which determines, and is equal to, the price ratio (since the commodity markets are assumed to be competitive), does not reflect the social ratio of marginal substitution.

FIGURE 2

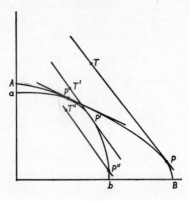

Now let us start from the same initial position P, but assume that a number of factors are immobile. The reason for the immobility may be technological or unwillingess to move. Then we get a more sharply curved transformation line, *aPb*, inside *APB*. This curve might well be regarded as a short-run curve, inasmuch as in the short run factor mobility is in all probability much less than in the long run. We assume, however, that factor prices are still in inelastic supply, and that competition prevails, all prices including wages being perfectly flexible.

This case is then, in principle, no different from the preceding one. The country will move by production from P to p', and from there to T' by trade. T' is inferior to T, but superior to P. The inferiority of T' compared with T is due to the fact that owing to the reduced mobility of factors or, in other words, due to the lower adaptability of production, the output of B cannot be expanded so much as previously when the output of A is reduced. It should be also observed that when the production of A contracts, it is quite likely that certain factors of production will become idle; but only after their prices (imputed value) have fallen to zero. Suppose A is wheat growing, then marginal pieces of land will be abandoned. (On the other hand, in the B industry extra marginal factors may be drawn into employment.) The existence of unused free goods, extra marginal land, machinery, buildings, mineral deposits or even labor does, however, not constitute unemployment, although its emergence may constitute extreme hardship for the owners of the factors which have become worthless. The hardship is, of course, especially conspicuous in the case of labor, but is not necessarily confined to it. In the case of labor there is the further complication that its supply is surely not inelastic at low wages. Therefore labor will become unemployed long before its price has fallen to zero. But we come to this point presently.

The third case is distinguished from the second by the fact that in addition to immobility we assume price rigidity for some factors. We ought, then, to draw a third transformation curve more sharply curved than, and inside, the second one. But for simplicity I use the curve aPb again. It, thus, illustrates two alternative cases.

If the price mechanism does not work competitively, if certain factors used in the production of A cannot shift to industry B *and* refuse to accept a price cut, but choose to become unemployed, the price line will cease to be tangent to the transformation curve. The country will move by production from P to (say) p'', and by trade from p'' to, say, T''.

T'' is inferior to P, and trade is therefore detrimental. What was said in the preceding section concerning the precise location of p'' and the possibility of T'' being superior to P applies also to the present case.

Why the two cases (the case of mere immobility and the case of price rigidity) lead to different results can be explained as follows. In the "ideal" case we have the following equilibrium conditions: the money prices of A and of B are equal to their respective marginal cost. Each factor is remunerated according to its marginal productivity, and all factors that are willing and able to move receive the same remuneration in both industries.

Now suppose that output of A is reduced by one unit. A marginal cost's worth of factors is thereby set free. But these factors produce the same value in industry B. It follows that the price ratio is equal to the marginal rate of transformation.[19] No factor released from industry A becomes unemployed unless its price has fallen to zero, i.e., unless its marginal productivity has vanished. Hence the existence or emergence of unutilised extramarginal factors does not affect the equality of the price and substitution ratio.

In the other case where some factor prices are rigid, factors become unemployed before their price has fallen to zero. Hence, when the production of A is curtailed by one unit, the production of B is expanded by less than the corresponding value because some of the factors go into unemployment rather than into employment in B. Therefore, the price ratio is not equal to the marginal rate of transformation. Expressed differently, the ratio of private marginal cost of A and B does not reflect

---

[19] This is, of course, true only if, as we assumed, the wage of those factors which can move is the same in both industries. Suppose factors can move freely, but that there exists a definite wage differential, wage-rates in one industry being, say, 20% higher than in the other; then the price ratio would not be equal to the marginal ratio of substitution. This is true whatever the cause for the existence of the wage differential. The welfare implications are, however, different according as to whether the wage differential is based: (*a*) on preferences of the workers (e.g., the one type of work being more disagreeable than the other) or (*b*) on an arbitrary regulation. (See Viner's critique of Mihail Manoïlesco's "The Theory of Protection and International Trade" in *Journal of Political Economy*, 1932, p. 121, and my *Theory of International Trade*, p. 197. This case could be analysed with the help of our diagrammatic apparatus. In fact Figure 3 below could be used without any change to portray this case.

the social ratio of marginal substitution, or, shorter, private and social cost deviate from one another.[20]

We have established the possibility (though not necessity) of detrimental effects of trade in case of rigid prices and of beneficial effects of protection in the case of unemployment. It should be remembered that unfavorable multiplier reactions are excluded and changes on the income distribution ignored.

How important is the case here analysed? Is it a theoretical curiosum or a matter of practical importance?

It is dangerous to jump from such an abstract model to practical application, and there is room in an article not even for a sketch of how to fill the gap. Still I venture to say that, at least in the short run, it is a matter of serious practical concern. However, even in the short run certain qualifications would have to be made, protection would not be more than a *pis aller* ["second best" it is now called] and rational policy should not be concerned entirely with short-term considerations. But we cannot pursue these thoughts any farther at this point.

V

In this section two other cases will be briefly analysed which give rise to a deviation of price ratio from the marginal rate of transformation. Unemployment is not involved in either case.

The first case is the much-discussed case of external economies or diseconomies.[21] It is usually thought to be connected with the case of de-

---

[20] In Pigou's terminology: Private and social marginal net product do not coincide.

The reader should remember that we have assumed inelastic supply of labor as far as the individual workers are concerned (as distinguished from the market supply as determined by collective action). This implies that our welfare scheme includes only alternative product cost and ignores other elements, e.g., possible differences in the "irksomeness of labor" in the two lines of employment. In other words, economic welfare (national income) is defined in terms of products A and B only. We could, of course, introduce in addition to that disutility of labor. If the rigidity of factor prices, i.e., elasticity of factor supply, were due to individual preference rather than to collective regulation, that is to say, if individuals preferred to go idle rather than to work below a certain wage, case 3 (T'') would not involve a welfare loss as compared with case 2 (T'), because the loss in terms of product would be voluntary: a certain amount of product would be voluntarily foregone in exchange either for more leisure or in order to avoid subjective or material cost of working.

To avoid misunderstanding, it should be emphasised that this construction does not neglect or minimise the hardship imposed on the owners of the factors whose income has fallen. These hardships may be severe, they may be socially intolerable. Compare what was said above concerning the neglect of income redistribution in the global welfare calculation. It is, of course, always possible to introduce additional value postulates concerning income distribution.

[21] The literature is fairly voluminous. See especially the famous controversy between F. P. Graham and F. H. Knight. Graham, "Some Aspects of Protection Further Considered" (*Quarterly Journal of Economics*, Vol. 37 (1923), p. 199 *et seq.*); Knight, "Some Fallacies in the Interpretation of Social Cost" (*ibid.*, Vol. 38 (1924), p. 582; Reply and Rejoinder, *ibid.*, Vol. 39). J. Viner has an illuminating review of the whole issue in his *Studies* (pp. 475–81). J. Tinbergen, *International*

creasing cost. Decreasing cost may be due to external economies. The assumption of external economies is, then, a way of making decreasing cost compatible with competition.

External economies (or diseconomies for that matter) need, however, not be associated with decreasing cost. Social as well as private costs may be increasing, and the underlying situation may therefore be quite stable and still there may be a deviation between social and private cost due to external economies or diseconomies, i.e., due to certain cost-raising or cost-reducing factors which would come into play if one industry expanded and the other contracted—factors which for some reason or other are not, or not sufficiently, allowed for in private cost calculations.

This situation is depicted in Figure 3. Production initially takes place

FIGURE 3

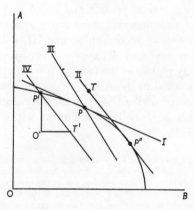

Economic Co-operation (Amsterdam–New York, 1945) devotes Appendix I, "Professor Graham's Case for Protection" (pp. 182–99) to a penetrating diagrammatic analysis of the subject.

On the broader issues about external and internal economies, private *vs.* social cost, the *locus classicus* is still Marshall's *Principles* and *Industry and Trade* and Pigou's *Economics of Welfare*. [As indicated earlier, the following analysis applies also to the case of differential wage rates, "the Manoïlesco case" which has received much attention recently. (See E. Hagen, "An Economic Justification of Protection," *Quarterly Journal of Economics*, Vol. 72, November 1958, and J. Bhagwati and V. K. Ramaswami, "Domestic Distortions, Tariffs and the Theory of Optimum Subsidy," *Journal of Political Economy*, Vol. 71, February 1963, Chapter 14 in this volume.) As pointed out by Hagen, this distortion, unlike the one treated above in my text, does not only shift the production point on the transformation curve away from the optimum but also pushes the transformation curve itself inward (towards the origin).

A point which seems to have been neglected in the literature cited is that wage differentials produced by trade union action do not always correspond to the Manoïlesco-Hagen-Bhagwati theory. Thus, if the union pursues a strict policy of closed shop, it creates two noncompeting groups. This changes the transformation curve, but does not justify protection on Manoïlesco grounds although it may create unemployment if the wage is set too high. Only if the union enforces a higher wage in industry while leaving entry of workers into industry from agriculture free do we have the Manoïlesco case.]

at *P*. The true, social ratio of transformation is given by the slope of the transformation curve (line I). The international exchange ratio (again for simplicity assumed to be fixed) is given by the slope of line II. Commodity *A* being cheaper abroad ought to be imported in exchange for *B*. The country should move to *P″* by production, and thence to (say) *T* by trade.

But now we assume that the ratio of private marginal cost of *A* and *B* and hence the domestic price ratio does not correspond to the true social-transformation ratio. Suppose it is given by the slope of line III. The exchange ratio overvalues *B* and undervalues *A*. This is due to external economies which could be realised and would lower the cost of production of *B*, if the *B* industry were expanded. These economies are, however, not recognised by *B* producers or for some other reasons fail to induce them to expand production.[22]

If the discrepancy between private and social cost is as large as assumed in Figure 3, the country will show a comparative price advantage in the "wrong" commodity. According to line III, *B* is cheaper abroad. Hence *B* will be imported and *A* exported. The production point will move to the left, to say *p′*, where the ratio of private marginal cost (slope of line IV) becomes equal to the international price ratio (slope of line II). *p′o′* of *A* is exported and *o′T′* imported. The new trading point, *T′*, is inferior to *P*. This is, I believe, a correct representation of what Graham really meant.[23]

---

[22] There is not enough space here for a thorough discussion of why this may be so. But let me say that it would be gratuitous simply to assume ignorance. The reason may be that investments would have to be made the fruits of which cannot be appropriated by private individuals (e.g., investment in the skill of the working population). On that point the literature mentioned above should be consulted. [In modern terminology we would now say "investment in human capital" is required and since in a nonslave economy it is not possible to "mortgage human beings" (Rosenstein-Rodan), private initiative often fails.]

It may be also noted, in parenthesis, that the existence of external economies involves a misallocation of resources in the absence of international trade. *P* would not be the optimum point. If I may be allowed to use briefly and inexactly community indifference curves, this could be demonstrated by pointing out that *P* is determined by the condition that an indifference line be tangent to line III, while the optimum point would be located at that point where an indifference curve is tangent to the transformation curve, that is somewhere to the right of *P*.

[23] If the discrepancy between the social and the private cost ratio is less extreme, i.e., if line III is steeper than line I, but less steep than line II, the country would specialise in the "right" direction but not sufficiently. It would after trade be better off than before, but it would not reach the optimum point *T*. In that case an export or import subsidy (rather than a tariff) would be indicated. [It should be added that if line III is less steep than line I, i.e., if it cuts the transformation curve at *P* "from below" (which implies that the external economies are in the *A*, the import competing industry, rather than in *B*, the export industry)—then the free trade production point will be located on the transformation curve beyond and below the optimum point *P*. The country will "overtrade" (rather than "undertrade") and an import *duty* will be indicated to bring production and trade to the optimum position, not a *subsidy* as in the case of "undertrading" discussed in the first paragraph of this footnote. This clears up, I believe, a point which bothered Bhagwati and Ramaswami, *loc. cit.*, p. 47. (The

It is one thing, however, and an easy one at that, to point out the possible consequences of a divergence of private and social cost and to cite instances in which such a divergence is likely to arise. It is an entirely different and infinitely more difficult task first to demonstrate that such discrepancies do in fact occur frequently, persistently and on a large scale and to indicate concretely how these cases can be recognised and evaluated.

Most economists who have given serious thought to these problems have reached the conclusion that roughly, and as a rule, the ratios of private money costs do reflect the true social real cost ratios. Practically all economists recognise that there are exceptions to the rule, but they would insist that the burden of proof is on those who maintain that the exceptions are numerous, persistent, large, and, last but not least, practically recognisable and calculable.[24]

The theory of external economies is related to the reasoning under-

---

analysis has been considerably sharpened and generalized by H. G. Johnson in "Optimal Trade Intervention in the Presence of Domestic Distortions," *Trade, Growth and the Balance of Payments*, Chicago, 1965.)]

It is not, however, a literal rendering of what Graham said. Such a literal interpretation is not attempted. It presents considerable difficulties, because Graham was not too clear and seems to have changed his position in the course of the controversy. Cf. the literature quoted above, especially Viner and Tinbergen.

[24] We may again turn to Dr. Balogh's convenient store of all sorts of confusions to find an exception which proves the rule. He says: "It is wholly illicit to assume that *money prices* are proportionate to *long run social real costs*. We know that private money costs are not proportionate to social real costs, and neither are prices proportionate to private money costs" (*loc. cit.*, pp. 189 and 190. Italics in original). Dr. Balogh is, of course, unable to give any proof; he just asserts and states impressions. I would not blame him for that, because such a statement as his could, in the nature of the case, not be proved within the frame of a few articles. But he accuses me of "invoking high authorities instead of proving" my contention that there is a rough correspondence between relative prices and real social cost. He seems to be not aware of the fact that the "high authorities," in fact practically all leading economists who have dealt with these matters, have, if not "proved" (such a theorem cannot be neatly proved like an arithmetical proposition), given plenty of reasons for accepting the contended proposition. They all treat deviations between private and social costs as exceptions to the rule of correspondence. This is, however, perfectly compatible with many shades of opinion about the relative importance or unimportance of these exceptions. Every leading economist who has dealt with these questions can be adduced (J. S. Mill, Marshall, Pigou, Taussig, Knight, Viner, etc.). Even Friedrich List could be read by Dr. Balogh with considerable profit. List was of the opinion that a manufacturing industry that cannot be kept alive on 20–30% tariff can be regarded as unsuited for the country concerned. (*Das Nationale System der Politischen Ökonomie*, Edition Berliner, 1930, p. 326.) Protection of 20–30% *ad valorem* has to be regarded as very moderate nowadays.

Dr. Balogh makes a lot of special risks attaching to foreign trade as an argument for protection and discrimination. It is true that the ultra-protectionist and chauvinistic economic policies advocated by Dr. Balogh which most countries have been now pursuing for many years (without waiting for Dr. Balogh's recommendations) have enormously increased the risk of investment abroad and at home for the purpose of building up export industries. But surely this fact cuts the other way than Dr. Balogh thinks. It increases the importance of expanding rather than of restricting international trade.

lying the infant-industry argument for protection, but the two are not identical.[25] The essence of the latter can, I think, be described with the help of our diagrammatic apparatus, as shown in Figure 4. We start this time with a situation where trade takes place, the production point being *P*, the trading point *T*. Suppose now that by means of an import tariff on *A*, production is shifted from *P* to *P'* and the new trading point is at *T'*.[26] The new situation is inferior to *T*, which represents the fact that, with the assumptions made, protection is necessarily detrimental.[27]

The essence of the infant-industry argument is that a movement on the transformation curve will bring about an irreversible shift of the curve itself. Concretely, if the *A*-industry is protected and expands,

FIGURE 4

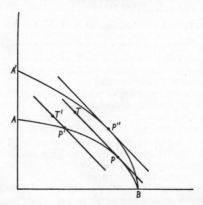

methods of production will gradually be perfected, skills will be acquired, and so the short-run curve *AB* will assume the long-run shape *A'B*. The production point will shift to *P''*. In the new situation trade may or may not take place, and the country may export either *A* or *B*, i.e., the trading

[25] On that I agree now with Viner (*Studies*, p. 482), while in my *Theory of International Trade* I held that Graham's case was but a variant of the infant-industry argument for protection. However, in view of the vagueness which attaches to much of the discussion and in view of the fact that different shades of each theory can be found, there would be not much point in a historical investigation about the closeness of their interrelation.

[26] The international terms are again assumed to be fixed. But that is not essential for the argument. The domestic terms of trade (internal price ratio including the tariff) is equal to the slope of the transformation curve at *P'*, and the height of the tariff is given by the difference between the slope of the transformation curve and the slope of the trading line.

[27] If we drop the assumption that foreign demand is infinitely elastic and assume instead that the terms of trade for the protected country improve, protection may be beneficial. This would be shown in our diagram by making the trading line steeper (not shown in the diagram). If it becomes sufficiently steep, *T'* may reach a position superior to *T*. In fact, as is well known, it can be shown that unless foreign demand is infinitely elastic there is always some tariff which makes *T'* superior to *T*.

point may be on either side of P'' depending upon "demand conditions."[28]

Again, it is an easy thing to state the assumptions, to derive the conclusions and to recognise that in principle the possibility must not be ignored that deliberate movement on the production-opportunity curve may shift the curve itself. But it should also be remembered that, in principle, the shifts may be in either direction; there may be external diseconomies as well as economies, and the possibility of favorable shifts in production-opportunity curve is not confined to import commodities. Improvements may just as well be realisable in the export industries, in which case the opposite of a trade restriction would be indicated. In other words, the argument may cut either way, and it is a little suspicious that the argument is practically always used in one direction, that is to say for the justification of protection rather than of freer trade.

To go beyond the statement of possibilities, to generalise about the overall importance of the infant-industry effect, and to evaluate it in concrete cases is an extremely difficult task which requires not only theoretical acumen, but intimate empirical knowledge of industrial development and, above all, historical perspective. Most leading economists, beginning from J. S. Mill, Marshall, Taussig to Pigou and Viner, accept the principle [of infant industry protection]. But those who made empirical studies, like Marshall and Taussig, became in the course of their studies somewhat sceptical with respect to the scope of the principle, and even more so concerning the chances of a rational application. It is to be hoped that the rapidly growing literature on the problem of developing underdeveloped countries will eventually add to our knowledge of these matters. But that is beyond the scope of the present paper.

---

[28] In terms of indifference curves: depending upon whether an indifference curve is tangent to the trading line at P'' or to the left or right of it.

14. Domestic Distortions, Tariffs, and the Theory of Optimum Subsidy [*][1]

By JAGDISH BHAGWATI and
V. K. RAMASWAMI[†]

THERE IS CONFUSION of varying degrees in the current literature on trade theory concerning the desirable form of intervention in foreign trade when the economy is characterized by domestic distortions (divergences of the commodity price ratios from the corresponding marginal rates of transformation). For instance, the age-old debate over whether tariffs or subsidies should be used to protect an infant industry is still carried on in terms of the respective political and psychological merits of the two forms of protection while their relative economic advantages are assumed not to point in the direction of a definite choice.[2]

Three questions about the use of tariffs when domestic distortions exist need to be distinguished here. (1) Is a tariff necessarily superior to free trade (that is, can a tariff rate always be found that yields a welfare position superior to that produced by free trade)? (2) Is a tariff policy necessarily superior to any other form of *trade* policy? (3) If the choice can be made from the entire range of policy instruments, which is the optimal economic policy?

In Section I we state the general theory that provides the answers to these three questions. In the light of this theory, we examine the propositions advanced in the two central contributions to trade theory in this field: Haberler's justly celebrated 1950 *Economic Journal* paper[3]

---

[*] *Journal of Political Economy*, Vol. LXXI, No. 1 (February, 1963), pp. 44–50.

[†] Delhi School of Economics; Ministry of Finance, Government of India.

[1] An early draft of this paper was read to seminars at Massachusetts Institute of Technology, the University of Chicago, and Stanford University by one of the authors. C. P. Kindleberger and H. G. Johnson have made useful suggestions.

[2] For instance, C. P. Kindleberger in his *International Economics* (Homewood, Ill.: Richard D. Irwin, Inc., 1958), as does also G. Haberler in his *Theory of International Trade* (Glasgow: William Hodge & Co., 1936), states the economic argument in favor of subsidies and tariffs without stating definitely that one is invariably superior to the other from the economic viewpoint.

[3] G. Haberler, "Some Problems in the Pure Theory of International Trade," *Economic Journal*, Vol. LX (June, 1950), pp. 223–40.

and Hagen's recent analysis of wage differentials.[4] Sections II and III examine these two analyses. Section IV concludes with some observations concerning the relative advantages of tariffs and subsidies from the practical viewpoint.

I. GENERAL THEORY

The three questions posed here can be effectively answered by analyzing the characteristics of an optimum solution. Thus, for instance, the optimum tariff argument can be stated elegantly in terms of these characteristics. The achievement of an optimum solution is characterized (assuming an interior maximum) by the equality of the foreign rate of transformation (FRT), the domestic rate of transformation in production (DRT), and the domestic rate of substitution in consumption (DRS). If the country has monopoly power in trade, a competitive free trade solution will be characterized by $DRS = DRT \neq FRT$. By introducing a suitable tariff, a country can achieve $DRS = DRT = FRT$. A subsidy (tax) on the domestic production of importables (exportables) could equalize DRT and FRT but would destroy the quality of DRS with DRT. Hence it is clear that a tax-cum-subsidy on domestic production is necessarily inferior to an optimum tariff. Moreover it may be impossible in any given empirical situation to devise a tax-cum-subsidy that would yield a solution superior to that arrived at under free trade.

By analogy we can argue that, in the case of domestic distortions, $DRS = FRT \neq DRT$ under free trade. A suitable tariff can equalize FRT and DRT but would destroy the equality between DRS and FRT. Hence it is clear that no tariff may exist that would yield a solution superior to that under free trade. A suitable tax-cum-subsidy on domestic production, however, would enable the policy-maker to secure $DRS = FRT = DRT$ and hence is necessarily the optimum solution. Hence a tariff policy is also necessarily inferior to an optimum tax-cum-subsidy policy. And the same argument must hold true of trade subsidies as well since they also, like tariffs, are directed at *foreign* trade whereas the problem to be tackled is one of *domestic* distortion.

Three propositions, therefore, follow in the case of domestic distortions. (a) A tariff is not necessarily superior to free trade. (b) A tariff is not necessarily superior to an export (or import) subsidy. (c) A policy permitting the attainment of maximum welfare involves a tax-cum-subsidy on domestic production. Just as there exists an optimum tariff policy for a divergence between foreign prices and FRT, so there exists an *optimum subsidy* (or an equivalent tax-cum-subsidy) policy for a divergence between domestic prices and DRT.

---

[4] E. Hagen, "An Economic Justification of Protectionism," *Quarterly Journal of Economics*, Vol. LXXII (November, 1958), pp. 496–514.

II. HABERLER ON EXTERNAL ECONOMIES

A divergence between the domestic commodity price ratios and the marginal rates of transformation between commodities may arise from what are usually described as "external economies." These may take various forms.[5] It is most fashionable at the moment to discuss the external economies arising from the interdependence of investment decisions.[6]

Haberler analyzes this problem in terms of the standard two-good, two-factor model of trade theory, using geometrical methods. Haberler is aware that a tariff is not necessarily superior to free trade. However, he is in error concerning the relative advantages of tariffs and trade subsidies. Further, he does not discuss the optimum economic policy under the circumstances.

Haberler distinguishes between two situations according to whether the domestic production of importables rises or falls (what he calls the direction of "specialization"). We shall analyze each case separately.

Case I. In the former case, illustrated here in Figure 1a, *AB* is the production possibility curve. The discrepancy between the domestic price ratio and the domestic rate of transformation (*DRT*) leads to self-sufficiency equilibrium at *S*. Free trade, at the *given* international price *PF*, leads to production at *P*, consumption at *F*, export of agricultural goods, and a deterioration in welfare.[7]

The following comments are warranted. First, although Haberler does not state this explicitly, it can be shown that prohibitive protection may make the country worse off (Figure 1b). Second, it follows from Section I that *no* tariff may be superior to free trade (this is implicit, we think, in Haberler's statements elsewhere in his paper). Finally, the optimum result could be achieved by a policy of tax-cum-subsidy on domestic production. Such a policy is illustrated in Figure 1c where the tax-cum-

---

[5] According to Haberler, "there may be a deviation between social and private cost due to external economies or diseconomies, i.e. due to certain cost-raising or cost-reduction factors which would come into play if one industry expanded and the other contracted—factors which for some reason or other are not, or not sufficiently, allowed for in private cost calculations" ("Some Problems . . . ," *op. cit.*, p. 236).

[6] This has been analyzed in the context of international trade by J. Bhagwati, "The Theory of Comparative Advantage in the Context of Under-development and Growth," *Pakistan Development Review*, Vol. II, No. 3 (Autumn, 1962), pp. 339–53. See also H. Chenery, "The Interdependence of Investment Decisions," in Moses Abramovitz *et al., The Allocation of Economic Resources* (Stanford, Calif.: Stanford University Press, 1959).

[7] Haberler wrongly seems to imply that the country must export agricultral goods in this case. There is no reason, *once there is a domestic distortion,* why a country should necessarily export the commodity that is cheaper than abroad in the absence of trade.

FIGURE 1a

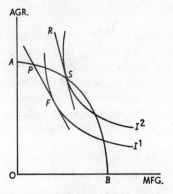

FIGURE 1b

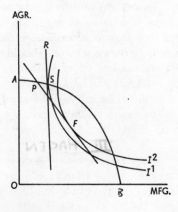

FIGURE 1c

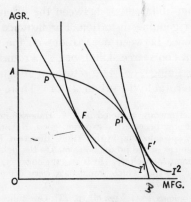

subsidy eliminates the divergence between commodity prices and *DRT* and brings production to P' and consumption to F'.

Case II.   Haberler distinguishes the other case by arguing that the self-sufficiency price ratio *RS* may be less steep than the *given* foreign price ratio *PF*. Here the production point is shifted to the right by free trade.[8] In this case, Haberler argues that "the country would specialize in the 'right' direction but not sufficiently. *It would after trade be better off than before, but it would not reach the optimum point. . . . In that case an export or import subsidy (rather than a tariff) would be indicated.*"[9]

✓   While Haberler is right in arguing that a movement to the right of *S*, when free trade is introduced, will necessarily be beneficial, his conclusion that an export (or import) subsidy is indicated and would be preferable to a tariff is erroneous in every rigorous sense in which it may be understood. First, it cannot be argued that the optimal solution when the policy used is an export (or import) subsidy will be necessarily superior to that when the policy used is a tariff. As argued in Section I, both policies are handicapped as they seek to affect *foreign* trade whereas the distortion is *domestic;* there is no reason why one should necessarily be better than the other. Second, nor can one maintain that an export (or import) subsidy will necessarily exist that will be superior to free trade, just as one cannot maintain that a tariff necessarily will be available that is superior to free trade. Third, the optimum solution again is to impose a tax-cum-subsidy on domestic production.

III HAGEN

Case III.   Hagen on Wage Differentials.   A divergence between *DRT*
✓ and the domestic price ratio, arising from factor-market imperfections in the form of intersectoral wage differentials, has been discussed in relation to trade policy by Hagen. Before we proceed to Hagen's analysis, certain observations concerning the circumstances in which differential remuneration causes a distortion are in order.

The observed wage differentials between the urban and rural sector may *not* represent a genuine distortion. For instance, they may reflect (1) a utility preference between occupations on the part of the wage-earners, or (2) a rent (on scarce skills), or (3) a return on investment in human capital (by training), or (4) a return on investment in the cost of movement (from the rural to the urban sector). There *would* be a distor-

---

[8] This, of course, is erroneous, as noted in n. 7. Haberler implies that under free trade manufactures will now become the exported good. Haberler also describes this case as characterized by specialization in the "right" direction. He is right if, by this, he means that the movement of the production point to the right of S, caused by free trade, will necessarily improve welfare. He is wrong, however, if he means that the commodity exported will be that which would have been exported if the divergence did not exist.

[9] Haberler, "Some Problems . . . ," *op. cit.*, p. 237. Our italics.

tion, however, where the differential is attributable to (5) trade-union intervention, or (6) prestige-cum-humanitarian grounds ("I must pay my man a decent wage") that fix wages at varying levels in different sectors. Two other types of explanations may also be discussed: (7) Hagen argues that the differential occurs in manufacture because this is the advancing sector and growing activities inevitably have to pay higher wages to draw labor away from other industries. While this "dynamic" argument appears to provide support for the distortionary character of the differential, there are difficulties with it. For instance, the fact that a differential has to be maintained to draw labor away may very well be due to the cost of movement.[10] (8) A more substantive argument is that the rural sector affords employment to non-adult members of the family whereas, in the urban sector, the adult alone gets employment (owing to institutional reasons such as factory acts). Hence, to migrate, an adult would need to be compensated for the loss of employment by the non-adult members of his family.[11] If this is the case, there is certainly a market imperfection (assuming that individual preferences rather than collective preferences, expressed in legislation, are relevant) and hence distortion.[12]

In the following analysis, we shall assume that the wage differential represents a genuine distortion while remaining skeptical about the degree to which such distortions obtain in the actual world.[13] We will also adopt Hagen's analytical framework of a two-commodity, two-factor model and a *constant* wage differential. The assumption of constancy of the wage differential raises some difficulties, probably with reasons (3) and (6) but certainly with reason (7), on which Hagen mainly relies. As will be seen presently, Hagen's analysis involves the *contraction* of manufactures after the introduction of trade; if the wage differential is due to the fact that manufactures are expanding and drawing labor away, it should surely reverse itself during the transition from autarky to free trade. The difficulty is that Hagen, in relying upon reason (7) while using traditional trade analysis, is illegitimately superimposing a dynamic argument upon a comparative statics framework. To analyze the distortion arising from

---

[10] Other difficulties also arise when the argument is used in conjunction with a static analysis. These will be discussed later.

[11] This hypothesis was suggested to us by D. Mazumdar.

[12] This "distortion," unlike the others, involves a contraction of the labor force as labor moves from one sector to another. Hence, the following analysis does not apply and a fresh solution, incorporating a changing labor supply, is called for. Note here also that the wage differential variety of distortion is quite distinct from the distortion caused when, although the wage is identical between sectors, it differs from the "shadow" optimal wage. This distinction has been blurred by recent analysts, especially W. A. Lewis, "Economic Development with Unlimited Supplies of Labor," *Manchester School*, Vol. XXII (May, 1959), and H. Myint, "Infant Industry Arguments for Assistance to Industries in the Setting of Dynamic Trade Theory" (paper presented to a conference on "Trade in a Developing World," International Economic Association, September, 1961). Also see Bhagwati, *op. cit.*

[13] A. Kafka, "A New Argument for Protectionism," *Quarterly Journal of Economics,* Vol. LXXVI (February, 1962), pp. 163–66.

reason (8) one needs an explicitly dynamic analysis. Hence, the following analysis applies, strictly speaking, only to distortions produced by reasons (5) and (6).

Hagen concludes that a tariff is superior to free trade when the *importable manufacturing* activity has to pay the higher wage.

> As a result of the wage disparity, manufacturing industry will be undersold by imports when the foreign exchanges are in equilibrium. Protection which permits such industry to exist will increase real income in the economy. However, a subsidy per unit of labour equal to the wage differential will increase real income further, and if combined with free trade will permit attaining an *optimum optimorum*.[14]

FIGURE 2a

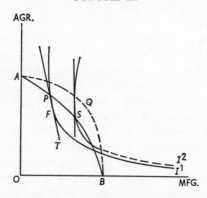

Hagen works successively with two models that differ only in the assumption concerning the number of factors of production. Since the first model has only one factor and is only a special case of the second, two-factor model, we shall concentrate here on the latter. It is assumed that all the standard Paretian conditions obtain except for the wage differential. We begin with Hagen's analysis and then comment on it.

In Figure 2a, *AQB* is the production possibility curve on the assumption of a wage uniform between the two sectors. *APB* is the production possibility curve, assuming the given wage differential.[15] The wage differen-

[14] *Op. cit.*, p. 498. Hagen himself does not state explicitly that he is confining the analysis to the case where the differential operates against the importable activity. If the differential were to work in the contrary direction, the results would naturally have to be modified radically.

[15] The reader can satisfy himself as to the "shrinking in" of the production possibility curve by manipulating the Edgeworth box diagram. The careful reader of Hagen's paper will note that Hagen draws the "shrunk-in" production possibility curve so that it is convex (in the mathematical sense). This, however, is a property that does not necessarily follow from the assumptions made, and it is possible to produce counter-examples of concavity, although we have not been able to produce a general mathematical proof. (When this paper was read at Stanford, Paul David drew attention to A. Fishlow and P. David's "Optimal Resource Allocation in an Imperfect

tial against manufactures, aside from reducing the production feasibilities, will make the commodity price ratio, at any production point on *APB*, steeper than the rate of transformation along *APB* so that the price ratio understates the profitability of transforming agriculture into manufactures. *PT* being the foreign price ratio, the economy produces at *P* and consumes at *F* under free trade. Under self-sufficiency, however, the relative price of manufactures being higher, the economy would produce and consume at *S* and be better off. From this, Hagen concludes: "Protection of manufacturing from foreign trade will increase real income."[16]

However, the conclusion must be rectified. First, as illustrated in Fig-

FIGURE 2b

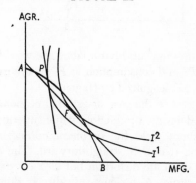

ure 2b, where the contrary possibility is shown, prohibitive protection is not necessarily superior to free trade. Second, it may further be impossible, as argued in Section I, to find any level of tariff (or trade subsidy) that is superior to free trade. Third, a tax-cum-subsidy on the domestic production of the commodities, which eliminates the divergence between the price ratio and *DRT* (along *APB*) would necessarily yield a better solution than protection. In Figure 2c, *F'* represents the consumption and *P'* the production reached by the pursuit of such a tax-cum-subsidy policy.[17]

Market Setting," *Journal of Political Economy*, Vol. LXIX [December, 1961], pp. 529–46, for a proof of this proposition. These writers have also anticipated our criticism concerning Hagen's confusion of statics and dynamics.) We shall use the convex curve, however, as it enables us to state our propositions in terms of equalities and without bothering about second-order conditions; the substance of the propositions *that interest us here* is unaffected by this complication. The divergence between the commodity price ratio and the domestic rate of transformation, which also results from the wage differential, needs a rigorous proof, which can be found by the reader in Hagen, *op. cit.*, pp. 507–8.

[16] Hagen, *op. cit.*, p. 510.

[17] In relation to this point, it is also worth noting that the standard procedure adopted by several tariff commissions, of choosing a tariff rate that just offsets the differential between the average domestic cost at some *arbitrary*, given production of the existing units and the landed (c.i.f.) cost, is not necessarily correct. There is no reason why the tariff rate which just offsets this differential is necessarily the tariff rate which is optimum from the viewpoint of economic policy.

FIGURE 2c

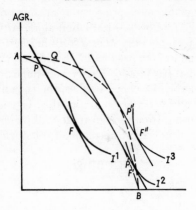

Finally, a policy of tax-cum-subsidy on labor use would achieve equilibrium production at P'' and consumption at F'' in Figure 2c and produce the "first-best" result, as recognized by Hagen.

Note that, in contrast to the case of external economies, the optimum tax-cum-subsidy on domestic production, while superior to protection or trade subsidy, does not yield the *optimum optimorum* in the wage-differential case. The reason is straightforward. The wage differential causes *not merely* a domestic distortion but *also* a restriction of the production possibility curve. A tax-cum-subsidy on domestic production measure will, therefore, merely eliminate the domestic distortion but not restore the economy to the Paretian production possibility curve (AQB). It will thus achieve the equality of FRT and DRS with DRT along *the restricted production possibility curve* (APB) and hence constitute the optimal solution when the wage differential cannot be directly eliminated. Where, however, a direct attack on the wage differential is permitted, the fully optimal, "first-best" solution can be achieved by a policy of tax-cum-subsidy on factor use.

IV. CONCLUSION

We have argued here that an optimum subsidy (or a tax-cum-subsidy equivalent) is necessarily superior to any tariff when the distortion is domestic. It may be questioned, however, whether this advantage would obtain in practice. This question, of course, cannot be settled purely at the economic level. A fully satisfactory treatment of this issue would necessarily involve disciplines ranging from politics to psychology. However, by way of conclusion, we think it would be useful to consider a few arguments that are relevant to the final, realistic choice of policy.

1. The contention that the payment of subsidies would involve the collection of taxes which in practice cannot be levied in a non-distortionary fashion is fallacious. A tax-cum-subsidy scheme could always be devised

that would *both* eliminate the estimated divergence and collect taxes sufficient to pay the subsidies.

2. The estimation problem is also easier with subsidies than with tariffs. The former involves estimating merely the divergence between the commodity price ratio and *DRT* (at the relevant production point). The latter must extend the exercises necessarily to the estimation of the relevant *DRS* (which involves locating both the right level of income *and* the relevant consumption point).

3. The political argument has usually been claimed by free traders to favor the payment of subsidies under external economy arguments like infant industries. It is thought that it would be difficult to pay a subsidy longer than strictly necessary whereas a tariff may be more difficult to abolish. It must be pointed out, however, that this argument also pulls the other way because, precisely for the reasons which make a subsidy difficult to continue, a subsidy is difficult to choose in preference to a tariff.

15. On Making the Best of Balance of

Payments Restrictions on Imports*

By J. MARCUS FLEMING†

PART I—THE THEORY

Introduction

1. The title of this paper very exactly describes its theme. No view is expressed or implied regarding the desirability, or otherwise, from the international standpoint, of the use of import restriction as a short- or medium-term stabiliser of the balance of payments. The fact that the principal stabilising device of the old system—variation in employment, production and incomes—is now generally regarded with disfavour, makes it necessary to lean more heavily on such alternative techniques as remain available, e.g., import restriction, flexible exchange rates, international short-term credit flows of a compensatory type and the use of substantial gold reserves. Economists will differ in the relative emphasis they lay upon the various alternatives. That issue is not examined here. Our theme is a more limited one; given that import restrictions continue to be rather widely employed as a means of meeting medium-term disequilibria in the balance of payments, how would they have to be applied in order to reduce to a minimum their admitted diseconomies?

Assumptions of the Economic Model

2. Assume that import restriction is the only method whereby a country can correct an adverse balance of payments. In each country full employment is maintained, and the level of factor prices is kept stable relative to the levels in other countries—thus excluding deflation and exchange depreciation as methods of restoring balance of payments equilibrium. Export subsidisation or restriction and any kind of manipulation of capital movements are also excluded. Currency reserves are negligible, so that any balance-of-payments disequilibrium has to be at once corrected. All currencies are convertible. Import restrictions, however, can be applied with varying degrees of severity according to commodity and country of origin. Perfect competition prevails within each country, so that the se-

* *Economic Journal,* Vol. LXI, No. 241 (March, 1951), pp. 48–71.

† International Monetary Fund.

verity of any import restriction is reflected in the margin between the price in the importing and that in the exporting country. Commodities exchange internationally at the prices prevailing in the country of export; any margin accrues to the importing country. The export-supply curves and the import-demand curves of the several commodities traded between the several pairs of countries are all given independently of each other and of the actual course of trade. (This assumption is later removed.) Export supply conditions are such as to ensure that any expansion in the demand for a country's exports increases the value as well as the quantity exported. Considerations of space prevent examination of the exceptional cases where these supply conditions do not obtain.

Welfare Conventions

3. It is assumed that there are no external economies of production or consumption, that producers equate value of marginal factor with product price for each factor and product, that consumers secure an equi-marginal return in private utility from all forms of expenditure, and that increments in the general utility or welfare are made up of the sum of the increments of the private utilities of individuals. This allows us henceforward to speak of "utility" without distinguishing whether it is private or general. Finally, it is assumed that the marginal utility of money expenditure is the same for each individual in whatever country he may live; or at least that it is, on the average, the same for those who gain by any given change in the economic situation as for those who lose. This implies that the marginal utility of any commodity to any individual can be measured by the price of that commodity within the country inhabited by the individual in question.

Criteria of "Optimisation" and "Improvement"

4. The problem is to define the characteristics of an optimal structure of restrictions on imports of each commodity into each country from each other country subject to the conditions of the model. In order to do this one has to be able to judge whether the change in the economic situation consequential on any alteration in an assumed initial structure of import restrictions is or is not an improvement.

5. Under the assumed conditions the net gain from any small change in the economic situation can be measured by: (*a*) any increments in output *minus*, (*b*) any increments in input *plus*, (*c*) any increments in goods, services or claims received by an individual *minus*, (*d*) any increments in goods, services or claims supplied by any individual, all such increments being valued at the prices prevailing in the countries inhabited by the firm or individual in question. Most of these items will cancel out. All transfers between individuals in the same country, or between individuals in countries having the same price for the commodity or claim in question (there being no trade barriers between the countries in

that commodity or claim) will count equally as gains and losses. Since we are here concerned with economic changes initiated by shifts in trade barriers, production changes are merely consequential and, since perfect competition prevails, each firm's increments of output will equal in value its increments in input. *The net gain from the whole operation can there-fore be measured by the sum of the increments of international trade in such items as are subject to import restriction, each increment being valued by the margin between the inland price in the importing country and that in the exporting country.* This margin will vary with the degree of restriction currently applied to the imports in question and will equal the specific import duty corresponding to that degree of restriction.[1]

6. The structure of import restrictions may be deemed optimal when no change in international trade quantities, capable of being brought about by a change in that structure, will yield a net gain by the above criterion. It is possible to define the characteristics of an optimal structure by considering a limited number of types of changes in international trade quantities or, as we shall call them, "trade adjustments."

Types of Equilibrated Trade Adjustment

7. Starting from an initial position in which each country is in balance-of-payments equilibrium with the others taken as a group, but only because some or all countries are applying restrictions on imports, consider the following types of adjustment, each of which is so applied as to leave each country's overall balance of payments unchanged.

a) A change in a certain country's import of a certain commodity and a change of opposite sign in its import of a second commodity, both from the same exporting country.

b) A change in a certain country's import of a certain commodity from a second country and a change of the same sign in the second country's import of a second commodity from the first country.

c) A change in a certain country's import of a certain commodity from a second country, a change of the same sign in second country's import of a second commodity from the third country and a change of the same sign in the third country's import of a third commodity from the first country.

d) A change in a certain country's import of a certain commodity from a second country, a change of the same sign in the second country's import of a second commodity from a third country and a change of opposite sign in the first country's import of a third commodity from the third country.

---

[1] This amounts to defining an improvement as any change which increases the value of world output less the value of world input at constant market prices. An alternative definition would have been "any change the gainers from which could (though they do not) over-compensate the losers." Where, as in the case examined here, the economic model is such that the payment or non-payment of compensation in itself affects real world output these criteria diverge. I hope to discuss the relative merits of the two criteria in such cases in a future paper.

Type (*a*) Adjustments (Unilateral)

8. Suppose that B's restrictions on imports of *m* from A are relaxed, while those on imports of *n* from A are intensified in such a way as to preserve unchanged any initial inequality of payments between A and B. The rise in the cost (at A prices) of imports of *m* must balance the fall in cost of imports of *n*. The gain, if any, from the adjustment is measured by the rise in imports of *m*, weighted by the margin between B prices and A prices of *m*, *less* the fall in imports of *n*, weighed by the price margin of *n*. There will be a net gain only if the ratio of *m*'s price margin to *n*'s price margin is higher than the rate at which imports of *n* fall as those of *m* rise. But the price margins of *m* and *n* depend on the severity of B's restrictions on imports of *m* and *n* respectively and the rate at which imports of *n* fall as those of *m* rise depends on the elasticities of supply from A to B of *n* and *m* respectively.

9. At this point it is convenient to introduce the notion of "responsiveness of supply" by which is meant the ratio of the proportionate increase in quantity sold to the proportionate increase in the seller's money receipts. "Responsiveness of supply" as thus defined is, of course, a function of the elasticity of supply with respect to price. Now, reverting to our example, the adjustment described will yield a net gain if, but only if, the ratio of the *ad valorem* tariff-equivalent of the import restriction on *m* to that of the import restriction on *n* exceeds the ratio of the responsiveness of supply (from A to B) of *n* to that of *m*. (In what follows, the expression "the 'tariff'" is used to signify "the tariff-equivalent of the import restriction.") The situation will be incapable of improvement by Type (*a*) adjustments when the ratio of the percentage "tariffs" on any pair of commodities imported by any country from any other country equals the reciprocal of the ratio of the corresponding export supply responsiveness.[2]

Type (*b*) Adjustments (Bilateral)

10. Suppose that A's restrictions on imports of *p* from B, and B's restrictions on imports of *q* from A are both relaxed in such a way as to leave unaffected A's balance of payments with B.

11. The mutual relaxation of import restrictions will give rise to an increase both in the value and in the volume of the exports both of *p* and *q*. So long as the price of each of these commodities in the importing country exceeds its price in the exporting country, i.e., so long as import restrictions are in force in both cases, the adjustment must, according to our criterion of meliorisation, be beneficial. The mutual relaxation of import restrictions can therefore be continued with advantage up to the point at which one or other of the commodities is being imported entirely without restriction. At this point, according to the conditions of our model,

---

[2] See Appendix, paragraph 1, page 258.

the adjustment must stop (though if import subsidisation had been permitted, it could have proceeded farther with advantage).

Type (c) Adjustments (Trilateral)

12. Suppose that A relaxes restrictions on imports of r from C, B relaxes restrictions on imports of s from A and C relaxes restrictions on imports of t from B in such a way as to leave unchanged the balance-of-payments surplus or deficit of each country *vis-à-vis* the other pair. There will ensue an expansion in the value and volume of exports of r, s and t which can continue with advantage up to the point at which one of the three commodities—say t—is being imported without restriction. At this point, according to the conditions of our model, the adjustment must stop.

Type (d) Adjustments (Trilateral)

13. Suppose that C intensifies restrictions on imports of x from A, and relaxes restrictions on imports of y from B, while B relaxes restrictions on imports of z from A, in such a way as to leave unchanged the balance-of-payments surplus or deficit of each country *vis-à-vis* the remaining pair taken together. This implies that the decline in value of C's imports of x must equal the increase in value of its imports of y, which in turn must equal the increase in value of B's imports of z. Starting from a point at which C's "tariff" on x is negligible, this type of adjustment can be carried either to a point at which it is abruptly brought to a stop by the disappearance of all import restrictions in B on z or in C on y, or to a point at which, thanks to the decline in B's "tariff" on z and C's "tariff" on y, and the increase in C's "tariff" on x, it ceases to show a net advantage. This optimal point will be attained when C's percentage "tariff" on x *times* the responsiveness of supply of x from A to C, *equals* C's percentage "tariff" on y times the responsiveness of supply of y from B to C, *plus* B's percentage "tariff" on z *times* the responsiveness of supply of z from A to B.[3]

Optimal Structure of Import Restrictions

14. By combining advantageous adjustments of Types (a) and (b), applying them to all commodities traded between all pairs of countries, and pushing them to the point of maximum advantage, we reach a situation in which in each pair of countries one country is importing all commodities from the other without restriction, while the second country is imposing on commodities imported from the first percentage "tariffs" inversely proportional to the corresponding responsivenesses of export supply.

15. By proceeding similarly, in addition, with advantageous adjustments of Types (c) and (d), and by pursuing the practice, whenever ad-

---

[3] See Appendix, paragraph 2, page 258.

vantageous adjustments are checked by the elimination of one country's restrictions on imports from another, of initiating a new set of adjustments involving the restriction of the second country's imports from the first, it is always possible to arrive at a situation of the following kind. *All countries are ranged in an order, which we may term an order of "strength," such that: (i) each country is importing freely from countries "weaker" than itself and restricting imports of all commodities from countries "stronger" than itself; (ii) the percentage "tariffs" imposed by any country on the various commodities imported from any "stronger" country are inversely proportional to the corresponding export supply responsivenesses; (iii) as between any three countries, the "weak" country will be imposing on any commodity imported from the "strong" country a percentage "tariff" which, when multiplied by the corresponding export supply responsiveness, will equal the sum of (a) the percentage "tariff" which it imposes on any commodity imported from the "intermediate" country, times the corresponding export supply responsiveness, and (b) the percentage "tariff" which the "intermediate" country imposes on any commodity imported from the "strong" country, times the corresponding export-supply responsiveness.*

16. Where all export-supply responsivenesses are equal each country should impose on all commodities imported from each "stronger" country a uniform percentage "tariff" equal to the sum of the percentage "tariffs" applied by itself and by each "intermediate" country on imports from the country immediately superior in order of "strength."

17. It could probably be demonstrated mathematically, given the relevant demand and supply conditions, that only one order of countries will satisfy the criteria set forth in paragraph 15 above, i.e., that any situation satisfying these criteria is not merely a "local" optimum but the absolute optimum subject to the conditions of the model. For suppose that, starting from a position which satisfies the criteria, a country is "promoted" to a higher place in the order over the heads of a number of other countries. The "promoted" country will have to remove any restrictions on imports from the "demoted" countries, while the latter will impose some restrictions on imports from the "promoted" country. Moreover, all countries of lower order will intensify their restrictions on imports from the "promoted" country relative to the restrictions on imports from the "demoted" countries. It seems impossible that both the "promoted" and the "demoted" countries will, under these conditions, maintain their overall balance-of-payments positions unchanged. The "promotion" will therefore not be permissible.

18. No advantage will be gained by proceeding to consider adjustments between four or more countries. Quadrilateral and multilateral adjustments can be resolved into a combination of notional trilateral adjustments of the kind already described, and can yield no improvement over the position already defined.

Inter-trade Repercussions

19. We must now consider to what extent the results so far attained will be affected by the removal of the simplifying assumption of paragraph 2 that each of the relevant export-supply curves and import-demand curves is unaffected by the volume of imports or exports in other commodities or with other countries.

20. The most important for our purpose of the possible interrelationships between particular trades are the following:

- (*i*) an increased export of a particular commodity from one country to another may raise the supply curves of other commodities exported by the first country to the second particularly in the short run;
- (*ii*) increased exports from one country to a second may raise the supply curves of exports from the first country to third countries, particularly of the same commodities, and particularly in the short run;
- (*iii*) increased imports by one country from a second country will tend to reduce the demand curves in the first country for imports from third countries, particularly imports of the same commodities.

Effect of Inter-trade Repercussions on the Optimal Structure of Import Restrictions

21. Repercussion (*i*) affects the optimal relative "tariffs" imposed by any one country on the various commodities imported from another. Any commodity which is highly substitutible in the export country for other commodities exported to the same importing country should be restricted more severely by the latter than its supply responsiveness would otherwise warrant. This will tend to make optimal relative percentage "tariffs" on different commodities imported from the same country more nearly equal than on the assumption of independent supply curves.

22. Repercussions (*ii*) and (*iii*) affect the desirability of carrying mutual trade between each pair of countries to the point at which only one of the two is restricting imports from the other. Suppose there are only three countries, A, B and C, ranged in that order, between which prevails a system of import restrictions of the type described in paragraph 15. A and B begin to restrict imports from each other without altering the initial inequality in their bilateral balance of payments. Can this be advantageous? Both A and B will tend, in accordance with (*iii*), to take additional imports from C in substitution for each other's products. Moreover, in accordance with (*ii*), the contraction in A's and B's mutual exports should tend to lower the supply prices of their exports to C. C will then be able to increase its imports from A and B without detriment to its balance of payments.

23. Up to a point the advantage of the expansion in C's imports from A and B might outweigh the disadvantage of the contraction of B's imports from A and also—though for small adjustments this is unimportant—

the contraction of A's imports from B. In the longer-run, however, the effects of (*ii*) will become negligible, and a contraction of A's and B's mutual trade, though justifiable in the short run, might well be unjustifiable in the long run.

24. Suppose, now, that starting from the position described in paragraph 15, countries B and C begin to contract their mutual imports while leaving their bilateral balance of payments unaltered. This will *not* lead automatically to any reduction in imports from A, since B's and C's imports from A are determined by their balance-of-payments position *vis-à-vis* A. It will, however, in the short-run at any rate, probably lead to a decline in the supply prices of B's and C's exports respectively to A. Everything now depends on the elasticity of demand in A for imports from B and C respectively. If, as will normally be the case, this elasticity is in both cases higher than unity, A will *increase* its expenditure on imports from B and C, which will therefore be in a position to expand their imports from A.

25. This operation will be advantageous only if the additional imports into C and B from A outweigh the fall in B's and C's mutual imports. It is clearly much less likely to be advantageous than the mutual restriction of imports between A and B previously considered. Import diversion plays no part in it. The effect of export diversion is indirect and is unlikely to be as beneficial as was export diversion in the case previously considered unless A's elasticity of demand for imports from B and C is at least 2. In the long-run, this elasticity of demand may well be substantially higher than 2, but by that time the fall in B's and C's export-supply prices, resulting from their mutual contraction of trade, may have become negligible. It therefore seems most unlikely that any mutual restriction of imports by B and C will prove to be advantageous. The same applies, in even greater measure, to a mutual restriction of imports between A and C.

26. Consider now the effect of inter-trade repercussions on the optimum for trilateral adjustments as previously established. Start once more with countries, A, B, C in that order of strength, with a structure of import restrictions as described in paragraph 15. Suppose that C imports more from A and less from B, thus forcing B to import less from A. A *small* trade adjustment of this sort, which leaves undisturbed each country's balance of payments with the other two combined, would, in the absence of the repercussions discussed below, have a negligible effect on welfare. Now the fall in B's imports from A will lead to an expansion in B's imports from C [repercussion (*iii*)] so that the fall of C's imports from B need no longer be so great in value as the rise of her imports from A. Moreover, the fall in B's exports to C may lead, in the short run, to a fall in the supply price of B's exports to A [repercussion (*ii*)] *and* (if A's demand is of more than unit elasticity) to an increase in B's export receipts from A, so that the fall in B's imports from A need no longer be as great in value as the fall of C's imports from B. These mitigations in the fall of C's imports

from B, and of B's imports from A, constitute, for small adjustments, a net advantage. An extension of such an adjustment, however, as it got farther from the position defined in paragraph 15 would create disadvantages which would, after a point, outweigh the advantages just mentioned.

27. To sum up, the examination of inter-trade repercussions alters our conception of an optimal structure of import barriers from that arrived at on the assumption of the independence of demand and supply curves,

   a) by mitigating the degree of inter-commodity discrimination in the restrictions to be imposed by any country on imports from a second country;
   b) by indicating a possible but doubtful advantage in some degree of mutual import restriction as between relatively "strong" countries, and
   c) by reducing the degree of preference to be given by "weaker" countries to imports from "intermediate" countries over imports from "stronger" countries.

PART II—THE THEORY APPLIED

28. Let us now examine to what extent various existing, projected, or possible trade-and-payments arrangements satisfy the requirements of an optimal structure so set forth in Part I.

Nondiscriminatory Import Restriction

29. Consider, first, the system under which balance-of-payments import restrictions are applied in a nondiscriminatory manner, so as to be equivalent to a uniform tariff *vis-à-vis* all supplying countries. If, as was assumed in Part I, all currencies were fully convertible, each country, in so far as it acted unilaterally without exchanging concessions with other countries, and without taking account of their supply elasticities or other indirect repercussions, would have an incentive to apply its import restrictions in this way.

30. In a world in which exchange rates or internal money cost levels were sufficiently flexible to dispense with the necessity for balance-of-payments restrictions on imports, the principle of nondiscrimination would undoubtedly be the right one. But, under the conditions of our model, which have to a considerable extent prevailed in reality in the postwar period, any system constructed on this principle would operate in a most unsatisfactory way. Starting from the supposition that, in the absence of import restrictions, one set of countries would be in balance-of-payments surplus and another set in deficit, imagine that the deficit countries seek to restore equilibrium in their external accounts by nondiscriminatory restrictions on imports from all other countries, including each other. Not merely will these restrictions reduce the export income of the original deficit countries and force them to intensify their restrictions, but they will also transform countries originally in approximate balance into deficit countries, and force them, in turn, to apply import re-

strictions. If nondiscriminatory import restrictions were the only way of correcting disequilibria, this process would continue until every country but one was applying import restrictions of a greater or lesser degree of severity.

31. Clearly, such a situation is very far removed from that described in paragraph 15 as optimal. Each country, other than the "strongest" country, will be withholding from each other country goods less valuable to itself than those which it could have obtained in exchange. "Strong" countries will be restricting imports from "weak" countries, thus enforcing unnecessary hardships on the latter without benefit to themselves. "Weak" countries will be giving no preference to imports from "intermediate" countries over imports from "strong" countries, thus imposing on "intermediate" countries a sacrifice which outweighs the benefit which they themselves derive from buying in the cheapest market.

Bilateral Balancing of Payments

32. Compared with this the regime of trade-and-payments bilateralism, which limited currency convertibility, as practised in Europe and South America since the war, has considerable advantages. Under such a regime payments between a pair of countries, or "monetary areas," are canalised ultimately through the two central banks concerned and, after offsetting, eventuate in a net addition to or subtraction from the balance held by one of the control banks with the other. If one of the pair has a continuing balance-of-payments surplus with the other, it accumulates in the other's currency a balance which it can use only if it can transform its surplus with the other into a deficit.

33. Such an arrangement gives each country an incentive to expand imports from the other, and particularly the surplus country from the deficit country, and thus tends to favour a bilateral expansion of trade, of the type discussed in paragraph 11, to the point at which one of the two countries has abandoned all balance-of-payments restrictions on imports from the other.

Mitigations of Bilateralism

34. The weakness of trade-and-payments bilateralism, of course, is in its failure to take advantage of trilateral adjustments, i.e., its tendency to eliminate or unduly to reduce bilateral surpluses and deficits. There are, however, three channels through which a measure of trade-and-payments multilateralism is frequently achieved within the general framework of the bilateral system:

(i) The existence of substantial or indefinite credit margins under bilateral agreements permits a—sometimes considerable—departure from strict bilateral balancing of payments. A country may be running a deficit with a second country, and a surplus with a third, both financed out of bilateral credit. Where, however, there is a persistent imbalance in bilateral accounts, the surplus country will probably seek to impose limits on the credit which it provides.

(*ii*) If a substantial proportion of a country's exports consist of "essentials" or "dollar-worthy" items it may succeed in maintaining bilateral surpluses without giving credit, by inducing its bilateral trading partners to settle their deficits in gold or hard currency. The second country, however, will desire, in these circumstances, to impose on imports from the first country restrictions which, if the first country is, from the "world" standpoint, relatively "weak" may be far more severe than is appropriate according to our formula. In practice, however, the second country may be deterred from applying the criterion of "dollar essentiality" to its purchases from the first country by fear that the latter may retaliate by ceasing to import freely from the former.

(*iii*) Under an arrangement which has assumed particular importance in connection with the use of sterling a country may permit the transfer of balances in its currency from holders resident in a second country to holders resident in a third country. The first country is likely to offer this facility provided that the currency of the second country is at least as scarce to it as that of the third country; the second country is likely to make the transfer provided that the currency of the third country is at least as scarce to it as that of the first country; and the third country is likely to accept the transfer provided that the currency of the first country is at least as scarce to it as that of the second country. In this connection the "scarcity" of a country's currency may be measured by the severity of the restrictions which it is necessary, on balance-of-payments grounds, to impose on imports from that country.

35. This device of "selective transferability" if fully exploited would enable all possible trilateral adjustments of Type (*c*), as defined in paragraph 12, to take place. Whenever country B is restricting imports from country A, country C from country B and country A from country C an expansion of exports from A to B, B to C and C to A will normally be advantageous to each of the countries concerned. The whole operation can be carried out in A-currency (with A allowing its transfer from C to B), in B-currency (with B allowing its transfer from A to C) or in C-currency (with C allowing its transfer from B to A).

36. Transferability of this kind will also enable trilateral adjustments of Type (*d*) to be carried to a certain point, though somewhat short of the optimum. Suppose, to start from the example in the previous paragraph, that the adjustment of Type (*c*) is brought to an end by the elimination of A's barriers against imports from C. Then C will probably find it worth while to start restricting imports from A if it is allowed to use its earnings of A-currency to purchase additional imports from B. B will be glad to accept A-currency, which will enable it to obtain additional imports from A. A will probably consent to the transfer of its currency from C to B, which will leave its aggregate exports and importing power unaffected;

unless, indeed, it had hoped to extract from B gold or some currency scarcer than its own. If we can assume that A will not withhold its consent to the transfer for the sake of earning scarce currency from countries "weaker" than itself, the Type (d) operation just described will continue to the point at which C is restricting imports from A as severely as from B.

37. As a result of selective transferability then, we might arrive at a situation in which countries are ranged in an unambiguous order of "strength" and "weakness" in which each country will have practically eliminated restrictions against imports from all countries "weaker" than itself, and in which each country, in restricting imports from countries "stronger" than itself, will restrict imports from a relatively "strong" supplier *at least* as severely as those from an "intermediate" supplier. This not unsatisfactory result is, however, dependent on relatively "strong" countries refraining from either restricting imports from, or refusing transfers to, relatively "weak" countries for the sake of earning gold or scarce currencies from them. In the post-war period countries have in fact refrained to a surprising extent from exercising their power to extract gold from bilateral debtors.

Group Discrimination Based on International Planning

38. Dissatisfaction with the contrasted evils of non-discriminatory restriction and of pure bilateralism has led to attempts to devise arrangements which would promote a modulated group discrimination of a desirable kind. The most intellectually audacious attempts of this sort are those by Professor Frisch in his articles "On the Need for Forecasting a Multilateral Balance of Payments" in the *American Economic Review* of September, 1947 and "The Problem of Multicompensatory Trade" in the *Review of Economics and Statistics* of November, 1948.

39. In the former article Frisch proposes:

   a) that information should be collected regarding the amounts of goods and services which countries would be able and willing to exchange with each other;

   b) that this information should be arranged in "matrices," i.e., square tables in which the columns show the amounts (in value terms) which particular importing countries would import from the various exporting countries, and the rows show the amounts which particular exporting countries would export to the various importing countries;

   c) that some international authority (e.g., the I.T.O.) should attempt, both by recommendatory and permissive action, to ensure that such cutting down in the various elements of this matrix of potential trade as is necessary to bring balance-of-payments surpluses and deficits within the limits permitted by international lending is carried out in such a way as to maximise the quantum of international trade.

40. This scheme is open to objection on grounds both of principle and practicability. It takes account only of the *quantum* of international

trade and neglects its *quality*—as measured by the (proportionate) margin between the price of the goods in question in the importing country and their price in the exporting country. The result is that no matter how essential may be the goods which a "weak" country imports from a "strong" country, the weak country must practically always be prepared to restrict them further if there is some intermediate country from which it can then expand its imports by an equal amount, thus enabling the latter in turn to expand imports from a "strong" country.[4] It is extremely doubtful whether the results of such a maximisation process would be preferable to the results of ordinary bilateralism qualified by "selective transferability" of currencies.

41. The practical difficulties are those of:

a) arriving at a matrix of potential trade, the elements of which are: (*i*) agreed between the importing and the exporting country and (*ii*) forecast with reasonable accuracy; and

b) inducing the countries concerned to take the action deemed desirable by the international authority.

42. The problem of providing an incentive to countries to implement an "optimal" structure of import restrictions arises, of course, whatever the principles on which the structure is designed. Where, as here, the pattern of trade is planned in quantitative terms, and if countries are unwilling to regulate their every import at the behest of an international authority, consideration might be given to a technique employed by the O.E.E.C., viz. the extension of drawing-rights on a bilateral basis. A "drawing-right" is a grant in the donor's more or less inconvertible currency and hence available for the purchase of only such imports as are normally purchasable with that currency. Since the right is liable to lapse or lose its value at the end of a stated period, the recipient has a strong incentive to develop a balance-of-payments deficit *vis-à-vis* the donor of an amount corresponding to the size of the grant. In the past this technique has been used in connection with the provision of United States aid to Europe. It could, however, be used as a method of implementing a planned pattern of bilateral surpluses and deficits without any country being on balance a donor or a recipient, i.e., each country would receive as large a sum in drawing rights from some countries as it extended to others. Of course, even this technique merely shifts the problem of incentive back one stage, since countries have to be induced to accept the pattern of drawing rights assigned to them.

43. A further difficulty about any attempt to bring about an optimal structure of import restrictions by quantitative planning is that the characteristics of an optimal structure of import restrictions set forth in paragraph 15 can be translated into quantitative terms only by making very

---

[4] This is what is implied in the priority which Frisch gives to "first-order" over "second-order" adjustments.

artificial assumptions about elasticities of import demand and export sup-ply. On the assumption that all export elasticities are infinite and all import elasticities equal and starting from an estimated trade pattern corresponding to universal free imports, each country would have to cut down its imports from each country stronger than itself by a proportion equal to the sum of the proportionate reductions imposed by any intermediate country on imports from the strong country and by the weak country on imports from the intermediate country.

Frisch's Multi-compensatory Trade System

44. In the second article referred to in paragraph 15, Frisch makes new proposals which purport to take account of the "quality" as well as of the quantity of trade. The essence of his scheme is as follows:

a) all trade to be subject to import licence:
b) all licence applications to be assigned a priority number (ranging from 9 to 0) by the exporting country and a priority number by the importing country and to be submitted for final approval to an International Bureau of Compensation;
c) the Compensation Bureau to approve or disapprove applications in such a way as to satisfy certain criteria.

45. The first criterion is that the value of each country's imports should equal the value of its exports (with a predetermined deviation). The second criterion is not very clearly formulated. After considering a number of alternatives Frisch concludes:

A plausible principle seems to be simply to put up as a goal the maximisation of the global surplus, i.e., the maximisation of the priority sum for import *minus* the priority sum for exports, both taken as a total for all countries, the figures for each country being normalised, so as to let only the relative, and not the absolute, magnitudes of the priority numbers influence the result.

The "priority sum" for imports (or exports) is the sum of the products of the import (or export) priority numbers *times* the value of the imports (or exports) falling within the corresponding priority class. Frisch illustrates this principle by a mathematical formula, which however, seems scarcely to correspond with the verbal description. According to the formula, what is to be maximised is the product of two terms, one of which is the aggregate value (at given prices) of the permitted trade, and the other is the sum of each country's "surplus" (as defined in the quotation above) expressed as a proportion of its "priority sum" for imports.[5]

46. The Frischian concepts cannot be compared with the formulæ developed earlier in this article unless the principles governments are to follow in assigning priority numbers to imports and exports are spe-

---

[5] See Appendix, paragraph 3, page 259.

cifically laid down and expressed in terms of market prices. Thus a given priority number (whether on imports or exports) might represent a given proportional excess of the value of the good in question in the internal market over its value in the international market. On this interpretation the appropriate criterion would be that of maximising the "global surplus," i.e., maximising the excess of the priority sum for imports over the priority sum for exports—prices and priority numbers both being treated as constants. Bearing in mind that, on the assumptions of my system, export subsidisation is not permitted and hence the priority number on exports must always be zero, this maximisation criterion is identical with the optimisation criterion employed elsewhere in this article.

47. Frisch's own verbal formulation appears to be vitiated by the "normalisation" procedure. This aims at preventing countries from gaining any advantage by manipulating the levels of their priority numbers, but could achieve this only by depriving the "weaker" countries of the benefit of the preference to which they are entitled in export competition with the "stronger" countries. Frisch's mathematical formula, on the other hand, reduces, when export priority numbers are taken as equal to zero, to the maximisation of the quantum of aggregate trade which is open, as shown in paragraph 40, to quite the opposite objection.

48. I take on trust Frisch's assurance that it is mathematically possible for the Compensation Bureau to tailor the import-licence applications originally submitted so as to satisfy both the balance-of-payments conditions and the maximisation criterion—and I assume this remains true when my criterion is substituted for his. Even so, the scheme is fraught with what are I fear overwhelming practical difficulties.

The Clearing Union Approach: International Control of National Import Duties

a) Variant One. 49. The methods so far discussed for bringing into effect an optimal structure of import restrictions have involved the regulation of trade as a quantitative basis. But the criteria for such an optimal structure are expressed in terms of rates of import duty having equivalent effect to the import restrictions in question, and it would be possible to get a much closer approximation to the ideal if import restrictions imposed for balance-of-payments reasons took the form of actual import duties. Schemes whereby such duties would be internationally controlled in the light of ideal criteria are most naturally conceived in the institutional framework of a clearing union, of the type, for example, of the recently founded European Payments Union.

50. In such a Union all surpluses and deficits arising out of bilateral payments arrangements are submitted periodically for offsetting, and the net deficits and surpluses thus accruing are settled by adjusting the accounts which each country keeps with the Union. Persistent net creditors accumulate credit balances, and persistent net debtors accumulate debit

balances on the Union's books. Suppose that all countries are members of a Union of this type and that to each country is assigned a quota, proportional to the value of its external trade. Defining a country's "normalised balance" as its balance, positive or negative, with the Union divided by its quota, it might be laid down that to each size of normalised balance should correspond a certain "basic percentage" which will be negative, zero, or positive according as the balance is negative, zero, or positive, and which should vary with the size of the "normalised balance," though not necessarily in proportion thereto. Countries would be deemed "stronger" or "weaker" according as their "basic percentages" were more or less positive. Now each country would be required:

a) to import without balance-of-payments restriction or import duty from any country "weaker" than, or equally "strong" with, itself;

b) to impose on imports from any country "stronger" than itself a percentage duty equal to the "basic percentage" of the country from which it is importing *less* its own "basic percentage."

51. In order to avoid constant fluctuation in import duties it would be expedient that basic percentages should vary with normalised balances only at discrete intervals. Thus to each basic percentage would correspond a certain "tranche" of credit which a country would have to run through before its "basic percentage" would be altered. Under this scheme a structure of import duties would be established corresponding roughly to the optimal criterion in paragraph 15, but making no allowance for differences in the responsiveness of supply of exports or for inter-trade repercussions. Short-term fluctuations in the balance of payments would be covered by the use of Union credit. Somewhat longer-term disequilibria, if not covered by international capital movements outside the Union, would be corrected by alterations in the structure of import duties.

52. Nothing has been said about any limits to the extent to which a country should be allowed to incur indebtedness to the Union. To set rigid limits would make it difficult to keep extreme net debtors within the system and would deprive the Union of its principal sanction for inducing "weak" countries to apply the desired degree of discrimination in favor of intermediate countries. Unlimited credit facilities would deprive the "weak" countries of any incentive to live within their means by the imposing of import duties appropriate to their position in the scale of "strong" and "weak" countries. The best solution might be to give the Union power to withhold further credit from countries which decline to adjust their import duties to the appropriate levels.

b) *Variant Two.*   53. To deny access to the resources of the Union is, however, something of a blunt instrument, and one which it would be difficult to apply to a country in a net creditor position in the Union. A more refined incentive to apply the correct degree of discrimination might be supplied by the following variant of the scheme outlined above.

54. For each country there would be a special rate called the "rate of equivalence" between its own currency and the unit of account in terms of which members' balances with the clearing union are expressed. Each country's rate of equivalence (expressed as a proportion of its par of exchange in clearing units) would rise or fall with the state of its "normalised balance" in a way rather similar to that previously described for the "basic percentage." When neither in debt nor in credit with the Union, a country's "equivalence" would be equal to unity.

55. While payments and receipts between countries would continue to be netted bilaterally at par, the equivalences would be used for turning net bilateral surpluses and deficits into clearing units for the purpose of multilateral offsetting as follows. Surpluses and deficits incurred by a country *vis-à-vis* "weaker" or equally "strong" countries would be converted into clearing units at the first country's own rate of equivalence. Surpluses or deficits incurred *vis-à-vis* "stronger" countries would be converted into clearing units at the rate of equivalence of the "stronger" country. Each country would be required to impose a percentage duty on imports from each "stronger" country equal to the proportionate excess of the "stronger" country's equivalence over that of the importing country.[6] Countries will have some incentive to apply the degree of import-discrimination required by this system in that it corresponds to the relative exchange rates actually effective for *marginal* transactions with the countries concerned.

The Clearing Union Approach, Combined with Quantitative Import Restrictions

56. Systems of the sort discussed in the last seven paragraphs, are, of course, far from being practical politics at the present time. Import duties are frequently bound under international trade agreements and in any event governments are reluctant to use them in defence of the balance of payments because of (*a*) the difficulty of anticipating their precise effects on that balance, (*b*) inflexibility resulting from parliamentary control over taxation and (*c*) their effect in raising the internal prices of imported goods. Quantitative restriction of imports by means of quotas and individual licensing is more convenient from all these standpoints, though in respect of the last point, its superiority depends on its being buttressed by internal price control and rationing.

57. An attempt might be made to use the clearing union device—for example, the system of variable "equivalence" described above—not to control import duties but merely to provide governments with an incentive to apply quantitative import restrictions with the right degree of severity and discrimination. The system, however, can provide the incentives for an appropriate discrimination only if countries are induced, by their

---

[6] See Appendix, paragraph 4, page 259.

shortage of clearing units to apply import restrictions of an adequate overall severity; and it would be very difficult for the Union management to determine whether a country's import restrictions were in fact falling so far short of the appropriate degree of severity as to warrant the denial of further access to the Union's resources.

The Question of Fundamental Disequilibrium

58. Any scheme for making the best of import restrictions involving as it must systematic discrimination in favour of "weak" countries, is open to the objection that it reduces the incentive to such countries to remedy (e.g., by the adjustment of exchange rates) what may be a fundamental disequilibrium. Recognition that this is so may well deter "stronger" countries from co-operating in building up the type of structure of import restrictions which would be optimal at current exchange rates. Yet it would be a pity if long-run adjustment could be secured only at the price of short-run frustration and waste.

59. The question therefore arises whether procedures for correcting fundamental disequilibrium could not be grafted on to the arrangements for ensuring that such import restrictions as are at any time necessary are applied with an optimal degree of discrimination. If some practicable system on clearing union lines could be devised for the latter purpose, it might also be made to serve the former. Countries which, in spite of the application of severe import restrictions, remain persistent net debtors are clearly marked out for devaluation, while persistent net creditors are equally clearly marked out for revaluation. Against the former at any rate, means of coercion lie to hand in the withdrawal both of credit facilities and of the preferential treatment hitherto accorded to their exports.

Conclusion

60. None of the arrangements examined in Part II of this paper have attempted to carry into effect *all* the features of an optimal system of import restrictions. They have in general ignored the desirability of adjusting the severity of import restrictions to the responsiveness of export supply of the commodities in question, and they have ignored the refinements rendered desirable by inter-trade repercussions. The system of bilateral agreements modified by selective currency transferability probably takes more account of these factors than the more formal multilateral arrangements subsequently examined.

61. The principal features of an optimal structure, however—the ordering of countries according to "strength" with free imports from "weaker" countries, and preference for "intermediate" over "strong" countries—are reproduced in all the schemes considered: (*i*) bilateralism *plus* selective transferability; (*ii*) international trade planning; (*iii*) Frisch's multi-compensatory system; and (*iv*) the various variants of the clearing union approach. My own preference is for schemes of type (*i*), as the most

practicable, and of type (*iv*), as the nearest approximation to the ideal. I have no illusions as to the immediate practicability of the various clearing union schemes suggested, culminating as they do in a streamlined I.M.F. *cum* I.T.O., but think it possible that some of the features roughly sketched in here may find a place in the international monetary and commercial system of the future—unless, indeed, that system is based on a much more continuous adjustment of exchange rates than has been assumed in the preparation of this paper.

MATHEMATICAL APPENDIX

1. Let—

q_m, q_n denote the quantity of m, n respectively imported by B from A.

$p_{m, \text{A}}, p_{m, \text{B}}$ denote the price of m in A and in B respectively.

$E = \dfrac{dq}{dp}\dfrac{p}{q}$ denote "elasticity of supply."

$R = \dfrac{dq}{d(pq)}\dfrac{pq}{q} = \dfrac{1}{1+\dfrac{1}{E}}$ denote "responsiveness of supply."

$T_m = \dfrac{p_{m,\,\text{B}} - p_{m,\,\text{A}}}{p_{m,\,\text{A}}}$ denote the *ad valorem* tariff equivalent restrictions in B on imports of m from A.

G denote the gain in welfare from the trade adjustment in question.

Then

$$G = p_{m,\text{A}}\, T_m\, \delta q_m + p_{n,\text{A}}\, T_n\, \delta q_n.$$

But the balance of payments must not be altered.

Therefore

$$\delta(p_{m,\text{A}}\, q_m) + \delta(p_{n,\text{A}}\, q_n) = 0$$

and

$$G = p_{m,\text{A}}\, \delta q_m \left(T_m - \frac{R_n}{R_m}\, T_n \right)$$

at the optimal point $G = 0$ and

$$\frac{T_m}{T_n} = \frac{R_n}{R_m}.$$

2. Adopting the same notation *mutatis mutandis* as in paragraph 1.

$$G = p_{x,\text{A}}\, T_x\, \delta q_x + p_{y,\text{B}}\, T_y\, \delta q_y + p_{z,\text{A}}\, T_z\, \delta q_z.$$

The balance-of-payments conditions are:

$$-\delta(p_{x,\text{A}}\, q_x) = \delta(p_{y,\text{B}}\, q_y) = \delta(p_{z,\text{A}}\, q_\text{A}).$$

Then

$$G = p_{x,\text{A}}\, \delta q_x \left(T_x - \frac{R_y}{R_x}\, T_y - \frac{R_z}{R_x}\, T_z \right).$$

The optimal point will be attained when

$$R_x T_x = R_y T_y + R_z T_z.$$

3. Frisch (*Review of Economics and Statistics*, November 1948) suggests maximising the following expression

$$(A_1 + A_2 + \ldots + A_n) \sum_{i=1}^{n} \frac{(1B_i^1 + 2B_i^2 + \ldots) - (1A_i^1 + 2A_i^2 + \ldots)}{(1B_i^1 + 2B_i^2 + \ldots)}$$

where $i = 1, 2, \ldots n$ designate the individual countries, A_i being the total multicompensatory export from i and B_i, the total multi-compensatory import into country i, the superscripts indicating the priority categories.

Using the same notation, and bearing in mind that my system admits no export subsidisation and thus no export priorities, I suggest maximising the following expression:

$$\sum_{i=1}^{n} 1B_i^1 + 2B_i^2 + \ldots nB_i^n.$$

4. C is restricting the import of x from A.
   C   ,,   ,,   ,, y ,, B.
   B   ,,   ,,   ,, z ,, A.

Let—
q_r denote the quantity of $r (= x, y, z)$ imported from the appropriate country to the appropriate country.
$p_{r,Q}$ denote the price of r in Q $(= A, B, C)$.
E_Q denote the rate of equivalence of Q's currency, expressed as a proportion of its par of exchange.
T_r denote the *ad valorem* tariff-equivalent of the restriction of imports of r.
$R = \dfrac{\delta q_r}{\delta (P_r q_r)} \cdot \dfrac{P_r q_r}{q_r}$ denote the responsiveness of supply of r from the appropriate country to the appropriate country.

The rule regarding import duties in paragraph 55 of the text is:

$$T_x = \frac{E_A - E_C}{E_C}$$

$$T_y = \frac{E_B - E_C}{E_C}$$

$$T_z = \frac{E_A - E_B}{E_B}$$

From which it follows that:

$$T_x = T_y + T_z + T_y T_z.$$

This, though it differs from the formula for an optimal tariff structure arrived at in paragraph 2 above, can be deduced from the same criterion of optimisation. The difference is due to the peculiar balance-of-payments conditions which characterise the system under consideration. The condition of optimisation is:

$$p_{x,\text{A}} T_x \, \delta q_x + p_{y,\text{B}} T_y \, \delta q_y + p_{z,\text{A}} T_z \, \delta q_z = 0.$$

And the balance of payments conditions are:

$$\delta(p_{x,\text{A}} \, q_x) = - \, \delta(p_{z,\text{A}} \, q_z),$$
$$\delta(p_{x,\text{A}} \, q_x) \, E_\text{A} = - \, \delta(p_{y,\text{B}} \, q_y) \, E_\text{B}.$$

From which it follows, if $R_x = R_y = R_z$, that

$$T_x = T_y + T_z + T_y T_z.$$

16. The Theory of Customs Unions:

A General Survey [1]

By R. G. LIPSEY[†]

THIS PAPER IS DEVOTED mainly to a survey of the development of customs-union theory from Viner to date; since, however, the theory must be meant at least as an aid in interpreting real-world data, some space is devoted to a summary of empirical evidence relating to the gains from European Economic Union. It is necessary first to define customs-union theory. In general, the tariff system of any country may discriminate between commodities and/or between countries. Commodity discrimination occurs when different rates of duty are levied on different commodities, while country discrimination occurs when the same commodity is subject to different rates of duty, the rate varying according to the country of origin. The theory of customs unions may be defined as that branch of tariff theory which deals with the effects of geographically discriminatory changes in trade barriers.

Next we must turn our attention to the scope of the existing theory. The theory has been confined mainly to a study of the effects of customs unions on welfare rather than, for example, on the level of economic activity, the balance of payments or the rate of inflation. These welfare gains and losses, which are the subject of the theory, may arise from a number of different sources: (1) the specialisation of production according to comparative advantage which is the basis of the classical case for the gains from trade; (2) economies of scale;[2] (3) changes in the terms of trade; (4) forced changes in efficiency due to increased foreign competition; and (5) a change in the rate of economic growth. The theory of customs unions has been almost completely confined to an investigation of (1) above, with some slight attention to (2) and (3), (5) not being dealt

Economic Journal, Vol. LXX, No. 279 (September, 1960), pp. 496–513.

† University of Essex.

1 An earlier version of this paper was read before the Conference of the Association of University Teachers of Economics at Southampton, January 1959. I am indebted for comments and suggestions to G. C. Archibald, K. Klappholz and Professor L. Robbins.

2 Points (1) and (2) are clearly related, for the existence of (1) is a *necessary* condition for (2), but they are more conveniently treated as separate points, since (1) is not a *sufficient* condition for the existence of (2).

with at all,[3] while (4) is ruled out of traditional theory by the assumption (often contradicted by the facts) that production is carried out by processes which are technically efficient.

Throughout the development of the theory of customs unions we will find an oscillation between the belief that it is possible to produce a general conclusion of the sort: "Customs unions will always, or nearly always, raise welfare," and the belief that, depending on the particular circumstances present, a customs union may have any imaginable effect on welfare. The earliest customs-union theory was largely embodied in the oral tradition, for it hardly seemed worthwhile to state it explicitly, and was an example of an attempt to produce the former sort of conclusion. It may be summarised quite briefly. Free trade maximises world welfare; a customs union reduces tariffs and is therefore a movement towards free trade; a customs union will, therefore, *increase* world welfare even if it does not lead to a world-welfare *maximum*.

Viner showed this argument to be incorrect. He introduced the now familiar concepts of trade creation and trade diversion[4] which are probably best recalled in terms of an example. Consider the figures in the following Table:

TABLE I

Money Prices (at Existing Exchange Rates) of a Single
Commodity (X) in Three Countries

Country	A	B	C
Price	35s.	26s.	20s.

A tariff of 100% levied by country A[5] will be sufficient to protect A's domestic industry producing commodity X. If A forms a customs union with either country B or country C she will be better off; if the union is with B she will get a unit of commodity X at an opportunity cost of 26 shillings-worth of exports instead of at the cost of 35 shillingsworth of other goods entailed by domestic production.[6] This is an example of trade creation.

---

[3] Since this article was written, considerable attention has been devoted to the "dynamic effects" of customs unions. See, e.g., B. Balassa, *Theory of Economic Integration* (London: Allen & Unwin, 1962). [This footnote added by author at the time of reprinting of this article.]

[4] Jacob Viner, *The Customs Union Issue* (New York: Carnegie Endowment for International Peace, 1950). See the whole of chap. 4, especially pp. 43–44.

[5] In everything that follows the "home country" will be labelled A, the "union partner" B and the rest of the world C.

[6] This argument presumes that relative prices in each country reflect real rates of transformation. It follows that the resources used to produce a unit of X in country A could produce any other good to the value of 35s. and, since a unit of X can be held from B by exporting goods to the value of only 26s., there will be a surplus of goods valued at 9s. accruing to A from the transfer of resources out of X when trade is opened with country B.

If A had been levying a somewhat lower tariff, a 50% tariff, for example,
she would already have been buying X from abroad before the formation
of any customs union. If A is buying a commodity from abroad, and if her
tariff is non-discriminatory, then she will be buying it from the lowest-
cost source—in this case country C. Now consider a customs union with
country B. B's X, now exempt from the tariff, sells for 26s., while C's X,
which must still pay the 50% tariff, must be sold for 30s. A will now buy
X from B at a price, in terms of the value of exports, of 26s., whereas she
was formerly buying it from C at a price of only 20s. This is a case of
Viner's trade diversion, and since it entails a movement from lower to
higher real cost sources of supply, it represents a movement from a
more to a less efficient allocation of resources.

This analysis is an example of what Mr. Lancaster and I have called
"The General Theory of Second Best":[7] if it is impossible to satisfy *all* the
optimum conditions (in this case to make all relative prices equal to all
rates of transformation in production), then a change which brings about
the satisfaction of *some* of the optimum conditions (in this case making
some relative prices equal to some rates of transformation in production)
may make things better or worse.[8]

Viner's analysis leads to the following classification of the possibilities
that arise from a customs union between two countries, A and B:

1. Neither A nor B may be producing a given commodity. In this case they
   will both be importing this commodity from some third country, and the
   removal of tariffs on trade between A and B can cause no change in the
   pattern of trade in this commodity; both countries will continue to import it from the cheapest possible source outside of the union.
2. One of the two countries may be producing the commodity inefficiently
   under tariff protection while the second country is a nonproducer. If
   country A is producing commodity X under tariff protection this means
   that her tariff is sufficient to eliminate competition from the cheapest
   possible source. Thus if A's tariff on X is adopted by the union the tariff
   will be high enough to secure B's market for A's inefficient industry.
3. Both countries may be producing the commodity inefficiently under tariff
   protection. In this case the customs union removes tariffs between country
   A and B and ensures that the least inefficient of the two will capture the
   union market.[9]

In case 2 above any change must be a trade-diverting one, while in case 3
any change must be a trade-creating one. If one wishes to predict the

[7] R. G. Lipsey and K. J. Lancaster, "The General Theory of Second Best," *Review
of Economic Studies*, Vol. XXIV (1), No. 63 (1956–57).

[8] The point may be made slightly more formally as follows: the conditions necessary for the maximising of *any* function do not, in general, provide conditions sufficient for an increase in the value of the function when the maximum value is not to be
obtained by the change.

[9] One of the two countries might be an efficient producer of this commodity
needing no tariff protection, in which case, *a fortiori*, there is gain.

welfare effects of a customs union it is necessary to predict the relative strengths of the forces causing trade creation and trade diversion.

This analysis leads to the conclusion that customs unions are likely to cause losses when the countries involved are complementary *in the range of commodities that are protected by tariffs*. Consider the class of commodities produced under tariff protection in each of the two countries. If these classes overlap to a large extent, then the most efficient of the two countries will capture the union market and there will be a re-allocation of resources in a more efficient direction. If these two classes do not overlap to any great extent, then the protected industry in one country is likely to capture the whole of the union market when the union is formed, and there is likely to be a re-allocation of resources in a less-efficient direction. This point of Viner's has often been misunderstood and read to say that, in some general sense, the economies of the two countries should be competitive and not complementary. A precise way of making the point is to say that the customs union is more likely to bring gain, the greater is the degree of overlapping between the class of commodities produced under tariff protection in the two countries.

A subsequent analysis of the conditions affecting the gains from union through trade creation and trade diversion was made by Drs. Makower and Morton.[10] They pointed out that, *given that trade creation was going to occur,* the gains would be larger the more dissimilar were the cost ratios in the two countries. (Clearly if two countries have almost identical cost ratios the gains from trade will be small.) They then defined competitive economies to be ones with similar cost ratios and complementary economies to be ones with dissimilar ratios, and were able to conclude that unions between complementary economies would, if they brought gain at all, bring large gains. The conclusions of Viner and Makower and Morton are in no sense contradictory. Stated in the simplest possible language, Viner showed that gains will arise from unions if both countries are producing the same commodity; Makower and Morton showed that these gains will be larger the larger is the difference between the costs at which the same commodity is produced in the two countries.[11]

We now come to the second major development in customs-union theory—the analysis of the welfare effects of *the substitution between commodities* resulting from the changes in relative prices which necessarily

[10] H. Makower and G. Morton, "A Contribution Towards a Theory of Customs Unions," *Economic Journal,* Vol. LXII, No. 249 (March, 1953), pp. 33–49.

[11] Care must be taken to distinguish between complementarity and competitiveness in costs and in tastes, both being possible. In the Makower–Morton model these relations exist only on the cost side. An example of the confusion which may arise when this distinction is not made can be seen in F. V. Meyer's article, "Complementarity and the Lowering of Tariffs," *American Economic Review,* Vol. XLVI, No. 3 (June, 1956). Meyer's definitions, if they are to mean anything, must refer to the demand side. Hence he is not entitled to contrast his results with those of Makower and Morton, or of Viner, all of whom were concerned with cost complementarity and competitiveness.

accompany a customs union. Viner's analysis implicitly assumed that commodities are consumed in some fixed proportion which is independent of the structure of relative prices. Having ruled out substitution between commodities, he was left to analyse only bodily shifts of trade from one country to another. The way in which Viner's conclusion that trade diversion necessarily lowers welfare depends on his implicit demand assumption is illustrated in Figure 1. Consider the case of a small country, A, specialised in the production of a single commodity, Y, and importing one commodity, X, at terms of trade independent of any taxes or tariffs levied

FIGURE 1

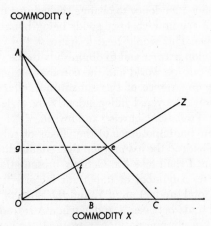

in A. The fixed proportion in which commodities are consumed is shown by the slope of the line *OZ*, which is the income- and price-consumption line for all (finite) prices and incomes. *OA* indicates country A's total production of commodity Y, and the slope of the line *AC* shows the terms of trade offered by country C, the lowest cost producer of X. Under conditions of free trade, country A's equilibrium will be at *e*, the point of intersection between *OZ* and *AC*. A will consume *Og* of Y, exporting *Ag* in return for *ge* of X. Now a tariff which does not affect A's terms of trade and is not high enough to protect a domestic industry producing Y will leave her equilibrium position unchanged at *e*.[12] The tariff changes relative prices, but consumers' purchases are completely insensitive to this change and, if foreign trade continues at terms indicated by the slope of the line *AC*, the community must remain in equilibrium at *e*. Now consider a case where country A forms a trade-diverting customs union with country B. This means that A must buy her imports of X at a price in

---

[12] It is assumed throughout all the subsequent analysis that the tariff revenue collected by the Government is either returned to individuals by means of lump-sum subsidies or spent by the Government on the same bundle of goods that consumers would have purchased.

terms of Y higher than she was paying before the union was formed. An example of this is shown in Figure 1 by the line *AB*. A's equilibrium is now at *f*, the point of intersection between *AB* and *OZ*; less of both commodities are consumed, and A's welfare has unambiguously diminished. We conclude therefore that, under the assumed demand conditions, trade diversion (which necessarily entails a deterioration in A's terms of trade) *necessarily* lowers A's welfare.

Viner's implicit assumption that commodities are consumed in fixed proportions independent of the structure of relative prices is indeed a very special one. A customs union necessarily changes relative prices and, in general, we should expect this to lead to some substitution between commodities, there being a tendency to change the volume of already existing trade with more of the now cheaper goods being bought and less of the now more expensive. This would tend to increase the volume of imports from a country's union partner and to diminish both the volume of imports obtained from the outside world and the consumption of home-produced commodities. The importance of this substitution effect in consumption seems to have been discovered independently by at least three people, Professor Meade,[13] Professor Gehrels[14] and myself. [15]

In order to show the importance of the effects of substitutions in consumption we merely drop the assumption that commodities are consumed in fixed proportions. I shall take Mr. Gehrels' presentation of this analysis because it illustrates a number of important factors. In Figure 2 *OA* is again country A's total production of Y, and the slope of the line *AC* indicates the terms of trade between X and Y when A is trading with country C. The free-trade equilibrium position is again at *e*, where an indifference curve is tangent to *AC*. In this case, however, the imposition of a tariff on imports of X, even if it does not shift the source of country A's imports, will cause a reduction in the quantity of these imports and an increase in the consumption of the domestic commodity Y. A tariff which changes the relative price in A's domestic market to, say, that indicated by the slope of the line *A'C'* will move A's equilibrium position to point *h*. At this point an indifference curve cuts *AC* with a slope equal to the line *A'C'*; consumers are thus adjusting their purchases to the market rate of transformation and the tariff has had the effect of reducing imports of X and increasing consumption of the home good Y. In these circumstances it is clearly pos-

---

[13] J. E. Meade, *The Theory of Customs Unions* (Amsterdam: North Holland Publishing Company, 1956).

[14] F. Gehrels, "Customs Unions from a Single Country Viewpoint," *Review of Economic Studies,* Vol. XXIV (1), No. 63 (1956–57).

[15] R. G. Lipsey, "The Theory of Customs Unions: Trade Diversion and Welfare," *Economica,* Vol. XXIV, No. 93 (February, 1957). My own paper was first written in 1954 as a criticism of the assumption of fixed ratios in consumption made by Dr. Ozga in his thesis (S. A. Ozga, "The Theory of Tariff Systems," University of London Ph.D. thesis, unpublished).

FIGURE 2

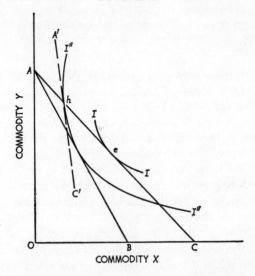

sible for country A to form a trade-diverting customs union and yet gain an increase in its welfare. To show this, construct a line through *A* tangent to the indifference curve *I″* to cut the *X* axis at some point *B*. If A forms a trade-diverting customs union with country B and buys her imports of X from B at terms of trade indicated by the slope of the line *AB*, her welfare will be unchanged. If, therefore, the terms of trade with B are worse than those given by C but better than those indicated by the slope of the line *AB*, A's welfare will be increased by the trade-diverting customs union. A's welfare will be diminished by this trade-diverting union with B only if B's terms of trade are worse than those indicated by the slope of *AB*.

The common-sense reason for this conclusion may be stated as follows:

The possibility stems from the fact that whenever imports are subject to a tariff, the position of equilibrium must be one where an indifference curve [surface or hyper-surface as the case may be] cuts (*not* is tangent to) the international price line. From this it follows that there will exist an area where indifference curves higher than the one achieved at equilibrium lie below the international price line. In Figure 2 this is the area above *I″* but below *AC*. As long as the final equilibrium position lies within this area, trade carried on in the absence of tariffs, at terms of trade worse than those indicated by *AC*, will increase welfare. In a verbal statement this possibility may be explained by referring to the two opposing effects of a trade-diverting customs union. First, A shifts her purchases from a lower to a higher cost source of supply. It now becomes necessary to export a larger quantity of goods in order to obtain any given quantity of imports. Secondly, the divergence between domestic and international prices is eliminated when the union is formed. The removal of the tariff has the effect of allowing . . . consumer[s] in A to adjust . . . purchases to a domestic price ratio which now is equal to the rate at which . . . [Y] can be transformed into . . . [X] by means of international trade. The final welfare effect of the trade-diverting customs union must be the net effect of these two opposing tendencies; the first working to lower welfare and the second to raise it.[16]

On this much there is general agreement. Professor Gehrels, however, concluded that his analysis established a general presumption in favour of gains from union rather than losses. He argued that "to examine customs unions in the light only of *production* effects, as Viner does, will give a biased judgment of their effect on countries joining them,"[17] and he went on to say that the analysis given above established a general presumption in favour of gains from union. Now we seemed to be back in the pre-Viner world, where economic analysis established a general case in favour of customs unions. In my article "Mr. Gehrels on Customs Unions"[18] I attempted to point out the mistake involved. The key is that Gehrels' model contains only two commodities: one domestic good and one import. There is thus only one optimum condition for consumption: that the relative price between X and Y equals the real rate of transformation (in domestic production or international trade, whichever is relevant) between these two commodities. The general problems raised by customs unions must, however, be analysed in a model containing a minimum of three types of commodities: domestic commodities (A), imports from the union partner (B) and imports from the outside world (C). When this change is made Gehrels' general presumption for gain from union disappears. Table II shows the three optimum conditions that domestic prices and international prices should bear the same relationship to each other for

TABLE II

Free Trade (*Col. 1*)	*Uniform* ad valorem *Tariff on All Imports* (*Col. 2*)	*Customs Union* *with Country B* (*Col. 3*)
$\dfrac{P_{Ad}}{P_{Bd}} = \dfrac{P_{Ai}}{P_{Bi}}$	$\dfrac{P_{Ad}}{P_{Bd}} < \dfrac{P_{Ai}}{P_{Bi}}$	$\dfrac{P_{Ad}}{P_{Bd}} = \dfrac{P_{Ai}}{P_{Bi}}$
$\dfrac{P_{Ad}}{P_{Cd}} = \dfrac{P_{Ai}}{P_{Ci}}$	$\dfrac{P_{Ad}}{P_{Cd}} < \dfrac{P_{Ai}}{P_{Ci}}$	$\dfrac{P_{Ad}}{P_{Cd}} < \dfrac{P_{Ai}}{P_{Ci}}$
$\dfrac{P_{Bd}}{P_{Cd}} = \dfrac{P_{Bi}}{P_{Ci}}$	$\dfrac{P_{Bd}}{P_{Cd}} = \dfrac{P_{Bi}}{P_{Ci}}$	$\dfrac{P_{Bd}}{P_{Cd}} < \dfrac{P_{Bi}}{P_{Ci}}$

Subscripts *A*, *B*, and *C* refer to countries of origin, *d* to prices in A's domestic market, and *i* to prices in the international market.

[16] R. G. Lipsey, "Trade Diversion and Welfare," *op. cit.*, pp. 43–44. The changes made in the quotation are minor ones necessary to make the notation in the example comparable to the one used in the present text.

[17] Gehrels, *op. cit.*, p. 61.

[18] R. G. Lipsey, "Mr. Gehrels on Customs Unions," *Review of Economic Studies,* Vol. XXIV (3), No. 65 (1956–57), pp. 211–14.

the three groups of commodities, A, B, and C.[19] In free trade all three optimum conditions will be fulfilled. If a uniform tariff is placed on both imports, then the relations shown in column 2 will obtain, for the price of goods from both B and C will be higher in A's domestic market than in the international market. When a customs union is formed, however, the prices of imports from the union partner, B, are reduced so that the first optimum condition is fulfilled, but the tariff remains on imports from abroad (C) so that the third optimum condition is no longer satisfied. The customs union thus moves country A from one non-optimal position to another, and in general it is impossible to say whether welfare will increase or diminish as a result. We are thus back to a position where the theory tells us that welfare may rise or fall, and a much more detailed study is necessary in order to establish the conditions under which one or the other result might obtain.

The above analysis has led both Mr. Gehrels and myself[20] to distinguish between *production effects* and *consumption effects* of customs unions. The reason for attempting this is not hard to find. Viner's analysis rules out substitution in consumption and looks to shifts in the location of production as the cause of welfare changes in customs unions. The analysis just completed emphasises the effects of substitution in consumption. The distinction on this basis, however, is not fully satisfactory, for consumption effects will themselves cause changes in production. A more satisfactory distinction would seem to be one between *inter-country substitution* and *inter-commodity substitution*. Inter-country substitution would be Viner's trade creation and trade diversion, when one country is substituted for another as the source of supply for some commodity. Inter-commodity substitution occurs when one commodity is substituted, at least at the margin, for some other commodity as a result of a relative price shift. This is the type of substitution we have just been analysing. In general, either of these changes will cause shifts in both consumption and production.

Now we come to Professor Meade's analysis. His approach is taxonomic in that he attempts to classify a large number of possible cases, showing the factors which would tend to cause welfare to increase when a union is formed and to isolate these from the factors which would tend to cause welfare to diminish.[21] Figure 3 (*i*) shows a demand and a supply

19 If we assume that consumers adjust their purchases to the relative prices ruling in their domestic markets, then the optimum conditions that rates of substitution in consumption should equal rates of transformation in trade can be stated in terms of equality between relative prices ruling in the domestic markets and those ruling in the international market.

20 Gehrels, *op. cit.*, p. 61, and Lipsey, "Trade Diversion and Welfare," *op. cit.*, pp. 40–41.

21 The point of his taxonomy or of any taxonomy of this sort, it seems to me, must be merely to illustrate how the model works. Once one has mastered the analysis it is possible to work through any particular case that may arise, and there would seem to be no need to work out all possible cases beforehand.

FIGURE 3 (*i*)   FIGURE 3 (*ii*)

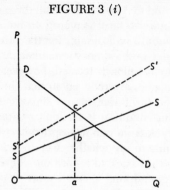
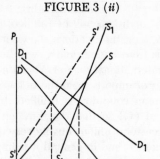

curve for any imported commodity. Meade observes that a tariff, like any tax, shifts the supply curve to the left (to S'S' in Figure 3) and raises the price of the imported commodity. At the new equilibrium the demand price differs from the supply price by the amount of the tariff. If the supply price indicates the utility of the commodity to the suppliers and the demand price its utility to the purchasers, it follows that the utility of the taxed import is higher to purchasers than to suppliers, and the money value of this difference in utility is the value of the tariff. Now assume that the marginal utility of money is the same for buyers and for sellers. It follows that, if one more *unit of expenditure* were devoted to the purchase of this commodity, there would be a net gain to society equal to the proportion of the selling price of the commodity composed of the tariff. In Figure 3 the rate of tariff is $cb/ab\%$, the supply price is ab and the demand price is ac, so that the money value of the "gain" ("loss") to society resulting from a marginal increase (decrease) in expenditure on this commodity is bc.

Now assume that the same *ad valorem* rate of tariff is imposed on all imports so that the tariff will be the same proportion of the market price of each import. Then the gain to society from a marginal increase in expenditure (say one more "dollar" is spent) on any import is the same for all imports, and this gain is equal to the loss resulting from a marginal reduction in expenditure (one less "dollar" spent) on any import. Now consider *a marginal reduction* in the tariff on one commodity. This will cause a readjustment of expenditure, in the various possible ways analysed by Meade, so that in general more of some imports and less of others will be purchased. Since, *at the margin*, the gain from devoting one more unit of expenditure to the purchase of any import is equal to the loss from devoting one less unit of expenditure to the purchase of any import, the welfare consequences of this discriminatory tariff reduction may be calculated by comparing the increase in the volume of imports (trade expansion) with the decrease in the volume of other imports (trade contraction). If there is a net increase in the volume of trade the customs union will have raised economic welfare. A study of the welfare consequences of customs unions can, therefore, be devoted to the factors which will increase or decrease the volume of international trade. If the influences which tend to cause trade expansion are found to predominate it may be predicted that a customs union will raise welfare. The main body of Meade's analysis is in fact devoted to a study of those factors which would tend to increase, and to those which would tend to decrease, the volume of trade. Complications can, of course, be introduced, but they do not affect the main drift of the argument.[22]

Meade's analysis, which makes use of demand and supply curves, suffers from one very serious, possibly crippling, limitation. It will be noted that we were careful to consider only *marginal reductions* in tariffs. For such changes Meade's analysis is undoubtedly correct. When, however, there are *large* changes in many tariffs, as there will be with most of the customs unions in which we are likely to be interested, it can no longer be assumed that the demand and supply curves will remain fixed; the *ceteris paribus* assumptions on which they are based will no longer hold, so that both demand and supply curves are likely to shift. When this happens it is no longer obvious how much welfare weight should be given to any particular change in the volume of trade (even if we are prepared to make all of the other assumptions necessary for the use of this type of classical welfare analysis). In Figure 3 (*ii*), for example, if the demand curve shifts to D_1D_1 and the supply curve to S_1S_1, what are we to say about the welfare gains or losses when trade changes from Oa to Oe?

There is not time to go through a great deal of Professor Meade's or my own analysis which attempts to discover the particular circumstances in which it is likely that a geographically discriminatory reduction in tariffs will raise welfare. I shall, therefore, take two of the general conclusions that emerge from various analyses and present these in order to illustrate the type of generalisation that it is possible to make in customs-union theory.

The first generalisation is one that emerges from Professor Meade's analysis and from my own. I choose it, first, because there seems to be general agreement on it and, second, although Professor Meade does not make this point, because it is an absolutely general proposition in the theory of second best; it applies to all sub-optimal positions, and customs-

---

[22] For example, the same rate of tariff might not be charged on all imports. In this case it is only necessary to weight each dollar's increase or decrease in trade by the proportion of this value that is made up by tariff—the greater is the rate of tariff the greater is the gain or loss. It is also possible, if one wishes to make inter-country comparisons, to weight a dollar's trade in one direction by a different amount than a dollar's trade in some other direction. These complications, however, do not affect the essence of Meade's analysis, which is to make a *small change* in some tariffs and then to observe that the welfare consequences depend on the net change in the volume of trade and to continue the study in order to discover in what circumstances an increase or a decrease in the net volume of trade is likely.

union theory only provides a particular example of its application. Stated in terms of customs unions, this generalisation runs as follows: when only some tariffs are to be changed, welfare is more likely to be raised if these tariffs are merely *reduced* than if they are completely *removed*. Proofs of this theorem can be found in both Meade[23] and Lipsey and Lancaster,[24] and we shall content ourselves here with an intuitive argument for the theorem in its most general context. Assume that there exist many taxes, subsidies, monopolies, etc., which prevent the satisfaction of optimum conditions. Further assume that all but one of these, say one tax, are fixed, and inquire into the second-best level for the tax that is allowed to vary. Finally, assume that there exists a unique second-best level for this tax.[25] Now a change in this one tax will either move the economy towards or away from a second-best optimum position. If it moves the economy away from a second-best position, then, no matter how large is the change in the tax, welfare will be lowered. If it moves the economy in the direction of the second-best optimum it may move it part of the way, all of the way or past it. If the economy is moved sufficiently far past the second-best optimum welfare will be lowered by the change. From this it follows that, if there is a unique second-best level for the tax being varied, a small variation is more likely to raise welfare than is a large variation.[26]

The next generalisation concerns the size of expenditure on the three classes of goods—those purchased domestically, from the union partner, and from the outside world—and is related to the gains from inter-commodity substitution. This generalisation follows from the analysis in my own thesis[27] and does not seem to have been stated in any of the existing customs-union literature. Consider what happens to the optimum conditions, which we discussed earlier, when the customs union is formed (see Table II). On the one hand, the tariff is taken off imports from the country's union partner, and the relative price between these imports and domestic goods is brought into conformity with the real rates of transformation. This, by itself, tends to increase welfare. On the other hand, the relative price between imports from the union partner and imports from

---

[23] *Op. cit.*, pp. 50–51.

[24] *Op. cit.*, Section V.

[25] A unique second-best level (i.e., the level which maximises welfare subject to the existence and invariability of all the other taxes, tariffs, etc.) for any one variable factor can be shown to exist in a large number of cases (see, for example, Lipsey and Lancaster, *op. cit.*, Sections V and VI), but cannot be proved to exist in general (*ibid.*, Section VIII).

[26] This may be given a more formal statement. Consider the direction of the change—towards or away from the second-best optimum position—caused by the change in the tax. Moving away from the second-best optimum is a sufficient, but not a necessary, condition for a reduction in welfare. Moving towards the second-best optimum is a *necessary*, but not a sufficient, condition for an increase in welfare.

[27] R. G. Lipsey, "The Theory of Customs Unions: A General Equilibrium Analysis," University of London Ph.D. thesis, unpublished, pp. 97–99, and Mathematical Appendix to chap. VI.

the outside world are moved away from equality with real rates of trans-formation. This by itself tends to reduce welfare. Now consider both of these changes. As far as the prices of the goods from a country's union partner are concerned, they are brought into equality with rates of trans-formation *vis à vis* domestic goods, but they are moved away from equality with rates of transformation *vis à vis* imports from the outside world. These imports from the union partner are thus involved in both a gain and a loss and their size is per se unimportant; what matters is the relation between imports from the outside world and expenditure on domestic commodities: the larger are purchases of domestic commodities and the smaller are purchases from the outside world, the more likely is it that the union will bring gain. Consider a simple example in which a country purchases from its union partner only eggs while it purchases from the outside world only shoes, all other commodities being produced and consumed at home. Now when the union is formed the "correct" price ratio (i.e., the one which conforms with the real rate of transformation) between eggs and shoes will be disturbed, but, on the other hand, eggs will be brought into the "correct" price relationship with all other com-modities—bacon, butter, cheese, meat, etc., and in these circumstances a customs union is very likely to bring gain, for the loss in distorting the price ratio between eggs and shoes will be small relative to the gain in establishing the correct price ratio between eggs and all other commodi-ties. Now, however, let us reverse the position of domestic trade and im-ports from the outside world, making shoes the only commodity produced and consumed at home, eggs still being imported from the union partner, while everything else is now bought from the outside world. In these circumstances the customs union is most likely to bring a loss; the gains in establishing the correct price ratio between eggs and shoes are indeed likely to be very small compared with the losses of distorting the price ratio between eggs and all other commodities. If, to take a third example, eggs are produced at home, shoes imported from the outside world, while everything else is obtained from the union partner, the union may bring neither gain nor loss; for the union disturbs the "correct" ratio between shoes and everything else except eggs, and establishes the "correct" one between eggs and everything else except shoes. This example serves to show that the size of trade with a union partner is not the important vari-able; it is the relation between imports from the outside world and pur-chases of domestic goods that matters.

This argument gives rise to two general conclusions, one of them ap-pealing immediately to common sense, one of them slightly surprising. The first is that, *given a country's volume of international trade,* a cus-toms union is more likely to raise welfare the higher is the proportion of trade with the country's union partner and the lower the proportion with the outside world. The second is that a customs union is more likely to raise welfare the lower is the total volume of foreign trade, for the lower is foreign trade, the lower must be purchases from the outside world relative to purchases of domestic commodities. This means that the sort of countries who ought to form customs unions are those doing a high proportion of their foreign trade with their union partner, and making a high proportion of their total expenditure on domestic trade. Countries which are likely to lose from a customs union, on the other hand, are those countries in which a low proportion of total trade is domestic, especially if the customs union does not include a high proportion of their foreign trade.

We may now pass to a very brief consideration of some of the empirical work. Undoubtedly a serious attempt to predict and measure the possible effects of a customs union is a very difficult task. Making all allowances for this, however, a surprisingly large proportion of the voluminous literature on the subject is devoted to guess and suspicion, and a very small proportion to serious attempts to measure. Let us consider what empirical work has been done in the European Common Market and the Free Trade Area, looking first at attempts to measure possible gains from specialisation. The theoretical analysis underlying these measurements is of the sort developed by Professor Meade and outlined previously.

The first study which we will mention is that made by the Dutch economist Verdoorn, subsequently quoted and used by Scitovsky.[28] The analysis assumes an elasticity of substitution between domestic goods and imports of minus one-half, and an elasticity of substitution between different imports of minus two. These estimates are based on some empirical measurements of an aggregate sort and the extremely radical assumption is made that the same elasticities apply to all commodities. The general assumption, then, is that one import is fairly easily substituted for another, while imports and domestic commodities are not particularly good substitutes for each other.[29]

Using this assumption, an estimate was made of the changes in trade when tariffs are reduced between the six Common Market countries, the United Kingdom and Scandinavia. The estimate is that intra-European trade will increase by approximately 17%, and, when this increase is weighted by the proportion of the purchase price of each commodity that is made up of tariff and estimates for the reduction in trade in other directions are also made, the final figure for the gains from trade to the European countries is equal to about one-twentieth of one per cent of their annual incomes. In considering this figure, the crude estimate of elasticities of substitution must cause some concern. The estimate of an increase in European trade of 17% is possibly rather small in the face of the known fact that Benelux trade increased by approximately 50% after the

---

[28] T. de Scitovsky, *Economic Theory and Western European Integration* (London: Allen and Unwin, 1958), pp. 64–78.

[29] Note also that everything is assumed to be a substitute for everything else; there are no relations of complementarity.

formation of that customs union. A possible check on the accuracy of the Verdoorn method would have been to apply it to the pre-customs union situation in the Benelux countries, to use the method to predict what would happen to Benelux trade and then to compare the prediction with what we actually know to have happened. Whatever allowances are made, however, Scitovsky's conclusion is not likely to be seriously challenged:

> The most surprising feature of these estimates is their smallness. . . . As estimates of the total increase in intra-European trade contingent upon economic union, Verdoorn's figures are probably underestimates; but if, by way of correction, we should raise them five- or even twenty-five-fold, that would still leave unchanged our basic conclusion that the gain from increased intra-European specialisation is likely to be insignificant.[30]

A second empirical investigation into the possible gains from trade, this time relating only to the United Kingdom, has been made by Professor Johnson.[31] Johnson bases his study on the estimates made by *The Economist* Intelligence Unit of the increases in the value of British trade which would result by 1970, first, if there were only the Common Market and, second, if there were the Common Market and the Free Trade Area. Professor Johnson then asks what will be the size of the possible gains to Britain of participation in the Free Trade Area? His theory is slightly different from that of Professor Meade, but since it arrives at the same answer, namely that the gain is equal to the increased quantity of trade times the proportion of the purchase price made up of tariff, we do not need to consider the details. From these estimates Johnson arrives at the answer that the possible gain to Britain from joining the Free Trade Area would be, *as an absolute maximum* 1% of the national income of the United Kingdom.[32]

Most people seem to be surprised at the size of these estimates, finding them smaller than expected. This leads us to ask: might there not be some inherent bias in this sort of estimate? and, might not a totally different approach yield quite different answers? One possible approach is to consider the proportion of British factors of production engaged in foreign trade. This can be taken to be roughly the percentage contribution made by trade to the value of the national product, which can be estimated to be roughly the value of total trade as a proportion of G.N.P., first subtracting the import content from the G.N.P. This produces a rough estimate of 18% of Britain's total resources engaged in foreign trade. The next step would be to ask how much increase in efficiency of utilisation for

---

[30] Scitovsky, *op. cit.*, p. 67.

[31] H. G. Johnson, "The Gains from Free Trade with Europe: An Estimate," *Manchester School*, Vol. XXVI (September, 1958).

[32] A third important empirical study was published after this article was written. See Wemelsfelder, "The Short Run Effects of the Lowering of Import Duties in Germany," *Economic Journal*, March, 1960. [This footnote added by the author at the time of reprinting of this article.]

these resources could we expect: (1) as a result of their re-allocation in the direction of their comparative advantage, and (2) as a result of a re-allocation among possible consumers of the commodities produced by these resources. Here is an outline for a possible study, but, in the absence of such a study, what would we guess? Would a 10% increase in efficiency not be a rather conservative estimate? Such a gain in efficiency would give a net increase in the national income of 1.8%. If the resources had a 20% increase in efficiency, then an increase in the national income of 3.6% would be possible. At this stage these figures can give nothing more than a common-sense check on the more detailed estimates of economists such as Verdoorn and Johnson. Until further detailed work has been done, it must be accepted that the best present estimates give figures of the net gain from trade amounting to something less than 1% of the national income (although we may not, of course, have a very high degree of confidence in these estimates).[33]

When we move on from the possible gains from new trade to the question of the economic benefits arising from other causes, such as economies of scale or enforced efficiency, we leave behind even such halting attempts at measurement as we have just considered. Some economists see considerable economies of scale emerging from European union. Others are sceptical. In what follows, I will confine my attention mainly to the arguments advanced by Professor H. G. Johnson.[34] His first argument runs as follows:

It is extremely difficult to believe that British industry offers substantial potential savings in cost which cannot be exploited in a densely-populated market of 51 million people with a G.N.P. of £18 billion, especially when account is taken of the much larger markets abroad in which British industry, in spite of restrictions of various kinds, has been able to sell its products.[35]

---

[33] Further reflection suggests that there are good general reasons for believing that the orders of magnitude obtained in these studies are the right ones. Typical European tariffs on manufactured goods are in the order of 20%. This means that industries from 1–20% less efficient than foreign competitors will be protected by these tariffs. If the costs of different industries are spread out evenly, some tariff-protected industries would be 20% less efficient than foreign competitors, but others would be only 1% less efficient, and their average inefficiency would be in the order of half the tariff rate, which is 10% less efficient than foreign competitors. Typically not much more than 10% of a country's resources would be devoted to producing behind tariff walls. This means that 10% of a country's resources would be producing 10% less efficiently than they would be if there were no tariffs, which makes a reduction in national income of something in the order of 1%. [This footnote added by author at the time of reprinting of this article.]

[34] In singling out Professor Johnson, I do not wish to imply that he is alone in practising the sort of economics which I am criticising. On the contrary, he is typical of a very large number of economists who have attempted to obtain quantitative conclusions from qualitative arguments.

[35] H. G. Johnson, "The Criteria of Economic Advantage," *Bulletin of the Oxford University Institute of Statistics,* Vol. 19 (February, 1957), p. 35. See also "The Economic Gains from Free Trade with Europe," *Three Banks Review,* September, 1958, for a similar argument.

Let us make only two points about Professor Johnson's observation. First, many markets will be very much less than the total population. What, for example, can we say about a product sold mainly to upper middle-class males living more than 20 miles away from an urban centre? Might there not be economies of scale remaining in the production of a commodity for such a market? Secondly, in the absence of some theory that tells us the statement is true for 51 and, say, 31, but not 21, million people, the argument must remain nothing more than an unsupported personal opinion. As another argument, Professor Johnson asks, "Why are these economies of scale, if they do exist, not already being exploited?"[36] It is, of course, well known that unexhausted economies of scale are incompatible with the existence of perfect competition, but it is equally well known that unexhausted economies of scale are compatible with the existence of imperfect competition as long as long-run marginal cost is declining faster than marginal revenue. Here it is worthwhile making a distinction, mentioned by Scitovsky,[37] between the long-run marginal cost of producing more goods, to which the economist is usually referring when he speaks of scale effects, and the marginal cost of making and selling more goods (which must include selling costs). This leads to a distinction between increasing sales when the whole market is expanding and increasing sales when the market is static, and thus increasing them at the expense of one's competitors. The former is undoubtedly very much easier than the latter. It is quite possible for the marginal costs of *production* to be declining while the marginal costs of *selling* in a static market are rising steeply. This would mean that production economies would not be exploited by the firms competing in the market, but that if the market were to expand so that *all* firms in a given industry could grow, then these economies would be realised.

Let us also consider an argument put forward in favour of economies of scale. Writing in 1955, Gehrels and Johnson argue that very large gains from economies of scale can be expected.[38] In evidence of this they quote the following facts: American productivity (i.e., output per man) is higher than United Kingdom productivity for most commodities; the differential is, however, greatest in those industries which use mass-production methods. From this they conclude that there are unexploited economies of mass production in the United Kingdom. Now this may well be so, but, before accepting the conclusion, we should be careful in interpreting this meagre piece of evidence. What else might it mean? Might it not mean, for example, that the ratios of capital to labour differed in the two countries so that, if we calculate the productivity of a factor

---

36 Johnson, "Economic Gains," *op. cit.*, p. 10, and "Economic Advantage," *op. cit.*, p. 35.

37 Scitovsky, *op. cit.*, pp. 42 ff.

38 Gehrels and Johnson, "The Economic Gains from European Integration," *Journal of Political Economy*, August, 1955.

by dividing total production by the quantity of one factor employed, we will necessarily find these differences? Secondly, would we not be very surprised if we did not find such differences in comparative costs between the two countries? Are we surprised when we find America's comparative advantage centred in the mass-producing industries, and, if this is the case, must we conclude that vast economies of mass production exist for Europe?

Finally, we come to the possible gains through forced efficiency. Business firms may not be adopting methods known to be technically more efficient than those now in use due to inertia, a dislike of risk-taking, a willingness to be content with moderate profits, or a whole host of other reasons. If these firms are thrown into competition with a number of firms in other countries who are not adopting this conservative policy, then the efficiency of the use of resources may increase because technically more efficient production methods are forced on the business-man now facing fierce foreign competition. Here no evidence has as yet been gathered, and, rather than report the opinions of others, I will close by recording the personal guess that this is a very large potential source of gain, that an increase in competition with foreign countries who are prepared to adopt new methods might have a most salutary effect on the efficiency of a very large number of British and European manufacturing concerns.[39]

---

[39] Milton Friedman's argument that survival of the fittest proves profit maximisation notwithstanding (see *Essays in Positive Economics* [Chicago: University of Chicago Press, 1953]). What seems to me to be a conclusive refutation of the Friedman argument is to be found in G. C. Archibald, "The State of Economic Science," *British Journal of the Philosophy of Science,* June, 1959.

IV | Trade, Growth, and Development

17. Economic Development and
International Trade*

By HARRY G. JOHNSON†

ECONOMIC GROWTH GIVES rise to many problems of international economic adjustment. This paper is concerned with the formal analysis of one group of such problems, the effects of economic growth of various kinds on the growing country's demand for imports and dependence on international trade. The analysis may be treated in either of two ways: as an analysis of the nature of the equilibrium adjustment which growth requires of the international economy; and as a preliminary to analysis of the monetary problems which arise if the mechanism of international adjustment prevents or inhibits the attainment of the required new international equilibrium. The argument employs the standard two-country two-factor model, assuming constant returns to scale in production and perfectly competitive conditions. When we come to analyse the effects of specific types of economic growth, the model will be "concretized" by making assumptions about the nature of the countries and the demand and supply conditions of the goods they produce.

To begin with, let us recapitulate the general nature of the equilibrium established in international trade. Two cases may be distinguished, corresponding to complete and incomplete specialization of the country in production: these are represented in Figures 1a and 1b. In both Figures quantities of commodities X and Y are measured along the axes, and I_1, I_2, I_3 represent community indifference curves. The domestic production possibilities are represented by the fixed quantity OP in the complete specialization case, and by the transformation curve TT in the incomplete specialization case: the terms of trade open to the country on the world market are represented by the slope of the line PC. In equilibrium, the terms-of-trade line is tangent to a community indifference curve at C; and also, in the incomplete specialization case, to the transformation curve at P; the country produces the quantities represented by P (OP of X in case a, OR of X and PR of Y in case b) and consumes the quantities

---

* *Nationaløkonomisk Tidsskrift*, 97 Bund 5–6 Hefte 1959, pp. 253–72. Also published in H. G. Johnson, *Money, Trade and Economic Growth* (Cambridge: Harvard University Press, 1962), pp. 75–103.

† The London School of Economics and the University of Chicago.

FIGURE 1a   FIGURE 1b

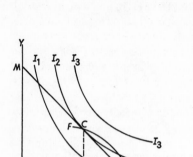

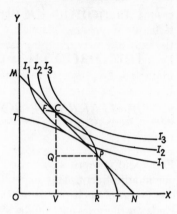

represented by C (OQ of X and CQ of Y in case a, OV of X and CV of Y in case b), exporting PQ of X to pay for imports of QC of Y. The value of the country's national product (national income), measured in terms of import goods, is represented by OM in each case; and the level of satisfaction enjoyed is I_2, as compared with the level I_1 that would be enjoyed if there were no international trade.

The foregoing account assumes that the country faces given terms of trade. In general, the terms of trade will not be given but will be variable and determined by the interaction in the market of the country's own willingness to trade, as determined by its preference system and production capacity (case a) or transformation curve (case b), and the willingness of the foreign country to trade, as determined by the same factors abroad. The foreign country's willingness to trade can be represented by an offer curve (PF in Figures 1a and 1b) showing the quantities of Y the foreign country would export in return for imports of various quantities of X, the price at which each exchange would occur being shown by the ratio of the quantities of X and Y exchanged. In case a, the foreign offer curve has a fixed origin at the point corresponding to the domestic country's productive capacity, and international trade equilibrium is determined by the condition that the point at which an indifference curve is tangent to the (variable) terms of trade line must lie on the foreign offer curve: in case b, the origin of the foreign offer curve shifts along the transformation curve, as domestic production alters; and international trade equilibrium requires, in addition to the condition just stated, that the terms-of-trade line be tangent to the transformation curve at the point from which the offer curve originates. With the insertion of the foreign offer curve PF, the "trade triangle" CPQ in Figures 1a and 1b represents the equilibrium of international trade when the terms of trade are variable.

The effect of economic growth is to shift the production point P outwards along *OX* in case *a*, and the transformation curve *TT* outwards in case *b*. The analysis of the effects of growth can be pursued in two alternative ways: by assuming a given foreign offer curve and analysing the new international trade equilibrium that will result from growth, or by considering the effect of growth on the domestic country's demand for imports at the initial terms of trade. The latter is the approach adopted here, both because it enables the isolation of the effects of the growth of the economy and the development of concepts for the analysis of these effects, concepts which are directly applicable to economies whose terms of trade are fixed by the world market, and because, if the foreign offer curve is unchanged, the direction of change of the terms and volume of

FIGURE 2a   FIGURE 2b

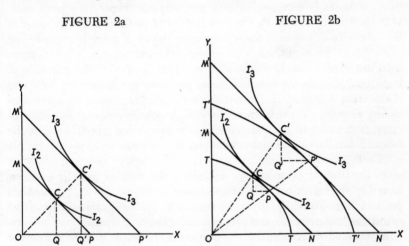

trade can be predicted from the effect of growth on the country's demand for imports at constant prices.

The general nature of the effect that economic growth would have on the growing country's demand for imports if growth occurred with unchanged terms of trade is illustrated in Figures 2a and 2b. In each case, the production point shifts from *P* to *P'*, national income (product) measured in terms of imports from *OM* to *OM'*, the consumption point from *C* to *C'*, and the level of satisfaction enjoyed from I_2 to I_3. Imports demanded increase from *CQ* to *C'Q'*, and exports supplied from *QP* to *Q'P'*.

The question of economic interest is whether growth will increase the demand for imports more than proportionally to the increase in the value of the national product, in the same proportion as, or less than proportionally to the increase in the value of the national product. From the growing country's point of view, the question is whether growth makes the country relatively less self-sufficient, no more or less dependent on trade, or relatively more self-sufficient. From the point of view of the foreign country, the question is whether the market for its exports expands more than proportionally to, at the same rate as, or less than proportionally to the growth of this country. The three possibilities can be conceptualized in terms of three types of growth: pro-trade-biased growth, which increases the country's demand for imports and supply of exports more than proportionally to output; "neutral" or unbiased growth, which increases the country's demand for imports and supply of exports in proportion to output; and anti-trade-biased growth, which increases the country's demand for imports and supply of exports less than proportionally to output. Figures 2a and 2b represent a particular type of unbiased growth, in which production and consumption of each of the two goods, and therefore exports and imports, expand proportionally with income—as shown by the fact that $M'M$, $C'C$, and $P'P$ all meet in the origin. In addition to the three general types of growth, two extreme cases can be distinguished: ultra-pro-trade-biased growth, in which more than the whole increase in national income is devoted to the purchase of imports so that the demand for home-produced goods actually falls and the country becomes absolutely less self-sufficient; and ultra-anti-trade-biased growth, in which more than the whole increase in national income is devoted to the purchase of home-produced goods, so that the demand for imports actually falls and the country becomes absolutely more self-sufficient.

In the case of complete specialization, the type of growth is determined by the behaviour of the consumption of importables as the national product rises. Formally, it can be related to the "output-elasticity of demand for importables"—the proportional change in quantity of importables demanded, divided by the proportional change in national output which causes the change in import demand: growth is pro-trade-biased, neutral, or anti-trade-biased according as this elasticity exceeds, equals, or falls short of one, ultra-anti-trade-biased if the elasticity is negative and ultra-pro-trade-biased if the elasticity exceeds the original ratio of national income to imports (an alternative way of expressing a negative output-elasticity of demand for exportables). The ranges of shift of the consumption point corresponding to the five possible types of growth are illustrated in Figure 3a.

If growth is due to some other cause than population change, income per head will rise, and the type of growth will depend on the average income-elasticity of demand for imports: if imports are luxury goods, growth will be pro-trade-biased, if they are necessary goods growth will be anti-trade-biased; if imports are inferior goods growth will be ultra-anti-trade-biased and if exports are inferior goods growth will be ultra-pro-trade-biased. If, on the other hand, growth is due to population increase alone, it may be presumed that income per head will fall, so that in aggregate demand luxury goods will behave like necessities and con-

FIGURE 3a   FIGURE 3b

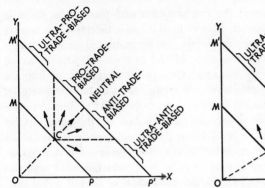
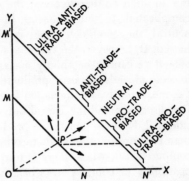

versely; the net effect of growth on demand will depend on the relations between population size and income per head, and between income per head and consumption per head of the good consumed, and a luxury good may even appear inferior in aggregate consumption. To simplify the following argument, and also because it seems reasonable to do so, cases of ultra-bias in the consumption shift will henceforth be ignored.

In the case of incomplete specialization, the effect of growth on the demand for imports depends on the combined behaviour of consumption and production. For analytical purposes it is convenient to consider separately the effects on the country's self-sufficiency of the consumption and production shifts associated with growth, before considering their combined effect. The consumption shift has already been analysed (the term "demand for importables" rather than "demand for imports" has been used deliberately to permit the argument to be extended to the case in which some importable goods are produced at home). The production shift can similarly be classified into five types, which can be formally described in terms of an "output-elasticity of supply of importables." If this elasticity exceeds one, so that domestic production of importables increases more than proportionally to national income and the country's production pattern becomes more self-sufficient, growth is anti-trade-biased; if the elasticity is negative, so that domestic production of importables falls, growth is ultra-pro-trade-biased; and so on. The ranges of shift of the production point corresponding to these types are shown in Figure 3b. The determinants of the production shift will be discussed later; it would be possible, but is not worth while, to develop an analysis of output-elasticity of supply in terms of luxury, necessary and inferior production paralleling the analysis of output-elasticity of demand in terms of luxury, necessary and inferior consumption already presented.

The effect of growth on the demand for imports is the combined result of its effects on consumption demand and domestic supply; and the addition of the effects of the consumption and production shifts is complicated. If both shifts are biased in the same direction, or one is neutral, the combined effect is clearly pro-trade-biased or anti-trade-biased. If, however, the two shifts are biased in opposite directions, the net effect cannot be simply assessed. Because consumption of imports initially exceeds domestic production of them, biases of the same degree (as measured by the deviation from unit output-elasticity) but in opposite directions will not cancel out; instead, the bias on the consumption side will dominate unless the production shift is sufficiently more biased than the consumption shift. In other words, the degrees of bias must be compared. But where there is ultra-bias in the production shift and the possibility of contrary ultra-bias in the consumption shift is ruled out, some simplification is possible: ultra-anti-trade-bias in the production shift is sufficient to make the effect of growth ultra-anti-trade-biased, and ultra-pro-trade-bias in the production shift is sufficient to prevent growth being ultra-anti-trade-biased on balance.

The relation between the output-elasticities of consumption and production of importables, the production and consumption biases, and the overall bias of growth can be shown geometrically in terms of Figure 4, which reproduces Figure 2b but for clarity omits the transformation and difference curves. The proportional changes in aggregate output, consumption of importables and production of importables are respectively:

$$\frac{MM'}{OM} = \frac{NN'}{ON}, \frac{CC'}{FC} = \frac{NN'}{FN}, \text{ and } \frac{PP'}{GP} = \frac{NN'}{GN}.$$

Hence the output-elasticity of consumption of importables is $CC'/FC \div MM'/OM = ON/FN$, and the output-elasticity of production of importables is $PP'/GP \div MM'/OM = ON/GN$. The proportional change in demand for imports is $CC'/HC = PP'/HP = QQ'/HQ$, and the output-elasticity of demand for imports is $CC'/HC \div NN'/ON$. The magnitude of the latter, and hence the overall bias of growth, can be determined simply by comparing the slopes of OH and MN. If OH and MN are parallel, as in Figure 4, $C'C/HC = NN'/ON$, the output-elasticity of demand for imports is unity and growth is neutral; if OH lies to the right of a line through O parallel to MN, $C'C/HC > NN'/ON$, the elasticity exceeds unity, and growth is pro-trade-biased; conversely, if OH lies to the left of the line through O parallel to MN, the elasticity is less than unity and growth is anti-trade-biased. By extension, if $C'C$ and $P'P$ meet in H at an obtuse angle growth is ultra-pro-trade-biased, while if H lies to the right of MN growth is ultra-anti-trade-biased. The bias of the consumption shift can be measured by the excess of the output-elasticity of consumption of importables over unity, and of the production shift by the excess of unity over the output-elasticity of production of importables (so that pro-

FIGURE 4

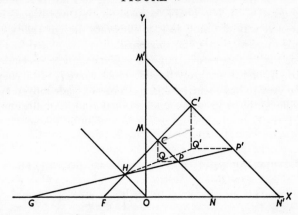

trade-bias is positive and anti-trade-bias negative in each case). On these definitions the consumption bias is represented in Figure 4 by *FO/FN* and the production bias by *GO/GN; GO/GN* is larger than *FO/FN*, thus demonstrating the point previously stated that where the biases are opposed the production bias must be larger than the consumption bias if the latter is not to predominate.

Ultra-pro-trade-biased growth and ultra-anti-trade-biased growth have been described as extreme cases, in terms of their effects on the growing country's self-sufficiency or dependence on trade. Before proceeding to discuss the likely effects on trade of growth due to particular causes, it seems appropriate to notice an alternative conception of extreme types of growth, a conception in terms of economic welfare which really belongs at a later stage of the argument but which it is convenient to introduce at this stage.

Let us assume that only the one country is growing, and consider the nature of the new international trade equilibrium that will result from its increased production, and the economic welfare that will be derived from it. Normally, at least so far as the argument up to this stage has taken us, we might expect that growth would increase the country's demand for imports, thereby worsening its equilibrium terms of trade and so imposing a loss of economic welfare as a partial offset to the gain in welfare associated with a higher level of production. This suggests two possible extreme cases. The first is the case in which the growing country's demand for imports falls instead of rises, so that its terms of trade improve and the benefit from increased production is augmented by a gain on the terms of trade; this case will occur when growth is ultra-anti-trade-biased, possible causes of which will appear in subsequent analysis. The other extreme is the case in which the terms of trade turn unfavourable to such an extent that the welfare loss from this cause more than offsets the gain from increased production, so that the country's growth leaves it worse off on balance. This is the case which Jagdish Bhagwati has described as "immiserizing growth";[1] it is probably a *curiosum,* but worth analysing.

The simplest way of doing so is to illustrate the possibility of growth which leads to no welfare gain; this possibility is depicted in Figures 5a and 5b, for the two cases of complete and incomplete specialization. In both figures, C_e on the pre-growth indifference curve I_2 is the consumption point when growth has occurred and the terms of trade moved against the country sufficiently to preserve international trade equilibrium; in Figure 5b, P_e is the new equilibrium production point on the new transformation curve.

FIGURE 5a   FIGURE 5b

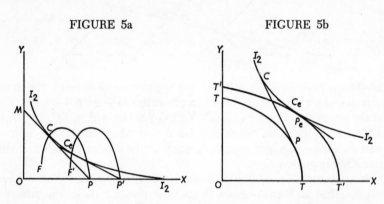

In the complete specialization case, zero-gain growth obviously requires that foreign demand for the country's exports be inelastic. With a higher price of imports and the same level of indifference, consumption of importables and therefore imports demanded must fall. For this to correspond to full international equilibrium, the foreigner must accordingly reduce the quantity of imports supplied when their price rises, or, what is the same thing, spend less of his goods on this country's exports when the price of the latter falls. This necessary condition for zero-gain growth in the complete specialization case is illustrated in Figure 5a, where PF and $P'F'$ represent the (given) foreign offer curve drawn through the pre-growth and post-growth production points. In the incomplete specialization case, consumption of importables must also fall; but the demand for imports does not necessarily fall, since domestic production of importables may fall by more than consumption of them. Thus, zero-gain growth in this case requires *either* that the foreign demand for the country's exports be inelastic *or* that the country's growth be ultra-pro-trade-biased.

To return to the main line of the argument, the concepts of neutral, pro-trade-biased, anti-trade-biased, and ultra-pro- and ultra-anti-trade-biased growth, together with the distinction between the consumption,

---

[1] Jagdish Bhagwati, "Immiserizing Growth: A Geometrical Note," *Review of Economic Studies,* Vol. XXV (3), No. 68 (June, 1958), pp. 201–5.

the production, and the overall effect of growth, must now be applied to analysing the effects of different types of growth. Following convention, we shall be concerned with three types of economic growth—technical progress, population increase, and capital accumulation—which are assumed to be analytically separable. And we shall consider their effects in two types of economy, one which exports manufactured goods in exchange for foodstuffs—a "manufacturing country"—and one which exports foodstuffs in exchange for manufactured goods—an "agricultural country." Both countries are assumed to be only partially specialized—this is the more interesting case, and can readily be adapted to the case of complete specialization.

To make the analysis more concrete, it is assumed that food is labour-intensive in production and a necessary good in consumption, while manufactures are capital-intensive in production and a luxury good in consumption. Further, it is assumed that capital is better off than labour, so that the average and marginal propensities to consume manufactures are higher for capital than for labour, and the average and marginal propensities to consume food are higher for labour than for capital.

In considering the effects of growth, it is convenient to distinguish between technical progress, which alters the production functions of the economy, and population increase and capital accumulation, which increase the quantity of a productive factor without altering the production function. The effects of factor accumulation are the simplest to deal with, and will therefore be discussed first. For reasons which will become clear in the course of the argument, it is necessary to consider the production effects before the consumption effects.

The production effect of factor accumulation, for the simple model we are using, is given by a rather simple proposition sometimes described as "the Rybczynski theorem";[2] if the terms of trade are constant, and one factor accumulates, there will be an absolute reduction in the production of the good which uses that factor less intensively, and the production of the good using that factor more intensively will increase by more than the value of the total increase in output. The proof of this proposition starts from the fact that, to keep the relative prices of the goods constant, it is necessary to keep factor prices constant, because an increase in the relative price of a factor will increase the relative cost of the good which uses that factor more intensively. To keep factor prices constant, it is necessary to keep the ratio of one factor to the other in each industry constant, since it is this ratio which determines the relative marginal productivities and therefore the relative prices of the factors.

How is this to be done when the amount of one factor increases? Suppose there is an increase in the quantity of capital: then if labour and

---

[2] T. M. Rybczynski, "Factor Endowment and Relative Commodity Prices," *Economica*, New series, Vol. XXII, No. 88 (November, 1955), pp. 336–41. I first encountered the argument in a paper read by W. M. Corden in November, 1954.

capital together are shifted out of the labour-intensive into the capital-intensive industry, labour will be released from the labour-intensive industry in greater quantities than are required to operate the released capital in the capital-intensive industry; and the surplus will be available to operate the additional capital.

This point can be illustrated by means of the production box-diagram, as in Figure 6. In the diagram AF represents the initial endowment of labour, and AM the initial endowment of capital; production indifference curves for food are drawn in the box with F as origin, and for manufactures with M as origin; the points of tangency of indifference curves from

FIGURE 6

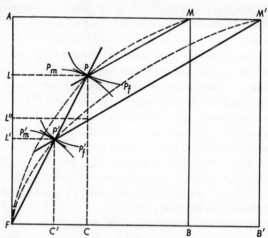

the two origins, which constitute efficient allocations of resources between the two industries, form the contract curve FPM. Suppose that P is the pre-growth production point, the economy producing P_f food by using FL of labour and FC of capital in agriculture, and P_m of manufactures by using LA of labour and BC of capital in manufacturing; the labour : capital ratios in food and manufactures respectively are shown by the slopes of FP and MP, and the exchange ratio between labour and capital is given by the slope of the common tangent to P_f and P_m at P.

Now suppose the capital increases to AM', shifting the origin of the manufactures production indifference curves to M' and altering the contract curve to $FP'M'$. At P', the point on the new contract curve with the same labour : capital ratio in each industry and therefore the same exchange ratio between factors as at P, production of food P'_f is lower than at P. The reduction of food production from P_f to P'_f releases LL' of labour and CC' of capital from agriculture; only $L'L''$ of the labour released is required to co-operate with CC' capital in manufactures, leaving LL'' free to operate the additional capital MM'.

It follows from the foregoing argument that capital accumulation will reduce agricultural production and increase manufacturing production at constant terms of trade. Capital accumulation in the manufacturing country will therefore have an ultra-pro-trade-biased production effect; whereas capital accumulation in the agricultural country will have an ultra-anti-trade-biased production effect. Conversely, population growth will reduce manufacturing output and increase agricultural output; thus the production effect of population growth will be ultra-anti-trade-biased in the manufacturing country and ultra-pro-trade-biased in the agricultural country.

It also follows from the previous argument that, at constant terms of trade (and so long as the country remains incompletely specialized), all of the increase in output goes as income to the factor which is accumulating. On our assumption of differing marginal and average propensities to consume the goods, capital accumulation will increase the average proportion of income spent on manufactures, and population growth will increase the average proportion of income spent on food. Hence the consumption effect of capital accumulation will be anti-trade-biased in the manufacturing country and pro-trade-biased in the agricultural country, while the consumption effect of population growth will be the reverse in the two countries. As explained earlier, an ultra-anti-trade-biased production effect will dominate the consumption effect while an ultra-pro-trade-biased production effect will rule out an ultra-anti-trade-biased total effect. Hence capital accumulation in the agricultural country and population growth in the manufacturing country will be ultra-anti-trade-biased, while the opposite type of factor accumulation in each country may be anything from ultra-pro-trade-biased to anti-trade-biased, but will not be ultra-anti-trade-biased.

Let us now turn to the effects of technical progress. This is a complex problem, because such progress may not only go on at different rates as between industries, but may also affect factors of production differentially in the industry in which it occurs, as well as in the economy as a whole. A technique for dealing with biased technical progress, which permits the whole problem to be dealt with in a relatively simple fashion, has only recently been published by two young American economists.[3] The following argument employs a somewhat modified version of their technique. As before, we begin with the production effect.

Let us begin with the simplest case of technical progress, "neutral" technical progress, defined as progress which reduces the quantities of the two factors required to produce a given quantity of output in the same proportion. Neutral technical progress has the initial effect of increasing the output of the industry in which it occurs, and lowering its cost of pro-

---

[3] R. Findlay and H. Grubert, "Factor Intensity, Technological Progress, and the Terms of Trade," *Oxford Economic Papers*, New Series, Vol. II, No. 1 (February, 1959).

duction at the initial factor prices. We are interested in the effect on production at constant relative prices and costs of the goods. In order to restore the initial relative prices, factors must shift from the other industry into this one: as they do so, the price of the factor used relatively intensively in this industry rises, and the price of the factor used relatively intensively in the other industry falls, so altering the relative costs of the goods and restoring the initial price ratio. Thus neutral technical progress in an industry leads to expansion of the output of that industry at the expense of the other, at given terms of trade; in other words, neutral progress is ultra-biased. It follows that neutral progress in manufacturing has an ultra-pro-trade-biased production effect in the manufacturing country, and an ultra-anti-trade-biased production effect in the agricultural country; while the effects of neutral progress in agriculture are exactly the reverse.

Now consider technical progress which is biased, in the sense that it alters the optimum ratio of one factor to the other employed at the initial factor prices in the industry in which progress occurs. Such progress may be described as saving the factor whose optimum ratio to the other is reduced.[4] Biased progress has a dual initial effect: it lowers the cost of production in the industry, and it releases a quantity of the factor it saves. Its effects are therefore the same as those of a neutral technical change,[5] combined with an increase in the supply of the factor which is saved by the biased progress.

Again we are interested in the effect on production at constant commodity prices. As in the case of neutral technical progress, the reduction in cost requires a shift of factors into the industry where the progress has occurred. As in the case of factor accumulation, the factor released by progress must be absorbed by an expansion of production of the good which uses the factor relatively intensively, at the expense of production of the other good.

It follows that if technical progress saves the factor which is used relatively intensively in the industry where the progress occurs, both factors operate in the same direction, and the production effect will be even more ultra-biased than if progress were neutral. But if progress saves the factor used relatively intensively in the other industry, the two effects—cost-reducing and factor-saving—work in opposite directions, and the production effect may vary from one to the other extreme of ultra-bias, depending on the balance of cost-reducing and factor-saving effects.

---

[4] The bias is defined in terms of the effect of progress on the optimum factor ratio, rather than in terms of the relative reductions in quantities of factors required per unit of output, because progress may increase the quantity of one factor required per unit of output.

[5] Neutral technical progress (increased output in the industry) if the cost-saving effect outweighs the bias effect so that less of both factors is required per unit of output than before, neutral technical regress (reduced output in the industry) if more of the other factor is required per unit of output than before.

The argument can be illustrated by reference to Figure 7, which is reproduced (with emendations) from Findlay and Grubert. Capital is measured on the vertical axis, labour on the horizontal. The country's factor-endowment ratio is OR. The line through P_m and P_f represents the pre-progress factor price ratio, tangent to a manufacturing production indifference curve at P_m and an agricultural production indifference curve at P_f, these curves representing quantities of equal cost and value at the initial price ratio. OP_m and OP_f are the optimum factor-ratios in the two industries; and the allocation of production between the industries must

FIGURE 7

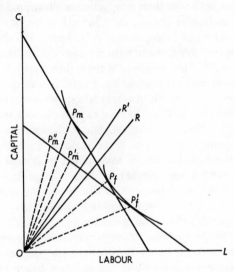

be such that the two ratios, each weighted by the proportion of the labour force in the industry where the ratio is used, average out to the endowment ratio OR.

This diagram, incidentally, can be used to establish the Rybczynski theorem. Suppose that capital is accumulated, increasing the endowment ratio to OR'; for OP_m and OP_f to average out to the higher level OR', the weight of OP_m must increase and that of OP_f decrease. That is, a larger proportion of the unchanged labour force must be employed in the capital-intensive manufacturing industry, and a smaller amount of labour in the labour-intensive food industry. Since capital : labour ratios are constant, production must vary with the amount of labour employed, falling in the labour-intensive industry.

To return to the effects of technical progress, suppose that there is technical progress in manufacturing, which shifts the production indifference curve for manufactures towards the origin O. At the initial factor prices, the cost of the quantity of manufactures represented by this indifference curve would now be less than the cost of the quantity of foodstuffs represented by the (unchanged) production indifference curve for agriculture. To keep the costs of the quantities of the goods equal, and so maintain the initial price ratio, factor prices must alter in favour of capital and against labour, to the factor-price ratio given by the new common tangent to the two production indifference curves, $P'_m P'_f$. As factor prices alter, labour will be substituted for capital in both industries.

The new capital : labour ratio in foodstuffs OP'_f is necessarily lower than the original one, owing to the substitution of cheaper labour for more expensive capital. If progress in manufacturing is capital-saving, neutral, or only slightly labour-saving, the capital : labour ratio in manufactures will also be lower than originally, as illustrated by P'_m. With a lower equilibrium capital : labour ratio in both industries, resources must have shifted out of the labour-intensive industry (foodstuffs) into the capital-intensive industry (manufactures) to maintain the overall average endowment ratio OR. Thus progress of these three types in manufacturing will be ultra-biased towards production of manufactures.

But if progress is sufficiently strongly labour-saving to offset the substitution effect of cheaper labour, the new capital : labour ratio in manufactures will be higher than the original. And with a higher capital : labour ratio in the one industry and a lower ratio in the other, the overall endowment ratio might have been maintained by a shift of resources in either direction (and to any extent) between the industries. Thus in this case the effect of technical progress in manufacturing may lie anywhere between the extremes of ultra-bias towards production of manufactures, and ultra-bias towards production of foodstuffs.

What about the consumption effect of technical progress? The restoration of the initial relative cost ratio involves lowering the relative price of the factor used less intensively in the industry where progress has occurred, and raising the price of the other. Thus more than the whole of the increase in national income due to progress goes to that factor which is used intensively in the industry in which the progress has occurred. In consequence, the proportion of expenditure out of national income on the good for which this factor's average and marginal propensity to consume is relatively high rises. It is even possible that total expenditure on the good preferred by the factor from which income is redistributed will fall; it will do so if the reduction in consumption due to straight income redistribution exceeds the increase in consumption due to the net increase in national income which accrues to the favoured factor. But it seems permissible to exclude this possibility of ultra-biased consumption effects through income-redistribution as an exceptional one. On this basis, it follows that progress in manufacturing, which reduces the income of labour and the proportional demand for food, will have an anti-trade-biased consumption effect in the manufacturing country and a pro-trade-biased consumption effect in the agricultural country; while the consumption effects of progress in agriculture will be the reverse.

Remembering that cases of ultra-anti-trade-biased and ultra-pro-trade-biased consumption effects have been excluded by assumption, the conclusions about the total effects of technical progress to which the foregoing analysis leads can be summarized as follows:

a) The following types of progress will be ultra-anti-trade-biased:

   (*i*) Neutral technical progress in agriculture in the manufacturing country;
   (*ii*) neutral technical progress in manufacturing in the agricultural country;
   (*iii*) capital-saving technical progress in manufacturing in the agricultural country;
   (*iv*) labour-saving technical progress in agriculture in the manufacturing country.

b) The following types of progress will be ultra-pro-trade-biased to anti-trade-biased, but not ultra-anti-trade-biased:

   (*i*) Neutral technical progress in manufacturing in the manufacturing country;
   (*ii*) neutral technical progress in agriculture in the agricultural country;
   (*iii*) capital-saving technical progress in manufacturing in the manufacturing country;
   (*iv*) labour-saving technical progress in agriculture in the agricultural country.

c) The following types of progress can be biased in any way whatever from ultra-pro-trade-biased to ultra-anti-trade-biased:

   (*i*) Capital-saving technical progress in manufacturing in either country;
   (*ii*) labour-saving technical progress in agriculture in either country.

In brief, progress which is neutral or saves the factor used relatively intensively in the industry in which it occurs will be ultra-anti-trade-biased if it occurs in a country's import-competing industry, and ultra-pro-trade-biased to anti-trade-biased but *not* ultra-anti-trade-biased if it occurs in a country's export industry; progress which saves the factor used relatively intensively in the other industry than that in which the progress occurs may have any effect whatsoever.

The production, consumption, and total effects of growth of the various types analysed in the argument so far on the growing country's demand for imports and supply of exports are summarized in the accompanying Table. The results in many cases are rather indefinite. It should perhaps be remarked that the chief reason why this is so lies in our original assumption that each factor prefers to consume the product in which it is employed intensively so that progress in that product, by redistributing

TABLE

The Effects of Economic Growth

Type of Growth	Manufacturing Country			Agricultural Country		
	Production Effect	Consumption Effect	Total Effect	Production Effect	Consumption Effect	Total Effect
Capital accumulation	UP	A	UP to A	UA	P	UA
Population growth	UA	P	UA	UP	A	UP to A
Neutral technical progress:						
(a) manufacturing	UP	A	UP to A	UA	P	UA
(b) agriculture	UA	P	UA	UP	A	UP to A
Capital-saving technical progress:						
(a) manufacturing	UP	A	UP to A	UA	P	UA
(b) agriculture	UA to UP	P	UA to UP	UP to UA	A	UP to UA
Labour-saving technical progress:						
(a) manufacturing	UP to UA	A	UP to UA	UA to UP	P	UA to UP
(b) agriculture	UA	P	UA	UP	A	UP to A

A: anti-trade-biased
P: pro-trade-biased
UA: ultra-anti-trade-biased
UP: ultra-pro-trade-biased

income towards that factor, increases the relative demand for the product. If each factor preferred the product in which it was used less intensively, the consumption and production effects of progress would work in the same direction in many cases, giving unambiguous results. This may be confirmed by scrutiny of the summary Table: if factors' preferences for goods were the opposite of those assumed, the effects of growth of the types discussed would be *either* ultra-anti-trade-biased, *or* pro-trade-biased to ultra-pro-trade-biased, except in cases of capital-saving progress in agriculture and labour-saving progress in manufactures.

There are two further possible results of technical progress, suggested by Figure 7, which should be mentioned, though it does not seem worth while to develop them in full. The first is that technical progress in one industry may reduce costs there so much that the country specializes completely on that product. In Figure 7, the production indifference curve shifts so far towards the origin that either no common tangent exists, or the common tangent implies factor ratios inconsistent with the endowment ratio and non-negative production. This case is simply the extreme example of an ultra-biased production effect.

The second possibility arises when progress is so saving of the factor used intensively in the industry in which it occurs as to make the optimum ratio of that factor to the other at the initial factor prices lower than the endowment ratio in both industries. In this case, the saved factor cannot be absorbed (at the initial factor price ratio) by a shift of factors between industries; its relative price must fall, so that the consumption effect of progress is biased against the industry in which it occurs. The production effect of this kind of progress will entail complete specialization on the good in which progress occurs, at the initial commodity prices, provided that it can be assumed that with the original technology, the relative factor-intensities of the two industries would be the same at any factor price ratio. This assumption ensures that, as the price of the saved factor falls, the relative cost of producing the product in which progress has occurred, using the pre-progress technique, will fall. Thus it will never pay to produce the other product.[6] But since the reduction in the price of the saved factor will reduce the cost of producing this product with the old technique more than it will reduce the cost of producing it with the new technique, it is possible that, before the optimum factor-intensity with the new technique is raised to the endowment ratio, the old and new techniques become cost-indifferent. In this case, specialization will be accompanied by the use of that mixture of old and new techniques which demands factors in the average proportion of the country's endowment ratio.

The next step is to analyse the effects of growth in the two countries together, that is, of the growth of the world economy. If growth of the same type is going on in the two countries, conclusions about the movement of the terms of trade between them (i.e., between manufactures and food) can be drawn directly from the Table in many cases. For example, capital accumulation and neutral or capital-saving technical progress in manufactures turn the terms of trade in favour of the agricultural country, population growth and neutral or labour-saving technical progress in food turns the terms of trade in favour of the manufacturing country. But capital-saving progress in agriculture and labour-saving progress in food may turn the terms of trade either way.

In the general case, with population increasing, capital accumulating, and technical progress being applied in both countries, the movement of the terms of trade will depend on the bias and the rate of growth in each country. This dependence can be expressed in the following formula:

$$R_{pm} = \frac{\epsilon_a R_a - \epsilon_m R_m}{\eta_a + \eta_m - 1} .$$

where R_{pm} is the rate of increase (decrease if negative) of the relative price of manufactures, R_a is the rate of growth of output in the agricultural

---

[6] If factor-intensities with the old technique can reverse as the price of the saved factor falls, it is possible for there to exist a common tangent to the new production indifference curve for the industry where progress has occurred and the production indifference curve for the other industry such that (a) the optimum factor ratios lie on opposite sides of the endowment ratio, (b) the cost of production with the new technique is lower than with the old, in the industry where progress has occurred. In this case the country remains incompletely specialized at the initial commodity prices, this being made possible by a reversal of relative factor intensities in the two industries; the production effect here may be anywhere between the extremes of bias. The writer is indebted to Messrs. Findlay and Grubert for pointing out in correspondence the importance of condition (b), and so permitting the correction of an error in the original formulation of the argument.

country and ϵ_a its output-elasticity of demand for imports, R_m *and* ϵ_m are the rate of growth and output-elasticity of demand for imports of the manufacturing country, η_a and η_m are the two countries' price-elasticities of demand for imports, and $\eta_a + \eta_m - 1$ is the "elasticity factor" which determines the proportion of the initial value of trade by which a country's trade balance would improve if the price of its export good fell. The sense of the formula is that $\epsilon_a R_a$ and $\epsilon_m R_m$ are the rates of increase in the countries' demands for each other's goods; if these are unequal, equilibrium must be maintained by a relative price change whose magnitude will vary inversely with the elasticity factor.

Consideration of the effects of growth on the terms of trade suggests a concept of "balanced growth"—growth of the two countries at rates which keep the terms of trade between them constant. Balance in this sense requires $\epsilon_a R_a = \epsilon_m R_m$; obviously, it is impossible if the output-elasticities of demand have opposite signs, the growth of one country being ultra-anti-trade-biased. In any case, the concept is of very limited usefulness, since "balance" does not imply equal rates of growth of total output, let alone output per head. All that is implied by growth not being "balanced" in this sense is that one of the countries is benefiting not only by the growth of its own output but by an improvement in its terms of trade, while the benefit the other derives from the growth of its output is reduced by a worsening of its terms of trade; it is even possible, as has been shown earlier, for a country to be worse off as the result of growth. If complete specialization is assumed, so that bias depends on consumption only, "balanced growth" implies slower growth in the agricultural country unless growth is due to population increase.

In conclusion, some remarks on the extension of the analysis beyond the confines of the two-country two-good two-factor model seem called for. In the first place, recognition of a third factor, land, used predominantly in agriculture, introduces the classical problem of diminishing returns. If returns diminish strongly enough, the conclusions concerning the effects of population growth may be reversed—if there is no outlet on the land, the growing population will be forced into manufacturing. Second, allowance for a multiplicity of products introduces a variety of complications: rising income may lead to demands for foreign products formerly considered not worth their cost as compared with domestic substitutes; technical progress may be random, leading to sudden reversals of comparative advantage—for example, giving a capital-rich country a comparative advantage in producing a formerly labour-intensive product; and capital accumulation or population increase may alter a country's comparative advantage in particular goods—so that, for example, it may shift from labour-intensive to capital-intensive products in both manufacturing and agriculture. Thirdly, recognition of intermediate products which may be traded, and of the network of intersectoral transactions, greatly complicates the simple connection assumed in the foregoing between domestic demand for and supply of final goods, and the volume of international trade. Fourthly, allowing for the presence of many countries means that the movement of the terms of trade between manufactures and agricultural products depends on the nature and rate of growth in all countries together. One consequence of this is as follows: in the two-country model, "general" growth of one country will tend to increase its demand for imports, so that if the other country does not grow or grows only slowly it will benefit from a favourable movement of its terms of trade; but if there are two groups of countries, the effect of world growth on a particular country depends not only on the relative rates of growth of the two groups, but also on its individual rate of growth as compared with the growth rates of others in its group. A country may lose by a low rate of growth because the rapid growth of others in its group turns the terms of trade against it.

18. Immiserizing Growth:

A Geometrical Note[*]

By JAGDISH BHAGWATI[†]

THE EFFECT OF ECONOMIC expansion on international trade has been receiving increasing attention from economic theorists since the publication of Professor Hicks' stimulating analysis of the "dollar problem."[1] It has, however, been insufficiently realised that, under certain circumstances, economic expansion may harm the growing country itself.[2] Economic expansion increases *output* which, however, might lead to a sufficient deterioration in the terms of trade to offset the beneficial effect of expansion and reduce the *real income* of the growing country. It is the purpose of this note to formulate the conditions under which immiserizing growth will occur. Section I sets out the analysis geometrically and arrives at the criterion for immiserizing growth. Section II discusses some of the implications of this criterion.

I

In the ensuing analysis we assume the traditional two-country, two-commodity "real" model where full-employment always obtains. We also assume, to simplify the analysis, that growth is confined to a single country so that the other country (i.e., the rest-of-the-world) is not experiencing any growth in *output;* this assumption enables us to assume the offer curve of the rest-of-the-world as "given" during the course of our

* *Review of Economic Studies*, Vol. XXV, No. 3 (June, 1958), pp. 201–5.

† Delhi School of Economics. The author wishes to thank Professor Harry Johnson for his generous assistance and encouragement in the writing of this paper. Thanks are also due to Sir Donald MacDougall and J. Black for helpful comments.

[1] J. R. Hicks, "An Inaugural Lecture," *Oxford Economic Papers*, N.S. Vol. 5, No. 2 (June, 1953). The following are of interest: H. G. Johnson, "Economic Expansion and International Trade," *Manchester School of Economic and Social Studies*, May, 1955; E. J. Mishan, "The Long-Run Dollar Problem: A Comment," *Oxford Economic Papers*, N.S. Vol. 7, No. 2 (June, 1955); and W. M. Corden, "Economic Expansion and International Trade: A Geometric Approach," *Oxford Economic Papers*, N.S. Vol. 8, No. 2 (June, 1956).

[2] Exception must be made, however, in the case of Professor Johnson, "Equilibrium Growth in An Expanding Economy," *Canadian Journal of Economics and Political Science*, Vol. XIX, No. 4 (Nov., 1953), p. 495; and also his *Manchester School*, May, 1955, article. It should also be mentioned that Prof. Johnson has independently worked out mathematically, in an unpublished note, a criterion for immiserizing growth which confirms the results derived geometrically in this note.

analysis. Finally, we simplify the problem by beginning with an investigation of the conditions under which growth would leave the country just as well off as before, and then determining whether the equilibrium actually realised would involve still less favourable terms of trade; this approach has the convenience of avoiding the need for an explicit analysis of the income effect of growth.

Consider now Figure 1 which represents the growing economy. C_0 is the pre-expansion consumption point, P_0 the pre-expansion production point, P_0C_0 the pre-expansion terms of trade or price-line, C_0R_0 the imports of Y into the country and R_0P_0 the exports of X from the country.

FIGURE 1

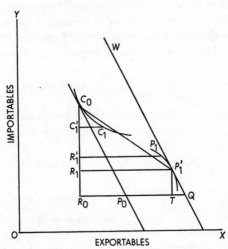

The production-possibility curve tangential to P_0C_0 has not been drawn in to avoid cluttering up the diagram; the indifference curve through C_0 is tangential to P_0C_0 at C_0 and has been drawn partially. Consider now growth which pushes the production-possibility curve outwards and which, at *constant terms of trade*, would bring production from P_0 to P'_1. Now assume that the terms of trade are changed just enough to offset indifference and the *new* production-possibility curve. We later assume, legitimately for infinitesimal changes, that $C_1 P_1$ coincides with $C_0 P'_1$.

The combined effect of the expansion and the compensating adjustment of the terms of trade is to reduce the demand for imports from C_0R_0 to $C'_1R'_1$. This reduction can be analysed into the sum of three effects:

(1) *The increase in production of importables due to the economic expansion:*

This increase (R_0R_1 in the diagram) may be analysed as follows. Let p_0 and p_1 be the original and the *zero-gain* prices respectively, measured as the number of units of exportables required to buy a unit of importables. Then the change in total output, valued at *initial* prices, is:

$$P_0 T + TQ = P_0 Q = SP_1'$$

And

$$SP_1' = \frac{P_1' R_1 - R_1 S}{C_0 R_1} \cdot C_0 R_1 = (p_1 - p_0) \cdot C_0 R_1$$

The change in the production of importables is:

$$R_0 R_1 = P_1 T = \frac{\delta Y}{\delta K} \cdot P_0 Q = \frac{\delta Y}{\delta K} \cdot SP_1'$$

where K is defined to be the country's productive capacity which is assumed to be kept fully employed and is measured by the value in terms of exportables of the output the country would produce at the initial terms of trade and Y is the domestic output of importables. Then,

$$R_0 R_1 = C_0 R_1 \cdot \frac{\delta Y}{\delta K} \cdot (p_1 - p_0)$$

Since we have assumed the changes to be infinitesimal, it follows that we can assume $C_0 R_1 = C_0 R_0$, the initial volume of imports, so that

$$R_0 R_1 = M \cdot \frac{\delta Y}{\delta K} \cdot dp \qquad (S_m \equiv M) \qquad (1)$$

where M is the quantity of imports.

This shows the change in the production of importables due to the economic expansion itself. The expression is normally positive, indicating that the output of importables increases, consequent on economic expansion, at constant terms of trade. It should be noted here, however, that, as argued in Section II, the output of importables may actually contract due to the expansion.

(2) *The decrease in consumption of importables due to the price-change:*

The price-change (from p_0 to p_1) shifts consumption *along* the indifference curve to C_1. The consumption of importables is then reduced by:

$$C_0 C_1' = -\frac{\delta C}{\delta p} \cdot dp \qquad (2)$$

where C is the total demand for importables.

(3) *The increase in production of importables due to the price-change:*

The price-change shifts production *along* the production-possibility curve to P_1. The production of importables is then increased by:

$$R_1 R_1' = \frac{\delta Y}{\delta p} \cdot dp \qquad (3)$$

The total decrease in the domestic demand for *imports*[3] is the sum of the three effects (1), (2) and (3):

$$\left(M \cdot \frac{\delta Y}{\delta K} + \frac{\delta Y}{\delta p} - \frac{\delta C}{\delta p} \right) \cdot dp \qquad (4)$$

This expression measures the decrease in demand for imports when the effect of growth on real income is exactly offset by an adverse movement of the terms of trade. In the abnormal case where output of importables *falls* as a result of growth, the expression may be negative, indicating an *increase* in the demand for imports.

Whether the country will actually be made worse off or not depends on what would happen to the quantity of imports supplied if the terms of trade were adjusted as assumed. The change in imports supplied as a result of such a price change is:

$$\frac{\delta S_m}{\delta p} \cdot dp \qquad (5)$$

The sum of (4) and (5) constitutes the excess supply of imports at the zero-gain terms of trade: if it is positive, the terms of trade will not move against the growing country enough to deprive it of all gain from growth; but if it is negative, the price of imports will have to rise still further to preserve equilibrium, and the growing country will actually be made worse off by growth.

The economic meaning of this criterion for immiserizing growth will be considered in the next section; for this purpose a neater formulation of the criterion is desirable, and this can be derived by subjecting it to some algebraic manipulation.

Multiplying (4) and (5) by $p/(M.dp)$, we get our criterion for immiserizing growth as:

$$\left(\frac{C}{M} \cdot \epsilon + \frac{Y}{M} \cdot \sigma + y + r_m \right) < 0 \qquad (6)$$

which may be written as:

$$\left(\frac{C}{M} \cdot \epsilon + \frac{Y}{M} \cdot \sigma + y \right) < -r_m \qquad (7)$$

where

$$\epsilon = -\frac{p}{C} \cdot \frac{\delta C}{\delta p}, \, r_m = \frac{p}{M} \cdot \frac{\delta S_m}{\delta p} \qquad (S_m \equiv M)$$

$$\sigma = \frac{p}{Y} \cdot \frac{\delta Y}{\delta p} \text{ and } y = p.\frac{\delta Y}{\delta K}$$

This criterion is also expressible in the alternative equivalent form:

$$\left(\frac{C}{M} \cdot \epsilon + \frac{Y}{M} \cdot \sigma + y \right) < 1 - \eta_x \qquad (8)$$

---

[3] As distinguished from *importables*.

where $\eta_x = p/X° \cdot \delta X°/\delta p$ and $X°$ is the quantity of exports. This follows from the fact that η_x and r_m are the *total* elasticities of the rest-of-the-world's offer curve; η_x being the elasticity of the rest-of-the-world's demand for imports (into the rest-of-the-world) in response to an infinitesimal change in the terms of trade and r_m being the elasticity of the rest-of-the-world's supply of (its) exports (to the growing country) in response to an infinitesimal shift in the terms of trade. It is a well-known proposition in the theory of international trade that $\eta_x - r_m = 1$; hence, $1 - \eta_x = -r_m$.

II

What are the implications of the criterion that we have derived in Section I? It will be remembered that $\sigma = (p/Y)(\delta Y/\delta p)$ and is thus necessarily positive and $\epsilon = -(p/C)(\delta C/\delta p)$ which again, being the constant-utility or expenditure-compensated demand-elasticity with respect to a change in the price of importables, is necessarily positive.[4] We can see from (6), (7) or (8) that the *possibility* of immiserizing growth is increased if:

(i) $\dfrac{Y}{M}$, the ratio of domestic production to import of importables is small. Since $C/M = 1 + Y/M$, it follows that C/M will also be small when Y/M is small;

(ii) ϵ, the constant-utility demand-elasticity for importables with respect to a change in the price of importables, is small; this would depend on the substitution effect against importables being negligible when the price of importables rises; and

(iii) σ, the elasticity in supply of importables when production shifts along the production-possibility curve in response to a change in the price of importables, is small.

These are, neither singly nor in combination, sufficient conditions for immiserizing growth. In fact, the *possibility* of immiserizing growth arises only when, with these conditions favourably fulfilled, either or both of the following crucial conditions are fulfilled: (*a*) the offer of the rest-of-the-world is inelastic (i.e., r_m is negative, which may be for the *extreme*, and by no means necessary, reason that the growing country's exports are Giffen goods abroad); and (*b*) growth actually reduces the domestic production of importables at constant relative commodity prices (i.e., y is negative).

Stringent as the latter condition may appear at first sight, recent analyses have shown that it is feasible under relatively simple assumptions. Thus the Rybczynski proposition states that under a two-commodity, two-factor model where, say, labour and land being the factors, one good

---

[4] This argument obviously rests on the assumption of "well-behaved" (convex) indifference curves and (concave) transformation curves, concavity being defined with reference to the origin and *not* in the strict mathematical sense.

is labour-intensive and the other land-intensive, if labour (land) increases in supply, then the output of the land-intensive (labour-intensive) industry must actually contract if the relative commodity prices are maintained constant.[5] Professor Johnson has recently advanced the proposition that under neutral technical progress in one industry, the technology of the other and the total factor endowment remaining unchanged, the output of the other industry must actually fall under constant relative commodity prices.[6] It may be of interest to note that under biased progress as well it is possible to establish conditions under which the output of the non-innovating industry will contract.[7]

---

[5] Rybczynski, "Factor endowments and Relative Commodity Prices," *Economica*, Nov., 1955. Linear homogeneity of the production functions and diminishing returns are *sufficient* conditions for the proposition to hold. The strong Samuelson notion of factor-intensity is not necessary.

[6] Johnson, *Manchester School, op. cit.* Diminishing returns are *sufficient* for this proposition to hold. The proposition can be readily extended to more than two goods and factors.

[7] The conditions under which this result will obtain can be established for specified production functions.

19. The Distribution of Gains between Investing and Borrowing Countries[*]

By H. W. SINGER[†][1]

INTERNATIONAL TRADE IS of very considerable importance to underdeveloped countries, and the benefits which they derive from trade and any variations in their trade affect their national incomes very deeply. The opposite view, which is frequent among economists, namely, that trade is less important to the underdeveloped countries than it is to industrialized countries, may be said to derive from a logical confusion—very easy to slip into—between the absolute amount of foreign trade which is known to be an increasing function of national income, and the ratio of foreign trade to national income. Foreign trade tends to be proportionately most important when incomes are lowest. Secondly, fluctuations in the volume and value of foreign trade tend to be proportionately more violent in that of underdeveloped countries and therefore *a fortiori* also more important in relation to national income. Thirdly, and *a fortissimo*, fluctuations in foreign trade tend to be immensely more important for underdeveloped countries in relation to that small margin of income over subsistence needs which forms the source of capital formation, for which they often depend on export surpluses over consumption goods required from abroad.

In addition to the logical confusion mentioned above, the great importance of foreign trade to underdeveloped countries may also have been obscured by a second factor; namely, by the great discrepancy in the productivity of labor in the underdeveloped countries as between the industries and occupations catering for export and those catering for domestic production. The export industries in underdeveloped countries, whether they be metal mines, plantations, etc., are often highly capital-

[*] *American Economic Review,* Vol. XL, No. 2 (May, 1950), pp. 473–85.

[†] United Nations.

[1] The author wishes to acknowledge help and advice received from many friends and colleagues; in particular Mr. Henry G. Aubrey, Dr. Harold Barger, of the National Bureau of Economic Research, Dr. Roberto de Oliveira Campos, of the Brazilian Delegation to the United Nations, Dr. A. G. B. Fisher, of the International Monetary Fund, Professor W. Arthur Lewis, of the University of Manchester (England), and Mr. James Kenny. He also had the inestimable advantage of a discussion of the subject matter of this paper in the Graduate Seminar at Harvard University, with Professors Haberler, Harris, and others participating.

intensive industries supported by a great deal of imported foreign technology. By contrast, production for domestic use, specially of food and clothing, is often of a very primitive subsistence nature. Thus the economy of the underdeveloped countries often presents the spectacle of a dualistic economic structure: a high productivity sector producing for export coexisting with a low productivity sector producing for the domestic market. Hence employment statistics in underdeveloped countries do not adequately reflect the importance of foreign trade, since the productivity of each person employed in the export sector tends to be a multiple of that of each person employed in the domestic sector. Since, however, employment statistics for underdeveloped countries are notoriously easier to compile than national income statistics, it is again easy to slip, from the fact that the proportion of persons employed in export trade is often lower in underdeveloped countries than in industrialized countries, to the conclusion that foreign trade is less important to them. This conclusion is fallacious, since it implicitly assumes rough equivalence of productivity in the export and domestic sectors. This equivalence may be safely assumed in the industrialized countries but not in the underdeveloped countries.

A third factor which has contributed to the view that foreign trade is unimportant in underdeveloped countries is the indisputable fact that in many underdeveloped countries there are large self-contained groups which are outside the monetary economy altogether and are therefore not affected by any changes in foreign trade. In industrialized countries, by contrast, it is true that repercussions from changes in foreign trade are more widely spread; but they are also more thinly spread.[2]

The previously mentioned fact, namely, the higher productivity of the foreign trade sector in underdeveloped countries might, at first sight, be considered as a cogent argument in favor of the view that foreign trade has been particularly beneficial to underdeveloped countries in raising their general standards of productivity, changing their economies in the direction of a monetary economy, and spreading knowledge of more capital-intensive methods of production and modern technology. That, however, is much less clearly established than might be thought. The question of ownership as well as of opportunity costs enters at this point. The productive facilities for producing export goods in underdeveloped countries are often foreign owned as a result of previous investment in these countries. Again we must beware of hasty conclusions. Our first reaction would be to argue that this fact further enhances the importance and benefits of trade to underdeveloped countries since trade has also led

---

[2] A more statistical factor might be mentioned. Some underdeveloped countries— Iran would be an illustration—exclude important parts of their exports and imports from their foreign trade statistics insofar as the transactions of foreign companies operating in the underdeveloped country are concerned. This is a tangible recognition of the fact that these pieces of foreign investments and their doings are not an integral part of the underdeveloped economy.

to foreign investment in those countries and has promoted capital formation with its cumulative and multiplier effects. This is also how the matter
is looked at in the economic textbooks—certainly those written by non-
socialist economists of the industrialized countries. That view, however,
has never been really accepted by the more articulate economists in the
underdeveloped countries themselves, not to mention popular opinion in
those countries; and it seems to the present writer that there is much more
in their view than is allowed for by the economic textbooks.

Can it be possible that we economists have become slaves to the geog-
raphers? Could it not be that in many cases the productive facilities for
export from underdeveloped countries, which were so largely a result of
foreign investment, never became a part of the internal economic structure of those underdeveloped countries themselves, except in the purely
geographical and physical sense? Economically speaking, they were really
an outpost of the economies of the more developed investing countries.
The main secondary multiplier effects, which the textbooks tell us to expect from investment, took place not where the investment was physically
or geographically located but (to the extent that the results of these investments returned directly home) they took place where the investment
came from.[3] I would suggest that if the proper economic test of investment
is the multiplier effect in the form of cumulative additions to income, employment, capital, technical knowledge, and growth of external economies,
then a good deal of the investment in underdeveloped countries which we
used to consider as "foreign" should in fact be considered as domestic
investment on the part of the industrialized countries.

Where the purpose and effect of the investments was to open up new
sources of food for the people and for the machines of industrialized
countries, we have strictly domestic investment in the relevant economic
sense, although for reasons of physical geography, climate, etc., it had to
be made overseas. Thus the fact that the opening up of underdeveloped
countries for trade has led to or been made possible by foreign investment
in those countries does not seem a generally valid proof that this combination has been of particular benefit to those countries. The very differential in productivity between the export sectors and the domestic sectors
of the underdeveloped countries, which was previously mentioned as an
indication of the importance of foreign trade to underdeveloped countries,
is also itself an indication that the more productive export sectors—often
foreign owned—have not become a real part of the economies of underdeveloped countries.

We may go even further. If we apply the principle of opportunity costs
to the development of nations, the import of capital into underdeveloped
countries for the purpose of making them into providers of food and raw

---

[3] Often underdeveloped countries had the chance, by the judicious use of royalties
or other income from foreign investment, to use them for the transformation of their
internal economic structure—a chance more often missed than caught by the forelock!

materials for the industrialized countries may have been not only rather ineffective in giving them the normal benefits of investment and trade but may have been positively harmful. The tea plantations of Ceylon, the oil wells of Iran, the copper mines of Chile, and the cocoa industry of the Gold Coast may all be more productive than domestic agriculture in these countries; but they may well be less productive than domestic industries in those countries which might have developed if those countries had not become specialized to the degree in which they now are to the export of food and raw materials, thus providing the means of producing manufactured goods elsewhere with superior efficiency. Admittedly, it is a matter of speculation whether in the absence of such highly specialized "export" development, any other kind of development would have taken its place. But the possibility cannot be assumed away. Could it be that the export development has absorbed what little entrepreneurial initiative and domestic investment there was, and even tempted domestic savings abroad? We must compare, not what is with what was, but what is with what would have been otherwise—a tantalizingly inconclusive business. All we can say is that the process of traditional investment taken by itself seems to have been insufficient to initiate domestic development, unless it appeared in the form of migration of persons.

The principle of specialization along the lines of static comparative advantages has never been generally accepted in the underdeveloped countries, and not even generally intellectually accepted in the industrialized countries themselves. Again it is difficult not to feel that there is more to be said on the subject than most of the textbooks will admit. In the economic life of a country and in its economic history, a most important element is the mechanism by which "one thing leads to another," and the most important contribution of an industry is not its immediate product (as is perforce assumed by economists and statisticians) and not even its effects on other industries and immediate social benefits (thus far economists have been led by Marshall and Pigou to go) but perhaps even further its effect on the general level of education, skill, way of life, inventiveness, habits, store of technology, creation of new demand, etc. And this is perhaps precisely the reason why manufacturing industries are so universally desired by underdeveloped countries; namely, that they provide the growing points for increased technical knowledge, urban education, the dynamism and resilience that goes with urban civilization, as well as the direct Marshallian external economies. No doubt under different circumstances commerce, farming, and plantation agriculture have proved capable of being such "growing points," but manufacturing industry is unmatched in our present age.

By specializing on exports of food and raw materials and thus making the underdeveloped countries further contribute to the concentration of industry in the already industrialized countries, foreign trade and the foreign investment which went with it may have spread present static benefits fairly over both. It may have had very different effects if we think of it not from the point of view of static comparative advantages but of the flow of history of a country. Of this latter school of thought the "infant" argument for protection is but a sickly and often illegitimate offspring.

To summarize, then, the position reached thus far, the specialization of underdeveloped countries on export of food and raw materials to industrialized countries, largely as a result of investment by the latter, has been unfortunate for the underdeveloped countries for two reasons: (*a*) because it removed most of the secondary and cumulative effects of investment from the country in which the investment took place to the investing country; and (*b*) because it diverted the underdeveloped countries into types of activity offering less scope for technical progress, internal and external economies taken by themselves, and withheld from the course of their economic history a central factor of dynamic radiation which has revolutionized society in the industrialized countries. But there is a third factor of perhaps even greater importance which has reduced the benefits to underdeveloped countries of foreign trade-*cum*-investment based on export specialization on food and raw materials. This third factor relates to terms of trade.

It is a matter of historical fact that ever since the seventies the trend of prices has been heavily against sellers of food and raw materials and in favor of the sellers of manufactured articles. The statistics are open to doubt and to objection in detail, but the general story which they tell is unmistakable.[4] What is the meaning of these changing price relations?

The possibility that these changing price relations simply reflect relative changes in the real costs of the manufactured exports of the industrialized countries to those of the food and primary materials of the underdeveloped countries can be dismissed. All the evidence is that productivity has increased if anything less fast in the production of food and raw materials, even in the industrialized countries[5] but most certainly in the underdeveloped countries, than has productivity in the manufacturing industries of the industrialized countries. The possibility that changing price relations could merely reflect relative trends in productivity may be considered as disposed of by the very fact that standards of living in indus-

---

[4] Reference may be made here to the publication by the Economic Affairs Department of the United Nations on "Relative Prices of Exports and Imports of Underdeveloped Countries."

[5] According to U.S. data of the WPA research project, output per wage earner in a sample of 54 manufacturing industries increased by 57 per cent during the twenty years, 1919–39; over the same period, agriculture increased only by 23 per cent, anthracite coal mining by 15 per cent, and bituminous coal mining by 35 per cent. In the various fields of mineral mining, however, progress was as fast as in manufacturing. According to data of the National Bureau of Economic Research, the rate of increase in output per worker was 1.8 per cent p.a. in manufacturing industries (1899–1939) but only 1.6 per cent in agriculture (1890–1940) and in mining, excluding petroleum (1902–39). In petroleum production, however, it was faster than in manufacturing.

trialized countries (largely governed by productivity in manufacturing industries) have risen demonstrably faster than standards of living in underdeveloped countries (generally governed by productivity in agriculture and primary production) over the last sixty or seventy years. However important foreign trade may be to underdeveloped countries, if deteriorated terms of trade (from the point of view of the underdeveloped countries) reflected relative trends of productivity, this could most assuredly not have failed to show in relative levels of internal real incomes as well.

Dismissing, then, changes in productivity as a governing factor in changing terms of trade, the following explanation presents itself: the fruits of technical progress may be distributed either to producers (in the form of rising incomes) or to consumers (in the form of lower prices). In the case of manufactured commodities produced in more developed countries, the former method, i.e., distribution to producers through higher incomes, was much more important relatively to the second method, while the second method prevailed more in the case of food and raw material production in the underdeveloped countries. Generalizing, we may say that technical progress in manufacturing industries showed in a rise in incomes while technical progress in the production of food and raw materials in underdeveloped countries showed in a fall in prices. Now, in the general case, there is no reason why one or the other method should be generally preferable. There may, indeed, be different employment, monetary, or distributive effects of the two methods; but this is not a matter which concerns us in the present argument where we are not concerned with internal income distribution. In a closed economy the general body of producers and the general body of consumers can be considered as identical, and the two methods of distributing the fruits of technical progress appear merely as two formally different ways of increasing real incomes.

When we consider foreign trade, however, the position is fundamentally changed. The producers and the consumers can no longer be considered as the same body of people. The producers are at home; the consumers are abroad. Rising incomes of home producers to the extent that they are in excess of increased productivity are an absolute burden on the foreign consumer. Even if the rise in the income of home producers is offset by increases in productivity so that prices remain constant or even fall by less than the gain in productivity, this is still a relative burden on foreign consumers, in the sense that they lose part or all of the potential fruits of technical progress in the form of lower prices. On the other hand, where the fruits of technical progress are passed on by reduced prices, the foreign consumer benefits alongside with the home consumer. Nor can it be said, in view of the notorious inelasticity of demand for primary commodities, that the fall in their relative prices has been compensated by its total revenue effects.

Other factors have also contributed to the falling long-term trend of prices of primary products in terms of manufactures, apart from the absence of pressure of producers for higher incomes. Technical progress, while it operates unequivocally in favor of manufactures—since the rise in real incomes generates a more than proportionate increase in the demand for manufactures—has not the same effect on the demand for food and raw materials. In the case of food, demand is not very sensitive to rises in real income, and in the case of raw materials, technical progress in manufacturing actually largely consists of a reduction in the amount of raw materials used per unit of output, which may compensate or even over-compensate the increase in the volume of manufacturing output. This lack of an automatic multiplication in demand, coupled with the low price elasticity of demand for both raw materials and food, results in large price falls, not only cyclical but also structural.

Thus it may be said that foreign investment of the traditional type which sought its repayment in the direct stimulation of exports of primary commodities either to the investing country directly or indirectly through multilateral relations, had not only its beneficial cumulative effects in the investing country, but the people of the latter, in their capacity as consumers, also enjoyed the fruits of technical progress in the manufacture of primary commodities thus stimulated, and at the same time in their capacity as producers also enjoyed the fruits of technical progress in the production of manufactured commodities. The industrialized countries have had the best of both worlds, both as consumers of primary commodities and as producers of manufactured articles, whereas the underdeveloped countries had the worst of both worlds, as consumers of manufactures and as producers of raw materials. This perhaps is the legitimate germ of truth in the charge that foreign investment of the traditional type formed part of a system of "economic imperialism" and of "exploitation."

Even if we disregard the theory of deliberately sinister machinations, there may be legitimate grounds in the arguments set out above on which it could be maintained that the benefits of foreign trade and investment have not been equally shared between the two groups of countries. The capital-exporting countries have received their repayment many times over in the following five forms: (a) possibility of building up exports of manufactures and thus transferring their population from low-productivity occupations to high-productivity occupations; (b) enjoyment of the internal economies of expanded manufacturing industries; (c) enjoyment of the general dynamic impulse radiating from industries in a progressive society; (d) enjoyment of the fruits of technical progress in primary production as main consumers of primary commodities; (e) enjoyment of a contribution from foreign consumers of manufactured articles, representing as it were their contribution to the rising incomes of the producers of manufactured articles.

By contrast, what the underdeveloped countries have to show cannot compare with this formidable list of benefits derived by the industrialized countries from the traditional trading-*cum*-investment system. Perhaps the widespread though inarticulate feeling in the underdeveloped countries that the dice have been loaded against them was not so devoid of foundation after all as the pure theory of exchange might have led one to believe.

It is, of course, true that there are transfer difficulties on the part of the underdeveloped countries which are avoided by production for export directly to the investing countries, but the above analysis may perhaps make a contribution to understanding why this traditional investment system broke down so rapidly and so irreparably in 1929 and 1930. The industrialized countries had already received real repayment from their foreign investments in the five forms described above, and in these ways they may have collected a pretty good return on their investments. When on top of the returns received in those five forms they also tried to "get their money back," they may perhaps have been asking (in the economic, though not in the legal, sense) for double payment; they may have been trying to get a quart out of a pint bottle.

There is a fairly widespread impression that this traditional trend towards deteriorating price relations for primary producers has been sharply reversed since prewar days, although this impression is not as strong now as it was in the middle of 1948. Even if we take that point of time, which represents the peak of postwar primary commodity prices up till now, a detailed analysis does not bear out the impression that terms of trade have significantly improved in favor of the underdeveloped countries since prewar days.[6]

It may be suggested that the impression that price relations have sharply improved for primary producers can be attributed partly to the abnormal composition of primary commodity imports into the U.S. where coffee plays a predominating part (coffee prices have increased particularly heavily in the immediate postwar period), and also specially to the widespread idea that foreign trade between underdeveloped countries and industrialized countries is an exchange of the primary commodities of the former for the capital goods of the latter. In fact, among the imports of the underdeveloped countries capital goods do not generally form the largest category, mainly because the import of capital goods from abroad requires a great deal of complementary domestic investment in those countries for which the domestic finance does not exist or is not mobilized.

The major proportion of the imports of the underdeveloped countries is in fact made up of manufactured food (especially in overpopulated underdeveloped countries), textile manufactures, and manufactured consumer

---

[6] For details see the above mentioned study of "Relative Prices of Exports and Imports of Under-developed Countries" (Economic Affairs Department of the United Nations).

L*

goods. The prices of the type of food imported by the underdeveloped countries, and particularly the prices of textile manufactures, have risen so heavily in the immediate postwar period that any advantage which the underdeveloped countries might have enjoyed in the postwar period from favorable prices realized on primary commodities and low prices of capital goods has been wiped out.

A further factor which has contributed to the impression that relative price trends have turned sharply in favor of primary producers since the war is the deterioration in British terms of trade and the publicity which this deterioration has received because of the strategic importance of the British balance of payments in the network of world trade. It should, however, not be forgotten that the changes in British postwar terms of trade do not merely represent *ceteris paribus* price changes but reflect considerable quantum changes; namely, an increase in the quantity exported and a decrease in the quantity imported. It may be suggested, perhaps, that these quantum changes rather than underlying price changes account for the adverse trend before devaluation of British terms of trade. Unless it is to be assumed that the elasticity of demand for British exports is infinite, it is obvious that an expansion in the volume of total exports of manufactured goods by almost 100 per cent will be reflected in lower unit prices for British exports; conversely, the reduction in the quantity of British imports is also reflected in higher prices paid than would otherwise have been the case, partly as a reflection of the diminishing bargaining strength of Britain in consequence of lower imports and partly as a necessary political concession to primary producers to enable them to maintain their incomes in the face of lower quantities sold. The supposition that the changed quantity relations in British trade (as well as deliberate colonial development policies) are largely responsible for the adverse trend in British terms of trade rather than price changes in world markets is greatly strengthened by the fact that other Western European exporters of manufactured goods did not only fail to experience any deterioration in their terms of trade, but on the contrary showed improved terms of trade.[7] The effect of quantum changes on British terms of trade is of course difficult to disentangle statistically. It is more in the nature of a gain missed through inability of exploiting the postwar sellers' market price-wise to the full. It is surely a remarkable fact that in a world hungry for capital goods, and with her two most important direct industrial competitors eliminated, England should have experienced adverse terms of trade in the years 1945 to 1948.

At this point it might be worth noting the curious ambivalence which price relations in foreign trade play for the underdeveloped countries. Good prices for their primary commodities, specially if coupled with a rise in quantities sold, as they are in a boom, give to the underdeveloped

---

[7] *Economic Survey of Europe in 1948* (United Nations, Department of Economic Affairs), pp. 93–106, especially 97, 98 and 99.

countries the necessary means for importing capital goods and financing their own industrial development; yet at the same time they take away the incentive to do so, and investment, both foreign and domestic, is directed into an expansion of primary commodity production, thus leaving no room for the domestic investment which is the required complement of any import of capital goods. Conversely, when the prices and sales of primary commodities fall off, the desire for industrialization is suddenly sharpened. Yet, at the same time, the means for carrying it out are sharply reduced. Here again it seems that the underdeveloped countries are in danger of falling between two stools: failing to industrialize in a boom because things are as good as they are, and failing to industrialize in a slump because things are as bad as they are.[8] It is no doubt true that failure to utilize high boom exports proceeds more determinedly for capital formation because of purely temporary price relations shows a deplorable lack of foresight, but this is hardly very apposite criticism of those underdeveloped countries which rely mainly on private development. All private activity tends to be governed by the price relations of the day.

If our view is accepted (namely, that the traditional type of foreign investment as it was known prior to 1929 was "foreign" only in the geographical sense and not in the relevant economic sense) does it then follow that foreign investment has failed to fulfill one of the functions traditionally ascribed to it (and hoped for from it for the future); i.e., ω spread industrialization more widely and more evenly throughout the world? It would be premature to jump to this conclusion. What has been maintained in the preceding part of this argument is that past foreign investment, and the type of foreign trade which went with it, failed to spread industrialization to the countries in which the investment took place. It may be, however, that for a full understanding of the process we have to consider not merely the investing and the invested countries but a third group of countries as well.

It is an interesting speculation that European investment overseas was the instrument by which industrialization was brought to North America. Roughly speaking, the supplies of food and raw materials pouring into Europe as the result of the investment-*cum*-trade system and the favorable terms of trade engendered by this system enabled Europe to feed, clothe, educate, train, and equip large numbers of emigrants sent overseas, principally to the United States and Canada. Thus the benefits to the investing countries of Europe arising out of the system described above were in turn passed on to the United States—the converse of the Marshall Plan—and were the main foundation of the enormous capital formation the result of which is now to be observed in North America. This "macro-

---

[8] This ambivalence of changing terms of trade has also been stressed in a different context by Professor Lloyd Metzler in his important article on "Tariffs, Terms of Trade and Distribution of National Income," in the *Journal of Political Economy*, February, 1949.

economic" analysis is, of course, in no way contradicted by the fact that the individual migrant was motivated by the prospect of raising his standards of living by the transfer.

Attention may be drawn to the interesting statistical computation of Corrado Gini that even the enormous capital stock characteristic of the United States economy is not more than the equivalent of the burden in consumption goods and in such services as health, education, and other provision for the immigrants—a burden which the United States was enabled to save by shifting it to the European mother countries of the immigrants. Perhaps in the final result it may be said that the ultimate benefits of the traditional investment-*cum*-trade system were not with the investing countries of Europe but with the new industrial countries of North America.[9]

If this analysis is correct, the industrialization of North America was made possible by the combination of migration and the opening up of underdeveloped overseas countries through European investment and trade. To that extent, Point Four and technical assistance on the part of the United States would be a gesture of historical justice and return of benefits received in the past.

It may be useful, rather than end on a wild historical speculation, to summarize the type of economic measures and economic policies which would result from the analysis presented in this paper. The first conclusion would be that in the interest of the underdeveloped countries, of world national income, and perhaps ultimately of the industrialized countries themselves, the purposes of foreign investment and foreign trade ought perhaps to be redefined as producing gradual changes in the structure of comparative advantages and of the comparative endowment of the different countries rather than to develop a world trading system based on existing comparative advantages and existing distribution of endowments. This perhaps is the real significance of the present movement towards giving technical assistance to underdeveloped countries not necessarily linked with actual trade or investment. The emphasis on technical assistance may be interpreted as a recognition that the present structure of comparative advantages and endowments is not such that it should be considered as a permanent basis for a future international division of labor.

Insofar as the underdeveloped countries continue to be the source of food and primary materials and insofar as trade, investment, and technical assistance are working in that direction by expanding primary production, the main requirement of underdeveloped countries would

---

[9] In more recent years, specially since 1924, U.S. capital accumulation had of course become quite independent from the original stimulus supplied by immigration, and proceeded without any visible check in spite of a heavy reduction in immigration. The argument put forward here is meant as a historical explanation rather than an analysis of the present sources of capital investment.

seem to be to provide for some method of income absorption to ensure that the results of technical progress are retained in the underdeveloped countries in a manner analogous to what occurs in the industrialized countries. Perhaps the most important measure required in this field is the reinvestment of profits in the underdeveloped countries themselves, or else the absorption of profits by fiscal measures and their utilization for the finance of economic development, and the absorption of rising productivity in primary production in rising real wages and other real incomes, provided that the increment is utilized for an increase in domestic savings and the growth of markets of a kind suitable for the development of domestic industries. Perhaps this last argument, namely, the necessity of some form of domestic absorption of the fruits of technical progress in primary production, provides the rationale for the concern which the underdeveloped countries show for the introduction of progressive social legislation. Higher standards of wages and social welfare, however, are not a highly commendable cure for bad terms of trade, except where the increment leads to domestic savings and investment. Where higher wages and social services are prematurely introduced and indiscriminately applied to export and domestic industries, they may in the end turn out a retarding factor in economic development and undermine the international bargaining strength of the primary producers. Absorption of the fruits of technical progress in primary production is not enough; what is wanted is absorption for reinvestment.

Finally, the argument put forward in this paper would point the lesson that a flow of international investment into the underdeveloped countries will contribute to their economic development only if it is absorbed into their economic system; i.e., if a good deal of complementary domestic investment is generated and the requisite domestic resources are found.

20. The "Classical Theory" of International Trade and the Underdeveloped Countries[*][1]

By HLA MYINT[†]

THERE HAS RECENTLY BEEN a considerable amount of controversy concerning the applicability of the "classical theory" of international trade to the underdeveloped countries.[2] The twists in this controversy may be set out as follows. The critics start with the intention of showing that the "nineteenth-century pattern" of international trade, whereby the underdeveloped countries export raw materials and import manufactured goods, has been unfavourable to the economic development of these countries. But instead of trying to show this directly, they concentrate their attacks on the "classical theory," which they believe to be responsible for the unfavourable pattern of trade. The orthodox economists then come to the defence of the classical theory by reiterating the principle of comparative costs which they claim to be applicable both to the developed and the underdeveloped countries. After this, the controversy shifts from the primary question whether or not the nineteenth-century pattern of international trade, as a historical reality, has been unfavourable to the underdeveloped countries to the different question whether or not the theoretical model assumed in the comparative-costs analysis is applicable to these countries. Both sides then tend to conduct their argument as though the two questions were the same and to identify the "classical theory" with the comparative-costs theory.

It will be argued in this paper that this has led to the neglect of those other elements in the classical theory of international trade which are much nearer to the realities and ideologies of the nineteenth-century ex-

[*] *Economic Journal*, Vol. LXVIII, No. 270 (June, 1958), pp. 317–37.

[†] The London School of Economics.

[1] This paper has benefited from comments by Sir Donald MacDougall, Professor H. G. Johnson, R. M. Sundrum and G. M. Meier.

[2] Of the very extensive literature on the subject, we may refer to two notable recent works, the first stating the orthodox position and the second the position of the critics: J. Viner, *International Trade and Economic Development*, and G. Myrdal, *An International Economy*.

pansion of international trade to the underdeveloped countries. In Sections I and II we shall outline these elements and show that they are traceable to Adam Smith and to some extent to J. S. Mill. In Section III we shall show how one of Adam Smith's lines of approach can be fruitfully developed to throw a more illuminating light on the past and present patterns of the international trade of the underdeveloped countries than the conventional theory. In Section IV we shall touch upon some policy implications of our analysis and show certain weaknesses in the position both of the orthodox economists and of their critics.

I

The neglected elements in the classical theory of international trade may be traced to Adam Smith, particularly to the following key passage in the *Wealth of Nations:*

Between whatever places foreign trade is carried on, they all of them derive two distinct benefits from it. It carries out that surplus part of the produce of their land and labour for which there is no demand among them, and brings back in return for it something else for which there is a demand. It gives a value to their superfluities, by exchanging them for something else, which may satisfy a part of their wants, and increase their enjoyments. By means of it, the narrowness of the home market does not hinder the division of labour in any particular branch of art or manufacture from being carried to the highest perfection. By opening a more extensive market for whatever part of the produce of their labour may exceed the home consumption, it encourages them to improve its productive powers, and to augment its annual produce to the utmost, and thereby to increase the real revenue and wealth of society (Vol. I, Cannan ed., p. 413).

There are two leading ideas here. (*i*) International trade overcomes the narrowness of the home market and provides an outlet for the surplus product above domestic requirements. This develops into what may be called the "vent for surplus"[3] theory of international trade. Later we hope to remove some of the prejudice aroused by this "mercantilist" sounding phrase. (*ii*) By widening the extent of the market, international trade also improves the division of labour and raises the general level of productivity within the country. This develops into what may be called the "productivity" theory. We shall be mainly concerned with the "vent for surplus" theory and the light it throws upon the growth of international trade in the underdeveloped countries in the nineteenth

---

[3] This term is borrowed from Professor J. H. Williams, who in turn quoted it from a passage in J. S. Mill's *Principles,* in which Mill was criticising this particular aspect of Smith's theory of international trade. Professor Williams is the only modern economist to sponsor this "crude" doctrine. While he is mainly concerned with the loss to a country on being deprived of the export market for its surplus product, we shall pay special attention to the gain to a hitherto isolated underdeveloped country on obtaining a "vent" for its surplus productive capacity. Cf. J. H. Williams, "The Theory of International Trade Reconsidered," *Economic Journal,* June, 1929, pp. 195–209.

century. But first it is necessary to consider the "productivity" theory briefly.

The "productivity" doctrine differs from the comparative-costs doctrine in the interpretation of "specialisation" for international trade. (*a*) In the comparative costs theory "specialisation" merely means a movement along a static "production possibility curve" constructed on the given resources and the *given techniques* of the trading country. In contrast, the "productivity" doctrine looks upon international trade as a dynamic force which, by widening the extent of the market and the scope of the division of labour, raises the skill and dexterity of the workmen, encourages technical innovations, overcomes technical indivisibilities and generally enables the trading country to enjoy increasing returns and economic development.[4] This distinction was clearly realised by J. S. Mill, who regarded the gains in terms of comparative-costs theory as direct gains and the gains in terms of Adam Smithian increases in productivity as "indirect effects, which must be counted as benefits of a high order." Mill even went on to extend this doctrine to countries at "an early stage of industrial advancement," where international trade by introducing new wants "sometimes works a sort of industrial revolution" (*Principles*, Ashley, ed., p. 581). (*b*) In the comparative costs theory "specialisation," conceived as a reallocation of resources, is a completely reversible process. The Adam Smithian process of specialisation, however, involves adapting and reshaping the productive structure of a country to meet the export demand, and is therefore not easily reversible. This means that a country specialising for the export market is more vulnerable to changes in the terms of trade than is allowed for in the comparative-costs theory. We shall come back to this point later.

In the expansive mental climate of the late nineteenth century the "productivity" aspect of international specialisation completely dominated the "vulnerability" aspect. At a semi-popular level, and particularly in its application to the underdeveloped countries, Smith's "productivity" doctrine developed beyond a free-trade argument into an export-drive argument. It was contended that since international trade was so beneficial in raising productivity and stimulating economic development, the State should go beyond a neutral and negative policy of removing barriers to trade and embark on a positive policy of encouraging international trade and economic development. Under its influence, many colonial governments went far beyond the strict *laissez-faire* policy in their attempts to promote the export trade of the colonies.[5] Further, although these

---

[4] Cf. *op. cit.*, chaps. II and III, Book I. This aspect of Smith's theory has been made familiar by Professor Allyn Young's article on "Increasing Returns and Economic Progress," *Economic Journal*, December, 1928, pp. 527–42.

[5] See for instance, L. C. A. Knowles, *The Economic Development of the British Overseas Empire*, Vol. I, pp. 119–20, 248–49 and 486–87. However, in Section IV below we shall argue that, in spite of the attention they have received, these export-drive policies were not successful enough to cause a significant "export-bias."

governments were frequently obliged to use "unclassical" methods, such as the granting of monopolistic privileges to the chartered companies or the taxing of the indigenous people to force them to take up wage labour or grow cash crops, they nevertheless sought to justify their policy by invoking the Adam Smithian doctrine of the benefits of international division of labour. This partly explains why some critics have associated the "classical theory" with "colonialism" and why they have frequently singled out Adam Smith for attack instead of Ricardo, the founder of the official classical free-trade theory.

It is fair to say that Smith's "productivity" doctrine is instructive more in relation to the ideological than to the actual economic forces which characterised the nineteenth-century expansion of international trade to the underdeveloped countries. It is true, as we shall see later,[6] that both the total value and the physical output of the exports of these countries expanded rapidly. In many cases the rate of increase in export production was well above any possible rate of increase in population, resulting in a considerable rise in output per head. But it is still true to say that this was achieved not quite in the way envisaged by Smith, viz., a better division of labour and specialisation leading on to innovations and cumulative improvements in skills and productivity per man-hour. Rather, the increase in output per head seems to have been due: (*i*) to once-for-all increases in productivity accompanying the transfer of labour from the subsistence economy to the mines and plantations, and (*ii*) what is more important, as we shall see later, to an increase in working hours and in the proportion of gainfully employed labour relatively to the semi-idle labour of the subsistence economy.

The transfer of labour from the subsistence economy to the mines and plantations with their much higher capital–output ratio and skilled management undoubtedly resulted in a considerable increase in productivity. But this was mostly of a once-for-all character for a number of reasons. To begin with, the indigenous labour emerging from the subsistence economy was raw and technically backward. Moreover, it was subject to high rates of turnover, and therefore not amenable to attempts to raise productivity. Unfortunately, this initial experience gave rise to or hardened the convention of "cheap labour," which regarded indigenous labour merely as an undifferentiated mass of low-grade man-power to be used with a minimum of capital outlay.[7] Thus when the local labour supply was ex-

---

[6] See footnotes 12 and 19 below. See also Sir Donald MacDougall's *The World Dollar Problem*, pp. 134–43. Sir Donald's argument that the productivity of labour in the underdeveloped countries has been rising faster than is generally assumed is mainly based on figures for productivity *per capita*. These figures are not inconsistent with our argument that on the whole the expansion of the export production has been achieved on more or less constant techniques and skills of indigenous labour, by increasing working hours and the proportion of gainfully employed labour rather than by a continuous rise in productivity per man-hour.

[7] Cf. S. H. Frankel, *Capital Investment in Africa*, pp. 142–46, and W. M. Macmillan, *Europe and West Africa*, pp. 48–50.

hausted the typical reaction was not to try to economise labour by install-
ing more machinery and by reorganising methods of production but to
seek farther afield for additional supplies of cheap labour. This is why
the nineteenth-century process of international trade in the underdeveloped countries was characterised by large-scale movements of cheap
labour from India and China.[8] This tendency was reinforced by the way
in which the world-market demand for raw materials expanded in a series
of waves. During the booms output had to be expanded as quickly as
possible along existing lines, and there was no time to introduce new
techniques or reorganise production; during the slumps it was difficult
to raise capital for such purposes.

This failure to achieve Adam Smith's ideal of specialisation leading on
to continuous improvements in skills can also be observed in the peasant
export sectors. Where the export crop happened to be a traditional crop
(e.g., rice in South-East Asia), the expansion in export production was
achieved simply by bringing more land under cultivation with the same
methods of cultivation used in the subsistence economy. Even where new
export crops were introduced, the essence of their success as peasant
export crops was that they could be produced by fairly simple methods
involving no radical departure from the traditional techniques of production employed in subsistence agriculture.[9]

Thus instead of a process of economic growth based on continuous
improvements in skills, more productive recombinations of factors and
increasing returns, the nineteenth-century expansion of international
trade in the underdeveloped countries seems to approximate to a simpler
process based on constant returns and fairly rigid combinations of factors.
Such a process of expansion could continue smoothly only if it could
feed on *additional* supplies of factors in the required proportions.

II

Let us now turn to Smith's "vent for surplus" theory of international
trade. It may be contrasted with the comparative-costs theory in two
ways.

(*a*) The comparative-costs theory assumes that the resources of a
country are given and fully employed before it enters into international

---

[8] Cf. Knowles, *op. cit.*, pp. viii and 182–201.

[9] Thus A. McPhee wrote about the palm-oil and ground-nut exports of West
Africa: "They made little demand on the energy and thought of the natives and they
effected no revolution in the society of West Africa. That was why they were so
readily grafted on the old economy and grew as they did" (*The Economic Revolution
in West·Africa*, pp. 39–40). Some writers argue that there was a studied neglect of
technical improvements in the peasant sector to facilitate the supply of cheap labour
to other sectors. Cf., for example, W. A. Lewis, "Economic Development with Unlimited Supplies of Labour," *Manchester School*, May, 1954, pp. 149–50. For a
description of imperfect specialisation in economic activity in West Africa see P. T.
Bauer and B. S. Yamey, "Economic Progress and Occupational Distribution," *Economic Journal*, December, 1951, p. 743.

trade. The function of trade is then to reallocate its given resources more efficiently between domestic and export production in the light of the new set of relative prices now open to the country. With given techniques and full employment, export production can be increased only at the cost of reducing the domestic production. In contrast, the "vent for surplus" theory assumes that a previously isolated country about to enter into international trade possesses a surplus productive capacity[10] of some sort or another. The function of trade here is not so much to reallocate the given resources as to provide the new effective demand for the output of the surplus resources which would have remained unused in the absence of trade. It follows that export production can be increased without necessarily reducing domestic production.

(*b*) The concept of a surplus productive capacity above the requirements of domestic consumption implies an inelastic domestic demand for the exportable commodity and/or a considerable degree of internal immobility and specificness of resources. In contrast, the comparative-costs theory assumes either a perfect or, at least, a much greater degree of internal mobility of factors and/or a greater degree of flexibility or elasticity both on the side of production and of consumption. Thus the resources not required for export production will not remain as a surplus productive capacity, but will be reabsorbed into domestic production, although this might take some time and entail a loss to the country.

These two points bring out clearly a peculiarity of the "vent-for-surplus" theory which may be used either as a free-trade argument or as an ·anti-trade argument, depending on the point of view adopted. (*a*) From the point of view of a previously isolated country, about to enter into trade, a surplus productive capacity suitable for the export market appears as a virtually "costless" means of acquiring imports and expanding domestic economic activity. This was how Adam Smith used it as a free-trade argument. (*b*) From the point of view of an established trading country faced with a fluctuating world market, a sizeable surplus productive capacity which cannot be easily switched from export to domestic production makes it "vulnerable" to external economic disturbances. This is in fact how the present-day writers on the underdeveloped countries use the same situation depicted by Smith's theory as a criticism of the nineteenth-century pattern of international trade. This concept of vulnerability may be distinguished from that which we have come across in discussing the "productivity" theory of trade. There, a country is considered "vulnerable" because it has adapted and reshaped its productive structure to meet the requirements of the export market through a genuine process of "specialisation." Here, the country is considered "vulnerable" simply because it happens to possess a sizeable surplus productive capacity which (even without any improvements and extensions) it cannot use for domestic production. This dis-

---

[10] A surplus over domestic requirements and *not* a surplus of exports over imports.

tinction may be blurred in border-line cases, particularly in under-developed countries with a large mining sector. But we hope to show that, on the whole, while the "vulnerability" of the advanced countries, such as those in Western Europe which have succeeded in building up large export trades to maintain their large populations, is of the first kind, the "vulnerability" of most of the underdeveloped countries is of the second kind.

Let us now consider the "vent-for-surplus" approach purely as a theoretical tool. There is a considerable amount of prejudice among economists against the "vent-for-surplus" theory, partly because of its technical crudeness and partly because of its mercantilist associations. This may be traced to J. S. Mill, who regarded Smith's "vent-for-surplus" doctrine as "a surviving relic of the Mercantile Theory" (*Principles*, p. 579).

The crux of the matter here is the question: why should a country isolated from international trade have a surplus productive capacity? The answer which suggests itself is that, given its random combination of natural resources, techniques of production, tastes and population, such an isolated country is bound to suffer from a certain imbalance or disproportion between its productive and consumption capacities. Thus, take the case of a country which starts with a sparse population in relation to its natural resources. This was broadly true not only of Western countries during their mercantilist period but also of the underdeveloped countries of South-East Asia, Latin America and Africa when they were opened up to international trade in the nineteenth century. Given this situation, the conventional international-trade theory (in its Ohlin version) would say that this initial disproportion between land and labour would have been equilibrated away by appropriate price adjustments: i.e., rents would be low and relatively land-using commodities would have low prices, whereas wages would be high and relatively labour-using commodities would have high prices. In equilibrium there would be no surplus productive capacity (although there might be surplus land by itself) because the scarce factor, labour, would have been fully employed. Thus when this country enters into international trade it can produce the exports only by drawing labour away from domestic production. Now this result is obtained only by introducing a highly developed price mechanism and economic organisation into a country which is supposed to have had no previous economic contacts with the outside world. This procedure may be instructive while dealing with the isolated economy as a theoretical model. But it is misleading when we are dealing with genuinely isolated economies in their proper historical setting; it is misleading, in particular, when we are dealing with the underdeveloped countries, many of which were subsistence economies when they were opened to international trade. In fact, it was the growth of international trade itself which introduced or extended the money economy in these countries. Given the genuine historical setting of an isolated economy, might not its initial disproportion between its resources, techniques, tastes and population show itself in the form of surplus productive capacity?

Adam Smith himself thought that the pre-existence of a surplus productive capacity in an isolated economy was such a matter of common observation that he assumed it implicitly without elaborating upon it. But he did give some hints suggesting how the "narrowness of the home market," which causes the surplus capacity, is bound up with the under-developed economic organisation of an isolated country, particularly the lack of a good internal transport system and of suitable investment opportunities.[11] Further his concept of surplus productive capacity is not merely a matter of surplus land by itself but surplus land combined with surplus labour; and the surplus labour is then linked up with his concept of "un-productive" labour. To avoid confusion, this latter should not be identified with the modern concept of "disguised unemployment" caused by an acute shortage of land in overpopulated countries. Although Smith described some cases of genuine "disguised unemployment" in the modern sense, particularly with reference to China, "unproductive" labour in his sense can arise even in thinly populated countries, provided their internal economic organisation is sufficiently underdeveloped. In fact, it is especially in relation to those underdeveloped countries which started off with sparse populations in relation to their natural resources that we shall find Smith's "vent-for-surplus" approach very illuminating.

III

Let us now try to relate the "vent-for-surplus" theory to the nineteenth-century process of expansion of international trade to the underdeveloped countries. Even from the somewhat meagre historical information about these countries, two broad features stand out very clearly. First the underdeveloped countries of South-East Asia, Latin America and Africa, which were to develop into important export economies, started off with sparse populations relatively to their natural resources. If North America and Australia could then be described as "empty," these countries were at least "semi-empty." Secondly, once the opening-up process had got into its stride, the export production of these countries expanded very rapidly, along a typical growth curve,[12] rising very sharply to begin with and tapering off afterwards. By the Great Depression of the 1930s, the

---

[11] *Op. cit.,* Vol. I, pp. 21 and 383. This is similar to what Mrs. J. Robinson has described as "primitive stagnation." Cf. *The Accumulation of Capital,* pp. 256–58.

[12] For instance, the annual value of Burma's exports, taking years of high and low prices, increased at a constant proportional rate of 5% per annum on the average between 1870 and 1900. Similar rates of expansion can be observed for Siam and Indonesia (cf. J. S. Furnivall, *Colonial Policy and Practice,* Appendix I; J. H. Boeke, *The Structure of Netherlands Indian Economy,* p. 184; and J. C. Ingram, *Economic Change in Thailand since 1850,* Appendix C). African export economies started their expansion phase after 1900, and the official trade returns for the Gold Coast, Nigeria and Uganda show similar rates of increase after that date, although the expansion process was arrested by the depression of the 1930s.

expansion process seems to have come to a stop in many countries; in others, which had a later start, the expansion process may still be continuing after the Second World War.

There are three reasons why the "vent-for-surplus" theory offers a more effective approach than the conventional theory to this type of expansion of international trade in the underdeveloped countries.

(*i*) The characteristically high rates of expansion which can be observed in the export production of many underdeveloped countries cannot really be explained in terms of the comparative-costs theory based on the assumption of given resources and given techniques. Nor can we attribute any significant part of the expansion to revolutionary changes in techniques and increases in productivity. As we have seen in Section I, peasant export production expanded by extension of cultivation using traditional methods of production, while mining and plantation sectors expanded on the basis of increasing supplies of cheap labour with a minimum of capital outlay. Thus the contributions of Western enterprise to the expansion process are mainly to be found in two spheres: the improvements of transport and communications[13] and the discoveries of new mineral resources. Both are methods of increasing the total volume of resources rather than methods of making the given volume of resources more productive. All these factors suggest an expansion process which kept itself going by drawing an increasing volume of hitherto unused or surplus resources into export production.

(*ii*) International trade between the tropical underdeveloped countries and the advanced countries of the temperate zone has grown out of sharp differences in geography and climate resulting in absolute differences of costs. In this context, the older comparative-costs theory, which is usually formulated in terms of qualitative differences[14] in the resources of the trading countries, tends to stress the obvious geographical differences to the neglect of the more interesting quantitative differences in the factor endowments of countries possessing approximately the same type of climate and geography. Thus while it is true enough to say that Burma is an exporter of rice because of her climate and geography, the more interesting question is why Burma should develop into a major rice exporter while the neighboring South India, with approximately the same type of climate and geography, should develop into a net importer of rice. Here the "vent-for-surplus" approach which directs our attention to population density as a major determinant of export capacity has an advantage over the conventional theory.[15]

---

[13] This is what Professor L. C. A. Knowles described as the "Unlocking of the Tropics" (*op. cit,* pp. 138–52).

[14] Cf. J. Viner, *International Trade and Economic Development,* pp. 14–16.

[15] Those who are used to handling the problem in terms of qualitative differences in factors and differential rent may ask: why not treat the surplus productive capacity as an extreme instance of "differential rent" where the transfer cost of the factors from the domestic to export production is zero? But this does not accurately portray the

(*iii*) Granted the importance of quantitative differences in factor endowments, there still remains the question why Smith's cruder "vent-for-surplus" approach should be preferable to the modern Ohlin variant of the comparative-costs theory. The main reason is that, according to the Ohlin theory, a country about to enter into international trade is supposed already to possess a highly developed and flexible economic system which can adjust its methods of production and factor combinations to cope with a wide range of possible variations in relative factor supplies (see Section II above). But in fact the economic framework of the underdeveloped countries is a much cruder apparatus which can make only rough-and-ready adjustments. In particular, with their meagre technical and capital resources, the underdeveloped countries operate under conditions nearer to those of fixed technical coefficients than of variable technical coefficients. Nor can they make important adjustments through changes in the outputs of different commodities requiring different proportions of factors because of the inelastic demand both for their domestic production, mainly consisting of basic foodstuff, and for their exportable commodities, mainly consisting of industrial raw materials. Here again the cruder "vent-for-surplus" approach turns out to be more suitable.

Our argument that, in general, the "vent-for-surplus" theory provides a more effective approach than the comparative-costs theory to the international trade of the underdeveloped countries does not mean that the "vent-for-surplus" theory will provide an exact fit to all the particular patterns of development in different types of export economies. No simple theoretical approach can be expected to do this. Thus if we interpret the concept of the surplus productive capacity strictly as pre-existing surplus productive capacity arising out of the original endowments of the factors, it needs to be qualified, especially in relation to the mining and plantation sectors of the underdeveloped countries. Here the surplus productive capacity which may have existed to some extent before the country was opened to international trade is usually greatly increased by the discovery of new mineral resources and by a considerable inflow of foreign capital and immigrant labour. While immigrant labour is the surplus population of other underdeveloped countries, notably India and China, the term "surplus" in the strict sense cannot be applied to foreign capital. But, of course, the existence of suitable surplus natural resources in an underdeveloped country is a pre-condition of attracting foreign investment into it. Two points may be noted here. First, the complication of foreign investment is not as damaging to the surplus-productive-capacity

---

situation here. The transfer cost of the factors is zero, not because land which is used for the export crop is not at all usable for domestic subsistence production but because with the sparse population in the early phase there is no demand for the surplus food which could have been produced on the land used for the export crop. As we shall see, at a later stage when population pressure begins to grow, as in Java, land which has been used for export is encroached upon by subsistence production.

approach as it appears at first sight, because the inflow of foreign investment into the tropical and semi-tropical underdeveloped countries has been relatively small both in the nineteenth century and the inter-war period.[16] Second, the nineteenth-century phenomenon of international mobility of capital and labour has been largely neglected by the comparative-costs theory, which is based on the assumption of perfect mobility of factors within a country and their imperfect mobility between different countries. The surplus-productive-capacity approach at least serves to remind us that the output of mining and plantation sectors can expand without necessarily contracting domestic subsistence output.

The use of the surplus-productive-capacity approach may prove in particular to be extremely treacherous in relation to certain parts of Africa, where mines, plantations and other European enterprises have taken away from the tribal economies the so-called "surplus" land and labour, which, on a closer analysis, prove to be no surplus at all. Here the extraction of these so-called "surplus" resources, by various forcible methods in which normal economic incentives play only a part, entails not merely a reduction in the subsistence output but also much heavier social costs in the form of the disruption of the tribal societies.[17]

When we turn to the peasant export sectors, however, the application of the "vent-for-surplus" theory is fairly straightforward. Here, unlike the mining and plantation sectors, there has not been a significant inflow of foreign investment and immigrant labour. The main function of the foreign export-import firms has been to act as middlemen between the world market and the peasants, and perhaps also to stimulate the peasants' wants for the new imported consumers' goods. As we have seen, peasant export production expanded by using methods of production more or less on the same technical level as those employed in the traditional subsistence culture. Thus the main effect of the innovations, such as improvements in transport and communications[18] and the introduction of the new crops, was to bring a greater area of surplus land under cultivation rather than to raise the physical productivity per unit of land and labour. Yet peasant export production usually managed to expand as rapidly as that of the other sectors while remaining self-sufficient with respect to basic food crops. Here, then, we have a fairly close approximation to the concept of a pre-existing surplus productive capacity which can be tapped by the world-market demand with a minimum addition of external resources.

---

[16] Cf. R. Nurkse, "International Investment To-day in the Light of Nineteenth Century Experience," *Economic Journal*, December, 1954, pp. 744–58, and the United Nations Report on *International Capital Movements during the Inter-war Period*.

[17] Cf. The United Nations Report on the *Enlargement of the Exchange Economy in Tropical Africa*, pp. 37 and 49–51.

[18] It may be noted that the expansion of some peasant export crops, notably rice in South-East Asia, depended to a much greater extent on pre-existing indigenous transport facilities, such as river boats and bullock carts, than is generally realised.

Even here, of course, there is room for differences in interpretation. For instance, there is evidence to suggest that, in the early decades of expansion, the rates of increase in peasant export production in South-East Asian and West African countries were well above the possible rates of growth in their working population.[19] Given the conditions of constant techniques, no significant inflow of immigrant foreign labour and continuing self-sufficiency with respect to the basic food crops, we are left with the question how these peasant economies managed to obtain the extra labour required to expand their export production so rapidly. A part of this labour may have been released by the decline in cottage industries and by the introduction of modern labour-saving forms of transport in place of porterage, but the gap in the explanation cannot be satisfactorily filled until we postulate that even those peasant economies which started off with abundant land relatively to their population must have had initially a considerable amount of underemployed or surplus labour. This surplus labour existed, not because of a shortage of co-operating factors, but because in the subsistence economies, with poor transport and little specialisation in production, each self-sufficient economic unit could not find any market outlet to dispose of its potential surplus output, and had therefore no incentive to produce more than its own requirements. Here, then, we have the archetypal form of Smith's "unproductive" labour locked up in a semi-idle state in the underdeveloped economy of a country isolated from outside economic contacts. In most peasant economies this surplus labour was mobilised, however, not by the spread of the money-wage system of employment, but by peasant economic units with their complement of "family" labour moving *en bloc* into the money economy and export production.

The need to postulate a surplus productive capacity to explain the rapid expansion in peasant export production is further strengthened when we reflect on the implications of the fact that this expansion process is inextricably bound up with the introduction of the money economy into the subsistence sectors. To the peasant on the threshold of international trade, the question whether or not to take up export production was not merely a question of growing a different type of crop but a far-reaching decision to step into the new and unfamiliar ways of the money economy.

Thus let us consider a community of self-sufficient peasants who, with

---

[19] For instance, cocoa output of the Gold Coast expanded over forty times during the twenty-five year period 1905–30. Even higher rates of expansion in cocoa production can be observed in Nigeria combined with a considerable expansion in the output of other export crops. Both have managed to remain self-sufficient with regard to basic food crops (cf. West African Institute of Economic Research, *Annual Conference*, Economic Section, Achimota, 1953, especially the chart between pp. 96 and 98; *The Native Economies of Nigeria*, ed. M. Perham, Vol. I, Part II). In Lower Burma, for the thirty-year period 1870–1900, the area under rice cultivation increased by more than three times, while the population, including immigrants from Upper Burma, doubled. (Cf. also, Furnivall, *op. cit.*, pp. 84–5.)

their existing techniques, have just sufficient land and labour to produce their minimum subsistence requirements, so that any export production can be achieved only by reducing the subsistence output below the
minimum level. Now, according to the conventional economic theory,
there is no reason why these peasants should not turn to export production if they have a differential advantage there, so that they could more
than make up for their food deficit by purchases out of their cash income
from the export crop. But, in practice, the peasants in this situation are
unlikely to turn to export production so readily. Nor is this "conservatism"
entirely irrational, for by taking up export production on such a slender
margin of reserves, the peasants would be facing the risk of a possible
food shortage for the sake of some gain in the form of imported consumers' goods which are "luxuries" to them. Moreover, this gain might be
wiped off by unfavourable changes in the prices of both the export crop
they would sell and the foodstuffs they would have to buy and by the
market imperfections, which would be considerable at this early stage.
Thus, where the margin of resources is very small above that required
for the minimum subsistence output, we should expect the spread of
export production to be inhibited or very slow, even if there were some
genuine possibilities of gains on the comparative costs principle.[20]

In contrast, the transition from subsistence agriculture to export production is made much easier when we assume that our peasants start
with some surplus resources which enable them to produce the export
crop *in addition* to their subsistence production. Here the surplus resources perform two functions: first, they enable the peasants to hedge
their position completely and secure their subsistence minimum before
entering into the risks of trading; and secondly, they enable them to look
upon the imported goods they obtain from trade in the nature of a clear
net gain obtainable merely for the effort of the extra labour in growing
the export crop. Both of these considerations are important in giving the
peasants just that extra push to facilitate their first plunge into the money
economy.

Starting from this first group of peasants, we may picture the growth
of export production and the money economy taking place in two ways.
Firstly, the money economy may grow extensively, with improvements in
transport and communications and law and order, bringing in more and
more groups of peasants with their complements of family labour into
export production on the same "part-time" basis as the first group of

---

[20] Of course, this argument can be countered by assuming the differences in
comparative costs to be very wide. But, so long as export production requires withdrawing some resources from subsistence production, some risks are unavoidable.
Further, remembering that the middlemen also require high profit margins at this
stage, the gains large enough to overcome the obstacles are likely to arise out of
surplus resources rather than from the differential advantages of the given fully
employed resources. The risk of crop-failure is, of course, present both in subsistence
and export production.

peasants. Secondly, the money economy may grow intensively by turning the first group of peasants from "part-time" into "whole-time" producers of the export crop.[21] In the first case, surplus resources are necessary as a lubricant to push more peasants into export production at each round of the widening circle of the money economy. Even in the second case, surplus resources are necessary if the whole-time export producers buy their food requirements locally from other peasants, who must then have surplus resources to produce the food crops above their own requirements. Logically, there is no reason why the first group of peasants who are now whole-time producers of the export crop should buy their food requirements locally instead of importing them. But, as it happens, few peasant export economies have specialised in export production to such an extent as to import their basic food requirements.

The average economist's reaction to our picture of discrete blocks of surplus productive capacity being drawn into a widening circle of money economy and international trade is to say that while this "crude" analysis may be good enough for the transition phase, the conventional analysis in terms of differential advantages and continuous marginal productivity curves must come into its own once the transition phase is over. Here it is necessary to distinguish between the expansion phase and the transition phase. It is true that in most peasant export economies the expansion process is tapering off or has come to a stop, as most of the surplus land suitable for the export crop has been brought under cultivation. This, of course, brings back the problem of allocating a fixed amount of resources, as we shall see in the next section when we consider issues of economic policy. But even so, the surplus-productive-capacity approach is not entirely superseded so long as the transition from a subsistence to a fully developed money economy remains incomplete. In most underdeveloped countries of Asia and Africa[22] this transition seems not likely to be over until they cease to be underdeveloped.

The continuing relevance of the surplus-productive-capacity approach

---

[21] In either case the expansion process may be looked upon as proceeding under conditions approximating to constant techniques and fixed combinations between land and labour once equilibrium is reached. The distinctive feature of peasant export economies is their failure to develop new and larger-scale or extensive methods of farming. It is true that in subsistence agriculture "fixed factors," such as a plough and a pair of bullocks, were frequently used below capacity, and one important effect of cash production was to increase the size of the holding to the full capacity of these "fixed factors." But this may be properly looked upon as equilibrium adjustments to make full use of surplus capacity rather than as the adoption of new and more land-using methods of production. Increasing the size of holding to make a more effective use of a pair of bullocks is different from the introduction of a tractor! Our assumption of constant techniques does not preclude the development of large-scale ownership of land as distinct from large-scale farming.

[22] Cf. the United Nations Report cited above on the *Enlargement of the Exchange Economy.* Even in the most developed peasant export economies the money economy has not spread to the same extent in the market for factors of production as in the market for products.

may be most clearly seen in the typical case of a peasant export economy which with its natural resources and methods of production has reached the limit of expansion in production while its population continues to grow rapidly. According to the surplus-productive-capacity approach, we should expect the export capacity of such a country to fall roughly in proportion as the domestic requirement of resources to feed a larger population increases. This common-sense result may, however, be contrasted with that obtainable from the conventional theory as formulated by Ohlin. First, it appears that the Ohlin theory puts to the forefront of the picture the *type* of export, i.e., whether it is more labour-using or land-using as distinct from the total export capacity measured by the ratio of total exports to the total national output of the trading country. Secondly, in the Ohlin theory there is no reason why a thickly populated country should not also possess a high ratio of (labour-intensive) exports to its total output.

The ideal pattern of trade suggested by the Ohlin theory has a real counterpart in the thickly populated advanced countries of Europe, which for that very reason are obliged to build up a large export trade in manufactures or even in agriculture as in the case of Holland. But when we turn to the thickly populated underdeveloped countries, however, the ideal and the actual patterns of international trade diverge widely from each other. Indeed, we may say that these countries remain underdeveloped precisely because they have not succeeded in building up a labour-intensive export trade to cope with their growing population. The ratio of their export to total production could, of course, be maintained at the same level and the pressure of population met in some other way. But given the existing conditions, even this neutral pattern may not be possible in many underdeveloped countries. Thus, in Indonesia there is some evidence to suggest that the volume of agricultural exports from the thickly populated Java and Madura is declining absolutely and also relatively to those of the Outer Islands, which are still sparsely populated.[23] Of course, there are other causes of this decline, but population pressure reducing the surplus productive capacity of Java seems to be a fundamental economic factor; and the decline spreads from peasant to plantation exports as more of the plantation lands, which were under sugar and rubber, are encroached upon by the peasants for subsistence production.[24] In general, given the social and economic conditions pre-

---

[23] Cf. J. H. Boeke, *Ontwikkelingsgang en toekomst van bevolkings-en ondern-emingslandbouw in Nederlandsch-Indie* (Leiden, 1948), p. 91. I owe this reference to an unpublished thesis by Mr. M. Kidron.

[24] The same tendency to transfer land from plantation to subsistence agriculture may be observed in Fiji with the growing population pressure created by the Indian immigrant labour originally introduced to work in the sugar plantations. The outline is blurred here by the decline in the sugar industry. The reason why this tendency does not seem to operate in the West Indies is complex. But it may be partly attributable to the tourist industry, which helps to pay for the food imports of some of the islands.

vailing in many underdeveloped countries, it seems fair to conclude that the trend in their export trade is likely to be nearer to that suggested by the surplus-productive-capacity approach than to that suggested by the theory of comparative costs.[25]

IV

This paper is mainly concerned with interpretation and analysis, but we may round off our argument by touching briefly upon some of its policy implications.

(*i*) We have seen that the effect of population pressure on many underdeveloped countries, given their existing social and economic organisation, is likely to reduce their export capacity by diverting natural resources from export to subsistence production. If we assume that these natural resources have a genuine differential advantage in export production, then population pressure inflicts a double loss: first, through simple diminishing returns, and secondly, by diverting resources from more to less productive use. Thus, if Java has a genuine differential advantage in growing rubber and sugar, she would obtain a greater amount of rice by maintaining her plantation estates instead of allowing them to be encroached upon by peasants for subsistence rice cultivation. The orthodox liberal economists, confronted with this situation, would, of course, strongly urge the removal of artificial obstacles to a more systematic development of the money economy and the price system. Now there are still many underdeveloped countries which are suffering acutely from the economic rigidities arising out of their traditional social structure and/or from discriminatory policies based on differences in race, religion and class. Here the removal of barriers, for instance, to the horizontal and vertical mobility of labour, freedom to own land and to enter any occupation, etc., may well prove to be a great liberating force.[26] But our analysis has suggested that it is much easier to promote the growth of the money economy in the early stage when a country is newly opened up to international trade and still has plenty of surplus land and labour rather than at a later stage, when there are no more surplus resources, particularly land, to feed the growth of the money economy. Thus in a country like Java there is a considerable amount of artificial restriction, customary or newly introduced, which the liberal economists can criticise, e.g., restriction on land ownership. But given the combina-

[25] The surplus-productive-capacity approach also partly helps to explain why underdeveloped countries, such as India, which started off with a thick population tend to retain large and persistent pockets of subsistence sectors in spite of their longer contacts with the world economy, while the subsistence sectors in thinly populated countries, such as those in West Africa, tend to disappear at a faster rate in spite of their much later start in international trade.

[26] This is why the case for the "liberal" solution is strong in places such as East and Central Africa, where due both to the general backwardness of the indigenous population and the presence of a white settler population, both types of rigidity prevail (cf. *The Royal Commission Report on East Africa*).

tion of population pressure, large pockets of subsistence economy and traditional methods of production which can no longer be made more labour-intensive, it seems very doubtful whether the mere removal of artificial restrictions can do much by itself without a more vigorous policy of state interference. The truth of the matter is that in the underdeveloped countries where, for various reasons described above, the exchange economy is still an extremely crude and imperfect apparatus which can make only rough-and-ready responses to economic differentials, it may require a considerable amount of state interference to move toward the comparative-costs equilibrium. Thus given that Java has genuine differential advantages in the production of rubber and sugar, a more optimal reallocation of her resources may require, for instance, the removal of her surplus population either to the thinly populated Outer Islands or to industries within Java and a vigorous export-drive policy supplemented by bulk purchase and subsidies on the imported rice. Here we come to a fundamental dilemma which is particularly acute for the orthodox liberal economists. On a closer examination it turns out that their free-trade argument, although ostensibly based on the comparative-costs principle, is buttressed by certain broad classical presumptions against protection and state interference:[27] e.g., the difficulty of selecting the right industry to protect, the virtual impossibility of withdrawing protection once given, the tendency of controls to spread promiscuously throughout the economic system strangling growth, and so on. These presumptions gain an added strength from the well-known administrative inefficiency and sometimes corruption of the governments of some underdeveloped countries. Thus even if we believe in the "nineteenth-century pattern" of international trade based on natural advantages, how can we be sure that the state is competent enough to select the right commodities for its export-drive policy when it is considered incompetent to select the right industry for protection?

(*ii*) We have seen that the rapid expansion in the export production of the underdeveloped countries in the nineteenth century cannot be satisfactorily explained without postulating that these countries started off with a considerable amount of surplus productive capacity consisting both of unused natural resources and under-employed labour. This gives us a common-sense argument for free trade which is especially relevant for the underdeveloped countries in the nineteenth century: the surplus productive capacity provided these countries with a virtually "costless" means of acquiring imports which did not require a withdrawal of resources from domestic production but merely a fuller employment for their semi-idle labour. Of course, one may point to the real cost incurred by the indigenous peoples in the form of extra effort and sacrifice of the

---

[27] Cf. J. Viner, *International Trade and Economic Development*, pp. 41–42. See also Sidgwick, *Principles of Political Economy*, Book III, chap. V.

traditional leisurely life[28] and also to the various social costs not normally considered in the comparative-costs theory, such as being sometimes subject to the pressure of taxation and even compulsory labour and frequently of having to accommodate a considerable inflow of immigrant labour creating difficult social and political problems later on. One may also point to a different type of cost which arises with the wasteful exploitation of natural resources.[29] But for the most part it is still true to say that the indigenous peoples of the underdeveloped countries took to export production on a voluntary basis and enjoyed a clear gain by being able to satisfy their developing wants for the new imported commodities. Thus our special argument for free trade in this particular context still remains largely intact. The orthodox economists, by rigidly insisting on applying the comparative-costs theory to the underdeveloped countries in the nineteenth century, have therefore missed this simpler and more powerful argument.

(*iii*) We have seen in Section I that the deep-rooted hostility of the critics towards the "classical theory" and the nineteenth-century pattern of international trade may be partly traced back to the time when Western colonial powers attempted to introduce export-drive policies in the tropical underdeveloped countries; and tried to justify these policies by invoking the "classical theory" of free trade and the Adam Smithian doctrine of international trade as a dynamic force generating a great upward surge in the general level of productivity of the trading countries. To the critics, this appears as a thinly disguised rationalisation of the advanced countries' desire for the markets for their manufactured products and for raw materials. Thus it has become a standard argument with the critics to say that the nineteenth-century process of international trade has introduced a large "export bias" into the economic structure of the underdeveloped countries which has increased their "vulnerability" to international economic fluctuations.

In Section II we have seen that once we leave the ideal world of the comparative costs theory in which the resources not required for the export market can be re-absorbed into domestic production, every country with a substantial export trade may be considered "vulnerable." Thus

---

[28] It may be formally possible to subsume the surplus-productive-capacity approach under the opportunity-cost theory, by treating leisure instead of foregone output as the main element of cost. But this would obscure the important fact that the underdeveloped countries have been able to expand their production very rapidly, not merely because the indigenous peoples were willing to sacrifice leisure but also because there were also surplus natural resources to work upon.

[29] The social cost of soil erosion can be very great, but this may be caused not merely by an expansion of export production but also by bad methods of cultivation and population pressure. The problem of adequately compensating the underdeveloped countries for the exploitation of their non-replaceable mineral resources belongs to the problem of the distribution of gains from trade. Here we are merely concerned with establishing that the indigenous peoples do obtain some gains from trade.

a country may be said to be vulnerable because it has built up a large ratio of export to its total production simply by making use of its pre-existing surplus productive capacity. *A fortiori,* it is vulnerable when it has genuinely improved upon its original surplus productive capacity. How does the idea of "export bias" fit into our picture?

The term "export bias" presumably means that the resources of the underdeveloped countries which could have been used for domestic production have been effectively diverted into export production by deliberate policy. The implication of our surplus-productive-capacity approach is to discount this notion of "export bias." In the peasant export sectors, at the early stage with sparse populations and plenty of surplus land, the real choice was not so much between using the resources for export production or for domestic production as between giving employment to the surplus resources in export production or leaving them idle. In the later stage, when the population pressure begins to increase as in the case of Java, we have seen that the bias is likely to develop against, rather than in favour of, the export sector. Even when we turn to the mining and plantation sectors, it is difficult to establish a significant "export bias" in the strict sense. Here the crucial question is: how far would it have been possible to divert the foreign capital and technical resources which have gone into these sectors into the domestic sector? The answer is clear. For a variety of reasons, notably the smallness of domestic markets, few governments of the underdeveloped countries, whether colonial or independent, have so far succeeded in attracting a significant amount of foreign investment away from the extractive export industries to the domestic industries. In criticising the colonial governments it should be remembered that the only choice open to them was whether to attract a greater or a smaller amount of foreign investment within the export sector and not whether to attract investment for the domestic or the export sector.

This is not to deny that the colonial governments had a strong motive for promoting export production. Apart from the interests of the mother country, the individual colonial governments themselves had a vested interest in the expansion of foreign trade because they derived the bulk of their revenues from it.[30] In their search for revenue they have pursued various policies designed to attract foreign investment to the mining and plantation sectors, such as granting favourable concessions and leases, favourable tariff rates for rail transport, taxation policy designed to facilitate the supply of labour, provision of various technical services, etc.[31] But on the whole it is still true to say that the most important con-

---

[30] This is true for the governments of most underdeveloped countries, whether colonial or independent, past or present.

[31] For a discussion of the question of the possible export bias through the operation of the 100% sterling exchange system of the colonies, see A. D. Hazlewood, "Economics of Colonial Monetary Arrangements," *Social and Economic Studies,* Jamaica, December, 1954.

tribution of the colonial governments towards the expansion of the colonial exports is to be found, not in these export-drive policies, but in their basic services, such as the establishment of law and order and the introduction of modern transport, which enabled the pre-existing surplus productive capacity of the colonies to be tapped by the world market demand. If we wish to criticise the export-drive policies of the colonial governments it would be more appropriate to do so, not on the ground of "export bias" but on the ground that they may have diverted too great a share of the gains from international trade and of the public services of the colonies to the foreign-owned mines and plantations at the expense of indigenous labour and peasant export producers.

It may be argued that we have given too strict an interpretation of the "export-bias" doctrine which is merely meant to convey the general proposition that, whatever the exact cause, the nineteenth-century process of international trade has landed many underdeveloped countries with a large ratio of raw materials exports to their total national products, making it desirable to reduce their "vulnerability" to international economic fluctuations. But the trouble is that the "export-bias" doctrine tends to suggest that the raw-materials export production of the underdeveloped countries has been artificially over-expanded, not merely in relation to their domestic sector, but absolutely. Given the strong feelings of economic nationalism and anti-colonialism in the underdeveloped countries, this can be a very mischievous doctrine strengthening the widespread belief that to go on producing raw materials for the export market is tantamount to preserving the "colonial" pattern of trade. Thus already many underdeveloped countries are giving too little encouragement to their peasant export sectors by diverting too much of their capital and technical resources to industrial-development projects, and are also crippling their mining and plantation export sectors by actual or threatened nationalisation and various restrictions and regulations. The effect is to reduce their foreign-exchange earnings so urgently needed for their economic development. Of course, no competent critic of the nineteenth-century pattern of international trade would ever suggest the drastic step of reducing exports absolutely; some would even concede the need for vigorous export drive policies.[32] But having built up a pervasive feeling of hostility and suspicion against the "nineteenth-century" or the "colonial" pattern of international trade, they are not in a position to ram home the obvious truths: (*a*) that, even on an optimistic estimate of the possibilities of international aid, the underdeveloped countries will have to pay for the larger part of the cost of their economic plans aiming either at a greater national self-sufficiency or at the export of manufactured goods; (*b*) that the necessary foreign exchange for these development plans can be earned by the underdeveloped countries at the present

---

[32] Cf., for example, Gunnar Myrdal, *An International Economy*, p. 274.

M

moment only by the export of raw materials (though not necessarily the same commodities for which they were supposed to have a differential advantage in the nineteenth century); and (c) that therefore to pursue their development plans successfully it is vitally important for them to carry out the "export-drive" policies, which in their technical properties may not be very different from those of the colonial governments in the past.[33] In trying to carry out their development plans on the foreign-exchange earnings from raw-materials export they would, of course, still be "vulnerable"; but this should be considered separately as a problem in short-term economic stability[34] and not as a criticism of the nineteenth-century pattern of international trade in relation to the long-term development of the underdeveloped countries. From a long-term point of view, even countries which have successfully industrialised themselves and are therefore able to maintain their population at a higher standard of living by building up a large export trade in manufactures, such as Japan or the thickly populated countries of Western Europe, will continue to be "vulnerable."[35]

[33] Colonial governments have frequently defended their export-drive policies as the means of taxing foreign trade to finance services needed for internal development. But because they were colonial governments, their motives were suspect. At first sight we might imagine that the new independent governments of the underdeveloped countries would be free from this disability. But unfortunately, given the atmosphere of intense nationalism and anti-colonialism, this is not true. In some cases the hands of the newly independent governments seem to be tied even more tightly, and economic policies admitted to be desirable are turned down as "politically impossible." Here those economists who regard themselves as the critics of the classical theory and the nineteenth-century pattern of international trade have a special responsibility. Instead of dealing tenderly with the "understandable" emotional reactions which they have partly helped to create, they ought to be emphatic in pointing out the conflicts between rational considerations and "understandable" mental attitudes. The under-developed countries are too poor to enjoy the luxury of harbouring their emotional resentments.

[34] Cf. the United Nations Report on *Measures for International Economic Stability* and Myrdal's comments on it, *op. cit.*, pp. 238–53.

[35] It is particularly in relation to the thickly populated advanced countries of Western Europe which have specialised and adapted their economic structure to the requirements of the export market that Professor J. H. Williams found Adam Smith's "vent-for-surplus" approach illuminating. We have, in this paper, interpreted the "surplus" more strictly in its pre-existing form without the improvements and augmentation in productive capacity due to genuine "specialisation." (Cf. J. H. Williams, "International Trade Theory and Policy—Some Current Issues," *American Economic Review, Papers and Proceedings*, 1951, pp. 426–27.)

V

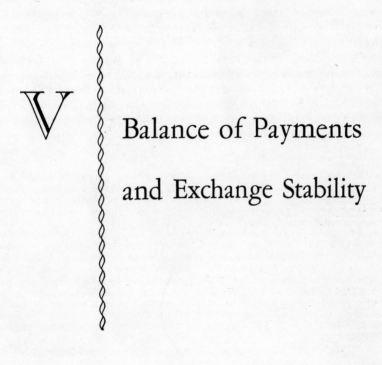

Balance of Payments

and Exchange Stability

21. Currency Depreciation, Income, and the Balance of Trade[*][1]

By ARNOLD C. HARBERGER[†][2]

I. INTRODUCTION

Existing discussions of the effects of depreciation on the balance of trade are framed in terms of a model in which incomes do not appear explicitly in the demand equations for imports and are thus implicitly assumed to be constant. Some writers have contended that the conditions for improvement in the balance of trade, obtained from such a model, are directly applicable to "Keynesian" models in which national incomes are variable. The purpose of the present paper is to investigate the validity of this contention; to make more precise the types of models for which various statements about the effects of depreciation on the balance of trade are valid; and to specify, for cases in which incomes are variable, the conditions under which income will increase as a result of depreciation.

In the discussion which follows, it will be assumed that the exchange rate is held fixed by means of national or international stabilization funds and is subject to change only through an alteration of the (national or international) policy governing the use of these funds. This assumption is in clear conformity with current institutional arrangements, and it permits us to consider a variation in the exchange rate as an independent cause leading to changes in the other variables of the system (as opposed to the alternative assumption of free exchanges, under which movements of the exchange rate are always induced by other causes, which also may have independent effects on the other variables of the system).

Furthermore, I shall assume that there are only two countries, each of

[*] *Journal of Political Economy*, Vol. LVIII, No. 1 (February, 1950), pp. 47–60.

[†] The University of Chicago.

[1] This paper was reprinted as "Cowles Commission Papers," New ser., No. 41, 1950.

[2] This paper was written while the author was affiliated with the Cowles Commission for Research in Economics. He is greatly indebted to L. A. Metzler, whose advice has been invaluable at many points, and to K. J. Arrow, F. Machlup, F. Modigliani, and the staff of the Cowles Commission for Research in Economics for many helpful comments and suggestions.

which produces only one good.[3] Income will be defined as the quantity of the national good currently produced (= production). For each country the quantity demanded of both its home-produced and the foreign-produced good will be taken to depend on current income (as defined above) and upon the ratio of the prices of the two goods (the terms of trade). I shall assume that all relations treated in this paper are linear.[4] For convenience, commodity units will be so chosen that the price of each good in terms of the currency of its country of production is initially equal to unity, and units of currency will similarly be chosen to make the initial exchange rate equal to 1.

II. A MODERN "FULL-EMPLOYMENT" MODEL

I shall first consider a case in which national income is held constant by government policy. This case conforms closely to an "ideal" policy, in that it presupposes that each government succeeds in stabilizing both the "full-employment" level of national output and the price of the good produced in its country. Such a policy could be pursued by the creation of a commodity standard in the national good in each country. Even if the supply curve of labor is a function of the terms of trade, so long as the desired output is attainable for all values of the exchange rate considered, the maintenance of demand at the desired output and of prices at fixed levels will lead to a wage adjustment sufficient to produce the desired output.

Under these conditions the demand for imports in each country can be written as a function of the exchange rate alone, thus:

$$x_1 = a_2 + b_2 k \text{ (demand of country 2 for the exports of country 1),} \quad (1)$$

$$x_2 = a_1 + \frac{b_1}{k} \text{ (demand of country 1 for the exports of country 2),} \quad (2)$$

where x_1 is exports of country 1; x_2 is exports of country 2; and k is the exchange rate (defined as that number by which the price of a good in country 1 must be multiplied to yield its price in country 2, with units of currency so chosen that, at the point of depreciation, $k = 1$). If we now let p_1 equal the stabilized price of the product of country 1 (= 1), and p_2 equal the stabilized price of the product of country 2 (= 1), we can

[3] The conditions of supply of each national good will vary among the models considered. Implicit in the assumed conditions of supply in the models treated are assumptions regarding the monetary policy, the production function, and the supply function for labor in each country. As each model is discussed, a set of such implicit conditions will be specified which is sufficient to generate the assumed supply function of the national good. Though sufficient, the specified conditions may not be necessary, and the reader may find alternative sets of assumptions which would equally justify the models presented.

[4] The assumption of linearity is justified by the fact that most functional relations can be approximated by linear relations when the range of contemplated variation is relatively small. The relevant linear approximation in all cases should be that one which connects the initial and ultimate equilibrium points.

write the balance of trade of country 1 in terms of the currency of country 2 as

$$B_1 = x_1 p_1 k - x_2 p_2. \tag{3}{}^5$$

The change in this balance of trade as a result of depreciation is then given by

$$\frac{dB_1}{dk} = x_1 + \frac{dx_1}{dk} - \frac{dx_2}{dk} = x_1 + b_2 + b_1. \tag{4}$$

We can now readily translate the price slopes (b) into price elasticities of demand (η), defined as < 0. Thus:

$$\eta_1 = \frac{b_1}{x_2} = \text{Price elasticity of demand for imports of country 1,}$$

$$\eta_2 = \frac{b_2}{x_1} = \text{Price elasticity of demand for imports of country 2.}$$

Then the change in B_1 resulting from depreciation can be written:

$$\frac{dB_1}{dk} = x_1 + x_1 \eta_2 + x_2 \eta_1; \tag{5}$$

and, if we let s equal the initial ratio of import expenditures to export receipts in country $1 = (x_2 p_2)/(x_1 p_1 k) = x_2/x_1$, we have

$$\frac{dB_1}{dk} = x_1 (1 + \eta_2 + s\eta_1). \tag{6}$$

On our definition of the exchange rate, depreciation by country 1 implies a decrease in k, so that, for improvement of the balance of trade of country 1 to result dB_1/dk must be negative. Thus our condition for improvement in the balance of trade in terms of foreign currency is that $|\eta_2 + s\eta_1| > 1$. If trade were initially balanced, the critical value of the (absolute) sum of the two elasticities of demand $|\eta_2 + \eta_1|$ would be 1, while, if country 1 had an initial deficit $(s > 1)$, this critical value would be somewhat less than 1.[6]

---

[5] Since both prices are, in this instance, assumed constant at unity, eq. (3) could alternatively be written $B_1 = x_1 k - x_2$.

[6] Only when trade is initially balanced is the critical value the same, regardless of whether the balance is written in terms of foreign currency or of home currency. For the case of an initial deficit, for example, the critical value is somewhat greater than 1 for improvement of the balance in terms of *home* currency, but less than 1 for improvement in terms of *foreign* currency (cf. A. O. Hirschman, "Devaluation and the Trade Balance: A Note," *Review of Economics and Statistics*, Vol. XXXI [February, 1949], pp. 50–53). The decision to consider the balance of trade in terms of foreign currency in this paper was not arbitrary, since it was felt that a deficiency in the supply of foreign currency is one of the primary incentives to depreciation. The other major incentive to depreciation is considered to be the desire to increase home income. While past discussions have used the change in the balance of trade in terms of home currency as an indicator of how home income will change as a result of depreciation, the change in income is given explicitly in our models with variable incomes. Thus,

These results are the same as those obtained by Marshall and Joan Robinson.[7] It is interesting to note, however, that these "traditional" conditions for improvement in the balance of trade follow so directly from the assumption that production is stabilized by Keynesian means. We can, alternatively, obtain a quasi-stability in national output by the use of a "classical model."

III. THE CLASSICAL MODEL

In a simple classical model for one country, output is determined by the equilibrium in the labor market, in which both supply of and demand for labor are functions of the real wage. In a two-country model, however, such precise determination cannot result, since not only the price of the home-produced good but also the price of the foreign good enter into workers' calculations of their "real wage." However, by considering the locus of equilibrium outputs for varying terms of trade, we can obtain output in each country as a function of the terms of trade. The terms of trade can then be looked upon as determining the level of national income in each country, and these levels of national income and the terms of trade as determining the total demand for the product of each country. Varying the terms of trade can succeed in equating total demand with total supply of one of the two national goods, but not both (except accidentally), since one price cannot generally be expected to equilibrate two markets.

The classical system avoided this over-determinacy by the assumption that in both countries all income is spent (Say's law). If this assumption holds true at all times (both *ex ante* and *ex post*) and in both countries, there will be some exchange rate which equilibrates the markets for both nations' goods; for now the demand functions for home goods and for imports in each country are related in a specific way, and we can eliminate the demand functions for, say, the product of country 1 by using Say's law and can find an exchange rate which will satisfy the equilibrium condition in the market for the product of country 2. Now, because Say's

---

for balance-of-trade problems, we consider B_1 (in terms of foreign currency) to be the relevant object of policy, while, for problems of income and employment, we consider income, and not the balance of trade in terms if domestic currency, as the relevant object of policy.

[7] Cf. Alfred Marshall, *Money, Credit, and Commerce* (London: Macmillan & Co., Ltd., 1923), pp. 355–56; and Joan Robinson, *Essays in the Theory of Employment* (2d ed.; Oxford: Basil Blackwell, 1947), pp. 142–43. Mrs. Robinson's more complicated expression for the effects of depreciation arises because she permits elasticities of supply of exports to be other than infinite. I shall discuss such a case below, where I permit the price of each national good to be a function of production. If each nation is assumed to produce more than one good, the conditions envisaged by Robinson might be still more closely approximated, and models which show the validity of Robinson's results when national incomes are assumed to be fixed by government policy can easily be constructed. However, when incomes are permitted to vary, the introduction of more than one commodity produced in each country leads to exceedingly complex models.

law implies not only that all income be spent but also that there is equilibrium in the balance of trade (see below), this exchange rate will also equilibrate the market for the product of country 1.[8]

Thus the classical two-country system can be regarded as determinate, once Say's law is introduced. But the introduction of Say's law implies equilibrium in the balance of trade; for the identity of income received with income spent implies equality of receipts from exports with payments for imports. Thus $x_1 p_1 k = x_2 p_2$, or $w = x_2/x_1$. Clearly, if trade is to be balanced in both the equilibrium position existing before and in that existing after depreciation, depreciation cannot improve the balance of trade. It will, in fact, lead only to a countervailing change in the ratio of the prices of the two goods, so as to leave the equilibrium terms of trade unchanged.

The fact that the classical system, if stable, implies that depreciation cannot affect the balance of trade does not mean that the Marshall-Robinson conditions have no applicability at all, for they remain as the conditions of stability in the system. This can be shown most easily by demonstrating that they characterize the case of "neutral" equilibrium (coincidence, over a certain range, of the reciprocal demand curves of the two countries). When this is true, trade will remain balanced even if the terms of trade change within the relevant range. For this range, then, $x_1 w \equiv x_2$, and

$$\frac{dx_1}{dw} \cdot \frac{w}{x_1} + 1 \equiv \frac{-dx_2}{d(1/w)} \cdot \frac{(1/w)}{x_2} .$$

This last identity can be written, in the notation used above, $\eta_2 + 1 \equiv -\eta_1$. These elasticities are the same as those used elsewhere in this paper when the supply of labor is affected only by the real wage in terms of the home-produced good in each country. They differ from those used above, however, when the supply of labor is affected by the terms of trade as well. Then they must be viewed as elasticities of demand, which take account of the indirect effect, through labor supply and national production, of changes in the terms of trade upon the demand for imports.

---

[8] Letting y, z, and x represent, respectively, total production, production for home consumption, and production for export and $w(=p_1 k/p_2)$ be the terms of trade, we have

$$y_1(w) = z_1(y_1, w) + x_1(y_2, w),$$
$$y_2(w) = z_2(y_2, w) + x_2(y_1, w).$$

From Say's law we obtain

$$x_2 \frac{p_2}{k} \equiv y_1 p_1 - z_1 p_1, \quad \text{i.e., } x_2 \equiv (y_1 - z_1)w;$$

$$z_2 p_2 \equiv y_2 p_2 - x_1 p_1 k, \quad z_2 \equiv y_2 - x_1 w;$$

hence we can find a value for w (w^0) which makes $x_2 + z_2 = y_2$. But this necessarily implies that

$$y_2 - x_1 w^0 + y_1 w^0 - z_1 w^0 = y_2,$$
$$\text{or } x_1 + z_1 = y_1.$$

IV. THE KEYNESIAN MODEL

Although the Marshall-Robinson conditions apply as conditions of stability in the classical model, the necessity that Say's law hold for this model to be consistent considerably reduces its short-run applicability to the real world. A Keynesian model can be constructed, however, which does not lead to inconsistency in the absence of Say's law. Such a case would arise if the supply of labor in each country were infinitely elastic at the prevailing real wage rate (in terms of the home-produced good) and if each national good were produced under competitive conditions with constant returns to labor input. Under these conditions we can, without loss of generality, consider the price of each national good to be the unit of currency in its country of production and to be stable. Production in each country would be determined by the equilibrium of total demand for its national good with its infinitely elastic supply, and, given the exchange rate, total demand for each good would be determined by the levels of production in both countries. The possibility of underemployment equilibrium, and of continued disequilibrium in the balance of trade, both characteristic of the "Keynesian" system, clearly exists here.

Such a case has been treated by Joan Robinson and A. J. Brown. They have reached the conclusion that the introduction of variable production leads to no change in the critical value of the sum of the elasticities of demand for imports but acts only to lower the absolute magnitude of the effect of depreciation on the balance of trade.[9] I propose to show that this conclusion does not follow from assumptions which I believe will be generally acceptable.

Consider any case in which, if production were stable, the elasticities of demand for imports would be precisely such as to leave the balance of trade unchanged as a result of depreciation. If, with such an initial situation, production were permitted to vary, the immediate effect of depreciation would be an increase in production in the depreciating country and a diminution of production abroad, both resulting from the substitution of the relatively cheaper product of the depreciating country for the relatively more expensive product of the nondepreciating country. These changes in production would, in turn, lead to an induced increase in demand for imports by the depreciating country and to an induced decrease in the demand for imports of the rest of the world. There would therefore ensue an induced deterioration of the trade balance of the depreciating country. Since in our example the initial effect of depreciation on the trade balance is, by hypothesis, zero, the "normal" total effect (initial plus induced) must be to worsen the balance.[10] Therefore, in order

---

[9] Cf. Robinson, *op. cit.*, p. 136, and A. J. Brown, "Trade Balances and Exchange Stability," *Oxford Economic Papers*, No. 6 (April, 1942), pp. 64–65.

[10] This analysis assumes that the elasticity of total (domestic plus foreign) demand for each country's product is negative. For a qualification of this assumption, which will be retained in the remainder of this paper, see the appendix, pp. 356–58.

for depreciation to have no net effect on the trade balance when production is variable, the sum of the elasticities of demand for imports of the two countries must normally be greater in absolute value than when production is fixed.

The "abnormal" cases in which our generalization would not hold follow readily from this example. Thus, if the induced effects led to a return of production in both countries to its initial levels, the critical value of the sum of the elasticities of demand for imports would be the same for the case of variable output as for the case of fixed output. But this would imply that production is not effectively variable as between "equilibrium" positions. Likewise, if the total effect of depreciation were to decrease production in the depreciating country and/or to increase production abroad, it might be true that the presence of variable production would lower rather than raise the critical value in question. But it would require a very special constellation of values of the marginal propensities to hoard and to import to invalidate the commonplace dictum that "unemployment can be exported by depreciation."

These conjectures can be proved rigorously within the framework of the following model:

$$\left.\begin{array}{l} y_1 = z_1 + x_1 \\ y_2 = z_2 + x_2 \end{array}\right\} \text{Income definitions and equilibrium conditions;} \qquad (7)$$

$$\left.\begin{array}{l} x_1 = a_2 + b_2 k + c_2 y_2 \\ x_2 = a_1 + \dfrac{b_1}{k} + c_1 y_1 \end{array}\right\} \text{Demand for imports;} \qquad (8)$$

$$\left.\begin{array}{l} z_1 = d_1 + e_1 k + f_1 y_1 \\ z_2 = d_2 + \dfrac{e_2}{k} + f_2 y_2 \end{array}\right\} \text{Demand for home goods,} \qquad (9)$$

where y_1 and y_2 represent production of the national goods of countries 1 and 2; z_1 and z_2 represent home demand in each country for its home-produced commodity; x_1 and x_2 represent exports of countries 1 and 2; c_1 and c_2 represent the marginal propensities to import in countries 1 and 2, and f_1 and f_2 represent the marginal propensities to consume home goods in countries 1 and 2. I shall additionally define $\eta_1 = b_1/x_2$ and $\eta_2 = b_2/x_1$ as the elasticities of demand for imports in countries 1 and 2; $h_1 = 1 - f_1 - c_1$ and $h_2 = 1 - f_2 - c_2$ as the marginal propensities to hoard in countries 1 and 2, and $s = x_2/x_1$ as the initial ratio of value of imports to value of exports in country 1.

From our assumptions it follows that production in each country of its national good is infinitely elastic (within the relevant range) with respect to the price of that good in terms of home currency. Thus, as before, prices do not appear explicitly in our model: their ratio (choosing commodity units so as to make each price = 1) is necessarily equal to the exchange rate. Again, as before, we choose units of currency so as to make the exchange rate $(k) = 1$ at the point of departure. In drawing conclusions from this model, I shall assume that all the marginal propensities involved are positive.[11]

From the definition of B_1 in equation (3) and from equations (8) it follows that

$$\frac{dB_1}{dk} = x_1 + b_2 + b_1 + \frac{c_2 dy_2}{dk} - \frac{c_1 dy_1}{dk} \tag{10}$$

We can determine dy_1/dk and dy_2/dk either directly (see n. 15 below) or indirectly. The latter approach has been chosen as a better indicator of the behavior relationships which underlie the system under consideration. The first fundamental assumption involved in the analysis which follows is that the marginal propensities to hoard, to import, and to consume home goods operate not on national production per se but on "real consumer income," of which national production is an adequate measure only when the exchange rate is constant. Let us therefore define $y_1' = y_1'(y_1, k)$; $y_2' = y_2'(y_2, k)$, where y' represents real consumer income and is made commensurable with production (y) by the requirement that $\partial y_1'/\partial y_1 = \partial y_2'/\partial y_2 = 1$ (i.e., that, as long as the terms of trade do not change, production can be used as a measure of real consumer income). Then

$$\frac{dy_1'}{dk} = \frac{dy_1}{dk} + \frac{\partial y_1'}{\partial k} ; \frac{dy_2'}{dk} = \frac{dy_2}{dk} + \frac{\partial y_2'}{\partial k} \tag{11}$$

The second fundamental assumption involved in the present analysis is that hoarding is a function of real consumer income *alone*. This assumption, together with the fact that the balance of trade in terms of home currency must be offset by hoarding (voluntary foreign investment is assumed to be included in the demand for imports), makes it possible for us to write

$$\frac{dB_1^\circ}{dk} = \frac{h_1 dy_1'}{dk} ; \frac{dB_2^\circ}{dk} = h_2 \frac{dy_2'}{dk}, \tag{12}$$

where B_1° and B_1° are the trade balances of countries 1 and 2 expressed in terms of home currency. From the definitions of B_1° and B_2° it is evident that $dB_2^\circ/dk = -dB_1/dk$, and that $dB_1^\circ/dk = (d/dk)(x_1 p_1 - x_2 p_2/k) = dB_1/dk + x_2 - x_1$. We can therefore substitute expressions in dB_1/dk and the initial balance of trade for dy_1'/dk and dy_2'/dk in equation (11), solve for dy_1/dk and dy_2/dk, and substitute the results in equation (10) to obtain

$$\frac{dB_1}{dk} = x_1 + b_2 + b_1 - \frac{c_2 dB_1}{h_2 dk} - c_2 \frac{\partial y_2'}{\partial k} - \frac{c_1}{h_1}\left(\frac{dB_1}{dk} + x_2 - x_1\right) + c_1 \frac{\partial y_1'}{\partial k} \tag{13}$$

[11] Both the above model and the present paper were suggested by a pioneering article by J. Tinbergen: "Modelli di commercio internazionale," *Giornale degli economisti*, Vol. VII (1948), pp. 627–48. Valuable comments by J. J. Polak led to the present formulation of the argument which follows.

In order to be able to express dB_1/dk in terms of the parameters and initial values of the variables of the system, we now need only to determine $\partial y'_1/\partial k$ and $\partial y'_2/\partial k$. It is easy to show, on the assumptions made above, however, that the change in "real consumer income" which would result if the exchange rate were to change while national production remained constant is equal to initial income times the percentage of income initially spent on imports times the change in the exchange rate (i.e., $\partial y'_1/\partial k = x_2; \partial y'_2/\partial k = -x_1$).[12] Equation (13) now becomes

$$\frac{dB_1}{dk} = \frac{h_1 h_2 [x_1 + b_2 + b_1 + c_2 x_1 + c_1 x_2 - (c_1/h_1) \ (x_2 - x_1)]}{h_1 h_2 + c_1 h_2 + c_2 h_1} \tag{14}$$

$$= \frac{h_1 h_2 x_1 \ [1 + \eta_2 + s\eta_1 + c_2 + c_1 s - (c_1/h_1) \ (s - 1)]}{h_1 h_2 + c_1 h_2 + c_2 h_1},$$

which, when trade is initially balanced, reduces to

$$\frac{dB_1}{dk} = \frac{h_1 h_2 x_1 \ (1 + \eta_2 + \eta_1 + c_2 + c_1)}{h_1 h_2 + c_1 h_2 + c_2 h_1}$$

Thus for the case of initial balance the critical (absolute) value of the sum of the elasticities of demand for imports is not unity when production is variable but unity plus the sum of the marginal propensities to import.[13]

---

[12] Letting v_1 represent money hoarding (in terms of home currency) in country 1, we can write the income identity $y_1 p_1 \equiv (x_2 p_2)/k + z_1 p_1 + v_1$. Differentiating this partially with respect to k, we obtain

$$\frac{\partial x_2}{\partial k} + \frac{\partial z_1}{\partial k} + \frac{\partial v_1}{\partial k} - x_2 = 0,$$

or

$$e_1 - b_1 + h_1 \frac{\partial y'_1}{\partial k} - x_2 = 0.$$

But e_1 and b_1 can be divided into substitution effects (e'_1, b'_1) and real-income effects ($f_1 \partial y'_1/\partial k$, $c_1 \partial y'_1/\partial [1/k]$), yielding the equation

$$e'_1 - b'_1 + f_1 \frac{\partial y'_1}{\partial k} + c_1 \frac{\partial y'_1}{\partial k} + h_1 \frac{\partial y'_1}{\partial k} - x_2 = 0.$$

Because e'_1 and b'_1 are slopes representing the pure substitution effect between home goods and imports, they must be equal (cf. Hicks, *Value and Capital* [2d ed.; Oxford: Clarendon Press, 1946], p. 310). Now, since $f_1 + c_1 + h_1 = 1$, our equation reduces to $\partial y' /\partial k = x_2$. Similarly, it can be shown that $\partial y'_2/\partial k = -x_1$.

[13] It may be noted that the critical values discussed thus far are critical values for elasticities of demand for imports (η) which contain income effects as well as substitution effects. We can alternatively consider critical values for elasticities (η') which contain substitution effects alone, by utilizing the equations

$$b_1 = b'_1 - c_1 \frac{\partial y'_1}{\partial k} = b'_1 - c_1 x_2;$$

$$b_2 = b'_2 + c_2 \frac{\partial y'_2}{\partial k} = b'_2 - c_2 x_1,$$

and defining $\eta'_1 = b'_1 /x_2; \ \eta'_2 = b'_2 /x_1$. The critical value for $| \eta'_1 + \eta'_2 |$ in the

Furthermore, since, when trade is initially balanced, $dB^*_1/dk = dB_1/dk$, this critical value also applies to the change in the balance of trade expressed in terms of domestic currency and to the change in "real consumer income" resulting from depreciation.

The effect of an initial deficit is, as in the fixed-production case, to reduce the critical value of the sum of the elasticities of demand for imports. It can further be stated that, for fixed values of the marginal propensities, there will be some initial deficit for which the critical value is the same for the fixed and variable production cases. This critical deficit is given by $s = 1 + (c_2/c_1)h_1/ (1 - h_1)$, which can be found by setting $c_2 + c_1s - (c_1/h_1) (s - 1) = 0$. Should s exceed this value, a set of elasticities of demand for imports such that depreciation, with fixed incomes, would lead to no change in the balance of trade would, with variable incomes, provide improvement in the balance of trade. This outcome would ensue because of a "perverse" effect of depreciation on the depreciating country's output (y_1), which would, in the new equilibrium established after depreciation, have fallen rather than risen from its initial value.[14]

The above example is probably unrepresentative of frequently encountered practical situations, but it points up clearly the fact that, under "reasonable" assumptions regarding production and tastes, it is possible for output to decline and the balance of trade to improve as a result of depreciation. The converse—an increase in output together with a deterioration of the balance of trade—is also possible, since, when trade is initially balanced, $dy_1/dk = (1/h_1)(dB_1/dk) - x_2$ and can therefore be negative even when dB_1/dk is positive. It is not possible, however, for production in both countries to move "perversely" as a result of de-

---

variable-production case when trade is initially balanced will then be unity. This cannot be compared, however, with the critical value of unity which we obtained for the fixed-production case in eq. (6), since the latter critical value refers to the sum of "total" elasticities $|\eta_2 + \eta_1|$. If we substitute for b_1 and b_2 in our fixed-production model, we obtain as the critical value for $|\eta' + s\eta'_1|$ not unity but $(1 - c_2 - c_1s)$. An interesting application of this fact arises in the interpretation of empirically estimated elasticities of demand for imports. Since these are usually obtained by using some measure of "real consumer income" (y') as the income variable in the demand equations, they are estimates of η' and not of η. The lowness of existing estimates is therefore at least partly counterbalanced by the fact that the critical value for $|\eta'_1 + s\eta'_1|$ is less than the traditionally accepted unity.

[14] For depreciation to be ineffective in the fixed-production case, $1 + \eta_2 + s\eta_1$ must equal 0. Then for the variable-production case

$$\frac{dB_1}{dk} = \frac{h_1 h_2 x_1 [c_2 + c_1 s - (s - 1)c_1/h_1]}{h_1 h_2 + c_1 h_2 + c_2 h_1}$$

which will be < 0 for $s > (1 + [c_2/c_1]h_1/[1 - h_1])$. But

$$\frac{dy_1}{dk} = \frac{dB_1}{h_1 dk} + \frac{x_2 - x_1 - x_2 h_1}{h_1} = \frac{h_2 x_1 [h_1 c_2 - c_1(s - 1 - sh_1)]}{h_1(h_1 h_2 + c_1 h_2 + c_2 h_1)} + \frac{x_1(s - 1 - sh_1)}{h_1},$$

which must be > 0 for $s \geqslant (1 + [c_2/c_1]h_1/[1 - h_1])$.

preciation, i.e., for production in the depreciating country to fall *and* for production in the rest of the world to rise.[15]

If the balance of trade in terms of domestic currency (B^*_1) is used in place of the balance in terms of foreign currency, our conclusions require only moderate revision. It is possible for this balance of trade to improve while production increases, or to deteriorate while production either increases or decreases, as a result of depreciation by country 1. It is impossible, however, for both an improvement in the trade balance in terms of domestic currency and a decrease in production to result from depreciation, since, from equations (11) and (12) and note 12, $dy_1/dk = h_1(dB^*_1/dk) - x_2$ and can therefore not be positive when dB^*_1/dk is negative.

When the trade balance is expressed in terms of domestic currency, the effect of an initial deficit is to raise rather than lower the value which the absolute sum of the elasticities of demand for imports must exceed if the balance is to improve with depreciation. Conversely, an initial surplus will lower this critical value, and if this surplus is great enough [$s < (1 - h_2)/(1 + [c_1h_2/c_2])$], the critical value will be lower rather than higher for the variable-income case than for the fixed-income case.[16]

The fact that an initial deficit has effects on the change in the balance of trade due to depreciation which are opposite in sign depending on whether the balance is expressed in terms of domestic or of foreign currency is not surprising. In this respect our conclusions merely represent the extension to the variable-income case of results which Hirschman has already shown to be true for the fixed-income case. Indeed, these relationships can be seen intuitively, once it is realized that $B^*_1 = -B_2$ (i.e., that the depreciating country's balance of trade in terms of its own currency is merely the negative of the nondepreciating country's balance of trade in terms of foreign currency).

V. A GENERAL MODEL

We can now generalize the Keynesian model specified by equations (7)–(9) by permitting the absolute price of each country's product to be a (presumably increasing) function of total production of that product.

---

[15] Direct solution of eqs. (7)–(9) yields alternative expressions for dy_1/dk and dy_2/dk:

$$\frac{dy_1}{dk} = \frac{(e_1 + b_2)(c_2 + h_2) - c_2(e_2 + b_1)}{h_1h_2 + c_1h_2 + c_2h_1} ;$$

$$\frac{dy_2}{dk} = \frac{(e_1 + b_2)c_1 - (e_2 + b_1)(c_1 + h_1)}{h_1h_2 + c_1h_2 + c_2h_1}$$

For output to decrease in the depreciating country ($dy_1/dk > 0$) and to increase abroad ($dy_2/dk < 0$) is impossible, since it requires that $(e_1 + b_2) > (e_2 + b_1)$ *and* $(e_2 + b_1) > (e_1 + b_2)$.

[16] These statements can be proved by deriving expressions analogous to eqs. (6) and (14) for dB^*/dk, and following, by analogy, the proof in n. 14.

Such conditions would arise if the supply of labor in each country were infinitely elastic at the ruling money wage and if diminishing returns to labor input prevailed or if, for any other reason, the supply of labor were characterized by "money illusion" on the part of workers. We must then substitute for k (the exchange rate), wherever it appears in equations $(7)-(9)$, an expression for the terms of trade, $w(= p_1 k/p_2)$, and add two equations expressing the price-income relationship:

$$\begin{matrix} p_1 = h_1 + m_1 y_1, \\ p_2 = h_2 + m_2 y_2. \end{matrix} \left. \right\} \begin{matrix} \text{Supply of products} \\ (m_1, m_2 > 0). \end{matrix} \qquad (15)$$

We now have released our assumption of constant prices in each country and can assume, instead, only such choice of units of commodities and currency that at the start $p_1 = p_2 = k = 1$. Differentiating the first six equations of this system with respect to w, we obtain the same expressions for dy_1/dw and dy_2/dw as we obtained in note 15 for dy_1/dk and dy_2/dk, respectively. Thus, so long as dw/dk is positive, only the magnitudes, but not the signs of the changes in incomes resulting from depreciation, will be affected.

If trade is not initially balanced, however, the expression for dB_1/dw will differ from that obtained for dB_1/dk in equation (14). This may be seen by rewriting equation (3) as

$$\frac{B_1}{p_2} = x_1 w - x_2 \qquad (16)$$

Then

$$\frac{dB_1}{dw} = x_1 + \frac{dx_1}{dw} - \frac{dx_2}{dw} + B_1 m_2 \frac{dy_2}{dw}. \qquad (17)$$

If trade is initially balanced ($B_2 = 0$) or if the price of the good produced in country 2 is stable ($m_2 = 0$), the last term in this equation will equal o, and the identity of dB_1/dw with the expression for dB_1/dk obtained earlier will be complete. Otherwise, in the "normal" case of a decrease in income in country 2, the critical value of the sum of the elasticities of demand for imports will be lower if an initial deficit, and higher if an initial surplus, prevailed in the balance of trade of country 1. However, the possibility of opposite directions of change in income and the balance of trade and the probability of a critical value other than that given by equation (6) for the sum of the elasticities of demand for imports remain as characteristics of this generalized model.

We must now investigate the conditions under which dw/dk will, in fact, be positive, i.e., in which the movement in terms of trade resulting from a change in the exchange rate will be in the same direction as the movement in the exchange rate itself. We can write the expression for dw/dk thus:

$$\frac{dw}{dk} = 1 + \frac{dp_1}{dk} - \frac{dp_2}{dk} \qquad (18)$$

$$= 1 + \left(m_1 \frac{dy_1}{dw} - m_2 \frac{dy_2}{dw} \right) \frac{dw}{dk}$$

$$= \frac{1}{1 + m_2 (dy_2/dw) - m_1 (dy_1/dw)}.$$

Obviously, this is uniformly positive for the normal case of an increase in income in country 1 ($[dy_1/dw] < 0$) and a decrease in income in country 2 ($[dy_2/dw] > 0$) as a result of depreciation by country 1. Only for cases in which incomes in both countries move in the same direction does any possibility exist that dw/dk might be negative.[17] Now in the normal case dw/dk is always < 1. In the other admissible cases it may be > 1, because here $m_2(dy_2/dw) - m_1(dy_1/dw)$ may be < 0. In these cases we should expect the effects of depreciation to be magnified rather than diminished by price flexibility, as $1 + m_2(dy_2/dw) - m_1(dy_1/dw)$ approaches zero. If this expression were equal to 0, dw/dk would equal ∞; and we should expect the system to be characterized by explosive instability. If, now, this expression were slightly less than zero, we should, at first glance, expect to observe explosive instability in the opposite direction. Yet the case of the negative multiplier (marginal propensity to consume > 1 implying explosive upward instability) leads to the conjecture that any $dw/dk < 0$ might imply explosive instability, the "multiplier" involved being "more than infinite." L. A. Metzler and Svend Laursen, in an unpublished paper,[18] have indeed shown this to be true. Thus the fact that such explosive instability is not observed can be accepted as demonstrating that, if the present model is considered sufficiently realistic for practical use, the sign of dw/dk can be taken as uniformly positive.

The introduction of flexible prices as functions of national production therefore destroys none of the qualitative conclusions which we reached in considering the Keynesian case above. In fact, all the models considered earlier are special cases of the present one, the Keynesian model arising when $m_1 = m_2 = 0$ and $dw/dk = 1$, the classical fixed-income model when $m_1 = m_2 = \infty$ and $dw/dk = 0$, and the case in which prices and incomes were fixed by government policy $m_1 = m_2 = 0$, $dw/dk = 1$, and $dy_1/dk = dy_2/dk = 0$.

VI. MODELS AND THE REAL WORLD

Though the application of the simple models considered in this paper to the real world is hazardous, it is nevertheless tempting. If we aver,

---

[17] The case of a decrease in income in the depreciating country, together with an increase in income in the nondepreciating country, is impossible (see n. 15 above).

[18] "Flexible Exchange Rates and the Theory of Employment" [subsequently published in *Review of Economics and Statistics*, Vol. XXXII (November, 1950), pp. 281–99].

with the classical economists, that the fundamental equilibrium relations of an economic system (national or international) are, within limits, determined by real variables and if we hold, with Pigou, that Keynesian underemployment equilibrium is, in fact, no equilibrium at all but only an important stage in one possible process of adjustment to disturbances, then we must retain the classical model set out in Section III as a fundamental guidepost to our economic thinking. The other models considered would then show methods, consistent with the policy and taste assumptions underlying them, of achieving equilibrium when, at the start, disequilibrium prevails or, in the hands of "hardhearted" governments, means of achieving a favorable (and reasonably lasting) disequilibrium in place of a pre-existing equilibrium.

If one is willing to grant that (in an approximate sense) governments are likely in the future to succeed, by monetary-fiscal measures, in maintaining both full employment and a stable price level, then the model of Section II becomes appropriate for analysis. Comparing this with the model of Section IV, which, in the same approximate sense, appears best to explain our experience in the 1930's, one can state that, if a significant fall in international demand for a country's exports should occur in spite of the successful maintenance of full employment at home and abroad, this fall in demand will no longer be partially equilibrated by movements in incomes at home and abroad. Rather, it will be reflected solely in the form of a balance-of-payments deficit—a deficit which will be larger than the one which would have arisen in the absence of policy-determined employment levels. Thus solution of the employment problem *implies* greater fluctuation in balances of payments arising out of shifts in international demand than would otherwise occur.

But the menace of balance-of-payments problems is not without compensation; for we have seen that a given amount of depreciation will generally be more effective in equilibrating the balance of payments if incomes are held stable than it would be if it were permitted to affect incomes as well as the balance of payments. In fact, so long as the ultimate equilibrium position is determined by real variables and so long as prices are stable in both countries, the amount of depreciation which will be necessary to reach this ultimate equilibrium after a given disturbance (e.g., a fall in foreign demand) will be the same, regardless of whether full-employment policies are successfully pursued in the countries concerned. The requisite amount of depreciation will, in the full-employment case, merely equilibrate the balance of payments. In the variable-income case the same amount of depreciation will succeed both in rectifying the (smaller) balance-of-payments deficit and in relieving the comcomitant unemployment resulting from the postulated disturbance.

Now if, in the future, full-employment policies are less than ideally successful and if unemployment is generally accompanied by a declining price level, while higher employment is found to be best stimulated by permitting the price level to rise, the general model of Section V becomes the appropriate tool of analysis. To the extent that full employment and stable price-level policies are effective, the generalizations made in the preceding paragraph will hold. However, to the extent that they do not hold, countries contemplating depreciation to eliminate balance-of-payments deficits should realize that depreciation will have repercussions on prices and employment which will tend to lessen its efficacy in equilibrating the balance of payments. When these repercussions are taken into account, the countries involved will find that the amount of depreciation necessary to restore equilibrium will be greater than would be estimated in abstraction from such repercussions.

The conclusions thus far presented could have been derived from the analyses of Robinson and Brown, with certain modifications for the case of variable price levels. I have as yet drawn no implications from the substantive conclusion of this paper that the critical value of the sum of the elasticities of demand for imports is lower, and may be substantially lower, when incomes are maintained by policy than when incomes are permitted to fluctuate. On this point I should like to suggest that the reluctance of so-called "practical" men in certain countries to contemplate depreciation may have been in part determined by the relative or complete ineffectiveness of exchange depreciations in the 1930's. This ineffectiveness was due partly to the fact that the depreciations of the 1930's were so widespread as to amount to little more than a world-wide change in the price of gold, and partly to the fact that the effect of the depreciations on incomes operated to lessen the absolute magnitude of the resulting changes in the balance of payments. But it may also be true that in some cases (e.g., where the relevant marginal propensities to import were high) the volatility of incomes made the critical value of the sum of the elasticities of demand for imports so high that depreciation led to a deterioration, not to an improvement, of the balance of payments. If this was the case with respect to certain countries in the 1930's, it should be pointed out to those countries that their situations need no longer be considered hopeless; for, if full-employment policies are successfully pursued at home and/or abroad, the critical values in question may now be significantly lower than they were in the 1930's; and depreciation, though ineffective in the last decade, may constitute the solution of their balance-of-payments problems in the present one.

VII. LIMITATIONS

The present simplifications of the theory of international trade reveal certain relationships of macro-economic magnitudes but conceal others, especially through the assumption of a homogeneous product and a single price level in each country. These limitations suggest that fruitful results might ensue if models were formulated which took into account (*a*) restraints on the substitution of one commodity for another in production, especially at levels of less than full employment,[19] and (*b*) the effects of differential movements in sectional price levels on the process of adjustment to disturbances under various assumptions and on the equilibria which would ultimately be approached.

APPENDIX

It has been assumed throughout this paper that, with production in both countries constant, the total quantity demanded (at home and

FIGURE 1

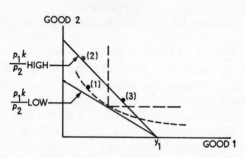

abroad) of each country's good was a decreasing function of the relative price of that good. This need not be the case, however, since (Hicksian) income effects are present in the situation postulated. This can be illustrated in the accompanying indifference diagram (Figure 1).

Since our price slopes b_1 and e_1 are defined as measuring the amounts by which consumption of imports and home goods, respectively, will change if p_1k/p_2 changes *with national production constant*, we are justified in making the two price lines converge at y_1.[20] Now one can easily see that, though the substitution effect will always lead toward negative price elasticities (point 1), the income effect will do the same only in the case in which the home-produced good is inferior (point 2). Under our assumption that neither good is inferior ($c_1, f_1 > 0$), the income effect will lead toward $b_1 < 0$, $e_1 > 0$ (point 3).

In order for the total demand for the product of country 1 to be an increasing function of its relative price (i.e., for $[e_1 + b_2]$ to be > 0), the (positive) income effect in e_1 must be strong enough to overcome three negative components: the income effect in b_2 and the substitution effects

---

[19] The classical full-employment model can easily be generalized to release the one-commodity assumption. In such cases the "elasticity of demand for imports" becomes a composite of elasticities of demand and elasticities of substitution in production.

[20] For simplicity, the hoarding effects, which are taken into account in the text, are neglected in the diagram.

in both e_1 and b_2. In the terminology of note 12, $(e_1 + b_2)$ will be > 0 only if $f_1 x_2 > |e'_1 + b'_2 - c_2 x_1|$ and $(e_2 + b_1)$ will be > 0 only if $f_2 x_1 > |e'_2 + b'_1 - c_1 x_2|$.

The inclusion of this (probably highly unlikely) case in our analysis destroys none of the conclusions reached above. The primary purpose of the present separate treatment is to point out that the perverse effects of depreciation upon the national production of either country, discussed in Section IV, are brought about entirely through the induced "repercussions" of production and demand. They do not require that the initial response of production to depreciation be perverse, which it would be if either $(e_1 + b_2)$ or $(e_2 + b_1)$ were > 0; nor do they require that either country have a negative marginal propensity to hoard, which is necessary for analogous perverse movements in production to take place when the disturbance is not depreciation but an international transfer of purchasing power at constant price and exchange-rate levels.

This fact can be demonstrated intuitively. Suppose that the initial increase in production in the depreciating country is large, while the initial fall in production abroad is very small. Then, if the marginal propensity to import of the depreciating country is sufficiently large, the increase of production abroad induced by the increased demand of the depreciating country may exceed the initial decrease, and the final equilibrium may thus be characterized by increased production in both countries. Conversely, if the initial decrease in foreign production were very large and the foreign marginal propensity to import were sufficiently high, the induced decrease in the depreciating country's production may exceed the initial increase, and the final equilibrium may thus be characterized by decreased production in both countries. One can also view depreciation as leading initially to increased hoarding abroad and to decreased hoarding in the depreciating country, owing to the initial effects of depreciation on "real consumer income." There may therefore result either an initial net increase or an initial net decrease in the total amount of active purchasing power in the international system. Net changes in active purchasing power, taken by themselves, will always, under our assumptions, lead to parallel movements in production in both countries, and, even when other effects of depreciation are present, this tendency to parallel movements of production may dominate.

These conclusions can be verified by reference to the equations of note 15, which show that dy_1/dk can be > 0 if $c_2 |e_2 + b_1| > (c_2 + h_2)|e_1 + b_2|$, and that dy_2/dk can be < 0 if $c_1 |e_1 + b_2| > (c_1 + h_1)|e_2 + b_1|$. Thus an ultimate decrease in production in the depreciating country will be the more likely, the larger is the initial decrease in production abroad compared to the initial increase in production at home (i.e., the larger is $|e_2 + b_1|/|e_1 + b_2|$), the larger is the marginal propensity to import of the foreign country, and the smaller is the marginal propensity to hoard of the foreign country. Similarly, an ultimate increase in production abroad will be the more likely, the larger is the initial increase of production in the depreciating country compared to the initial decrease in production abroad, the larger is the marginal propensity to import of the depreciating country, and the smaller is the marginal propensity to hoard of the depreciating country.

22. Effects of a Devaluation

on a Trade Balance[*]

By SIDNEY S. ALEXANDER[†]

THE CONVENTIONAL ANSWER to the question, what is the effect of a devaluation on the trade balance of the devaluing country, runs in terms of the supply and demand conditions in the devaluing country and in the rest of the world. It is presumed that the devaluation initially tends to reduce the foreign prices of the country's exports in proportion to the devaluation. At these reduced prices, foreign demand for the country's exports will be increased, thus tending to bid up the foreign prices of these exports part-way back toward their predevaluation levels. How much the foreign currency proceeds of the country's exports will change then depends upon the elasticity of foreign demand for the country's exports and the elasticity of domestic supply of export goods. Similarly, on the import side, the initial effect of the devaluation is to raise the domestic price of imports, presumably leading to some reduction in the country's demand for imports, which in turn may tend to reduce the world price of the imported goods. The size of these reactions on imports depends upon the elasticity of domestic demand for imports and the elasticity of foreign supply of imports. The effect of the devaluation on the foreign trade balance can accordingly be expressed in a formula which involves principally the four elasticities mentioned above.[1]

In the present paper, it is suggested that a more fruitful line of approach can be based on a concentration on the relationships of real expenditure to real income and on the relationships of both of these to the price levels, rather than on the more traditional supply and demand analysis.

---

[*] IMF Staff Papers, Vol. II (April, 1952), pp. 263–78.

[†] Massachusetts Institute of Technology.

[1] See A. P. Lerner, The Economics of Control (New York, 1946), p. 378; Joan Robinson, "The Foreign Exchanges," Essays in the Theory of Employment (2d ed.; Oxford, 1947), p. 143, fn., reprinted in Readings in the Theory of International Trade, H. S. Ellis and L. Metzler (eds.) (Philadelphia, 1949), p. 93, fn. 10; A. J. Brown, "Trade Balances and Exchange Stability," Oxford Economic Papers, No. 6 (1942), pp. 57–76; Lloyd Metzler, "The Theory of International Trade," A Survey of Contemporary Economics, H. S. Ellis (ed.) (Philadelphia, 1948), p. 226.

THE ELASTICITIES APPROACH

The conventional analysis is an extension, to imports and to exports as a whole, of the familiar Marshallian supply and demand analysis of the price and production of a single commodity. While supply and demand curves are very useful tools for analyzing the factors that determine price and output for a single good, their value is much more questionable when applied to imports and exports as a whole. Similarly, the extension of the Marshallian partial equilibrium analysis to the determination of total employment and output has been found to be of limited use. The most important reservation against the use of the Marshallian supply and demand curves in the analysis of the effects of a devaluation arises from the complexity of the relationships which govern supply and demand conditions in international trade. The elasticities for which the conventional formulas are valid must be defined as total elasticities and not as partial elasticities.

Partial elasticities measure the effect of a change of price on the quantity supplied or demanded when all other things remain equal. Total elasticities relevant to a devaluation measure the corresponding relationship when the other things have changed that are likely to change as a result of the devaluation. Accordingly, a total elasticity does not measure the direct effects of price changes on quantity, but the co-variation of price and quantity as the whole economic system seeks a new equilibrium. A total elasticity is the ratio of a percentage change in quantity to a percentage change in price. But the percentage change in quantity is the result not only of the price change to which it is related, but also of many other price and income changes which are themselves direct and indirect effects of devaluation. The percentage change in price is not generally equal to the percentage devaluation, but itself depends on the same complicated set of relationships. Therefore the total elasticities appropriate for the analysis of the effects of a devaluation depend on the behavior of the whole economic system, and the statement that the effect of a devaluation depends on the elasticities boils down to the statement that it depends on how the economic system behaves.

THE INCOME-ABSORPTION APPROACH

In examining the relationships of real expenditure to real income and of both of these to price levels, the analysis of the effects of devaluation should, of course, be applied to both the devaluing country and the rest of the world. It is generally recognized that a country's net foreign trade balance is equal to the difference between the total goods and services produced in that country and the total goods and services taken off the market domestically. For brevity, the taking of goods and services off the market will be referred to here as absorption. Absorption then equals the sum of consumption plus investment as usually defined (including in

investment any change in the holding of inventories). If a devaluation is
to affect the foreign balance, it can do so in only two ways: (1) It can
lead to a change in the production of goods and services in the country;
this change will have associated with it an induced change in the absorption of goods and services so that the foreign balance will be altered
by the difference between the change in income and the income-induced
change in absorption. (2) The devaluation may change the amount of
real absorption associated with any given level of real income.

In order to simplify the discussion, any factors affecting the foreign
balance of a country other than those connected with trade in goods and
services will be ignored. Also, it will be assumed that there are no restrictions on trade and payments, although that assumption is not
necessary for the validity of the subsequent analysis. Furthermore, only
the simplest forms of the various relationships involved will be considered. For example, only one price level will be considered, and the
change in that level will be denoted by p. The reader who wishes to
think of a more complex and realistic model may consider p as denoting
a whole set of price changes that might be represented by a vector.
Similarly, y will denote the change in the aggregate net production of
goods and services, i.e., in national income.[2] Finally, the relationships in
the devaluing country will be examined; to complete the picture, a similar
analysis, with some of the terms reversed, would have to be applied to
the rest of the world.

A starting point is the identity that the foreign balance, B, is equal to
the difference between the total production of goods and services, Y,[3]
and the total absorption of goods and services, A:

$$B = Y - A.$$

Changes in these quantities may be denoted by the corresponding
small letters, so that

$$b = y - a \qquad (1)$$

is our fundamental identity. It indicates that the change in the foreign
balance equals the difference between the change in output and the
change in absorption of goods and services. It shows that the first question
to be investigated is how the devaluation will affect the two terms, y and

---

[2] This might be taken by the ambitious reader to mean the whole set of changes in
the output of various goods and services each taken separately. Any linear coefficient,
such as the propensity to absorb, which appears as a simple constant in this discussion
could also be re-interpreted as an appropriate vector or matrix which multiplies the
income or price vector. In short, the analysis will proceed in terms of a highly
simplified model which could be made much broader by a re-interpretation of the
symbols.

[3] It makes no difference for the formal analysis whether Y is taken net or gross, i.e.,
whether it is national income or gross national product, provided A is correspondingly
defined as net or gross. For convenience, Y will subsequently be referred to as national
income, or, more briefly, income.

a. The above relationships hold, of course, both in real and in money terms. The present discussion will deal only with real quantities, not with money values.

Account may first be taken of the fact that the absorption of goods and services depends, at least in part, on real income, which itself is equal to the output of goods and services. Absorption may also depend on the price level, or other factors related to the devaluation, so that

$$a = cy - d \tag{2}$$

where c is the propensity to absorb, equal to the propensity to consume plus an analogous effect of income on investment, which may be called the propensity to invest. The term d may be called the direct effect of the devaluation on absorption. It expresses whatever tendency there may be for the devaluation to induce a change in the amount of real absorption at any given level of real income.

Equation (2) therefore states that the change in the absorption of goods and services in real terms as a result of devaluation is made up of two parts. The first, cy, is the change in real consumption plus real investment that is induced by the change in real income that results from the devaluation. The other part, d, is the change in absorption which results other than through the income effect.

A combination of the functional relationship (2) with the fundamental identity (1) yields

$$b = (1 - c)\,y + d. \tag{3}$$

This formulation is useful in that it directs the investigation to three basic questions: How does the devaluation affect income? How does a change in the level of income affect absorption, i.e., how large is c? How does the devaluation directly affect absorption at any given level of income, i.e., how large is d? In order to analyze these questions in precise terms, the entire economic structure of the devaluing country and of the rest of the world would have to be considered. Such an analysis would be far more complicated than is desirable for the presentation of the main ideas of this paper. Consequently, what follows is a summary of these main ideas, rather than a precise formulation of the relationships.

EFFECT OF DEVALUATION ON INCOME

Idle Resources Effect

The principal effect of a devaluation on income is associated with the increased exports of the devaluing country and the induced stimulation of domestic demand through the familiar multiplier relationship, provided there are unemployed resources.[4] In addition to the multiplier

---

[4] Fritz Machlup, *International Trade and the National Income Multiplier* (Philadelphia, 1943) and J. E. Meade, *The Balance of Payments* (London, 1951).

itself, the limiting factors on the process of inducing enlarged output are (1) the degree to which an increased output of goods and services is forthcoming without an extensive price rise in the devaluing country, and (2) the degree to which the rest of the world can absorb the increase in exports that is associated with the decline in the foreign prices of exports made possible by the devaluation—after allowance for the counteracting upward movement of the domestic prices of export goods, which occurs as the demand for these goods expands. These considerations are familiar in the literature.

It must be emphasized that the net effect of the recovery of income and production on the foreign balance is not the total amount of additional production induced, but merely the difference between that amount and the induced increase in absorption. This difference between the real production or income and the real expenditure on goods and services may be termed real hoarding. The foreign balance is, by the fundamental identity, equal to the aggregate real hoarding of the economy as a whole. The income-induced change in the balance, b, is accordingly equal to the income-induced change in real hoarding, i.e., the change in income, y, multiplied by the propensity to hoard, $1-c$. The existence of the business cycle makes it plausible that c may be greater than unity, that an increase in income may stimulate an even greater increment in the absorption of goods and services into consumption and investment. Many of the current theories of the business cycle do depend on the assumption that c is greater than unity. If c is equal to or greater than unity, the foreign balance will not be improved as a result of the increased output. Under such circumstances, the devaluation might be effective in stimulating recovery but not in improving the foreign balance except possibly through direct effects, which will be considered below.

At any rate, under conditions of unemployment, devaluation may be expected to exert a favorable effect on production and employment. This fact became evident in the devaluations of the thirties, and was recognized even before the promulgation of the Keynesian theory, though not in so systematic or analytic a framework.[5] The competitive depreciations of the thirties were largely associated with the recognition of the income effects of a devaluation, a recognition that was perhaps dim and intuitive on the part of many of those responsible for the devaluations, but nevertheless clear enough to motivate those devaluations. Of course, to the extent that the additional exports of the devaluing country displace those of its competitors, the levels of production and income in the competitor countries will be adversely affected. Recognition of this fact, as well as direct balance of payments considerations, must lie behind the opposition to competitive devaluation from an international point of

---

[5] See Seymour Harris, *Exchange Depreciation* (Cambridge, Massachusetts, 1936), especially pages 6 and 7.

view, as reflected in the International Monetary Fund's Articles of Agreement, I (*iii*).

From the point of view of a devaluing country that has unemployed resources, the effect on income, as well as the favorable effect on the balance of payments if c is less than unity, must constitute the most attractive potentiality of a devaluation. If the country is at full employment, this potentiality does not exist and the effects of a devaluaion must depend on the more tenuous and less attractive direct effects on absorption.[6]

Terms of Trade Effect

Another income effect frequently considered as influencing the foreign balance is that of the terms of trade. It is usually presumed, frequently with justification, that a devaluation will result in a decline of export prices in foreign currency greater than the decline of import prices in foreign currency. This presumption is based on the fact that a country's exports are usually more specialized than its imports, so that the price of exports will be much more subject to the influence of devaluation than will the price of imports. There may be some compensation, though probably only to a minor degree, if imports greatly exceed exports prior to the devaluation. Thus, if before the devaluation the country concerned was importing twice as much as it was exporting, and if as a result of the devaluation the fall in foreign prices of exports is 2 per cent and of imports 1 per cent, the deficit in foreign currency would be unchanged if the physical values of imports and exports were unchanged. It may, however, be assumed that the normal result of a devaluation will be such a deterioration of the terms of trade of the devaluing country as to make the balance of payments deteriorate by the amount t. That is, t is the measure of the reduction of the country's real income associated with the deterioration of the terms of trade.

A fallacious argument, frequently encountered, is that a deterioration of the terms of trade on account of devaluation will improve the foreign balance since it reduces the real income of the country and hence the demand for imports. It is true that the reduced income associated with a deterioration of the terms of trade will reduce the demand for imports

---

[6] See J. J. Polak and T. C. Chang, "Effect of Exchange Depreciation on a Country's Export Price Level," *Staff Papers*, Vol. I (February, 1950), pp. 49–70 for statistical evidence that, as far as effectiveness in altering export prices relative to those of competitors is concerned, the effects of a devaluation tend to be much stronger in depression than in full prosperity or inflation. However, Barend de Vries, in an unpublished paper, found that there was little difference in the competitive price effects of important devaluations as between the extreme depression period 1931–33 and the recovery years 1935–36. Deflation in nondevaluing countries in the earlier period tended somewhat to reduce the competitive advantages gained by the devaluers, while presumably in the later period the rise of domestic prices in the devaluing countries themselves also tended to reduce the competitive price effect of the devaluation.

as well as for domestic goods. Thus the decline in income, t, resulting from the changed terms of trade will induce a reduction of absorption by the amount ct, which will permit an equivalent improvement in the foreign balance partly through the direct reduction of imports included in ct and partly through the eventual transfer to the production of exports or of import substitutes of the resources formerly used to produce the domestic components of ct. The effects of the deterioration of the terms of trade accordingly will be, after resources are transferred, an improvement of the amount, ct. But the entire deterioration, t, of the national income as a result of the changed terms of trade is initially a reduction in the foreign balance. That is, the change of the terms of trade initially imposes a reduction, t, in the foreign balance and then has the effect of stimulating an improvement, ct, so that the change in the balance associated with the initial terms of trade effect on income, t, is $t\text{-}ct$ or $(1\text{-}c)t$. This might have been seen directly from equation (3). If t is negative, as assumed, and if c is less than unity, then a deterioration in the terms of trade also implies a deterioration in the foreign balance. Only if c is greater than unity will the adverse terms of trade effect improve the foreign balance.

The aggregate income effects may then be expressed as $(1\text{-}c)$ multiplied by the change of income. That change of income will have two components. One, presumably positive, is the idle resources effect, i.e., the increased production stimulated by the devaluation. The other, presumably negative, is the effect on income of the change in the terms of trade. The resulting change in income, y, will induce a change in absorption, cy, so that it will, according to equation (1), result in a change of the foreign balance equal to $y\text{-}cy$ or $(1\text{-}c)y$.

DIRECT EFFECT ON ABSORPTION

If there is initially full employment, or if c is almost unity or greater than unity, the principal favorable influence of a devaluation on the foreign balance is through the direct effect on absorption. This direct effect is largely associated with a tendency for a high or rising price level to discourage consumption or investment out of a given level of real income. It is important to recognize that this effect is not connected with any tendency for higher prices to force a reduction of consumption or investment out of a given money income. That would be an effect through real income, since if prices go up relative to money income, real income goes down. Except for the terms of trade effect on income, the real income of the devaluing country should not be expected to decline; at full employment, money income and money prices can be expected to move together. The direct effect on absorption is any influence toward lower real expenditure as money income and money prices rise together as a result of the devaluation.

In order most clearly to illustrate the nature of the forces behind d, the direct effect on absorption, certain assumptions which imply that all other effects are absent can be made. Accordingly, assume that the devaluing country is at full employment so that real income produced cannot be increased as a result of devaluation. Furthermore, assume that the foreign supply of imports and the foreign demand for exports are perfectly elastic, so that the foreign currency prices of imports and exports, and hence the terms of trade, will be unchanged. Thus there will be no income effects, either through increased production or through a change in the terms of trade.

The higher import and export prices in domestic currency resulting from devaluation will initially induce an attempt by individuals and enterprises in the devaluing country to shift their demand from imports to the home market and to export more. The resulting increased demand for the country's production would tend to raise domestic prices and money incomes to the point where the increased demands are choked off by the combined operation of the direct absorption effect and the narrowing price differential between the foreign and the domestic markets. If there were no direct absorption effect, domestic prices would continue to rise until there was no longer any tendency to substitute domestic goods for imports, or to try to export more, and there would be no change of the foreign balance as a result of the devaluation.

The relationship involved may be illustrated by a crude example. Suppose, under the assumed conditions of full employment and perfectly elastic foreign supply and demand, that there is a 10 per cent devaluation and an elasticity of direct absorption of 0.1. This would mean that a 1 per cent increase in the general price level would induce a 0.1 per cent reduction of absorption at a given level of real income. It may also be assumed that the substitutability of domestic goods for imports in consumption, and of resources as between the production of domestic goods and exports, is such as to link the domestic price level to the prices of foreign goods by a factor of 0.5, so that the 10 per cent increase of import and export prices in domestic currency leads to a 5 per cent rise of the general domestic price level. Then the devaluation would lead to a reduction of absorption by one-half of one per cent of total absorption. If imports furnish about 20 per cent of total absorption, the improvement of the foreign balance would amount to 2½ per cent of imports. In terms of the conventional analysis, the inelasticity of domestic supply of exports and of import substitutes reduces the effect of the devaluation in spite of the perfect elasticities of foreign supply and demand. At full employment, the elasticity of domestic supply for import substitutes and exports taken together must be just another way of expressing the direct absorption effect.

It is frequently taken for granted that, even when the devaluing country is at full employment, a devaluation will lead to increased exports and reduced imports. If it does so, then clearly domestic absorption will have been reduced. The question to be explored is why, with a given real income, when money incomes and prices rise in the same proportion there should be a reduction of real consumption or investment.

The direct absorption effect can be divided into a cash balance effect, an income redistribution effect, a money illusion effect, and possibly into other, miscellaneous direct absorption effects.

Cash Balance Effect

The cash balance effect is perhaps the best known of the direct absorption effects. If the money supply is inflexible, and if moneyholders desire to maintain cash holdings of a certain real value, they must, as prices rise, accumulate more cash. This will require a reduction in their real expenditures relative to their real incomes. It might be possible for any individual to increase his cash holdings by selling other assets, but this is clearly impossible for the country as a whole as long as the banking system or government does not create more money, except to the extent that goods or services may be sold abroad and the domestic money supply thereby increased. Capital movements are ruled out here; if they were allowed they might change or eliminate the cash balance effect.

One result of the attempt to maintain real cash balances by increasing their money amounts while prices rise may be to drive down the prices of assets, i.e., to increase the rate of interest. This in turn might have some effect on real consumption or investment relative to real income: thus the cash balance effect may operate *directly* on the income-expenditure relationship through the foregoing of expenditure in order to build up cash, or *indirectly* through the rate of interest as the result of an attempt to shift from other assets into cash—an attempt that can be discouraged only by a rise in the rate of interest. Clearly, one of the most important components of the direct absorption effect would be the cash balance effect. A hypothetical example applied to the United Kingdom may illustrate the possible magnitude of that effect. Suppose that in the United Kingdom the total money supply is £5 billion, and that a devaluation raises domestic prices by 5 per cent and thus cuts the real value of cash balances by about 5 per cent or £250 million. Suppose that cash balances were previously in adjustment with the level of real incomes, and that for each £10 that they are out of adjustment there is a cut of expenditure of £1 to rebuild them. There would then be a cash balance effect (ignoring any repercussions through the rate of interest and assuming no change in real income) of about £25 million per year on absorption, and therefore on the foreign balance.

It is possible that the reduction of absorption on account of the cash balance effect, or of the other direct absorption effects, might be directed toward certain domestic goods and services, from whose production it is not easy to transfer resources to the production of exports or import substitutes; therefore, some unemployment might result. The results of this unemployment might then be traced throughout the economy. If c is less than one, the net result of this adverse effect on income produced would be a deterioration of the foreign balance which would tend to counteract the improvement from the direct absorption effects.

It is pointed out below that, before any of the analysis of this paper is applied to a practical case, it is necessary to abandon the oversimplification here adopted and to recognize that y, a, p, and c are sets of quantities, i.e., that they must be regarded as vectors or matrices. The economic content of this fact is that it will make a difference, in view of immobility of resources and other imperfections, in what sector of the economy a particular reduction of absorption, or change of income, takes place.

Redistribution of Income

The redistribution of income effect is also well recognized. There may be a long lag of wages behind prices, and profits might therefore gain at the expense of wages as a result of the devaluation. Rising prices will transfer income from fixed money income groups to the rest of the economy. Taxes, at least in advanced countries, can be expected to take a larger share of a given real income when the price level is higher. To the extent that income is shifted from those with a high marginal propensity to absorb to those with a low propensity, the foreign balance will be improved by the devaluation. It must be remembered, however, that absorption includes both consumption and investment, so that it is by no means certain that a shift to profits will lead to reduced absorption. Although the proportion of any increment of income consumed by the profit recipient may be smaller than the proportion consumed by the wage earner, the higher profits may stimulate investment demand. The government can, in advanced countries, usually be expected to have a low marginal propensity to absorb, so that the tax shift might be a significant factor influencing the relationship of absorption to income, and so affecting the foreign balance.

Money Illusion

The money illusion may contribute a favorable effect to a devaluation if it actually leads people to pay more attention to money prices than to money incomes. If at higher prices people choose to buy and consume less even though their money income has increased in proportion, over and above what can be attributed to the cash balance effect, the result on the balance of payments will be favorable. But rising money incomes and rising prices may actually operate in the opposite manner; for example, annual savings may be calculated in money terms and may fail to rise in proportion to money incomes and prices.

Miscellaneous Direct Absorption Effects

There may be other direct absorption effects, some working toward a favorable, others toward an unfavorable, change in the foreign balance.

Expectations of price rises may be inspired, leading to increased absorption with adverse effects on the foreign balance, at least in the short run. If investment goods come largely from abroad, investment may be much less attractive after the devaluation than before because of the rise in the domestic price of investment goods, provided no close substitutes are produced domestically. More generally, the goods imported may be such that when the domestic prices rise, the domestic purchasers cut their expenditures on those goods but save or hoard the difference, rather than shift the expenditures to other goods. The importance of such a tendency in any actual case is open to doubt, but it is a theoretical possibility.

Impermanence and Non-Proportionality of Effects

Many of the direct absorption effects may be transitory. Thus the money supply may respond to the increased demand for cash balances, so that the cash balance effect may gradually disappear or be counterbalanced by additional absorption financed by credit creation. Similarly, some of the income-distribution effects are associated with lags, but the lagged income may eventually catch up, e.g., wages may eventually rise to restore the predevaluation wage-profit relationship. Other effects depend on dynamic movements, on rising prices rather than on high prices. As the rise in prices comes to a halt, these effects will tend to disappear.

Furthermore, some of the effects may be non-proportional. A small devaluation may take advantage of the money illusion, or of wage inertia; a large devaluation may shatter the money illusion, or impart a dynamic momentum to the wage inertia, or lead to modifications of tax rates, etc.

In general, then, many of the effects of a devaluation on the balance of payments through the direct absorption effects may be expected to be transitory and non-proportional. It does not necessarily follow that, in the absence of unemployment, a devaluation cannot have a strong influence on the balance of payments; that depends on the strength of the various effects discussed above. The author's impression, however, is that in many cases, in which the question of devaluation is likely to become a live issue under conditions of full employment, the favorable direct absorption effects are likely to be weak. It would seem to be much more effective to operate on absorption directly through monetary and credit policy—limitation of government expenditures, of private investment and, possibly, of private consumption—provided these can be brought to bear on the foreign balance without adversely affecting income and employment. They must, of course, "adversely" affect absorption, since, at full employment, it is possible to improve the foreign balance only through reducing absorption.[7]

This practical conclusion is not, however, the main conclusion of this paper. The main conclusion is that the most fruitful approach to the

---

[7] Theoretically it is also possible through improving the terms of trade as well.

N

general problem of obtaining a satisfactory foreign balance, and in particular of appraising the effects on the foreign balance of a devaluation, is via the analysis of the income-absorption relationship. It is theoretically possible to obtain the same answers in terms of supply and demand elasticities, but one is more likely to be misled. It seems more in accord with the realities of the situation to recognize that, if the foreign balance is to be improved, the community as a whole must reduce its absorption of goods and services relative to its income. The inquiry can then best follow the line of asking who is to cut his absorption relative to his income, or what is to be the shift of income from those who, on the margin, absorb more to those who absorb less. Supply and demand conditions, in the sense of partial elasticities, may be useful tools in this analysis. But the total elasticities, for which the conventional formulas alone are valid, are not only poor tools; they may mislead, or at least obscure the analysis.

DEVALUATION COMPARED WITH OTHER METHODS

If an improvement of the foreign balance is required, it may possibly be achieved either through a devaluation or through some other method of reducing absorption relative to production. The general alternative to devaluation is sometimes referred to as deflation, but that term has a narrower connotation than it is desirable to give to the alternatives to devaluation. These alternatives, which may for brevity be referred to as disabsorption, may be characterized as the discouragement of absorption relative to income by means other than devaluation. Disabsorption may be attained through monetary policy, as for example, by discouraging investment and consumption through tightening credit. It may be achieved by direct controls, such as investment licensing or rationing of consumers goods. It may be applied over the whole economy, as in the form of a sales tax or income tax, or in selected spheres, as in the form of investment licensing or import controls. The means to disabsorption are many and varied, but they may all be characterized as domestic measures calculated to change the relationship of absorption to income, and hence to affect the foreign balance.

An analysis of the relative advantages, from the point of view of a single country, of devaluation and trade restrictions has been presented elsewhere.[8] That analysis is appropriate only to conditions of full employment. It can be extended to any other domestic measure for achieving a given balance of trade at full employment. Measures tending to reduce imports are of benefit to the country concerned as long as the relative domestic welfare value of import goods relative to export goods does not exceed the marginal terms of trade, i.e., the rate at which export goods

---

[8] See Sidney S. Alexander, "Devaluation versus Import Restriction as an Instrument for Improving Foreign Trade Balance," *Staff Papers*, Vol. I (April, 1951), pp. 379–96.

can be exchanged for import goods at the margin on foreign markets, account being taken of any tendency for the prices of exports to fall relative to imports as more exports are offered and imports demanded.

When consideration is given to measures to improve the foreign balance under conditions of widespread unemployment, the above criterion must be so modified as to be abandoned for all practical purposes. That criterion is based on the proposition that, if the marginal rate of exchange of export goods for import goods in the foreign market is less favorable than their domestic welfare values, it would pay to cut back on imports and thus gain a greater welfare value in the export goods saved for the domestic economy. But if the resources used to make those export goods would, under those conditions, become unemployed, then there would be no gain from the restriction but rather a considerable loss. It is generally recognized that under conditions of widespread unemployment a domestic expansion policy is appropriate. Any adverse effects on the foreign balance can, except in extreme cases of inelasticity of foreign demand and supply, be appropriately handled by devaluation rather than by disabsorption under such circumstances. Disabsorption becomes an attractive policy only as full employment is approached.

If disabsorption of a general nature, say through a broad deflationary policy, should lead from full employment to the idleness of certain resources which cannot be expected to be transferred to the production of exports or import substitutes, it is to that extent undesirable. It is well recognized that when deflation leads to unemployment it is an undesirable measure for improving the foreign balance. Other means, such as import restriction or devaluation, would be preferable. In actual practice, therefore, the choice between devaluation and disabsorption will be affected not only by the considerations of the terms of trade on which the above criterion is based, but more immediately by considerations of other effects of any particular measure on the domestic economy. Considerations of the desirability of the resulting changes in the distribution of income as among individuals are ignored here, although in practice these considerations may be important and sometimes governing. One of the most important effects of any measure to improve the foreign balance is the influence it has on production as well as on absorption.

In the analysis both of devaluation and of disabsorption, the issues turn largely on the price rigidities and general inflexibilities of the economy. A satisfactory analysis of the problems depends on the identification and the appraisal of these inflexibilities. This is strictly analogous to the familiar question of whether, for stimulating employment, a reduction of wages can be as effective as an increase in aggregate monetary demand. That question hinges on whether the supply of labor is related to real wages or to money wages; that is, whether the effect of a given change in real wages that comes from a reduction of the general price level differs from that which comes from an increase in money wages.

Similarly, in evaluating various measures likely to affect the balance of payments, an identification of the rigidities and inflexibilities is vital to the conclusions. Thus, in the foregoing theory no attempt was made to distinguish between those components of a reduction in total absorption, a, which actually provide additional exports or import substitutes and those which do not. This constituted an implicit assumption that the resources freed by a reduction in absorption anywhere in the economy could be applied anywhere else, and in particular to the production of exports or import substitutes. It is, accordingly, necessary in any actual case to deal with a far more complicated set of components of the quantities, such as income and absorption, than have been used in this discussion. It must first be ascertained whether the contemplated measure will actually bring about the desired disabsorption and whether there may not merely be a shift of absorption to other objects, e.g., to clothing if food is rationed. It is further necessary to consider whether the resources to be set free by any contemplated disabsorption will in fact find their way into the production of exports or import substitutes. Thus what is required is a highly detailed analysis of the locus of impact of the contemplated measure and the nature of the adjustments in absorption and in production that will consequently be made.

Even where some form of disabsorption—for example, restriction of investments through licensing—can be achieved in such a manner that the investment goods can then be exported, the choice between that measure and devaluation must depend on whether the economy can spare the investment goods better than the different set of goods that would be foregone as the result of a devaluation or a restriction on imports. At this level of generality, it is possible to distinguish between two important lines of inquiry that must be followed in evaluating the relative merits of various possible measures to improve the balance of payments. The first concerns the effects on income, the second the relative welfare value of the absorption that must be foregone. These two considerations must be appraised jointly. Thus, for example, an import restriction may not reduce income at all but merely change the level of absorption in the country concerned. A devaluation at full employment that achieved an equal improvement in the foreign balance might have a tendency to reduce the real income by the terms of trade effect. Imports may, however, have a domestic welfare value sufficiently above that of exports so that the reduction in real income associated with a more desirable composition of absorption is preferable to the higher real income but less desirable composition of absorption associated with import restrictions. This paradox contains an implicit criticism of the measure of real income used here, it implies that a lower real income can have a higher welfare value. The paradox could be eliminated by an improved method of measuring real income, but the fundamental principle remains. In evaluating alternative measures for improving the balance of payments, the final criterion must be the welfare value of the goods and services absorbed at the given balance of payments to be achieved. This will depend not only on the level of employment and production but also on the composition of that production, and on the level and composition of trade.

23. Towards a General Theory of the Balance of Payments[*][1]

By HARRY G. JOHNSON[†]

THE THEORY OF the balance of payments is concerned with the economic determinants of the balance of payments, and specifically with the analysis of policies for preserving balance-of-payments equilibrium. So defined, the theory of the balance of payments is essentially a post-war development. Prior to the Keynesian Revolution, problems of international disequilibrium were discussed within the classical conceptual framework of "the mechanism of adjustment"—the way in which the balance of payments adjusts to equilibrium under alternative systems of international monetary relations—the actions of the monetary and other policy-making authorities being subsumed in the system under consideration. While the Keynesian Revolution introduced the notion of chronic disequilibrium into the analysis of international adjustment, early Keynesian writing on the subject tended to remain within the classical framework of analysis in terms of international monetary systems—the gold standard, the inconvertible paper standard—and to be concerned with the role and adequacy in the adjustment process of automatic variations in income and employment through the foreign trade multiplier. Moreover, the applicability of the analysis to policy problems was severely restricted by its assumption of general under-employment, which implied an elastic supply of aggregate output, and allowed the domestic-currency wage or price level to be treated as *given*, independently of the balance of payments and variations in it.

The pre-war approach to international monetary theory reflected the way in which balance-of-payments problems tended to appear at the time, namely as problems of international monetary adjustment. Since

---

[*] In H. G. Johnson, *International Trade and Economic Growth: Studies in Pure Theory* (Cambridge: Harvard University Press, 1961), pp. 153–68.

[†] The London School of Economics and the University of Chicago.

[1] This paper embodies ideas developed in lecture courses at Cambridge and elsewhere; part of the argument is reproduced from an earlier paper, "Sketch of a Generalization of Keynesian Balance-of-Payments Theory," *Indian Journal of Economics,* Vol. XXXVII, No. 144 (July, 1956), pp. 49–56. The writer is grateful to the Institut de Science Économique Appliquée for providing him with both the opportunity and the incentive to attempt a more extensive exposition of these ideas.

the war, for reasons which need not be elaborated here, the balance of payments has come to be a major problem for economic policy in many countries. Correspondingly, a new (though still Keynesian) theoretical approach to balance-of-payments theory has been emerging, an approach which is better adapted to post-war conditions than the "foreign trade multiplier theory" and "elasticity analysis" of the pre-war period in two major respects: it poses the problems of balance-of-payments adjustment in a way which highlights their policy implications, and it allows for conditions of full employment and inflation.

The essence of this approach, which has been termed "the absorption approach," is to view the balance of payments as a relation between the aggregate receipts and expenditures of the economy, rather than as a relation between the country's credits and debits on international account. This approach has been implicit to an important extent in the thinking of practical policy-makers concerned with balance-of-payments problems in post-war conditions. Its main formal development is to be found in the works of Meade, Tinbergen and Alexander, though many others have contributed.[2] The purpose of this paper is to synthesize and generalize the work of these writers, and to use their approach to clarify certain aspects of the balance-of-payments policy problem.

Let us first summarize the traditional approach to balance-of-payments theory. The balance of payments must necessarily balance, when all international transactions are taken into account; for imbalance or disequilibrium to be possible, it is necessary to distinguish between "autonomous" international transactions—those which are the result of the free and voluntary choices of individual transactors, within whatever restrictions are imposed by economic variables or policy on their behaviour—and "induced" or "accommodating" international transactions—those which are undertaken by the foreign exchange authorities to reconcile the free choices of the individual transactors—and to define the "balance of payments" to include only autonomous transactions. To put the point

---

[2] See in particular J. E. Meade, *The Theory of International Economic Policy. Vol. I: The Balance of Payments* (London, 1951); J. Tinbergen, *On the Theory of Economic Policy* (Amsterdam, 1952); S. Alexander, "The Effects of a Devaluation on a Trade Balance," *International Monetary Fund Staff Papers*, Vol. II, No. 2 (April, 1952), pp. 263–78; also G. Stuvel, *The Exchange Stability Problem* (Oxford, 1951); A. C. Harberger, "Currency Depreciation, Income, and the Balance of Trade," *Journal of Political Economy*, Vol. LVIII, No. 1 (February, 1950), pp. 47–60; S. Laursen and L. A. Metzler, "Flexible Exchange Rates and the Theory of Employment," *Review of Economics and Statistics*, Vol. XXXII, No. 4 (November, 1950), pp. 281–99; R. F. Harrod, "Currency Depreciation as an Anti-Inflationary Device: Comment," *Quarterly Journal of Economics*, Vol. LXVI, No. 1 (February, 1952), pp. 102–16. The terminology of "absorption" was initiated by Alexander; Machlup's criticisms of Alexander's argument (F. Machlup, "The Analysis of Devaluation," *American Economic Review*, Vol. XLV, No. 3 [June, 1955], pp. 255–78), though valid in detail, miss the main point of Alexander's contribution, a point obscured by Alexander's own emphasis on the contrast between the "elasticity" and the "absorption" approaches to devaluation and his attack on the former. The later argument of this paper attempts a reconciliation of the two approaches in a broader framework of analysis.

another way, balance-of-payments problems presuppose the presence of an official foreign exchange authority which is prepared to operate in the foreign exchange market by the use of official reserves so as to influence the exchange rate; and "disequilibrium" is defined by changes in the official reserves, associated with imbalance between the foreign receipts and foreign payments of residents of the country, where "resident" is defined to include all economic units domiciled in the country *except* the foreign exchange authority.[3]

The "balance of payments" appropriate to economic analysis may then be defined as

$$B = R_f - P_f \tag{1}$$

where R_f represents aggregate receipts by residents from foreigners, and P_f represents aggregate payments by residents to foreigners. The difference between the two constitutes a surplus (if positive) or a deficit (if negative); a surplus is accompanied by sales of foreign currency to the exchange authority by residents or foreigners in exchange for domestic currency, and conversely a deficit is financed by sales of domestic currency by residents or foreigners to the authority in exchange for foreign currency. To remedy a deficit, some action must be taken to increase receipts from foreigners and reduce payments to foreigners, or increase receipts more than payments, or reduce payments more than receipts; and conversely with a surplus (though the rectification of a surplus is not generally regarded as a "balance-of-payments problem").

The "balance of payments" can, however, be defined in another way, by making use of the fact that all payments by residents to residents are simultaneously receipts by residents from residents; in symbols $R_r \equiv P_r$. Hence the balance of payments may be written

$$B = R_f + R_r - P_f - P_r = R - P. \tag{2}$$

monetary nature

That is, the balance of payments is the difference between aggregate receipts by residents and aggregate payments by residents. A deficit implies an excess of payments over receipts, and its rectification requires that receipts be increased and payments decreased, or that receipts increase more than payments, or that receipts decrease less than payments; and conversely with a surplus. In what follows, however, surpluses will be ignored, and the argument will be concerned only with deficits.

The formulation of a balance-of-payments deficit in terms of an excess of aggregate payments by residents over aggregate receipts by residents constitutes the starting point for the generalization of the "absorption

---

[3] Where the central bank or other monetary authority also holds the foreign exchange reserves, it is necessary for the purposes of this paper to separate its functions conceptually into two parts, and to class its transactions as monetary authority (including those with itself as exchange authority) among transactions of residents.

approach" to balance-of-payments theory—what might be termed a "payments approach"—which is the purpose of this paper. It directs attention to two important aspects of a deficit—its monetary implications, and its relation with the aggregate activity of the economy—from which attention tends to be diverted by the traditional sectoral approach, and neglect of which can lead to fallacious analysis. These two aspects will be discussed in turn, beginning with the monetary implications of a deficit.

The excess of payments by residents over receipts by residents inherent in a balance-of-payments deficit necessarily implies one or other of two alternatives. The first is that cash balances of residents are running down, as domestic money is transferred to the foreign exchange authority.[4] This can, obviously, only continue for a limited period, as eventually cash balances would approach the minimum that the community wished to hold and in the process the disequilibrium would cure itself, through the mechanism of rising interest rates, tighter credit conditions, reduction of aggregate expenditure and possibly an increase in aggregate receipts. In this case, where the deficit is financed by dishoarding, it would be self-correcting in time; but the economic policy authorities may well be unable to allow the self-correcting process to run its course, since the international reserves of the country may be such a small fraction of the domestic money supply that they would be exhausted well before the running down of money balances had any significant corrective effect. The authorities might therefore have to take action of some kind to reinforce and accelerate the effects of diminishing money balances.

This last consideration provides the chief valid argument for larger international reserves. The case for larger international reserves is usually argued on the ground that larger reserves provide more time for the economic policy authorities to make adjustments to correct a balance-of-payments disequilibrium. But, as Friedman has argued in criticism of Meade,[5] there is no presumption that adjustment spread over a longer period is to be preferred—the argument could indeed be inverted into the proposition that, the larger the reserves, the more power the authorities have to resist desirable adjustments. The acceptable argument would seem to be that, the larger the international reserves in relation to the domestic money supply, the less the probability that the profit- or utility-maximizing decisions of individuals to move out of cash into commodities or securities will have to be frustrated by the monetary authorities for fear of a balance-of-payments crisis.

The second alternative is that the cash balances of residents are being replenished by open market purchases of securities by the monetary or

---

[4] Where monetary authority and exchange authority are one and the same institution, domestic monetary liabilities may simply be extinguished by sales of foreign exchange.

[5] Milton Friedman, "The Case for Flexible Exchange Rates," 157–203 in *Essays in Positive Economics* (Chicago, 1953), especially 186, n. 11.

foreign exchange authority, as would happen automatically if the monetary authority followed a policy of pegging interest rates or the exchange authority (as in the British case) automatically re-lent to residents any domestic currency it received from residents or foreigners in return for sales of foreign exchange. In this case, the money supply in domestic circulation is being maintained by credit creation, so that the excess of payments over receipts by residents could continue indefinitely without generating any corrective process—until dwindling reserves forced the economic policy authorities to change their policy in some respect.

To summarize the argument so far, a balance-of-payments deficit implies *either* dishoarding by residents, *or* credit creation by the monetary authorities—either an increase in V, or the maintenance of M. Further, since a deficit associated with increasing velocity of circulation will tend to be self-correcting (though the authorities may be unable to rely on this alone), a continuing balance-of-payments deficit of the type usually discussed in balance-of-payments theory ultimately requires credit creation to keep it going. This in turn implies that balance-of-payments deficits and difficulties are essentially monetary phenomena, traceable to either of two causes: too low a ratio of international reserves relative to the domestic money supply, so that the economic policy authorities cannot rely on the natural self-correcting process; or the pursuit of governmental policies which oblige the authorities to feed the deficit by credit creation. In both cases, the problem is associated fundamentally with the power of national banking systems to create money which has no internationally acceptable backing.

To conclude that balance-of-payments problems are essentially monetary is not, of course, to assert that they are attributable to monetary mismanagement—they may be, or they may be the result of "real" forces in the face of which the monetary authorities play a passive role. The conclusion does mean, however, that the distinctions which have sometimes been drawn between monetary and real disequilibria, for example by concepts of "structural disequilibrium," are not logically valid—though such concepts, carefully used, may be helpful in isolating the initiating causes of disequilibrium or the most appropriate type of remedial policy to follow.

Formulation of the balance of payments as the difference between aggregate payments and aggregate receipts thus illuminates the monetary aspects of balance-of-payments disequilibrium, and emphasizes its essentially monetary nature. More important and interesting is the light which this approach sheds on the policy problem of correcting a deficit, by relating the balance of payments to the overall operation of the economy rather than treating it as one sector of the economy to be analysed by itself.

An excess of aggregate payments by residents over aggregate receipts by residents is the net outcome of economic decisions taken by all the individual economic units composing the economy. These decisions may usefully be analysed in terms of an "aggregate decision" taken by the community of residents considered as a group (excluding, as always, the foreign exchange authority), though it must be recognized that this technique ignores many of the complications that would have to be investigated in a more detailed analysis.

Two sorts of aggregate decision leading to a balance-of-payments deficit may be distinguished in principle, corresponding to the distinction drawn in monetary theory between "stock" decisions and "flow" decisions: a (stock) decision to alter the composition of the community's assets by substituting other assets for domestic money,[6] and a (flow) decision to spend currently in excess of current receipts. Since both real goods and securities are alternative assets to domestic money, and current expenditure may consist in the purchase of either goods or securities, the balance-of-payments deficit resulting from either type of aggregate decision may show itself on either current or capital account. That is, a current account deficit may reflect either a community decision to shift out of cash balances into stocks of goods, or a decision to use goods in excess of the community's current rate of production, while a capital account deficit may reflect either a decision to shift out of domestic money into securities or a decision to lend in excess of the current rate of saving.

The distinction between "stock" and "flow" balance-of-payments deficits is important for both theory and practical policy, though refined theoretical analysis has generally been concerned with "flow" deficits, without making the distinction explicit. The importance of the distinction stems from the fact that a "stock" deficit is inherently temporary and implies no real worsening of the country's economic position, whereas a "flow" deficit is not inherently temporary and may imply a worsening of the country's economic position.

Since a stock decision entails a once-for-all change in the composition of a given aggregate of capital assets, a "stock" deficit must necessarily be a temporary affair;[7] and in itself it implies no deterioration (but rather the reverse) in the country's economic position and prospects.[8] Neverthe-

---

[6] With the community defined to include the monetary authority, a substitution of securities for domestic money can only be effected by drawing securities from abroad in exchange for international reserves.

[7] A temporary deficit of this kind must be distinguished from a deficit which is "temporary" in the sense that the causal factors behind it will reverse themselves, leading to a later compensating surplus: e.g. a deficit due to a bad harvest.

[8] The deficit involves the replacement of international reserves by stocks of exportable or importable goods and/or by holdings of internationally marketable securities, the change being motivated by private profit considerations. For this to constitute a deterioration from the national point of view, the alternatives facing private asset-holders must be assumed not to reflect true social alternative opportunities, or private asset-holders must be assumed to act less rationally than the economic policy authorities, or the national interest must be defined so as to exclude their welfare from counting. If any of these assumptions is valid, it indicates the need for a

less, if the country's international reserves are small, the economic policy authorities may be obliged to check such a deficit by a change in economic policy. The policy methods available are familiar, but it may be useful to review them briefly in relation to the framework of analysis developed here.

To discourage the substitution of stocks of goods for domestic currency, the economic policy authorities may either raise the cost of stock-holding by credit restriction or reduce its attractiveness by currency depreciation.[9] Under both policies, the magnitude of the effect is uncertain—depreciation, by stimulating de-stabilizing expectations, may even promote stock accumulation—while unavoidable repercussions on the flow equilibrium of the economy are set up. These considerations provide a strong argument for the use of the alternative method of direct controls on stock-holding, an indirect and partial form of which is quantitative import restriction.

To discourage the substitution of securities for domestic currency, the same broad alternatives are available: credit restriction, which amounts to the monetary authority substituting domestic currency for securities to offset substitution of securities for domestic currency by the rest of the community; devaluation, which affects the relative attractiveness of securities only through expectations and may work either way; and exchange controls restricting the acquisition of securities from abroad. Considerations similar to those of the previous paragraph would seem to argue in favour of the use of controls on international capital movements as against the alternative methods available.

In both cases, evaluation of the policy alternatives suggests the use of control rather than price system methods. It should be recalled, though, that the problem is created by the assumed inadequacy of the country's international reserves. In the longer run, the choice for economic policy lies, not between the three alternatives discussed, but between the necessity of having to choose between them and the cost of investing in the accumulation of reserves large enough to finance potential "stock" deficits. Also, nothing has been said about the practical difficulties of maintaining effective control over international transactions, especially capital movements.

In contrast to a "stock" deficit, a "flow" deficit is not inherently of limited duration. It will be so if the monetary authority is not prepared to create credit, but this is because its existence will then set up monetary repercussions which will eventually alter the collective decision responsi-

---

remedial policy, but not one conditional on the existence of a deficit or to be applied through the balance of payments. This point is argued more fully below, in connection with import restrictions.

[9] Stocks are built up by withholding goods from export or by increasing imports; depreciation makes both of these less attractive. A third policy might be increased taxation, either of stocks or of home-market sales of goods.

ble for it, not because the initial decision implied a temporary deficit. If the decision not to create credit is regarded as a specific act of policy equivalent to a decision to raise interest rates,[10] it follows that the termination of a "flow" deficit requires a deliberate change of economic policy. Further, a "flow" deficit may imply a worsening of the country's capital position, providing an economic as well as a monetary incentive to terminate the disequilibrium.[11]

In analysing the policy problems posed by "flow" deficits, it is convenient to begin by abstracting altogether from international capital movements (other than reserve transactions between foreign exchange authorities) and considering the case of a current account deficit. In this case, if intermediate transactions are excluded, the balance of payments becomes the difference between the value of the country's output (its national income) and its total expenditure, i.e.

$$B = Y - E.$$

To facilitate analysis by avoiding certain complications associated with the possibility of changes in the domestic price level, income and expenditure are conceived of as being valued in units of domestic output. A deficit then consists in an excess of real expenditure over real income, and the problem of correcting a deficit is to bring real national income (output) and real national expenditure into equality.

This formulation suggests that policies for correcting current-account deficits can be classified broadly into two types: those which aim at (or rely on) increasing output, and those which aim at reducing expenditure. The distinction must, of course, relate to the initial impact of the policy, since income and expenditure are interdependent: expenditure depends on and varies with income, and income depends on and varies with expenditure (because part of expenditure is devoted to home-produced goods). Consequently any change in either income or expenditure will initiate multiplier changes in both. It can, however, readily be shown that, so long as an increase in income induces a smaller change in aggregate expenditure, the multiplier repercussions will not be large enough to offset the impact effect of a change, so that an impact increase in output

---

[10] This assumption, which is slightly inconsistent with the argument above concerning the monetary implications of a deficit, is made here to avoid the necessity of repeating the analysis for the case where limited reserves prevent the authorities from allowing a deficit to solve itself.

[11] Whether this is so depends on the use to which the finance provided by the deficit is put, which involves comparison with what would have happened in the absence of the deficit. If the deficit finances additional investment in productive domestic capital or income-yielding foreign assets the net effect on the capital position may be favourable; if it finances additional consumption it is likely to be unfavourable, though even additional consumption may sometimes increase productive capacity.

or decrease in expenditure will always improve the balance on current account.[12]

The distinction between output-increasing and expenditure-reducing policies may usefully be put in another way. Since output is governed by the demand for it, a change in output can only be brought about by a change in the demand for it; a policy of increasing domestic output can only be effected by operating on expenditure (either foreign or domestic) on that output. Given the level of expenditure, this in turn involves effecting a switch of expenditure (by residents and foreigners) from foreign output to domestic output. The distinction between output-increasing and expenditure-decreasing policies, which rests on the *effects* of the policies, may therefore be replaced by a distinction between expenditure-switching policies and expenditure-reducing policies, which rests on the *method* by which the effects are achieved.

A policy of expenditure-reduction may be applied through a variety of means—monetary restriction, budgetary policy, or even a sufficiently comprehensive battery of direct controls. Since any such policy will tend to reduce income and employment, it will have an additional attraction if the country is suffering from inflationary pressure as well as a balance-of-payments deficit, but a corresponding disadvantage if the country is suffering from unemployment. Moreover, since the impact reduction in expenditure and the total reduction in income and output required to correct a given deficit are larger the larger the proportion of the expenditure reduction falling on home-produced goods, and since different methods of expenditure-reduction may differ in this respect, the choice between alternative methods may depend on the inflationary-deflationary situation of the economy. Finally, since the accompanying reduction in income may lead to some reduction in the domestic price level, and/or a greater eagerness of domestic producers to compete with foreign pro-

---

[12] Differentiating the equation in the text, we obtain $dB = (1 - e)dY + dE$, where e is the marginal propensity to spend out of income, dY is the total *increase* in output (including multiplier effects) and dE is the autonomous *decrease* in expenditure. If multiplier effects through foreign incomes are ignored,

$$dY = \frac{1}{1 - e(1 - m)} \, dA,$$

where dA is an autonomous change in demand for domestic output and m is the proportion of marginal expenditure leaking into imports. Splitting dA into two components, dO for output-increasing policies and $-hdE$ for expenditure-reducing policies (where h is the proportion of expenditure reduction falling on domestic output), gives the result

$$dB = \frac{1 - e}{1 - e + em} \, dO + \left(1 - \frac{(1 - e)h}{1 - e + em}\right) dE.$$

Hence either an output-increasing or an expenditure-reducing policy will improve the balance, so long as e is less than unity. (Alexander has argued that since e includes induced investment it may well exceed unity; this possibility is ignored in the argument of the text.) Expenditure reduction will in fact improve the balance so long as multiplier stability is present.

ducers both at home and abroad, expenditure-reducing policies may have incidental expenditure-switching effects.

Expenditure-switching policies may be divided into two types, according to whether the policy instrument employed is general or selective: devaluation (which may be taken to include the case of a deflation-induced reduction of the domestic price level under fixed exchange rates), and trade controls (including both tariffs and subsidies and quantitative restrictions). Devaluation aims at switching both domestic and foreign expenditure towards domestic output; controls are usually imposed on imports, and aim at (or have the effect of) switching domestic expenditure away from imports towards home goods, though sometimes they are used to stimulate exports and aim at switching foreigners' expenditure towards domestic output.

Both types of expenditure-switching policy may have direct impact-effects on residents' expenditure. Devaluation may result in increased expenditure from the initial income level, through the so-called "terms-of-trade effect" of an adverse terms-of-trade movement in reducing real income and therefore the proportion of income saved. Trade controls will tend to have the same effect, via the reduction in real income resulting from constriction of freedom of choice.[13] In addition, trade controls must alter the real expenditure corresponding to the initial output level if they take the form of import duties or export subsidies uncompensated by other fiscal changes; this case should, however, be classed as a combined policy of expenditure-change (unfavourable in the case of the export subsidy) and expenditure-switch.

Whether general or selective in nature, an expenditure-switching policy seeks to correct a deficit by switching demand away from foreign towards domestic goods; and it depends for success not only on switching demand in the right direction, but also on the capacity of the economy to make available the extra output required to satisfy the additional demand. Such policies therefore pose two problems for economic analysis: the conditions

---

[13] These arguments conflict with the assumption, more frequently made in connection with trade controls than with devaluation, that the public will consume less because it cannot obtain the goods it prefers as readily as before. That assumption may well be valid in the case of a policy expected to be applied for a short period only, after which goods will become as available as before, or in the analysis of the short run during which the economy is adjusting to the change in policy; but it is invalid in the present context of flow disequilibrium, since it overlooks the effect of the policy change in reducing the future value of savings and hence the incentive to save. An example of this type of faulty reasoning is the assertion sometimes made that quantitative import restriction is particularly effective in under-developed countries because their economic structure allows little possibility of substitution for imported goods in either production or consumption.

One qualification to the argument of the text, which also applies to the final sentence of the paragraph, is that if the goods towards which domestic expenditure is switched are more heavily taxed than those from which expenditure is diverted (a type of complication which is ignored in the general argument of the text), real expenditure may fall rather than rise.

required for expenditure to be switched in the desired direction, and the source of the additional output required to meet the additional demand.

As to the first question, the possibilities of failure for both devaluation and controls have been investigated at length by international trade theorists, and require only summary treatment here.[14] Export promotion will divert foreign expenditure away from the country's output if the foreign demand is inelastic, while import restriction will divert domestic expenditure abroad if demand for imports is inelastic and the technique of restriction allows the foreigner the benefit of the increased value of imports to domestic consumers. Devaluation has the partial effect of diverting domestic expenditure abroad, via the increased cost of the initial volume of imports, and this adverse switch will not be offset by the favourable effect of substitution of domestic for foreign goods at home and abroad, if import demand elasticities average less than one half.

While the elasticity requirement for successful devaluation just cited is familiar, the approach developed in this paper throws additional light on what non-fulfilment of the requirement implies. From the equation $B = Y - E$, it is clear that, if direct effects on expenditure from the initial income level are neglected, devaluation can worsen the balance only if it reduces total world demand for the country's output. This implies that the country's output is in a sense a "Giffen case" in world consumption; and that the market for at least one of the commodities it produces is in unstable equilibrium.[15] Neither of these ways of stating the conditions for exchange instability makes the possibility of instability as plausible *a priori* as their equivalent, reached through sectoral analysis, in terms of elasticities of import demand.

The second, and more interesting, analytical problem relates to the source of the additional domestic output required to satisfy the demand for it created by the expenditure-switching policy. Here it is necessary to distinguish two cases, that in which the economy is under-employed and that in which it is fully employed, for both the relevant technique of analysis and the factors on which the outcome of the policy depend differ between the two.

If the economy has unemployed resources available, the additional output required to meet the additional demand can be provided by the re-absorption of these resources into employment: in this case the switch policy has the additional attraction of increasing employment and income. The increase in domestic output may tend to raise the domestic

---

[14] Impact effects on the level of expenditure from a given income level of the type discussed in the next-but-one paragraph preceding this one are ignored in this paragraph.

[15] *Cf.* E. V. Morgan, "The Theory of Flexible Exchange Rates," *American Economic Review*, Vol. XLV, No. 3 (June, 1955), pp. 279–95. Morgan's statement (p. 285) that instability requires "very strong and perverse income effects" is fallacious— all that is strictly necessary is a preference in each country for home-produced goods.

price level, through the operation of increasing marginal real costs of production, and conversely the foreign price level may tend to fall, thus partially counteracting the initial effects of the switch policy; but such repercussions can legitimately be analysed in terms of elasticity concepts, since under-employment implies that additional factors are available at the ruling price.

If the economy is already fully employed, however, the additional output required cannot be provided by increasing production; it can only be provided through a reduction in the previous level of real expenditure.[16] This reduction may be brought about either by a deliberate expenditure-reducing policy introduced along with the switch policy, or by the inflationary consequences of the switch policy itself in the assumed full-employment conditions.[17]

If the increased output is provided by a deliberate expenditure-reducing policy, the nature of this policy will obviously influence the effects of the expenditure-switching policy, since the composition of the output it releases may be more or less substitutable for foreign output in world demand. Thus, for example, an expenditure-reducing policy which reduces domestic demand for imports and exportable goods will be more favourable to expenditure-switching than one which reduces domestic demand for non-traded goods. The analysis of the effects of an expenditure-switching policy supported by an expenditure-reducing policy must therefore comprise the effects of the latter in determining the composition of the productive capacity available to meet the increased demand created by the former, as well as the elasticity relations which govern the effects of the interaction of increased demand with increased production capacity on the prices and volumes of goods traded.

If the expenditure-switching policy is not accompanied by an expenditure-reducing policy, its effect will be to create an inflationary excess of aggregate demand over supply, leading to price increases tending to counteract the policy's expenditure-switching effects. Inflation, however, may work towards curing the deficit, through various effects tending to reduce the level of real expenditure from the full employment level of output. These effects, which are familiar and have been analysed in detail by Alexander, include the effect of high marginal tax rates in increasing the proportion of real income absorbed by taxation as wages

---

[16] Recognition of this point may be regarded as the fundamental contribution of the absorption approach, though none of the authors cited seems to have appreciated all its implications: Meade, for example, analyses the case on the assumption that an appropriate expenditure-reducing policy is in effect, without examining the interdependence between the two policies or the alternative of inflation, while Alexander does not recognize that the effects of inflation on absorption could be achieved by policy.

[17] For analytical simplicity, both the possibility of increased production through "over-full employment" and of direct expenditure-reducing effects of a switch policy (discussed earlier in this paper) are ignored here.

and prices rise, the possibility of a swing to profits increasing the proportion of income saved, and the effect of rising prices in reducing the real purchasing power of cash and government bonds held by the public, so reducing their wealth and propensity to consume. All of these effects, it may be noted, depend on particular asymmetries in the reactions of the sectors affected to the redistributive effects of inflation on real income or wealth, which may not in fact be present. The important point, however, is that these factors, on which the success of an expenditure-switching policy depends in this case, are monetary factors, and that the analysis required employs monetary concepts rather than elasticity concepts. As in the previous case, the elasticity factors are subordinate to the factors governing the reduction in aggregate real expenditure, in determining the consequences of the expenditure-switching policy for the balance of payments.

The argument of the previous paragraph—that in full employment conditions the success of expenditure-switching policies depends mainly on the effectiveness of the consequent inflation in reducing real expenditure—helps to explain both the prevalence of scepticism about, and hostility towards, exchange rate adjustment as a means of curing balance-of-payments disequilibria, and the fact that historical experience can be adduced in support of the proposition that devaluation is a doubtful remedy. The argument does not, however, support the conclusion frequently drawn from the analysis of devaluation in these circumstances, that import restrictions are to be preferred; this is a *non sequitur*, since import restrictions are equally an expenditure-switching policy. Rather, the proper conclusion is that expenditure-switching policies are inappropriate to full employment conditions, except when used in conjunction with an expenditure-reducing policy as a means of correcting the employment-reducing effects of the latter.

But what of the choice between devaluation and selective trade controls, to which reference has just been made? So far, it has not been necessary to distinguish between them, since from the point of view of the balance of payments both can be treated as expenditure-switching policies. It is from the point of view of economic welfare that they differ; and the arguments on their relative merits have nothing to do with the state of the balance of payments, except that if controls are preferable a deficit may offer an opportunity for introducing them with less risk of foreign retaliation than if trade were balanced.

The welfare arguments for controls on a country's international trade may be divided into two groups, those centring on controls as a means of influencing the internal distribution of real income, by discouraging imports consumed by the rich and encouraging those consumed by the poor, and those centring on controls as a means of increasing the country's gains from trade through exploiting its monopoly/monopsony power in foreign markets. The former are of doubtful validity, both because the ethics of disguising a real income policy as a trade policy are suspect, and because both the efficiency and the effectiveness of trade controls as instruments for governing real income distribution are dubious. The latter are valid, to the extent that the country has powers to exploit the foreigner and can use them without provoking sufficient retaliation to nullify the gains.

This is the familiar optimum tariff argument. Its application to balance-of-payments policy depends on the level of trade restrictions already in force, as compared with the optimum level of restrictions.[18] If an expenditure-switching policy is required to correct a deficit, and the level of trade restrictions is below the optimum, restriction[19] is preferable to devaluation until the optimum level is reached; in the opposite case, devaluation is perferable. But it is the relation of actual to optimum restrictions, and not the state of the trade balance, which determines whether restriction is desirable or not.

This concludes the analysis of alternative policies for correcting a "flow" balance-of-payments deficit on current account. To complete the analysis of "flow" disequilibria, it would be necessary to relax the assumption that international capital movements are confined to reserve movements between foreign exchange authorities, and to consider alternative policies for correcting a deficit on current and capital account combined. The central problem in this case is to determine the level of current account surplus or deficit, capital export or import, at which economic policy should aim. This raises two further problems too difficult to pursue here: the optimum rate of accumulation of capital for the community as a whole, and the degree to which it is desirable to discriminate in favour of investment at home and against investment abroad.

In conclusion, the argument of this paper may be summarized as follows: formulation of the balance of payments as the difference between aggregate receipts and payments, rather than receipts and payments on international account only, has two major advantages. It brings out the essentially monetary nature of a deficit, which must be accompanied by dishoarding of domestic money or credit creation; and it relates the deficit to the operation of the economy as a whole. A deficit may reflect a "stock" decision or a "flow" decision by the community. The conditions which make a "stock" deficit a policy problem indicate the use of direct control methods as against price system methods of correction. Policies for deal-

---

[18] See S. Alexander, "Devaluation versus Import Restriction as an Instrument for Improving Foreign Trade Balance," *International Monetary Fund Staff Papers*, Vol. I, No. 3 (April, 1951), pp. 379–96, for a lucid and pioneering exposition of this principle.

[19] Generally, optimum trade restriction entails restriction of both imports and exports; but if the country's currency is over-valued it may imply subsidization of some or even all exports, and if the currency is under-valued it may imply subsidization of some or even all imports. (These conclusions follow from the fact that a devaluation is equivalent to an all-round export subsidy and import duty).

ing with "flow" deficits on current account may be divided into expenditure-reducing and expenditure-switching policies; in full employment conditions the latter must be supported by the former, or rely on inflation for their effect, which in either case cannot be analysed adequately in terms of elasticities. When capital account transactions are introduced into the analysis, the choice between policy alternatives requires reference to growth considerations not readily susceptible to economic analysis.

24. The Role of Money in Trade-Balance Stability: Synthesis of the Elasticity and Absorption Approaches[*]

By S. C. TSIANG[†]

THE SPIRITED CONTROVERSY between S. S. Alexander [1] [2] and Fritz Machlup [13] [14] on the relative merits of the relative prices (or elasticities) and aggregate spending (absorption) approaches to the problem of determining the effect of devaluation appears to have ended, for the time being, in a rather disappointing anticlimax. After having witnessed the mutual accusation of the rival approaches as consisting of implicit theorizing based upon purely definitional tautologies [13, pp. 268–71] [2, pp. 22–24], one feels somewhat let down by the compromise which Alexander now proposes [2, pp. 26–34]: that the result obtained by the traditional elasticities approach may be treated as the "initial" (or primary) effect of a devaluation to which a sort of "multiplier" (normally less than unity), computed from the propensities to hoard, to import, etc., is to be applied to yield the final effect of the devaluation.

The extension of the elasticity approach by a superimposition of a multiplier analysis in this manner is essentially the same as what A. J. Brown had already done in 1942.[1] Indeed, it was already indicated by J. Robinson [18, esp. p. 93] in her pioneering article on the foreign exchanges first published in 1937.

The superimposition of a multiplier upon the elasticities solution of the effect of a devaluation usually glosses over the following difficulty: Unless the supplies of exportable and domestic goods in both countries concerned are all infinitely elastic, so that prices in both countries (except prices of imports) will remain constant, the multiplier effect of the initial change in the trade balance will bring about further changes in relative prices, and hence further substitution between imports and domestically

[*] American Economic Review, Vol. LI, No. 5 (December, 1961), pp. 912–36.

[†] The author is professor of economics at the University of Rochester. He is indebted to T. C. Liu and E. Zabel for discussion at different stages of the preparation of this paper, and to Fritz Machlup, J. J. Polak, J. M. Fleming, and R. A. Mundell for reading the manuscript and making a number of valuable suggestions.

[1] See [6, esp. pp. 64–66]; also Allen [3].

produced goods in both countries. Thus if the conventional elasticities solution is treated as a sort of multiplicand, to which a multiplier (or a damping coefficient) is to be applied to obtain the final effect, then the multiplier itself should again involve the relevant elasticities that are in the multiplicand. There can be no neat dichotomy of the final effect of a devaluation into a part that consists of the elasticities solution and another that consists of the multiplier (or absorption) solution. The total effect of a devaluation must be analyzed in a comprehensive system in which changes in incomes, prices and outputs are all taken into consideration. In fact, even before Alexander raised the outcry against the elasticities approach and proposed the substitution of the absorption approach, a number of attempts had already been made to analyze the effect of a devaluation with more or less comprehensive mathematical systems that allow for both income and price changes, notably those by Meade [15], Harberger [7], Laursen and Metzler [12], and Stuvel [22]. If the controversy between the relative-prices and aggregate-spending approaches merely leads to a synthesis which had already been worked out before the controversy, what then has been gained by the debate?

If anything of enduring value has come out of Alexander's proposal of the absorption approach, it is the fact that the simple identity:

$$
\begin{array}{ccccc}
B & \equiv & Y & - & A \\
\text{Trade} & & \text{National} & & \text{Absorption} \\
\text{Balance} & & \text{Income} & & \text{or National} \\
& & & & \text{Expenditure}
\end{array}
$$

which he pushed to the forefront in the analysis of the effect of a devalua-. tion, has brought out in strong relief a fundamental fact, viz., that a negative trade balance necessarily implies national expenditure in excess of national income. This obvious truth was underscored by Machlup [13, pp. 272–73] who therefore emphasized the role played by credit creation in sustaining the excess expenditure in the case of a trade deficit (a negative B) and concluded that "nothing can be said about the effects of a devaluation unless exact specifications are made regarding the supply of money and credit." The highlighting of the monetary implications of a balance-of-payments deficit or surplus was also stressed by Johnson [10, pp. 156–58] as the major contribution of the absorption approach. More recently, Michaely, in an attempt to reconcile the relative-prices and absorption approaches under the assumption of full employment, also naturally resorted to the "real balance effect" of devaluation-induced price changes with the money supply kept constant [16]. Thus as a by-product of Alexander's attack on the elasticities approach, the much neglected role played by the supply of money and credit in working out the effect of a devaluation and the stability of the trade balance is once more being recognized.[2]

---

[2] Monetary factors were certainly not overlooked by classical economists, who regarded the contraction or expansion of the money supply under the gold standard as

The rediscovery of the significance of monetary factors, however, has not yet been reflected in the formulae and mathematical models for the analysis of the effect of a devaluation on the balance of trade. Not only did the conventional elasticities formulae of the effect of devaluation take no account of the monetary factors (since implicitly they generally assume a constant money income), but in the various attempts to combine the elasticities approach with a multiplier analysis (e.g., those of Brown [6] and Allen [3], and even in most of the more or less comprehensive models of Harberger [7], Laursen and Metzler [12], Stuvel [22],[3] and Jones [11]), the role of money and credit was also totally disregarded. In a quite recent attempt to marry the elasticity and the absorption approaches, Brems also did not include either the money supply or the rate of interest in his otherwise rather complicated mathematical model [5]. Even Alexander himself tends to neglect the role of money; for in his discussion of the multiplier process engendered by the initial change in the trade balance, a process supposed to be determined by the propensities to hoard and to spend on imports and exportables, the monetary mechanism of income expansion was never brought in at all. It was only in his discussion of the cash balance effects at full employment that the money supply was briefly mentioned [2, p. 33].

In this respect, Meade's model for the analysis of the balance of payments stands out as a splendid exception; for he alone included the money supply and the rate of interest as variables in his model and always clearly stated the specific assumptions he made about monetary and fiscal policies. Unfortunately, however, Meade worked out the solution for the effect of a devaluation from his model only under the assumption of either a so-called "Keynesian neutral economy" or that of a monetary policy that ensures "internal balance." Under the "neutral economy" assumption, the monetary authorities are supposed to keep the supply of money infinitely elastic at a constant interest rate, so that the supply of money will passively adapt itself to whatever the demand for money might be at the constant interest rate [15, pp. 31, 49]. This in effect obliterates all possible influences the supply of money and the interest rate might have on his solution for the effect of a devaluation. On the other hand, the assumption of a monetary policy that ensures "internal balance" (i.e., a constant level of employment [15, pp. 33, 56–57]), coupled with the assumptions that money wage rates are exogenously given and that prices always equal marginal labor cost, in effect implies that money

the automatic mechanism for the adjustment of the balance of payments. It is with the advent of the "new economics" and the breakdown of the gold standard that monetary factors came to be disregarded in the discussion of the balance of trade and devaluation.

[3] Harberger, in his review article [8, esp. pp. 858–59], strongly criticized Stuvel for not even mentioning the amount of money or the rate of interest in his analysis, nor stating what kind of monetary or fiscal policy he assumes. Harberger also admitted that he himself committed the same omission in his own earlier attempt at model construction.

income is somehow effectively kept constant, provided money wage rates remain constant. This again eliminates all the positive influences the money supply and the interest rate might exert on the effect of a devaluation, as they are assumed to adjust themselves passively to the requirements of the policy objective of maintaining money income constant [15, pp. 68–72; Table 4, p. 150].

The purpose of this paper is to demonstrate the crucial role that could be played by monetary factors and thus to show in a more comprehensive way how relative prices and income-expenditure adjustments combine to determine the effect of a devaluation. To avoid further proliferation of models, each with the idiosyncrasies of its creator fully displayed in the choice of variables and notation system, I shall adopt Meade's simplified two-country, two-commodity model, which seems by far the most economically sound, and shall only make a slight modification to make good an omission (viz., that of the effect of changes in the terms of trade on aggregate expenditure) which has been much discussed since Harberger, Laursen and Metzler pointed out its possible significance. I shall also trim his model of all nonessential policy variables, such as tariff rates and various shift variables, which he adopted to represent controlled or uncontrolled shifts in various functional relationships, so as to make the system intelligible to the reader without overtaxing his perseverance.[4]

I. THE MODEL

We shall adopt Meade's notation throughout so as to facilitate comparison between his results and ours. In Meade's notation, a subscript a refers to country A and a subscript b to country B. The subscript ab for a term indicates that it is the sum of a corresponding A-term and B-term (e.g., $\pi_{ab} = \pi_a + \pi_b$). Capital italic letters refer to total quantities; small italic letters to small increments (or differentials) of those qualities; and a bar over a term means a price corresponding to that term. The small Greek letters stand for functional relationships between the differentials (i.e., either partial derivatives or elasticities obtained from such partial derivatives). Thus:

Q_a = A's product.

$\bar{Q}_a$ = the price of A's product, which is put equal to 1 at the initial position by using the appropriate unit for Q_a.

H_a = volume of employment in country A.

$\bar{H}_a$ = the money wage rate in country A, which is put equal to 1 at the initial position by choosing the appropriate unit for H_a.

I_a = the physical volume of A's imports, which constitute B's exports.

---

[4] The popularity of Meade's excellent work has suffered a great deal from the overcomplicated model and its formidable list of variables, which he presented at the very beginning of his book, but which he himself abandoned later as too cumbersome to yield any definite result. Even Alexander complained that Meade's model is "unintelligible to any but the most dogged readers" [2, p. 24].

D_a = domestic expenditures in A in terms of domestic currency.
R_a = the rate of interest in A.
M_a = the amount of money in A.

The corresponding terms for country B with the subscript b are similarly defined.

E = the rate of exchange expressed as the number of units of A's currency per unit of B's currency, which is again put equal to 1 at the initial position by choosing the appropriate unit for B's currency.
T = the balance of trade, i.e., the net excess of A's receipts from exports valued in A's currency.

It is assumed that at the initial position:

$$I_a \bar{Q}_b E = I_b \bar{Q}_a = I_a = I_b = I.$$

The differentials of these terms are represented by the corresponding small italic letters with the same subscripts, thus $dQ_a = q_a$, $d\bar{Q}_a = \bar{q}_a$, etc.

Meade's system as simplified for our purpose may be represented by the following system of equations in differentials. First, we have a pair of identities for the increments in domestic expenditures for the two countries:

$$d_a \equiv q_a - i_b + i_a + (Q_a - I)\bar{q}_a + I\bar{q}_b + Ie, \tag{1}$$

$$d_b \equiv q_b - i_a + i_b + (Q_b - I)\bar{q}_b + I\bar{q}_a - Ie, \tag{2}$$

which are obtained by differentiating the following definitional expenditure identities:

$$D_a \equiv \bar{Q}_a(Q_a - I_b) + \bar{Q}_b E I_a,$$

$$D_b \equiv \bar{Q}_b(Q_b - I_a) + \bar{Q}_a \frac{1}{E} I_b.$$

Next Meade gives us the two domestic expenditure functions in differentials:

$$d_a = (1 - \lambda_a)q_a - \rho_a r_a + D_a \bar{q}_a, \tag{3}$$

$$d_b = (1 - \lambda_b)q_b - \rho_b r_b + D_b \bar{q}_b, \tag{4}$$

where $(1 - \lambda_a)$ and $(1 - \lambda_b)$ are the partial derivatives of domestic expenditures with respect to domestic money incomes, and hence λ_a and λ_b are the marginal propensities to hoard, and ρ_a and ρ_b are the partial derivatives of domestic expenditures with respect to the interest rate in the two countries, respectively. The terms $D_a \bar{q}_a$ and $D_b \bar{q}_b$ are introduced to indicate that these expenditures functions are "real functions" in the sense that domestic expenditure in real terms is a function of real income, so that a change in the general price level would bring about a proportionate change in money expenditures. Here for the sake of simplicity, Meade has taken the change in the price level of domestic products to represent the change in the general price level so that the effect of a change in the terms of trade on the price level and on the level of aggregate domestic expenditures is neglected.[5]

However, the effect upon domestic expenditure of a change in the terms of trade produced by a devaluation has been emphasized by both Harberger [7, pp. 50–55] and Laursen and Metzler [12, pp. 295–97] as having the effect of making the stability condition for the exchange rate more stringent. To assume away with Meade the effect of the terms of trade on domestic expenditure would, therefore, seem to gloss over a potentially significant factor. In fact, Meade has been strongly criticized by H. Johnson for this omission [10A, pp. 816–18 and 830–32]. Actually, Meade could have allowed for the effect of a change in the terms of trade on domestic expenditure without making the aggregate expenditure functions too complicated to handle. For if we assume with Meade that the relationship between domestic expenditure and its determinants is a "real" and not a "money" relationship and that there is no money illusion (so that the money expenditure function is homogeneous of degree 1 in money income and all prices, including prices of imports), then the two equations for changes in aggregate expenditures, taking into consideration the effect of the terms of trade, would be no more complicated than:

$$d_a = (1 - \lambda_a)q_a - \rho_a r_a + D_a \bar{q}_a - \lambda_a I(\bar{q}_a - \bar{q}_b - e) \qquad (3a)$$

and

$$d_b = (1 - \lambda_b)q_b - \rho_b r_b + D_b \bar{q}_b - \lambda_b I(\bar{q}_b - \bar{q}_a + e).[6] \qquad (4a)$$

---

[5] In effect, (3) and (4) are derived by differentiating aggregate expenditure functions of the type:

$$D_a = D_a \{Q_a \bar{Q}_a, \bar{Q}_a, R_a\} \qquad (i)$$

which is supposed to be homogeneous of degree 1 in $Q_a \bar{Q}_a$ and $\bar{Q}_a$. By Euler's Theorem,

$$D_a = \frac{\partial D_a}{\partial (Q_a \bar{Q}_a)} \cdot Q_a \bar{Q}_a + \frac{\partial D_a}{\partial \bar{Q}_a} \bar{Q}_a$$

$$= (1 - \lambda_a)Q_a + \frac{\partial D_a}{\partial \bar{Q}_a} \qquad (ii)$$

$$\therefore \frac{\partial D_a}{\partial \bar{Q}_a} = D_a - (1 - \lambda_a)Q_a.$$

Substitute (ii) in the differentiation of (i), we get:

$$d_a = (1 - \lambda_a)q_a + D_a \bar{q}_a - p_a r_a.$$

Alternatively, (3) and (4) may be regarded as derived from expenditure functions of the form:

$$\frac{D_a}{\bar{Q}_a} = D_a \circ \left\{ \frac{Q_a \bar{Q}_a}{\bar{Q}_a}, R_a \right\}, \qquad (iii)$$

which, upon differentiation, yields directly the same result.

[6] This was first pointed out to me by T. C. Liu of Cornell University.

In view of the lively controversy over the possible effect of a change in the terms of trade upon aggregate domestic expenditure,[7] I shall try to derive (3a) and (4a) in the most unsophisticated and least controversial way. Let us suppose that in the absence of money illusion and dynamic price expectations, domestic expenditure in real terms is a function of domestic real income and the interest rate, i.e.,

$$\frac{D_a}{P_a} = D_a\left\{\frac{Q_a\bar{Q}_a}{P_a}, R_a\right\} \tag{5}$$

where P_a is the general price level in country A, defined as:

$$P_a = \frac{D_a - I_a}{D_a} \cdot \bar{Q}_a + \frac{I_a}{D_a} \cdot \bar{Q}_b E, \tag{6}$$

which is equal to 1 at the initial position, since $\bar{Q}_a = \bar{Q}_b = E = 1$. Equation (5) indicates that domestic money expenditure is homogeneous of degree 1 in money income and all prices.[8]

Differentiating (5) and (6) and substituting, we get:

$$d_a - (D_a - I)\bar{q}_a - I(\bar{q}_b + e)$$
$$= (1 - \lambda_a)\left[q_a + Q_a\bar{q}_a - \frac{Q_a(D_a - I)}{D_a}\bar{q}_a - \frac{Q_aI}{D_a}(\bar{q}_b + e)\right] - \rho_a r_a.$$

Since at the initial position $Q_a = D_a$, therefore,

$$d_a = (1 - \lambda_a)q_a + D_a\bar{q}_a - \lambda_aI(\bar{q}_a - \bar{q}_b - e) - \rho_a r_a.$$

By a similar procedure, (4a) may be obtained.[9] Equations (3a) and (4a) clearly indicate that the partial derivative of domestic expenditure with respect to a change in the terms of trade (an improvement is here to be treated as a positive change and a worsening a negative change) is

---

[7] See, for example, [25] [21] [17] and [11]. Although Laursen and Metzler have specifically discussed the effect of a change in the exchange rate upon domestic money expenditure, including investment as well as consumption, later participants in this discussion have concentrated exclusively on the effect upon consumption expenditure to the total neglect of the effect upon investment expenditure, as if the latter may be assumed to be fixed in money terms with a change in import prices. Actually, under the assumptions of no money illusion and no dynamic price expectations, there is as much reason·to assume money expenditure on investment to be homogeneous of degree 1 in all prices and money income as to assume the same for money expenditure on consumption.

[8] The money balances effect (or the Pigou effect) of a proportionate rise in money income and all prices may preclude the homogeneity of the money expenditure function. However, an increase in the relative scarcity of cash balances implies a rise in the marginal convenience yield of money balances and hence would lead to a rise in the interest rate, which is included as another determining variable of the expenditure function. The Pigou effect of a proportionate rise in all prices is therefore taken care of in the term $\rho_a r_a$, and hence would not interfere with the homogeneity of the expenditure function in money income and all prices, exclusive of the interest rate.

[9] A crucial assumption here is that $Q_a\bar{Q}_a = Q_a = D_a$ and $Q_b\bar{Q}_b = Q_b = D_b$ at the initial position which is implied in the assumption that trade is initially balanced.

equal to minus the marginal propensity to hoard times the initial amount of imports of the country concerned (i.e., $-\lambda_a I$ or $-\lambda_b I$).[10]

The two import functions are written by Meade in differentials as follows: For country A,

$$i_a = \pi_a d_a + [-(Q_a - I)\pi_a + I\epsilon_a]\bar{q}_a - I(\pi_a + \epsilon_a)(\bar{q}_b + e) \qquad (7)$$

$$= \pi_a d_a - \pi_a Q_a \bar{q}_a + I(\pi_a + \epsilon_a)(\bar{q}_a - \bar{q}_b - e)$$

where π_a is A's propensity to import defined with reference to A's aggregate national expenditure instead of national income; ϵ_a is what he calls "the expenditure compensated price elasticity of demand for imports in A" (or in other words, the elasticity of the pure substitution effect on A's import demand with respect to the relative price ratio between domestic products and imports); and hence $-(Q_a - I)\pi_a \bar{q}_a$ and $-I\pi_a(\bar{q}_b + e)$ are the familiar Slutsky-Hicksian income effect on A's demand for imports of a change in the price of A's domestic products and a change in A's import prices, respectively, and $I\epsilon_a(\bar{q}_a - \bar{q}_b - e)$ the pure substitution effect on A's import demand of the change in the relative price ratio in A between domestic products and imports.[11]

---

[10] This result agrees fully with those obtained by Harberger and Jones. Harberger, in whose model there is no investment, has shown that the effect of the terms of trade (an adverse change is treated as a positive change) is equal to the propensity to save times the initial amount of imports [7, pp. 52–53]. Jones, by a more general and elegant method, has shown that the partial derivative of consumption expenditure with respect to a rise in import prices is equal to: (1 minus the ratio of the marginal propensity to consume to the average propensity to consume) times the initial amount of imports [11, pp. 78–79]. Substituting total expenditure and the propensity to spend for consumption expenditure and the propensity to consume, respectively, and taking into account the assumption that in our model the average propensity to spend is 1 in the initial position (trade initially balanced), their results can be readily converted to ours.

[11] The Slutsky-Hicksian way of splitting off the income effect of a price change presumes that the effect on real income of a change in the price of a commodity, with money income fixed, is equal to the initial volume of that commodity purchased times the change in its price. In his criticism of Harberger, however, Spraos has rightly pointed out that in so far as there is a part of income which is neither spent on domestic products nor on imports, the loss in real income out of a fixed money income implied by, say, a rise in import prices is greater than the initial amount of imports consumed times the rise in import prices; for the loss in real value of the part of income that was initially not spent must also be compensated. Otherwise the demand function would imply some degree of money-illusion. In the present case, however, it is assumed that trade was initially balanced so that all income must have been spent initially either on imports or on domestic products. Hence, as Spraos himself has conceded, his objection would not apply to the present case [21, p. 144, esp. fn. 4].

Meade's import demand equations, i.e., (7) and (8), certainly cannot be accused of implying the presence of money illusion, because it can be shown that the partial derivatives of the demand for imports in these two equations satisfy Euler's theorem for a homogeneous equation of degree zero in all the determining variables; for from, say, equation (7) we have:

$$\frac{\partial I_a}{\partial D_a} = \pi_a; \quad \frac{\partial I_a}{\partial \bar{Q}_a} = [-(Q_a - I)\pi_a + I\epsilon_a]$$

Similarly, for country B, we have

$$i_b = \pi_b d_b - \pi_b Q_b \bar{q}_b + I(\pi_b + \epsilon_b)(\bar{q}_b - \bar{q}_a + e) \tag{8}$$

The income effect components of the effect on import demand of a change in domestic prices or import prices perhaps require a little further explanation. Since Meade has defined π_a as the partial derivative of imports with respect to domestic expenditure instead of national income, it might be thought that in formulating these import functions, Meade has not been consistent with his definition of the propensity to import. For it might be questioned that if π_a (or π_b) is defined as the marginal propensity to import with reference to aggregate money expenditures, should not the income effect on the demand for imports of a change in, say, domestic prices be written as $-(Q_a - 1)\pi_a(1 - \lambda_a)\bar{q}_a$, since out of the equivalent implicit increase in money income only $(1 - \lambda_a)$ part of it will result in new expenditure and only π_a times the new expenditure concerned will be on additional imports? This inconsistency, however, is only apparent; for if the decrease in domestic prices should result in a net decrease in aggregate money expenditure (a net hoarding) equal to $\lambda_a(Q_a - I)$, its effect on import demand is already taken care of by the term $\pi_a d_a$. When aggregate money expenditure is included as a separate determining variable of import demand, therefore, we may assume, in formulating the income effect of a change in domestic prices (or in import prices), that all the implicit increase in income will be spent or that all the implicit decrease in income will be borne by a cut in expenditure.

Meade's definition of the propensity to import with reference to aggregate expenditure must be regarded as an improvement over the conventional one which related the demand for imports to domestic national income. For the demand for imports, in so far as they are finished products, as is tacitly assumed in this model, is clearly primarily a function of total expenditure and, hence, is correlated with national income only at one remove (i.e., through the correlation between income and expenditure). Since in the present model the relationship between income and expenditure is subject to the influence of both the interest rate and the terms of trade, the relationship between income and demand for imports may also be expected to change under the influences of these factors. Such influences on the functional relationship between income and import demand can only be taken into account when the propensity

---

and

$$\frac{\partial I_a}{\partial(\bar{Q}_b E)} = -I(\pi_a + \epsilon_a).$$

Thus

$$\pi_a D_a + [-(Q_a - I)\pi_a + I\epsilon_a]\bar{Q}_a - I(\pi_a + \epsilon_a)\bar{Q}_b E = 0,$$

since at the initial position $\bar{Q}_a = \bar{Q}_b = E = 1$, and $D_a = Q_a$.

to import is defined as Meade did, i.e., with respect to expenditures instead of income.

Next we shall adopt Meade's equations for the changes in domestic prices simplified by the assumption of constant money wages, viz:

$$\bar{q}_a = \frac{1}{\eta_a} \frac{q_a}{Q_a} \tag{9}$$

$$\bar{q}_b = \frac{1}{\eta_b} \frac{q_b}{Q_b} \tag{10}$$

where η_a and η_b are the elasticities of supply of A and B's products, respectively, in terms of real labor cost (i.e., in terms of wage units).[12]

When full employment is reached, the expressions on the right-hand side of (9) and (10) would automatically become indeterminate forms, with q and η both approaching zero, and thus would leave it entirely to the other equations of the system to determine the changes in domestic prices with no change in domestic products (i.e., a zero q).

We shall also simplify the demand-for-money equations in Meade's model by getting rid of the assumed link between money supply and gold or foreign exchange reserves, as there is hardly any country that mechanically follows this rule of the gold standard game. Thus we shall simply state that:

$$m_a = \xi_a(q_a + Q_a\bar{q}_a) - \zeta_a r_a \tag{13}$$

$$m_b = \xi_b(q_b + Q_b\bar{q}_b) - \zeta_b r_b \tag{14}$$

were ξ_a and ξ_b are redefined, as distinct from Meade's own usage, as the partial derivatives of the demand for money with respect to money in-

---

[12] These are derived from the condition that the prices of domestic products in both countries must equal the marginal costs of those products, i.e.,

$$\bar{Q}_a = \bar{H}_a \frac{h_a}{q_a}, \tag{11}$$

$$\bar{Q}_b = \bar{H}_b \frac{h_b}{q_b}. \tag{12}$$

Differentiating (11), we get:

$$\bar{q}_a = \bar{H}_a d\left(\frac{h_a}{q_a}\right) + \frac{h_a}{q_a}\bar{h}_a = d\left(\frac{h_a}{q_a}\right)$$

since $\bar{H}_a$ is assumed constant and put equal to 1 at the initial position. By definition,

$$\eta_a = \frac{\frac{h_a}{q_a}}{Q_a} \frac{q_a}{d\left(\frac{h_a}{q_a}\right)}$$

By (11), however, when $\bar{Q}_a$ and $\bar{H}_a$ are put equal to 1, h_a/q_a must also equal 1.

$$\therefore \bar{q}_a = d\left(\frac{h_a}{q_a}\right) = \frac{1}{\eta_a}\frac{q_a}{Q_a}.$$

The derivation of (10) is exactly the same.

come in countries A and B, respectively, and ζ_a and ζ_b are redefined as the partial derivatives of their demand for money with respect to domestic interest rates, respectively.

Finally, the balance-of-trade equation in differentials and in terms of A's currency may be stated as:

$$t = i_b - i_a + I\bar{q}_a - I(\bar{q}_b + e). \tag{15}$$

The eleven equations (1), (2), (3), (4), or alternatively (3a) and (4a) as we have amended them, (7)–(10) and (13)–(15) should normally be sufficient to determine the eleven variables, d_a, d_b, $\bar{q}_a$, $\bar{q}_b$, i_a, i_b, r_a, r_b, and t. The variables m_a, m_b and e will be treated as exogenous policy variables. In particular, when we want to examine the effect of a devaluation on the trade balance, we shall determine the value of t in terms of e and the parameters when all the other dependent variables have adjusted to the new situation.[13]

II. EFFECT OF A DEVALUATION

A. Internal Balance Assumed

As pointed out above, the effect of a devaluation was examined by Meade only under the assumption of either a Keynesian neutral monetary policy or a monetary policy that assures internal balance. The assumption of a monetary policy that ensures internal balance for both countries concerned implies that q_a and q_b are both zero. With the additional assumption that money wages are given, $\bar{q}_a$ and $\bar{q}_b$ may also be taken as zero. Thus equations (9) and (10) may be dropped and the rest of the

---

[13] It should be noted that substituting (15) into (1) and (2) in turn, we get:

$$t = q_a + Q_a\bar{q}_a - d_a \tag{1'}$$
$$t = d_b - (q_b + Q_b\bar{q}_b) \tag{2'}$$

Furthermore, by substituting (3) into (1') and (4) into (2'), we get:

$$t = \lambda_a q_a + \rho_a r_a \tag{3'}$$
$$t = -\lambda_b q_b - \rho_b r_b \tag{4'}$$

and similarly, by substituting (3a) into (1') and (4a) into (2') we get:

$$t = \lambda_a q_a + \rho_a r_a + \lambda_a I(\bar{q}_a - \bar{q}_b - e) \tag{3'a}$$
$$t = -\lambda_b q_b - \rho_b r_b - \lambda_b I(\bar{q}_b - \bar{q}_a + e). \tag{4'a}$$

These equations facilitate the solution of t in terms of e, i.e., the ascertainment of the effect of a small devaluation on the trade balance, which we shall presently proceed to do.

(1') and (2') indicate that the change in the trade balance must be equal to the change in the gap between national product and expenditure (absorption). (3') and (4'), or (3'a) and (4'a), further tell us that the improvement in the trade balance must equal the increase in hoardings, which are either income-induced, or interest-induced, or terms-of-trade-induced—the last mentioned item being shown only in (3'a) and (4'a). These equations, however, provide only partial solutions for the effect of devaluation on the trade balance; for q_a, q_b, r_a, r_b, $\bar{q}_a$ and $\bar{q}_b$ will all be affected by e, and the total effect on t will depend on how they in their turn are affected. This is, however, as far as the absorption approach can carry us. To obtain a full solution for the effect of a devaluation, the elasticity approach must be called in.

equations greatly simplified. The solution for t/e obtained from equations
(1), (2), (7), (8) and (15) is:

$$\frac{t}{e} = \frac{dT}{dE} = \frac{(\pi_{ab} + \epsilon_{ab} - 1)I}{1 - \pi_a - \pi_b} \qquad (16)$$

where

$$\pi_{ab} = \pi_a + \pi_b \text{ and } \epsilon_{ab} = \epsilon_a + \epsilon_b.[14]$$

The solution is different from the Marshall-Lerner formula in that it
has a denominator of $1 - \pi_a - \pi_b$. This is solely due to the fact that the
propensities to import are defined here with respect to aggregate expenditures instead of incomes, so that the effect on the demand for imports of changes in aggregate expenditures cannot be excluded even
though incomes in both countries are, by assumption, kept constant.[15]

For stability of the exchange rate, it is necessary that t/e should be
positive, i.e., that a devaluation should bring about an improvement in
the balance of trade. Since the denominator $(1 - \pi_a - \pi_b)$ can normally
be assumed to be positive, the stability-condition for the exchange rate is
the same as that implied in the Marshall-Lerner formula, viz., that the
sum of the elasticities of demand for imports in both countries (including
both the income effect and the substitution effect) should be greater than
unity.

Also note that under Meade's assumption of internal balance, the
introduction of the terms-of-trade effect on aggregate expenditure would
make no difference at all in the effect of a devaluation on the trade balance. In other words, substituting (3a) and (4a) for (3) and (4) in the
above system of 9 equations would yield exactly the same solution for
t/e as (16). This is because the additional effect on expenditure of a
change in the terms of trade would be automatically compensated by
monetary policy which is assumed to offset any tendency of deviation
from full employment.[16]

Under such an implicit assumption of internal balance, the influence

---

[14] From (1') and (2') in footnote 13 above, we can see directly that, when internal balance is maintained in both countries,

$$t = -d_a = d_b.$$

Substitute this result into (7), (8) and (15), we get the result (16).

[15] It can be shown that when the propensities to import of both A and B are
defined with respect to their respective money incomes, as is usually done, so that
the import demand functions may be written as:

$$i_a = \pi_a^* q_a + I(\pi_a^* + \epsilon_a)(\bar{q}_a - \bar{q}_b - e) \qquad (7a)$$

and

$$i_b = \pi_b^* q_b + I(\pi_b^* + \epsilon_b)(\bar{q}_b - \bar{q}_a + e) \qquad (8a)$$

the denominator would disappear.

[16] In fact the solution (16) for t/e can be derived without reference to equations
(3) and (4). The substitution of (3a) and (4a) for (3) and (4), respectively, merely
affects the monetary changes that will be required for the maintenance of internal
balance.

of monetary factors is not observable at all from the equation for the effect of a devaluation, because changes in monetary factors are assumed to happen implicitly. It is therefore rather uninteresting for the study of the rôle played by monetary factors.

B. Keynesian Neutral Monetary Policy

The alternative policy assumption made by Meade is that of a neutral policy combination, under which, in addition to the assumed absence of direct government efforts to influence imports, exports and domestic expenditures by commercial and fiscal policies, the domestic rate of interest is specifically assumed to be kept constant by the monetary authorities by maintaining the supply of money and credit infinitely elastic at the existing rate of interest. According to Meade, this neutral monetary policy is the type generally assumed in "what may be called Keynesian analysis." Indeed, it is tacitly taken for granted by all economists who apply the multiplier analysis to international trade without any explicit mention of monetary factors at all.

To distinguish this type of neutral monetary policy from the more orthodox type of neutral money policy, we shall call the former the Keynesian neutral monetary policy. The latter will be called the orthodox neutral monetary policy, which, in the absence of long-run growth of population and real productive capacity of the economy, may be described simply as the monetary policy that keeps the money supply of the economy constant.

When Keynesian neutral monetary policy is assumed for both countries A and B, r_a and r_b are *ex hypothesi* zero and equations for the demand for money, i.e., (13) and (14), can be omitted altogether in the solution for the change in the balance of trade t. Using Meade's own domestic expenditure functions, i.e., (3) and (4), together with the other seven equations (1), (2), (7)–(10), and (15), the result obtained is:

$$\frac{t}{e} = \frac{dT}{dE} = \frac{\lambda_a \lambda_b (\pi_{ab} + \epsilon_{ab} - 1)I}{\Delta_1}, \qquad (17)$$

where

$$\Delta_1 = \lambda_a \lambda_b \left\{ 1 + \frac{\pi_a(1 - \lambda_a)}{\lambda_a} + \frac{\pi_b(1 - \lambda_b)}{\lambda_b} \right.$$
$$\left. + (\pi_{ab} + \epsilon_{ab} - 1)\left(\frac{\Pi_a}{\lambda_a \eta_a} + \frac{\Pi_b}{\lambda_b \eta_b} \right) \right\}, \qquad (18)$$

and Π_a and Π_b are the proportions of national expenditures (hence of national incomes, since with initial balance assumed to be zero, national incomes and expenditures are identical) initially spent on imports in countries A and B, respectively.[17]

---

[17] The method of solution is simply successive substitution to eliminate all other variables than t and e. While the order in which these other variables are eliminated

Again the stability of the exchange rate requires that $t/e > 0$. However, since it is by no means unlikely that either one or both of the two propensities to hoard (i.e., λ_a and λ_b) should be negative, we need to be more specific about this stability condition. For it has been pointed out by Samuelson that for an equation system such as the nine equations (1)–(4), (7)–(10) and (15), to be dynamically stable, it is necessary that Δ_1 (which is the determinant of the system with the sign reversed) be positive too.[18] Since it is impossible for the exchange rate to be stable when the whole system is dynamically unstable, we must conclude that it is necessary, for the stability of the exchange rate, that both (17) and (18) be positive.[19] This is what Samuelson calls "the correspondence principle" which enables us to narrow down the necessary stability conditions in comparative static analysis with dynamic stability requirements.

We shall leave for later discussion the more complicated cases where one or both of λ_a and λ_b might be negative, and for the time being concern ourselves with the simple case where they are both positive. As long as λ_a and λ_b are both positive, (17) and (18) will both be positive when $(\pi_{ab} + \epsilon_{ab} - 1) > 0$. In other words, the critical value for the sum of the elasticities of demand for imports in the two countries concerned is 1 in this Keynesian case of variable income, just as in the classical case of constant money incomes. The only difference is that the effect of devaluation will be much dampened by the changes in incomes and prices in both countries.

C. The Terms-of-Trade Effect

Let us now allow for the terms-of-trade effect upon aggregate expenditures by substituting equations (3a) and (4a) for (3) and (4) in the above system of nine equations. The solution for t/e then becomes:

$$\frac{t}{e} = \frac{dT}{dE} = \frac{\lambda_a \lambda_b (\epsilon_{ab} - 1)I}{\Delta_2} \tag{19}$$

---

is quite immaterial, the particular procedure used was first to reduce the variables $\bar{q}$'s, d's, and i's to expressions in terms of the q's only, and then, making use of equations (3′) and (4′) in footnote 13, to solve for the q's. Then t can be readily solved as $t = \lambda_a q_a$, using (3′) in footnote 13 and assuming $r_a = 0$.

[18] The number of equations being odd in this case, it is a necessary condition, for all the eigenvalues of the matrix of the system to be negative, that the determinant of the system be negative also [19] [20]. For an excellent lucid exposition of this principle, see also Baumol [4, pp. 373–78].

[19] This point was glossed over by Meade, who, after canceling out $\lambda_a \lambda_b$ from both the numerator and the denominator, observed that the denominator (with $\lambda_a \lambda_b$ canceled out) "is certainly positive if $\epsilon_{ab} + \pi_{ab} > 1$, which we shall assume normally to be the case" [15, p. 50]. This point appears also to have been overlooked by Stuvel who, after obtaining a similar expression for the effect of a devaluation on the balance of payments, asserted that it is only the sign of the whole expression that matters for stability, regardless of the sign of the denominator. See [22, Ch. 4, esp. Math. App., pp. 233–35].

where

$$\Delta_2 = \lambda_a \lambda_b \cdot \left\{ \left[1 + \frac{\pi_a(1-\lambda_a)}{\lambda_a} + \frac{\pi_b(1-\lambda_b)}{\lambda_b} \right] \left(1 + \frac{\Pi_a}{\eta_a} + \frac{\Pi_b}{\eta_b} \right) \right. \tag{20}$$
$$\left. + (\epsilon_{ab} - 1)\left(\frac{\Pi_a}{\lambda_a \eta_a} + \frac{\Pi_b}{\lambda_b \eta_b} \right) \right\}.^{20}$$

Again Samuelson's correspondence principle would require that for the stability of the exchange market it is necessary that both (19) and (20) be greater than zero.

Again assuming for the time being that λ_a and λ_b are both positive, the crucial stability condition is now $(\epsilon_{ab} - 1) > 0$, i.e., the sum of the components of the pure substitution effect alone in the two elasticities of demand for imports must be greater than 1.

A comparison of (17) and (19) therefore confirms the findings of Harberger as well as Laursen and Metzler that when the effects of the terms of trade on aggregate expenditures are taken into consideration, the stability condition for the exchange rate becomes more stringent. The crucial stability condition implied in (19), when λ_a and λ_b are both assumed to be positive, i.e., $(\epsilon_{ab} - 1) > 0$, although apparently much simpler, is in fact identical to the stability conditions obtained by Harberger and Laursen and Metzler.[21] This simpler form, however, shows more clearly the true magnitude of this bugbear, which, according to Laursen and Metzler, might require the crucial value of the sum of the two elasticities of demand for imports to "exceed unity by a considerable amount" [12, p. 296]. Equation (19) clearly shows that the result of allowing for the terms-of-trade effect on aggregate expenditures is merely

---

[20] The method of solution adopted here is again successive elimination, and the particular procedure is first to reduce the $\bar{q}$'s, d's, and i's to expressions in terms of the q's only and then solve for the q's. The solution for t can then be obtained from those for q_a and q_b.

[21] Harberger's stability condition is:

$$(\eta_1 + \eta_2) > (1 + c_1 + c_2),$$

where η_1 and η_2, the two elasticities of demand for imports, correspond to our $(\pi_a + \epsilon_a)$ and $(\pi_b + \epsilon_b)$, respectively; and c_1 and c_2, the two propensities to import, correspond to our π_a and π_b, respectively. Thus his condition can be easily converted to our form, viz. $(\epsilon_{ab} - 1) > 0$ [7, p. 53, esp. fn. 13].

Laursen and Metzler's condition is given in the form:

$$\{(1 - w_1)(1 - w_2)v_1(\eta_1 + \eta_2 - 1) - s_1 m_1(1 - w_2) - s_2 m_2(1 - w_1)\} > 0,$$

where w_1 and w_2 are the propensities to spend, and hence $(1 - w_1)$ and $(1 - w_2)$ correspond to our λ_a and λ_b; v_1, the initial volume of imports (assumed to be the same for both countries), corresponds to our I; η_1 and η_2 to our $(\pi_a + \epsilon_a)$ and $(\pi_b + \epsilon_b)$, respectively; m_1 and m_2 to our π_a and π_b, respectively; and s_1 and s_2 are partial derivatives of the aggregate expenditures with respect to the exchange rate for the two countries, respectively. In our notation, $s_1 = \partial D_a / \partial E$ and $s_2 = \partial D_b / \partial (1/E)$, which, according to equations (3a) and (4a) above, are respectively equal to $\lambda_a I$ and $\lambda_b I$. Thus written in our notation, Laursen and Metzler's condition becomes:

$$\{\lambda_a \lambda_b I(\pi_{ab} + \epsilon_{ab} - 1) - \lambda_a I \pi_a \lambda_b - \lambda_b I \pi_b \lambda_a\} = \lambda_a \lambda_b I(\epsilon_{ab} - 1) > 0,$$

which is exactly the same as implied in equation (19).

to cancel out the components of the income effect in the crucial sum of the two elasticities of demand for imports. If the proportion of the national income spent on imports is high so that the terms-of-trade effect on expenditure may be expected to be of some significance, so also would be the income effect component in the elasticity of demand for imports which offsets it. Conversely, if the income effect component in the elasticity of import demand is negligible, then the terms-of-trade effect upon aggregate expenditure, that is supposed to cause difficulty, would also be of negligible significance. Therefore, the existence of the terms-of-trade effect upon aggregate expenditure is not likely to make the stability condition of the exchange rate so dangerously stringent as was at first suggested.

D. Instability of the Keynesian Neutral Monetary Policy

This observation about the significance of the terms-of-trade effect upon aggregate expenditure, however, is rather a digression from our main purpose in this paper, which is to achieve a synthesis of the elasticity and the absorption approaches and to highlight the role played by monetary factors. More pertinent to the main purpose of this paper are the following facts about the effect of a devaluation, as may be observed from (17) and (18) or (19) and (20):

1. It is impossible to dichotomize the effect of a devaluation into two clear-cut components, viz. a relative-price effect and an absorption or multiplier effect which constitutes a damping coefficient to the former; for as soon as we abandon the usual assumption of constant costs and prices of domestic products in both countries, the multiplier process would again involve changes in relative prices and hence the relative-price effect on the trade balance.[22] It is quite naive, therefore, to claim that the absorption approach is a superior new tool that could supersede entirely the relative-price approach.

2. The absorption approach is right in the case of a Keynesian neutral monetary policy in pointing out that unless there is a positive propensity to hoard in both countries, the balance of trade is unlikely to be stable even if the sum of the elasticities of demand for imports of the two countries is greater than 1. For if one of the propensities to hoard is negative while the sum of the elasticities of demand for imports is greater than 1,

---

[22] If we make the usual simplifying assumption that the elasticities of supply of products of A and B are both infinite, i.e., $\eta_a = \eta_b = \infty$, so that prices of domestic products will remain constant, then (19), for instance, can be simplified to:

$$\frac{t}{e} = \frac{\lambda_a\lambda_b(\epsilon_{ab}-1)I}{\lambda_a\lambda_b + \pi_a(1-\lambda_a)\lambda_b + \pi_b(1-\lambda_b)\lambda_b} \tag{21}$$

In this case, it is indeed permissible to say that the relative-price effect determines the initial change in trade balance to which a damping coefficient, determined by propensities to hoard and import is to be applied. Too often, however, analyses of the effect of a devaluation stop with such simple cases.

then (17) or (19) cannot be positive, when the necessary condition for the dynamic stability of the system is satisfied, i.e., when Δ_1 or $\Delta_2 > 0$.

If one of the propensities to hoard is zero, t/e would be zero, which implies that the effect of a devaluation would be zero. If both λ_a and λ_b are negative, it might seem that it is not impossible for both (17) and (18), or (19) and (20), to be positive as required for stability, and hence for the exchange rate to be stable, provided the absolute values of the negative λ_a and λ_b are large enough relatively to π_a and π_b, respectively, and η_a and η_b are also large. This is, however, illusory; for it must be remembered that Δ_1 (or Δ_2) > 0 is only a necessary condition for the dynamic stability of the system. By direct economic reasoning, it can be shown that there can be no stability for the system if the marginal propensities to spend in both countries are greater than 1. For with marginal propensities to spend greater than 1 and the supplies of money infinitely elastic at constant interest rates as assumed under the Keynesian neutral monetary policy, both countries would be unstable in isolation. It is therefore impossible that the two countries would become stable when joined together in mutual trade, since there is no possibility for the instability of the one being compensated by the stability of the other.[23]

In the actual state of affairs, it is not at all unlikely that the marginal propensity to hoard, in the sense of 1 minus the marginal propensity to spend (on both investment and consumption), should be zero or negative. Thus it would appear that the stability of the exchange rate and the balance to trade is frequently in a very precarious state, even if the sum of the elasticities of demand for imports is well above 1.

We shall soon see, however, that only under the Keynesian neutral monetary policy that eliminates all the stabilizing influences of monetary factors is the stability of the exchange rate so precarious. Under a different monetary policy, say, the orthodox neutral monetary policy, it would not be necessary at all for the stability of the exchange rate and the dynamic system that the propensity to hoard of either country be greater than zero.

3. Furthermore, even if the sum of the elasticities of demand for imports is well above 1 and the marginal propensities to hoard of both countries are greater than zero, the exchange rate would at best be in a sort of "indifferent" or "neutral" equilibrium under the Keynesian neutral monetary policy, as soon as full employment is reached in the devaluing country. For when full employment is reached in country A, η_a approaches

---

[23] There seems to be a possibility that, if one of the propensities to hoard is negative and at the same time the sum of the elasticities of demand for imports is smaller than its critical value, the necessary condition for the stability of the dynamic system as well as the exchange rate might be satisfied. I am not sure, however, whether the sufficient condition for dynamic stability can be satisfied by such a combination since I have not worked out fully the sufficient condition for dynamic stability. Furthermore it seems that in such cases, the relative speed of price and income adjustments will have to be taken into consideration.

0 as a limit and equations (17) and (19) would also approach zero as a limit, i.e.,

$$\frac{dT}{dE} = \frac{t}{e} \to 0, \qquad \text{as } \eta_a \to 0;$$

for Δ_1 and $\Delta_2 \to \infty$, as $\eta_a \to 0$. In other words, the effect of devaluation on the balance of trade would be zero.[24] Thus if a freely fluctuating exchange rate system is adopted in a country with full employment and a Keynesian neutral monetary policy, any slight chance imbalance in trade could cause violent depreciation of the currency as the exchange rate would be entirely indeterminate.[25]

4. So far we have abstracted from money-wage changes due to trade union pressure and speculative capital movements. We have reached the conclusion that a full-employment economy with a Keynesian neutral monetary policy would imply instability in the balance of trade and the exchange rate without taking into consideration the possibilities of a wage-price spiral and a destabilizing speculative capital movement.

When these possibilities are taken into consideration, the instability implied in the Keynesian monetary policy will certainly be aggravated. I have shown elsewhere [23] [24] that the Keynesian monetary policy—i.e., the pegging of the interest rate at a fixed level with an infinitely elastic supply of money—provides precisely the monetary condition that is most conducive to the generation of a cumulative (self-aggravating) speculative capital movement; and that the instability of the French franc due to speculative capital flights in the 'twenties, a case which has been much

---

[24] The fact that the other country is fully employed is not a menace to the stability of the trade balance and exchange rate for a devaluing country. For under full employment, the elasticity of aggregate supply is likely to take on different values according to the direction in which aggregate demand is changing. The elasticity of aggregate supply is zero when confronted with an increase in aggregate demand, but it is not likely to be zero when confronted with a decrease in aggregate demand, particularly when money wages in the country concerned are rigid. Since the aggregate demand for the products of the country whose currency has relatively appreciated is likely to fall, the relevant elasticity of supply of its products is not likely to be zero, even when it is enjoying full employment.

[25] So far we have assumed a balanced trade position as the starting point. It has been pointed out by A. O. Hirschman that if there is a trade deficit to start with, the necessary and sufficient condition for a devaluation to improve the balance of trade becomes easier to fulfill [9]. However, in a sense, the condition for $dT/dE > 0$, assuming no initial trade deficit, is still the basic stability condition; for if $dT/dE > 0$ only when there is an initial trade deficit, but < 0 when there is no initial deficit, then the country concerned may use devaluation to improve its balance of trade to some extent when it has an initial trade deficit, but it cannot use devaluation to eliminate its deficit; for when its deficit gets smaller, further devaluation may begin to have an adverse effect on its trade balance. If $dT/dE > 0$ when there is an initial deficit, but equals 0 when trade is balanced, then theoretically it is not impossible for the country eventually to eliminate its initial trade deficit by keeping on devaluing its currency. But once the trade deficit is eliminated, the momentum of devaluation may carry it further and further; for then the exchange rate becomes indeterminate (being in an indifferent equilibrium).

cited as the evidence of the inherent instability of a floating exchange rate system, was really made possible and stimulated by the French monetary policy at the time of pegging the interest rate on the large amount of floating debt then in existence and being issued. Those economists with a Keynesian inclination, who decry the traditional reliance on exchange rate adjustment to restore the balance of payments, often forget that one of the chief reasons why devaluation may fail to improve the balance of trade, particularly in the postwar world of full or overfull employment, is precisely the monetary policy which they either take for granted or are actively advocating.

E. Orthodox Neutral Money Policy

That monetary factors can play a vital stabilizing role in the exchange market can be clearly shown by substituting the orthodox neutral money policy as defined above for the Keynesian neutral monetary policy. Under the assumption of an orthodox neutral money policy, changes in money supply, i.e., m_a and m_b, may be put equal to zero, whereas interest rates would be permitted to change freely. The effect of a devaluation can then be obtained by solving the system of 11 equations, consisting either of (1)–(4), (7)–(10), and (13)–(15) or (1), (2), (3a), (4a), (7)–(10) and (13)–(15), for t in terms of e after putting m_a and m_b equal to zero.

The result obtained with the first set of equations, i.e., the set of equations that do not allow for the terms-of-trade effect on aggregate expenditures, is:

$$\frac{t}{e} = \frac{dT}{dE} = a\beta \frac{(\pi_{ab} + \epsilon_{ab} - 1)I}{\Delta_3} \tag{22}$$

where

$$\Delta_3 = a\beta \left\{ 1 + \frac{\pi_a(1-a)}{a} + \frac{\pi_b(1-\beta)}{\beta} \right.$$
$$\left. + (\pi_{ab} + \epsilon_{ab} - 1)\left(\frac{\Pi_a}{a\eta_a} + \frac{\Pi_b}{\beta\eta_b}\right) \right\} \tag{23}$$

$$a = \lambda_a + \left(1 + \frac{1}{\eta_a}\right)\frac{\rho_a\xi_a}{\zeta_a} \tag{24}$$

and

$$\beta = \lambda_b + \left(1 + \frac{1}{\eta_b}\right)\frac{\rho_b\xi_b}{\zeta_b}.{}^{26} \tag{25}$$

Equations (22) and (23) are of exactly the same form as (17) and (18) respectively; the only difference is that in (22) and (23) a and β are substituted for λ_a and λ_b of (17) and (18). The terms a or β may be re-

---

[26] The procedure adopted here is again to reduce the $\bar{q}$'s, r's, d's and i's to expressions in terms of the q's only and then solve for q_a and q_b. The solution for t is then obtained from those for q_a and q_b.

garded as consisting of two components: First, there is the usual marginal propensity to hoard directly induced by real-income changes (viz., λ_a or λ_b, respectively). Secondly, we have the interest-induced marginal propensity to hoard brought about by changes in the interest rate resulting from changes in the demand for transaction balances in connection with changes in money income, viz.,

$$\left(1 + \frac{1}{\eta_a}\right)\frac{\rho_a\xi_a}{\zeta_a} \text{ or } \left(1 + \frac{1}{\eta_b}\right)\frac{\rho_b\xi_b}{\zeta_b},$$

respectively. As long as the interest-elasticity of the demand for money is not infinitely large (in absolute value) and the interest elasticity of aggregate expenditure is not zero, the interest-induced marginal propensity to hoard is always positive. Moreover, if there is a practical limit to the velocity of circulation of money, ζ_a or ζ_b would approach zero as the limit of the velocity of circulation is gradually approached.

Thus unless we start from a position deep down in the liquidity trap, the second component is bound eventually to overwhelm the first, regardless of whether the latter is positive or negative. The danger of instability due to a negative propensity to hoard (or a greater than unity propensity to spend), which is after all quite a normal phenomenon, will, therefore, be quite under control if an orthodox neutral monetary policy is adopted instead of the Keynesian neutral monetary policy.

Furthermore, and what is more important for the current world, full employment at home need not imply instability in the balance of trade and the exchange rate. For when full employment is reached in country A, and hence η_a approaches zero, t/e would not approach zero as under the Keynesian neutral monetary policy. For equations (22)–(25) indicate that, as $\eta_a \to 0$,

$$\frac{t}{e} \to \frac{(\pi_{ab} + \epsilon_{ab} - 1)I}{1 - \pi_a + \dfrac{\pi_b(1 - \beta)}{\beta} + (\pi_{ab} + \epsilon_{ab} - 1)\left(\dfrac{\Pi_a\zeta_a}{\rho_a\xi_a} + \dfrac{\Pi_b}{\beta\eta_b}\right)} \qquad (26)$$

since

$$a = \lambda_a + \left(1 + \frac{1}{\eta_a}\right)\frac{\rho_a\xi_a}{\zeta_a} \to \infty, \quad a\eta_a \to \frac{\rho_a\xi_a}{\zeta_a}, \quad \text{as} \quad \eta_a \to 0.$$

The limit for t/e as $\eta_a \to 0$ will be greater than zero as long as the primary stability condition $\pi_{ab} + \epsilon_{ab} > 1$ is fulfilled. Thus full employment at home and a marginal propensity to spend equal to or greater than 1 are no threat to the stability of the balance of trade and the exchange rate under an orthodox neutral money policy.[27]

---

[27] I have shown elsewhere [23, pp. 410–12] that so long as the interest elasticity of supply of money is zero (as is implied by the orthodox neutral monetary policy) and the interest elasticity of demand for money is fairly small, as it would be when the prevailing interest rate is well above the minimum set by the liquidity trap, it is highly unlikely that the speculative demand for foreign exchange will be unstable or self-aggravating.

The introduction of the effect of terms-of-trade changes on aggregate expenditures would make no difference to the substance of the above conclusions. In addition it may be shown that the significance for exchange rate stability of the terms-of-trade effect on expenditure is less under an orthodox neutral money policy than under a Keynesian monetary policy. For by substituting equations (3a) and (4a) for (3) and (4) in the system and putting m_a and m_b equal to zero as before, we get

$$\frac{t}{e} = \frac{\alpha\beta\left(\pi_{ab} + \epsilon_{ab} - 1 - \frac{\lambda_a\pi_a}{\alpha} - \frac{\lambda_b\pi_b}{\beta}\right)I}{\Delta_4} \qquad (27)$$

where

$$\Delta_4 = \alpha\beta\left\{1 + \frac{\pi_a(1-\alpha)}{\alpha} + \frac{\pi_b(1-\beta)}{\beta} \right. \qquad (28)$$

$$+ \left[\pi_{ab} + \epsilon_{ab} - 1 + \lambda_a(1-\pi_{ab}) - \frac{\pi_b(\lambda_a - \lambda_b)}{\beta}\right]\frac{\Pi_a}{\alpha\eta_a}$$

$$\left. + \left[\pi_{ab} + \epsilon_{ab} - 1 + \lambda_b(1-\pi_{ab}) - \frac{\pi_a(\lambda_b - \lambda_a)}{\alpha}\right]\frac{\Pi_b}{\beta\eta_b}\right\}.[28]$$

Comparison of equation (27) with (22) again indicates that, as pointed out by Harberger, and Laursen and Metzler, if λ_a and λ_b are positive so that a worsening of the terms of trade has a stimulating effect on the aggregate spending of the country concerned, the terms-of-trade effect upon aggregate expenditure would make the stability condition for the exchange rate more stringent. On the other hand, comparison of (27) with (19) shows that the significance for exchange stability of the terms-of-trade effect on expenditure is clearly reduced under an orthodox neutral monetary policy. For whereas under the Keynesian neutral monetary policy the effect of the terms-of-trade changes on expenditure would exactly cancel out the income-effect components of the elasticities of demand for imports, thus making the stability condition $\epsilon_{ab} > 1$, under an orthodox neutral money policy it will normally fall short of doing this. Given that α and β are both positive, which is practically always ensured under such a monetary policy, the crucial stability condition for the balance of trade is now:

$$\left(\pi_{ab} + \epsilon_{ab} - 1 - \frac{\lambda_a\pi_a}{\alpha} - \frac{\lambda_b\pi_b}{\beta}\right) > 0. \qquad (29)$$

Since α and β are normally greater than λ_a and λ_b, respectively, the influence of the terms-of-trade effect on expenditure will not be big enough to offset completely the income-effect components in the elasticities of import demands. Thus the terms-of-trade effect on expenditure appears to be a much exaggerated bugbear in the eyes of elasticity pessimists.

It also can be shown that under an orthodox neutral money policy full employment at home will cause no difficulty to exchange rate stability

---

[28] The procedure adopted here is similar to the one used in the preceding case.

even if the terms-of-trade effect on expenditure is allowed for. For as $\eta_a \to 0$, equation (27) becomes:

$$\frac{t}{e} \to \frac{\left(\pi_{ab} + \epsilon_{ab} - 1 - \frac{\lambda_b \pi_b}{\beta}\right) I}{\Delta_5}, \tag{30}$$

where

$$\Delta_5 = 1 - \pi_a + \frac{\pi_b(1-\beta)}{\beta} + \left[\pi_{ab} + \epsilon_{ab} - 1 + \lambda_a(1 - \pi_{ab}) \right. \tag{31}$$

$$\left. - \frac{\pi_b(\lambda_a - \lambda_b)}{\beta} \right] \frac{\Pi_a \zeta_a}{\rho_a \xi_a} + \left[\pi_{ab} + \epsilon_{ab} - 1 + \lambda_b(1 - \pi_{ab}) \right] \frac{\Pi_b}{\beta \eta_b}.$$

When λ_a is positive, the stability condition implied in (30), i.e.,

$$\left(\pi_{ab} + \epsilon_{ab} - 1 - \frac{\lambda_b \pi_b}{\beta} \right) > 0,$$

is certainly fulfilled, when that implied in (27) is fulfilled.

When $\lambda_a < 0$, it implies that the terms-of-trade effect on expenditure in country A will give a boost to, instead of detracting from, the stability of the balance of trade. Equation (30) would then merely indicate that when full employment at home is attained, this possible boost to stability would disappear. In any case, the stability condition

$$\left(\pi_{ab} + \epsilon_{ab} - 1 - \frac{\lambda_b \pi_b}{\beta} \right) > 0$$

is not substantially different from the traditional Marshall-Lerner stability condition of $(\pi_{ab} + \epsilon_{ab} - 1) > 0$.[29]

III. CONCLUDING REMARKS

We conclude that the absorption approach to the analysis of the effects of devaluation has contributed to our understanding of the prob-

---

[29] In fact a comparison of (22) and (23) with (17) and (18), or of (27) and (28) with (19) and (20), shows that the dampening influence of income variation on the effect of a devaluation is generally reduced by the adoption of an orthodox, instead of a Keynesian, neutral monetary policy.

In the extreme case, where the interest elasticity of demand for money is zero in both countries (i.e., $\zeta_a = \zeta_b = 0$, which implies that the velocities of circulation of money are constant in both countries), a and β would approach infinitely. Then (22), (26), (27) and (30) would all become the same as (16); i.e.,

$$\frac{t}{e} = \frac{(\pi_{ab} + \epsilon_{ab} - 1)I}{1 - \pi_a - \pi_b},$$

which is the solution we obtained under the assumption of internal balance in both countries (see above p. 399).

Thus the neglect of the dampening influence of income variation by the neoclassical economists is probably due partly to their customary assumption of zero interest elasticity of demand for money (or constant velocity of circulation of money). Alexander's characterization of the neoclassical elasticity approach as part tautological theorizing is, therefore, quite unjustified.

lem only in emphasizing the fundamental facts that a positive trade balance implies the presence of hoarding (nonspending) of incomes or credit contraction and that a negative trade balance implies the presence of dishoarding or credit expansion, and that a more comprehensive analysis, including in particular an analysis of the effect on income and expenditure, is needed than is implied in the classical elasticity approach As an independent analytical tool, in substitution for the traditional elasticity approach, however, it is quite inadequate; for we have shown that not only is the primary effect of a devaluation determined by the elasticities, but the secondary damping factor also depends on the relevant elasticities, once domestic prices are recognized as liable to change with the changes in income.

The significance of monetary factors, the role of which is clearly indicated by the fundamental identity of the absorption approach, is however entirely obliterated by the usual assumption of constant interest rates supported by infinitely elastic supply of or demand for money with respect to the interest rate, an assumption explicitly or implicitly made in practically all modern Keynesian analyses. Such a monetary assumption, however, would imply instability in the exchange rate as soon as full employment is reached at home, even without allowing for the destabilizing influence of speculative capital movements and the possibility of a wage-price spiral. To take for granted such a monetary policy may have been justified in the deep depression years of the 'thirties, but it is hardly appropriate in the current world of prosperity and high-level employment.

It is high time that we abandoned this ubiquitous underlying assumption in our aggregate analysis lest we should scare ourselves out of our own wits in "discovering" dangerous instability lurking everywhere in our economy (notably, for example, the supposed razor-edge instability of our growth path) and thus clamor for more and more government controls on our economic life.

REFERENCES

1. S. S. ALEXANDER. "Effects of a Devaluation on a Trade Balance," Internat. Mon. Fund *Staff Papers*, Vol. 2 (April, 1952), pp. 263–78.
2. ———. "Effects of a Devaluation: A Simplified Synthesis of Elasticities and Absorption Approaches," *Am. Econ. Rev.*, Vol. 49 (March, 1959), pp. 23–42.
3. W. R. ALLEN. "A Note on the Money Income Effect of Devaluation," *Kyklos*, Vol. 9 (1956), pp. 372–80.
4. W. J. BAUMOL. *Economic Dynamics*. 2nd ed. New York, 1959.
5. H. BREMS. "Devaluation, A Marriage of the Elasticity and Absorption Approaches," *Econ. Jour.*, Vol. 67 (March, 1957), pp. 49–64.
6. A. J. BROWN. "Trade Balances and Exchange Stability," *Oxford Econ. Papers*, No. 6 (April, 1942), pp. 57–75.

7. A. C. HARBERGER. "Currency Depreciation, Income and the Balance of Trade," *Jour. Pol. Econ.*, Vol. 58 (Feb., 1950), pp. 47–60.

8. ———. "Pitfalls in Mathematical Model Building," *Am. Econ. Rev.*, Vol. 42 (Dec., 1952), pp. 856–65.

9. A. O. HIRSCHMAN. "Devaluation and Trade Balance—A Note," *Rev. Econ. Stat.*, Vol. 31 (Feb., 1949), pp. 50–53.

10. H. G. JOHNSON. "Towards a General Theory of the Balance of Payments," *International Trade and Economic Growth*, ch. 6. London, 1958.

10A. ———. "The Taxonomic Approach to Economic Policy," *Econ. Jour.*, Vol. 61 (Dec., 1951), pp. 812–32.

11. R. W. JONES. "Depreciation and the Dampening Effect of Income Changes," *Rev. Econ. Stat.*, Vol. 42 (Feb., 1960), pp. 74–80.

12. S. LAURSEN and L. A. METZLER. "Flexible Exchange Rates and the Theory of Employment," *Rev. Econ. Stat.*, Vol. 32 (Nov., 1950), pp. 281–99.

13. F. MACHLUP. "Relative Prices and Aggregate Spending in the Analysis of Devaluation," *Am. Econ. Rev.*, Vol. 45 (June, 1955), pp. 255–78.

14. ———. "The Terms of Trade Effects of Devaluation upon Real Income and the Balance of Trade," *Kyklos*, Vol. 9, No. 4 (1956), pp. 417–52.

15. J. E. MEADE. *The Balance of Payments, Mathematical Supplement*. London, 1951.

16. M. MICHAELY. "Relative Prices and Income Absorption Approaches to Devaluation: A Partial Reconciliation," *Am. Econ. Rev.*, Vol. 50 (Mar., 1960), pp. 144–47.

17. I. F. PEARCE. "A Note on Mr. Spraos' Paper," *Economica*, N.S. Vol. 22 (May, 1955), pp. 147–51.

18. J. ROBINSON. "The Foreign Exchanges," *Essays in the Theory of Employment*. New York, 1937. Pt. III, Ch. 1, reprinted in *Readings in the Theory of International Trade*, H. S. ELLIS and L. A. METZLER (eds.). Philadelphia, 1949, pp. 83–103.

19. P. A. SAMUELSON. "The Stability of Equilibrium: Comparative Statics and Dynamics," *Econometrica*, Vol. 9 (April, 1941), pp. 97–120.

20. ———. *Foundations of Economic Analysis*. Cambridge, 1953.

21. J. SPRAOS. "Consumers' Behaviour and the Conditions for Exchange Stability," *Economica*, N.S. Vol. 22 (May, 1955), pp. 137–47.

22. G. STUVEL. *The Exchange Stability Problem*. Oxford, 1951.

23. S. C. TSIANG. "A Theory of Foreign Exchange Speculation under a Floating Exchange System," *Jour. Pol. Econ.*, Vol. 66 (Oct., 1958), pp. 399–418.

24. ———. "Floating Exchange Rate System in Countries with Relatively Stable Economies: Some European Experience After World War I," *Internat. Mon. Fund Staff Papers*, Vol. 7 (Oct., 1959), pp. 244–73.

25. W. H. WHITE. "The Employment-Insulating Advantages of Flexible Exchange Rates: A Comment on Professors Laursen and Metzler," *Rev. Econ. Stat.*, Vol. 36 (May, 1954), pp. 225–28.

25. The Case for Flexible Exchange Rates*

By MILTON FRIEDMAN†

THE WESTERN NATIONS seem committed to a system of international payments based on exchange rates between their national currencies fixed by governments and maintained rigid except for occasional changes to new levels. This system is embodied in the statutes of the International Monetary Fund, which provides for changes in exchange rates of less than 10 per cent by individual governments without approval of the Fund and for larger changes only with approval; it is implicit in the European Payments Union; and it is taken for granted in almost all discussions of international economic policy.

Whatever may have been the merits of this system for another day, it is ill suited to current economic and political conditions. These conditions make a system of flexible or floating exchange rates—exchange rates freely determined in an open market primarily by private dealings and, like other market prices, varying from day to day—absolutely essential for the fulfilment of our basic economic objective: the achievement and maintenance of a free and prosperous world community engaging in unrestricted multilateral trade. There is scarcely a facet of international economic policy for which the implicit acceptance of a system of rigid exchange rates does not create serious and unnecessary difficulties. Promotion of rearmament, liberalization of trade, avoidance of allocations and other direct controls both internal and external, harmonization of internal monetary and fiscal policies—all these problems take on a different cast .and become far easier to solve in a world of flexible exchange rates and its corollary, free convertibility of currencies. The sooner a system of flexible exchange rates is established, the sooner unrestricted multilateral trade will become a real possibility. And it will become one

* This paper had its origin in a memorandum written in the fall of 1950 when I was a consultant to the Finance and Trade Division of the Office of Special Representative for Europe, United States Economic Cooperation Administration. Needless to say, the views it expresses are entirely my own. I am grateful to Joel Bernstein and Maxwell Obst for criticism of the original memorandum and to Earl J. Hamilton and Lloyd A. Metzler for criticism of a subsequent draft. The paper owes much, also, to extensive discussion of the general problem with a number of friends, particularly Aaron Director, James Meade, Lloyd Mints, and Lionel Robbins. Unfortunately, these discussions failed to produce sufficient agreement to make a disclaimer of their responsibility unnecessary. [Abridged from M. Friedman, Essays in Positive Economics (Chicago: University of Chicago Press, 1953), pp. 157–203.]

† The University of Chicago.

without in any way interfering with the pursuit by each nation of domestic economic stability according to its own lights.[1]

Before proceeding to defend this thesis in detail, I should perhaps emphasize two points to avoid misunderstanding. First, advocacy of flexible exchange rates is *not* equivalent to advocacy of unstable exchange rates. The ultimate objective is a world in which exchange rates, while *free* to vary, are in fact highly stable. Instability of exchange rates is a symptom of instability in the underlying economic structure. Elimination of this symptom by administrative freezing of exchange rates cures none of the underlying difficulties and only makes adjustment to them more painful. Second, by unrestricted multilateral trade, I shall mean a system in which there are no direct quantitative controls over imports or exports, in which any tariffs or export bounties are reasonably stable and nondiscriminatory and are not subject to manipulation to affect the balance of payments, and in which a substantial fraction of international trade is in private (nongovernmental) hands. Though admittedly vague and subject to considerable ambiguity, this definition will do for our purposes. I shall take for granted without detailed examination that unrestricted multilateral trade in this sense[2] is a desirable objective of economic policy.[3] However, many of the arguments for flexible exchange rates remain valid even if this premise is not accepted.

I. ALTERNATIVE METHODS OF ADJUSTING TO CHANGES AFFECTING INTERNATIONAL PAYMENTS

Changes affecting the international trade and the balance of payments of various countries are always occurring. Some are in the "real" conditions determining international trade, such as the weather, technical conditions of production, consumer tastes, and the like. Some are in monetary conditions, such as divergent degrees of inflation or deflation in various countries.

These changes affect some commodities more than others and so tend to produce changes in the structure of relative prices—for example, rearmament by the United States impinges particularly on selected raw materials and tends to raise their prices relatively to other prices. Such

---

[1] Indeed, I have elsewhere argued that flexible exchange rates are the logical international counterpart of the monetary and fiscal framework for economic stability that seems to me the most promising. See "A Monetary and Fiscal Framework for Economic Stability," *American Economic Review,* Vol. XXXVIII (June, 1948), pp. 245–64, reprinted in M. Friedman, *Essays in Positive Economics,* pp. 133–56.

[2] And indeed in the even more extreme sense of trade free from all barriers, including tariffs and export bounties.

[3] In brief, it is desirable in its own right as one of the basic freedoms we cherish; it promotes the efficient use of resources through an appropriate international division of labor and increases consumer welfare by maximizing the range of alternatives on which consumers can spend their incomes; it facilitates international political amity by removing potent sources of conflict between governments.

effects on the relative price structure are likely to be much the same whether exchange rates are rigid or flexible and to raise much the same problem of adjustment in either case and so will receive little attention in what follows.

But, over and above these effects on particular commodities and prices, the changes in question affect each country's balance of payments, taken as a whole. Holders of foreign currencies want to exchange them for the currency of a particular country in order to purchase commodities produced in that country, or to purchase securities or other capital assets in that country, or to pay interest on or repay debts to that country, or to make gifts to citizens of that country, or simply to hold for one of these uses or for resale. The amount of currency of a particular country that is demanded per unit of time for each of these purposes will, of course, depend in the first instance on the exchange rate—the number of units of a foreign currency that must be paid to acquire one unit of the domestic currency. Other things the same, the more expensive a given currency, that is, the higher the exchange rate, the less of that currency will in general be demanded for each of these purposes. Similarly, holders of the currency of the country in question want to exchange that currency for foreign currencies for the corresponding purposes; and, again, the amount they want to exchange depends, in the first instance, on the price which they can get. The changes continuously taking place in the conditions of international trade alter the "other things" and so the desirability of using the currencies of various countries for each of the purposes listed. The aggregate effect is at one time to increase, at another to decrease, the amount of a country's currency demanded at any given rate of exchange relative to the amount offered for sale at that rate. Of course, after the event, the amount of a particular currency purchased must equal the amount sold—this is a question simply of double-entry bookkeeping. But, in advance, the amount people want to buy need not equal the amount people want to sell. The *ex post* equality involves a reconciliation of these divergent desires, either through changes in the desires themselves or through their frustration.

There is no way of avoiding this reconciliation; inconsistent desires cannot simultaneously be satisfied. The crucial question of policy is the mechanism whereby this reconciliation is brought about. Suppose the aggregate effect of changes in the conditions affecting international payments has been to increase the amount of a country's currency people want to buy with foreign currency relatively to the amount other people want to sell for foreign currency at the pre-existing exchange rate—to create an incipient surplus in the balance of payments. How can these inconsistent desires be reconciled? (1) The country's currency may be bid up, or put up, in price. This increase in the exchange rate will tend to make the currency less desirable relative to the currency of other countries and so eliminate the excess demand at the pre-existing rate.[4] (2) Prices within the country may rise, thus making its goods less desirable relative to goods in other countries, or incomes within the country may rise, thus increasing the demand for foreign currencies. (3) Direct controls over transactions involving foreign exchange may prevent holders of foreign balances from acquiring as much domestic exchange as they would otherwise like to; for example, they may be prevented from buying domestic goods by the inability to get a required export license. (4) The excess amount of domestic currency desired may be provided out of monetary reserves, the foreign currency acquired being added to reserves of foreign currencies—the monetary authorities (or exchange equalization fund or the like) may step in with a "desire" to buy or sell the difference between the amounts demanded and supplied by others.

Each of these four methods has its obvious counterpart if the effect of the changes is to create an incipient deficit. Aside from purely frictional frustrations of desires (the inability of a buyer to find a seller because of imperfections of the market), these are fundamentally the only four ways in which an *ex ante* divergence between the amount of a country's currency demanded and the amount supplied can be converted into the *ex post* equality that necessarily prevails. Let us consider each in turn.

A. Changes in Exchange Rates

Two different mechanisms whereby exchange-rate changes may be used to maintain equilibrium in the balance of payments must be sharply distinguished: (1) flexible exchange rates as defined above and (2) official changes in temporarily rigid rates.

1. *Flexible Exchange Rates.* Under flexible exchange rates freely determined in open markets, the first impact of any tendency toward a surplus or deficit in the balance of payments is on the exchange rate. If a country has an incipient surplus of receipts over payments—an excess demand for its currency—the exchange rate will tend to rise. If it has an incipient deficit, the exchange rate will tend to fall. If the conditions responsible for the rise or the fall in the exchange rate are generally re-

---

[4] It is conceivable that, under some conditions and for some range of exchange rates, a rise in exchange rates would increase the excess demand. Though this possibility has received considerable attention, it will be neglected in what follows as of little practical relevance. As a purely theoretical matter, there will always be some set or sets of rates that will clear the market, and, in the neighborhood of at least one of the sets of rates a rise in the rate will mean a decline in excess demand (i.e., a negative excess demand); a fall, a rise in excess demand. Exchange rates can remain in a region in which this is not true only if they are not free to move and if some non-price mechanism is used to ration domestic or foreign currency. As a practical matter, the conditions necessary for any relevant range of rates to have the property that a rise increases excess demand seem to me highly unlikely to occur. But, if they should occur, it would merely mean that there might be two possible positions of equilibrium, one above, the other below, the existing controlled rate. If the higher is regarded as preferable, the implication for policy would be first to appreciate the controlled rate and then to set it free.

garded as temporary, actual or potential holders of the country's currency will tend to change their holdings in such a way as to moderate the movement in the exchange rate. If a rise in the exchange rate, for example, is expected to be temporary, there is an incentive for holders of the country's currency to sell some of their holdings for foreign currency in order to buy the currency back later on at a lower price. Conversely, if a decline is expected to be temporary, there is an incentive to buy domestic currency for resale at a higher price. In this way, such "speculative" transactions in effect provide the country with reserves to absorb temporary surpluses or to meet temporary deficits. On the other hand, if the change in the exchange rate is generally regarded as produced by fundamental factors that are likely to be permanent, the incentives are the reverse of those listed above, and speculative transactions will speed up the rise or decline in the exchange rate and thus hasten its approach to its final position.

This final position depends on the effect that changes in exchange rates have on the demand for and supply of a country's currency, not to hold as balances, but for other purposes. A rise in the exchange rate produced by a tendency toward a surplus makes foreign goods cheaper in terms of domestic currency, even though their prices are unchanged in terms of their own currency, and domestic goods more expensive in terms of foreign currency, even though their prices are unchanged in terms of domestic currency. This tends to increase imports, reduce exports, and so offset the incipient surplus. Conversely, a decline in the exchange rate produced by a tendency toward a deficit makes imports more expensive to home consumers, and exports less expensive to foreigners, and so tends to offset the incipient deficit.

Because money imparts general purchasing power and is used for such a wide variety of purposes abroad as well as at home, the demand for and supply of any one country's currency is widely spread and comes from many sources. In consequence, broad, active, and nearly perfect markets have developed in foreign exchange whenever they have been permitted— and usually even when they have not been. The exchange rate is therefore potentially an extremely sensitive price. Changes in it occur rapidly, automatically, and continuously and so tend to produce corrective movements before tensions can accumulate and a crisis develop.

The recurrent foreign-exchange crises of the United Kingdom in the postwar period are perhaps a dramatic example of the kind of crises that could not develop under a system of flexible exchange rates. In each case no significant corrective action was taken until large disequilibriums had been allowed to cumulate, and then the action had to be drastic. The rigidities and discontinuities introduced by substituting administrative action for automatic market forces have seldom been demonstrated so clearly or more impressively.

 2. *Official Changes in Exchange Rates.* This example suggests the sharp difference between flexible exchange rates and exchange rates held temporarily rigid but subject to change by government action to meet substantial difficulties. While these exchange-rate changes have the same kind of effect on commodity trade and the like as those produced automatically under a system of flexible exchange rates, they have very different effects on speculative transactions. Partly for this reason, partly because of their innate discontinuity, each exchange-rate change tends to become the occasion for a crisis. There is no mechanism for producing changes in exchange rates of the required magnitude or for correcting mistakes, and some other mechanism must be used to maintain equilibrium during the period between exchange-rate changes—either internal price or income changes, direct controls, or monetary reserves.

 Even though an exchange-rate change would not otherwise be the occasion for a crisis, speculative movements are highly likely to convert it into one, for this system practically insures a maximum of destabilizing speculation. Because the exchange rate is changed infrequently and only to meet substantial difficulties, a change tends to come well after the onset of difficulty, to be postponed as long as possible, and to be made only after substantial pressure on the exchange rate has accumulated. In consequence, there is seldom any doubt about the direction in which an exchange rate will be changed, if it is changed. In the interim between the suspicion of a possible change in the rate and the actual change, there is every incentive to sell the country's currency if devaluation is expected (to export "capital" from the country) or to buy it if an appreciation is expected (to bring in "capital"); either can be done without an exchange loss and will mean an exchange gain when and if the rate is changed. This is in sharp contrast with the situation under flexible exchange rates when the decline in the exchange rate takes place along with, and as a consequence of, the sales of a currency and so discourages or penalizes sales, and conversely for purchases. With rigid rates, if the exchange rate is not changed, the only cost to the speculators is a possible loss of interest earnings from an interest-rate differential. It is no answer to this argument to say that capital flows can be restricted by direct controls, since our ultimate objective in using this method is precisely to avoid such restrictions.

 In short, the system of occasional changes in temporarily rigid exchange rates seems to me the worst of two worlds: it provides neither the stability of expectations that a genuinely rigid and stable exchange rate could provide in a world of unrestricted trade and willingness and ability to adjust the internal price structure to external conditions nor the continuous sensitivity of a flexible exchange rate.

B. Changes in Internal Prices or Income

 In principle, changes in internal prices could produce the same effects on trade as changes in the exchange rate. For example, a decline of 10 per cent in every internal price in Germany (including wages, rents, etc.) with an unchanged dollar price of the mark would clearly have identically the same effects on the relative costs of domestic and foreign goods as a decline of 10 per cent in the dollar price of the mark, with all internal prices unchanged. Similarly, such price changes could have the same effects on speculative transactions. If expected to be temporary, a decline in prices would stimulate speculative purchases of goods to avoid future higher prices, thus moderating the price movement.

If internal prices were as flexible as exchange rates, it would make little economic difference whether adjustments were brought about by changes in exchange rates or by equivalent changes in internal prices. But this condition is clearly not fulfilled. The exchange rate is potentially flexible in the absence of administrative action to freeze it. At least in the modern world, internal prices are highly inflexible. They are more flexible upward than downward, but even on the upswing all prices are not equally flexible. The inflexibility of prices, or different degrees of flexibility, means a distortion of adjustments in response to changes in external conditions. The adjustment takes the form primarily of price changes in some sectors, primarily of output changes in others.

Wage rates tend to be among the less flexible prices. In consequence, an incipient deficit that is countered by a policy of permitting or forcing prices to decline is likely to produce unemployment rather than, or in addition to, wage decreases. The consequent decline in real income reduces the domestic demand for foreign goods and thus the demand for foreign currency with which to purchase these goods. In this way, it offsets the incipient deficit. But this is clearly a highly inefficient method of adjusting to external changes. If the external changes are deep-seated and persistent, the unemployment produces steady downward pressure on prices and wages, and the adjustment will not have been completed until the deflation has run its sorry course.

Despite these difficulties, the use of changes in internal prices might not be undesirable if they were called for only rarely and only as a result of changes in the real underlying conditions of trade. Such changes in underlying conditions are likely in any event to require considerable changes in relative prices of particular goods and services and only changes of a much smaller order of magnitude in the general level of internal prices. But neither condition is likely to be satisfied in the modern world. Adjustments are required continuously, and many are called for by essentially monetary phenomena, which, if promptly offset by a movement in the exchange rate, would require no change in the actual allocation of resources.

Changes in interest rates are perhaps best classified under this heading of changes in internal prices. Interest-rate changes have in the past played a particularly important role in adjustment to external changes, partly because they have been susceptible to direct influence by the monetary authorities, and partly because, under a gold standard, the initial impact of a tendency toward a deficit or surplus was a loss or gain of gold and a consequent tightening or ease in the money market. The rise in the interest rate produced in this way by an incipient deficit increased the demand for the currency for capital purposes and so offset part or all of the deficit. This reduced the rate at which the deficit had to be met by a decline in internal prices, which was itself set in motion by the loss of gold and associated decrease in the stock of money responsible for the rise in interest rates. Conversely, an incipient surplus increased the stock of gold and eased the money market. The resulting decline in the interest rate reduced the demand for the currency for capital purposes and so offset part or all of the surplus, reducing the rate at which the surplus had to be met by the rise in internal prices set in motion by the gain of gold and associated rise in the stock of money.

These interest-induced capital movements are a desirable part of a system relying primarily on changes in internal prices, since they tend to smooth out the adjustment process. They cannot, however, be relied on alone, since they come into operation only incidentally to the adjustment of internal prices.

Primary reliance on changes in internal prices and incomes was tolerable in the nineteenth century partly because the key countries of the Western world placed much heavier emphasis on freedom from government interference at home and unrestricted multilateral trade abroad than on domestic stability; thus they were willing to allow domestic economic policy to be dominated by the requirements of fixed exchange rates and free convertibility of currencies. But, equally important, this very emphasis gave holders of balances confidence in the maintenance of the system and so made them willing to let small differences in interest rates determine the currency in which they held their balances. Furthermore, the emphasis on freedom from government interference at home gave less scope to internal monetary management and so meant that most changes affecting international trade reflected real changes in underlying conditions, or else monetary changes, such as gold discoveries, more or less common to the major nations. Modern conditions, with the widespread emphasis on full employment at home and the extensive intervention of government into economic affairs, are clearly very different and much less favorable to this method of adjustment.

C. Direct Controls

In principle, direct controls on imports, exports, and capital movements could bring about the same effects on trade and the balance of payments as changes in exchange rates or in internal prices and incomes. The final adjustment will, after all, involve a change in the composition of imports and exports, along with specifiable capital transactions. If these could be predicted in advance, and if it were technically possible to control selectively each category of imports, exports, and capital transactions, direct controls could be used to produce the required adjustment.

It is clear, however, that the changes in imports and exports and the required capital transactions cannot be predicted; the fact that each new foreign-exchange crisis in a country like Britain is officially regarded as a bolt from the blue is ample evidence for this proposition. Even if they could be predicted, direct control of imports, exports, and capital transactions by techniques other than the price system[5] necessarily means extending such control to many internal matters and interfering with the efficiency of the distribution and production of goods—some means must be found for rationing imports that are being held down in amount or disposing of increased imports and for allocating reduced exports or getting increased exports.

Aside from the many unfortunate results of such a process which are by now abundantly clear, it has a perverse effect on the foreign-payments problem itself, particularly when direct controls are used, as they have been primarily, to counter an actual or incipient deficit. The apparent deficit that has to be closed by direct controls is larger than the deficit that would emerge at the same exchange rate without the direct controls and, indeed, might be eliminated entirely or converted into a surplus if the direct controls on imports and exports and their inevitable domestic accompaniments were removed. The mere existence of the direct controls makes the currency less desirable for many purposes because of the limitations it places on what holders of the currency may do with it, and this is likely to reduce the demand for the currency more than it would be reduced by the fluctuations in exchange rates or other adaptive mechanisms substituted for the direct controls. In addition, permitted imports are generally distributed at prices lower than those that would clear the market and so are used wastefully and in the wrong places, increasing apparent import "requirements"; similarly, the composition of imports is determined by administrative decisions that tend to have the same effect. Both of these are particularly important in hindering exports, because export industries are not likely to get so large a fraction of the imports as they would bid away in a free market, even if the government supposedly favors export industries, and cannot make their influence fully felt in determining the composition of imports; and the direct controls have a tendency to make the incentive to export lower than it would otherwise be.[6]

---

[5] Note that a tariff of a uniform percentage on all imports used to pay a subsidy of a uniform percentage on all exports is equivalent to a depreciation in the exchange rate by the corresponding percentage; and, similarly, a subsidy of a uniform percentage; and, similarly, a subsidy of a uniform percentage on all imports financed by a tax of a uniform percentage on all exports is equivalent to an appreciation in the exchange rate by the corresponding percentage. Thus devices such as these should be classified under exchange-rate changes rather than direct controls.

[6] Selling import licenses at a price that would clear the market would eliminate the first effect; it would not eliminate the second and third unless the permits were not for specific commodities but for foreign exchange to be used in any way desired. Even this would not eliminate the fourth unless the proceeds were used to pay a percentage subsidy to exports and other transactions leading to the acquisition of foreign

Finally, whatever the desirability of direct controls, there are political and administrative limits to the extent to which it is possible to impose and enforce such controls. These limits are narrower in some countries than in others, but they are present in all. Given sufficient incentive to do so, ways will be found to evade or avoid the controls. A race develops between officials seeking to plug legal loopholes and to discover and punish illegal evasions of the controls and the ever numerous individuals whose inventive talents are directed toward discovering or opening up new loopholes by the opportunities for large returns or whose respect for law and fear of punishment are overcome by the same opportunities. And the race is by no means always to the officials, even when they are honest and able. In particular, it has proved extremely difficult in all countries to prevent capital movements by direct controls.

D. Use of Monetary Reserves

Given adequate reserves, tendencies toward a surplus or a deficit can be allowed to produce an actual surplus or deficit in transactions other than those of the monetary authority (or exchange equalization fund, or whatever the name may be) without a change in exchange rates, internal prices or incomes, or direct controls, the additional domestic or foreign currency demanded being supplied by the monetary authority. This device is feasible and not undesirable for movements that are small and temporary, though, if it is clear that the movements are small and temporary, it is largely unnecessary, since, with flexible exchange rates, private speculative transactions will provide the additional domestic or foreign currency demanded with only minor movements in exchange rates.

The exclusive use of reserves is much less desirable, if possible at all, for movements of large magnitude and long duration. If the problem is a deficit, the ability of the monetary authorities to meet the deficit is immediately limited by the size of their reserves of foreign currency or the equivalent plus whatever additional sums they can or are willing to borrow or acquire in other ways from holders of foreign currency. Moreover, if the internal price level (or level of employment) is to be kept stable, the proceeds from the sales of foreign-exchange reserves must not be impounded or used in other deflationary ways. This assumes, of course, that the deficit is not itself produced by internal inflationary policies but occurs despite a stable internal price level. The proceeds must be used to retire debt or to finance a deficit in the budget to whatever extent is necessary to prevent a price decline.

If the problem is a surplus, the monetary authorities must be pre-

---

exchange. This final system is, as indicated in the preceding note, identical with a change in the exchange rate. If the price of permits to use foreign exchange and the subsidy for acquiring it were determined in a free market so as to make total receipts equal total payments, the result is equivalent to or identical with a system of flexible exchange rates.

pared to accumulate foreign exchange indefinitely, providing all the domestic currency that is demanded. Moreover, if the internal price level is to be maintained constant, it must obtain the domestic currency it sells for foreign currency in noninflationary ways. It can print or create the currency only to the extent that is consistent with stable prices. For the rest it must get the amount required by borrowing at whatever interest rates are necessary to keep domestic prices stable or from a surplus of the appropriate amount in the government budget. Entirely aside from the technical problems of monetary management involved, the community is unlikely to be willing to exchange indefinitely part of its product for unproductive currency hoards, particularly if the source of the surplus is monetary inflation abroad, and thus the foreign currency is decreasing in real value.

Traditionally, of course, monetary reserves have not been used as the primary method of adjusting to changes in external conditions but as a shock absorber pending changes in internal prices and incomes. A deficit has been met out of monetary reserves in the first instance, but the proceeds or even a multiple of the proceeds have been, as it were, impounded; that is, the stock of money has been allowed or made to decrease as a result of the decline of monetary reserves, with a consequent rise in interest rates and downward pressure on internal prices. Similarly, the domestic currency exchanged for a surplus of foreign currency has, as it were, been created and allowed to or made to increase the stock of money by the same amount or a multiple of that amount, with a consequent decline in interest rates and upward pressure on internal prices.[7]

Since the end of the first World War, nations have become increasingly unwilling to use reserves in this way and to allow the effect to be transmitted directly and immediately to internal monetary conditions and prices. Already during the 1920's, the United States, to cite one outstanding and critical example, refused to allow its surplus, which took the form of gold imports, to raise domestic prices in the way the supposed rules of the gold standard demanded; instead, it "sterilized" gold imports. Especially after the Great Depression completed the elevation of full employment to the primary goal of economic policy, nations have been unwilling to allow deficits to exert any deflationary effect.

The use of monetary reserves as the sole reliance to meet small and temporary strains on balances of payments and of other devices to meet larger and more extended or more basic strains is an understandable objective of economic policy and comes close to summarizing the philosophy underlying the International Monetary Fund. Unfortunately, it is not a realistic, feasible, or desirable policy. It is seldom possible to know in advance or even soon after the event whether any given strain in the

---

[7] Under a pure gold standard, these effects follow automatically, since any international claims not settled otherwise are settled by gold, which, in case of a deficit, is bodily extracted from the monetary stock and, in case of a surplus, bodily added to it.

balance of payments is likely to be reversed rapidly or not; that is, whether it is a result of temporary or permanent factors. Reserves must be very large indeed if they are to be the sole reliance in meeting changes in external conditions until the magnitude and probable duration of the changes can be diagnosed with confidence and more fundamental correctives undertaken in light of the diagnosis, far larger than if they serve the function they did under the classical gold standard. Except perhaps for the United States, and even for the United States only so long as gold is freely acceptable as an international currency, reserves are nothing like this large. Under the circumstances there is a strong tendency to rely on reserves too long for comfort yet not long enough for confident diagnosis and reasoned action. Corrective steps are postponed in the hope that things will right themselves until the state of the reserves forces drastic and frequently ill-advised action.

E. A Comparison

One or another of the methods of adjustment just described must in fact be used to meet changes in conditions affecting external trade; there is no avoiding this necessity short of the complete elimination of external trade, and even this would be an extreme form of direct controls over imports and exports. On the basis of the analysis so far, flexible exchange rates seem clearly the technique of adjustment best suited to current conditions: the use of reserves is not by itself a feasible device; direct controls are cumbrous and inefficient and, I venture to predict, will utimately prove ineffective in a free society; changes in internal prices and incomes are undesirable because of rigidities in internal prices, especially wages, and the emergence of full employment—or independence of internal monetary policy—as a major goal of policy.

The argument for flexible exchange rates is, strange to say, very nearly identical with the argument for daylight saving time. Isn't it absurd to change the clock in summer when exactly the same result could be achieved by having each individual change his habits? All that is required is that everyone decide to come to his office an hour earlier, have lunch an hour earlier, etc. But obviously it is much simpler to change the clock that guides all than to have each individual separately change his pattern of reaction to the clock, even though all want to do so. The situation is exactly the same in the exchange market. It is far simpler to allow one price to change, namely, the price of foreign exchange, than to rely upon changes in the multitude of prices that together constitute the internal price structure.

II. OBJECTIONS TO FLEXIBLE EXCHANGE RATES

Three major criticisms have been made of the proposal to establish a system of flexible exchange rates: first, that flexible exchange rates may increase the degree of uncertainty in the economic scene; second, that flexible exchange rates will not work because they will produce offsetting changes in domestic prices; and, third, that flexible exchange rates will not produce the best attainable timing or pace of adjustment. The first objection takes many different forms, and it will promote clarity to deal with some of these separately, even though this means considerable overlapping.

A. Flexible Exchange Rates and Uncertainty

1. *Flexible Exchange Rates Mean Instability Rather Than Stability.* On the naïve level on which this objection is frequently made, it involves the already-mentioned mistake of confusing the symptom of difficulties with the difficulties themselves. A flexible exchange rate need not be an unstable exchange rate. If it is, it is primarily because there is underlying instability in the economic conditions governing international trade. And a rigid exchange rate may, while itself nominally stable, perpetuate and accentuate other elements of instability in the economy. The mere fact that a rigid official exchange rate does not change while a flexible rate does is no evidence that the former means greater stability in any more fundamental sense. If it does, it is for one or more of the reasons considered in the points that follow.

2. *Flexible Exchange Rates Make It Impossible for Exporters and Importers to Be Certain about the Price They Will Have to Pay or Receive for Foreign Exchange.* Under flexible exchange rates traders can almost always protect themselves against changes in the rate by hedging in a futures market. Such futures markets in foreign currency readily develop when exchange rates are flexible. Any uncertainty about returns will then be borne by speculators. The most that can be said for this argument, therefore, is that flexible exchange rates impose a cost of hedging on traders, namely, the price that must be paid to speculators for assuming the risk of future changes in exchange rates. But this is saying too much. The substitution of flexible for rigid exchange rates changes the form in which uncertainty in the foreign-exchange market is manifested; it may not change the extent of uncertainty at all and, indeed, may even decrease uncertainty. For example, conditions that would tend to produce a decline in a flexible exchange rate will produce a shortage of exchange with a rigid exchange rate. This in turn will produce either internal adjustments of uncertain character or administrative allocation of exchange. Traders will then be certain about the rate but uncertain about either internal conditions or the availability of exchange. The uncertainty can be removed for some transactions by advance commitments by the authorities dispensing exchange; it clearly cannot be removed for all transactions in view of the uncertainty about the total amount of exchange available; the reduction in uncertainty for some transactions therefore involves increased uncertainty for others, since all the risk is now concen-

trated on them. Further, such administrative allocation of exchange is always surrounded by uncertainty about the policy that will be followed. It is by no means clear whether the uncertainty associated with a flexible rate or the uncertainty associated with a rigid rate is likely to be more disruptive to trade.

3. *Speculation in Foreign-Exchange Markets Tends to Be Destabilizing.* This point is, of course, closely related to the preceding one. It is said that speculators will take a decline in the exchange rate as a signal for a further decline and will thus tend to make the movements in the exchange rate sharper than they would be in the absence of speculation. The special fear in this connection is of capital flight in response to political uncertainty or simply to movements in the exchange rate. Despite the prevailing opinion to the contrary, I am very dubious that in fact speculation in foreign exchange would be destabilizing. Evidence from some earlier experiences and from current free markets in currency in Switzerland, Tangiers, and elsewhere seems to me to suggest that, in general, speculation is stabilizing rather than the reverse, though the evidence has not yet been analyzed in sufficient detail to establish this conclusion with any confidence. People who argue that speculation is generally destabilizing seldom realize that this is largely equivalent to saying that speculators lose money, since speculation can be destabilizing in general only if speculators on the average sell when the currency is low in price and buy when it is high.[8] It does not, of course, follow that speculation is not destabilizing; professional speculators might on the average make money while a changing body of amateurs regularly lost larger sums. But, while this may happen, it is hard to see why there is any presumption that it will; the presumption is rather the opposite. To put the same point differently, if speculation were persistently destabilizing, a government body like the Exchange Equalization Fund in England in the 1930's could make a good deal of money by speculating in exchange and in the process almost certainly eliminate the destabilizing speculation. But to suppose that speculation by governments would generally be profitable is in most cases equivalent to supposing that government officials risking funds that they do not themselves own are better judges of the likely movements in foreign-exchange markets than private individuals risking their own funds.

The widespread belief that speculation is likely to be destabilizing is doubtless a major factor accounting for the cavalier rejection of a system of flexible exchange rates in the immediate postwar period. Yet this belief does not seem to be founded on any systematic analysis of the available

---

[8] A warning is perhaps in order that this is a simplified generalization on a complex problem. A full analysis encounters difficulties in separating "speculative" from other transactions, defining precisely and satisfactorily "destabilizing speculation," and taking account of the effects of the mere existence of a system of flexible rates as contrasted with the effects of actual speculative transactions under such a system.

empirical evidence.[9] It rests rather, I believe, primarily on an oversimplified interpretation of the movements of so-called "hot" money during the 1930's. At the time, any speculative movements which threatened a depreciation of a currency (i.e., which threatened a *change* in an exchange rate) were regarded as destabilizing, and hence these movements were so considered. In retrospect, it is clear that the speculators were "right"; that forces were at work making for depreciation in the value of most European currencies relative to the dollar independently of speculative activity; that the speculative movements were anticipating this change; and, hence, that there is at least as much reason to call them "stabilizing" as to call them "destabilizing."

In addition, the interpretation of this evidence has been marred by a failure to distinguish between a system of exchange rates held temporarily rigid but subject to change from time to time by government action and a system of flexible exchange rates. Many of the capital movements regarded as demonstrating that foreign-exchange speculation is destabilizing were stimulated by the existence of rigid rates subject to change by government action and are to be attributed primarily to the absence of flexibility of rates and hence of any incentive to avoid the capital movements. This is equally true of post–World War II experience with wide swings in foreign-payments positions. For reasons noted earlier, this experience has little direct bearing on the character of the speculative movements to be expected under a regime of genuinely flexible exchange rates.

4. *Flexible Exchange Rates Involve Increased Uncertainty in the Internal Economy.* It is argued that in many countries there is a great fear

---

[9] Perhaps the most ambitious attempt to summarize the evidence is that by Ragnar Nurkse, *International Currency Experience* (Geneva: League of Nations, 1944), pp. 117–22. Nurkse concludes from interwar experience that speculation can be expected in general to be destabilizing. However, the evidence he cites is by itself inadequate to justify any conclusion. Nurkse examines only one episode in anything approaching the required detail, the depreciation of the French franc from 1922 to 1926. For the rest, he simply lists episodes during which exchange rates were flexible and asserts that in each case speculation was destabilizing. These episodes may or may not support his conclusion; it is impossible to tell from his discussion of them; and the list is clearly highly selective, excluding some cases that seem prima facie to point in the opposite direction.

Even for the French episode, the evidence given by Nurkse does not justify any firm conclusion. Indeed, so far as it goes, it seems to me clearly less favorable to the conclusion Nurkse draws, that speculation was destabilizing, than to the opposite conclusion, that speculation was stabilizing.

In general, Nurkse's discussion of the effects of speculation is thoroughly unsatisfactory. At times, he seems to regard any transactions which threaten the existing value of a currency as destabilizing even if underlying forces would produce a changed value in the absence of speculation. At another point, he asserts that destabilizing transactions may occur on *both* capital and current account simultaneously, in a context in which these two accounts exhaust the balance of payments, so that his statement is an arithmetical impossibility (pp. 210–11). It is a sorry reflection on the scientific basis for generally held economic beliefs that Nurkse's analysis is so often cited as the basis or "proof" of the belief in destabilizing speculation.

of inflation and that people have come to regard the exchange rate as an indicator of inflation and are highly sensitive to variations in it. Exchange crises, such as would tend to occur under rigid exchange rates, will pass unnoticed, it is argued, except by people directly connected with international trade, whereas a decline in the exchange rate would attract much attention, be taken as a signal of a future inflation, and produce anticipatory movements by the public at large. In this way a flexible exchange rate might produce additional uncertainty rather than merely change the form in which uncertainty is manifested. There is some merit to this argument, but it does not seem to me to be a substantial reason for avoiding a flexible exchange rate.

Very nearly the opposite of this argument is also sometimes made against flexible exchange rates. It is said that, with a flexible exchange rate, governments will have less incentive and be in a less strong position to take firm internal action to prevent inflation. A rigid exchange rate, it is said, gives the government a symbol to fight for—it can nail its flag to the mast of a specified exchange rate and resist political pressure to take action that would be inflationary in the name of defending the exchange rate. Dramatic foreign-exchange crises establish an atmosphere in which drastic if unpopular action is possible. On the other hand, it is said, with a flexible exchange rate, there is no definite sticking point; inflationary action will simply mean a decline in the exchange rate but no dramatic crisis, and people are little affected by a change in a price, the exchange rate, in a market in which relatively few have direct dealings.

Of course, it is not impossible for both these arguments to be valid—the first in countries like Germany, which have recently experienced hyperinflations and violently fluctuating exchange rates, the second in countries like Great Britain, which have not. But, even in countries like Britain, it is far from clear that a rigid exchange rate is more conducive under present conditions to noninflationary internal economic policy than a flexible exchange rate. A rigid exchange rate thwarts any immediate manifestation of a deterioration in the foreign-payments position as a result of inflationary internal policy. With an independent monetary standard, the loss of exchange reserves does not automatically reduce the stock of money or prevent its continued increase; yet it does temporarily reduce domestic inflationary pressure by providing goods in return for the foreign-exchange reserves without any simultaneous creation of domestic income. The deterioration shows up only sometime later, in the dull tables of statistics summarizing the state of foreign-exchange reserves. Even then, the authorities in the modern world have the alternative—or think they have—of suppressing a deficit by more stringent direct controls and thus postponing still longer the necessity for taking the appropriate internal measures; and they can always find any number of special reasons for the particular deterioration other than their internal policy. While the possibilities of using direct controls and of finding plausible excuses are present equally with flexible exchange rates, at least the deterioration in the foreign-payments position shows up promptly in the more readily understandable and simpler form of a decline in the exchange rates, and there is no emergency, no suddenly discovered decline in monetary reserves to dangerous levels, to force the imposition of supposedly unavoidable direct controls.

These arguments are modern versions of an argument that no longer has much merit but was at one time a valid and potent objection to flexible exchange rates, namely, the greater scope they give for government "tampering" with the currency. When rigid exchange rates were taken seriously, and when the armory of direct controls over international trade had not yet been resurrected, the maintenance of rigid rates left little scope for independent domestic monetary policy. This was the great virtue of the gold standard and the basic, albeit hidden, source of its emotional appeal; it provided an effective defense against hyperinflation, against government intervention of a kind that had time and again led to the debasement and depreciation of once-proud currencies. This argument may still be a source of emotional resistance to flexible exchange rates; it is clear that it does not deserve to be. Governments of "advanced" nations are no longer willing to submit themselves to the harsh discipline of the gold standard or any other standard involving rigid exchange rates. They will evade its discipline by direct controls over trade if that will suffice and will change exchange rates before they will surrender control over domestic monetary policy. Perhaps a few modern inflations will establish a climate in which such behavior does not qualify as "advanced"; in the meantime we had best recognize the necessity of allowing exchange rates to adjust to internal policies rather than the reverse.

The positive side of the reluctance to use changes in internal price levels and employment to meet external changes is the promotion of internal monetary stability—the avoidance of either inflation or deflation. This is clearly a highly desirable objective for each country separately. But, under a system of rigid exchange rates and unrestricted trade, no country can attain this objective unless *every* other important country with which it is linked directly or indirectly by trade does so as well. If any one country inflates, for example, this tends to increase its imports and reduce its exports. Other countries now start to accumulate currency balances of the inflating country. They must either be willing to accumulate such balances indefinitely—which means they must be willing to continue shipping out goods without a return flow and thus in effect subsidize the inflating country—or they must follow the inflation themselves (or impose import controls). Hence the strong pressure to achieve harmonization of internal monetary policies.

But this pressure has understandably not been matched by a willingness of all countries to submit their internal policy to external control. Why should a country do so when the failure of any one country to co-operate or to behave "properly" would destroy the whole structure and permit it to transmit its difficulties to its neighbors? Really effective "co-ordination" would require essentially either that nations adopt a common commodity monetary standard like gold and agree to submit unwaveringly to its discipline or that some international body control the supply of money in each country, which in turn implies control over at least interest-rate policy and budgetary policy. The first alternative is neither currently feasible nor particularly desirable in the light of our past experience with the gold standard.[10] As to the second alternative, whether feasible or not, is it desirable that such far-reaching powers be surrendered to any authority other than an effective federal government democratically elected and responsible to the electorate?

A system of flexible exchange rates eliminates the necessity for such far-reaching co-ordination of internal monetary and fiscal policy in order for any country separately to follow a stable internal monetary policy. If, under such a system, any one country inflates, the primary effect is a depreciation in its exchange rate. This offsets the effect of internal infla-tion on its international trade position and weakens or eliminates the tendency for the inflation to be transmitted to its neighbors; and con-versely with deflation. Inflation and deflation in any one country will then affect other countries primarily in so far as it affects the real income posi-tion of the initial country; there will be little or no effect through purely monetary channels.

In effect, flexible exchange rates are a means of combining interde-pendence among countries through trade with a maximum of internal monetary independence; they are a means of permitting each country to seek for monetary stability according to its own lights, without either imposing its mistakes on its neighbors or having their mistakes imposed on it. If all countries succeeded, the result would be a system of reasonably stable exchange rates; the substance of effective harmonization would be attained without the risks of formal but ineffective harmonization.

The chance that all countries would succeed is far greater with flexible exchange rates than with a system of rigid exchange rates that is not also a strict commodity standard. For not only do the laggards tend to call the tune under rigid exchange rates by infecting the other countries with which they are linked but also the very existence of this link gives each country an incentive to engage in inflationary action that it would not otherwise have. For, at least in the initial stages, inflationary currency issue enables the issuers to acquire resources not only from within the country but also from without: the rigid rates mean, as we have seen, that other countries accumulate balances of the currency of the inflating coun-

---

[10] See my "Commodity-Reserve Currency," *Journal of Political Economy*, Vol. LIX, No. 3 (June, 1951), pp. 203–32; also reprinted in M. Friedman, *Essays in Positive Economics*, for a more extensive discussion of the advantages and disadvan-tages of a commodity standard.

try. Under reasonably stable but not rigid rates, this incentive is largely removed, since the rates will remain stable only so long as countries avoid inflationary action. Once they embark on it, a decline in the exchange rates for their currency will replace the accumulation of balances that would have to take place to keep the rates rigid.

B. Flexible Exchange Rates and Internal Prices

While I have just used the primacy of internal policy as an argument for flexible exchange rates, it has also been used as an argument against flexible exchange rates. As we have seen, flexible exchange rates promote adjustments to changes in external circumstances by producing changes in the relation between the prices of foreign and domestic goods. A decline in an exchange rate produced by a tendency toward a deficit in the balance of payments tends to make the prices of foreign goods higher in terms of domestic currency than they would otherwise have been. If domestic prices are unaffected—or affected less—this means a higher price of foreign goods relative to domestic goods, which stimulates exports and discourages imports.

The rise in prices of foreign goods will, it is argued, mean a rise in the cost of living, and this, in turn, will give rise to a demand for wage increases, setting off what is typically referred to as a "wage-price spiral"— a term that is impressive enough to conceal the emptiness of the argument that it generally adorns. In consequence, so the argument continues, prices of domestic goods rise as much as prices of foreign goods, relative prices remain unchanged, there are no market forces working toward the elimination of the deficit that initially caused the decline in the exchange rate, and so further declines in the exchange rate are inevitable until nonmarket forces are brought into play. But these might as well have been used before as after the decline in the exchange rate.

This argument clearly applies only to rather special circumstances. At most, it may be an objection to a particular country at a particular time allowing its currency to go free; it is not a general objection to a *system* of flexible exchange rates as a long-run structure. It does not apply to circumstances making for the appreciation of a currency and applies only to some circumstances making for depreciation. Suppose, for example, that the tendency toward a deficit were produced by monetary deflations in other countries. The depreciation of the currency would then prevent the fall in external prices from being transmitted to the country in question; it would prevent prices of foreign goods from being forced down in terms of domestic currency. There is no way of eliminating the effect of the lowered "real" income of other countries; flexible exchange rates prevent this effect from being magnified by monetary disturbances. Similarly, the argument has little relevance if the decline in exchange rates reflects an open inflationary movement at home; the depreciation is then an obvious result of inflation rather than a cause. The argument has perhaps most relevance in either of two cases: an inflationary situation being repressed by direct controls or a depreciation produced by a change in the "real" conditions of trade.

Even in these cases, however, the argument cannot be fully granted. The crucial fallacy is the so-called "wage-price spiral." The rise in prices of foreign goods may add to the always plentiful list of excuses for wage increases; it does not in and of itself provide the economic conditions for a wage rise—or, at any rate, for a wage rise without unemployment. A general wage rise—or a general rise in domestic prices—becomes possible only if the monetary authorities create the additional money to finance the higher level of prices.[11] But if the monetary authorities are ready to do so to validate any rise in particular prices or wages, then the situation is fundamentally unstable without a change in the exchange rate, since a wage rise for any other excuse would lead to similar consequences. The assumption is that to him who asks will be given, and there is never a shortage of willingness to ask under such circumstances.

It will be answered that this innate instability is held in check by some sort of political compromise and that this compromise would be disturbed by the change in the exchange rate. This is a special case of the general argument considered earlier that the government is more likely to resist political pressure to take inflationary action if it nails its flag to the mast of a rigid exchange rate than if it lets the exchange rate fluctuate. But note that the forces leading to a changed exchange rate are not eliminated by freezing the rate; foreign exchange will have to be acquired or economized somehow. The "real" adjustment must be made in one way or another; the question is only how. Why should this way of making the adjustment destroy the compromise while other ways do not? Or, if this is true for a time, can it be expected to continue to be true? If, as we have argued, flexible exchange rates are the least costly way of making the adjustment, will not other methods be even more likely to destroy a tenuous political compromise?

C. Flexible Exchange Rates and the Timing of Adjustment

The ultimate adjustment to a change in external circumstances will consist of a change in the allocation of productive resources and in the composition of the goods available for consumption and investment. But this ultimate change will not be achieved immediately. It takes time to shift from the production of goods for domestic consumption to the production of goods for export, or conversely; it takes time to establish new markets abroad or to persuade consumers to substitute a foreign for a domestic good to which they have been accustomed; and so on in endless variety. The time required will vary widely: some types of adaptations can take

---

[11] In principle, there are other possibilities related to the "velocity of circulation" of money that I neglect to simplify the argument; they do not change its essence.

place instantaneously (e.g., curtailment by a high price of the purchase of imported cheese, though even here the price rise required to achieve a given curtailment will be higher at first than after a time when people have had a chance to adapt their habitual pattern of consumption to the new price); other types of adaptation may take a generation (e.g., the development of a new domestic industry to produce goods formerly imported).

Suppose a substantial change in (real) external circumstances to occur and, to keep matters simple, circumstances thereafter to remain essentially unchanged for a lengthy period, so that we can (conceptually) isolate the adaptation to this one change. Suppose, further, that exchange rates are flexible and that international "capital" or "speculative" transactions are impossible, so that payments on current account must balance—a condition it is admittedly difficult to define precisely in any way susceptible to observation. It is clear that the initial change in exchange rates will be greater than the ultimate change required, for, to begin with, all the adjustment will have to be borne in those directions in which prompt adjustment is possible and relatively easy. As time passes, the slower-moving adjustments will take over part of the burden, permitting exchange rates to rebound toward a final position which is between the position prior to the external change and the position shortly thereafter. This is, of course, a highly oversimplified picture: the actual path of adjustment may involve repeated overshooting and undershooting of the final position, giving rise to a series of cycles around it or to a variety of other patterns. We are here entering into an area of economics about which we know very little, so it is fortunate that a precise discussion of the path is not essential for our purposes.

Under these circumstances it clearly might be in the interests of the community to pay something to avoid some of the initial temporary adjustments: if the exchange rate depreciates, to borrow from abroad at the going interest rate to pay for an excess of imports while the slower-moving adjustments take place rather than making the full immediate adjustment by curtailing those imports that can be readily curtailed and forcing out those exports that can be readily increased; if the exchange rate appreciates, to lend abroad at the going interest rate to finance an excess of exports while the slower-moving adjustments take place rather than making the full immediate adjustment by expanding those imports that can be readily expanded and curtailing those exports that can be readily curtailed. It would not, however, be worth doing this indefinitely, even if it were possible. For, if it were carried to the point at which the exchange rate remained unchanged, no other adjustments at all would take place. Yet the change in external circumstances makes a new allocation of resources and composition of goods optimal for the country concerned. That is, there is some optimum pace and timing of adjustment through exchange-rate-induced changes in the allocation of resources

P

which is neither at the extreme of full immediate adjustment in this way alone nor at the other extreme of complete avoidance of adjustment.

Under a flexible exchange-rate system with a reasonably broad and free market in foreign exchange and with correct foresight on the part of speculators, just such an intermediate pace and timing of adjustment is produced even if there is no explicit negotiation of foreign loans. If the exchange rate depreciates, for example, the tendency for the exchange rate to fall further initially than ultimately offers an opportunity to make a profit by buying the currency now and reselling it later at a higher price. But this is precisely equivalent to lending by speculators to the country whose currency has depreciated. The return to the speculators is equal to the rate at which the currency they hold appreciates. In a free market with correct foresight, this will tend, aside from the minor costs of buying or selling the foreign exchange, to approach the interest rate that speculators could earn in other ways. If the currency appreciates at more than this rate, speculators still have an incentive to add to their holdings; if it appreciates at less than this rate, it is costing the speculators more in foregone interest to hold the balances than they are gaining in the appreciation of the exchange rate. In this way, speculation with a flexible exchange rate produces the same effect as explicit borrowing by a country whose currency has depreciated or explicit lending by one whose currency has appreciated. In practice, of course, there will be both explicit lending or borrowing and implicit lending or borrowing through exchange speculation. Moreover, the prospect of appreciation of a currency is equivalent to a higher interest rate for loans to the country and thus serves the same function in attracting capital to that country as the rises in interest rate that took place under the gold standard when a country was losing gold. There is, however, this important difference: under flexible exchange rates the inducement to foreign lenders need involve no change in the interest rate on domestic loans; under the gold standard, it did—a particular example of the independence of domestic monetary policy under flexible exchange rates.

But is the pace and timing of adjustment achieved in this way under flexible exchange rates an approximation to the optimum? This is an exceedingly difficult question to answer, depending as it does on whether the interest rate implicitly paid in the form of the appreciation or depreciation of the currency reflects the full relevant costs of too rapid or too slow adjustment. About all one can say without much more extensive analysis, and perhaps even with such analysis, is that there seems no reason to expect the timing or pace of adjustment under the assumed conditions to be systematically biased in one direction or the other from the optimum or to expect that other techniques of adaptation—through internal price changes, direct controls, and the use of monetary reserves with rigid exchange rates—would lead to a more nearly optimum pace and timing of adjustment.

This much would probably be granted by most persons who argue that flexible exchange rates lead to an undesirable pace and timing of adjustment. But, they would maintain, the foreign-exchange market is not nearly so perfect, or the foresight of speculators so good, as has been assumed to this point. The argument already considered, that speculation in foreign exchanges is destabilizing, is an extreme form of this objection. For, in that case, the immediate change in the foreign-exchange rate must go far enough to produce an immediate adaptation sufficient not only to balance current transactions but also to provide payment in foreign currencies for the balances of domestic currency that speculators perversely insist on liquidating when the exchange rate falls, or to provide the domestic currency for the balances speculators perversely insist on accumulating when the exchange rate rises. The country lends, as it were, when it should be borrowing and borrows when it should be lending.

But one need not go this far. Speculation may be stabilizing on balance, yet the market for foreign exchange, it can be said, is so narrow, foresight so imperfect, and private speculation so dominated by socially irrelevant political considerations that there is an insufficient smoothing-out of the adjustment process. For this to be a valid argument against flexible exchange rates, even if true, there must be some alternative that promises a better pace and timing of adjustment. We have already considered several other possibilities. We have seen that direct controls with a rigid exchange rate and the official use of monetary reserves have striking defects of their own, at least under modern conditions; they are likely to produce a highly erratic pace and timing of adjustment with alternate fits of unduly slow and unduly rapid adjustments, and direct controls are besides likely to produce the wrong kind of adjustments. Private capital movements in response to interest-rate differentials were at one time a real alternative but have been rendered largely unavailable by the unwillingness of monetary authorities to permit the required changes in interest rates, by the loss of confidence in the indefinite maintenance of the fixed exchange rates, and by the fear of restrictions on the use of exchange. In any event, such capital movements are, as we have seen, available and at least as likely to take place under flexible exchange rates.

The plausibility of the view that private exchange speculation produces too little smoothing of exchange-rate fluctuations derives, I believe, primarily from an implicit tendency to regard any slowing-down of the adjustment process as an improvement; that is, implicitly to regard no adjustment at all or an indefinitely prolonged one as the ideal.[12] This is the

---

[12] An interesting example is provided by an argument for 100 per cent banking reserves under a gold standard given by James E. Meade, *The Balance of Payments*, Vol. I of *The Theory of International Economic Policy* (Oxford: Oxford University Press, 1951), p. 185. Meade argues correctly that with 100 per cent reserves the internal adaptations consequent on an external change of any given size will be at a slower rate than with a lower reserve ratio. On this ground, he says, 100 per cent reserves are better than fractional reserves. But this conclusion follows only if any slowing-down in the rate of internal adaptation is an improvement, in which case 200 per cent reserves or their equivalent ("sterilization" of gold imports and exports) would be better than 100 per cent, and so on indefinitely. Given that there is some

counterpart of the tendency to believe that internal monetary policy can and should avoid all internal adjustments in the level of income.[13] And both, I suspect, are a manifestation of the urge for security that is so outstanding a feature of the modern world and that is itself a major source of insecurity by promoting measures that reduce the adaptability of our economic systems to change without eliminating the changes themselves.

III. CONCLUSION

The nations of the world cannot prevent changes from occurring in the circumstances affecting international transactions. And they would not if they could. For many changes reflect natural changes in weather conditions and the like; others arise from the freedom of countless individuals to order their lives as they will, which it is our ultimate goal to preserve and widen; and yet others contain the seeds of progress and development. The prison and the graveyard alone provide even a close approximation to certainty.

The major aim of policy is not to prevent such changes from occurring but to develop an efficient system of adapting to them—of using their potentialities for good while minimizing their disruptive effects. There is widespread agreement, at least in the Western world, that relatively free and unrestricted multilateral trade is a major component of such a system, besides having political advantages of a rather different kind. Yet resounding failure has so far marked repeated attempts to eliminate or reduce the extensive and complex restrictions on international trade that proliferated during and immediately after World War II. Failure will continue to mark such attempts so long as we allow implicit acceptance of an essentially minor goal—rigid exchange rates—to prevent simultaneous attainment of two major goals: unrestricted multilateral trade and freedom of each country to pursue internal stability after its own lights.

There are, after all, only four ways in which the pressures on balances of payments produced by changes in the circumstances affecting international transactions can be met: (1) by counterbalancing changes in currency reserves; (2) by adjustments in the general level of internal prices and incomes; (3) by adjustments in exchange rates; and (4) by direct controls over transactions involving foreign exchange.

The paucity of existing currency reserves makes the first impractical for all but very minor changes unless some means can be found to increase

---

optimum rate of adjustment, all one can say is that there exists some reserve ratio that would tend to produce this rate of adjustment and so be optimal on these grounds alone; I see no way of knowing on the basis of the considerations Meade presents whether this ratio would be 5 per cent or 500 per cent.

[13] See "The Effects of a Full-Employment Policy on Economic Stability: A Formal Analysis," in M. Friedman, *Essays in Positive Economics*, pp. 117–32, for a more detailed consideration of the formal problem involved in both internal and external policy and for some examples of this tendency.

the currency reserves of the world enormously. The failure of several noble experiments in this direction is testimony to the difficulty of this solution.

The primacy everywhere attached to internal stability makes the second method one that would not be permitted to operate; the institutional rigidities in internal price structures make it undesirable that it should be the major means of adjustment.

The third—at least in the form of a thoroughgoing system of flexible rates—has been ruled out in recent years without extensive explicit consideration, partly because of a questionable interpretation of limited historical evidence; partly, I believe, because it was condemned alike by traditionalists, whose ideal was a gold standard that either ran itself or was run by international central bankers but in either case determined internal policy, and by the dominant strain of reformers, who distrusted the price system in all its manifestations—a curious coalition of the most unreconstructed believers in the price system, in all its other roles, and its most extreme opponents.

The fourth method—direct controls over transactions involving foreign exchange—has in this way, by default rather than intention, been left the only avenue whereby pressures on balances of payments can be met. Little wonder that these controls have so stubbornly resisted elimination despite the repeated protestations that they would be eliminated. Yet this method is, in my view, by all odds the least desirable of the four.

There are no major economic difficulties to prevent the prompt establishment by countries separately or jointly of a system of exchange rates freely determined in open markets, primarily by private transactions, and the simultaneous abandonment of direct controls over exchange transactions. A move in this direction is the fundamental prerequisite for the economic integration of the free world through multilateral trade.

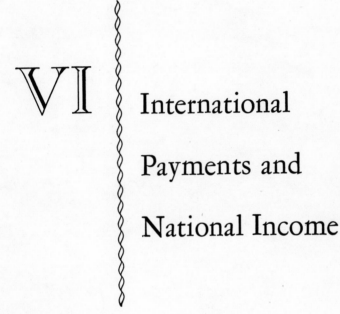

VI | International
Payments and
National Income

26. The Long-Run Dollar Problem[*]

By J. R. HICKS[†]

I HAVE CHOSEN TO DEVOTE this lecture to the discussion of a particular problem, instead of attempting a broad survey of the current state of economics; but I do not think that I need to apologize for the choice which I have made. The problem which I propose to examine is of the first importance to all of us; it is perhaps the fundamental economic problem confronting this country. There are some simple and significant things which can be said about it by a proper application of the best-established methods of economic theory. With so good an opportunity to hand of showing the potentiality of my subject, it has not seemed necessary to look farther.

The particular line of thought about the dollar problem which I shall be developing was suggested to me by a passage in the Stamp Memorial Lecture, given in London last November by Professor J. H. Williams of Harvard, under the title *Economic Stability in the Modern World*. What Professor Williams there did was to draw a striking picture of the rate at which productivity has been increasing in the United States—not merely during the last decade but during the whole of the present century; he then went on to offer as his main explanation of dollar shortage the disparity between the *rate* of economic advance which America has been able to achieve and that which has been achieved by most other countries. Professor Williams is distinguished among American economists for his imaginative understanding of the problems of countries outside America; I believe that his diagnosis is substantially correct. As he rightly observed, the problems raised by such a disparity were insufficiently examined by "classical" or traditional economists; but it does not follow that these problems are incapable of being treated in the classical manner. I think I can show that the classical methods are very well suited to the study of these modern problems. I shall therefore begin by asking what is the correct theory of the effects on international trade of disparate changes in productivity; I shall then say something about the bearing of the results I get upon the practical case of British relations with the United States.

This disparity with which we are to be concerned is a long-run phe-

* Abridged slightly from "An Inaugural Lecture," *Oxford Economic Papers*, Vol. V, No. 2 (June, 1953), pp. 117–35. A revision of these views is published in J. R. Hicks, *Essays on World Economics* (Clarendon Press, 1959), pp. 251–59.

† All Souls College, Oxford.

nomenon; thus the theory we are looking for must be a long-run theory. Since the disparate increases in productivity are to be thought of as going on all the time, there can be no state of equilibrium; but since we are to be interested in the process as a whole, not in particular incidents of the process, we need pay no attention to effects that are bound to be episodic. In practice, when a country experiences adverse trading conditions, it begins by running a deficit on its balance of payments—a deficit which is covered by loss of reserves (whether held in gold or in some other form) or in some other temporary way. But the extent to which such temporary expedients can be used is always limited; they can therefore do no more than provide breathing-time, without affording any permanent means of adjustment to an enduring difficulty. We are here to be concerned with permanent adjustments; we may therefore look across all such temporary expedients, and make it a rule that the balance of payments of every country goes on being balanced—somehow. The only countries which can export gold, so long as this rule holds, are the gold-producers; import of gold can only take place to the extent of the gold-producers' exports. Balance of payments deficits and surpluses also (for one country's surplus spells another's deficit) are otherwise ruled out.

This assumption of continuous balance is undoubtedly the right approach to the problem before us; it is justified in itself, but it is at the same time an immense convenience. It enables us to cut straight through a vast tangle of complications, which in practice occupies the whole foreground, and may easily prevent us from seeing the real issues. And it is not the only simplification which we are at liberty to make. Since our inquiry is concerned with the effect of productivity changes, we can also cut out the "geometrical" complications which bothered the generation of Marshall and Edgeworth; we can go straight back to the basic simplicities of Ricardo and Senior.

The distinguishing assumption of the Ricardian theory was the hypothesis of *constant cost*—that all commodities (or at least all manufactured commodities) are produced at a cost per unit which is independent of the amount produced. Dubious as this assumption may be in many connexions, in this place it is a very harmless simplification. For what makes cost curves slope upwards or downwards is changes in productivity *induced* by changes in the scale of output; in this inquiry, where we are concerned with the *effects* of changes in productivity, we should give ourselves unnecessary trouble if we bothered to sort out the spontaneous and induced changes into separate boxes. The assumption of constant cost merely enables us to treat all changes in productivity as spontaneous —and in the present context that does no harm at all.

I therefore assert with some confidence the perfect applicability of Ricardian theory to the problem which I have undertaken to examine. We can, indeed, not merely make Ricardo's assumptions, we can also ask some of Ricardo's questions. In particular, we must still distinguish between the real (or barter) effects of productivity changes and the monetary effects by which they are in practice so greatly complicated.

What I mean by barter effects are those which persist whatever the course of money incomes—those which remain even if we suppose that money incomes in the various countries can be changed in whatever way is necessary to make adjustment as simple as possible. By monetary effects I mean those which arise out of difficulties in the adjustment of money incomes. Nineteenth-century economists studied these monetary effects in terms of a particular "monetary mechanism"; we are nowadays obliged to take a different view. But the changed approach to monetary problems does not prevent the distinction between real and monetary effects from holding good; it is, indeed, of crucial importance. For monetary difficulties are in principle capable of being eased, if not wholly dissipated, by appropriate institutions. Thus if the difficulty which we find is purely monetary, it ought to be possible to find a means of doing something about it; but if the monetary problem hides a real problem, no monetary wizardry can conjure it away.

The decks are now cleared, and we can get to work. I shall begin by setting out my analysis in rather formal terms.

Let us consider two countries, A and B, which are trading together, and which are such that productivity in A is increasing more rapidly than productivity in B. It will, I think, make little difference to the essence of the argument (and will certainly facilitate its exposition) if we neglect the expansion of productivity in B, and simply assume that productivity in A is increasing while that in B remains constant. We begin from a position in which the balance of payments between the two countries is in balance, as we are bound to do by our assumptions; but it does not matter how the balance has been brought about. It may be due to the classical forces which were thought to operate under free trade, or to changes in the volume of employment, or to import restrictions. On any of these suppositions the argument would be substantially unaffected.

I begin by laying down a proposition of central (though in relation to practical problems rather limited) significance. If productivity in A is increasing *uniformly*—at the same rate in all of A's industries—the barter effects of the development are most unlikely to be harmful to B. The simplest way of proving this proposition is to see what would happen if money incomes in B remained unchanged, while money incomes in A rose to the full extent of the rise in productivity. Then the cheapening of A-products would be wiped out by the rise in A-incomes, so that the prices of A-products would be unchanged. The prices of B-products are of course unchanged, so that all prices are unchanged. Money income in B is unchanged, so that there is no reason why B should buy any more or less of A-exports than before. But A-income has risen, and this will affect A's demand for B-exports. Though it is possible to construct weird cases in which the conclusion would not follow, we can surely be confident that in

444 *Readings in International Economics*

practice a rise in *A*-incomes, with all prices constant, would cause *A*'s demand for *B*-exports to *rise*. This means that if *A*-incomes rose to the full extent of the rise in *A*-productivity, the balance of payments would turn in *B*'s favour. If it is not to turn in *B*'s favour, but to remain in balance, the rise in *A*-incomes must accordingly be less than the rise in productivity. But if *A*-incomes rise by less than the rise in productivity, there will be some reduction (however small it may be) in the prices of *A*-exports. Money income in *B* can remain constant, and the prices of *B*-products can remain constant; nevertheless the balance of payments can remain balanced, while *B* gets her imports from *A* rather more cheaply than before. The real income of the *B*-population must be somewhat improved.

Thus, so far as barter effects are concerned, a *uniform* increase in productivity in *A* is almost certain to redound to *B*'s advantage. So far, the classical optimism is justified; some part of the improvement in *A* will slop over to *B*.

What, however, of the monetary effect? It is an essential element in the story we have been telling that *A*-incomes rise relatively to *B*-incomes. There is a fall in the prices of *A*-products relatively to *B*-products, so that the commodity terms of trade (what are ordinarily called the terms of trade) move in *B*'s favour. But the factorial terms of trade (to use Professor Viner's convenient expression for the ratio of money incomes, which is the relative value of *A*'s factors of production and *B*'s factors of production) move in favour of *A*. Now a strong movement of the factorial terms in *A*'s favour—and it will be a strong movement, if the change in productivity is considerable—is only consistent with a steady level of money incomes in *B* if money incomes in *A* are rising rapidly. So far we have simply assumed that *A*-incomes do rise sufficiently rapidly; but though it is possible that the requisite rise in *A*-incomes may come about from some extraneous cause, it is difficult to think of any automatic mechanism which will have the desired effect. The classical mechanism of gold flows has been discredited, not only by modern theory but directly by modern experience; yet even if one believed in that mechanism, it could only do the job which is here in question to quite a limited extent. Deflation in *B* would only be prevented if there was a sufficient output of new gold to support the requisite rise in *A*-incomes; otherwise, the 'inflation' in *A* would have to be matched by a deflation in *B*. Even on the basis of this now outmoded theory, it would be expected that money income in *B* would decline, unless indeed there were a sufficient output of newly mined gold to come to the rescue.

A more modern approach would, in substance, confirm the same conclusion, though the qualifications which it would introduce would be different. We should now expect that an employer would be constrained to raise the weekly wages of his employees to some extent when they (or he) achieved greater productivity; but the initial gain which accrues to the employer from the introduction of more productive methods would be wiped out if he could not expect to secure a substantial net reduction in money cost from the improvement. It is further to be expected that when costs are reduced, then (by one or other competitive or semi-competitive mechanism) prices will soon follow. In the course of this adjustment there will be effects on saving (which are fairly clear) and effects on investment (which are not). I shall not attempt to discuss these in detail, but shall merely conclude (as I think most economists would do) that while there may be some "natural" increase in money incomes in A, in consequence of the rise in A-productivity, it is most unlikely (in the absence of extraneous factors) that this increase will be sufficient to prevent the appearance of a downward pressure upon the level of money incomes in B.

It has therefore to be expected, if the rate of increase in productivity in A is rapid (or rapid relatively to the increase in productivity in B), that there will be a deflationary effect on B, assuming that there is a stable rate of exchange between A's and B's currency, and that B takes no special measures to counteract the deflation. This is what has to be expected if the level of money incomes in A moves in what we may call a 'natural' manner. It is of course perfectly possible that special causes, such as rearmament, or a flood of specially capital-using inventions, may cause money incomes in A to rise more rapidly than has been assumed. If so, the monetary pressure on B would be relieved. But no reason has been advanced which would justify us in regarding such relief as anything more than a temporary exception to a general rule.

It does nevertheless remain true, under the assumptions that we have been making, that the only reason why B gets into trouble is that A-incomes fail to rise with sufficient rapidity. There will, we may say, be some *appropriate* rate of rise in A-incomes (less, but perhaps not much less, than the rate of increase in productivity) which will keep trade between the two countries in balance, even though the level of B-incomes remains in money terms completely unchanged. If A-incomes do rise at this appropriate rate, there need be no deflation in B, while B is actually benefited by a certain change in the commodity terms of trade in its favour. It is only when A-incomes rise at less than the appropriate rate that B gets into difficulties.

Now, at this point, instead of tracing out consequences any farther, I want to ask you to stand back from the picture I have been drawing, and ask: Is it right? Does it in fact describe the kind of thing we have been experiencing? Surely the answer is that it does not.

I have nevertheless chosen to draw it out in some detail, both because it is a useful basis for further investigation and because it has so evidently been in the minds of many people who have given advice on economic policy during these last years. I think that this was especially the case just after the war. One remembers very well how we used to be told (even by Lord Keynes[1]) that inflation in America was a very good thing from the point of view of this country—that it would help to get us out of our difficulties. It might not last for ever, but it would be a help to us so long as it lasted. Now if America and Britain were the A and B of our example, and if our picture was drawn correctly, that would be true. All that would have been necessary would have been that we should have stopped our wages from rising, while American wages continued to rise; we should then have been freed from balance of payments troubles, while we could have continued to enjoy our own modest rate of real economic progress. All we should have needed to do would have been to control our own inflation; in the conditions supposed, that should not have been particularly difficult. That is the story we used to be told; but after the experiences we have had, it can hardly go on being told to us any longer.

What is it that has gone wrong? Not, I think, that the whole theory is wrong—though that is a conclusion to which people are only too ready to jump when they find a discrepancy between theory and fact. All that has happened is that a little assumption has crept in—an assumption which (unlike most writers on the subject) I have made explicit. It is the assumption that productivity in A is increasing *uniformly* in all industries.

No one, of course, has ever supposed that productivity does ever increase at a uniform rate in all industries; what has been implied is that differences between industries in this respect do not matter. There are indeed some sorts of differences which would not much matter; if the non-uniformity was quite random, it would certainly make little difference to the preceding argument. But it makes a very great difference if the non-uniformity is biased, so that the improvement in productivity is concentrated upon industries that have a special relation to foreign trade. There are two sorts of bias which come into question here, of which one is much more relevant to present discontents than the other. But we need to consider both sorts in order to get a balanced picture.

Let us accordingly take as our next subject of study the case in which the improvement in productivity is concentrated upon the goods which A exports; or, as we shall find it convenient to say, when the improvement is export-biased. In order to simplify the argument, let us say that there is a uniform improvement in productivity in A's export industries, but no improvement at all elsewhere. This, we shall find, is a case which is extremely favourable for B. For suppose that incomes remain constant in both countries; the prices of B-exports will then remain constant (for there has been no change in productivity in B), while the prices of A-exports are reduced. There is not much reason why the quantity of B-exports to A (and therefore their value, since their prices are constant) should be much affected; the quantity of A-exports to B must increase,

[1] I refer to Keynes's posthumous article, "The Balance of Payments of the United States," *Economic Journal*, 1946.

but since their prices are reduced, it is by no means certain that their total value will rise. With suitable (and quite possible) demand conditions in B, it is perfectly possible that trade will continue to balance at unchanged money incomes in both countries—that is to say, at unchanged factorial terms of trade. Thus in this case there may be no monetary difficulty; and even if there is some, it will be fairly small. The commodity terms of trade must, however, turn in favour of B, so that in this case there is bound to be a real gain to B, which is greater than the gain which occurs in the case of all-round uniformity.

This, you may say, is a sweet story; but it is matched by the ugliness of what happens in the corresponding case of an improvement that is "import-biased"—one, that is, that is concentrated upon the A-industries which compete most closely with B-exports. In this case it is certain that the factorial terms of trade must turn against B (so that there are the same monetary difficulties as in the case of uniformity); but B is now afflicted with a *real* (or barter) loss as well. We can show this in the same manner as before. If incomes in both countries remained constant, the prices of A-products which competed with B-exports would fall, so that A's demand for B-exports would decline; and this would itself be enough to cause a deficit in B's balance of payments, for there would be no reason why B's demand for A-exports should be affected. Thus in order to maintain a trade balance there must be a rise in A-incomes relatively to B-incomes; the factorial terms of trade must turn adversely to B. Further, since there has been no improvement in productivity in A's export in-industries, a rise in A-incomes implies a rise in the prices of A-exports, so that the commodity terms of trade must turn adversely to B. Whatever are the monetary arrangements, whatever the course of money incomes, an improvement in A-productivity that is *import-biased* must make B worse off.

A balanced view of the matter we are discussing would therefore distinguish three cases: (1) that in which the improvement is export-biased, which is the least likely to lead to monetary difficulties, the least favourable from the point of view of the improving country, and the most favourable for the foreigner; (2) that in which the improvement is more or less uniformly distributed, when there may well be monetary difficulties, but in which (if the monetary difficulties can be overcome) some part of the gain goes to the foreigner; (3) that in which the improvement is import-biased, when there are monetary difficulties as in the second case, and a real loss for the foreigner as well. This is a pure classification of cases; but it is a natural common-sense classification, with nothing academic or artificial about it. It is the kind of classification which one would expect to be able to use for the analysis of historical and contemporary experience.

It is, indeed, tempting to hazard the guess that it can be translated, rather directly, into terms of historical categories. Those periods of history which have seen a great growth of *trade* must nearly always have been periods in which productivity, in some sense, was increasing; it is much easier to see how improvements in productivity should lead to a growth of *trade* if the improvements that are taking place are export-biased. Export-biased improvements increase the advantages of foreign trade relatively to those of domestic production; the growth of trade is thereby directly stimulated. It is, indeed, possible to argue that any great growth of trade, which is not purely due to geographical exploration, must be due to export-biased improvements; for it should be noticed that improvements in transport and in the art of merchanting reckon as export-biased on our classification. But it is, of course, not necessary that the rate of improvement should be very different in the various countries that are trading together—though it would be surprising if such disparities were not in practice a pretty general rule.

We should further expect to find that the improvements which *start* a process of development will be export-biased. This is little more than a deduction from the general principle of the division of labour. Countries, like people, are most likely to make their improvements in those sorts of production which they already do relatively well than in those they do relatively badly; though not an infallible rule, it is one that is likely to hold unless there is special reason to the contrary. Since it is the things which they make relatively well which they will be exporting, or on the point of exporting, improvements in these industries will be export-biased. But all this means is that the first stage in a process of development is very likely to be export-biased. It is a stage which will be marked by growth of trade, by growth in the international division of labour. Though the division of labour will be limited, in Adam Smith's famous phrase, by the extent of the market—or, as we should say, by the inelasticity of foreign demand—such relative inelasticity is at this stage a stabilizing factor. It prevents the advancing countries from advancing too rapidly in relation to the rest, and thus from upsetting the international equilibrium.

But if our analysis is right, this will, in general, be no more than the first stage of the process. The very improvements upon which the expansion is based set up forces which tend to change its character. Even though the improvements are likely to be made, in the first place, in those countries which already have a comparative advantage for the industries mainly affected, the mere fact that improvements have been made, that the techniques and organization of production have been altered, sets up forces which tend to change the pattern of comparative advantages. It is certainly true that the change which then ensues may take a long time to declare itself fully. Even though the ideal location of production, from the point of view of such things as natural resources and transport costs, has shifted away from the old centres—so that if the whole production system had to be started anew it would no longer be sensible to specialize in the old way—nevertheless the old centres still retain their accumulated skill, and may be able to retain a lead on that basis, even when the geographical factors have turned against them. But once this point is reached, the position of the old centres has become very vulnerable. It has to be expected that some of the countries which were formerly their customers, but which possess the right natural resources for home production of the things they used to import, when production is organized according to the new methods, will in time acquire the skills which will enable them to compete. When this happens on a large scale, the process passes into its second stage—notice that it is still a stage of development for the world economy, taken as a whole—in which the lead is taken by new centres, which are now making improvements that are import-biased. Thus when our analysis is put into an historical dress, it suggests as a normal sequence the succession of an export-biased by an import-biased phase.

I am no historical determinist; and it is no part of my intention to suggest that historical phenomena will ever fit very neatly into any such logical pattern. But I do think that we see the shadows of such patterns across the face of history. Western Europe is not the first metropolis of trade and industry which has suffered from the competition of the new lands which it has itself developed; there was, I fancy, an element of this same process in the decline of ancient Greece; we ourselves in this island grew great in the fifteenth century and later at the expense of the Flemish and Italian centres on which we had formerly depended. But though such historical examples warn us that the process under discussion is not at all uncommon, they also indicate that there is nothing inevitable about its denouement. After the general expansion of the first phase has given place to the expansion here, contraction there, of the second, it may happen that the troubles of the contracting countries lay so heavy a burden upon the whole international economy that its general progress is brought to a halt. It may happen that the contraction remains localized, and that the expanding centres of the second phase establish a new leadership. It may happen that the centres which have lost their old comparative advantages develop new ones and begin a new expansion of their own. If Professor Postan is right,[2] the history of the Netherlands in the fifteenth and sixteenth centuries affords a remarkable example of this happier outcome.

But I must return to my immediate topic. Whatever the applicability of my analysis to remoter history, its application to the age in which we live is clear and direct. The distinction which I have been making provides a simple and fundamental explanation of the change in economic atmosphere between the nineteenth and twentieth centuries. Once we

---

[2] *Cambridge Economic History of Europe*, Vol. ii, ch. 4, especially pp. 251–56. The somewhat different version of the story which is told by Miss Carus-Wilson in ch. 6 of the same volume will also repay attention.

assume (and such facts as are readily available offer fair direct confirmation of the assumption) that nineteenth-century improvements were mainly export-biased, while those of our day have a predominant bias in the other direction, the whole story begins to make sense. And the dollar problem fits into its place as an episode, albeit a critical episode, in a wider evolution.

It is true that the forms in which the dollar problem has actually appeared have constantly tempted us to regard it as something much less deep-rooted. In the nineteen-twenties it was entangled with war debts; in the nineteen-thirties with world depression and the flight of capital before Hitler; in the nineteen-forties with war damage, more war debts, and the Cold War in international trade. A special explanation of the difficulties which were being experienced by European countries in settling their dollar debts could always be found. But the continuance of the same consequence, the same dollar shortage, as the result of these various "causes," has by now become very striking. That there is some general influence underlying these particular manifestations can now no longer be doubted. It is hard to see that there is any other general force which would account for what has been happening than the disparity in growth of productivity which we have been discussing.

Looking at our own case, it is no novelty in British history for the development of America to be as important for us as anything going on outside our island. The political independence of the United States did not break the economic links which bound us to them; throughout the nineteenth century the Anglo-American nexus remained a key to the economic development of both countries. The general characteristic of the trade throughout that time was an exchange of the products of American farms for those of British factories. In spite of the high productivity of American manufacturing (which began very early), it was possible for British manufacturers to compete with American on the basis of lower wages; in spite of the high wages in America, Britain could still import American farm-products advantageously to herself, because the exceedingly high productivity of American agriculture kept American farm-products very reasonably cheap. During the age of mainly export-biased improvements this mutually advantageous trade continued to grow. Export-biased improvements continued to be made on both sides of the Atlantic, not indeed quite synchronously—so that the rate at which the gain from trade was increasing swung sometimes to one side, sometimes to the other—but evenly enough to ensure a continuing gain to both sides. Especially in the railway age, when nearly the whole of the United States and much of Canada were made into possible sources of exports, British dependence on North American agriculture was carried so far as to be a major characteristic of the British economy.

The time came (probably it had to come) when the rate of growth of productivity in Britain fell behind that in America. This in itself, as we have seen, must have caused monetary difficulties—manageable so long as the discrepancy remained small, serious as it became wider. In the first phase of the dollar shortage (say the nineteen-twenties) the difficulties which arose may indeed be said to have been almost exclusively monetary. So long as British wages (under the restored gold standard) remained fixed in terms of dollars, British industry found difficulty in competing with American; but the productivity of agriculture (in North America and elsewhere) was still increasing so rapidly that a moderate devaluation would have restored our earning-power without imposing more than a very temporary sacrifice upon the British consumer. Thus at this stage it was quite right to think of the problem in monetary terms —to analyse it as Keynes did in fact analyse it at the time.

Since then things have become more difficult, mainly because the rate of growth in productivity in agriculture has slowed up. As things are today, it may still be necessary to reduce the dollar value of British wages in order to keep British manufactures competitive with American manufactures, but we can no longer count upon the real sacrifice involved being slight or temporary. Increasing productivity of our agricultural suppliers can no longer be relied upon to come to the rescue. If a monetary adjustment is needed to keep trade in balance it now requires a fall in British wages in terms of British imports, or a rise in the prices of British imports relatively to British wages.[3]

It is still true that the core of the whole matter is to find a way of paying for the agricultural imports from the United States and Canada (raw materials as well as foodstuffs) on which the standard of living of the British people has come to depend. It has long been impossible to pay for them, save to a small extent, by direct export of British goods to the "dollar area." For this the American tariff must bear some part of the blame; but since the same difficulty is felt in Canada as in the United States, it is clear that the increasing productivity of American industry must be regarded as mainly responsible. Yet even when the mass export of British goods to America became a thing of the past, it was still possible for us to pay for our imports from America by triangular trade. America still requires some products (tropical and mineral) which she cannot produce within her own borders; if America will buy from (say) Africa and Africa will buy from Britain, Britain can still buy from America and pay for what she buys, handing on the "dollars" which she has received

[3] The particular mechanism by which the relative rise in import prices is transmitted to the British consumer is an internal question, rather independent of the main conclusion. It is possible that the prices of imported goods may just be allowed to rise on the home market; or their prices may be kept down by subsidy and the demand for them kept down by rationing. If sufficient taxes are imposed to offset the effect of the subsidies, the difference between the two techniques is a matter of the internal distribution of the burden which has to be endured. For an admirable study of the relation between this burden and the others under which post-war Britain has laboured, see Harry Johnson, *The Overloaded Economy* (University of Toronto Press, 1952).

from Africa. But this indirect solution, though we have come to depend upon it, is itself threatened by the same forces as destroyed the bilateral balance. Unless British manufacturers can compete with American in the markets of third countries, trade between these third countries and America will settle down into a bilateral exchange of third-country products against American manufactures, with Britain left out in the cold. Political influence, and propaganda based upon the alleged "instability" of the American market, will fight a losing battle unless British exports are competitive, unless (that is) the triangular trade is more advantageous from the point of view of the third countries than direct bilateral trade with America would be. Though protective devices may do something to put off the evil day, the trend is bound to be in the direction of American— "African" bilateralism, unless British costs fall as fast as American costs may be expected to fall.[4]

If the rate of increase in productivity in British export industry falls behind that in American export industry, British costs can only remain competitive if there is a fall in British wages relatively to American wages, when both are measured in the same currency. But if the costs of American and Canadian farm-produce are not falling in terms of American wages, this must mean that the British consumer is made less able to buy the North American farm-produce to which he has become accustomed. This, again, would not much matter if there were other suppliers of farm-produce which were making export-biased improvements, so that the imports which were becoming harder to get from North America could be replaced from other sources at a cost which was not getting out of reach. But in a world where improvements are turning import-biased, such relief cannot be taken for granted. Thus the change in relative wages, however it is brought about (whether directly, or by some monetary trick such as devaluation), must be expected to mean a real loss for the British consumer.

This, of course, is the real reason why the devaluation of 1949 was a failure. It was put over as a trick which would enable the balance of payments to be righted without real sacrifice. Thus when the sterling prices of imported commodities began to rise in order to enforce a real sacrifice, wages chased after the rising prices, and the rise in wages made the devaluation largely ineffective. If we devalue again in the same delu-

---

[4] In making the above statements, I am begging the much-debated question of the world elasticity of demand for British exports, which I assume (in opposition to much important opinion, and to some alleged evidence) to be quite high. I must therefore emphasize (1) that I am talking about long-run elasticity, which all would admit to be higher than short-run elasticity; (2) that for the "curve" to be elastic upwards —so that a moderate excess of our prices over those of our competitors will cause us to be pushed out of the market—does not imply that it is elastic downwards—for the domestic producer may well secure additional protection if his market is invaded too drastically. The theory of the "kinked demand curve" may well have a more important application to international trade than to other branches of economics.

sion, the same thing will doubtless happen again, and may happen even more quickly. Along that road there is no way out.[5]

If the rate of growth of productivity in British industry remains behind that in American industry (and it would be optimistic to hope that such a disparity can now be avoided), there is no way of avoiding a long-run fall in the British standard of living *unless our essential imports become easier to get*. Improvements in primary production have now become quite vital to us, but they will help us wherever they occur. If they occur in North America itself, they will help us to acquire supplies from America by offering them to us at a reduced cost in terms of American wages; if they occur in this country, they will make it possible for us to reduce our imports without sacrifice; if they occur in other countries, they will enable us to replace our imports from North America by imports from these other countries, which will then be offered to us on more favourable terms. But all these are in a sense part of the same problem; it is only by some kind of attack upon that problem that we can hope in the end for a solution of our difficulties.

The present check to the process of cost-reduction in world agriculture is partly a consequence of the long-run forces which I discussed at an earlier point of this lecture; but it is due in part to causes which may be of a more temporary character. Some of these are political causes, which I shall not attempt to consider; but there is one that is economic, and which deserves a mention because it may be removable. It is the common fate of all large-scale agricultural improvements to run up against obstacles (perhaps temporary obstacles) to the profitable disposal of an increased product. But even in cases where it is quite impossible to increase sales by lowering prices, reductions in cost remain desirable in the general interest of economic progress, since they enable a given product to be produced with a smaller application of resources (usually, with less labour) and accordingly set labour free for increased production of other things. Nevertheless, in the short run, while unnecessary numbers of workers are attached to the production in question, the incomes of producers are abnormally low. The consumer is then deriving an advantage, not only

---

[5] In a world of full employment and cost-of-living inflation, the above is the strongest objection to the devaluation "remedy"; but I do not desire to suggest that it is the only objection. To adjust the value of money as a once-for-all measure to meet a single identifiable change (such as that caused by a world war) seems to me to be one thing; a continuing policy of depreciation, to deal with a continuing failure of competitive power, to be quite another. If currency depreciation is adopted as a regular policy, people must come to foresee it. If they do so, they will decline to hold the depreciating currency; for it is more profitable to hold a stable money than one which is depreciating. Even though the "soft" currency is fortified by exchange restrictions, the objection is not wholly met; for it is doubtful if any practicable exchange restrictions will suffice to protect a currency, depreciation of which has become a habit. In our own case, in view of the advantages which we gain from the use of sterling as an international medium, this argument is particularly powerful. We may be put to great straits in order to maintain the exchange value of sterling (at least to the outsider); but I doubt if we have any alternative but to bear our cross.

from the technical reduction in cost (this is an advantage to which, in a sense, he is entitled), but also from the temporary lowness of the producers' incomes (and the gain which he gets from that is hardly one to which he is entitled in the same sense). Throughout the twenties and thirties agricultural incomes were abnormally low from this cause; and the British consumer derived a corresponding advantage, which masked the weakening of his own economic position. He has now lost that advantage, as he was bound to do sooner or later; but he has not merely lost an advantage—he is suffering from a disadvantage that runs the other way. Primary producers, through their own organizations and through their governments, are taking measures to protect themselves from further over-production; but in so doing they are slowing up the cost-reducing process itself. The arrested development of world agriculture is therefore not wholly natural—it is in part contrived; importing countries could hardly be blamed if they reacted against such contriving in any way that was open to them. Our own bulk purchase of agricultural supplies has in fact been used for the underpinning of the "stabilization" schemes of primary producers, though stabilization of supplies is against our own interest. It might not be impossible to make some agreements in a form which would encourage increases of production from particular regions[6]; even though the costs of such a policy were for a time considerable, it might be sensible to make some sacrifice for it if it helped to break the jam and gave us a better prospect for the further future.

---

[6] I am thinking, for instance, of the proposals put forward by Mr. Kaldor (*Economics of the International Wheat Agreement*, F.A.O. 1952).

27. Longer-Run Problems of the Balance of Payments[*]

By T. W. SWAN[†]

I. INTRODUCTION

Since Keynes published *The General Theory* in 1936, it has been widely accepted that the two fundamental propositions of a full employment policy are (*a*) that incomes and employment depend on the level of spending; and (*b*) that there is no automatic mechanism to keep spending near its full employment level, without conscious action by economic and financial authorities. But the balance of payments equally depends on the level of spending. Must it be only a happy chance if the "internal balance" and "external balance" levels of spending coincide? Is there an automatic mechanism to ensure this, or what kind of conscious action by the authorities is required?

The 1945 White Paper "Full Employment in Australia" gave some partial answers:

a) "Minor fluctuations in export income" should be borne by international reserves. (Par. 89.)

b) A loss of export income which "although prolonged and severe, is not permanent," should be met by quantitative import restrictions (which would incidentally help maintain employment in Australia, but would only be imposed if the balance of payments required them). (Pars. 91 and 49.)

c) A "permanent" loss of export income should be met by exchange depreciation. (Par. 91.)

d) "The tariff and other methods of protection are legitimate devices for building up industries appropriate to our economy," but would be used only to protect "efficient" industries on the advice of the Tariff Board. (Par. 72.)

e) The "normal upward trend" of productivity, resulting chiefly from technical progress and development, should be reflected in the level of

[*] Paper presented to Section G of the Congress of the Australian and New Zealand Association for the Advancement of Science, Melbourne 1955. Published in H. W. Arndt and M. W. Corden (eds.), *The Australian Economy: A Volume of Readings* (Melbourne: Chesire Press, 1963), pp. 384–95.

[†] The Australian National University.

real wages, by means of a periodical review of the basic wage standard. (Par. 77.)

f) The Government would collaborate in international measures to expand and stabilise world trade, would actively help to develop the export trade in primary and manufactured goods, and would encourage "shifts of productive resources" which might become necessary to meet changing world demands for Australian products. (Pars. 46, 86, 87, 91.)

This programme does not recognise the possibility of balance of payments deficits arising from Australian over-spending. The connexion between wages policy, tariff policy, and the balance of payments is only implicitly recognised, if at all, in (d) and (e). The conflict between real wages tied to physical productivity trends under (e) and effective action by depreciation under (c) is not noticed. Nevertheless, if over-spending is ruled out; if "loss of export income" is generalised to include all changes in the terms of trade, whether from the export or import side: if "productivity" is measured after due allowance for "permanent" changes in the terms of trade; if the word "permanent" is not taken too literally; and if somehow we start from a position in which the level of real wages is properly adjusted to whatever length of run is regarded as "permanent"—then, on these assumptions, the White Paper programme does broadly provide a prescription for reconciling full employment with long-run external balance. It is not an automatic mechanism: "conscious action by the authorities" is required to prevent over-spending, to keep real wages in line with long-run movements of productivity and the terms of trade, and to impose temporary quantitative restrictions during (and only during) middle-run troughs of the terms of trade.

Fears about the future, which are shared by many economists, arise from a suspicion that in all these three directions the will and/or the means to the required policy action are lacking, and that we are therefore faced with a persistent tendency towards over-spending, excessive wage costs, balance of payments deficits, and more or less permanent import restrictions with a consequent bias towards inflation and a "distortion" (in some sense) of patterns of investment and production.

These notes are intended merely to serve as a basis for discussion of these suspicions, with particular reference to the problem of wages policy in the current context of the Australian economy.

II. HOW EMPLOYMENT AND THE BALANCE OF PAYMENTS ARE JOINTLY DETERMINED

Take productivity, the terms of trade, capital movements and other financial transfers as given, and assume no special import restrictions imposed on balance of payments grounds. Then Diagram 1 shows how employment and the balance of payments both depend on the level of spending *and* on the Australian relative cost situation. "Real Expenditure" is total domestic investment and consumption (private and public) at con-

DIAGRAM 1

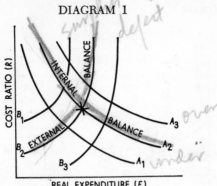

stant prices, hereafter called E for short. The "Cost Ratio," hereafter called R, is some sort of index measuring the competitive position of Australian industries—e.g., the ratio of an index of international prices (prices of imports and exports) to an index of local wages, with weights reflecting the sensitivity of supply and demand for different commodities to changes in relative costs.

A given level of employment can be sustained with E very low if R is high enough (i.e., if our costs are so favourable that we export a great deal and import very little), and vice versa. This is shown in the A curves —A_1 for a given amount of unemployment, A_2 for "full employment," A_3 for a given amount of "over-employment." On the other hand, a given balance of payments requires a combination of low E and low R, or high E and high R. This is shown in the B curves—B_1 for a surplus, B_2 for zero (equilibrium), B_3 for a deficit. The B curves all turn up steeply near and beyond the A_2 curve of full employment, because as local resources are over-strained more and more of further increases in E must "spill" overseas, till in the end an "infinite" improvement in R is needed to off-set any increase in E (i.e., an increasing deficit cannot be prevented by any cost adjustment whatever). There are, of course, as many A and B curves as we like to draw, for different levels of employment and the balance of payments.

Any combination of E and R along A_2 gives internal balance; any combination along B_2 gives external balance; only at their point of intersection do we have both internal and external balance. The two curves of internal balance and external balance divide existence into four zones of economic unhappiness (Diagram 2).

However, between the two halves of each zone, as divided by the broken straight lines, the causes of disequilibrium differ. Only in Zones II and IV is the level of spending unequivocally too low or too high; only in Zones I and III are costs unequivocally too low or too high. Thus in each zone the necessary direction of adjustment of one of the two factors, E and R, is apparent, whereas the other may be either too high or too

DIAGRAM 2

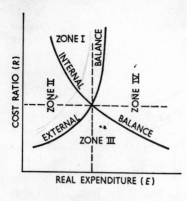

REAL EXPENDITURE (E)

Zone I: Over-full employment and balance of payments surplus.
Zone II: Under-full employment and balance of payments surplus.
Zone III: Under-full employment and balance of payments deficit.
Zone IV: Over-full employment and balance of payments deficit.

low, depending on our precise position in the zone. Conversely, over-spending is consistent with both unemployment and over-employment, and with both a balance of payments surplus and a deficit (but not with under-employment and a surplus together); and so on. This is the source of many of the problems and errors of economic policy—if one factor is substantially out of line, the "natural" indications for the other may be quite misleading. For policy, we need to know which *quadrant* we are in, whereas the mere facts of the employment situation and the balance of payments can tell us only which *zone* we are in.

Even these "facts" fail to tell us anything directly, in the short-run, if for policy we want to distinguish between short- and long-run situations—e.g., if the terms of trade are temporarily better than their long-run average, we may appear to be in Zone I, although from a long-run viewpoint we are in Zone III. For the curves shift bodily with any change in the factors "taken as given" at the beginning of the first paragraph in Section II. Thus an improvement in the terms of trade or in capital inflow, etc., shifts all the B curves, including the curve of external balance, to the right and downwards, permitting equilibrium with E higher and R lower. An improvement in productivity shifts all the A curves to the right and upwards as well as all the B curves to the right and downwards, permitting equilibrium with E higher and R probably lower (R higher if the productivity increase is concentrated in "sheltered" home industries or if people insist on spending too high a proportion of their extra incomes on imports and exportables).

However, for many purposes it is convenient to think of the position of the curves as unchanged, while changes in the terms of trade, etc., shift the economic situation in the diagram in relation to the curves.

III. SHORT-RUN POLICIES

The importance of the policy distinction between the short- and the long-run arises from the fact that both the A curves and the B curves are much "flatter" in the long-run than in the short-run over most of their range (but even in the long-run the B curves are still vertical or nearly vertical in the region where over-full employment has already strained local resources to the limit). This is because the longer is the time allowed for adjustments in the patterns of production and spending, the more sensitive are supplies and demands to different levels of R, whereas the effect of different levels of E is always immediate. Hence attempts to maintain short-run equilibrium by movements in R might involve violent and wasteful instability in the cost structure and distribution of incomes. Presumably the ideal would be (since we can hardly divide history into a series of discrete prospective long-runs) that R should respond very slowly to short-run changes in the economic situation, so that its level would reflect a sort of long-run moving average. This implies the use of international reserves as a buffer against the short-run fluctuations, and therefore the average size of these reserves will determine how long-run the adjustments of R can be.

This is the basic rationale of the use of quantitative import restrictions —as a short-run device to buy time for external balance, by economising on the average level of reserves needed to permit effective long-run relative cost adjustments to be made.

If restrictions are imposed only for sufficiently short and isolated periods and are sufficiently moderate in their impact, we may reasonably assume—

a) that established trading habits will prevent any great element of "profiteering" in licences and licenced goods, and that at the same time problems of the rationing of goods in short supply will not become acute;

b) that recurrent periods of free importation or liberal allocation of new quotas will prevent ossification of the importing business and of trade connexions;

c) that the prospect of early removal of restrictions will prevent any significant long-term investment in import-replacing industries; and

d) that the margin of uncertainty, as to how serious a balance of payments deficit has to be before restrictions will be imposed, can be used to discourage speculative buying in anticipation of restrictions.

With these assumptions, import restrictions do not differ in their effects from the running down of international reserves, except that we do not get the imports and that we still keep both the international reserves and their counterpart in domestic liquidity. There is, therefore, everything to be said for imposing import restrictions if otherwise we would be temporarily in Zone III, with unemployment and a balance of payments deficit (provided that we make sure that the imposition of the restrictions does not itself carry us into a position of over-full employment). The resulting diversion of demand to domestic products and retention of domestic liquidity both help to sustain employment, without loss of international reserves, and without the upheaval of costs and incomes that would be otherwise needed to preserve short-run external balance.

But if we try to use import restrictions as a substitute for cuts in expenditure—in Zone IV, with over-employment and deficit—then the fact that we are keeping out goods and keeping in liquidity means that the problems of excess demand are made more acute than ever, local costs are driven up, and we move still further away from equilibrium: with little prospect of ending the restrictions unless we not only mend our ways and make the expenditure cuts that we hoped to dodge, but also take steps to undo the damage done to the relative cost situation in the meantime.

At the same time, we must notice that an attempt to use exchange depreciation or tariff increases to protect reserves in Zone IV must have similar unfortunate results: for in this zone, so long as expenditure is kept too high external balance requires a more or less unlimited improvement in the relative cost situation, whereas internal balance requires, and over-full employment tends to produce, a movement in the opposite direction. And import restrictions do have the merit that they at least protect the reserves, while exchange depreciation and tariff increases, alongside rising money wages, might not do even that.

The moral is that there is no substitute, even in the short-run, for an effective limitation of expenditure to the level of the goods and services available from full employment output plus the maximum import surplus that we can afford after allowing for a temporary run-down of reserves. But if expenditure is effectively limited, then import restrictions are not merely a good substitute for, but a preferable alternative to, *temporary* cost adjustments which would otherwise be necessary. Indeed, import restrictions may often rightly be used in circumstances in which "temporary" money wage cuts, depreciation, or tariff increases would be plain nonsense.

However, even in such circumstances, import restrictions should not be resorted to so readily and frequently that the assumptions given above are seriously undermined. (Penicillin cream for impetigo?) This is not an argument for trying to make what are essentially long-run adjustments do a short-run job, but rather an argument on the one hand for very careful consideration before quantitative restrictions are imposed and on the other hand for seizing every opportunity to build up reserves and to adjust relative costs in the long-run to a level which will make restrictions only rarely necessary.

In passing, we may note that the logic of quantitative restrictions as a device for temporarily short-circuiting the price mechanism, in circumstances in which it is ineffective, seems to rule out any case for the various proposals which have been made for the auctioning of licences, which would restore the price mechanism by the back door.

IV. LONG-RUN COST ADJUSTMENTS

The argument of the preceding section implies that effective *short-run* control of Real Expenditure (E) and effective *long-run* adjustments of the Cost Ratio (R) are both necessary to reconcile full employment with long-run external balance. The cost adjustments required are essentially adjustments of real wage rates (as we see, for instance, in the familiar propositions that exchange depreciation and money wage cuts are alternative routes to the same end, and that depreciation will not be effective if money wages rise proportionally with international prices in local currency, so as to preserve real wage rates unchanged). If long-run relative cost adjustments are not made, then import restrictions, imposed as a short-run device to eke out international reserves in specially "bad" years (for the terms of trade), may have to become a permanent feature of the economy in "good" years as well as "bad." Does this mean that the necessity for cost adjustments—for relating real wage rates to movements in productivity and the terms of trade—can be indefinitely postponed if only we can put up with quantitative restrictions of imports as a long-run institution?

The illusion of real wage rates might indeed be sustained in these circumstances with a certain amount of statistical success if with systematic price control and rationing the prices of permanently restricted imports were kept down to a cost-plus basis—but "real wages" would have to be measured in terms of purchasing power over a basket of commodities consisting in part of empty import boxes, whereas actual wages would be spent on more expensive or less preferred home substitutes. The higher "real wages" in this sense (as compared with their equilibrium level without import restrictions) the more empty boxes there would be, since export industries would be gradually squeezed out, till in the limit we could balance our international payments "with nought on both sides and all of us flat on our backs."

In practice, we must expect long-continued import restrictions (realistically assuming no price control and rationing) to lead inevitably to "profiteering" in licences and imported goods to the extent of charging "what the traffic will bear." Thus if in the long-run real wages are not well regulated so as to make import restrictions unnecessary, they will be clipped to the necessary extent by the "profiteering" of the importers and the dearness of available home substitutes—again, a process which reaches its limit with zero exports and imports.

Long-run quantitative restrictions are in fact almost precisely the equivalent of a tariff, except that the licence-holder collects the duties instead of the Government. If the licences are interchangeable commodity-wise (as in Category B) the equivalent is a uniform *ad valorem* tariff; if they are specific (as in Category A), the equivalent is a tariff with differential *ad valorem* rates.

We should not complain if import restrictions encourage investment biased towards import-replacement. If the restrictions are really temporary, there is little danger of "distortion"; if they are needed in the long-run, import-replacing investment is just what is called for and would anyway be encouraged by wage-cuts, depreciation, or tariff increases. But we may reasonably complain that both tariffs and quantitative restrictions (unlike wage-cuts and depreciation) encourage import-replacement without encouraging export-expansion; and perhaps we may complain also that quantitative restrictions, as usually administered, encourage in particular "non-essential" import-replacement.

Certainly, tariffs are from almost every point of view preferable to long-run quantitative restrictions—if we must have one or the other. But we have been taught, on very respectable authority, that tariffs offer a way of sustaining real wages (at the expense of rural rents). Is there then still a hope of avoiding long-run relative cost adjustments in terms of real wages? It is true that a required adjustment of R may be made more "economically," in terms of real wages, by raising only the relative price of imports (by means of a tariff) than by reducing domestic wages all round or by raising export and import prices all round, if the price of exportables is a significant element in real wages but their production is insensitive to changes in relative costs. (If exportables are not an element in the cost of living, a tariff which does not reduce real wages will neither encourage domestic industry nor reduce imports; if export production is sensitive to relative cost changes, a tariff may worsen the balance of payments even though it promotes import replacement.) This argument is strong in the short-run, but its force diminishes in the long-run, especially if we allow for the "imperfections" which make investment in export industries depend to a considerable extent on average rather than marginal returns. In any case, the argument obviously cannot be carried too far, and once we have exploited its possibilities we are back with the necessity for real wage adjustments.

The only obvious mechanism of real wage adjustment works in terms of the bargaining power of the trade unions, which depends largely on the state of the labour market. But whether this latter mechanism can be made to work in the direction of producing the necessary cost adjustments depends on how far the employment situation can be allowed to vary without departing too far from "acceptable" standards of "full employment."

If there is no direct way of regulating real wages, other than through the state of the labour market, then official control of E must seek simultaneously to do two jobs—to keep the economy close to "full employment," but sufficiently on one side or the other of it to keep real wages moving in proper harmony with the long-run trends of productivity and the terms of trade. The experience of recent years provides some reason to think that the acceptable range of "full employment" is fairly wide, and that towards the lower limit of that range real wages can perhaps be restrained from increasing.

V. CONTROL OF SPENDING

It is evident that without proper control of the level of E it is useless to talk about the scope for other policies, such as quantitative import restrictions, tariff policy, or wages policy. All can be good or bad, meaningful or nugatory, according to what steps are being taken to regulate expenditure.

If there is a "persistent tendency to over-spend," there seem to be at least two possible interpretations of it:

a) That it springs from the magnitude of investment opportunities and needs which are largely associated with the migration programme, and which require more capital each year than we are willing to set aside in private and public saving. It probably takes 10–15 years for the savings out of a migrant's contribution to current production to add up to the cost of the capital equipment "needed" directly and indirectly as a result of his presence; the capital needs of 100,000 migrants may be £100–£200 m. On this view, if we reduced or abolished migration, or alternatively if we secured enough capital from overseas to support it, the tendency to over-spend should disappear.

b) That it springs from a spendthrift disposition of the body politic which makes us unwilling to set limits to our expenditure until we are faced with sufficiently hard facts in the form of labour shortages, dwindling international reserves, etc. On this view, cuts in migration, or heavy borrowing abroad, would soon be followed by a loosening of financial restraints and new expenditures on a scale sufficient to ensure as much embarrassment as before (much as the traffic across a bridge may be limited only by the inconvenience of over-crowding, so that adding an extra lane or two would not diminish the over-crowding). If this is the case, a programme of political and popular education, may be the only remedy.

Perhaps in either case it would help if we could devise a more acceptable form and pattern for the limitation of expenditure. For example, is there any way of tightening the money market which does not hit mainly housing and hospitals etc., while scarcely touching hire-purchase?

If we cannot hope for complete rectitude in avoiding over-spending perhaps we may still hope for a policy which will keep us fairly close to the boundary of Zone IV—spending on a scale which will give over-full employment when there is balance of payments surplus or equilibrium (in the upper half of Diagram 2) but will avoid over-full employment when there is a deficit or when import restrictions are in operation (in the lower half of Diagram 2). Such a policy would have a definite inflationary bias, and would require exchange depreciation from time to time as rising costs began to press heavily on the export industries, unless our long-run terms of trade were improving fairly rapidly. But it would avoid the worst dangers of instability (e.g., depreciation in Zone IV) and unless our terms of trade were worsening fairly rapidly might not be utterly disastrous.

28. The Process of International Adjustment under Conditions of Full Employment: A Keynesian View[*]

By LLOYD A. METZLER[†]

CONTEMPORARY IDEAS ABOUT the way in which an even balance of payments is achieved have always been closely related to the prevailing theories of money and prices. Thus, in the pre-Keynesian era, when the quantity theory of money was the accepted version, the balancing process was described largely in terms of movements in money and the level of prices. Later, under the influence of Lord Keynes' *General Theory of Employment, Interest and Money*, these monetary variables were replaced by changes in the circular flow of income or by movements in the level of output and employment. To some extent the *General Theory* reflected a condition of deep depression and widely fluctuating output; it was therefore not applicable to the prosperous conditions which prevail today. Nevertheless, in modifying his concepts of monetary theory to allow for conditions of depression and fluctuating output, Keynes made a contribution to the traditional theory which will have a profound influence on the theory of international adjustment even when full employment prevails. Specifically, he introduced the concept of a monetary rate of interest which altered the foundation upon which the traditional theory was based, namely, the quantity theory of money.

The purpose of my paper is to consider a situation where full employment prevails but where the Keynesian monetary rate of interest is also taken into account. I shall assume that prices are governed by the demand for goods and services compared with the supply so that a rise of prices indicates an excess demand while a fall indicates an excess supply. Further, I shall assume that we are dealing with trade between two countries, an advanced country and an underdeveloped one. The characteristic of the advanced country, of course, is that it possesses a larger amount of capital per worker so that the marginal return on investment is smaller than in the underdeveloped country while produc-

[*] Unpublished, delivered before the Econometric Society, December, 1960.

[†] The University of Chicago.

tivity and the rate of saving are higher. I shall assume that in both countries the level of demand is high enough so that, at some point in the saving and investment schedules, a rate of interest exists at which potential saving at full employment equals potential investment. Thus the two-country economy with which I shall be dealing represents a reconciliation of two monetary theories which a generation ago were the subject of lively controversy among economists: first, the traditional theory which recognized changes in the quantity of money and prices as the principal regulators of the system; and secondly, the Keynesian theory which emphasized the movements of the circular flow of income as the determinants of a country's balance of payments.

FIGURE 1a   FIGURE 1b

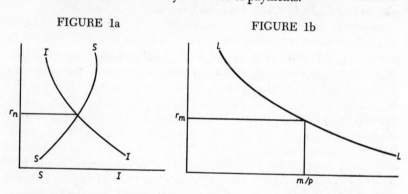

Before elaborating further, however, a word should be said about the general consensus which has now developed concerning the relations between the monetary rate of Keynes and the traditional theory. And in order to simplify the relationships as much as possible, I shall start with an economy which is isolated from the rest of the world. Consider, for example, Figures 1a and 1b below. Figure 1a represents potential saving and net investment at a full employment level of income. On the vertical axis the rate of interest on newly issued securities is represented while on the horizontal axis the variables are real investment and real saving. Looking at the matter from the point of view of newly issued securities, we may say that the saving line SS, represents a demand for these securities. The investment line, *II*, on the other hand, represents a supply of new securities issued by entrepreneurs to finance their planned investment. We may thus look upon the SS and *II* schedules from two points of view: from the point of view of the new securities market, they depict the supply of and demand for such securities. And from the point of view of the goods and services market, the intersection of the saving and investment schedules at the interest rate r_n may be said to represent a condition where the total demand for such goods and services *equals* the economy's full employment capacity.

By contrast with 1a, 1b represents the *monetary* conditions of balance, or the market for existing securities. If r_n is the natural rate or the rate which creates a balance between the *flow* of real saving and the flow of investment, r_m is the monetary rate or the rate which satisfies the asset owners with their existing *stocks* of securities and real cash balances. Thus, at any point along LL of Figure 1b the asset owners are holding real cash balances in a manner which gives them no incentive to shift from cash to securities or from securities to cash. The analogy which is suggested by these comparisons is that between a profit and loss statement and a balance sheet. Figure 1a describes the flow of income per unit of time and shows how this flow is distributed between saving and investment. Figure 1b, on the other hand, presents the ownership of assets and the distribution of such assets between securities and cash.

As of the moment of time for which Figure 1b represents the balance sheet, the amount of existing securities is a fixed quantity, governed by past investments. Moreover, the capitalized value of these security holdings is higher the lower the rate of interest. We may assume, as Keynes does, that as the rate of interest falls, the asset owner wishes to hold a larger ratio of real cash balances to securities. The higher degree of desired liquidity will be a result of three considerations. First, as the rate of interest falls, the opportunity cost of holding cash rather than securities becomes smaller; second, a fall in security yields, which means a rise in security prices, may eventually create an expectation that security prices will fall and their yields will therefore rise. And third, a fall in interest rates increases the capitalized value of existing securities.

But all of this is by now a well-accepted part of monetary theory. What I wish to concentrate upon is the relation between the monetary rate and the natural rate. Clearly, there can be no difference between the one and the other for both types of securities, once issued, are the same. What happens, then, when the real value of cash balances together with the demand for these balances is such that the natural rate differs from the monetary? This situation is depicted in Figures 2a and 2b. The natural rate—the rate which balances the new-securities market—is r_n, which is lower than the monetary rate, r_m. Under these conditions, both markets cannot be in equilibrium simultaneously. Whenever a discrepancy exists between the monetary rate and the natural rate, there is a general agreement, I believe, that in the short run, the prevailing rate will be dominated by monetary conditions, regardless of the discrepancies which may arise between saving and investment at the monetary rate. This conclusion is based upon the fact that the stock of assets which governs the monetary rate is normally large relative to the flow of saving and investment which determines the demand for goods and services and hence the movement of prices. Consider, for example, an economy where the amount of saving represents approximately 10 percent of the national income per year. And suppose that the capital supply or the stock of capitalized wealth is four times the national income. This means that the market for existing securities will be roughly 40 times the size of the flow of saving and investment. Moreover, we can make the predominance of existing securities as large as we please by reducing the period of time upon which the tentative figures given above were based. Thus, if we consider saving and investment on a semiannual basis, these variables will be only half of what I have described, while the stock of assets, which has no time dimension, will be the same as before; and if we consider saving and investment on a monthly basis, we can further reduce the significance of the market for goods and services, or the new-securities market.

FIGURE 2a   FIGURE 2b

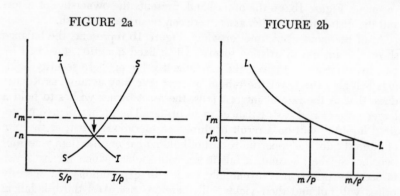

Paradoxically, although the monetary rate determines the actual rate of interest in a very short period of time, over a longer period the monetary rate eventually adapts itself to the natural rate through changes in the price level which alter the real value of cash balances. Consider again the situation represented by Figures 2a and 2b. With a nominal quantity of money equal to m and a price level of p, the real value of cash balances, m/p, is such that the monetary rate, r_m, is larger than the natural rate, r_n. Suppose, now, that the period of time is short enough so that the prevailing rate is governed by monetary conditions and therefore lies at r_m. At the higher rate, r_m, potential saving at full employment exceeds potential investment. This means that the demand created by a full employment level of output falls short of productive capacity. In other words, a deflationary gap exists in the demand for goods and services, and the general level of prices, costs, and income accordingly tends to fall. Assuming that the nominal quantity of money remains fixed, the deflation will increase the real value of cash balances or the purchasing power of money. Since the economy is now more liquid, the rate of interest which satisfies the asset holders with their portfolios will have to fall. In short, the real value of cash balances in Figure 2b increases from m/p to m/p' where p' represents the lower price index, and the monetary rate of interest accordingly falls.

This process of adaptation of the money rate to the natural rate must continue until r'_m is again equal to r_m, as indicated in Figure 2b. For as long as the monetary rate is above the natural rate, a deflationary situation will continue to exist and the deflation, by increasing the real value of cash balances, will push the monetary rate of interest downward.

A careful examination of the foregoing argument will show that, under conditions of full employment, Keynes' *General Theory of Employment, Interest and Money* does not differ substantially from his *Treatise on Money*. The pendulum has made a full swing and we are back where we started, despite liquidity preference. Keynes himself would no doubt have been the first to recognize this fact. In the preface to his *General Theory* he said:

> The relation between this book and my *Treatise on Money* which I published five years ago is probably clearer to myself than it will be to others; and what in my own mind is a natural evolution in a line of thought which I have been pursuing for several years, may sometimes strike the reader as a confusing change of view. . . . This book . . . has evolved into what is primarily a study of the forces which determine changes in the scale of output as a whole; and whilst it is found that money enters into the economic scheme in an essential and peculiar manner, technical monetary detail falls into the background.

The fact that the monetary rate of interest eventually adapts itself to the natural rate under conditions of full employment enables us to simplify the theory of international adjustment to a great extent, for we can express the conditions of international balance entirely in terms of the saving and investment schedules. Since I am concerned, here, with the monetary process of adjustment, however, I shall introduce the demand for money at a later stage of the process. It will be found, then, that liquidity preference determines not the final position of equilibrium after our economy has been disturbed but rather the amount of money flow required to create a condition where the natural rate and the monetary rate are equal under the new conditions. And the money flow, in turn, will determine the length of time during which the economy has a deficit or surplus in its balance of payments.

Apart from the condition of monetary equilibrium, there are three markets I wish to describe: the market for goods and services, the market for foreign exchange, and the market for new securities. One can demonstrate, however, that if any two of these markets is in balance, the third market must also be in balance. Thus we need not consider all markets simultaneously but may choose any two that we please. I shall begin with the market for goods and services.

The components which comprise the demand for a country's output may be classified into three parts as follows:

$$\text{Net output} = \text{Domestic consumption} + \text{Domestic investment} \\ + \text{Exports} - \text{Imports}.$$

The negative correction for imports is necessary because domestic consumption, domestic investment, and exports all contain items, such as imported raw materials, which do not represent a direct demand on the country's resources. Moreover, in defining domestic consumption and domestic investment I have considered the total demand of residents, whether purchased at home or abroad. In other words, the criterion of domesticity is the location of the spender, not the location of the goods upon which income was spent. To avoid double counting, a correction must therefore be made for imports of finished goods, including the raw material content of these imports, and for the imported raw materials contained in domestic expenditures and exports. But this correction obviously includes the total of all imports.

FIGURE 3

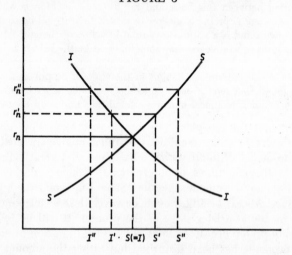

Transposing domestic consumption and domestic investment to the left-hand side of the above equation, and changing signs, we have

$$\text{Net output} - \text{Domestic consumption} - \text{Domestic investment}$$
$$= \text{Exports} - \text{Imports}.$$

Since net output minus domestic consumption is a measure of domestic saving, the foregoing equation may be written in the following form:

$$\text{Saving} - \text{Investment} = \text{Exports} - \text{Imports}.$$

Thus, if a country has an excess of saving over investment, at a given rate of interest, the resulting deflationary pressure can be eliminated, provided the country has an export surplus equal to its excess saving. Moreover, a market mechanism exists by which the country will eventually achieve the balance of trade needed to give it an equilibrium in the commodities market. Consider, for example, the schedules of savings and investment depicted by Figure 3.

Suppose that the quantity of money in real terms is such that the prevailing rate of interest is at r_n, where saving and investment are equal.

At this point, the commodities market will not balance unless prices are at a level, relative to prices in the rest of the world, where the value of the country's exports is equal to the value of its imports. Suppose, now, that the quantity of money is reduced, and the rate of interest in the short run rises from r_n to r'_n. At the old prices the value of exports continues to be equal to the value of imports. Since saving now exceeds investment at the higher rate of interest, the result of the contraction in money and the rise of interest rates is a deficient demand for goods and services. Inventories therefore rise and prices as well as costs tend to

FIGURE 4a   FIGURE 4b

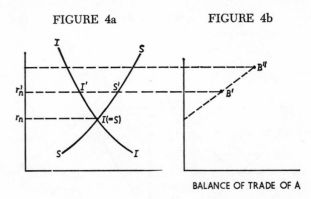

BALANCE OF TRADE OF A

fall. As prices fall, the country becomes a cheaper place in which to purchase and the balance of trade improves. This process must continue until the country has an export surplus equal to the amount of its excess saving. Thus, in Figure 3, if the rate of interest is r'_n the country's export surplus must be $S' - I'$. Continuing this line of reasoning, we may suppose that the rate of interest is further increased by a contraction of the money supply, until it reaches the level of r''_n. At this higher rate an even larger export surplus will be required to create a balance in the goods-and-services market, for the excess of real saving over real investment will be larger at r''_n than at r'_n. And again, market forces will create the necessary export surplus through a movement of prices.

I have now shown that corresponding to any given rate of interest there exists a unique balance of trade at which the demand for our country's goods and services is equal to its productive capacity at full employment. I shall call this relationship a schedule of the "natural balance of trade." The method of deriving this schedule is indicated in Figures 4a and 4b. For any given rate of interest, the equilibrium balance of trade is represented in Figure 4b as the balance which makes the difference between saving and investment equal to the difference between exports and imports. The schedule of the natural balance of trade will prove to be a valuable tool in describing the process of international adjustment. But before carrying the analysis further I must ask the reader's indulgence while the interdependence between the various markets in a trading country is examined.

I have already described the market for goods and services. The market for newly issued securities must now be considered. Even if the banking system supplies the required degree of liquidity through open market purchases, the excess demand for new domestic securities cannot be represented entirely as an excess of saving over investment. For, quite apart from the demand for liquidity, a portion of current saving will be devoted to the purchase of foreign rather than domestic securities. This assumes, of course, that interest rates are higher in the foreign country than abroad. At this point, in order to make ideas explicit, I shall present

FIGURE 5a   FIGURE 5b

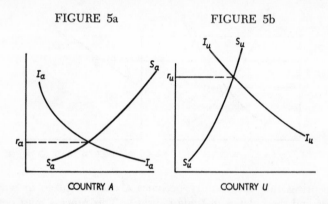

COUNTRY A   COUNTRY U

a diagrammatic representation of the saving and investment relations between the two countries mentioned earlier, namely an advanced country with a large amount of capital per worker, and an undeveloped country with a small amount of capital per worker. Let the advanced country and the undeveloped country be called "Country A" and "Country U" respectively. Schedules of saving and investment are given below for each of these countries in Figures 5a and 5b.

If both countries were isolated, the natural rate of interest would be r_a in Country A and r_u in Country U. A presumption thus exists that the rate of return on securities will be higher in the undeveloped country than in the advanced one.

Suppose, now, that we are describing the demand for and supply of new securities in the advanced country. Apart from liquidity considerations, the demand for new domestic securities will fall short of saving to the extent that a part of such saving is devoted to the purchase of U securities where the return is higher. Thus the net domestic demand for new securities in A will be saving *less* purchase of securities in U. A similar adjustment must of course be made for the fact that some investors in U will sell their securities in A and convert their A currency into U currency on the foreign exchange market. But in order to simplify the problem I shall assume that the only element in capital movements is the purchase of foreign securities by A savers, which represents a capital outflow. The condition of balance in newly issued A securities will then be

$$\text{Saving} - \text{Capital outflow} = \text{Investment,}$$

or

$$\text{Saving} - \text{Investment} = \text{Capital outflow.}$$

With this relationship in mind, the interrelations between our three markets may now be discussed. Specifically, I wish to show that if the market for goods and services and the market for new domestic securities are in equilibrium, the market for foreign exchange must also be in balance. I shall begin with a tabulation which represents, on the left side, the type of market, and on the right side the conditions of equilibrium for that market.

Type of Market	*Conditions of Equilibrium*	
Goods and services:	Saving — Investment = Exports — Imports.	(1)
New domestic securities:	Saving — Investment = Capital outflow.	(2)

From (1) and (2) the export surplus and the capital outflow are both equal to the excess of saving over investment. Since two quantities equal to the same thing (saving minus investment) must be equal to each other it follows that

$$\text{Exports} - \text{Imports} = \text{Capital outflow.} \qquad (3)$$

But this condition is the condition for balance in the country's foreign exchange market; the export surplus creates a supply of foreign exchange, while the capital outflow represents a demand. Thus a balance in the foreign exchange market is achieved when the former is equal to the latter. It follows that if both the new securities market and the market for goods and services are in balance, the third market, or the market for foreign exchange, must also be in equilibrium. This is a special application of Walras' well-known proposition that in a general equilibrium involving n markets, if $n - 1$ of these markets is balanced, the nth market must also balance. And it is a slightly generalized treatment of Professor Alexander's conception of "income absorption," which states that currency devaluation will not be effective in improving a country's balance of payments unless it is accompanied by measures to reduce the demand for goods and services. All such ideas are derived from the basic tautology that a business man's costs represent an income earner's revenue and are therefore closely linked to the notion of a circular flow of income.

Bearing in mind the interrelations among the various markets in an open economy, it is now possible to consider the conditions of international balance between two countries as well as the process by which such an adjustment is achieved. And, as before, I shall describe a situation of trade between an advanced country and an undeveloped one.

In depicting international trade between two countries, a minor complication arises which might as well be settled at once. In explaining the state of a country's balance of trade, the important consideration was the absolute level of interest rates which determines the saving-investment relation or the surplus available for export, assuming that prices are adjusted both at home and abroad so that the foreign demand absorbs the required surplus. But in considering the balance of payments as a whole the capital inflow or outflow must be taken into account as well as the balance of trade; the awkwardness of putting capital movements into the balance of payments arises from the fact that they do not depend upon absolute interest rates, as the balance of trade does, but upon the *difference* of interest rates between the two countries. Thus savers in

FIGURE 6a   FIGURE 6b   FIGURE 6c

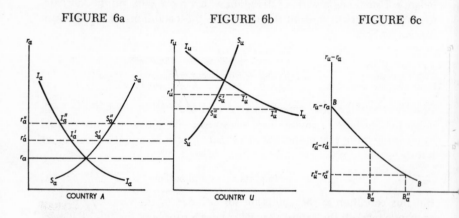

Country A purchase securities in U because the rate of return is greater in U than in A. To avoid this difficulty, I shall define the schedule of the natural balance of payments in such a way that it can be expressed in terms of differences in interest rates between the two countries. In doing so, a certain amount of information will be lost but this can easily be picked up at the end of the demonstration.

The basic ideas are presented in Figures 6a and 6b and 6c. Suppose we start with an interest rate of r_a in Country A, where saving is equal to investment. At this rate, internal balance in A's goods and services market requires that exports *equal* imports; for, as we have seen, the excess of saving over investment must be equal to the excess of exports over imports. But if Country A's balance of trade is zero, Country U's balance of trade must likewise be zero, for in our two-country economy the exports of one country are imports of another; and if U's balance of trade is zero her natural rate of interest must be r_u, to preserve internal balance in the goods and services market, for r_u is the rate where saving is equal to investment. Thus, for a given interest rate, r_a, in A, there exists another rate r_u, in U and a balance of trade between the two countries at which both trading countries will have a full employment demand for goods and services.

Continuing in this direction, we may suppose that the prevailing rate of interest in A is increased from r_a to r'_a. At r'_a, Country A's saving exceeds her investment and full-employment equilibrium in the goods and services market cannot exist until the resulting deflation increases that country's export surplus to the amount of her excess saving. Again, if A has an export surplus of $S'_a - I'_a$ in Figure 6a, U will have an import surplus of the same amount. But if full-employment equilibrium is to exist in U's market her import surplus must be offset by an excess of investment over saving exactly equal to the amount of her import surplus. Thus, for any given interest rate, r'_a in A there is another, and lower interest rate r'_u in U at which both countries have a state of full employment with an

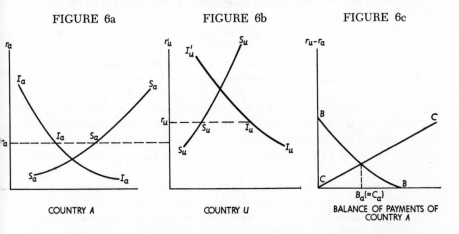

FIGURE 6a   FIGURE 6b   FIGURE 6c

COUNTRY A   COUNTRY U   BALANCE OF PAYMENTS OF
                                          COUNTRY A

export surplus in A equal to $S'_a - I'_a$. In general the higher the interest rate in A the lower will be the interest rate in U; "tight money" in the one country creates "easy money" in the other. Thus we have a pattern of interest rates in the two countries and a balance of trade between them which is consistent with full employment in both Country A and Country U. This relationship is presented in Figure 6c as the line BB. As before, I shall call the revised schedule BB, expressed in differentials, a schedule of the "natural balance of trade." Any point along BB involves an implicit price level between A and U; with given tastes, the price ratio required for full employment will be lower as the interest rate differentials are narrowed. Moreover, the ordinary operations of the market mechanism will establish the natural balance of trade required for full employment. Since BB is expressed as a function of interest rate differentials it is necessary to show how the differentials can be translated into absolute interest rates. In order to avoid confusion I shall repeat Figures 6a, 6b and 6c without the broken lines required to derive the BB schedule.

As far as Country A's balance of payments is concerned the conditions of equilibrium are represented in Figure 6c. Here we see that the advanced country has an export surplus of B_a, exactly offset by a capital out-

476   *Readings in International Economics*

flow, C_a, of the same amount. (The capital outflow does not entirely equalize interest rates because some interest rate differential is required to induce it.) The equality between a country's balance of trade and its capital outflow, as shown by Figure 6c is achieved when the interest rates differential is $r_u - r_a$. I propose to show how this difference in rates can be transformed into actual rates in the two countries. The key to such a transformation lies in the fact that at any point along the BB schedule the export surplus of A is equal to her excess of saving over investment. Thus, in Figures 6c and 6a the absolute interest rate r_a is found at a point where $B = S_a - I_a$. And likewise, for Country U the interest rate r_u is the rate at which the import surplus, $-B$, is the (negative) difference between saving and investment. In the notation of 6b and 6c, $-B = s_u - I_u$ or $B = I_u - S_u$.

To summarize the results of the Figures 6a, 6b and 6c we may say that international trade, combined with a capital outflow from A to U, has the effect of raising the natural rate in Country A and lowering that rate in U, compared with the situation where the two countries are isolated. At the same time, since A has an export surplus after trade, her price level must be somewhat lower than it would have been if capital movements did not exist. Conversely in Country U the interest rate will be reduced by the existence of trade and capital movements, while the price level will be increased in order to give U the required import surplus, $-B$.

Suppose, then, that we start from the position of equilibrium represented by Figures 6a, 6b and 6c. And suppose, further that this equilibrium is disturbed by some event which gives the advanced country a potential deficit in its balance of payments. What is the process by which this deficit will eventually be eliminated and how does the new equilibrium in the balance of payments compare with the old? And finally, what part does the monetary system—i.e., the movement in the stock of real cash balances—play in the process of adjustment? A complete answer to these questions must take account of two elements, interest rates and the balance of capital movements, and prices and the balance of trade. Thus, the deficit country, if it is pledged to buy and sell foreign currencies at fixed rates, will find that the demand exceeds supply so that its foreign currency reserves decline, together with a corresponding decline in the nominal quantity of money. And of course the surplus country will find its quantity of money increasing because the supply of foreign exchange exceeds the demand. Thus the monetary rate of interest, which governs the actual rate in the short run, will tend to rise in the deficit country and to fall in the surplus. The differences between interest rates will therefore be narrowed and any capital outflow which may have taken place will be discouraged. At the same time, the temporary rise in interest rates in the deficit country will have a deflationary effect on demand and prices will fall with the result that the balance of trade will improve; and conversely in the surplus country. The deficit will accordingly be altered partly by a movement of interest rates with a corresponding backflow of capital and partly by a change in prices which will improve the balance of trade in the deficit country. The question that needs to be explored is whether most of the adjustment will take the form of interest rate changes and a backflow of capital or whether changes in prices and an improvement in the deficit country's balance of trade will be the dominant factor in creating an even balance of payments. One might suppose that banking policy would have a considerable influence upon the nature of this adjustment. But it can be shown that if the banks wish to maintain equilibrium both externally and internally they have no choice as to how a given disturbance will ultimately affect their position. We have seen that in an isolated economy the banking system can affect neither the natural rate of interest nor the real value of cash balances; the same proposition holds true in an open economy.

Before exploring this avenue further, however, I wish to emphasize that the nature of the adjustment process is determined largely by the type of initial disturbance. For some types of disturbance the balance of trade will do most if not all of the adjustment while for others interest and capital flows will be more significant. I propose to consider two types of disturbances. The first of these is a change of tastes of such a nature that with the given price structure, income earners in A prefer to buy a larger amount of U goods and a smaller amount of their own goods; in other words the disturbance consists of a shift in demand from A goods to U goods. The second is an increased awareness of A citizens of the advantages of buying securities in U, or an increase in the amount of A's capital outflow corresponding to a given difference in interest rates between U and A.

The simpler of these disturbances is a change of tastes and this is the one with which I shall begin. The initial effect of the increased desire of A income earners to purchase goods from U will be to increase the amount of A's imports. If we start from a position where A's export surplus is just equal to her capital outflow, the initial effect of the shift in demand will be to reduce A's export surplus to a point where it is less than her given capital outflow. Country A, then, has a deficit in her balance of payments, and money flows from A to U. As a result of the changes in the quantity of money, the monetary rate, which governs the natural rate, tends to rise in A and to fall in U. This discourages the capital outflow from A to U and also creates a deflationary gap in A and an inflationary gap in U. The process continues until the potential deficit is ultimately eliminated. Note, however, that the type of disturbance I am here considering does not affect either the saving and investment schedules in A or U or the capital outflow from A to U. This means that, in the new position of equilibrium the schedule of the natural balance of payments,

BB, as well as the schedule of capital outflows, *CC,* will remain unchanged. As a consequence the amount of capital outflow, the rates of interest, and the balance of trade are the same as before. In other words, for the type of disturbance now being considered—i.e., an increase in the desire of income earners in A to buy goods from U—the process of adjustment takes place entirely through a change in money and prices, and an adaptation of A's balance of trade to a fixed capital movement. In the final equilibrium, interest rates remain in their original positions. The rise of the interest rate in A is only temporary; it is the means by which the deflation needed to improve the balance of trade is brought about. Like-

FIGURE 7

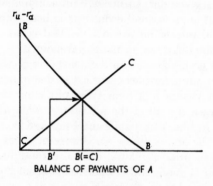

BALANCE OF PAYMENTS OF A

wise, the temporary reduction in Country U's interest rate is the method of achieving a rise in prices there.

The process of adjustment is presented in Figure 7. Initially, Country A's balance of payments is in equilibrium; an export surplus of B is offset by a capital outflow of the same amount. When her demand for imports from U rises the value of imports also rises. As a result, the export surplus of Country A falls (from B to b' in Figure 7). The advanced country now has a deficit in her balance of payments; the supply of foreign exchange arising from her export surplus is no longer large enough to offset the capital outflow. As a result both the quantity of money and foreign reserves decline in A and the monetary interest rate, which governs the natural rate in the short run, tends to rise. The rise in the interest rate, by increasing the excess of saving over investment, creates a deflationary gap which leads to a fall in prices and costs. As a consequence of the fall in prices, Country A becomes a cheap place in which to buy and her export surplus expands. From Figure 7 we see that the shift in demand leaves the *BB* schedule unchanged because it does not affect the saving and investment schedules in either country. Thus the difference in interest rates, $r_u - r_a$, the balance of trade, B, and the absolute rates, r_u and r_a, remain where they were before the change in demand created a deficit.

In this case Country A's deficit has obviously been eliminated, through changes in relative prices, by an adaptation in the balance of trade to a given level of capital outflows.

In the later stages of the adjustment, when the economic system begins to adapt itself to the deficit, something also happens to the monetary rate of interest. We have seen, before, that in the long run the monetary rate adapts itself to the natural rate. And since the natural rate is unchanged, as shown in Figure 7, the monetary rate must likewise remain unchanged. Given the demand for real cash balances, this means that the change in the price level needed to give A an export surplus of B (again in Figure 7) must be proportionate to the loss of nominal balances attributable to the deficit. If prices fall by 15 percent, the nominal quantity of money must fall by the same amount. And conversely in Country U, where lower interest rates create an inflationary situation, while a surplus in the balance of payments increases the nominal quantity of money, the monetary rate must again adapt itself to the unaltered natural rate. And, given the demand for real cash balances, this means that the relative increase of prices must be proportionate to the relative increases in the nominal quantity of money. For the type of disturbance I have been considering, a reasonably good case could thus be made out for the classical, quantity theory of money. In spite of saving and investment, liquidity preference, and all the rest, the system seems to behave rather like the traditional theory in which the balance of trade adjusted itself to fluctuations in capital movements through movements in the quantity of money and corresponding changes in prices.

The example is misleading, however, for a change in the demand for imports is only one of the possible disturbances which may create a deficit or surplus in a country's balance of payments; and for other disturbances, the quantity theory does not fare so well.

Consider, for example, the case where Country A's deficit is the result of an increase of capital outflows from A to U. If we start, again, from a position of international balance where Country A's export surplus is offset by capital outflows, the increase in capital outflow will create a situation where A has a deficit in her balance of payments; the demand by A for U currency in order to purchase securities in that country will now exceed the supply of such currency arising from an export surplus. Money will flow from the deficit country, A, to the surplus country, U. The stock of money will accordingly fall in A and rise in U. As a result, the monetary rate which governs the natural rate in the short run will rise in A and fall in U. As a consequence of these changes in interest rates, Country A, the deficit country, will have a deflationary gap while U will experience inflationary pressures. Prices will therefore fall in A and rise in U, and the export surplus of A will increase. Thus far, the mechanism of adjustment to A's deficit seems quite like the first case where the disturbing element was an increased demand in A for the imports of U.

In the early stages, at least, the deficit is reduced partly by a narrowing of interest rates and a backflow of capital, partly by a fall of prices in A relative to prices in U and an increase in A's export surplus. When a final adjustment has been made, however, we can see from Figure 8 that, after the system has adapted itself to the increase in capital outflows, the rate of interest, rather than being a temporary force to get the required changes in prices in A and U, is a permanent part of the new adaptation. Interest rates remain higher in A even after the balance of payments has reached a new equilibrium and the flow of money has ceased. The higher interest

FIGURE 8

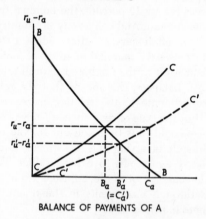

BALANCE OF PAYMENTS OF A

rates are attributable to the fact that under the new conditions country A's balance of trade has increased from B to B'. In order to preserve balance in the internal demand for goods and services, A must have an increase in her excess of saving over investment and this will occur automatically as a result of the operations of the market.

In eliminating the deficit, the importance of changes in interest rates and capital movements, compared with changes in prices and the balance of trade, obviously depends upon the slope of the capital outflow schedule CC, relative to the slope of the BB schedule. In general, interest rates and capital movements will play a significant role if the CC schedule is relatively flat while the BB schedule is steep. And conversely prices and the balance of trade will be the dominant influence if the BB schedule is flat while the CC schedule is steep. In Figure 9a a situation is shown in which most of the adjustment takes place through interest rates and movements of capital, with the balance of trade playing a minor role. In Figure 9b, on the other hand, the movement of the balance of trade adapts itself to a relatively rigid level of capital movements. But apart from these differences the most important condition to notice is that an increase of capital outflows entails a permanent alteration of interest rates. In A, the interest

FIGURE 9a   FIGURE 9b

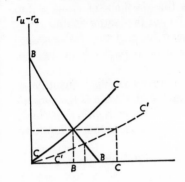

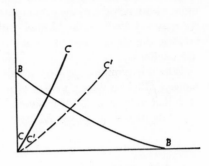

rate rises; and, unlike the previous case it remains higher even after a balance has been achieved. Likewise in Country U the interest rate falls and continues to be somewhat lower even after the balance of payments between the two countries is again in equilibrium.

I turn now from the real aspects of the problem to a discussion of the monetary process of adjustment. We have seen that when the initial disturbance is an increased demand in A for the imports of U, the monetary adjustment is quite like the quantity theory of money. The quantity of money and the level of prices both fall in the deficit Country A and rise in U. And the changes in the quantity of money are proportional to the price movements in both countries. Apart from movements in the terms of trade, the real value of cash balances thus remains unchanged in both countries.

When the initial disturbance is an increase of capital outflows from A to U, this conclusion no longer holds true. For the movement of capital outflows has altered the rate of interest in both countries and the change in interest rates affects the demand for real cash balances. In Country A, for example, the rate of interest rises and the demand for real cash balances therefore falls. This means that if adjustment of the balance of payments in A calls for a 15 percent reduction in prices the monetary rate will not be in line with the natural rate unless the nominal quantity of money has been reduced, through A's deficit, by something more than 15 percent. (The reduction in nominal balances might be 25 percent for example.) Likewise, in Country U the rate of interest falls and this means that the monetary rate will not be in line with the new natural rate unless the real value of cash balances has risen. In short, the nominal quantity of money must rise more than the level of prices has risen. If equilibrium in the balance of payments calls for a 15 percent rise in U's prices, for example, the nominal quantity of money must rise by more than 15 percent.

Thus, the introduction of liquidity preference creates a certain inertia in the system. Prices do not react as readily to movements in the nominal quantity of money as they would in the classical system. Moreover, the degree of inertia is higher, the higher is the elasticity of demand for money with respect to the rate of interest. To put the matter another way, we may say that, as the elasticity of demand for real cash balances increases, the significance of money movements as a regulator of the system declines.

What determines the rise or fall in a country's nominal quantity of money? Obviously for a system of pegged exchange rates it is the surplus or deficit in its balance of trade *and the length of time required to eliminate this surplus or deficit.* In view of this fact it is clear that as liquidity

FIGURE 10a   FIGURE 10b

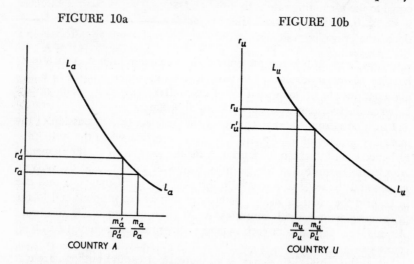

COUNTRY A   COUNTRY U

preference becomes more elastic in both countries the time interval of adjustment will become longer for the entire system. The situation is described in Figures 10a and 10b for Countries A and U respectively.

When we were considering the relations between the monetary rate and the natural rate in an isolated state, we started with the supposition that the banking system stabilized the nominal quantity of money; in this system, fluctuations in the real value of cash balances were a result of movements in the level of prices. In an open economy, however, there are two influences which alter the real value of cash balances. In Country A, for example, the deficit reduces the nominal quantity of money, and the reduction in nominal balances must continue as long as the deficit exists. At the same time, the fall in prices induced by a rise of interest rates increases the real value of the lower nominal balances. If the real value of cash balances is to be reduced in A, in order to adapt the monetary rate to the higher natural rate, it is obvious that the deficit-effect on nominal balances must overshadow the price-effect on real balances. Conversely, in Country U, the surplus in that country's balance of payments increases the nominal quantity of money while the inflation arising from the fall of interest rates reduces the real value of this increased stock of money. And again, if the real value of cash balances is to rise, as it must to adjust the demand for real cash balances to the lower interest rate, the rise in nominal balances attributable to the surplus must be larger, relatively, than the fall in real value attributable to the inflation.

Referring again to Figure 10b, the absolute rates of interest in Country U at the original position of equilibrium, is r_u. The price level is p_u—determined by income earners' tastes and the size of the equilibrium balance of trade. The quantity of money which makes the monetary rate equal to the prevailing rate is thus m_u, and the real value of cash balances is m_u/p_u. In the new position, after the increase of capital outflows has reduced the prevailing rate of interest to r'_u the real value of cash balances has increased to m'_u/p'_u. Thus the money inflow exceeds the rise of prices. In Country A, on the other hand, the real value of cash balances falls from m_a/p_a to m'_a/p'_a. And again this means that the reduction of nominal balances is greater than the reduction of prices. At first glance one might suppose that the system, including the demand for money, is overdetermined. For p'_u and p'_a are governed by the condition that an equilibrium balance of payments be achieved. And if the banking system is one in which no money is created except through deficits and surpluses in the balance of payments, the total quantity of money is restricted to the condition that $m'_a + m'_u = M$, where M represents the total quantity of nominal balances in the two-economy system. Thus it might seem that since m'_a and m'_u are restricted by bank policies, while p'_a and p'_u are governed by conditions of equilibrium in the balance of payments, it might be impossible to find an m'_a/p'_a for A and an m'_u/p'_u for U, such that the monetary rate of interest would be in line with the natural rate for both countries.

In reality however, the possibility of having an overdetermined system does not arise. What matters for the balance of trade is not the separate absolute prices p'_a and p'_u but the relative price ratio p'_a/p'_u. And the absolute levels at which the two prices settle will be determined by the size of M in the equation $m'_a + m'_u = M$. Nevertheless, an interesting question arises when the elasticity of liquidity preference differs as between the two countries. In view of the fact that the position of equilibrium ultimately depends upon relative prices, or the terms of trade, rather than absolute prices, the question naturally arises as to whether most of the adjustment will take place in one country or the other.

One can demonstrate that, other things being equal, most of the price adjustment will fall upon the country which has the smaller elasticity of demand for real cash balances. Consider again, for example, the situation where the disturbance is an increase in capital outflows. And suppose, as in Figures 10a and 10b above, that the natural rate of interest rises from r_a to r'_a in Country A and falls from r_u to r'_u in Country U. Suppose, further, that the demand for real cash balances is less elastic in U than in A. This situation is presented in Figures 11a and 11b.

As a result of the capital outflow from A to U, the prevailing rate of interest rises in A and falls in U. In A the rise is from r_a to r'_a in Figure 11a; in U the fall is from r_u to r'_u in Figure 11b. Because U's demand for real cash balances has a small elasticity with respect to the interest rate, a relatively small increase in cash balances is sufficient to align the monetary rate with the prevailing rate. In Figure 11b, the increase is from m_u/p_u to m'_u/p'_u. This means that the rise in nominal cash balances attributable

FIGURE 11a   FIGURE 11b

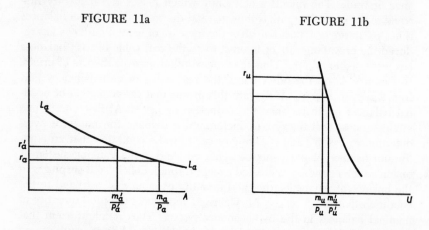

to the surplus is only slightly larger than the rise in the price level attributable to the interest rate. On the other hand, in Figure 11a the elasticity of A's liquidity preference schedule is high and the reduction in real cash balances required to equalize the monetary rate with the prevailing higher rate r'_a is therefore significant. Now the total decline in the nominal stock of money in A $(m_a - m'_a)$ must be exactly the same as the total rise in the nominal stock in U $(m_u - m'_u)$. Since the change in real balances in U $(r_u/p_u - r'_u/p'_u)$ is considerably smaller than the decline in A's real balances $(r_a/p_a - r'_a/p'_a)$ a presumption exists that the change in relative prices required to improve A's balance of trade will consist largely of a rise in prices in U and a comparatively small decrease of prices in A. The degree of inertia of the adjustment process may thus be unevenly divided between the two countries because of differences in their elasticity of demand for liquidity. The fact that A has a relatively elastic demand for real cash balances enables her to put most of the adjustment process on the shoulders of U.

An opposite situation is shown in Figures 12a and 12b. Here the elasticity of demand for liquidity is low in A and high in U. Without going into details concerning the role of money in the process of adjustment I believe it should be obvious from the earlier discussion that the high

FIGURE 12a

FIGURE 12b

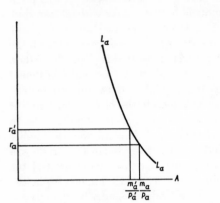

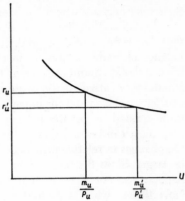

elasticity of liquidity preference in U and the low elasticity in A means that the price adjustments will take place largely through A; i.e., prices will fall to a considerable extent in A and rise only slightly in U.

The time has come for a summing up of the results of this paper. In a few words, what is the significance of introducing liquidity preference into the process of international adjustment? I believe that I have demonstrated a number of things. In the first place, when a final balance has been achieved the real variables of the system—terms of trade, interest rates, etc.—are unaffected by the demand for money. It remains true that a country which has a deficit in its balance of payments will eliminate this deficit partly by a rise of interest rates, relative to interest rates in the the rest of the world, which will lead to a capital backflow, and partly by an outflow of money which will lead to a deflation at home, inflation abroad, and an improvement in the country's balance of trade. But all this is common knowledge, at least since Keynes' *Treatise on Money*. What changes have been made, then, by introducing liquidity preference?

In the first place, I have shown that, by introducing liquidity preference, a degree of inertia is added to the equilibrating process. A larger flow of money is required to achieve a new balance; moreover, this degree of inertia is larger the more elastic is the liquidity preference. And if we consider differences in elasticity of demand for real balances, the country with the larger elasticity is able to force a larger part of the necessary price movement onto the country with the relatively small elasticity of demand for money. The way in which relative prices are transformed into absolute prices thus depends in an important way upon the nature of the demand for money.

With respect to the real variables I have shown that whether most of a deficit is eliminated through prices and the balance of trade or whether it is eliminated through interest rates and the balance of capital movements does not depend upon the external conditions of the demand for imports but upon the internal conditions of saving and investment. At this point the reader may ask why it has been possible to go so far without introducing the demand for imports at all. In answer to this question I would say that the elasticity of demand does not determine the degree to which the balance of trade expands to meet a given deficit; this depends, rather, upon internal conditions such as the slopes of the saving and investment schedules, relative to the slope of the capital outflow formation. The elasticities of demand for imports govern merely the changes in terms of trade needed to get the balance of trade required for equilibrium. In general, it can be said that as the elasticities of demand become smaller the changes in relative prices needed to get a given balance of trade will be larger. Since the terms of trade were implicit throughout most of the paper, it was not necessary to introduce the demand for imports explicitly. Nevertheless, with regard to these terms of trade the paper is by no means complete. A change in the terms of trade, for example, can alter the real value of a given capital outflow to the borrowing country without altering its value to the lending country. Likewise, a change in the terms of trade can alter the real value of cash balances without changing domestic prices. I cannot say with certainty how much the general conclusions would be modified if some of these terms-of-trade effects were taken into account, but I suspect the changes would not be of great importance. In any event a few constructive criticisms along these lines should go far toward deciding whether Keynes' ideas have made a substantial contribution to the concept of monetary adjustment.

29. Capital Mobility and Stabilization

Policy under Fixed and

Flexible Exchange Rates*

By *ROBERT A. MUNDELL*†

THE WORLD IS STILL a closed economy, but its regions and countries are becoming increasingly open. The trend, which has been manifested in both freer movement of goods and increased mobility of capital, has been stimulated by the dismantling of trade and exchange controls in Europe, the gradual erosion of the real burden of tariff protection, and the stability, unparalleled since 1914, of the exchange rates. The international economic climate has changed in the direction of financial integration[1] and this has important implications for economic policy.

My paper concerns the theoretical and practical implications of the increased mobility of capital. In order to present my conclusions in the simplest possible way, and to bring the implications for policy into sharpest relief, I assume the extreme degree of mobility that prevails when a country cannot maintain an interest rate different from the general level prevailing abroad. This assumption will overstate the case but it has the

* This paper was presented at the annual meeting of the Canadian Political Science Association in Quebec on June 6, 1963. It was written while the author was a member of the staff of the International Monetary Fund, but it does not, of course, necessarily reflect the Fund's official position. [*Canadian Journal of Economics and Political Science*, Vol. XXIX, No. 4 (November, 1963), pp. 475–85. For a generalization of the results of this paper in the context of a world model see R. A. Mundell, "Capital Mobility and Size: Reply," *Canadian Journal of Economics and Political Science*, Vol. XXX, No. 3 (August, 1964), pp. 421–31, especially 424–31.]

† The University of Chicago.

[1] See James C. Ingram, "A Proposal for Financial Integration in the Atlantic Community," Joint Economic Committee print, Nov., 1962, for a valuable analysis of financial integration under fixed exchange rates; Harry G. Johnson, "Equilibrium under Fixed Exchange Rates," *American Economic Review*, Vol. LIII (May, 1963), pp. 112–19, for a discussion of some of the advantages of closing the exchange rate margins; C. P. Kindleberger, "European Economic Integration and the Development of a Single Financial Center for Long-Term Capital," *Weltwirtschaftliches Archiv*, Band 90, 1963, Heft 2, pp. 189–210, for a discussion of competition among financial centres as integration proceeds; and A. N. McLeod, "Credit Expansion in an Open Economy," *Economic Journal*, Vol. LXII (Sept., 1962), pp. 611–40, for a theoretical discussion of related topics.

merit of posing a stereotype towards which international financial relations seem to be heading. At the same time it might be argued that the assumption is not far from the truth in those financial centers, of which Zurich, Amsterdam, and Brussels may be taken as examples, where the authorities already recognize their lessening ability to dominate money market conditions and insulate them from foreign influences. It should also have a high degree of relevance to a country like Canada whose financial markets are dominated to a great degree by the vast New York market.

I. METHOD OF ANALYSIS

The assumption of perfect capital mobility can be taken to mean that all securities in the system are perfect substitutes. Since different currencies are involved this implies that existing exchange rates are expected to persist indefinitely (even when the exchange rate is not pegged) and that spot and forward exchange rates are identical. All the complications associated with speculation, the forward market, and exchange rate margins are thereby assumed not to exist.

In order to focus attention on policies affecting the level of employment, I assume unemployed resources, constant returns to scale, and fixed money wage rates; this means that the supply of domestic output is elastic and its price level constant. I further assume that saving and taxes

TABLE 1

Sector \ Market	Goods		Securities		Money		International Reserves	
Government ..	$T - G$	+	Government borrowing	+	Government dishoarding	+	*1	= 0
	+		+		+		+	+
Private	$S - I$	+	Private borrowing	+	Private dishoarding	+	*2	= 0
	+		+		+		+	+
Foreign	$M - X$	+	Capital outflow	+	*3	+	Increase in reserves	= 0
	+		+		+		+	+
Banking	*4	+	Open market sales	+	Monetary expansion	+	Foreign exchange sales	= 0
	‖	+	‖	+	‖	+	‖	‖
	0		0		0		0	= 0

* Negligible or ignored items: (1) would refer to Treasury holdings of foreign exchange; (2) to the non-bank public's holdings of foreign exchange; (3) to foreigners' holdings of domestic money (domestic currency is not a "key" currency); and (4) to the net contribution of the banking system to goods account. In the analysis government dishoarding will also be assumed zero.

Note that if the entries are defined as *ex ante* or *planned* magnitudes both the horizontal and vertical sums to zero are *equilibrium conditions*, but if they are defined as *ex post* or *realized* magnitudes the sums to zero are *identities*. Note also that the rows could be disaggregated, making special distinctions between households and firms, commercial and central banks, etc., down to each individual spending unit, just as the columns could be multiplied to distinguish between different classes of goods, money, and securities.

rise with income, that the balance of trade depends only on income and the exchange rate, that investment depends on the rate of interest, and that the demand for money depends only on income and the rate of interest. My last assumption is that the country under consideration is too small to influence foreign incomes or the world level of interest rates.

Monetary policy will be assumed to take the form of open market purchases of securities, and *fiscal policy* the form of an increase in government spending (on home goods) financed by an increase in the public debt. Floating exchange rates result when the monetary authorities do not intervene in the exchange market, and fixed exchange rates when they intervene to buy and sell international reserves at a fixed price.

It will be helpful, in the following discussion, to bear in mind the distinction between conditions of *sectoral* and *market* equilibria (illustrated in the table). There is a set of sectoral restraints (described by the rows in the table) which show how expenditure in each sector of the open economy is financed: a budget deficit $(G - T)$ in the *government* sector is financed by an increase in the public debt or a reduction in government cash balances (dishoarding); an excess of investment over saving $(I - S)$ in the *private* sector is financed by net private borrowing or a reduction in privately-held money balances; a trade balance deficit $(M - X)$ in the *foreign* sector[2] is financed by capital imports or a reduction in international reserves; and, finally, an excess of purchases over sales of domestic assets of the banking sector is financed by an increase in the monetary liabilities of the banking system (the money supply) or by a reduction in foreign exchange reserves. For simplicity of exposition, I shall assume that there is, initially, no lending between the sectors.

There is also a set of market restraints (described by columns in the table) which refer to the condition that demand and supply of each object of exchange be equal. The *goods and services* market is in equilibrium when the difference between investment and saving is equal to the sum of the budget surplus and the trade balance deficit. The *capital* market is in equilibrium when foreigners and domestic banks are willing to accumulate the increase in net debt of the government and the public. The *foreign exchange* market is in equilibrium when the actual increase in reserves is equal to the rate (which may be positive or negative) at which the central bank wants to buy reserves.[3] And the *money* market is in equilibrium when the community is willing to accumulate the increase in the money supply offered by the banking system. I shall also assume that, initially, each market is in equilibrium.

---

[2] The foreign sector refers to all the transactions of the country as a whole with respect to the outside world.

[3] For certain purposes it would be more elegant to define a separate market for foreign goods as distinct from domestic goods, but the present approach is satisfactory for the purpose on hand.

II. POLICIES UNDER FLEXIBLE EXCHANGE RATES

Under flexible exchange rates the central bank does not intervene to fix a given exchange rate, although this need not preclude autonomous purchases and sales of foreign exchange.

Monetary Policy.   Consider the effect of an open market purchase of domestic securities in the context of a flexible exchange rate system. This results in an increase in bank reserves, a multiple expansion of money and credit, and downward pressure on the rate of interest. But the interest rate is prevented from falling by an outflow of capital, which causes a deficit in the balance of payments, and a depreciation of the exchange rate. In turn, the exchange rate depreciation (normally) improves the balance of trade and stimulates, by the multiplier process, income and employment. A new equilibrium is established when income has risen sufficiently to induce the domestic community to hold the increased stock of money created by the banking system. Since interest rates are unaltered this means that income must rise in proportion to the increase in the money supply, the factor of proportionality being the given ratio of income and money (income velocity).

In the new equilibrium private saving and taxes will have increased as a consequence of the increase in income, and this implies both net private lending and retirement of government debt. Equilibrium in the capital market then requires equality between the sum of net private lending plus debt retirement, and the rate of capital exports, which in conjunction with the requirement of balance of payments equilibrium, implies a balance of trade surplus. Monetary policy therefore has a strong effect on the level of income and employment, not because it alters the rate of interest, but because it induces a capital outflow, depreciates the exchange rate, and causes an export surplus.[4]

It will now be shown that central bank operations in the foreign exchange market ("open market operations" in foreign exchange) can be considered an alternative form of monetary policy. Suppose the central bank buys foreign reserves (gold or foreign currency) with domestic money. This increases bank reserves, causing a multiple expansion of the money supply. The monetary expansion puts downward pressure on the interest rate and induces a capital outflow, further depreciating the exchange rate and creating an export surplus, which in turn increases, through the multiplier effect, income and employment. Eventually, when income has increased sufficiently to induce the community to hold the increased stock of money, the income-generating process ceases and all sectors are again in equilibrium, with the increased saving and taxes financing the capital outflow. This conclusion is virtually the same as the

---

[4] Richard E. Caves arrives at essentially the same result in his paper, "Flexible Exchange Rates," *American Economic Review*, Vol. LIII (May, 1963), pp. 120–29.

conclusion earlier reached regarding monetary policy, with the single important difference that *foreign* assets of the banks are increased in the case of foreign exchange policy while *domestic* assets are increased in the case of monetary policy. Foreign exchange policy, like monetary policy, becomes a forceful tool of stabilization policy under flexible exchange rates.

Fiscal Policy. Assume an increase in government spending financed by government borrowing. The increased spending creates an excess demand for goods and tends to raise income. But this would increase the demand for money, raise interest rates, attract a capital inflow, and appreciate the exchange rate, which in turn would have a depressing effect on income. In fact, therefore, the negative effect on income of exchange rate appreciation has to offset exactly the positive multiplier effect on income of the original increase in government spending. Income cannot change unless the money supply or interest rates change, and since the former is constant in the absence of central bank action and the latter is fixed by the world level of interest rates, income remains fixed. Since income is constant, saving and taxes are unchanged, which means, because of the condition that the goods market be in equilibrium, that the change in government spending is equal to the import surplus. In turn, the flexible exchange rate implies balance of payments equilibrium and therefore a capital inflow equal to the import surplus. Thus, both capital and goods market equilibria are assured by equality between the rate of increase in the public debt and the rate of capital imports, and between the budget deficit and the import surplus. Fiscal policy thus completely loses its force as a domestic stabilizer when the exchange rate is allowed to fluctuate and the money supply is held constant. Just as monetary policy derives its importance as a domestic stabilizer from its influence on capital flows and the exchange rate, so fiscal policy is frustrated in its effects by these same considerations.

III. POLICIES UNDER FIXED EXCHANGE RATES

Under fixed exchange rates the central bank intervenes in the exchange market by buying and selling reserves at the exchange parity; as already noted the exchange margins are assumed to be zero.

Monetary Policy. A central bank purchase of securities creates excess reserves and puts downward pressure on the interest rate. But a fall in the interest rate is prevented by a capital outflow, and this worsens the balance of payments. To prevent the exchange rate from falling the central bank intervenes in the market, selling foreign exchange and buying domestic money. The process continues until the accumulated foreign exchange deficit is equal to the open market purchase and the money supply is restored to its original level.

This shows that monetary policy under fixed exchange rates has no sustainable effect on the level of income. The increase in the money supply arising from open market purchases is returned to the central bank through its exchange stabilization operations. What the central bank has in fact done is to purchase securities initially for money, and then buy money with foreign exchange, the monetary effects of the combined operations cancelling. The only final effect of the open market purchase is an equivalent fall in foreign exchange reserves: the central bank has simply traded domestic assets for foreign assets.

Fiscal Policy.   Assume an increase in government spending superimposed on the foreign exchange policy of pegging the exchange rate. The increased spending has a multiplier effect upon income, increasing saving, taxes, and imports. Taxes increase by less than the increase in government spending so the government supplies securities at a rate equal to the budget deficit, whereas the private sector absorbs securities at a rate equal to the increase in saving.

After the new equilibrium is established both the goods and capital markets must be in balance. In the goods market the budget deficit has as its counterpart the sum of the excess of private saving over investment and the balance of trade deficit, which implies that the induced balance of trade deficit is less than the budget deficit. In the capital market the private and foreign sectors must be willing to accumulate the new flow of government issues. But since the excess private saving is equal to the flow of private lending, and since the budget deficit equals the flow of new government issues, capital market equilibrium requires that the import deficit be exactly balanced by a capital inflow, so that there is balance of payments equilibrium after all adjustments have taken place.

There will nevertheless be a change in foreign exchange reserves. Before the flow equilibrium is established the demand for money will increase, at a constant interest rate, in proportion to the increase in income. To acquire the needed liquidity the private sector sells securities and this puts upward pressure on the interest rate, and attracts foreign capital. This improves the balance of payments temporarily, forcing the central bank to intervene by buying foreign reserves and increasing the money supply. The money supply is therefore increased directly through the back door of exchange rate policy. Foreign exchange reserves accumulate by the full amount of the increased cash reserves needed by the banking system to supply the increased money demanded by the public as a consequence of the increase in income.

IV. OTHER POLICY COMBINATIONS

Other cases deserve attention in view of their prominence in policy discussions. In the following cases it is assumed that exchange rates are fixed.

Central Bank Financing of Fiscal Deficits.   An important special case of combined operations of monetary, fiscal, and exchange policies is central bank financing of budget deficits under fixed exchange rates. As before, the increase in government spending yields a multiplier effect on income. In the new equilibrium there is a budget deficit, an excess of saving over investment, and a balance of trade deficit. The government issues securities at a rate equal to the budget deficit and these are (by assumption) taken up by the central bank. Capital market equilibrium therefore requires that the net flow demand for securities on the part of the private sector be equal to the net capital outflow.

It is easy to see that in the new equilibrium the balance of payments deficit and the consequent rate at which reserves are falling is exactly equal to the budget deficit and to the rate at which the central bank is buying government securities. Since the capital outflow is equal to the excess of saving over investment, and the loss of reserves is equal to the balance of payments deficit, which is the sum of the trade deficit and the capital outflow, reserves fall at a rate equal to the sum of the import deficit and the excess of saving over investment. Then since this sum equals the budget deficit, by the condition of equilibrium in the goods market, it follows that reserves fall at a rate equal to the budget deficit. The budget deficit is entirely at the expense of reserves.

There is, however, in this instance too an initial stock adjustment process. As income increases the demand for money grows, the private sector dispenses with stocks of securities, causing a capital inflow and an increase in reserves. This increase in reserves is a once-for-all inflow equal to the increase in cash reserves necessary for the banks to satisfy the increased demand for money. The rate of fall in reserves takes place, therefore, from a higher initial level.

The Special Case of Sterilization Operations. Sterilization (or neutralization) policy is a specific combination of monetary and exchange policy. When the central bank buys or sells foreign exchange the money supply increases or decreases, and the purpose of sterilization policy is to offset this effect. The mechanism is for the central bank to sell securities at the same rate that it is buying foreign exchange, and to buy securities at the same rate that it is selling foreign exchange. In reality, therefore, neutralization policy involves an exchange of foreign reserves and bonds. The exchange rate is stabilized by buying and selling reserves in exchange for securities.

Suppose the government increases spending during a time when neutralization policy is being followed. The increase in spending would normally have a multiplier effect on income. But this would increase the demand for money and put upward pressure on interest rates as the private sector dispenses with holdings of securities; this would cause a capital inflow and induce a balance of payments surplus. But now the authorities, in their rate-pegging operation, buy foreign exchange and simultaneously sell securities, thus putting added pressure on interest rates and accelerating the inflow of capital without satisfying the increased demand for money. The system has now become inconsistent, for goods market equilibrium requires an increase in income, but an increase in income can only take place if either the money supply expands or interest rates rise. The capital inflow prevents interest rates from rising and the neutralization policy inhibits the money supply from expanding. Something has to give, and it must either be the money supply or the exchange rate. If the central bank sells securities at the same rate as it is buying reserves, it cannot buy reserves at a rate fast enough to keep the exchange rate from appreciating. And if the central bank buys reserves at a rate fast enough to stabilize the exchange rate, it cannot sell securities fast enough to keep the money supply constant. Either the exchange rate appreciates or money income rises.

In a similar way it can be shown that, from an initial position of equilibrium, open market operations (monetary policy) lead to an inconsistent and overdetermined result. A purchase of securities by the central bank would cause a capital outflow, balance of payments deficit, and sales of foreign exchange by the central bank. The restrictive monetary impact of the foreign exchange sales are then offset by further open market purchases which induce further sales of foreign exchange. The process repeats itself at an accelerating speed. There is no new equilibrium because the public wants to hold just so much money, and the central bank's attempt to alter this equilibrium simply results in a fall in reserves. The sterilization procedures merely perpetuate the self-generating process until exchange reserves are exhausted, or until the world level of interest rates falls.

V. DIAGRAMMATIC ILLUSTRATION

These results can be illustrated by diagrams similar to those I have used for analysis of related problems.[5] In the top quadrant of both Figures

---

[5] "The Appropriate Use of Monetary and Fiscal Policy for Internal and External Stability," *IMF Staff Papers*, Vol. IX, No. 1 (March, 1962); "The International Disequilibrium System," *Kyklos*, Vol. XIV, No. 2 (1961), pp. 153–72; and "Employment Policy under Flexible Exchange Rates," *Canadian Journal of Economics and Political Science*, Vol. XXVII, No. 4 (Nov., 1961), pp. 509–17. In the latter paper (the main purpose of which was to show that commercial policy—import restriction or export promotion—was ineffective under flexible exchange rates) it was argued that *both* monetary and fiscal policies are more effective under flexible exchange rates than under fixed exchange rates. The apparent conflict with the present analysis lies in the different definition of monetary and fiscal policy and in the extreme assumption in the present paper of perfect capital mobility. In the earlier paper fiscal policy was taken to be an increase in government spending with interest rates maintained constant by the central bank, while capital inflows were assumed to be a function of the rate of interest alone; in other words no capital inflow takes place (because the domestic interest rate is constant) while the money supply is allowed to expand in proportion to the increase in income induced by the more expansive fiscal policy. In the present paper, I have defined fiscal policy as an increase in government spending financed by government bond issues with *no* change in the money supply. In both cases the underlying model is (in essence) the same and would yield the same results if the same assumptions were made about capital mobility and the same definitions were used.

1 and 2, XX plots the relation between the interest rate and income (given the exchange rate) along which there is no excess demand in the goods and services market (internal balance); LL describes a similar relation for the money market; and FF gives the external balance condition which is dominated by the world level of interest rates. Analogously in the bottom quadrants, XX plots internal balance, and FF external balance as a function of income and the exchange rate. The internal balance line in the top quadrant applies only for the given exchange rate represented by π_0 in the bottom quadrant, and the external balance schedule in the bottom quadrant applies only for the initial rate of capital imports (assumed to be zero).

Consider the effects of monetary policy (Figure 1). From Q an increase in the money supply shifts LL in the upper quadrant to $L'L'$, implying at the original interest rate and income level (at Q) excess liquidity; this causes a capital outflow. Under flexible exchange rates FF in the lower quadrant shifts downward to $F'F'$, and the improvement in the trade balance increases income and employment as XX in the top quadrant is pushed by the devaluation towards $X'X'$. The new equilibrium is at P, with an improved trade balance and greater capital outflow (or lessened inflow).

With the exchange rate fixed at π_0, however, the increase in the money supply merely creates excess liquidity, an export of capital, a balance of payments deficit, and a reduction in the money supply with no shift in XX in the top quadrant. The line $L'L'$ returns to its original position and Q is restored as equilibrium at a lower level of reserves; Q is the only possible equilibrium consistent with both FF and XX so the money supply

---

It may puzzle the reader why I went to some length to alter the definitions of monetary and fiscal policy and thus to bring about a seemingly artificial difference between the conclusions based purely upon different definitions. The reason is that monetary policy cannot in any meaningful sense be defined as an alteration in the interest rate when capital is perfectly mobile, since the authorities cannot change the market rate of interest. Nor can monetary policy be defined, under conditions of perfect capital mobility, as an increase in the money supply, since the central bank has no power over the money supply either (except in transitory positions of disequilibrium) when the exchange rate is fixed. The central bank has, on the other hand, the ability to conduct an open market operation (which only temporarily changes the money supply) and that is the basis of my choice of this definition of monetary policy for the present analysis.

In an earlier paper I analysed some of the purely dynamic aspects of the adjustment process ("The Monetary Dynamics of International Adjustment under Fixed and Flexible Exchange Rates," *Quarterly Journal of Economics*, May, 1960, pp. 227–57) on varying assumptions regarding capital mobility, but the treatment of the perfect capital mobility case in that paper suffers from the defects I have tried to avoid in this paper by my different definition of "monetary policy." However, the basic conclusions of that paper are not vitiated by the present analysis since the basic problem posed, in the flexible exchange rate case, that "monetary policy" exerts its influence on domestic incomes only indirectly through the exchange rate, still remains, with possibilities of cyclicity and even instability depending on the adjustment speeds; in the present case it can be shown that instability at least would be ruled out if the exchange rate adapted virtually instantaneously.

FIGURE 1
Monetary Policy

FIGURE 2
Fiscal Policy

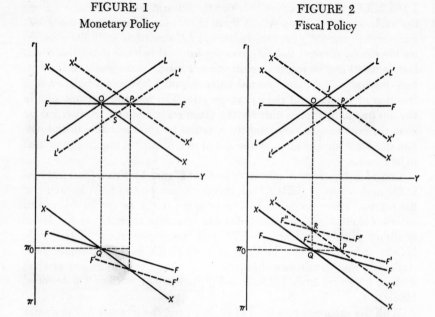

will adapt to it if it is allowed to. But if the increase in the money supply is accompanied by *sterilization* operations, that is, if $L'L'$ is maintained, there can be no equilibrium. The central bank buys securities, gold flows out, and the central bank buys more securities. Since the exchange rate is maintained at π_0, XX in the top quadrant is unaffected, as is FF. The attempt of the central bank to maintain $L'L'$ cannot satisfy both the conditions that the interest rate remains at the world level and that the new equilibrium be on XX. Either the exchange rate must change (shifting XX to $X'X'$) or the attempt to maintain $L'L'$ by sterilization operations must be abandoned.

Consider next the case of fiscal policy (Figure 2). An increase in government spending shifts XX to $X'X'$ in both quadrants. At the fixed exchange rate π_0 this increases income and increases the demand for money. Interest rates tend to rise, capital is attracted from abroad, the balance of payments improves and the money supply increases, eventually establishing $L'L'$ as the new money curve. After this instantaneous "stock adjustment," process capital is attracted from abroad sufficiently to establish $F'F'$ as the new foreign balance line, with the equilibrium P in both quadrants.

Under flexible rates, however, the money supply remains constant. The increased spending puts upward pressure on interest rates and appreciates the exchange rate. FF therefore shifts downward to $F''F''$ establishing R as the new equilibrium. At R the price of foreign exchange is lower but output and employment are unchanged.

Again, if the exchange rate is fixed *and* the authorities attempt to sterilize the initial gold inflow one of the policies must fail. This is because the new equilibrium (P) on FF and $X'X'$ in the upper quadrant is only consistent if the money supply is allowed to expand. Obviously the points J and P cannot be maintained simultaneously.

Certain qualifications or extensions to the analysis should be mentioned. The demand for money is likely to depend upon the exchange rate in addition to the interest rate and the level of income; this would slightly reduce the effectiveness of a given change in the quantity of money, and slightly increase the effectiveness of fiscal policy on income and employment under flexible exchange rates, while, of course, it has no significance in the case of fixed exchange rates.

Another possible influence is the real balance effect, but this cannot alter in any essential way the final result: income rises, under flexible exchange rates, in proportion to the increase in the money supply, whereas income remains unchanged, in the case of fixed exchange rates, because the quantity of money does not increase.

A further factor that might be considered is the negative effect of changes in the exchange rate upon the level of saving, but again there is no important alteration in the results: although the budget deficit arising from increased government spending under flexible exchange rates is then partly financed by an increase in saving of the private sector the conclusions regarding changes in the level of output and employment are unaltered.

The conclusions of course have not made any allowance for growth. Because of growth the money supply would normally be increased at a rate more or less commensurate with the actual or desired growth of the economy; my conclusions are, so to speak, superimposed on the growth situation. Moreover, many of our actual observations about the economic world are observations of disequilibrium positions; it is clearly possible to alter the money supply (under fixed exchange rates) if there is excess or deficient liquidity, although even this is in practice unnecessary since we can be assured, as we were as long ago as the days of Ricardo, that the money supply would automatically settle down to its equilibrium level. In any case these observations do not vitiate the principles I have been trying to elucidate.

CONCLUSIONS

I have demonstrated that perfect capital mobility implies different concepts of stabilization policy from those to which we have become accustomed in the post-war period. Monetary policy has no impact on employment under fixed exchange rates while fiscal policy has no effect on employment under flexible exchange rates. On the other hand, fiscal policy has a strong effect on employment under fixed exchange rates (simple Keynesian conclusions hold) while monetary policy has a strong effect on employment under flexible exchange rates (classical quantity theory conclusions hold).

A further implication of the analysis is that monetary policy under fixed exchange rates becomes a device for altering the levels of reserves, while fiscal policy under flexible exchange rates becomes a device for altering the balance of trade, both policies leaving unaffected the level of output and employment. Under fixed exchange rates, open market operations by the central bank result in equal changes in the gold stock, open market purchases causing it to decline and open market sales causing it to increase. And under flexible exchange rates, budget deficits or surpluses induced by changes in taxes or government spending cause corresponding changes in the trade balance.

Gold sterilization policies make no sense in a world of fixed exchange rates and perfect capital mobility and will ultimately lead to the breakdown of the fixed exchange system. In the absence of gold sterilization, as we have seen, an attempt of the central bank to alter the money supply is frustrated by capital outflows and automatically offsetting monetary changes through the exchange equalization operations; this is running water into a sink that is filled to the brim, causing the water to spill over the edges at the same rate that it is coming out of the tap.[6] But sterilization operations are analogous to trying to prevent the water from spilling out, even though the sink is full and water is still pouring out of the tap.

If my assumptions about capital mobility were valid in Canada,[7] it would mean that expansive fiscal policy under flexible exchange rates was of little help in increasing employment because of the ensuing inflow of capital which kept the exchange rate high and induced a balance of trade deficit: we should have observed a zero or very small multiplier. By the same token, now that Canada has adopted a fixed exchange system, we should not reason from earlier negative experience about the size of the multiplier and conclude that the multiplier is *now* low: while a reduction in the budget deficit under flexible rates would have helped the trade balance without too much damage to employment, a reduction in the budget deficit today could be expected to have a sizable impact on excess demand and unemployment.

---

[6] John Exter used a reservoir simile in "The Gold Losses," a speech delivered before the Economic Club of Detroit, May 7, 1962.

[7] See the accounts of the Canadian experience by Clarence Barber in his submission to the Royal Commission on Banking and Finance, April, 1962, "The Canadian Economy in Trouble," and by Harry Johnson from his speech to the Canadian Club of Toronto, November, 1962, "Canada in a Changing World." Perhaps the most complete verification of the applicability of the conclusions to the Canadian case is provided in an econometric paper by R. Rhomberg published in the *Journal of Political Economy*.

Of course the assumption of perfect capital mobility is not literally valid; my conclusions are black and white rather than dark and light grey. To the extent that Canada can maintain an interest rate equilibrium different from that of the United States, without strong capital inflows, fiscal expansion can be expected to play *some* role in employment policy under flexible exchange rates, and monetary policy can have *some* influence on employment and output under fixed exchange rates. But if this possibility exists for us today, we can conjecture that it will exist to a lesser extent in the future.

VII

Empirical

Investigations

of International

Trade and Payments

30. Domestic Production and Foreign Trade; the American Capital Position Re-examined[*][1]

By WASSILY LEONTIEF[†]

I. THE STRUCTURAL BASIS OF INTERNATIONAL TRADE

Countries trade with each other because this enables them to participate in and profit from the international division of labor. Not unlike businesses and individuals, each area specializes in those lines of economic activity to which it happens to be best suited and then trades some of its own outputs for commodities and services in the production of which other countries have a comparative advantage. The word comparative is in this connection of particular significance.

The United States, for example, exports automobiles and imports newsprint. It does so because the quantity of Canadian paper which we can obtain in exchange for, say, a million dollars' worth of American cars is larger than the additional amount of newsprint which we would be able to produce at home if we withdrew the capital, labor and other resources now absorbed in the manufacture of one million dollars' worth of automobiles and used it instead to increase the output of our domestic paper industry. Canada, for analogous but in a sense opposite reasons, finds it advantageous to obtain its automobiles from the United States in exchange for newsprint rather than to divert resources from their present employment in its paper industry into an increased domestic production of cars.

This explanation of the international exchange of goods and services

[*] Paper read on April 24, 1953, before the American Philosophical Society in Philadelphia, Pennsylvania. *Economia Internazionale*, Vol. VII, No. 1 (February, 1954), pp. 3–32. [Condensed by the author, at the request of the editors, by deletion of the sixth section of the original article.]

[†] Harvard University.

[1] The study described in this paper constitutes a part of the systematic analysis of *Structure of the American Economy* conducted by the Harvard Economic Research Project. Miss Sue Smulekoff, assisted by Mrs. Nancy Bromberger, has prepared the statistical tables presented in this paper and performed the numerical computations underlying these tables.

in terms of the comparative advantage of the alternative allocation of resources in each of the trading countries, was originally developed in the writings of David Ricardo and other so-called classical economists of the late eighteenth and the early nineteenth centuries. It still constitutes the basis of the modern theory of international trade. The theory of comparative costs—as many other economic theories—reigns, however, in the pages of college text books without actually governing the practice of empirical economic analysis.

Until recently, we had so little systematic knowledge of the productive structure of our own or of any other national economy that the application of such general theoretical principles to the analysis and explanation of actual foreign trade relationships has been practically out of the question. Most of what has been said on that subject consisted of reasonable common sense conjectures or of plausible examples which—like the automobile and newsprint reference used above—serves well enough to illustrate the logic of the theoretical argument, but had hardly any specific base in detailed facts and figures.[2]

A widely shared view on the nature of the trade between the United States and the rest of the world is derived from what appears to be a common sense assumption that this country has a comparative advantage in the production of commodities which require for their manufacture large quantities of capital and relatively small amounts of labor. Our economic relationships with other countries are supposed to be based mainly on the export of such "capital intensive" goods in exchange for foreign products which—if we were to make them at home—would require little capital but large quantities of American labor. Since the United States possesses a relatively large amount of capital—so goes this oft repeated argument—and a comparatively small amount of labor, direct domestic production of such "labor intensive" products would be uneconomical; we can much more advantageously obtain them from abroad in exchange for our capital intensive products.

Recent progress in the collection and systematic organization of detailed quantitative information on the structure of all the various branches of the American economy, accompanied by a parallel advance in the technique of large scale numerical computation, now enables us to narrow the frustrating gap between theory and observation.[3]

---

[2] As an example of the recent empirical studies in that field see G. D. A. Macdougall, "British and American Exports: A Study Suggested by the Theory of Comparative Costs. Part I," *Economic Journal*, Vol. LXI (December 1951); also G. D. A. Macdougall, "British and American Exports: A Study Suggested by the Theory of Comparative Costs. Part II," *Economic Journal*, Vol. LXII (September, 1952). A succinct discussion of the theoretical problems involved can be found in P. A. Samuelson, "International Trade and the Equalisation of Factor Prices," *Economic Journal*, Vol. LVIII (June, 1948); and "International Factor-Price Equalisation Once Again," *Economic Journal*, Vol. LIX (June, 1949).

[3] For description of the so-called input-output approach to structural economic analysis, see Wassily Leontief, and members of the Harvard Economic Research

This is the first preliminary progress report on a study designed to analyze the structural basis of trade relationships between the United States and the rest of the world.

II. DIRECT AND INDIRECT INPUT REQUIREMENTS

None of the basic factual information used here had to be collected especially for this particular inquiry. Both the statistical data and the analytical procedure employed constitute an integral part of the so-called input-output or inter-industry research program jointly conducted by various agencies of the government and private institutions, of which the Harvard Economic Research Project is one.

The factual information referred to above comprises many sets of figures of which the largest and in a sense the most important is organized in terms of a so-called input-output table.[4] This table describes the actual flow of commodities and services among all the different parts of the American economy. Specifically, it shows how each one of our manufacturing industries, each branch of agriculture, each kind of transportation and distribution—in short each sector of the American economy—depends upon every other sector. A single column of an input-output table, shows, for example, how many steel sheets, steel bars, and other steel products automobile manufacturers buy from the steel industry for every million dollars' worth of cars they produce; it also shows how many yards (or dollars' worth) they need of upholstery material, how much paint from the chemical industry and so on. Similarly, the "steel industry column" of the same table describes the various kinds of inputs, such as, coal, ore, etc., which the steel industry must obtain from the other sectors of the economy in order to produce an additional million dollars' worth of its own output which, of course, consists of various steel products. The table contains as many columns as there are separate industries so that it presents each link connecting any two sections of the economy.

On the basis of the statistical information contained in an input-output table one can determine the effect of any given increase or decrease in the level of output in any one sector of the economy upon the rate of production in all the other sectors.

Using the 1947 input-output structure of the American economy as the basis of such computations, one finds that to produce an additional million dollars' worth of automobiles the output of steel would have to increase by 235 thousand dollars, the output of chemicals by 58 thousand dollars, while raising the production of non-ferrous metals by 79, of textiles by 39 thousand dollars and so on. Even the communication

Project, *Studies in the Structure of the American Economy* (N.Y.: Oxford Univ. Press, 1952).

[4] W. Duane Evans and Marvin Hoffenberg, "The Interindustry Relations Study for 1947," *Review of Economics and Statistics,* Vol. XXXIV (May, 1952).

R*

services—telephone and telegraph—would have to contribute indirectly to the production of a million dollars' worth of additional automobiles.

Column 2 in our Table 1 shows the result of this particular computation. Without entering into the discussion of technical details it may be sufficient to observe that the magnitude of every one of the entries depends upon all the input-output relationships among all the sectors of the economy, and that the computation of each one of these figures is equivalent to the solution of a system of as many simultaneous equations as there are distinct sectors in the economy.

The more minute the breakdown of industries in the basic input-output table, the more detailed the final results will be. The following analysis is based on a 200 industry breakdown consolidated in some of its stages —for purposes of computation and simplified presentation—into fifty sectors (38 of which trade their products directly on the international market).

TABLE 1

Capital and Labor Requirements for the Final Output of
One Million Dollars' Worth of Motor Vehicles

Industry[a]	Output Require- ments[b]	Requirements per Million Dollars of Output of Industry Listed on Left		Requirements per Million Dollars of Final Output of Motor Vehicles	
		Capital	Labor	Capital	Labor
1	2	3	4	5	6
		(in 000's)	(Man years)	(in 000's)	(Man years)
26. Motor vehicles (145)	$1,457.45[c]	$ 565.8	60.340	$ 824.6	87.942
15. Iron and steel	235.14	1,026.3	77.777	241.3	18.288
19. Other fabricated metal products	118.25	713.5	95.335	84.5	11.273
16. Nonferrous metals	78.69	1,001.6	55.715	78.8	4.384
25. Other electrical machinery	75.50	551.1	102.638	41.6	7.749
22. Other non-electric machinery	60.70	775.7	96.579	47.1	5.862
10. Chemicals	57.95	592.7	49.779	34.3	2.885
12. Rubber products	56.19	493.1	90.172	27.7	5.067
31. Railroad transportation ...	50.18	3,343.3	153.640	167.8	7.710
11. Products of petroleum and coal	46.85	1,397.2	29.843	65.5	1.398
4. Textile mill products	39.29	493.6	110.563	19.4	4.344
14. Stone, clay and glass products	33.64	1,026.3	128.539	34.5	4.324
8. Paper and allied products	31.95	564.1	64.805	18.0	2.071
34. Trade	31.82	984.8	165.876	31.3	5.278
30. Coal, gas and electric power	29.50	2,222.6	99.318	65.6	2.930
1. Agriculture and fisheries ..	27.53	2,524.4	82.025	69.5	2.258

TABLE 1 (Continued)

Industry^a	Output Require-ments^b	Requirements per Million Dollars of Output of Industry Listed on Left		Requirements per Million Dollars of Final Output of Motor Vehicles	
		Capital	Labor	Capital	Labor
1	2	3	4	5	6
21. Metalworking machinery ..	27.48	1,246.9	130.705	34.3	3.592
33. Other transportation	23.88	928.3	121.576	22.2	2.903
9. Printing and publishing ...	19.72	436.0	114.038	8.6	2.249
38. Business services	18.44	144.5	97.543	2.7	1.799
39. Personal and repair services	18.10	681.8	183.503	12.3	3.321
6. Lumber and wood products	15.98	537.9	141.540	8.6	2.262
5. Apparel	13.74	262.2	108.795	3.6	1.495
29. Miscellaneous manu-facturing	11.26	439.4	100.364	4.9	1.130
37. Rental	10.68	8,156.5	16.324	87.1	.174
28. Professional and scientific equipment	10.35	841.8	133.129	8.7	1.378
2. Food and kindred products	9.98	361.9	43.143	3.6	.431
36. Finance and insurance ...	9.83	28.2	92.242	.3	.907
35. Communications	6.21	4,645.4	163.097	28.8	1.013
44. Eating and drinking places	6.02	688.0	125.365	4.1	.755
27. Other transportation equipment	5.11	759.0	122.419	3.9	.626
13. Leather and leather products	5.06	264.0	109.629	1.3	.555
23. Motors and generators	4.99	404.3	117.771	2.0	.588
24. Radios	4.65	449.0	124.097	2.1	.577
7. Furniture and fixtures	4.28	485.1	116.923	2.1	.500
18. Fabricated structural metals products	3.79	441.9	83.300	1.7	.316
20. Agriculture, mining and construction machinery ...	3.65	838.6	87.794	3.1	.320
17. Plumbing and heating supplies	2.67	509.9	99.388	1.4	.265
40. Medical, educational and nonprofit org's.	2.05	2,689.5	253.044	5.5	.519
3. Tobacco manufactures	.53	557.6	40.539	.3	.021
41. Amusements	.10	1,082.9	166.899	.1	.017
Total requirements in all industries per million dollars of final output of motor vehicles				2,104.8	201.476

^a See footnote † for Table 2.
^b The output required from each industry in order to produce one million dollars' worth of motor vehicles for export or domestic consumption. See Evans and Hoffenberg, "The Interindustry Relations Study for 1947," *Review of Economics and Statistics*, Vol. XXXIV (May, 1952), Table 6.
^c This figure includes the "back feed" within this industry, i.e., the automotive industry's purchases from itself, as well as the million dollars' worth of motor vehicles going to final consumers and the amounts needed by the various other industries to meet their output requirements. For detailed explanation of the technical point involved, see W. Duane Evans and Marvin Hoffenberg, *loc. cit.*, pp. 137 and 140.

III. CAPITAL AND LABOR INPUTS

The second and the third sets of our statistical data (columns 3 and 4, Table 1) show the direct capital and labor requirements of each industry. These figures are based on detailed information which tells us, for example, that to produce an additional million dollars' worth of finished cars, our automobile industry would have to invest in 175 thousand dollars' worth of new buildings, 266 thousand of additional machinery and many other fixed items. It also would have to increase its inventories of raw materials and "goods in process" by 124 thousand dollars. All together this adds up to 566 thousand dollars which represent the total additional capital (in 1947 prices) which would have to be invested in the American automobile industry if its capacity were raised so as to enable us to produce an additional million dollars' worth of cars per year.

But this is only one part of the total additional capital which would have to be invested in the American economy in order to enable it to produce—say, for export purposes—these additional automobiles. As we saw before, the input of steel into the automobile industry will have to increase by 235 thousand dollars and the input of textiles by 39 thousand. This, of course, means additional investment in both the steel and textile industries. The magnitude of each of these capital requirements can be computed. To do so one must simply multiply the amount of capital which each of these two industries requires per million dollars of its capacity by the additional demand for its product indirectly generated by the million dollar rise in automobile output. The amounts of additional capital which each one of the various sectors of the economy would need in order to enable the United States to increase its automobile export by one million dollars are listed in column 5 of Table 1. These add up to 2,105 thousand dollars which is the total amount of capital which the United States economy of 1947 had to invest for every million dollars' worth of cars produced for export or final domestic use.

Like the top of an iceberg, visible above the surface of the water, the part invested in the automobile industry itself constitutes only a small portion of the total—26 per cent to be exact; the rest is distributed among the other 42 productive sectors of the economy. Similar computations have been performed for each category of commodities and services which we export or import (in competition with domestic output).

Labor is the other primary factor, the availability of which must obviously have a decisive role in establishing the pattern specialization which determines the composition of our foreign trade. Not unlike capital, the man years which go into the production of, say, one million dollars' worth of automobiles are partly absorbed by the automobile industry itself but are partly employed also by all the other sectors of the economy. The computation of such direct and indirect labor requirements is quite analogous to the computation of the direct and indirect demand for capital (see columns 3 and 5, Table 1).

The summary of total quantities of capital and labor required for domestic production of each of the many types of commodities exported and imported by the United States is entered in columns 2 and 3, Table 2.

In this table most of the 38 large industry and commodity groups are broken down into their components, described in terms of the more detailed 200 industry input-output classification.

The figures entered in columns 2 and 3 were actually arrived at in two steps. First the indirect capital and labor requirements generated by one million dollars' worth of demand for the product of each of the composite 38 sectors were computed. This computation (essentially a solution of corresponding system of linear equations) was performed in terms of the consolidated 50 industry input-output table. Next, the *total* capital and labor requirements respectively of each *particular* commodity type within the sector were obtained by adding its *specific direct* requirements to the previously computed (in a sense average) *indirect* requirements of the consolidated sector as a whole. Thus, the differences between the total capital and labor requirements of the industrial products belonging to the same consolidated sector are due entirely to the difference in their *direct* requirements, since their *indirect* requirements are assumed to be the same.

The main reason for such a two-stage procedure is economic. If based throughout on the 200 × 200 input-output table the computation of direct and indirect requirements would cost a thousand dollars more. The errors caused by the short cut are not likely to be of decisive importance since the similarity of their structural relationship to the rest of the economy constituted the guiding principle in the aggregation of the individual industries into the larger sectors. What is even more important, whatever errors do occur in these basic computations, can have no biasing effect on the final results of our numerical analysis. The disregard of differences between the *indirect* capital and labor requirements of industries belonging to the same group has, furthermore, a theoretical reason which will become clear in the course of the later argument.

IV. COMPUTATION OF EXPORT AND OF IMPORT REPLACEMENT COSTS

Now we are ready to find out whether it is true that the United States exports commodities the domestic production of which absorb relatively large amounts of capital and little labor and imports foreign goods and services which—if we had produced them at home—would employ a great quantity of indigenous labor but a small amount of domestic capital.

Let us imagine a situation in which the United States for some reason wanted to reduce its dependence on foreign countries and, to achieve

TABLE 2

Capital and Labor Requirements per Million Dollars of U.S. Exports and Import Replacements[a]—1947

Industry[b]	Direct and indirect requirements per million dollars of final output		Exports per million dollars of total exports[e]	Imports per million dollars of total imports[f]	Requirements per million dollars of exports and import replacements of average (1947) composition				Comparison of export and imports requirements[g]	
					Capital		Labor			
	Capital[c]	Labor[d]			Exports	Import replacements	Exports	Import replacements	Capital	Labor
1	2	3	4	5	6	7	8	9	10	11
	(Millions of dollars)	(Man years)	(Dollars)	(Dollars)	(Dollars)	(Dollars)	(Man years)	(Man years)		
All industries			1,000,000	1,000,000	2,550,780	3,091,339	182.313	170.004	≦	≦
1. Agriculture and fisheries (1–10a)	4.7120	158.710	100,987	257,526	475,851	1,213,463	16.028	40.872		
2. Food and kindred products			105,701	98,045	3,119,593[h]	3,349,599	159.847	183.508	<	<
Meat packing and poultry (21)	3.0158	149.032	17,568	7,189	52,982	21,681	2.618	1.071		
Processed dairy products (22)	3.1334	165.081	15,217	2,429	47,681	7,611	2.512	.401		
Canning, preserving and freezing (23)	3.2287	206.505	11,446	48,043	36,956	155,116	2.364	9.921		
Grain mill products (24)	3.0375	146.371	45,928	1,522	139,506	4,623	6.723	.223		
Bakery products (25)	3.2447	221.331	468	32	1,519	104	.104	.007		
Miscellaneous food products (26)	3.2610	175.271	10,553	8,825	34,413	28,778	1.850	1.547		
Sugar (27)	4.1953	148.850	1,997	12,970	8,378	54,413	.297	1.931		
Alcoholic beverages (28)	3.2923	169.712	2,524	17,035	8,310	56,084	.428	2.891		
3. Tobacco manufactures (29)	3.2887	173.472	13,245	21,439	43,559	70,506	2.298	3.719		
4. Textile mill products			56,810	23,657	2,308,032	2,327,539	213.202	206.662	≦	>
Spinning, weaving and dyeing (30)	2.3114	215.250	53,758	9,796	124,256	22,643	11.571	2.109		
Special textile products (31) ..	2.3420	201.558	684	8,922	1,602	20,895	.138	1.798		

Industry									
Jute, linen, cordage and twine (32)	2.3412	200.639	815	4,728	1,908	11,069	.164	.949	
Floor coverings (35a)	2.1591	154.206	1,553	211	3,353	456	.239	.033	∧ ∨
5. Apparel			21,129	36,029	1,661,527	2,213,875	233.802	207.139	
Canvas products (33)	1.6106	237.848	174	0	280	0	.041	0	
Apparel except furs (34)	1.6050	250.169	15,493	12,630	24,866	20,271	3.876	3.160	
House furnishings, etc. (35b)	1.6492	188.151	4,479	1,814	7,387	2,992	.843	.341	
Furs (hunting and trapping) (10b)	2.6176	183.571	983	21,585	2,573	56,501	.180	3.962	∧ ∨
6. Lumber and wood products	1.6383	188.365	10,223	31,787	1,560,785	1,617,910	242.003	231.636	
Logging (36)			378	9,149	619	14,989	.071	1.723	
Sawmills, planing and veneer mills (37)	1.6383	251.604	7,153	20,435	11,719	33,479	1.800	5.142	
Plywood (38)	1.3366	209.125	863	761	1,154	1,017	.180	.159	
Fabricated wood products (39)	1.3465	226.188	1,217	632	1,639	851	.275	.143	
Wood containers and cooperage (40)	1.3491	242.168	612	810	826	1,093	.148	.196	∧ ∨
7. Furniture and fixtures (41–43)	1.6821	233.687	2,075	437	3,490	735	.485	.102	
8. Paper and allied products			9,743	103,616	1,726,891	1,859,722	165.764	161.346	
Pulp mills (44)	1.8611	152.803	1,337	42,732	2,488	79,529	.204	6.530	
Paper and paper board mills (45)	1.8611	167.325	4,401	60,447	8,191	112,498	.736	10.114	
Converted paper products (46)	1.5346	169.389	4,005	437	6,146	671	.678	.074	∧ ∨
9. Printing and publishing (47)	1.3216	196.597	4,329	1,425	5,721	1,883	.851	.280	
10. Chemicals			49,153	105,398	2,337,851	2,390,120	167.681	147.602	
Industrial inorganic chemicals (48)	2.2968	171.293	7,693	9,748	17,669	22,389	1.318	1.670	
Industrial organic chemicals (49)	2.8055	161.081	7,303	4,340	20,489	12,176	1.176	.699	
Plastic materials (50)	2.5614	159.740	3,082	97	7,894	249	.492	.015	
Rubber (51)	2.5208	141.238	342	55,751	862	140,537	.048	7.874	
Synthetic fiber (52)	2.9200	212.841	1,739	2,720	5,078	7,942	.370	.579	
Explosives (53)	2.2814	197.963	342	0	780	0	.068	0	
Drugs and medicines (54)	2.1666	184.150	9,329	1,457	20,212	3,157	1.718	.268	
Soap and related products (55)	2.1417	146.365	2,524	405	5,406	867	.369	.059	

TABLE 2 (Continued)

Industry[b]	Direct and indirect requirements per million dollars of final output		Exports per million dollars of total exports[e]	Imports per million dollars of total imports[f]	Requirements per million dollars of exports and import replacements of average (1947) composition				Comparison of export and imports requirements[g]	
	Capital[c]	Labor[d]			Capital		Labor		Capital	Labor
					Exports	Import replacements	Exports	Import replacements		
1	2	3	4	5	6	7	8	9	10	11
	(Millions of dollars)	(Man years)	(Dollars)	(Dollars)	(Dollars)	(Dollars)	(Man years)	(Man years)		
Paints and allied products (56)	2.0430	152.411	3,663	340	7,484	695	.558	.052		
Gum and wood chemicals (57)	2.4267	184.907	2,140	3,854	5,193	9,353	.396	.713		
Fertilizers (58)	2.3700	180.631	450	356	1,067	844	.081	.064		
Vegetable oils (59)	2.0071	128.889	2,734	20,063	5,487	40,268	.352	2.586		
Animal oils (60)	2.0062	136.738	1,079	2,672	2,165	5,361	.148	.365		
Miscellaneous chemical industries (61)	2.2467	170.497	6,733	3,595	15,127	8,077	1.148	.613		
11a. Crude petroleum and natural gas (17)	3.2118	108.844	6,248	37,372	20,067	120,031	.680	4.068		
11b. Products of petroleum and coal			34,566	21,730	2,600,946	2,674,929	94.110	93.465	<	>
Petroleum products (62)	2.5514	94.011	32,881	19,658	83,893	50,155	3.091	1.848		
Coke and products (63)	3.8708	87.760	1,355	2,040	5,245	7,896	.119	.179		
Paving and roofing materials (64)	2.3237	131.557	330	32	767	74	.043	.004		
12. Rubber products			10,199	389	1,817,051	1,801,799	194.823	205.656	≧	<
Tires and inner tubes (65)	1.8305	185.087	6,044	49	11,064	90	1.119	.009		
Miscellaneous rubber products (66)	1.7975	208.989	4,155	340	7,469	611	.868	.071		

Industry										
13. Leather and leather products			5,054	5,974	1,667,016	1,668,681	233.874	227.151	∧	≦
Tanning and finishing (67)	1.6900	183.095	1,901	2,817	3,213	4,761	.348	.516		
Other leather products (68)	1.6395	271.302	749	1,360	1,228	2,230	.203	.369		
Nonrubber footwear (69)	1.6574	262.612	2,404	1,797	3,984	2,978	.631	.472		
14. Stone, clay and glass products			12,788	27,560	1,961,425	2,345,091	192.211	177.794	∧	∨
Stone, sand, clay and abrasives (18)	2.5821	226.822	330	3,854	852	9,951	.075	.874		
Sulphur (19)	2.5821	139.703	1,385	0	3,576	0	.193	0		
Other nonmetallic minerals (20)	2.5821	154.790	881	17,456	2,275	45,073	.136	2.702		
Glass (70)	1.9293	199.932	4,419	1,295	8,526	2,498	.883	.259		
Cement (71)	2.4944	167.940	1,043	0	2,602	0	.175	0		
Structural clay products (72)	1.7718	271.334	959	49	1,699	87	.260	.013		
Pottery and related products (73)	1.3682	261.934	929	2,477	1,271	3,389	.243	.649		
Concrete and plaster products (74)	1.6727	205.466	246	65	412	109	.051	.013		
Abrasive products (75)	1.4890	159.882	1,127	1,765	1,678	2,628	.180	.282		
Asbestos products (76)	1.4890	176.167	600	32	893	48	.106	.006		
Other miscellaneous non-metallic minerals (77)	1.4948	179.324	869	567	1,299	848	.156	.102		
15a. Iron ore mining (11)	3.1683	212.434	552	7,675	1,749	24,317	.117	1.630		
15b. Iron and steel			37,732	4,695	2,724,880	2,655,654	118.305	151.438	∧	∧
Blast furnaces (78)	2.6394	142.525	396	3,676	1,045	9,702	.056	.524		
Steel works and rolling mills (79)	2.7599	180.703	35,585	955	98,211	2,636	6.430	.173		
Iron foundries (80)	2.0344	232.540	672	32	1,367	65	.156	.007		
Steel foundries (81)	2.0349	236.564	90	16	183	33	.021	.004		
Iron and steel forgings (92)	2.0311	179.672	989	16	2,009	33	.178	.003		
16a. Nonferrous metal mining			468	47,154	4,402,991	4,372,254	286.325	281.885	⫽	⫽
Copper mining (12)	3.2280	197.862	0	5,263	0	16,989	0	1.041		
Lead and zinc mining (13)	2.6210	230.618	12	5,360	32	14,049	.003	1.236		
Bauxite mining (14)	2.6948	221.395	114	3,757	307	10,124	.025	.832		
Other nonferrous mining (15)	5.0347	310.689	342	32,774	1,722	165,007	.106	10.183		

TABLE 2 (Continued)

Industry[b]	Direct and indirect requirements per million dollars of final output		Exports per million dollars of total exports[e]	Imports per million dollars of total imports[f]	Requirements per million dollars of exports and import replacements of average (1947) composition				Comparison of export and imports requirements[g]	
	Capital[c] 2	Labor[a] 3	4	5	Capital		Labor		Capital 10	Labor 11
					Exports 6	Import replacements 7	Exports 8	Import replacements 9		
1	(Millions of dollars)	(Man years)	(Dollars)	(Dollars)	(Dollars)	(Dollars)	(Man years)	(Man years)		
16b. Processing nonferrous metals ..			9,516	57,759	2,402,427	2,445,386	149.222	127.461	≦	>
Primary copper (82)	2.4334	121.184	2,788	22,216	6,784	54,060	.338	2.692		
Copper rolling and drawing (83)	2.4348	155.831	1,565	49	3,811	119	.244	.008		
Primary lead (84)	2.4340	120.806	30	6,720	73	16,357	.004	.812		
Primary zinc (85)	2.4350	166.224	1,379	2,672	3,358	6,506	.052	.444		
Primary metals, n.e.c. (86) ...	2.4348	131.553	396	18,913	964	46,049	.052	2.488		
Nonferrous metal rolling, n.e.c. (87)	2.4349	148.977	983	16	2,394	39	.146	.002		
Primary aluminum (88)	3.2849	144.156	204	761	670	2,500	.029	.110		
Aluminum rolling and drawing (89)	2.1816	177.628	1,769	0	3,859	0	.314	0		
Secondary nonferrous metals (90)	2.4355	125.398	282	6,396	687	15,578	.035	.802		
Nonferrous foundries (91)	2.1821	244.406	120	16	262	35	.029	.004		
17. Plumbing and heating supplies .			3,202	49	2,048,157	2,046,700	211.118	204.647	≧	≧
Metal plumbing and vitreous fixtures (97)	2.0510	223.913	1,085	0	2,225	0	.243	0		
Heating equipment (98)	2.0467	204.647	2,117	49	4,333	100	.433	.010		
18. Fabricated structural metal products			4,053	179	1,748,187	1,796,648	182.087	178.771	≧	<

Industry	(1)	(2)	(3)	(4)	(5)	(6)	(7)	(8)	
Structural metal products (99)	1.6954	183.767	2,518	49	4,269	83	.463	.009	
Boiler shop products (100a)	1.8348	178.945	1,535	130	2,816	239	.275	.023	≦
19. Other fabricated metal products			16,531	1,262	2,011,342	1,971,712	203.738	207.607	≦
Tin cans and other tinware (93)	2.1458	174.998	791	32	1,697	69	.138	.006	
Cutlery (94)	2.0414	241.579	1,229	178	2,509	363	.297	.043	
Tools and general hardware (95)	2.0421	227.946	3,130	259	6,392	529	.713	.059	
Hardware, n.e.c. (96)	2.0459	228.406	1,811	16	3,705	33	.414	.004	
Metal stampings (101)	1.8530	202.075	2,075	453	3,845	839	.419	.092	
Metal coating and engraving (102)	2.0457	264.165	0	0	0	0	0	0	
Lighting fixtures (103)	2.0419	195.244	2,140	16	4,370	33	.418	.003	
Fabricated wire products (104)	2.0401	169.167	3,286	49	6,704	100	.556	.008	
Metal barrels, drums, etc. (105)	2.0397	164.918	486	130	991	265	.080	.021	
Tubes and foils (106)	2.0399	206.580	282	32	575	65	.058	.007	
Miscellaneous fabricated metal products (107)	2.0406	190.366	258	65	527	133	.049	.012	
Steel springs (108)	2.0397	172.761	0	0	0	0	0	0	
Nuts, bolts and screw machine products (109)	1.8550	216.333	1,043	32	1,935	59	.226	.007	∨
20. Agriculture, mining and construction machinery			34,518	5,667	2,083,252	2,115,952	193.059	202.400	≦
Tractors (112a)	2.1098	185.783	11,722	1,457	24,731	3,074	2.178	.271	
Farm equipment (113)	2.1183	208.218	5,504	4,194	11,659	8,884	1.146	.873	
Construction and mining machinery (114)	2.0541	188.271	12,081	16	24,816	33	2.275	.003	
Oil field machinery and tools (115)	2.0541	204.419	5,211	0	10,704	0	1.065	0	
21. Metal working machinery (116–117)	2.1793	212.211	12,633	227	27,531	495	2.681	.048	≦
22. Other non-electric machinery			58,836	3,238	1,907,679	1,978,413	195.442	192.712	∨
Fabricated pipe (100b)	1.6724	176.071	0	0	0	0	0	0	

TABLE 2 (Continued)

Industry[b]	Direct and indirect requirements per million dollars of final output		Exports per million dollars of total exports[e]	Imports per million dollars of total imports[f]	Requirements per million dollars of exports and import replacements of average (1947) composition				Comparison of export and imports requirements[g]	
	Capital[c]	Labor[a]			Capital		Labor		Capi-tal	La-bor
					Exports	Import replacements	Exports	Import replacements		
1	2	3	4	5	6	7	8	9	10	11
	(Millions of dollars)	(Man years)	(Dollars)	(Dollars)	(Dollars)	(Dollars)	(Man years)	(Man years)		
22. (Continued)										
Steam engines and turbines (110)	1.6334	234.085	1,409	16	2,302	26	.330	.004		
Internal combustion engines (111)	1.6334	183.850	6,212	389	10,147	635	1.142	.072		
Industrial trucks (112b)	1.8509	175.047	851	0	1,575	0	.149	0		
Special industrial machinery (118)	2.1146	202.576	19,684	1,943	41,624	4,109	3.988	.394		
Pumps and compressors (119)	1.8797	179.349	4,335	0	8,149	0	.777	0		
Elevators and conveyors (120)	1.8754	181.040	2,452	0	4,599	0	.444	0		
Blowers and fans (121)	1.8744	182.857	396	0	742	0	.072	0		
Power transmission equipment (122)	1.8749	204.820	162	0	304	0	.033	0		
Industrial machinery, n.e.c. (123)	1.8748	170.428	2,494	648	4,676	1,215	.425	.110		
Commercial machines and equipment, n.e.c. (124)	1.8185	224.616	7,051	32	12,822	58	1.584	.007		
Refrigeration equipment (125)	1.6074	169.170	6,697	0	10,765	0	1.133	0		
Valves and fittings (126)	2.2257	211.626	2,782	0	6,192	0	.589	0		
Ball and roller bearings (127)	2.2110	233.258	1,457	32	3,221	71	.340	.007		
Machine shops (128)	2.2131	212.277	156	0	345	0	.033	0		
Electrical appliances (135a)	1.6404	170.386	2,698	178	4,426	292	.460	.030		

Industry									
23. Motors and generators (131)	1.3747	202.568	4,383	97	6,025	133	.888	.020	
24. Radios and related products (139)	1.5768	249.783	6,763	130	10,664	205	1.689	.032	
25. Other electrical machinery									>
Wiring devices and graphite products (129)	1.7708	200.531	15,794	193	1,767,716	1,771,503	218.121	202.073	≧
Measuring instruments (130)	1.7748	224.339	1,745	16	3,090	28	.350	.003	
Transformers (132)	1.7713	204.589	714	16	1,267	28	.160	.004	
Control apparatus (133)	1.7731	214.419	971	0	1,720	0	.190	0	
Welding apparatus (134)	1.7717	183.887	1,679	0	2,977	0	.360	0	
Heating appliances (135b)	1.7181	179.511	1,289	49	2,284	87	.237	.009	
Insulated wire and cable (136)	1.7663	172.350	1,163	0	1,998	0	.209	0	
Engine electrical equipment (137)	1.7690	297.422	1,457	16	2,574	28	.251	.003	
Electric lamps (138)	1.7678	226.812	971	0	1,718	0	.289	0	
Tubes (140)	1.7763	297.568	726	32	1,283	57	.165	.007	
Communication equipment (141)	1.7744	231.621	947	0	1,682	0	.282	0	
Storage batteries (142)	1.7695	154.318	2,147	32	3,810	57	.497	.007	
Primary batteries (143)	1.7697	209.119	576	16	1,019	28	.089	.002	
X-ray apparatus (144)	1.7742	276.505	486	0	860	0	.102	0	
26. Motor vehicles (145)	2.1048	201.476	923	16	1,638	28	.255	.004	∥
Motor vehicles (145)	2.1048	216.227	61,151	1,085	2,104,799	2,104,799	201.779	201.476	>
Truck trailers (146)	2.1048	210.641	59,892	1,085	126,061	2,284	12.067	.219	
Automobile trailers (147)			1,259	0	2,650	0	.272	0	
27a. Other transportation equipment			0	0	0	0	0	0	=
Aircraft and parts (148)	1.7328	235.024	20,236	1,247	1,678,459	1,528,148	189.761	169.206	>
Locomotives (150)	1.6663	170.126	7,525	130	13,039	225	1.769	.031	
Railroad equipment (151)	1.6663	158.126	4,731	16	7,883	27	.805	.003	
Motorcycles and bicycles (152)	1.5019	161.216	6,433	0	10,719	0	1.017	0	
27b. Ships and boats (149)	2.1404	263.615	1,547	1,101	2,323	1,654	.249	.177	
28a. Professional and scientific equipment			5,360	810	11,473	1,734	1.413	.214	
			6,566	11,529	1,844,913	1,840,559	251.904	238.442	

TABLE 2 (Continued)

Industry[b]	Direct and indirect requirements per million dollars of final output		Exports per million dollars of total exports[e]	Imports per million dollars of total imports[f]	Requirements per million dollars of exports and import replacements of average (1947) composition				Comparison of export and imports requirements[g]	
	Capital[c]	Labor[d]			Capital		Labor		Capital	Labor
					Exports	Import replacements	Exports	Import replacements		
1	2	3	4	5	6	7	8	9	10	11
	(Millions of dollars)	(Man years)	(Dollars)	(Dollars)	(Dollars)	(Dollars)	(Man years)	(Man years)		
Scientific instruments (153)	1.8465	266.625	3,748	65	6,921	120	.999	.017		
Medical and dental instruments and supplies (155)	1.8437	229.939	2,039	97	3,759	179	.469	.022		
Watches and clocks (156)	1.8405	238.387	779	11,367	1,434	20,921	.186	2.710		
28b. Optical, ophthalmic and photo equipment (154)	1.8465	311.213	4,707	680	8,692	1,256	1.465	.212		
29. Miscellaneous manufacturing (157–163)	1.4382	186.429	10,762	23,771	15,478	34,188	2.006	4.432		
30. Coal, gas and electric power			22,083	1,133	1,790,214	3,702,030	209.573	136.805	∨	∧
Coal mining (16)	1.7821	209.883	22,011	259	39,226	462	4.620	.054		
Electric light and power (167)	4.2709	115.066	72	874	308	3,733	.008	.101		
Natural, manufactured and mixed gas (168)	2.2676	97.194	0	0	0	0	0	0		
31. Railroad transportation (169)	3.9285	186.879	40,957	0	160,900	0	7.654	0		
32. Ocean transportation (172)	2.6324	165.090	80,361	40,157	211,542	105,709	13.267	6.630		
33. Other transportation			20,068	2,364	2,007,843	2,151,946	165.238	150.592	∨	∧
Trucking (170)	1.1152	152.922	9,018	0	10,057	0	1.379	0		
Warehousing and storage (171)	3.9155	376.255	1,529	0	5,987	0	.575	0		

Industry								
Other water transportation (173)	4.2776	119.141	3,933	696	16,824	2,977	.469	.083
Air transportation (174)	1.2650	163.866	4,976	1,668	6,295	2,110	.815	.273
Pipeline transportation (175)	1.8485	127.555	612	0	1,131	0	.078	0
Local and highway transportation (178)	1.0436	173.106	0	0	0	0	0	0
34. Trade			62,302	0	1,417,208	0	185.452	0
Wholesale trade (176)	1.4157	185.346	62,158	0	87,997	0	11.521	0
Retail trade (177)	2.0683	228.730	144	0	298	0	.033	0
35. Communications			2,272	0	5,097,887	0	246.360	0
Telephone and telegraph (179)	5.0979	246.360	2,272	0	11,582	0	.560	0
Radio broadcasting (186a)	.8310	57.460	0	0	0	0	0	0
36. Banking, finance and insurance (181)	.4699	134.774	8,106	16,516	3,809	7,761	1.092	2.226
37. Business services[i] (186b–187)	1.6345	240.990	156	0	255	0	.038	0
38. Amusements[j] (190)	2.2801	237.204	7,687	0	17,527	0	1.823	0

[a] All figures refer to 1947.

[b] The thirty-eight composite industries are found in W. Duane Evans and Marvin Hoffenberg, "The Interindustry Relations Study for 1947," *Review of Economics and Statistics*, Vol. XXXIV (May, 1952). The component industries are based on Bureau of Labor Statistics, Division of Interindustry Economics, *Interindustry Relations Study, 1947 Emergency Model Classification*; 1–25, 1952. In column 1, the numbers in parentheses correspond to this latter classification.

[c] The derivation of these figures is given in the text (see page 508). The basic data on the direct capital requirements (capital coefficients) of individual industries were computed by the Harvard Economic Research Project. For a general description of methods, see Wassily Leontief and members of the Harvard Economic Research Project, *Studies in the Structure of the American Economy* (New York: Oxford University Press, 1952), chap. 6.

[d] See text, pp. 508–09, for the derivation of these figures. The direct labor requirements (labor coefficients) were computed by the Harvard Economic Research Project from B. L. S. and census data.

[e] Export figures are based on Bureau of Labor Statistics, Division of Interindustry Economics, Table 1–Interindustry flow of goods and services by industry of origin and destination, section 6, October, 1952. Exports are valued at producer's value: transportation, insurance and trade margins are charged separately as export items. The total value of exports in 1947 was $16,678.4 million; the actual value of the exports of each industry can be obtained by multiplying each item in column 4 by $16,678.4.

[f] Import figures are based on Bureau of Labor Statistics, *op. cit.* All import figures refer to competitive imports only. Imports are valued at domestic import value, i.e., foreign port value plus transportation, insurance, etc, plus duties. The total value of competitive imports in 1947 was $6,175.7 million; column 5 times $6,175.7 million gives the actual value of each type of competitive import.

[g] The sign > indicates that the export requirement exceeds the corresponding requirements for import replacement; < shows the opposite. The signs ≥ and ≤ mark differences amounting to less than 2 per cent of the larger of the two italicized figures.

[h] For the meaning of the italicized figures, see Section VI of the original (*Economia Internazionale*) article.

[i] These two industries are numbered 38 and 41, respectively, in Table 1. They are numbered consecutively here because the intervening industries do not directly participate in international trade.

[j] Both the capital and labor coefficients for "Other nonferrous mining" (15) must be considered unreliable (too high) since they were based on output statistics which probably did not include operations performed under the authority of the Atomic Energy Commission.

this end, decided to decrease both its imports and exports by one million dollars each. Let us, in particular, examine the rather plausible case in which the reduction of exports is to be achieved by an equal proportional cut in each export commodity so that after the reduction the percentage composition of exports remains unchanged. The same procedure can be applied to so-called competitive imports, i.e., imports of commodities which can be and are, at least in part, actually produced by domestic industries. The level of non-competitive imports which, conventionally, are taken to comprise coffee, tea, jute (but not rubber, which can now be commercially synthesized) and a few other minor items, is assumed to remain at the same time unchanged. Such an exemption obviously has a good common sense basis. Moreover, within the context of the present analysis, it also has the closely related reason that labor and capital requirements for the domestic production of, say, coffee, cannot be realistically assessed. For later reference, one might observe that hot houses and heating installations would in any case require inordinately large capital investment per million dollars' worth of competitively produced Florida or California coffee.

To replace a million dollars' worth of imports we would have to raise the output of the corresponding United States industries. If competitive imports were, as has been assumed, cut proportionally all along the line, the domestic production of the specific goods involved would have to expand by the amounts equal to the reduction in the corresponding imports, i.e., by the same proportional amounts. If, for example, newsprint constituted 20 per cent of all competitive imports, and woollens ten, then in replacing the total of one million dollars' worth of competitive imports, the domestic output of newsprint would have to be increased by two hundred thousand dollars and the production of woollens by one hundred thousand dollars.

Such domestic production for replacing imports would mean additional direct and indirect capital and labor requirements. These can be determined in the following way.

The large 200 industries input-output table of the American economy for the year 1947 shows the competitive imports for that year classified by the commodity groups into which they would fall if they had been produced by our domestic industries. Dividing each one of these figures by the aggregate dollar value of all competitive imports gives us the amounts by which the domestic outputs of these goods and services would have to be increased if our economy proceeded to replace commodity by commodity an aggregate million dollars' worth of (proportionally reduced) competitive imports. Column 5 in Table 2 shows the composition of an average million dollars' worth of competitive imports. To compute the total amount of capital which would be required to produce domestically this particular collection of commodities, one has only to multiply each of these figures by the corresponding capital requirements listed in column 2 and then find the sum total of the resulting products. The products—one for each kind of the competitive imports—are entered in column 7.

An analogous computation yields the corresponding labor requirements. Column 9 shows the number of American man years which, in combination with the capital entered in column 7, would have to be employed to replace the foreign goods and services listed in column 3 with similar goods produced domestically.[5]

---

[5] For the purposes of the present analysis, we were able to utilize the previously completed computation which shows the effects of any given change in "final demands" on the levels of output of all American industries. (See Evans and Hoffenberg, *ibid.*) The results of these original computations must, however, be subjected to a quantitatively not very significant but in principle very important adjustment.

Common sense reasoning as well as actual experience shows that whenever any one of the American industries expands or contracts, the level of its operation tends to increase (or to decrease) its demand for imported inputs in a way analogous to the increases (or decreases) in its requirements for materials and services of domestic origin. An increase in the rate of our domestic outputs will, therefore, in general, lead to a rise in the volume of the dependent imports. The usual input-output computations thus present the United States' imports as depending on the level of final demand which, in particular, implies that any rise in exports would necessarily require an increase in imports.

For the purposes of the present analysis, this conclusion should certainly be retained in respect to inputs which are unlikely to be replaced by a supply coming from domestic sources. Coffee, jute, tin, and a number of other raw materials can be safely included in this "non-competitive" category. In evaluating the effect of increased exports on domestic capital requirements, it seems to be reasonable to assume that whatever additional indirect demand for the above type of goods will arise, it will be satisfied by foreign sources. In other words, in contemplating any possible changes in the level and the composition of our exports and imports—as they would result from alternative patterns of American foreign economic policy—it is reasonable to assume that the volume of such *non-competitive* imports will be in the future as in the past directly determined by structurally conditioned domestic requirements.

With the typical competitive imports—such as cars, most other highly manufactured products, and also some raw materials such as, for example, crude oil—the situation is entirely different. If the problem of comparative costs, i.e., the question of possible alternative patterns of trade is to have any meaning in respect to such commodities, one must explicitly consider stepped-up domestic production as being an alternative to imports and *vice versa*. In this context, an increase in final demand and particularly an increase in export demand should not be assumed to result in an automatic rise in competitive imports. On the contrary, the domestic repercussion—for example, the change in domestic capital and labor requirements—of additional exports must first of all be computed on the assumption that whatever virtual demand for competitive importation might arise, it will be satisfied entirely and only through expansion of domestic output. The possibility of increasing the imports of such competitive commodities has to be considered as a separate alternative. The capital saving effects of such imports are explicitly taken into account when one separately postulates the expected changes in the level of specific competitive imports and computes the repercussion of such imports on domestic capital requirements.

In a very open economy, such, for example, as the British, the difference between the domestic reactions computed first on the assumption of an automatically induced change in the level of competing imports and then without such induced changes might be quite large; in the case of the United States—the most self-sufficient of the modern western economies—such discrepancy will be quite small. It was still, however, taken into account in the present study.

The quantities of capital and of labor absorbed by the American economy per million dollars of its 1947 exports can be determined exactly in the same way. Column 4 in Table 2 shows the composition of an average million dollars' worth of the United States' exports. The quantities of capital and labor required to produce the indicated amount of each export—obtained by multiplying each figure in column 4 by the corresponding figure in columns 2 and 3—are entered in columns 6 and 8, respectively.

VI. EMPIRICAL FINDINGS AND THEIR INTERPRETATION

The principal findings of the quantitative factual analysis described above are summarized in the following figures:

Domestic Capital and Labor Requirements per Million Dollars of
U.S. Exports and of Competitive Import Replacements
(of Average 1947 Composition)

	Exports	Import Replacements
Capital (dollars, in 1947 prices)	2,550,780	3,091,339
Labor (man years)	182.313	170.004

These figures show that an average million dollars' worth of our exports embodies considerably less capital and somewhat more labor[6] than would be required to replace from domestic production an equivalent amount of our competitive imports. America's participation in the inter-

---

[6] There exists a good reason to believe that the excess of the labor requirements per million dollars' worth of American exports over the labor requirements for the equivalent amount of imports replacing output is actually larger than our computations show it to be.

Part of the labor input entering in both of these figures consists of agricultural labor. Agricultural employment figures are well-known to be biased in the upward direction partly because many persons living on the farms do not actually work on them and partly because a very large portion of agricultural labor input is absorbed, one could nearly say wasted, in marginal subsistence farming.

Since the agricultural employment contributes less to the labor requirement of our exports than it does to the replacement requirements for our competitive imports, any downward revision in that figure would tend to increase the difference between the two figures.

The labor requirements shown in the summary table presented above are split between the agricultural and all other labor as follows:

Agricultural and Non-Agricultural Labor Requirements per Million
Dollars of U.S. Exports and of Competitive Import-Replacement
(of Average 1947 Composition)

	Exports	Import Replacements
Agricultural labor (man years)	22.436	40.934
Non-Agricultural (man years)	159.872	129.069
Total	182.308	170.003

national division of labor is based on its specialization on labor intensive, rather than capital intensive, lines of production. In other words, this country resorts to foreign trade in order to economize its capital and dispose of its surplus labor, rather than vice versa. The widely held opinion that—as compared with the rest of the world—the United States' economy is characterized by a relative surplus of capital and a relative shortage of labor proves to be wrong. As a matter of fact, the opposite is true.

What is the explanation of this somewhat unexpected result? The conventional view of the position which the United States occupies today in the world economy is based—as has been previously explained —first, on an empirical observation and second, on a factual assumption. The observation is that the United States possesses more productive capital per worker than any other country. It can hardly be disputed.

To reach the conclusion that this means that there exists a comparative surplus of capital and a scarcity of labor in this country, the conventional argument must combine the foregoing observation with the implicit assumption that the *relative* productivity of capital and labor—if compared industry by industry—is the same here and abroad. Concretely, this assertion means that if in the United States we can transform ten pounds of yarn into a corresponding amount of finished cloth by using, say, one man year and two thousand dollars' worth of machinery, and transform a barrel of oil into gasoline by using one man year and twenty thousand dollars' worth of equipment, the corresponding foreign industries can perform each of these two operations either with exactly identical inputs of capital and labor or—if this is not the case—at least with inputs differing in both (and all the other) industries in the same proportion. So, for example, if in India one could weave ten pounds of yarn by using two man years and four thousand dollars' worth of machinery (instead of one man year and two thousand dollars as in the United States) the cracking of one barrel of oil could also be accomplished by using a double quantity of both factors, i.e., two man years and forty thousand dollars' worth of equipment.

Only on the basis of such an assumption, will the comparative costs argument necessarily lead to the conclusion that a country possessing a large stock of capital and a relatively small number of workers will find it advantageous to specialize in industries which, in terms of its own productive possibilities, require much capital and relatively little labor.

Let us, however, reject the simple but tenuous postulate of comparative technological parity and make the plausible alternative assumption that in any combination with a given quantity of capital, one man year of American labor is equivalent to, say, three man years of foreign labor. Then, in comparing the relative amounts of capital and labor possessed by the United States and the rest of the world—a comparison used for the explanation of their respective specialization in capital or labor intensive industries respectively—the total number of American workers must be multiplied by three, which would increase our 1947 labor force from 65 million to three times that number, i.e., 195 million of "equivalent" foreign man years. Spread thrice as thinly as the unadjusted figures suggest the American capital supply per "equivalent worker" turns out to be comparatively smaller, rather than larger, than that of many other countries.

This, I submit, is the analytical explanation of the results of our empirical findings. In terms of the relative production possibilities here and abroad, the United States is rich in man power and poor in capital. This country resorts to foreign trade to save its capital and to dispose of its relative surplus labor.

Our data obviously cannot explain why American labor is more productive than foreign labor. The problem of productivity is so intricate and has been so thoroughly discussed elsewhere that no casual remarks can possibly advance its solution. The following negative observation, however, has a direct bearing on the subject of the present analysis and on the possible interpretation of its principal findings.

The extent to which the high relative efficiency of American man power causes this country to exchange goods which absorb relatively little capital for those which would require more capital if we chose to produce them at home, *cannot* be due simply to the large amount of capital which American industry uses per employed worker.

The fact that workers are frequently replaced by machines cannot be denied. But such technological substitution, if profitable in the United States, would in general be profitable also in the corresponding industries abroad. The argument that the comparative shortage of capital might prevent the use of the same labor-saving technology by foreign countries would only hold if international trade, i.e., the international division of labor, did not exist. Actually, it does take place and if it were simply the problem of substituting capital for labor, foreign countries could and would imitate the American production practice industry by industry. At the same time, their production would be concentrated on those commodities which, both there as well as in the United States, require relatively little capital and large amounts of labor. The United States would for similar reasons concentrate on capital intensive industries and the trade between it and the rest of the world would consist in an exchange of American capital intensive against foreign labor intensive goods.[7] Our empirical findings indicate that in fact the opposite is true.

---

[7] To clarify the internal logic of the argument leading to this assertion, let us consider—from the point of view of the world as a whole—the double problem of, first, allocating capital and labor between the various industries and, second, of locating the various industries in specific countries endowed with different relative amounts of capital and labor.

If in accordance with the conventional argument, but in contradiction to the argument presented in this paper, one considers the technological possibilities to be the same throughout the world, i.e., if one assumes that with a given amount of capital and a given number of indigenous man years, every industry in England, in

Thus, without denying that capital can be substituted for labor, we must still look for some other reason in explaining the high productivity of labor in America as compared with the labor employed by similar industries abroad.

Entrepreneurship and superior organization have often been mentioned in this connection. In accepting this most plausible explanation, we must, however, make the following comment. Both these, as well as such other factors as education or the general climate of our production oriented society do certainly make the American economy more efficient in the sense that it is able to achieve the same output of finished commodities and services with smaller inputs of capital and labor. There exists a definite statistical evidence that the man hour and the capital investment both measured per unit of output have been reduced in many of our industries through better utilization of equipment and more rational use of labor.[8] To explain the comparative surplus of labor which our figures unmistakably reveal, we must, however, also infer that entre-

---

India or anywhere else is able to produce an output equal to that which the corresponding American industry *could* achieve with the *same* amount of capital and an equal number of (American) man years, that double task can be accomplished in the following two steps.

First, considering the total stock of capital and the combined supply of labor of all countries and taking in account the total world demand for various commodities and services, the proverbial "invisible hand" of competitive adjustment would determine on the basis of the uniform technological possibilities of the world as a whole—the proper amounts of capital and labor which each industry would best use per, say, every million dollars' worth of its respective output. Barring certain special, unusual situations, this decision could and would be made without any regard to the actual distribution of the combined labor and capital resources of the world between the different countries. This distribution could be taken into account separately in the next step in which all the individual industries would be actually assigned to the separate countries. In accordance with the "comparative supply of factors" considerations described in the first section of this paper, this second step will result in placing the industries requiring relatively large amount of capital into the countries comparatively well supplied with that particular factor and in locating the labor intensive lines of production in the areas having a comparatively larger supply of labor.

As a final result of such efficient "comparative costs" allocation, the capital rich countries must specialize on the production and export of capital intensive goods, while the labor rich areas will produce and export labor intensive commodities, while importing goods which, when produced at home, would absorb comparatively large amounts of capital and little labor.

It is particularly important to observe that under the assumption of technological parity the combination of capital and labor used in each industry—having been decided in the first stage of the two stage allocation procedure described above—will necessarily be the same in all the countries. For example, any specific textile product requiring much capital and little labor when made in the United States would require the same combination of these two factors also, if it had been produced in England, in India or in any other country. Being short of capital, i.e., of the factor which this product uses most, these other countries would, however, manufacture only relatively small amounts of that particular textile or even none at all.

[8] See Wassily Leontief, "Machines and Man," *Scientific American*, 1952, pp. 150–60. A different point of view is presented in the detailed factual study by L. Rostas, *Comparative Productivity in British and American Industry* (Cambridge: Cambridge Univ. Press, 1948).

preneurship, superior organization and favorable environment must have increased—in comparison with other countries—the productivity of American labor much more than they have raised the efficiency of American capital.

From the point of view of sheer arithmetic, the American comparative capital shortage and labor surplus—as revealed in our figures—could, of course, be equally well explained if instead of assuming that American man years are more productive than foreign man years we took the labor productivity to be the same here and abroad, but at the same time assumed the United States' capital to be less productive than its dollar equivalent in foreign countries. Such an alternative explanation, implying an absolute inferiority of the American productive technology, hardly would pass the test of empirical scrutiny; it is plainly contradicted by the fact an average American man year receives a much higher remuneration than the man year of labor employed in most other countries.

VI. SOME GENERAL IMPLICATIONS

This study has been designed to ascertain the structural basis of the United States' trade with the rest of the world. We find that, contrary to widely held opinion, our exchange of domestically produced goods for competitive imports serves as a means to compensate for the comparative shortage of our domestic capital supply and a corresponding oversupply of American labor.

Without attempting a systematic exploration of the possible widereaching implications of these empirical findings, let me merely mention here a few questions, the answers to which might be seriously affected by the results of this preliminary investigation.

Foremost among them is the problem of the changing position of the United States in the world economy. A richly abundant supply of natural resources—as compared with capital and labor—dominated our early development and our trade relations with foreign countries up to about 1910. From the fact that at the present time capital appears to be comparatively more scarce than labor, one might surmise that this scarcity has dominated our entire economic development until now. This would mean that—in terms of a comparison with the rest of the world—our capital supply, while steadily growing, has still not caught up with the increase in our labor force, if the peculiarly high effectiveness of that labor force is taken into account. A larger supply of domestic capital, if not matched by a corresponding increase in domestic man power, will, in any case, reduce rather than increase the comparative advantage in labor supply on which our present exchange of goods and services with foreign countries seems to be based. In other words, a more rapid rise in our average productive investment per worker would diminish rather than increase the advantage derived by the United States from its foreign trade. Only a spectacular additional increase in domestic capital stock could tip the balance of comparative advantage to the other side and thus bring about conditions which by common assumption are already supposed to exist, i.e., a situation in which the United States would actually find it advantageous to use its foreign trade as a means to save American labor and to dispose of surplus American capital. In view of the determined effort of many so-called backward countries to increase their own capital stock, such tipping of the scale will take some time. On the other hand, the factors, whatever they may be, which are responsible for the peculiarly high relative productivity of American labor might soon become operative in other economies and thus accelerate the elimination of disparity between the effective comparative supply of capital and labor here and in foreign countries. This signifies, of course, a reduced incentive to the continued exchange of commodities and services between the United States and the rest of the world.

Since no discussion of foreign trade is considered to be well rounded off without some mention of free trade and protection, I conclude with an observation on that timeless subject. An increase in the United States' tariff must obviously reduce the volume of our competitive imports below what it otherwise would have been; by restricting the effective foreign demand for American goods, it would bring about also a corresponding cut in our exports. Since the exchange of goods and services with foreign countries serves as a means to relieve the pressure of our domestic labor surplus and our capital shortage, a partial closing of that valve will tend to increase such pressure. In other words, protectionist policies are bound to weaken the bargaining position of American labor and correspondingly strengthen that of the owners of capital.

31. Measurement of Price Elasticities

in International Trade[*][1]

By GUY H. ORCUTT[†]

THE STATISTICAL ESTIMATES recently calculated for price elasticities of demand for imports and exports have been widely accepted as supporting the view that a depreciation would be ineffective. In this paper we first point out that prior to the availability of these rather recent statistical estimates it had been rather generally believed, in the prewar period at least, that in the absence of retaliatory action, such as devaluation or increased restrictions on imports, depreciation would be highly effective in improving the trade balances of the depreciating countries. After a brief discussion of why this is a reasonable belief, we attempt to prove that, not only are the existing statistically estimated price elasticities unreliable for the purpose of predicting the effects of such a depreciation, but that there is a strong presumption that these estimates lead to a considerable underestimation of its effectiveness. We attempt to point out some possible lines of approach to the problem of predicting the effects of an exchange depreciation. However, it cannot be emphasized too strongly that there are no estimates of elasticities of supply of exports, and that the statistical techniques used in estimating elasticities of demand could very well have indicated demand to be inelastic even in cases in which it was almost infinitely elastic.

INTRODUCTION

Although price elasticities of imports and exports of between -0.5 and -1.0 are sufficient to insure that under favorable conditions depreciation would be effective in improving the trade balances of the depreciating

[*] The Review of Economics and Statistics, Vol. XXXII, No. 2 (May, 1950), pp. 117–32.

[†] University of Wisconsin.

[1] The substance of this paper was originally prepared as a research memorandum for the International Monetary Fund, August 1949. It was entitled "Why the Statistically Estimated Price Elasticities of Demand for Imports and Exports Do Not Imply That Depreciation Would Be Ineffective." The author is grateful to Irving Friedman for starting him on this project and for encouragement in completing it. Considerable thanks are also due to Margaret Garritsen, W. John R. Woodley, Roger Anderson, and William White.

countries, recent statistically estimated price elasticities of demand for imports and exports have been widely accepted as supporting the view that depreciation would be ineffective, or at best nearly neutral.[2] Favorable conditions, in this context, include the absence of retaliatory actions, such as devaluation or increased restriction on imports, and the avoidance of inflation in the depreciating countries. That these estimates should have been so interpreted is not surprising since many of the estimated price elasticities of demand for imports and exports are between zero and −0.5 and since some of the individuals making the estimates have taken their estimates as an indication that depreciation would be ineffective.[3]

The highest estimated price elasticity of demand for the total quantity of imports of any country is −1.84 for Latvia (Chang 1948a), and the highest estimated price elasticity of demand for the total quantity of exports of any country is −1.34 for Canada (Chang 1945–46). The highest estimate for the total quantity of United States imports is −0.97 (Chang 1945–46), and the lowest estimate is −0.01 (Chang 1948b). The estimate for the demand for total United States exports is −0.43 (Chang 1948a).

At least three major types of price elasticity of demand for imports and exports have been estimated. They are partial elasticity, substitution elasticity, and what might be called total or semi-total elasticity. The latter is supposed to indicate the percentage change in the quantity imported per percentage change in the price of the import, with allowance made for the full response of domestic competitors. It is the one we shall always have directly in mind throughout this paper. A partial elasticity of demand for an import is supposed to indicate the percentage change in the quantity imported per percentage change in the ratio of its price to the price of the domestic substitute. It is partial in the sense that it is supposed to measure what would happen if the price of domestic substi-

[2] Robinson (1947), Brown (1942), Liu (1949), White (1949), and others have investigated under somewhat different assumptions what price elasticities of demand and supply of imports and exports are required if exchange depreciation is to be effective. The results obtained depend to some extent on what is assumed about secondary effects and whether or not exports are equal to imports. Nevertheless it is fairly certain that, if for a country or group of countries, the sum of the price elasticities of demand for their imports and for their exports is greater than something close to one, then a depreciation will be effective in improving its trade balance in terms of either foreign or domestic currency. This is particularly certain if it can be assumed that effective steps are taken to insure stability of internal price and income levels so that adverse secondary effects are prevented or at least minimized.

[3] A bibliography is given in Appendix 4, where detailed information will be found for references indicated in parentheses throughout the text. In writing this paper the author has in mind estimates of the type made by Adler (1945, 1946), Chang (1945–46, 1946, 1947, 1948a, 1948b), Derksen and Rombouts (1939), Hinshaw (1945, 1946), Holzman (1949), Neisser (1945, 1948a, 1948b), Polak and Chang (1949), Tinbergen (1937, 1946, 1947, 1948a, 1948b), de Vegh (1941), and others, although it is believed that the ideas set forth in this paper are relevant to a somewhat broader field of studies.

8

tutes were held constant. A substitution elasticity is supposed to indicate the percentage change in the share of the domestic market of an import per percentage change in the ratio of the price of the import to the price of the domestic substitute. Each of these tells us something about how competitive an import is but nothing, directly at least, about what would happen if the price of imports went down by, say, 10 per cent. Estimates of these first two types will be subject to most of the same difficulties, but in greater degree, as the estimates of total elasticities discussed in this paper. We have omitted a direct discussion of these two types because they appear to have only an indirect bearing on the effectiveness of depreciation. These two types have generally been estimated for particular commodities, while total or semi-total elasticities have been estimated for all, or large groups, of imports lumped together.

NONSTATISTICAL EVIDENCE

Surveys of informed opinion such as reported in "The Market for United Kingdom Consumer Goods in the United States" prepared by Time, Incorporated give a strong impression that sales of imported goods are sensitive to price. The reliance that is to be placed on such surveys is open to question, but certainly the opinion of people close to the actual market situations for various commodities should be given some consideration. Stronger support is given to the belief in high price elasticities of demand for imports and exports by the following considerations.

It is widely recognized that the demand schedule for the product of an individual producer has, in general, far greater price elasticity than the aggregate demand schedule for the entire output of the product. A classic case is the demand schedule for wheat as seen by an individual wheat grower compared with the total demand schedule for wheat.

The demand for imports (or exports) is usually a demand for products which are either produced domestically or at least have close substitutes which are so produced. This is particularly true if one is considering depreciation of most of the nondollar area versus the dollar area, since each of these areas is very large and very diverse and imports are frequently small relative to the domestic production of the same products or of close substitutes. Thus we would expect the demand schedule for imports or exports to be very elastic for the same reasons that we believe the demand for the products of individual producers to be highly elastic. If the price of imports falls as a result of depreciation, the demand for imports (and similarly for exports) should be highly elastic since the quantity imported rises, both to supply the additional amount of the product demanded at lower prices and to replace the amount by which the domestic producers reduce their output as the price is forced down. Since these increases in imports are to be taken relative to the volume of imports and not the total sales of the good or of the good and its close substitutes, the price elasticity of demand for imports (or exports) would in general be expected to be some multiple of the sum (in absolute terms) of the total elasticities of demand and domestic supply of the same or closely competing products.[4]

PROBLEMS OF PREDICTION

Prediction is based upon reasoning by analogy. On the basis of relations that have been found to hold between observable phenomena, predictions are made in new situations which appear to be analogous in important respects to the old. The real difficulty is, of course, in knowing what aspects of any situation are essential if the analogy is to hold. It is only by experience that we may gradually hope to learn which aspects are essential and thus minimize this difficulty. Nevertheless this difficulty can never be overcome with complete assurance and hence all predictions involve some risk.

In the particular case in hand, we are dealing with attempts to predict the effects of depreciations. In a number of studies a statistical relation between the quantity of imports or exports and unlagged relative import prices and incomes of the consumers has been estimated. The quantities of imports "predicted" on the basis of the historical price and income series agree fairly well with the big movements of the historical import series, and therefore the hope naturally arises that the present situation is analogous enough to the interwar period so that we may expect to find the same type of relation between quantities of imports and prices and incomes as was found to exist for the interwar period. This would not, in general, seem an unreasonable hope. However, we shall attempt to prove that in a situation where relative prices of imports change due to a depreciation that is not retaliated against, we cannot place much reliance on the existing statistically estimated demand for imports relations and the associated estimates of price elasticities of demand.

Depreciation by, let us say, the nondollar area versus the dollar area will result in a downward shift, in terms of dollar prices, of the supply schedules of exporters to the dollar area. In other words, exporters to the dollar area would be willing to supply the same amounts at lower dollar prices or more at the same dollar prices. Such a depreciation would also result in an upward shift, in terms of devalued currencies, of the supply schedules of exporters to the nondollar areas. What we need to know to estimate the effects of depreciation is the slopes, or at least the average slopes in the relevant range, of the supply and demand schedules, and also the extent of the supply schedule shifts. This paper deals with estimates of demand schedules. Perhaps the extent of supply schedule shifts may be taken as given. However, as far as I am aware, we lack any serious estimates of the needed supply schedules.

In the following discussion we shall first point out that the historical data used contain only a very limited amount of information about this point, and then we shall go on to discuss five reasons why the quantity

---

[4]See Appendix 1.

changes associated with price changes in the interwar period cannot be considered as even approximate estimates of the effects of a price change due almost solely to a large shift in the supply schedules. It so happens that in the case of each of these reasons the presumption is that the existing estimates have substantially underestimated the effectiveness of such a price change.

HISTORICAL DATA USED

Early attempts at measuring price elasticities involved the use of historical price and quantity time series in order to obtain estimates of the way in which the quantity demanded of a particular product depended on its price.[5] Thus, for example, the price and quantity sold each year might be represented as a single point on a diagram, having price measured along the vertical axis and quantity along the horizontal axis. The historical data for a number of years might then be represented as a set of points on a scatter diagram. A line would then be passed through these points in such a way as to obtain the best fit in some sense.[6]

It was, of course, soon realized that only under rather special circumstances would the points obtained from historical price and quantity data fall along the demand curve. This is so because there is not only a demand relation but also a relation between the price and the amount producers are willing to supply. If the quantity demanded and supplied depended exclusively on the price, the point of intersection of the demand and supply curves would be the only point at which they would match, and history would never give us anything but this one point. Since any line passing through this one point would fit perfectly, we obviously could not determine either the demand or supply relation. Fortunately, however, prices and quantities do in general show changes over time, so that the investigation of consumers' demand does not usually founder on this point. If the amount demanded depended solely on prices, the demand curve would remain fixed; and if the supply depended extensively on other variables which moved somewhat independently of price, the supply schedule would move up and down. Then the historical points generated by the intersection of the shifting supply schedule and fixed demand

---

[5] The literature on demand analysis is very extensive; however, good discussions of many of the problems involved may be found in Henry Schultz, *The Theory and Measurement of Demand* (1938), and in the more recent study by Richard Stone, *The Analysis of Market Demand* (1945).

[6] The shape of the line fitted to the data is of course of some importance, but this question is largely irrelevant to our main line of argument. Usually either linear or logarithmic relations have been fitted to the data. The logarithmic curves have the property of being of constant elasticity at all points on the same curve. The linear relations have a constant slope and therefore varying elasticity as one moves along the straight lines. However, for convenience we shall talk in terms of linear relations and it need only be remembered that the more nearly vertical the line, the more inelastic the demand. The usual criterion by which a line of best fit is chosen is that of minimizing the sum of the squares of the points from the line in a direction parallel to the axis along which the dependent variable is measured.

schedule would be scattered along the demand curve. Thus fitting a line to these points would yield the true relationship between quantity demanded and price. If, on the other hand, the amount that producers were willing to supply depended solely on the price, whereas the amount demanded depended also on one or more other variables, the points of intersection would have all fallen along the supply curve. Fitting a line to the points representing the historical price and quantity data would have yielded the supply schedule and not the demand schedule. Even if the demand were perfectly elastic, it would be possible to obtain a line fitting the historical data which was not only inelastic but actually sloped upward to the right. If both the amount demanded and supplied depended on other variables, the historical time series would yield points which did not fall along either line. They might either be randomly scattered or, if the shifts of the supply and demand schedules were correlated, they would be scattered along some entirely different line. In the latter case a good, or even perfect, fit of the line to the observational points would not be indicative that either a demand or supply curve had been even approximately fitted.

From the above it should be clear why Henry Schultz primarily limited his attempts to estimating demand elasticities of such things as total United States demand for various agricultural products. By doing this, he obtained cases in which he could be somewhat assured, because of the large role played by weather conditions, that the major historical price and quantity variations were due to shifts in the supply schedules.

One way of dealing with situations in which both the demand and supply schedules shift over time is that of incorporating the other variables influencing demand into the relation which is to be fitted to the data and thus attempt to fit a surface in several variables instead of a straight line to the data. By this means a demand surface which has not shifted materially over the historical time period studied might be obtained. Then as the supply schedule shifts about, a series of observations are generated which will supply points lying on or near the demand surface. For illustrative purposes, let us suppose that the amount demanded, Q, depends linearly upon the price, P, of the product and the income, Y, of the consumers. Then the demand surface, or plane, in this case, might be represented as in Chart 1, by the plane passing through the three solid lines marked A, B and C. Arrows are used in the Chart to indicate the direction in which each variable increases. In particular, it is to be noted that income, Y, increases as we move along the Y axis from left to right. If the amount which producers are willing to supply at any price depends upon factors other than the price and income, supply schedule shifts and income variations will give points scattered over the demand plane. Then the historical data will give the demand surface relating the quantity consumers are willing to take to price and income. The slope of the intercept in the P, Q plane, indicated by line B, will then indicate how the amount demanded depends on price for a given income. The price elasticity of

CHART 1

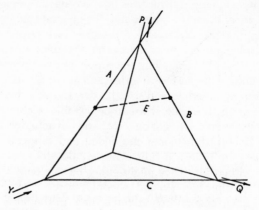

demand at any price and quantity will then be the percentage change in quantity demanded per percentage change in price.

Since the prices of other commodities are also likely to influence the amount bought of the commodities in question, some account needs to be taken of their behavior. In most cases what is done is to take the price of the product in question relative to some general price level.

In practice, instead of the observational points being scattered nicely over a plane, they are more nearly scattered around or along a line represented by, say, the dotted line E in Chart 1. If all the points fell exactly on this line, then of course any plane passing through this line would do as well as any other and the situation would be exactly analogous to the two-dimensional case in which neither the demand nor supply schedules shifted and the historical data yielded a single point. The difficulty is that as the two explanatory variables, relative price and income, are highly correlated, it is very difficult to separate out the influence of price (or the influence of income). Putting this another way, the range of relevant price variation (i.e., after correcting for income changes) has been very narrow. The range of relative price variation by itself is not large, and the only relevant part of this variation is that which is independent of income. In many cases, it is only 5 or 10 per cent. If, now, in Chart 1, all of the observational points were projected in a direction parallel to the dotted line E onto the reference plane containing the price and quantity axis, we might obtain a picture something like the dotted area in Chart 2. The line DD is the intercept (B of Chart 1) of the demand plane in the price, quantity reference plane. It is thus the demand schedule at a given income level, and it is the slope and position of this line that is needed. This scatter diagram would then show the evidence that was available for determining DD (the relation between quantity and price at a given income level). The range of price variation would be very small relative to a range over which we wish to predict, and relative to the magnitude of the errors that are likely to be present in the data.

CHART 2

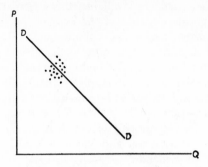

In this section we have emphasized the limited range of relevant experience that has been brought to bear on determining the way in which the quantity of imports or exports demanded would be affected by relatively large price changes at nearly constant incomes and price levels. These considerations are sufficient to indicate that the existing statistical estimates are very uncertain.

In the next section we shall present a number of reasons why even this limited amount of conceivably relevant information may be very misleading for purposes of predicting the effectiveness of a noncompetitive exchange depreciation, and why there is a strong presumption that the statistical estimates derived from it are substantially too low.[7]

SOURCES OF ERROR AND BIAS

A. Errors and Bias Due to Shifts in the Demand Surface During the Interwar Period[8]

If the demand for imports or exports depended solely on the income of the importing area and on the price of the imports relative to the price

---

[7] There is another type of argument not developed in this paper which also would lead to the conclusion that the existing statistically estimated price elasticities of demand are not very reliable. It is based upon the fact that, although yearly observations may be available for something approaching twenty years, these yearly observations are not independent observations but are highly autocorrelated. That is, each successive value of nearly any economic time series is usually much more nearly equal to the preceding item than it is to the mean of the whole series. Under these conditions, it has been shown that the effective number of observations will be substantially less than the actual number of observations and may very probably be between five and ten. The interested reader is referred to the article by Orcutt and James (1948), and the article by Cochrane and Orcutt (1949).

[8] See Appendix 2 for a mathematical treatment of this subject.

The complication that arises when there exists more than one relationship between the economic time series being studied was forcefully brought to the attention of economists by Frisch (1934) and Haavelmo (1943, 1944), and much work has since been done on this problem by Koopmans (1945, 1947) and others. See, for example, the studies by Girshick and Haavelmo (1947), Marschak and Andrews (1944), and Orcutt and Cochrane (1949).

536 *Readings in International Economics*

level of the importing area, then, although only a very limited amount of relevant information would be available, this information might tell us something about the dependence of the demand on independent price changes over a narrow price range Unfortunately, this assumption can hardly be justified. It must be remembered that the demand for imports depends both upon all the usual demand factors and upon all the factors affecting the competing domestic supply. It is clearly unreasonable to assume that changes in tastes and also in technology have been so minor over a twenty-year period as not to have shifted the demand surface by enough to account for a large part of the small relevant price variation that took place. World-wide war and major political upheaval must also have left their mark on demand.

This line of argument is reinforced when, for example, it is considered that large internal migrations of the United States population took place during the interwar period, and that sizable changes took place in the size and age distribution of the populations of many countries. Nor is it reasonable to assume that the influence of income on demand for imports has been completely removed by use of a linear relation. Income distribution is likely to be important as well as its over-all magnitude. Thus, although the major variations in demand were probably due to variations in the relative price of the imports and the income of the importing country, minor variations were due to other factors. Even though minor, these variations must have been large relative to the influence of the price variation which was independent of income.

It is difficult to deal with three dimensional diagrams, but the problem can be reduced, for purposes of presentation, to a two dimensional one by assuming that the relations of quantities and prices to income are known. Then instead of plotting quantity against income and price we can plot that part of the quantity variation not explained by income, Q', against that part of the price variation not explained by income, P'. This is equivalent to projecting, as we discussed previously, the observational points in the three dimensional space represented in Chart 1 in a direction parallel to the dotted line, E, onto a Q, P reference plane.

Now, at best, we are forced to assume that the demand schedule shifted up and down in a random way and independently of shifts in the supply schedule. We are here and in the rest of the paper talking about shifts not linearly explainable by income variations. It should also be remembered that the price variable represents the ratio of the price of the imports to the price level of the importing country. It can be shown (and is shown in Appendix 2) that even random shifts of the demand schedule will result in an estimated price elasticity which is lower than the true price elasticity. For illustration, assume that the demand schedule shifted up and down in a random way between the limits imposed by the lines DD and $D'D'$, in Chart 3. Also suppose that the supply schedule shifted up and down in a random way between the limits imposed by the lines

CHART 3

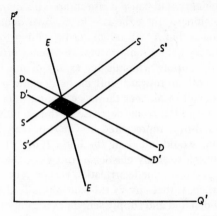

SS and S'S'. Then the points of intersection of the supply and demand curves would be scattered over the enclosed parallelogram. Now if we fit a line EE to these points in such a way as to minimize the sums of squares of deviations, in a horizontal direction, of these points from the line, the line so obtained will have a steeper slope (i.e., will show less elasticity) than the slope of the true demand schedule. It is this steeper line, however, that is obtained by the statistical methods of fitting that have been used. If the shifts in the demand schedule were large relative to those of the supply schedule, a line approximating the supply schedule would be obtained. If they were small relative to shifts of the supply schedule, a line between the supply and demand schedules, but closer to the demand schedule, would be obtained. No attempt at estimating the relative magnitude of such shifts appears to have been made.

For a number of reasons it seems likely that shifts in demand schedules have not in general been independent of shifts in supply schedules. Rather it seems that in general when the demand-for-imports schedule shifted upward the supply schedule for these imports also shifted upwards. As pointed out previously, the demand for imports is increased by anything which increases the demand for the type of products imported, and is reduced by anything which increases the amount which competing domestic producers are prepared to offer at given prices and incomes. Likewise, the supply of exports depends inversely upon factors affecting the internal demand for the product and directly upon factors affecting the total supply schedules for the type of product exported by the producers. This kind of situation is almost bound to result in the supply schedule for imports shifting up at the same time as the demand schedule for imports. Because of world wars, to take one case, the demand schedules for particular kinds of goods, machinery for example, will rise, relative to demand in general, all over the world at about the same time. Let us suppose that area A exports machinery to area B. In B the rise in the demand schedule for machinery will cause a rise in area B's demand schedule for the import of machinery. In A the rise in A's own demand schedule for machinery will mean that A will no longer be willing to export the same amount of machinery at the same prices. In other words, it will mean a shift upward in A's supply schedule for export of machinery to area B. The net result of both an upward shift in the demand and supply schedule of B's imports will mean that the price of machinery imported by B will rise sharply with little or no decrease in the quantity exported to B. This situation can also be represented by Chart 3. Here it is obvious that the observed points would fall along the line *EE* even if the demand-for-import schedule was extremely elastic. In this case, the fitted line would be *EE* even though the obtained correlation was perfect.

The position, then, is that any world-wide shifts in demand or in technology will cause demand and supply schedules for imports to shift up and down together, and so make misleading even the very limited information that might have been relevant. To predict the effect of a noncompetitive depreciation, we need to know the true demand schedules, since presumably only the supply schedules will be shifted by depreciation. However, over the historical period used, both the supply and demand schedules must have shifted, and they most likely shifted up and down together. Because of this, our estimated elasticities of demand for imports are probably much lower than the true values, and so far as this evidence goes we would not even be justified in saying that the true values were less than infinity, however unrealistic such a figure might be on other grounds.

B. Errors and Bias Due to Errors of Observation[9]

It is obvious that errors of observation will in any case reduce the accuracy of estimated demand for import or export relations. It would also probably be generally granted that the errors involved in available statistics of quantities and prices of imports and exports are not reliable within, say, a 5 per cent or 10 per cent range. The sources of error in such measurements are many and include not only such obvious sources as falsification and misclassification, but also faulty methods of index construction. In addition, the data collected are seldom precisely what is wanted, while it is not only the year-to-year errors that are important but also the cumulation of such errors over the entire period studied. It is thus reasonable to suppose that the magnitude of the errors of observation is as large as the range of relevant price variation present in the statistical studies of import elasticities. Indeed, it would seem difficult to prove that it is not substantially greater.

---

[9] See Appendix 2 for a mathematical treatment of this subject.

The complication that arises when the variables are subject to errors of observations has received consideration in the work of Frisch (1934), Koopmans (1937), Tintner (1948), Reiersøl (1945), Geary (1949), and others.

The implication of this, as far as accuracy of estimation is concerned, is unequivocal, but it may not be so evident that these errors of observation are likely to result in a substantial underestimation of the price elasticities. Very little appears to be known about the nature of these errors. To be completely certain about the direction of the resulting bias it would be necessary to know the precise way in which errors of observation in the observed quantities, incomes, and prices are correlated with each other and with the true values of the quantity, income, and price series. It has not been possible to construct a reasonable case supporting either negative or positive correlations between the errors or between the errors

CHART 4

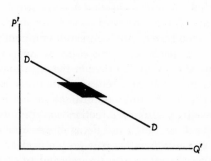

and the true values of the variables. In view of this, it has seemed reasonable to assume that the errors of observation in the quantity, price, and income series are essentially uncorrelated with each other and with the true values of these series. For purposes of illustration it is assumed that there is an exact linear relation between the true quantities and prices. If there were no errors in the price variable but only in the quantity variable, then the situation might be illustrated by Chart 4. Here DD represents the line along which the "true" points would lie. Since the observed prices are assumed to be correct, each observed point will be the same distance up from the Q' axis as the corresponding "true" point on the line, DD. On the other hand, the observed quantities are assumed to be in error, so the observational points will be scattered in a horizontal direction about the line and would fall in some such parallelogram as shown. In this case, fitting a line so as to minimize the sums of the squares of the deviations of the points from the line would result in obtaining an unbiased estimate of the line DD. The estimate would be subject to a wide margin of error with only 20 observations, but the line obtained would at least be just as likely to be too steep as too flat.

On the other hand, suppose that errors of observation were limited to the price variable and that the quantities imported were known exactly. This situation might be illustrated by Chart 5. Here DD again represents the line along which the "true" points would lie. Since the observed quan-

CHART 5

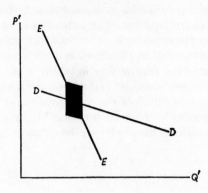

tities are assumed to be correct, each observed point will be the same distance to the right of the price axis as the corresponding "true" point on the
line. However, since the observed prices are in error they are scattered in
a vertical direction about the line and would fall in some such parallelogram as shown in Chart 5. In this case fitting a line so as to minimize the
sums of the squares in a horizontal direction would result in a line such as
EE which is steeper than the "true" demand schedule *DD*. How much
steeper the observed line is than the true line depends upon how large the
errors of observation are relative to the relevant price variations. If the
true demand schedule were perfectly elastic (*DD* horizontal), there
would have been no relevant price changes but this would not be obvious
from the observed data and it would still be possible to obtain estimated
elasticities which were close to zero.

If the errors of observation were limited to the income variable, then
it could be shown that the estimated income and price elasticities would
both be biased toward zero.[10] It can also be shown that any combination
of errors of the type assumed in the price and income series will bias the
estimated price and income elasticities toward zero, whether or not such
errors are present in the quantity series.

C. Historical Price and Quantity Indices Reflect Price Changes of Commodities with Very Different Price Elasticities

Most of the estimated price elasticities dealt with in this paper relate
to the total demand for imports, or at least to the combined demand for
imports of a wide variety of types. However, it seems reasonable to assume
that historical price changes have been largest for those goods that admittedly have low price elasticities of demand. Thus we expect raw material and agricultural prices to show a wider range of price fluctuations
than do products in general. This means that most of the price changes in

---

[10] See Appendix 2.

the historical price indices of imports lumped together were due to price changes of commodities with inelastic demands. Since these price changes were associated with only small quantity adjustments, the estimated price elasticity of all imports might well be low. However if, as is usually assumed, the price elasticities of supply of exports are very high, at least in the long run, then it follows that a depreciation would result in sizable and more or less uniform price declines for imports of nondepreciating areas. The effect on quantity of imports or exports of a more or less uniform price change would evidently be substantially greater than in a situation in which most of the price changes were for products with inelastic demands or supplies.

D. Short-Run Instead of Long-Run Price Elasticities Have Been Estimated[11]

Since it is evident that industries do not grow up or fade away in six months or a year, it has been widely recognized that on the supply side short-run price elasticities are likely to be much smaller than long-run price elasticities and that a fairly full adjustment to a price change may take several years. However, as has already been pointed out a number of times in this paper and elsewhere, the demand for imports depends upon the supply schedules of domestic competitors as well as on the demand schedule of consumers. It follows from this that long-run price elasticities of imports and exports are probably substantially larger than short-run price elasticities.

The existing statistical estimates have been based on relating the volume of current imports (yearly averages) to current prices (yearly averages). If part of the quantity adjustment to a price change comes in the two or three or more years following the price change, then since current years are compared not only will the explanation be inadequate but the apparent effect of price changes on quantity will be less than the true, long-run effect.

E. The Price Elasticity of Demand for Imports or Exports Is Probably Much Larger for Large Price Changes Than for Small Price Changes

During the interwar period dealt with in obtaining the statistically estimated price elasticities of demand for imports and exports, the range of price variation, which was independent of income variation, was small compared with what might be expected under a depreciation of the nondollar areas. Extrapolations are always risky and subject to substantial error, and this case does not have the appearance of being an exception.

In addition to the large margin of uncertainty which the narrow range of experience creates, there are several reasons to expect the demand schedule for imports to be more inelastic for small than for large price

---

[11] See Appendix 3 for a mathematical treatment of this point.

variations. One major reason for believing this is that there are usually some costs to the consumer involved in shifting from one source of supply to another. These costs may be psychological or economic. Consumers are slow to change their habits. Producers incur costs in establishing new trade connections or in modifying the machinery and techniques by which the imported product is used. Thus either oil or gas may do equally well for many heating purposes, but costs are involved in switching. Again, flour manufacturers can probably blend, with nearly equal success, flour with different proportions of Canadian, Australian and Argentine wheat, but some cost will be involved in adjusting the process and recipes to different proportions. Thus small price changes and particularly those which appear to be of a temporary nature will be ignored. Little shifting will take place until the differential is at least sufficient to cover the costs of switching, whereas a large and fairly permanent change produced by depreciation would result in substantial substitution.

A second reason for believing that demand schedules for imports or exports are more elastic for large than for small price changes is that entirely new commodities may be brought into international trade by large price shifts, and also existing products may become competitive in mass rather than luxury markets.

REMOVAL OF SOURCES OF ERROR AND BIAS

If the arguments of this paper are accepted, it is clear that little light is likely to be thrown on the effectiveness of depreciation by the grinding out of more regression analyses on the same general type of time series. It is also believed that it is unlikely that any greater success can be achieved by an application of some of the newer statistical techniques to these time series; for example, those designed to deal with the problems arising from the existence of several relations between the time series, or with the presence of errors of observations.[12] No approach seems certain, and any realistic approach to this problem will almost undoubtedly be far more laborious than the type of studies already made. Nevertheless, certain possibilities for further study are promising.

By studying the dependence of quantities on price for individual commodities it should be possible to avoid the difficulty described, under C, above, concerning the structure of import or export price changes, since if the individual elasticities are known, they could be combined in an appropriate way for any structure of price changes. However, it would seem reasonable to put the emphasis on obtaining for individual commodities total elasticities rather than the partial or substitution elasticities which have been sought in the past.

By studying the history of individual commodities it might be possible to separate out cases in which it was almost certain that the price and quantity shifts were due to shifts in the supply schedule. A close study

---

[12] For a partial justification of this belief, see Orcutt and Cochrane (1949).

of such cases should be more illuminating than a study of the behavior of time series for which there is practically no information as to the causes of individual price and quantity shifts.

By studying individual commodities it might also be possible to group them into classes such that all members of a class might be expected to have experienced nearly the same demand influences. Then differences in their price and quantity behavior might possibly be ascribed to differences in the movement of their respective supply schedules.

By studying individual commodities one might likewise be able to find a number of cases in which relatively large price changes took place. If so, then the problem of errors of observation might be reduced to minor proportions and more could be discovered about the effect of big price changes. The field of tariff changes is one obviously fertile and nearly unexplored field that should be thoroughly examined for likely cases.

Some progress could probably be made in obtaining long-run, instead of short-run, price elasticities by looking for cumulative instead of current effects of price changes. However, the longer the interval between a price change and its effect and the more attenuated the effect, the greater is bound to be the difficulty of showing that the quantity movements are in fact related to the price movements which caused them.

APPENDIX 1

Relation of Elasticity of Demand for Imports to Elasticity of Domestic Demand and Supply[13]

Assume that area A both imports and produces domestically a given product. Let the domestic demand and supply schedules (for given income) be represented by

$$\text{Demand schedule} \qquad Q_d = F_1(P) \qquad\qquad (1)$$

$$\text{Supply schedule} \qquad Q_s = F_2(P) \qquad\qquad (2)$$

The demand schedule for imports, Q_m, will be

$$Q_m = Q_d - Q_s = F_1(P) - F_2(P) \qquad\qquad (3)$$

and the price elasticity of demand for imports, e_m, will be

$$e_m = \frac{dQ_m}{dP} \cdot \frac{P}{Q_m} = \frac{P}{Q_m}\left(\frac{dF_1}{dP} - \frac{dF_2}{dP}\right) \qquad\qquad (4)$$

or

$$e_m = \frac{Q_d}{Q_m}\, e_d - \frac{Q_s}{Q_m}\, e_s \qquad\qquad (5)$$

The price elasticity of A's demand for the given product, e_d, will be negative, and the price elasticity of A's domestic supply, e_s, will be positive. For example, if the quantity imported, Q_m, is equal to one third of

---

[13] See Yntema (1932), pp. 43–45, for a derivation of this result.

the quantity domestically supplied, Q_s, and remembering that, $Q_d = Q_m + Q_s$, we obtain

$$e_m = 4\,e_d - 3\,e_s \tag{6}$$

Thus, if the domestic demand and supply have elasticities of -1 and $+1$, respectively, the price elasticity of demand for imports will be -7.

APPENDIX 2

Mathematical Appendix on Errors and Bias Due to Shifts in the Demand Surface and to Errors of Observation

A. *General Formulation of Problem.* Assume that the true demand surface is given by an equation of the following type:

$$X'_1 = A_1 + B_{12}X'_2 + B_{13}X'_3 + B_{14}X'_4 + + + \tag{1}$$

X'_1 is the exact value, indicated by a prime, of the dependent variable, and X'_2, X'_3, X'_4, . . . are the exact values, indicated by primes, of the explanatory variables. In our particular case, X'_1 may be considered as either the quantity of exports or imports or as any single valued function of the quantity of exports or imports. The explanatory variables may be any economic or noneconomic variables, or any single valued functions of them. Thus while our model involves only a linear relation it is general enough to include any type of relation which can be put in this form. In particular, it includes logarithmic formulations based upon the assumption of demand surfaces of constant elasticities.

Some of the explanatory variables must, because of ignorance or absence of data, be omitted in any concrete or statistical formulation of the demand surface. Let us represent the omitted part by V. In terms of our notation

$$V = B_{14}X'_4 + B_{15}X'_5 + + + \tag{2}$$

when two explanatory variables are included in the statistical explanation of X'_1. V is, of course, never known.

In addition to being forced to omit variables we are also usually forced to use inaccurate data. Let us represent the observed value of a variable by the same symbol as the exact value but with the prime omitted. That is

$$X_i = X'_i + E_i \text{ for all values of } i. \tag{3}$$

E_i is therefore the error of observation in the observed value of the variable X_i.

Using equations 2 and 3, we may rewrite equation (1) as either (4) or (5) below:

$$X_1 - E_1 = A_1 + B_{12}(X_2 - E_2) + B_{13}(X_3 - E_3) + V \tag{4}$$

$$X_1 = A_1 + B_{12}X_2 + B_{13}X_3 + (E_1 - B_{12}E_2 - B_{13}E_3 + V) \tag{5}$$

where the quantity in parentheses at the right is unobservable.

Expressing each variable in terms of deviations from its sample mean, we can eliminate the constant A_1. Thus we have:

$$x_i = X_i - \bar{X}_i \text{ where } \bar{X}_i = \frac{\sum\limits_{t=1}^{n} X_{it}}{n} \tag{6}$$

Using equation (6) we may rewrite equation (5) as

$$(x_1 + \bar{X}_1) = A_1 + B_{12}(x_2 + \bar{X}_2) + B_{13}(x_3 + \bar{X}_3) + \tag{7}$$
$$(e_1 + E_1) - B_{12}(e_2 + E_2) - B_{13}(e_3 + E_3) + (v + V)$$

or

$$x_1 = B_{12}x_2 + B_{13}x_3 + v + e_1 - B_{12}e_2 - B_{13}e_3 + K \tag{8}$$

where $K = (A_1 - \bar{X}_1 + B_{12}\bar{X}_2 + B_{13}\bar{X}_3 + E_1 - B_{12}E_2 - B_{13}E_3 + V)$

Multiplying equation (8) through by x_2, we obtain:

$$x_1 x_2 = B_{12}x^2{}_2 + B_{13}x_2 x_3 + x_2(v + e_1 - B_{12}e_2 - B_{13}e_3) + x_2 K \tag{9}$$

and therefore:

$$\Sigma x_1 x_2 = B_{12}\Sigma x^2{}_2 + B_{13}\Sigma x_2 x_3 + \Sigma x_2(v + e_1 - B_{12}e_2 - B_{13}e_3) \tag{10}$$

since $\Sigma x_2 K = 0$

In the same manner we obtain

$$\Sigma x_1 x_3 = B_{12}\Sigma x_2 x_3 + B_{13}\Sigma x^2{}_3 + \Sigma x_3(v + e_1 - B_{12}e_2 - B_{13}e_3) \tag{11}$$

Let $b_{12.3}$ be the least squares estimate of B_{12}, and $b_{13.2}$ be the least squares estimate of B_{13}. Then, as is well known, the least squares estimates, $b_{12.3}$ and $b_{13.2}$ are obtained by solving simultaneously the following two equations:

$$\Sigma x_1 x_2 = b_{12.3}\Sigma x^2{}_2 + b_{13.2}\Sigma x_2 x_3 \tag{12}$$

$$\Sigma x_1 x_3 = b_{12.3}\Sigma x_2 x_3 + b_{13.2}\Sigma x^2{}_3 \tag{13}$$

Subtracting equation 12 from equation 10, and 13 from 11, we obtain

$$0 = (B_{12} - b_{12.3})\Sigma x^2{}_2 + (B_{13} - b_{13.2})\Sigma x_2 x_3 \tag{14}$$
$$+ \Sigma x_2(v + e_1 - B_{12}e_2 - B_{13}e_3)$$

and

$$0 = (B_{12} - b_{12.3})\Sigma x_2 x_3 + (B_{13} - b_{13.2}) \tag{15}$$
$$\Sigma x^2{}_3 + \Sigma x_3(v + e_1 - B_{12}e_2 - B_{13}e_3)$$

Or, rewriting, we have

$$(B_{12} - b_{12.3}) + b_{32}(B_{13} - b_{13.2}) = C_1 \qquad (16)$$
$$\text{(Line I of Chart 6)}$$

and

$$b_{23}(B_{12} - b_{12.3}) + (B_{13} - b_{13.2}) = C_2 \qquad (17)$$
$$\text{(Line II of Chart 6)}$$

where b_{32} and b_{23} are the sample values of the two zero order regression coefficients between the two explanatory variables x_2 and x_3. C_1 and C_2 are given by the following equations:

$$
\begin{aligned}
C_1 &= -\frac{\Sigma x_2(v + e_1 - B_{12}e_2 - B_{13}e_3)}{\Sigma x^2_2} \qquad (18) \\
&= -\frac{\Sigma(x'_2 + e_2)\ (v + e_1 - B_{12}e_2 - B_{13}e_3)}{\Sigma x^2_2}
\end{aligned}
$$

and

$$
\begin{aligned}
C_2 &= -\frac{\Sigma x_3(v + e_1 - B_{12}e_2 - B_{13}e_3)}{\Sigma x^2_3} \qquad (19) \\
&= -\frac{\Sigma(x'_3 + e_3)\ (v + e_1 - B_{12}e_2 - B_{13}e_3)}{\Sigma x^2_3}
\end{aligned}
$$

The two lines represented by equations (16) and (17) are shown in Chart 6. In any concrete case the slopes of these two lines can be calculated so that the point of intersection, which determines the magnitude of $(B_{12} - b_{12.3})$ and $(B_{13} - b_{13.2})$ will depend on C_1 and C_2, and the problem becomes one of estimating the probable signs and possible magnitudes of C_1 and C_2. It is, of course, evident that, as the correlation between x_2 and x_3 increases toward plus (or minus) unity, the two lines become nearer and nearer to being parallel so that even small divergencies of C_1 and C_2 from zero may result in large values of $(B_{12} - b_{12.3})$ and $(B_{13} - b_{13.2})$.

B. *Application to Evaluation of Statistically Estimated Demand for Imports or Exports Relations.* For the purposes of this application of our theoretical analysis, we will identify X_1 with the observed quantity of imports variable, X_2 with the observed income variable, X_3 with the observed relative price variable. x_1, x_2, and x_3 will then be deviations from sample means of X_1, X_2, and X_3, respectively. e_1, e_2, and e_3 represent the deviations from the mean errors of observation of X_1, X_2, and X_3, respectively, and are thus the errors of observation present in x_1, x_2, and x_3. v represents the deviations from the mean of the omitted part of the true demand relationship.

Case 1. Assume that all variables are measured without errors of observation, and that income is uncorrelated with the omitted part, v, of the

CHART 6

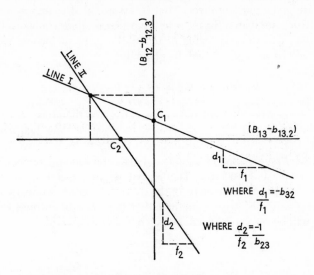

complete explanation of demand. Then C_1 will be zero and C_2 will be given by

$$C_2 = -\frac{\Sigma x'_3 v}{\Sigma x^2_3} \tag{20}$$

In this situation we are fairly certain that there must exist a supply relation which relates the price charged to the quantity sold. Since the quantity sold depends in part on v, it follows that, due to the supply relation, the price variable, x_3, will on this account be positively correlated with v. This will make C_2 negative and so make $(B_{13} - b_{13.2})$ negative and $(B_{12} - b_{12.3})$ positive. Since B_{13} is a negative number, this will mean that the estimated price effect will be biased toward zero. Likewise, since B_{12} should be positive, it will also mean that the estimated income effect will be biased toward zero. It is also rather apparent that if the price and income variables have been standardized, the bias in the estimated price effect will be larger than in the estimated income effect. If, as we have argued in the text, the shifts in price, due to shifts in other than the quantity variable, are positively correlated with shifts in the statistical demand surface, then the value of C_2 will be even more negative and the above biases even more pronounced.

The assumption that income is essentially uncorrelated with the omitted part, v, of the demand relations may, of course, not be true and thus a further measure of uncertainty is introduced. However, a lot more work would seem to be required before it will be possible to make any reasonable argument about the sign or magnitude of the correlation of income, x_2, with v.

Case 2. Assume that v is zero and that the amount demanded and income are given without error. That is, assume that e_1 and e_2 are equal to zero. Also assume that the error in the price variables is uncorrelated, in the sample, with the true value of either the price or income variables. Then C_1 will be zero and C_2 will be given by

$$C_2 = \frac{B_{13}\Sigma e^2_3}{\Sigma x^2_3} \qquad (21)$$

Since B_{13} is negative, this will make C_2 negative and therefore $(B_{13} - b_{13.2})$ will be negative and $(B_{12} - b_{12.3})$ will be positive thus again result in biasing both the estimated price and income effects toward zero.

Case 3. Assume that v is zero and that the amount demanded and price are given without error. That is, we assume e_1 and e_3 are equal to zero. Also assume that the error in the income variable is uncorrelated, in the sample, with the true value of either the price or income variables. Then C_2 will be zero and C_1 will be given by

$$C_1 = \frac{B_{12}\Sigma e^2_2}{\Sigma x^2_2} \qquad (22)$$

Since B_{12} is presumably positive, C_1 will be positive and again the estimated price and income effects will each be biased toward zero.

These three cases have all given biases in the same direction and any combination of them would also result in biases in the same direction. Errors in the quantity variable will not result in any biases so long as they are uncorrelated with the observed price and income variables. Undoubtedly there are many other conceivable assumptions that might be made in addition to those in the above three cases. This adds to the uncertainty of any estimate, but until some case can be given supporting them as likely possibilities these conceivable cases do not lead to any presumption about the likely direction of biases.

APPENDIX 3

Mathematical Note on Bias and Error Due to Neglect of Lagged Prices

Let us suppose that

$$Q_t = A + B_1 P_t + B_2 P_{t-1} + B_3 P_{t-2} \qquad (1)$$

where Q_t represents the quantity of imports, at time t adjusted for the influence of all variables except P_t, P_{t-1}, and P_{t-2}; and P_t represents the relative import price at time t. Then if the price remains constant for three or more periods we have

$$Q_t = A + (B_1 + B_2 + B_3)P_t = A + BP_t \qquad (2)$$

where $B = (B_1 + B_2 + B_3)$ is the coefficient relating Q to P, allowing sufficient time for a full adjustment of quantity to price.

If the effect of P_{t-1} and P_{t-2} is neglected, then we may write

$$Q_t = A + B_1 P_t + E \tag{3}$$

where

$$E = (B_2 P_{t-1} + B_3 P_{t-2}) \tag{4}$$

and thus represents the omitted part of the demand relation.

Expressing the deviations of each variable from the sample mean by a small, rather than a capital, letter, we may rewrite equation (3) as

$$q_t = B_1 p_t + e_t \tag{5}$$

Multiplying through by p_t and summing over the sample, we obtain

$$\Sigma q_t p_t = B_1 \Sigma p^2{}_t + \Sigma p_t e_t \tag{6}$$

The normal equation giving the least squares estimate of B_1, denoted by b_1 is

$$\Sigma q_t p_t = b_1 \Sigma p^2{}_t \tag{7}$$

Subtracting equation (7) from equation (6) we obtain

$$(B_1 - b_1)\, \Sigma p^2{}_t + \Sigma p_t e_t = 0 \tag{8}$$

or

$$(B_1 - b_1) = -\,\frac{\Sigma p_t (B_2 p_{t-1} + B_3 p_{t-2})}{\Sigma p^2{}_t} \tag{9}$$

Since $B = B_1 + B_2 + B_3$, we may rewrite equation (9) as:

$$b_1 = B + B_2 \left(\frac{\Sigma p_t p_{t-1}}{\Sigma p^2{}_t} - 1 \right) \tag{10}$$

$$+ B_3 \left(\frac{\Sigma p_t p_{t-2}}{\Sigma p^2{}_t} - 1 \right)$$

From equation (10) it can be seen that b_1 will in general be biased toward zero. This follows since B_2 and B_3 are presumably negative and the two quantities in brackets are also negative.

$$\frac{\Sigma p_t p_{t-1}}{\Sigma p^2{}_t}$$

is very nearly equal to the correlation of p_t with p_{t-1}, and likewise

$$\frac{\Sigma p_t p_{t-2}}{\Sigma p^2{}_t}$$

is very nearly equal to the correlation of p_t with p_{t-1}. By definition they cannot exceed one for infinite series and can only exceed one by very small amounts for short series. In practice, they are almost certainly well below one for any choice of price variable that has been made. If these auto-correlations of the price series were negative, then b_1, compared with B, would be biased toward zero by an amount greater than the absolute value of $(B_2 + B_3)$. If the price series were random in time, then the bias toward zero would be equal to the absolute value of $(B_2 + B_3)$. And if the price series is positively autocorrelated, then the bias toward zero would be greater than zero but less than the absolute value of $(B_2 + B_3)$.

The extension of the above case to a model involving values of p lagged more than two time periods is straightforward, and the results are of a similar nature.

APPENDIX 4

Bibliography

A. *Theoretical and Statistical Works.*

BROWN, A. J. (1942). "Trade Balances and Exchange Stability," *Oxford Economic Papers,* No. 6, pp. 57–76.

COCHRANE, D. and ORCUTT, G. H. (1949). "Application of Least Squares Regression to Relationships Containing Autocorrelated Error Terms," *Journal of the American Statistical Association,* Vol. 44, pp. 32–61.

FRISCH, R. (1934). *Statistical Confluence Analysis by Means of Complete Regression Systems.* Oslo.

GEARY, R. C. (1949). "Determination of Unbiased Linear Relations between the Systematic Parts of Variables with Errors of Observations," *Econometrica,* Vol. 17, pp. 30–58.

GIRSCHICK, M. A. and HAAVELMO, T. (1947). "Statistical Analyses of the Demand for Food: Examples of Simultaneous Estimation of Structural Equations," *Econometrica,* Vol. 15, pp. 79–110.

HAAVELMO, T. (1943). "The Statistical Implications of a System of Simultaneous Equations," *Econometrica,* Vol. 11, pp. 1–12.

HAAVELMO, T. (1944). "The Probability Approach in Econometrics," *Econometrica,* Vol. 12, Supplement.

KOOPMANS, T. (1937). *Linear Regression Analysis of Economic Time Series.* Netherlands Economic Institute, Haarlem.

KOOPMANS, T. (1945). "Statistical Estimation of Simultaneous Economic Relations," *Journal of the American Statistical Association,* Vol. 40, pp. 448–66.

KOOPMANS, T. (1947). "Statistical Methods of Measuring Economic Relationships," *Cowles Commission Discussion Papers,* Statistics No. 310 (mimeographed copy of lectures delivered at the University of Chicago).

LIU, T. C. (1949). "Exchange Depreciation and the Balance of Trade," International Monetary Fund, RD–876.

MARSCHAK, J. and ANDREWS, W. H. (1944). "Random Simultaneous Equations and the Theory of Production," *Econometrica,* Vol. 12, pp. 143–205.

ORCUTT, G. H. and COCHRANE, D. (1949). "A Sampling Study of the Merits of Autoregressive and Reduced Form Transformations in Regression Analysis," *Journal of the American Statistical Association,* Vol. 44, pp. 356–72.

ORCUTT, G. H. and JAMES, S. F. (1948). "Testing the Significance of Correlation between Time Series," *Biometrika,* Vol. 35, pp. 1–17.

REIERSØL, O. (1945). "Confluence Analysis by Means of Instrumental Sets of Variables," *Arkiv för Matematik, Astronomi Och Fysik,* Band 32A, No. 4.

ROBINSON, J. (1947). "The Foreign Exchanges," *Essays in the Theory of Employment*. 2nd ed. Oxford, pp. 134–55.

SCHULTZ, H. (1938). *The Theory and Measurement of Demand*. University of Chicago Press.

STONE, R. (1945). "The Analysis of Market Demand," *Journal of the Royal Statistical Society*, Vol. 108, pp. 286–391.

TINTNER, G. (1946). "Some Applications of Multivariate Analysis to Economic Data," *Journal of the American Statistical Association*, Vol. 41, pp. 472–500.

WHITE, W. H. (1949). "Import Demand Elasticities and the Effectiveness of Exchange Depreciation," unpublished paper.

YNTEMA, T. O. (1932). *A Mathematical Reformulation of the General Theory of International Trade*. University of Chicago Press.

B. *Statistical or Inductive Studies of the Determinants of Imports or Exports.*

ADLER, J. H. (1945). "United States Import Demand during the Interwar Period," *American Economic Review*, Vol. xxxv, pp. 418–30.

ADLER, J. H. (1946). "The Postwar Demand for United States Exports," *Review of Economic Statistics*, Vol. xxviii, pp. 23–33.

CHANG, T. C. (1945–46). "International Comparison of Demand for Imports," *Review of Economic Studies*, Vol. xiii, pp. 53–67.

CHANG, T. C. (1946). "The British Demand for Imports in the Interwar Period," *Economic Journal*, Vol. lvi, pp. 188–207.

CHANG, T. C. (1947). "A Note on Exports and National Income in Canada," *Canadian Journal of Economics and Political Science*, Vol. 13, 276–80.

CHANG, T. C. (1948a). "A Statistical Note on World Demand for Exports," *Review of Economics and Statistics*, Vol. xxx, pp. 106–16.

CHANG, T. C. (1948b). "The Demand for Imports of the United States in the Interwar Period," International Monetary Fund, RD–511.

DERKSEN AND ROMBOUTS (1939). "The Influence of Prices on Exports," *De Nederlandsche Conjunctuur*, Special Memorandum No. 1.

HINSHAW, R. (1945). "American Prosperity and the British Balance of Payments Problems," *Review of Economic Statistics*, Vol. xxvii, pp. 1–9.

HINSHAW, R. (1946). "Effect of Income Changes on American Imports of Goods and Services," mimeographed, Board of Governors of Federal Reserve System.

HOLZMAN, M. (1949). "The U.S. Demand for Imports of Certain Individual Commodities in the Interwar Period," International Monetary Fund, RD–811.

NEISSER, HANS (1945). "The Propensity of Industrial Countries to Import Raw Materials" (mimeographed), Institute of World Affairs, New School for Social Research, New York.

NEISSER, HANS (1948a). "The Propensity of Industrial Countries to Import Food" (mimeographed), Institute of World Affairs, New School for Social Research, New York.

NEISSER, HANS (1948b). "The Propensity of Industrial Countries to Import Manufactured Goods" (mimeographed), Institute of World Affairs, New School for Social Research, New York.

POLAK, J. J. and CHANG, T. C. (1949). "An International Economic System," International Monetary Fund, RD–853.

TIME, INCORPORATED (1948). *The Market for United Kingdom Consumer Goods in the United States,* New York.

TINBERGEN, J. (1937). *An Econometric Approach to Business Cycle Problems.* Paris.

TINBERGEN, J. (1946). "Some Measurements of Elasticities of Substitution," *Review of Economic Statistics,* Vol. xxviii, pp. 109–16.

TINBERGEN, J. (1947). "Quelques Estimations de l'Influence des Contingentements 1933–1938 sur l'Emploi aux Pays-Bas," *Revue de l'Institut International de Statistique,* Vol. 15, pp. 1–16.

TINBERGEN, J. (1948a). "Some Remarks on the Problem of Dollar Scarcity," mimeographed paper, in English, for World Statistical Congress 1947; and published in French in *Revue d'Economic Politique,* Vol. 58, No. 1 (1948).

TINBERGEN, J. (1948b). "The Fluctuations of the Netherlands Imports, 1923–1938," in *Statistische en Econometrische Onderzockingen,* aflevering 2, published by the Centraal Bureau voor Statistiek (in Dutch with English summary).

DE VEGH, IMRE (1941). "Imports and Income in the United States and Canada," *Review of Economic Statistics,* Vol. xxiii, pp. 130–46.

32. British and American Exports: A Study Suggested by the Theory of Comparative Costs[*][1]

By G. D. A. MACDOUGALL[†]

A. EXPORTS AND LABOUR COSTS

The Labour Theory of Comparative Costs

The work of Mr. Rostas[2] and others on the productivity of British and American industries makes it possible to test some aspects of the theory of comparative costs. According to that theory, when based on a labour theory of value and assuming two countries, each will export those goods for which the ratio of its output per worker to that of the other exceeds the ratio of its money wage-rate to that of the other. Before the war, American weekly wages in manufacturing were roughly double the British,[3] and we find that, where American output per worker was

[*] *Economic Journal*, Vol. LXI, No. 244 (December, 1951), pp. 697–724. The second part of the article, which could not be included in this volume due to limitation of space, was published in the *Economic Journal*, Vol. LXII, No. 247 (September, 1952), pp. 487–521; it used the data to measure elasticities of substitution between British and American exports and the influence of nonprice factors on market shares.

[†] Department of Economic Affairs.

[1] I am indebted to Messrs. Corner, Dehn, Donnison, Lisle and Thackeray, Mrs. Little, Miss Brotman and Miss Orton for statistical assistance, and particularly indebted to Miss Verry, who performed a large part of the calculations. I am grateful for technical and other services provided by the Oxford University Institute of Statistics and for financial assistance from the Oxford University Social Studies Research Fund. Professors D. G. Champernowne and J. E. Meade, Messrs. A. I. Bloomfield, H. Klemmer, D. J. Morgan, R. V. Rosa, L. Rostas, R. L. Sammons, J. R. N. Stone, C. Winsten and others have kindly given valuable advice, but are, of course, in no way responsible for any shortcomings in this paper.

[2] L. Rostas, *Comparative Productivity in British and American Industry*.

[3] The Ministry of Labour's figure (*Ministry of Labour Gazette*, March 1951, p. 92) for average weekly earnings in manufacturing industries only in the United Kingdom in October 1938 is 50s. 4d. = $12 (at £1 = $4.769). The Department of Labour's figure for United States manufacturing for October 1938 is $23.98, and the N.I.C.B. figure $26.14. These are respectively 2·0 and 2·2 times the British figure. A comparison of the United States and United Kingdom Censuses of Production for 1935 suggests a

more than twice the British, the United States had in general the bulk
of the export market, while for products where it was less than twice as
high the bulk of the market was held by Britain. This is shown clearly
in Table I, and more detailed figures are given in Table II. Out of twenty-
five products taken, twenty (covering 97% of the sample by value) obey
the general rule, and two of the remaining five would cease to be exceptions if a different measure of output per worker were chosen.[4]

TABLE I

U.S. and U.K. pre-war Output per Worker and Quantity of Exports in 1937

U.S. output per worker more than twice the British:

Wireless sets and valves	U.S. exports	8 times	U.K.	exports	
Pig iron	"	" 5.	"	"	"
Motor cars	"	" 4	"	"	"
Glass containers	"	" 3½	"	"	"
Tin cans	"	" 3.	"	"	"
Machinery	"	" 1½	"	"	"
Paper	"	1.	"	"	"

U.S. output per worker 1·4–2·0 times the British:

Cigarettes	U.K. exports	2 times	U.S.	exports	
Linoleum, oilcloth, etc.	"	" 3	"	"	"
Hosiery	"	" 3	"	"	"
Leather footwear	"	" 3.	"	"	"
Coke	"	" 5	"	"	"
Rayon weaving	"	" 5.	"	"	"
Cotton goods	"	" 9	"	"	"
Rayon making	"	" 11	"	"	"
Beer	"	" 16	"	"	"

U.S. output per worker less than 1·4 times the British:

Cement	"	" 11	"	"	"
Men's and boy's outer clothing of wool	"	" 23	"	"	"
Margarine	"	" 32	"	"	"
Woollen and worsted	"	" 250	"	"	"

Exceptions (U.S. output per worker more than twice the British, but U.K. exports
exceeded U.S. exports): Electric lamps, rubber tyres, soap, biscuits, matches.

See Table II for further details.

---

figure nearer 1¾. The British and American figures are not, of course, strictly
comparable, and the weights given to the various industries are not the same.

[4] See footnote 34 to Table II.

The following industries for which Mr. Rostas made estimates were omitted from
the analysis: pipe tobacco, cigars and fish-curing, where it is Mr. Rostas's estimates are
particularly liable to error; steelworks, foundries, bricks and seed crushing, where it is
hard to find comparable export figures; manufactured ice (no recorded exports from
either country); grain-milling and beet sugar.

The sample used covered nearly half United Kingdom exports in 1937 of "articles
wholly or mainly manufactured" plus "tobacco, manufactured" and nearly half United
States exports of "finished manufactures." It also included a small value of manufactured foodstuffs (biscuits, margarine and beer), and a small part of the exports
classified in the United States returns as "semi-manufactures."

But while in the normal text-book examples the exports of each country go to each other, the great bulk of the exports of the United States and the United Kingdom in 1937 went to third countries—more than 95% of British exports of all our sample products but three, more than 95% of American exports of all the products but six (see columns (4) and (5) of Table II). It is true that each country was nearly always a net exporter to the other of products in which it had a comparative advantage (see column (9) of Table II), but this is of limited interest, since trade between them was in general a negligible proportion of their total consumption, despite the large differences in the ratio of productivity, which enabled some British industries to sweep the board in third markets, while in other industries America swept the board. The lower part of column (8) of Table II shows that, even where Britain had a comparative advantage, and could undersell American producers in third markets, her exports to America were usually a small fraction of 1% of total American consumption. The upper part of column (8) shows that, where America had the comparative advantage, her exports to Britain were, in general, more substantial, but never more than a few per cent of total British consumption.

Tariffs

Why was this so? Apart from costs of transport and the many difficulties of selling in a foreign country where there are rival domestic producers, there seems little doubt that tariffs were a decisive obstacle. The approximate *ad valorem* incidence of the American tariffs (adjusted where necessary for internal revenue taxes[5]) is shown in column (6) of Table II,[6] and Figure 1 shows how far they offset Britain's comparative advantages. This diagram (drawn on a double logarithmic scale for reasons to be explained later) shows the ratio of American to British output per worker in each industry—measured vertically—and the ratio of American to British exports—measured horizontally—for all products in our sample save the exceptions noted above. Where United States output per worker is

---

[5] Such adjustments were necessary only for beer (where the internal revenue tax was levied only on home production) and for margarine (where the internal revenue tax was higher for imports than it was for home production). Where internal revenue taxes were levied on other items, they applied equally to home production and to imports, and were additional to Customs duty.

[6] The tariff rate (before adjusting for internal revenue tax) was obtained by expressing the calculated duty on the relevant categories of imports from the United Kingdom as a percentage of the value, excluding duty, of imports from the United Kingdom. This states correctly the protective effect of the tariff where (as with motor cars) one rate of duty applies to all sub-categories and the rate is *ad valorem*. But where the rate is wholly or partly specific, or where there is more than one rate, the protective effect tends to be understated, since imports of types and qualities on which the *ad valorem* incidence of the tariff is highest will tend to be the most restricted and may even be eliminated; it is shown in the text that potential imports from the United Kingdom were in large part kept out by the United States tariff.

FIGURE 1
Productivity, Exports, and Tariffs

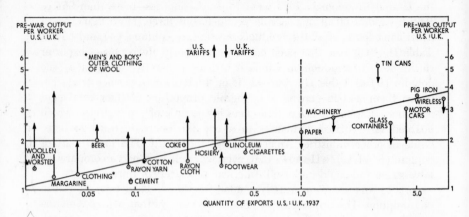

QUANTITY OF EXPORTS U.S. : U.K. 1937

not more than twice the British (items on or below the horizontal line marked 2) the incidence of the American tariff is shown by an upward-pointing arrow. In cotton spinning and weaving, for example, United States output per worker is estimated at 1·5 times the British, and since the United States tariff was on average about 35%, the arrow extends upwards to just over 2·0. This means that, assuming a labour theory of value and American weekly wages double the British, the price of United Kingdom goods would be three-quarters of the American in the world market, but as dear as the American in the American market after paying the tariff. Thus the tariff almost exactly offset Britain's comparative advantage in cotton goods, even ignoring the cost of transport.[7]

It will be seen that the American tariff fully offset Britain's comparative advantage in every product except cement and coke (where the cost of transport is high), and footwear, where the remaining margin was not large in relation to the transport and other special costs involved. (Figures given later show that the United States tariff also offset Britain's advantage as measured by *export prices* in every product save cement, coke, footwear and beer.[8]) It is perhaps significant that the American tariff was, in general, much higher on products where Britain had a comparative advantage than it was on the others. The unweighted average was 61% *ad*

---

[7] It will be seen later that the United States tariff on cotton goods offset, with a more substantial margin to spare, Britain's advantage as measured both by wage costs per unit of output and by export price.

[8] If, however, the *ad valorem* incidence of the (specific) beer duties is reckoned on the average value of the United Kingdom's total exports of beer, rather than on that of United States imports from the United Kingdom, the United States tariff (even after allowing for the internal revenue tax levied only on American-produced beer) fully offset Britain's price advantage.

valorem where Britain had a comparative advantage, 28% where she had not.[9]

(It must be emphasised that all these conclusions refer to pre-war conditions. Since then, the *ad valorem* incidence of the U.S. tariff on many items has been substantially reduced, both through the reduction of rates and through the rise in prices, which has reduced the incidence of specific duties. There has, moreover, been a large rise in the ratio of American to British average dollar weekly earnings in manufacturing, from about 2 in October 1938 to nearly 3½ in April 1951. While in many industries output per worker may also have risen faster in the United States, there seems little doubt that, in most, American labour cost per unit of output must have risen in relation to the British. It seems likely, therefore, that the importance of the United States tariff in offsetting Britain's comparative advantages has in general been reduced.)

The British 1937 tariffs (Column (7) of Table II) were generally lower than the American; the unweighted average was 24% *ad valorem*[10] com-, pared with an American average of 45%. The downward-pointing arrows in the diagram[11] show that the British tariffs fully offset America's comparative advantage in only paper and glass containers; British imports of these products from the United States were a negligible part of her total consumption. The British tariff failed to offset America's comparative advantage in machinery, motor cars, wireless sets and valves, pig iron and tin cans; in all but the last, where the cost of transport is high because of stowage difficulties, Britain's imports from the United States were a significant but still a small part of her consumption, ranging from 2½ to 8%. That they were not larger may perhaps be partly explained by transport and other special costs. The margins remaining after the tariff were small for machinery and motor cars, and for pig iron the cost of transport is heavy. Another possible reason will be given later for the low imports of these products into Britain.[12]

The more protective nature of the United States than of the United

---

[9] Groups II and I respectively in Table II.

Similar calculations covering 155 commodities showed that the average American tariff was 40% where the British *export price* was lower than the American and 26% where it was higher. They also showed that, in a (bare) majority of the cases where the British export price was lower than the American, the American tariff offset the British price advantage. (In these calculations, the *ad valorem* incidence of the American tariff was, for simplicity in computation, based on American imports from all sources, rather than on imports from the United Kingdom only.)

[10] Omitting tin cans, for which no American figure was found.

[11] If the United Kingdom tariff was 100 t% and the ratio of United States to United Kingdom productivity R, the downward-pointing arrow brings the point down to $R/(1 + t)$

[12] See Section on "Indirect Labour."

Figures given later show that America's advantage as measured by *export price* was fully offset by the United Kingdom tariff on motor cars, and the margins remaining after the tariff are reduced on tin cans, pig iron and wireless sets and valves. (For glass containers and paper, however, the American advantage is no longer offset.)

TABLE II

	(1) Output per Worker U.S.:U.K., Pre-war.	(2) Quantity of Exports U.S.:U.K., 1937.	(3) Price of Exports U.S.:U.K., 1937.	(4) U.S. Exports to U.K. as % of Exports to all Countries, 1937.	(5) U.K. Exports to U.S. as % of Exports to all Countries, 1937.	(6) U.S. Tariff %, 1937.	(7) U.K. Tariff %, 1937.	(8)	(9) A = U.S. Export Surplus to U.K.; B = U.K. Export Surplus to U.S., 1937.
I. U.S. output per worker more than twice U.K.:[1]								*U.K. Imports from U.S. as % of U.K. Consumption, 1935.*	
Tin cans	5·25	3·0	0·68	—	—	[s1]	20	0·005	A
Pig iron	3·6	5·1[3]	0·84	30	—	5	Nil[4]	2·4[5]	A
Wireless receiving sets and valves	3·5[6]	7·6[7]	0·64	10	—	35	25[8]	{ 4·7 sets 8·2 valves	A
Motor cars	3·1	4·3[9]	0·91[s1]	3	—	10	33⅓	2·7[5]	A
Machinery	2·7[10]	1·5[11]	—	13[11]	2[11]	20	20[12]	3·2	A
Glass containers	2·4	3·5	0·69	2	—	75	25	0·2	A
Paper	2·2	1·0[13]	0·72	8	1	25	20	0·06	A
II. U.S. output per worker not more than twice U.K.:[1]								*U.S. Imports from U.K. as % of U.S. Consumption, 1939.*	
Beer	2·0[16]	0·056	1·30	—	2	20[40]	30[17]	0·01	B
Linoleum, oilcloth, etc.	1·9[10]	0·34[18]	1·04	4	9	40	20	2·0	B
Coke	1·9	0·19	1·08	—	1	Nil	Nil	0·03	B
Hosiery	1·8	0·30[19]	1·24	6	10	65	20[20]	0·4	B
Cigarettes	1·7	0·47	1·08	2	—	115	70[21]	0·004	A
Rayon weaving	1·5	0·20	1·19	2	1	80	40[22]	0·0023	B
Cotton spinning and weaving	1·5[23]	0·11[24]	1·03	—	1	35	20[25]	{ 0·04 yarn 0·14 cloth	B

	(1)	(2)	(3)	(4)	(5)	(6)	(7)	(8)	(9)
Leather footwear	1·4	0·32[25]	1·31	11	4	20	20	0·03	A[38]
Rayon making	1·4	0·091	1·53	—	—	55	55[26]	0·0014	B
Woollen and worsted	1·35	0·004[27]	1·42	2	4	85	20[28]	{0·08 yarn / 1·8 cloth}	B
Men's and boys' outer clothing of wool	1·25[29]	0·044[30]	[31]	—	16[30]	60[14]	20	[31]	B
Margarine	1·2	0·031	1·34	2	—	210[39]	10	—	B
Cement	1·1[33]	0·091	2·12	2	—	5	10	0·007	B
III. Exceptions:[2]									
Electric lamps	5·4[6]	0·94[33]	0·51	1	—	20	10		A
Biscuits	3·1	0·23	1·01	4	2	30	10		B
Matches	3·1[34]	0·09[35]	0·86	—[35]	—	30	45[36]		A
Rubber tyres	2·7[34]	0·74[37]	1·12[37]	1	—	10	33⅓		A
Soap	2·7	0·35	1·24	3	1	25	20		B

Sources and General Notes on each Column

Column (1). Rostas, *Comparative Productivity in British and American Industry*, except where otherwise stated. Rounded figures.

Column (2). *Foreign Commerce and Navigation of the United States; Annual Statement of the Trade of the United Kingdom*. An attempt was made to find categories comparable to those used by Mr. Rostas. Weighted averages of sub-items have been calculated in several cases.

Column (3). Same sources as for column (2). Obtained by dividing index of value (in dollars) by index of quantity as in column (2). Price differences may reflect partly differences of quality, etc.

Columns (4) and (5). Same sources as for column (2). Quantity ratios, in some cases weighted averages of sub-items. The sign — in these columns means less than one-half of 1%. Some of the figures in column (5) may be underestimated where no United States exports to the United Kingdom trade accounts although some took place.

Column (6). *Foreign Commerce and Navigation of the United States; Annual Reports of the Commissioner of Internal Revenue*. Calculated duty on relevant categories of imports from the United Kingdom as percentage of value of imports from the United Kingdom, excluding duty. Allowance made where necessary for internal revenue taxes. Rounded figures.

Column (7). *Annual Statement of the Trade of the United Kingdom; Customs and Excise Tariff of the United Kingdom, 1937*. Average non-preferential rates in round figures. Since it was not always very clear into which tariff category a product fell, some errors may have arisen. Allowance was made so far as possible for excise taxes on British-produced goods.

Column (8). *United Kingdom Census of Production, 1935; Annual Statement of the Trade of the United Kingdom*; British Iron and Steel Federation, *Statistics of the Iron and Steel Industries*; Society of Motor Manufacturers and Traders, Ltd., *The Motor Industry of Great Britain; Foreign Commerce and Navigation of the United States*; U.S. Tariff Commission, *Post-War Imports and Domestic Production of Major Commodities*, 1945. The categories covered do not always correspond exactly with those used in other parts of the table.

Column (9). Same sources as for column (2).

Footnotes to Table II.

1 American prewar weekly wages were roughly twice as high as the British.

2 American output per worker more than twice British, but British exports greater than American.

3 This ratio is typical of the years 1937–39, but much higher than in earlier years.

4 A duty of 33⅓% was removed during 1937.

5 1937.

6 United Kingdom, 1935; United States, 1939.

7 Weighted average of sets and valves.

8 Weighted average of sets (20%) and valves (33⅓%).

9 Weighted average of private and commercial vehicles.

10 United Kingdom, 1935; United States, 1937.

11 Based on value; approximately same coverage in the United States and the United Kingdom; includes electrical machinery and locomotives.

12 Typical rate of duty; the average incidence was probably lower, allowing for imports exempt from duty.

13 Partly estimated.

14 Based on figures for miscellaneous woollen wearing apparel, not knit or crocheted.

15 Weighted average of main types.

16 Beer is included in Group II, although Mr. Rostas's index is 2·01.

17 Customs (approximately 130% of import value) less excise (approximately 100% on equivalent beer). Based on imports from all foreign countries. No imports from the United States are separately recorded.

18 Weighted average of various types (linoleum, oilcloth, felt base floor covering, etc.).

19 Weighted average of stockings, knitted underwear, knitted outerwear (approximate).

20 Excluding silk and rayon duty.

21 Customs duty was 14/7d. per lb. There was no excise duty on home-produced cigarettes as such, but that on home-grown tobacco was equivalent to an excise duty of 11/5d. per lb. The difference, 3/2d. per lb., is about 70% of the import value of U.S. cigarettes.

22 Rough figure for printed rayon tissues only, from all foreign countries, allowing for excise duty on home-produced yarn.

23 Adjusted to 1937 in each country.

24 Weighted average of yarn and cloth.

25 Rate on tissues.

26 Customs (approximately 75% of import value) less excise (approximately 20%). Based on imports from all foreign countries. No imports from the United States are separately recorded.

27 Weighted average of yarn, cloth, carpets, felt.

28 Rate on tissues and carpets.

29 1946. *Heavy Clothing Industry Working Party Report*, p. 153.

30 Based on value; quantity data inadequate.

31 Not available.

32 United Kingdom, 1938; United States, 1939.

33 This ratio would be lower if allowance were made for the higher proportion of larger bulbs in United Kingdom exports.

34 In terms of value of net output per worker, the ratios are 1·0 for matches and 1·7 for rubber tyres and the two items cease to be exceptions.

35 1935.

36 Customs (approximately 370% of import value) less excise (approximately 325%). Women's shoes—large United States export surplus to United Kingdom. No imports from the United States are separately recorded.

37 Automobile outer covers only.

38 Men's shoes—large United Kingdom export surplus to United States. Women's shoes—large United States export surplus to United Kingdom.

39 Imports paid customs duty of 14 cents per lb. and internal revenue tax of 15 cents per lb., making a total of 29 cents per lb. Margarine produced in the United States paid internal revenue tax of 10 cents per lb. if coloured and of ¼ cent per lb. if uncoloured. Assuming that all imports from the United Kingdom were coloured, the extra tax paid by them was 19 cents per lb., equivalent to approximately 210% of the average value of imports from the United Kingdom. On uncoloured imports the extra tax would be still higher.

40 Customs (approximately 29% of import value) less internal revenue tax (approximately 9%), which was levied on beer produced in the United States, but not on imported beer.

Kingdom tariff may help to explain the following facts: in 1937, only
4½% of Britain's exports of manufactures were sold in the United States,
although that country accounted for about one-third of the world's consumption (not imports) of manufactures outside the United Kingdom;
but as much as 11% of the United States' exports of manufactures were sold
in the United Kingdom, roughly equal to the proportion which Britain
represented of the world's consumption of manufactures outside the
United States.[13]

Varying Relative Wages

So far we have assumed that American weekly wages were roughly
double the British in all the industries considered. In fact, there was some
variation. It is, however, difficult to make allowance for this since the industrial classifications used by the two countries for the purpose of wage
statistics differ considerably, and do not agree very closely with the classifications used in the productivity comparisons quoted. It was thought desirable, nevertheless, to make some very rough estimates of relative wage
costs per unit of output, allowing for varying wage ratios, to test the
validity of the general conclusions so far reached. The results for thirteen
industries are shown in Table III. The "exceptional" cases are excluded
as before, together with other industries for which it seemed impossible
to make even rough estimates of relative wages.

It was found that American weekly earnings ranged between about
1½ and 2½ times the British (see column (2)). Column (3) gives rough
estimates of relative wage costs per unit of output, calculated from the
relative output per worker and wage figures. It will be seen that, in all
industries save cigarettes, American wage costs per unit of output were
less than or greater than the British, according as American output per
worker was or was not more than twice the British. There is also a clear
inverse relation between relative wage costs per unit of output (column
(3)) and relative exports (column (4)), rather clearer in fact than that
between relative output per worker and relative exports. The earlier generalisations on tariffs also remain valid.[14]

Owing to the unsatisfactory nature of the statistics, no great significance
should be attached to the detailed results shown, but the general impres-

---

[13] The figures in this paragraph are not all strictly comparable. The proportion of
Britain's exports of manufactures sold in the United States is based on the United
Kingdom's recorded exports of "articles wholly or mainly manufactured." The
proportion of the United States' exports of manufactures sold in the United Kingdom
is based on American recorded exports of "finished manufactures" plus "semi-
manufactures." The other two proportions quoted are calculated mainly from *Indus-
trialisation and Foreign Trade*, League of Nations, 1945, and are based broadly on the
classification "manufactured articles" in the International (Brussels) Classification of
1913.

[14] The only differences are that the American tariff now offsets the British
advantage in leather footwear and fails to offset it in beer and in men's and boys'
outer clothing of wool (but only by around 10% in each case).

TABLE III

	(1) *Output per* *Worker* *U.S. : U.K.* *Pre-war*	(2) *Weekly* *Dollar* *Earnings* *U.S. : U.K.* *Oct. 1938*	(3) *Wage Costs* *Per Unit of* *Output* *U.S. : U.K.* *(2) ÷ (1)*	(4) *Quantity of* *Exports* *U.S. : U.K.* *1937*
Pig iron	3·6	1·5	0·4	5·1
Motor cars	3·1	2·0	0·6	4·3
Machinery	2·7	1·9	0·7	1·5
Glass containers	2·4	2·0	0·8	3·5
Paper	2·2	2·0	0·9	1·0
Cigarettes	1·7	1·5	0·9	0·47
Leather footwear	1·4	1·5	1·1	0·32
Hosiery	1·8	1·9	1·1	0·30
Cotton spinning and weaving	1·5	1·7	1·1	0·11
Beer	2·0	2·6	1·3	0·056
Cement	1·1	1·7	1·5	0·091
Woollen and worsted	1·35	2·0	1·5	0·004
Men's and boys' outer clothing of wool	1·25	2·3	1·8	0·044

Sources: Columns (1) and (4): from Table II. Column (2): *Ministry of Labour Gazette*, November and December, 1940, and *Monthly Labour Review*, February, 1939 (U.S. Dept. of Labour; Bureau of Labour Statistics). The figures are rough orders of magnitude only and subject to a considerable margin of error. They often refer to industry groups that are neither exactly comparable in the two countries nor identical with those used in deriving the figures in columns (1) and (4).

sion derived from Table III is that the main conclusions reached earlier in the paper are unaffected by the fact that American wages were not exactly double the British in all industries.

The Ohlin Theory

The figures given so far tend to confirm the theory of comparative costs, even when based on a labour theory of value, so far as exports to third countries are concerned, and the small volume of trade in manufactures between Britain and America can be largely explained by tariffs that offset comparative advantages. The theory, as developed by Ohlin, that countries will export goods requiring a relatively high proportion of the factors with which they are well endowed, is not, however, confirmed by the statistics given by Mr. Rostas. If horse-power is taken as a rough index of capital employed, there is little tendency for Britain to export more than America of products requiring a low ratio of capital to labour, and vice versa. We find, for example, that Britain had the larger export market in linoleum, cement and coke, where the ratio of horse-power to labour is above the average for all factory trades in both countries, while the United States had the larger export market in tin cans, wireless, motor cars, machinery and glass containers, where the ratio of horse-power to labour is below the average.[15] Since, however, horse-power is probably an inadequate measure of capital employed, these negative results must not be taken as a refutation of the Ohlin theory.

Imperfect Markets

The usual labour theory of comparative costs assumes perfect markets and homogeneous products. If there were also no transport costs, Britain and America could both export the same commodity only where the productivity ratio equalled the wage ratio. Where either country had any comparative advantage, however small, she would get the whole export market. We find that, in fact, neither Britain nor American ever got the whole of the market (although this might be the case if we could take very narrow categories of goods). Each country tended rather to get the larger share of the market where it had a comparative advantage. But the figures show more than this. There is also a tendency for each country to get a larger and larger share of the market the greater its comparative advantage, especially when allowance is made for varying relative wages. This is what we should expect when there are imperfect markets, non-homogeneous products and transport costs, and the data thus tend to confirm the labour theory of comparative costs when these more realistic conditions are introduced.

A feature revealed by Figure 1 that would not have been expected *a priori* is that the points lie fairly close to a straight line when plotted on a double logarithmic scale. The implications will be discussed later, but it may be well to consider for a moment the fact that the regression line passes through the horizontal line marked 2 (American output per worker twice the British) at a point well to the left of the vertical line marked 1·0 (American and British exports the same). This means that America tended to export considerably less than Britain (less than two-fifths as much) even in industries where her output per worker was double the British and so exceeded the British by as much as her wage level. America tended to export as much as Britain only when her output per worker was about 2½ times the British.[16] One possible reason is that Britain had on balance an advantage in the imperfect world market, including the advantage of Imperial Preference. But there is another possible reason which must now be mentioned.

Indirect Labour

It seems likely that, where Mr. Rostas's figures show the Americans using half as much labour *within the factory* per unit of output, they were using more than half as much labour indirectly, to produce the goods

---

[15] See Rostas, *op. cit.*, pp. 68–70.

[16] If the "exceptional" cases are included, the line is shifted still farther to the left.

and to transport them to the ports, in other sectors of the economy such as building, transport, distribution, commercial and other services. Even if in some non-manufacturing sectors, such as coal-mining, the Americans used less than half as much indirect labour per unit of output, it seems likely that on balance the figures of Mr. Rostas exaggerate the overall American superiority, except perhaps in products where they show American output per worker in the factory as considerably less than twice the British; in such cases the American superiority in output per worker may be less in the factory than in other sectors, and Mr. Rostas's figures may therefore understate the overall American superiority.[17]

If we could re-draw our diagram in terms of output per worker, including indirect workers, we should therefore expect the points on the right, referring to products where America had a comparative advantage, to be brought down nearer to the horizontal line marked 2; this would help to explain the small scale of Britain's imports even where her tariff did not appear to offset America's comparative advantage. On the left of the diagram, the higher points would tend to be lowered and some of the lower points might be raised. It seems that, in general, our conclusions on the protective nature of the American tariff would be unaffected. It is not unlikely that the regression line would be lowered and would cut the horizontal line marked 2 farther to the right, thus reducing the apparent disadvantage of the United States in the imperfect world markets.

It is likely that the regression line, besides being shifted downwards, would also become flatter, not only because the relative amounts of indirect labour per unit of output used in transport, distribution, etc., are largely independent of relative productivity in the factory,[18] but also in

---

[17] Mr. Rostas (*op. cit.*, p. 89) suggests the following rough relative productivities per worker (United States: United Kingdom) in certain non-manufacturing sectors:

Transport of goods	1·0	(ignoring distance, which seems appropriate for this analysis)
Commercial and other services	1·0	
Distribution	1·5	
Building	1·15	
Gas	1·7	
Electricity	1·9	
Communications	2·7	
Mining	4·15	

To find the indirect labour used in a manufactured product it is, of course, necessary to estimate also the amount of fuel, commercial services, etc., used per unit of output, but it is not thought that this would substantially alter the conclusions reached in the text. As regards labour used indirectly in replacing capital equipment, Mr. Rostas (*op. cit.*, pp. 56–8) finds no reason for supposing that this would greatly alter the average 2:1 superiority of United States industry in output per worker.

[18] It also seems that there is no observable relation between the relative amounts of capital (at least as measured by horse-power) used per unit of output and the relative productivities (see Rostas, *op. cit.*, p. 54). In so far as relatively high output per worker goes with relatively high capital per unit of output, the range of overall relative productivity would be still further reduced by the inclusion of labour used in capital replacement.

so far as individual factories used semi-finished products from a random selection of manufacturing industries in which the American relative superiority in output per worker tended to average 2 : 1. The importance of this latter consideration must not, however, be exaggerated. Textile factories, for example, tend to use the semi-finished products of other textile factories, and Britain tended to have a comparative advantage over most of the textile field. Similarly, engineering works tend to use the products of other engineering works, and the United States had a comparative advantage over much of this field.

This may also help to explain the fairly good correlation between relative output per worker in the factory and relative exports. It is, after all, total cost and price rather than output per worker that is of importance in determining exports,[19] and, since the wage bill of the average British factory was only about one-fifth of the total value of the output, it might have been thought that the differences in other costs would swamp differences in wage costs.[20] But there is in fact, as we shall see, a distinct correlation between relative output per worker in the factory and relative export price, and this may well be because a large part of the semi-manufactures bought by the average firm comes from industries with an output per worker, in relation to America, similar to its own.

B. EXPORTS AND PRICES

We have already mentioned the rather surprising fact that, if relative output per worker is plotted against relative exports, the points tend to lie about a straight line if a double logarithmic scale is used. The correlation coefficient is $0 \cdot 8$, and the steeper of the two regression lines (that minimising the sum of the squares of the deviations in a horizontal direction) has a slope of about 4.[21] This is the regression line shown in Figure 1. (If the "exceptional" items are included the correlation coefficient is $0 \cdot 7$ and the slope is about 3.[22]) In other words, we find that, if the ratio of British to American output per worker in the factory was 1% higher for commodity A than for commodity B, the ratio of exports, according to the regression line shown, tended to be 3–4% higher. If *prices* in each country were proportional to direct *factory* labour used per unit of output the plotting of relative export prices against relative export quantities would show a downward slope of exactly the same magnitude, but if, as is less unlikely, prices were proportional to the *total* amount of labour used per

[19] Except in so far as high productivity includes the ability to keep up to date, etc.

[20] In round figures, the gross output of factory trades in the 1935 Census of Production was made up of 20% wages, 55% raw materials, etc., 25% other costs and profits.

[21] Throughout this paper, for simplicity of exposition, dx/dy is used as a measure of slopes, not dy/dx, the more usual measure.

[22] The slope of the regression line, when the sum of the squares of the *vertical* deviations is minimised, is considerably flatter ($5 \cdot 7$ excluding the exceptional cases and $6 \cdot 0$ including them).

unit of output, including indirect labour, we would expect the slope to be flatter for the reasons given above. The range of prices would, moreover, be still further reduced, and the curve still further flattened, if we took account of the use of raw materials entering into world trade and coming from neither the United States nor the United Kingdom, since their cost would tend to be the same for British and American manufacturers.

We do in fact find (in column (3) of Table II) that, disregarding our exceptional cases as before, the American export price was always lower than the British where America had a comparative advantage (output per worker in the factory more than twice the British) and exported more than Britain. Similarly, British export prices were always lower than the American where Britain had a comparative advantage and exported more than America.[23] The inverse relation between relative price and relative quantity is clearly illustrated in Table IV.[24] When relative exports are plotted against relative prices, rather than against relative output per

TABLE IV

Price and Quantity of American and British Exports, 1937

American price less than the British:

Wireless sets and valves	U.S. exports 8 times U.K. exports
Pig iron	,, ,, 5 ,, ,, ,,
Motor cars	,, ,, 4 ,, ,, ,,
Glass containers	,, ,, 3½ ,, ,, ,,
Tin cans	,, ,, 3 ,, ,, ,,
Paper	,, ,, 1 ,, ,, ,,

American price 1–1¼ times the British:

Rubber tyres	U.K. exports 1½ times U.S. exports
Cigarettes	,, ,, 2 ,, ,, ,,
Linoleum, oilcloth, etc.	,, ,, 3 ,, ,, ,,
Hosiery	,, ,, 3 ,, ,, ,,
Soap	,, ,, 3 ,, ,, ,,
Biscuits	,, ,, 4 ,, ,, ,,
Rayon weaving	,, ,, 5 ,, ,, ,,
Coke	,, ,, 5 ,, ,, ,,
Cotton goods	,, ,, 9 ,, ,, ,,

American price over 1¼ times the British:

Leather footwear	,, ,, 3 ,, ,, ,,
Rayon making	,, ,, 11 ,, ,, ,,
Cement	,, ,, 11 ,, ,, ,,
Beer	,, ,, 18 ,, ,, ,,
Margarine	,, ,, 32 ,, ,, ,,
Woollen and worsted	,, ,, 250 ,, ,, ,,

[23] No figures of price were available for machinery or for men's and boys' outer clothing of wool. Omitting these, the coefficient of correlation between the logarithms of relative output per worker and relative price was −0·83 excluding the exceptional cases and −0·70 including them.

[24] This table includes three of the five "exceptional" cases: rubber tyres, soap and biscuits. It excludes the remaining two (electric lamps and matches), American exports of which were less than the British although American prices were lower.

worker in the factory, on a double logarithmic scale, the correlation coefficient is −0·8 and the steeper regression line has a slope of about −5.
(If the five "exceptional" cases are included, the correlation coefficient is
−0·7 and the slope about −4.[25]) The slope of the line is flattened as we
had expected.[26] A difference of 1% in relative price tends to be associated
with a difference of 4–5% in relative quantity of exports. This result, and
those that follow, are based on the steeper of the two regression lines.
Reasons will be given later for supposing that such results tend to underestimate the true difference in relative quantity associated with a 1%
difference in relative price. In the same way, the flatter of the two regression lines tends to give an overestimate.

The term "price" is, of course, a misnomer in this context. It should,
strictly, be replaced by "average value" to take account of differing qualities and the like. This matter will be further discussed below. It is likely
that, in other respects, some of the figures quoted so far give a misleading
picture of particular products. For this, apologies are due to experts in
the various industries. It should be emphasised that the study is concerned only with an attempt to establish certain general conclusions, and
it is hoped that these will not be upset by technical errors in the various
fields. The detailed figures given should be interpreted in this light, and
should not be taken as establishing anything about any particular industry
or product; this would require more intensive study. In the rest of the
paper no mention will be made of specific products.

A Larger Sample

The results given so far are based on a sample covering a substantial
part of the British and American export trade in manufactures by value,
but the number of observations is comparatively small. If, however, we
leave productivity comparisons and the labour theory of value—the validity of which is in any case limited—we are no longer bound to the industrial groups for which Mr. Rostas and others have calculated figures. We
can delve into the greater detail of the export trade returns.

This has been done, again for 1937, and 171 manufactures (including
some semi-manufactures and manufactured foodstuffs) were found that
seemed reasonably comparable and for which suitable quantity and value
figures were given in the trade accounts of the two countries.[27] A correla-

---

25 The slope of the other regression line is −7.6, both including and excluding
the exceptional cases.

26 The regression and correlation coefficients given here are broadly comparable
with those in the previous paragraph, since the latter are hardly affected by the exclusion of machinery and clothing.

27 These covered approximately 40% of British exports of "articles wholly or
mainly manufactured" plus "tobacco, manufactured," 30% of American exports of
"finished manufactures" and 10% of American exports of "semi-manufactures." They
also included a small number of manufactured foodstuffs. For statistical reasons, very
few observations were possible in the important field of machinery.

tion of the logarithms of relative dollar prices and relative quantities of
exports gave a correlation coefficient of $-0\cdot62$, and the regression line had
a slope of $-2\cdot9$, steeper than that derived from the smaller sample even
when the "exceptional" cases were included.

To test whether this result for 1937 was typical, similar calculations
were made for each of the years 1922 to 1938. Owing to changes of classification in the trade accounts, it was impossible to get data for the same
171 products in each year. Reasonably comparable figures were, however,
found for 109 items in each of the years 1928–38, for ninety-seven items
in each of the years 1925–28 and for eighty-six items in each of the years
1922–25. (For the years before 1922, classification problems greatly reduced the number of comparable figures available.) The results are
shown in Table V. Bearing in mind the changed coverage introduced in
1925 and 1928, for which years figures were calculated for both the
smaller and the larger number of items, it is possible to analyse the
trends over the whole period 1922–38.

When only 109 items are used, rather than 171, the correlation for 1937
is slightly better ($-0\cdot65$) and the slope slightly flatter ($-3\cdot1$). These
figures turned out to be typical of the years 1934–38, each of which
showed a correlation coefficient of between $-0\cdot64$ and $-0\cdot68$, and a slope
of between $-2\cdot9$ and $-3\cdot2$. For the earlier years the slope was steeper
and the correlation, at least before 1931, poorer. Neither the correlation
nor the slope show any tendency to vary with the trade cycle. There is,
however, a steady increase in the correlation coefficient and a fairly steady
flattening of the slope from about 1924 until 1931. This may reflect the
slow emergence of a new pattern of trade after the war and the gradual
readjustment to a new price structure during a period of comparative
exchange-rate stability following the post-war exchange-rate fluctuations,
which no doubt upset price–quantity relationships. In February 1920 the
pound had fallen, at its lowest point, to two-thirds of its pre-war dollar
value; by 1922 it had recovered to about 90%, and subsequent fluctuations
were comparatively small until the return to the gold standard in 1925
ensured exchange-rate stability until September, 1931.

In 1932 there was a reversal of the previous upward trend in both correlation coefficient and slope. Both fell, no doubt because of Britain's
abandonment of the gold standard and the sharp fall in the dollar value
of the pound, which might have been expected temporarily to upset price–
quantity relationships.

Both correlation coefficient and slope increased again in 1933 and 1934,
and from 1934 to 1938 remained generally at higher levels than previously,
but showed no upward or downward trend. The flatter slope and higher
correlation in these last five years is consistent with the trend observed in
earlier years. It might have been thought that the Ottawa Agreements
would have tended to weaken, rather than to strengthen, the relationship
between relative prices (f.o.b. Britain and the United States) and relative

quantities of exports to third countries, but, as will be seen later, the increased preference granted to British exports was probably not of great quantitative importance. The rather violent changes in exchange rates between September 1931 and the end of 1933 might have been expected to

TABLE V

Correlation between Logarithms of Relative Quantities (q) and Logarithms of Relative Dollar Prices (p) of United States and United Kingdom Exports of Individual Manufactured Products[*]

	(1) Number of Manufactures.	(2) Correlation Coefficient (r).	(3) Regression Coefficient (Slope) (b_{qp}).	(4) Rate of Exchange, Pounds to dollars 1929 = 100.
1913[†]	32	−0·54	−3·2	100
1922	86	−0·41	−2·0	91
1923	86	−0·40	−1·8	94
1924	86	−0·43	−1·9	91
1925	86	−0·47	−2·2	99
1925	97	−0·48	−2·1	99
1926	97	−0·50	−2·4	100
1927	97	−0·54	−2·4	100
1928	97	−0·55	−2·5	100
1928	109	−0·56	−2·5	100
1929	109	−0·57	−2·6	100
1930	109	−0·58	−2·6	100
1931	109	−0·66	−2·7	93
1932	109	−0·62	−2·6	72
1933	109	−0·65	−2·8	87
1934	109	−0·68	−3·2	104
1935	109	−0·64	−3·0	101
1936	109	−0·67	−2·9	102
1937	109 (171)	−0·65 (−0·62)	−3·1 (−2·9)	102
1938	109	−0·68	−3·1	101
1934–38[‡]	109	−0·73	−3·6	102
1937	118	−0·62	−3·0	102
1948	118	−0·34	−1·6	83

[*] Including some semi-manufactures and manufactured foodstuffs.
[†] Mid-1912 to mid-1913 for the United States.
[‡] See text.

upset, at least temporarily, the price–quantity relationship, but, as the dollar–sterling rate had returned by 1934 to approximately the old parity, and as it varied little between 1934 and 1938, it may be that the fluctuations between September 1931 and the end of 1933 merely served to increase the price-consciousness of importers able to buy either British or American goods, and that this is one reason for the flatter slope in the later thirties. The fact that the exchange rate returned to approximately its old level may also help to explain the comparative stability of the slope and the correlation from 1934 onwards. After a substantial change in exchange rates that was *not* reversed, time might be required for a new pattern of trade to emerge, and during this period one might expect the correlation gradually to improve and the slope to flatten. It may be, of course, that such a tendency between 1934 and 1938 was offset by the growth of exchange and trade controls which weakened the relation between price and quantity. It is by no means easy to explain the observed changes in the correlation coefficient and in the slope. The suggestions made above are highly tentative.

Similar calculations were made for the years 1913 and 1948. For 1913 only thirty-two comparable products could be found. The correlation coefficient was $-0 \cdot 54$ and the slope $-3 \cdot 2$, but, in view of the much smaller number of observations, these results cannot be compared with those for the later years; nor should any great significance be attached to them. The calculation for 1948 covered 118 products.[28] The correlation coefficient was low ($-0 \cdot 34$) and the slope only $-1 \cdot 6$. Such a weak relation between relative price and relative quantity was to be expected. Discriminatory regulation of trade was widespread, and the demand for many goods (particularly of British origin) at the ruling price was unsatisfied in varying degree owing to shortage of supply.

Similar calculations were also made, for 1929, for eight other pairs of the five major exporters of manufactures (the United Kingdom, the United States, Germany, Japan, France). The year 1929 was chosen rather than one in the late thirties, since by that time : (*a*) the German official rate of exchange was of doubtful value for conversion purposes, (*b*) German trade policy was such as to weaken greatly the relation between price and quantity, (*c*) the French franc was depreciating rapidly. The results are shown in Table VI, together with that for the United States and the United Kingdom for comparison. The number of observations obtainable was smaller than in the comparison of British and American exports. The data used were also, in general, less comparable. This may account for the lower slopes generally obtained. These ranged from $-1 \cdot 6$ to $-2 \cdot 8$, with a mean of $-2 \cdot 1$, compared with $-2 \cdot 6$ for the United States: United Kingdom comparison. The four comparisons of American exports with those of the other industrial countries gave very similar results, with slopes ranging between $-2 \cdot 4$ and $-2 \cdot 8$.

The calculations so far described were all made for single years. It was, however, observed that, in the United States : United Kingdom comparison, the price–quantity relationship for certain manufactures, although consistent over most years, went astray in particular years. In an attempt

---

[28] It was impossible to obtain figures for the 109 products used in the calculations for 1928–38. The 118 products are, however, all included in the 171 used in the original calculation for 1937.

TABLE VI

Correlation between Logarithms of Relative Quantities and Relative Dollar
Prices of Exports of Manufactures, 1929

	Number of Observations	Correlation Coefficient	Slope of Regression Line
U.S.: U.K.	109	−0·57	−2·6
U.S.: Japan	41	−0·62	−2·8
U.S.: Germany	51	−0·60	−2·4
U.S.: France	56	−0·54	−2·4
U.K.: France	58	−0·48	−2·2
France: Japan	40	−0·52	−2·2
France: Germany	81	−0·47	−1·7
U.K.: Japan	44	−0·61	−1·6
U.K.: Germany	77	−0·43	−1·6

to iron out these erratic movements, calculations were also made for the period 1934–38 as a whole.[29] This gave a better correlation (−0·73) and a considerably flatter slope (−3·6). The regression line is shown in Figure 2. Almost identical results (correlation −0·71; slope −3·6). were obtained by correlating relative quantities in 1938 with relative prices in 1934–38, suggesting that relative quantities in a given year are rather better explained by relative prices over a period of years ending in that year than by relative prices in that year alone, and that a 1% difference in relative price over a period of years is associated with a larger difference in relative quantity in the last year than is a 1% difference in relative price in the last year only. This is what we might expect where relative prices have changed in the last year, assuming that time is required for relative quantities to be adjusted. As, however, relative prices in 1938 were highly correlated with relative prices in earlier years, the difference is not very great.[30]

---

[29] The correlation was between:

$$\frac{\text{Total quantity of U.S. exports, 1934–38}}{\text{Total quantity of U.K. exports, 1934–38}}$$

and

$$\frac{\text{Average value of U.S. exports, 1934–38}}{\text{Average value of U.K. exports, 1934–38}}$$

for each of the 109 manufactures. The average value of United States exports of manufacture X was obtained by dividing the total value of United States exports of X, over the period 1934 to 1938, by the total quantity exported.

[30] Several attempts were also made, using multiple correlation analysis, to explain relative quantity in one year by relative price (a) in that year, (b) in one or more earlier years, but this did not greatly improve the explanation; the correlation between relative prices in the various years was high. However, the sum of the partial regression coefficients was generally somewhat higher than the simple regression coefficient obtained by correlating relative price and quantity in the last year only. This suggests that a 1% difference in relative price *maintained* over a period of years is associated with a somewhat larger difference in relative quantity than is a 1% difference in relative price in the year in question alone.

Bias Due to Errors of Observation

The slopes of the regression lines derived from the data available are consistent with flatter "real" slopes, *i.e.*, with a larger difference in relative quantity associated with a 1% difference in relative price, if only truly comparable figures could be obtained.

FIGURE 2

Relative Prices and Quantities of U.S. & U.K. Exports
of 109 Manufactures 1934–38

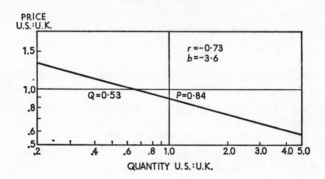

One trouble is that the quality, design, etc., of products falling into comparable categories in the two trade returns are not always the same, and the proportion of different qualities exported by each country may differ. If sufficient information were available the figures could, in principle, be adjusted. In some cases this could be done fairly precisely, e.g., where there were well-established grades (as with wheat), with fairly constant price differentials; but with many manufactures the adjustment could only be rough and ready. The adjustments would affect both the relative price and the relative quantity figures, but in opposite senses. If, for example, it was known that the iron-ore exports[31] of country A had a 50% iron content and those of B a 25% iron content, and that importers were interested primarily in the iron content, the adjusted figures would show a relative price (A : B) half as great as the unadjusted relative price per ton of ore, and a relative quantity (A : B) twice as great as the unadjusted figure.[32]

A second difficulty is that a classification used by one country may

---

[31] Iron ore is not, of course, included in our sample of manufactures.

[32] This would mean that, on a double logarithmic scale, the adjustment would involve a shift in the point downwards and to the right, or upwards and to the left, along a line at an angle of 45° to the horizontal. In terms of logarithms the absolute price and quantity errors in the unadjusted figures would be equal. The implications are developed in Appendix A.

include commodities not included at all in the most closely corresponding classification (or classifications) of the other. In this case, the required adjustment would change the figure of relative quantity, and might or might not change the figure of relative price either in the same or in the opposite sense.[33]

There is no reason why errors in the relative quantities (which are measured horizontally) should alter, in any particular sense, the slope of the regression line (which minimises the sum of the squares of the deviations in a horizontal direction). But errors in the relative prices (which are measured vertically) will tend to steepen the slope. This has been well illustrated by Mr. Orcutt,[34] and the matter is discussed in more detail in Appendix A to the present article. The following simple illustration of an extreme case may help to make the matter clear.

Suppose the figures were completely comparable and fully adjusted for differences in quality and the like, and suppose also that the market were perfect, with no transport costs. The observed points would then look like this:[35]

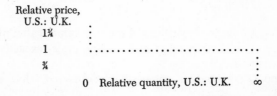

Relative price,
U.S.: U.K.

Where America's price was above the British, she would export nothing; where it was less, Britain would export nothing; where it was the same, both could export. But if the observations were imperfect for the reasons given, the points might look like this:

Relative price,
U.S.: U.K.

0   Relative quantity, U.S.: U.K.   ∞

---

[33] Suppose the adjustment excluded a product from A's recorded exports within a certain category. This would increase, reduce or leave unaltered A's relative price, according as the product excluded had a price lower than, higher than or equal to that of the other products in the category.

[34] G. H. Orcutt, "Measurement of Price Elasticities in International Trade," *Review of Economics and Statistics*, May, 1950.

[35] Nought and infinity cannot in fact, of course, be shown on a logarithmic scale.

The correlation would be very low and the regression line minimising the sum of the squares of the deviations in a horizontal direction nearly vertical. The imperfection of the data might thus lead us to suppose that there was little or no relationship between relative price and relative quantity when in fact a small difference in relative price was associated with a very large difference in relative quantity.

It may, therefore, be the "real" slopes are flatter than those given by the calculations described above. The discussion in Appendix A gives reasons for believing that the slope of $-3 \cdot 6$ for the years 1934–38 might easily have become -4 to $-4\frac{1}{2}$ if the observed data could have been corrected for errors of the type described, i.e., that a 1% difference in relative price may well have been associated, in those years, with a difference of, say, 4–4½% in relative quantity.

APPENDIX A: EFFECTS OF ERRORS OF OBSERVATION ON THE SLOPES OF THE REGRESSION LINES[36]

Suppose the true relationship between relative quantity and relative price of each product is given by the equation

$$X_1' = A + BX_2' \tag{1}$$

where X_1' and X_2' are the logarithms of the true values (after all necessary adjustments) of relative quantity and relative price respectively, and A and B are constants.

Let X_1 and X_2 (without the primes) be the observed values, and let

$$X_1 = X_1' + E_1 \text{ and } X_2 = X_2' + E_2 \tag{2}$$

so that E_1 and E_2 are errors of observation.

From (1) and (2) we have

$$X_1 = A + BX_2 + E_1 - BE_2 \tag{3}$$

Let $\bar{X}_1$, $\bar{X}_2$, E_1 and E_2 be means and x_1, x_2, e_1 and e_2 the deviations from them, so that

$$X_1 = \bar{X}_1 + x_1, \text{ etc.} \tag{4}$$

(3) can then be re-written:

$$x_1 = Bx_2 + e_1 - Be_2 + (A - \bar{X}_1 + B\bar{X}_2 + E_1 - BE_2) \tag{5}$$

Multiplying through by x_2 and summing, we get

$$\Sigma x_1 x_2 = B\Sigma x_2^2 + \Sigma e_1 x_2 - B\Sigma e_2 x_2 \tag{6}$$

(Σx_2 multiplied by the constant expression in brackets in (5) is zero.)

Whence

$$B = \frac{\Sigma x_1 x_2 - \Sigma e_1 x_2}{\Sigma x_2{}^2 - \Sigma e_2 x_2} \tag{7}$$

---

[36] It will be evident that this Appendix owes much to Mr. Orcutt, *op. cit.*

i.e.,
$$B = \frac{\Sigma x_1 x_2 - \Sigma e_1 x_2' - \Sigma e_1 e_2}{\Sigma x_2{}^2 - \Sigma e_2 x_2' - \Sigma e_2{}^2} \tag{8}$$

This is the true slope we wish to find. The slope obtained by the method of least squares from the observed data (minimising the sum of the squares of the deviations of the logarithms of relative *quantity*) is, however,

$$b = \frac{\Sigma x_1 x_2}{\Sigma x_2{}^2} \tag{9}$$

We now compare the values of B and b. Four cases are considered.

I. Errors in Observed Values of Relative Quantities but Not in Observed Values of Relative Prices

$e_2 = 0$, and hence, from (8),

$$B = \frac{\Sigma x_1 x_2 - \Sigma e_1 x_2'}{\Sigma x_2{}^2} \tag{10}$$

i.e.,
$$B = b - \frac{\Sigma e_1 x_2'}{\Sigma x_2{}^2} \tag{11}$$

If there is no reason to assume correlation between the true relative price (X_2') and the error in the relative quantity (E_1), there is no reason to expect the second term in (11) to be positive rather than negative, or vice versa. The value of b derived from the observed values is thus unbiased.

II. Errors in Relative Price but Not in Relative Quantity

$e_1 = 0$ and, assuming no correlation between true relative price (X_2') and the error in relative price (E_2), equation (8) becomes

$$B = \frac{\Sigma x_1 x_2}{\Sigma x_2{}^2 - \Sigma e_2{}^2} \tag{12}$$

$$\therefore \frac{b}{B} = \frac{\Sigma x_2{}^2 - \Sigma e_2{}^2}{\Sigma x_2{}^2} \tag{13}$$

$$= 1 - \frac{\Sigma e_2{}^2}{\Sigma x_2{}^2} \tag{14}$$

$$\therefore \frac{b}{B} < 1 \tag{15}$$

Since b is negative, and we assume that B is negative, B is numerically greater than b, which is thus biased towards zero.

III. Errors Both in Relative Quantity and in Relative Price, but No Correlation between These Errors

Then
$$B = \frac{\Sigma x_1 x_2}{\Sigma x_2{}^2 - \Sigma e_2{}^2} \tag{16}$$

as in equation (12), and b is biased towards zero, as in II.

IV. Errors in Logarithms of Relative Quantity and Relative Price of Equal Magnitude but Opposite Sign

This is the case described on pp. 572–73 of the text.

From (8), since $E_1 = -E_2$, and, therefore, $e_1 = -e_2$,

$$B = \frac{\Sigma x_1 x_2 + \Sigma e_2^2}{\Sigma x_2^2 - \Sigma e_2^2} \tag{17}$$

assuming no correlation between E_1 and X_2' or between E_2 and X_2'.

Starting with $b = \Sigma x_1 x_2 / \Sigma x_2$, where $\Sigma x_1 x_2$ is negative, we are, in (17), reducing the negative quantity in the numerator by the same amount as the positive quantity in the denominator. Since $|\Sigma x_1 x_2| > \Sigma x_2^2$ in the results described in the text, B is therefore numerically greater than b, on the assumption that

$$\Sigma x_2^2 \geqslant \Sigma e_2^2 \ {}^{37}$$

i.e., that $\Sigma (x_2' + e_2)^2 \geqslant \Sigma e_2^2$

i.e., that $\Sigma x_2'^2 + 2\Sigma x_2' e_2 \geqslant 0.$

This is so, assuming no correlation between X_2' and E_2. Hence b is biased towards zero.

It was shown in the text (pp. 572–73) that errors of types III and IV exist in the data used. We may now consider what bias these may exercise on the regression coefficient obtained in the analysis of the five years, 1934–38. In this case there were 109 observations and

$$\Sigma x_1 x_2 = -12.25$$
$$\Sigma x_2^2 = 3.38$$
$$b = -3.624.$$

Using equations (16) and (17), we may calculate B for various values of Σe_2^2.

Thus, for example, if $\Sigma e_2^2 = 0 \cdot 6$, B is $-4 \cdot 4$ or $-4 \cdot 2$ according as the errors are wholly of type III or wholly of type IV. Columns (2) and (3) of Table VII show the values of B on these assumptions for values of Σe_2^2 between $0 \cdot 1$ and $1 \cdot 0$.

Given Σe_2^2, the (arithmetic) *average* value of e_2 lies between $\sqrt{2\Sigma e_2^2/109}$ (the case where only two observed relative prices have errors different from the mean error[38]) and $\sqrt{\Sigma e_2^2/109}$ (the case where all the

---

[37] If $\Sigma x_2^2 < \Sigma e_2^2 \leqslant |\Sigma x_1 x_2|$, B would be positive or zero, and if $\Sigma x_2^2 < \Sigma e_2^2 > |\Sigma x_1 x_2|$, B would be negative, but numerically less than unity, and therefore numerically less than b.

[38] It is impossible for only one observed price to have an error different from the mean error.

errors differ from the mean by the same numerical amount[39]). If $\Sigma e_2{}^2$ were equal to $0\cdot6$, the average difference from the mean error of the logarithms of relative prices would lie between $0\cdot01$ and $0\cdot0742$, equivalent to between $2\cdot3$ and $18\cdot7\%$ of the observed value (or of the true value plus the mean error if smaller), and in practice well within these limits, say between 5 and 15%. Columns (4) to (7) of Table VII show the range of average difference from the mean error, measured in these two ways, for the various values of $\Sigma e_2{}^2$.

Now an average difference from the mean error of 5–15%, which means, assuming no biased errors in the observations, an average error of 5–15%, seems quite likely in the data used (the standard deviation of the 109 relative prices was $0\cdot1761$ in logarithms, equivalent to 50% in the original

TABLE VII

109 Products, 1934–38 ($b = -3.624$)

$\Sigma e_2{}^2$.	Value of B.		Range of Average Values of $\lvert e_2 \rvert$.		Equivalent Average Difference from the Mean Error in Original Relative Price Data, %.‡	
	Errors of Type III Only.*	Errors of Type IV Only.†	Minimum $\dfrac{\sqrt{2\Sigma e_2{}^2}}{109}$	Maximum $\sqrt{\dfrac{\Sigma e_2{}^2}{109}}.$	Minimum	Maximum
(1)	(2)	(3)	(4)	(5)	(6)	(7)
$0\cdot1$	$-3\cdot7$	$-3\cdot7$	$0\cdot0041$	$0\cdot0303$	$0\cdot9$	$7\cdot3$
$0\cdot2$	$-3\cdot9$	$-3\cdot8$	$0\cdot0058$	$0\cdot0428$	$1\cdot4$	$10\cdot4$
$0\cdot3$	$-4\cdot0$	$-3\cdot9$	$0\cdot0071$	$0\cdot0525$	$1\cdot6$	$12\cdot8$
$0\cdot4$	$-4\cdot1$	$-4\cdot0$	$0\cdot0082$	$0\cdot0606$	$1\cdot9$	$15\cdot0$
$0\cdot5$	$-4\cdot3$	$-4\cdot1$	$0\cdot0092$	$0\cdot0677$	$2\cdot1$	$16\cdot9$
$0\cdot6$	$-4\cdot4$	$-4\cdot2$	$0\cdot0100$	$0\cdot0742$	$2\cdot3$	$18\cdot7$
$0\cdot7$	$-4\cdot6$	$-4\cdot3$	$0\cdot0109$	$0\cdot0801$	$2\cdot5$	$20\cdot2$
$0\cdot8$	$-4\cdot7$	$-4\cdot4$	$0\cdot0116$	$0\cdot0857$	$2\cdot7$	$21\cdot8$
$0\cdot9$	$-4\cdot9$	$-4\cdot6$	$0\cdot0123$	$0\cdot0909$	$2\cdot9$	$23\cdot3$
$1\cdot0$	$-5\cdot1$	$-4\cdot7$	$0\cdot0130$	$0\cdot0958$	$3\cdot0$	$24\cdot7$

* $B = \dfrac{\Sigma x_1 x_2}{\Sigma x_2{}^2 - \Sigma e_2{}^2}\cdot$ (Equation (16).)

† $B = \dfrac{\Sigma x_1 x_2 + \Sigma e_2{}^2}{\Sigma x_2{}^2 - \Sigma e_2{}^2}\cdot$ (Equation (17).)

‡ As per cent of observed value or true value adjusted for the mean error if smaller.

Col. (6) is 100 (antilog $\dfrac{\sqrt{\Sigma e_2{}^2}}{109} - 1$).

Col. (7) is 100 (antilog $\sqrt{\dfrac{\Sigma e_2{}^2}{109}} - 1$).

data). It thus seems quite possible that, if the observed data could have been corrected for errors of the type described, the slope of the regression line might have been of the order of -4 to $-4\frac{1}{2}$.

It may be mentioned in this connection that the slope of the other regression line, minimising the sum of the squares of the deviations in a

---

[39] Strictly not possible with an odd number of observations.

vertical direction, was −6·9 and that the diagonal regression (the geometric mean of the slopes of the two regression lines) was −5·0. The diagonal regressions for the individual years 1922–38 ranged from −4·1 to −4·9.

33. Tariff Protection in Industrial

Countries: An Evaluation[*][1]

By BELA BALASSA[†]

I

Viner expressed the opinion in 1950 that "there is no way in which the 'height' of a tariff as an index of its restrictive effect can be even approximately measured, or, for that matter, even defined with any degree of significant precision."[2] Undaunted by Viner's and others' critical remarks, a long 'line of investigators, using more or less ingenious methods, have made attempts to compare the height of tariff levels in industrial countries.[3] More recently, these inquiries have been given added impetus by the establishment of the European Common Market[4] and tariff negotiations undertaken in the framework of the Kennedy round.[5]

[*] *Journal of Political Economy*, Vol. LXXIII, No. 6 (December, 1965), pp. 573–94.

[†] Johns Hopkins University.

[1] Data collection and calculations have been carried out within the framework of the Atlantic Trade Project, sponsored by the Council on Foreign Relations and directed by the present author. He is indebted to G. Basevi, R. N. Cooper, and W. M. Corden for comments on an earlier draft. Special thanks are due to Harry G. Johnson, whose advice and suggestions have been of great help in improving the argument of the paper.

[2] Jacob Viner, *The Customs Union Issue* (New York: Carnegie Endowment for International Peace, 1950), pp. 66–67.

[3] The earliest efforts were: United Kingdom Board of Trade, *Publications* (2d ser., Cd. 2.337 [1905]; League of Nations, *Tariff Level Indices, 1927* (Geneva, 1927); and J. G. Crawford, "Tariff Level Indices," *Economic Record* (December, 1934), pp. 213–21.

[4] Raymond Bertrand, "Comparison du niveau des tarifs douaniers des pays du Marché Commun," *Cahiers de l'Institut de Science Économique Appliquée*, Series R, No. 2 (February, 1958); and H. C. Binswanger, "Der Zollschutz in den Ländern der Europäischen Wirtschaftsgemeinschaft und in der Schweiz," *Aussenwirtschaft* (March–June, 1958), pp. 119–46.

[5] See, e.g., M. Mesnage, "Comparaison statistique du tarif douanier commun de la CEE, du tarif des États-Unis d'Amerique et du tarif du Royaume-Uni de Grande-Bretagne de d'Irelande du Nord," *Informàtions Statistiques* (Office Statistique des Communautés Européennes), No. 3 (1963), pp. 101–23, and Research and Policy Committee of the Committee for Economic Development, "The Height of United States and EEC Tariffs," *Trade Negotiations for a Better Free World Economy: A Statement on National Policy* (Washington, 1964).

Estimates of the height of national tariff levels are designed to give expression to the restrictive effect of duties on trade flows.[6] In a general equilibrium framework, the restrictive effect of a country's tariff can be indicated by the difference between potential and actual trade, when the former refers to trade flows that would take place under *ceteris paribus* assumptions if the country in question eliminated all of its duties. Tariffs affect the pattern of production and consumption and generally reduce imports *and* exports under full employment conditions as changes in relative prices associated with the imposition of tariffs lead to resource shifts from export industries to import-competing industries. In empirical investigations, however, attention is focused on imports, so that the difference between potential and actual imports is presumed to express the restrictive effect of duties.[7]

Among the *ceteris paribus* assumptions, two are of special interest: the assumption of given exchange rates and of given tariffs in other countries. For one thing, the maintenance of balance-of-payments equilibrium would probably necessitate a devaluation in the country that unilaterally reduced its tariffs;[8] for another, actual changes in trade flows would depend on the changes that occurred in all the national tariffs. To avoid the complications associated with changing more than one variable, in the following discussion we will consider the restrictive effects of national tariffs under the assumption that exchange rates (and domestic prices) remain unchanged, and we will disregard at the earlier stages of the argument the interaction of tariffs imposed in individual countries.

II

In international comparisons of the height of tariff levels, two procedures have been generally employed: the calculation of weighted and unweighted averages of duties. Under the first alternative, duties on individual commodities are often weighted by the imports of the country in question, which is equivalent to expressing the amount of duty paid

---

[6] While the terms-of-trade effects of tariffs occupy a central place in the theory of tariffs, these are largely disregarded in empirical investigations that have used a partial-equilibrium framework and have, explicitly or implicitly, assumed infinite export-supply elasticities. Cf., e.g., R. N. Cooper, "Tariff Dispersion and Trade Negotiations," *Journal of Political Economy* (December, 1964), pp. 597–606. See, however, M. E. Kreinen, "Effect of Tariff Changes on the Prices and Volume of Imports," *American Economic Review* (June, 1961), pp. 310–24.

[7] The decline in imports following the imposition of duties will generally be associated with a fall in the consumption and an increase in the domestic production of the protected commodities; the latter is customarily referred to as the protective effect of the tariff.

[8] Correspondingly, if exchange rates vary over time, an international comparison of national tariff levels will have little meaning. For a recent attempt, see E. Lerdau, "On the Measurement of Tariffs: The U.S. over Forty Years," *Economia Internazionale* (1957), pp. 232–47.

in a given year as a percentage of the value of total imports. In turn, the second procedure entails calculating a simple average of all duties from national tariff schedules.

Although there are several recent examples of weighting with own imports,[9] this approach should not claim our attention since it has been repeatedly shown to provide distorted results: low duties associated with high levels of imports are given large weights, whereas high duties that restrict imports have small weight and prohibitive duties zero weight. Thus, while on the basis of a comparison of tariff averages weighted by own imports France would have been classified among low-tariff countries in 1955, this result appears to have been due to the restrictive effect of high duties on the imports of various categories of products.[10]

To remedy these deficiencies, it has been suggested that domestic production or consumption should be used as weights.[11] But these choices, too, are open to several objections. The composition of imports under free trade will differ from the composition of consumption under protection, in part because of the distorting effects of duties on consumer's choice, and in part because of intercommodity differences in "tradeability," when the latter depends, among other things, on the relative importance of specific inputs and the ratio of transportation costs to the value of output. Thus, over nine-tenths of the world production of coffee and tin enters international trade, but only a small fraction of the output of construction materials is traded.[12]

In turn, following the suggestions made in a League of Nations report (see n. 3), Raymond Bertrand has calculated an unweighted average of duties for the approximately 1,100 four-digit headings of the Brussels Tariff Nomenclature (BTN). This method has also been applied by the Commission of the European Economic Community (EEC) in comparing tariff levels in the United States, the United Kingdom, and the Common Market.[13] Actually, the calculation of unweighted averages involves giving equal weights to all BTN headings under the assumption that the "law of large numbers" will lend meaning to the results. But the relative importance of the individual BTN headings differs considerably. In the Common Market countries, for example, imports of automobiles (BTN

---

[9] See, e.g., European Economic Community, Commission, *Third General Report on the Activities of the Community* (Brussels, 1960); and Joint Economic Committee, U.S. Congress, *Trade Restrictions in the Western Community* (Washington, 1961).

[10] See my *The Theory of Economic Integration* (Homewood, Ill.: Richard D. Irwin, Inc., 1961), pp. 45–46; see also K. Bieda, "Trade Restrictions in the Western Community," *American Economic Review* (March, 1963), pp. 130–32.

[11] Swedish Customs Tariff Commission, *Revision of the Swedish Customs Tariff* (Stockholm, 1957), pp. 33–36.

[12] Production (consumption) weights would be of use, however, in measuring the production (consumption) cost of protection.

[13] See nn. 3, 4, and 5.

87.02) amounted to $667.6 million in 1962 as against imports of zinc articles for construction (BTN 79.05) of $14 thousand.[14]

To give expression to the relative importance of individual products in international exchange, one may instead weight tariffs by the value of world trade. We will thereby escape, in a large part, the distorting effects of the idiosyncrasies of national tariffs on imports, although inter-country similarities in the structure of tariffs will still affect the commodity composition of international exchange. At the same time, weighting by the value of world trade will offer further advantages over the use of unweighted averages if we consider groups of commodities rather than all goods taken together.

This last observation brings us to the question whether one should calculate an average of tariffs on *all* commodities entering international trade. Calculations of this type have a long history, and an over-all average has recently been used in evaluating the protectiveness of the U.S. and Common Market tariffs by the Committee for Economic Development.[15] In turn, the EEC Commission has suggested restricting the investigation to non-agricultural products.

There are good reasons for excluding food, beverages, and tobacco, since the tariff is only one of the protective measures employed in the case of these commodities. A comparison of tariffs on agricultural commodities in the Common Market and the United Kingdom would make little sense, for example, since the former employs duties and the latter subsidies to protect domestic agriculture. Neither would comparisons with the United States be meaningful, given that the latter's system of agricultural protection involves the use of price-support measures and quotas.[16] Finally, revenue duties on coffee, tea, alcoholic beverages, and tobacco further complicate the picture.

These considerations suggest that the usefulness of tariff comparisons will be enhanced if we excluded from the scope of the investigation

---

[14] A further difficulty with the commission's study is that in cases when a range rather than a single figure is indicated for a BTN heading in the U.S. or United Kingdom tariff classification, the lower and upper limits have been taken separately, and the BTN heading in question has been assigned double weight. Since in these two countries duties are generally given in terms of a range for commodities that are protected by relatively high tariffs, the tariff averages calculated by the use of this method are subject to an upward bias.

[15] *Trade Negotiations for a Better Free World Economy* (cited in n. 5); see also R. N. Cooper, *op. cit.*

[16] The difficulties associated with the international comparison of duties on agricultural commodities are exemplified by a calculation made in the Committee for Economic Development study. According to the latter, using U.S. imports as weights, the EEC tariff averages at 12.1 per cent if sugar is included and 9.6 percent without sugar (*Trade Negotiations for a Better Free World Economy*, p. 72). And, whatever the weights, the tariff average of the Common Market will be affected by its high duty on sugar imports, while U.S. sugar production is protected by quotas. Thus, using combined U.S.-EEC imports as weights, the average of EEC tariffs is 8.6 excluding sugar and 10.2 including sugar.

agricultural products that are subject to non-tariff measures. Adjustments would also have to be made for non-agricultural commodities that are protected by quotas or receive domestic subsidies.[17] But aside from the effects of non-tariff measures, we face a further problem that has been largely disregarded in making international tariff comparisons: the implications of duties on raw materials and intermediate products for the protection of goods at a higher level of fabrication.[18] It is easy to see that high duties on materials and intermediate products will raise the average level of tariffs on non-agricultural commodities but will reduce the degree of protection accorded to final goods by increasing the cost of inputs.

We have to distinguish, therefore, between nominal and effective rates of tariffs when the latter will take account of duties levied on material inputs.[19] Under the usual assumptions of the international immobility of labor and capital, the effective rate of duty will indicate the degree of protection of value added in the manufacturing process.[20] If input coefficients are constant in the relevant range, the effective rate of duty (z) for any commodity can be expressed in the framework of an input-output system. Let t denote the nominal rate of tariffs, a the material

---

[17] Petroleum, petroleum products, lead and zinc, and steel flatware are subject to import quotas in the United States, while the United States as well as the Common Market relies on formal and informal agreements to limit imports of some manufactures from Japan, Hong Kong, and India. Finally, subsidies are given to shipbuilding in most industrial countries.

[18] Several writers have considered this problem in a national context in regard to Canada and Australia. The most important contributions are: Clarence L. Barber, "Canadian Tariff Policy," *Canadian Journal of Economics and Political Science* (November, 1955), pp. 513–30, and W. M. Corden, "The Tariff," in Alex Hunter (ed.), *The Economics of Australian Industry* (Melbourne: Melbourne University Press, 1963).

More recently, the effects of protection in the presence of intermediate goods have attracted the attention of several economists. After the first version of this paper had been completed, I had the occasion to see Harry G. Johnson's "The Theory of Tariff Structure, with Special Reference to World Trade and Development," *Trade and Development* ("Études et Travaux de l'Institut Universitaire de Hautes Études Internationales" [Geneva: Librairie Droz, 1965]); and G. Basevi, "The U.S. Tariff Structure: Estimates of Effective Rates of Protection of U.S. Industries and Industrial Labor," *Review of Economics and Statistics* (in press). Also, W. M. Corden is engaged in research on the theoretical aspects of tariff structures.

[19] At the same time, there is no need to take account of tariffs paid at earlier stages of production, since material inputs are available to the domestic producer at the world-market price, inclusive of transportation costs, plus the duty.

[20] Similar calculations should be made for estimating the effective duty on the exports of manufactures from less-developed areas. I have noted elsewhere that, from the point of view of the entrepreneur's decision to transform a raw material into semifinished or finished products for exportation to developed countries, the tariff burden on value added in the production process rather than the nominal rate of duty is relevant (*Trade Prospects for Developing Countries* [Homewood, Ill.: Richard D. Irwin, Inc., 1964], p. 116). See also Harry G. Johnson, "Tariffs and Economic Development: Some Theoretical Issues," *Journal of Development Studies*, October, 1964.

input coefficients, and v the proportion of value added to output, all measured at world-market prices. For commodity i we have, then, equation (1):

$$z_i = \frac{(1+t_i) - \sum_j a_{ji}(1+t_j) - \left(1 - \sum_j a_{ji}\right)}{1 - \sum_j a_{ji}} = \frac{t_i - \sum_j a_{ji}t_j}{v_i}. \quad (1)$$

For given world-market prices, this formula will indicate the excess in domestic value added, obtainable by reason of the imposition of tariffs, as a percentage of value added in a free-trade situation. It is easy to see that the effective and the nominal rates of duty will be identical if the weighted average of duties on material inputs is the same as the tariff on the final product; the effective tariff will be higher than the nominal rate of duty if the product bears a higher tariff than its inputs, and vice versa.

These relationships can also find application in international comparisons. Assume, for example, that material inputs account for 60 per cent of the value of output of a given commodity in a free-trade situation, and country A levies a 10 per cent duty on the materials and 20 per cent on the product itself, while B admits the materials duty free and applies a 16 per cent tariff to the final product. Now, according to the conventional analysis, the higher rate of duty in country A would provide a greater degree of protection to the final product than B's lower tariff does, and the average of nominal rates of tariffs will also be higher in country A, regardless of the system of weighting. On the other hand, the effective tariff on the final product will be 40 per cent in country B as against 35 per cent in country A. It appears, then, that the protectiveness of national tariffs cannot be indicated by comparing nominal rates of duties and averages of these duties—weighted or unweighted.[21]

III

We have concluded that, in international comparisons of the protective effect of national tariffs, one should use effective rather than nominal rates of duties. In the present paper, effective tariffs have been calculated for the United States, the European Common Market, the United Kingdom, Sweden, and Japan. These countries are the main participants in the Kennedy round of tariff negotiations and account for about 80 per cent of world exports and over 40 per cent of world imports of manufactured goods. The investigation has been limited to manufactured products, and raw materials have been considered only as inputs.

---

[21] Nominal tariffs will continue to have relevance for the consumer's choice between domestic goods and imports, however. The effects of nominal duties on the domestic consumption of protected commodities will be considered in Section VI below.

This solution has been chosen in part because the countries in question compete largely in the field of manufactures and in part because tariffs provide the principal means of protection in the case of manufactured goods, while quotas and subsidies predominate in agriculture.

In order to calculate the effective rates of tariffs, we need comparable data on nominal tariff rates and input-output coefficients *net* of duties. Input-output tables using a common system of classification that also insures comparability with trade statistics, have been published for the five Common Market countries (Belgium, France, Germany, Italy, Netherlands), pertaining generally to the year 1959.[22] Comparable tables for the other countries under consideration are not available, however, and we have chosen to use "standardized" input-output coefficients in all cases. In deriving these coefficients, we have relied largely on the input-output tables for Belgium and the Netherlands.[23] The choice has been made for these countries because they had nil or low duties on most commodities in 1959, and hence the distortion in input-output relationships, due to the existence of duties, is relatively small.

The application of identical input-output coefficients for all countries is justified if the countries in question have identical production functions with unitary substitution elasticity in all industries, or if intercountry differences in efficiency are neutral in the sense that production functions differ only by a multiplicative constant. Under these assumptions, differences in the relative prices of inputs would not affect the coefficients.[24]

While the above assumptions have often been made in empirical research,[25] they may not be fulfilled in the real world. One may argue, however, that we can abstract from non-neutral differences in production functions, since firms in the industrial countries under consideration presumably have the same "technological horizon." At the same time, the use of standardized coefficients has the important advantage that the results will not be affected by international differences in the composition of output·in individual industries.

Standardized input-output coefficients have been derived for thirty-six industries, including all of manufacturing except for food processing. In the system of classification applied we have been constrained by the breakdown used in the input-output tables of the Common Market coun-

---

[22] Office Statistique des Communautés Européennes, *Tableaux "Entrées-Sorties" pour les pays de la Communauté Européenne Économique,* October, 1964.

[23] The input-output tables of the other three countries have served as a basis, however, in regard to automobiles, aircraft, and precision instruments that are not produced in substantial quantities in Belgium and the Netherlands.

[24] The reader will note that the coefficients derived from input-output tables are expressed in value rather than in quantity terms and hence indicate relative shares.

[25] Cf., e.g., Kenneth Arrow, H. B. Chenery, B. Minhas, and R. M. Solow, "Capital-Labor Substitution and Economic Efficiency," *Review of Economics and Statistics* (August, 1960), pp. 225–50.

tries which provide a rather narrow definition of some industries (e.g., cleansing agents and perfumes) while a number of diverse commodities are included in others (e.g., miscellaneous chemical products). A more detailed breakdown has been employed in regard to inputs, however, whenever the use of a specific input could be ascertained. For example, from the category "synthetic materials" we have selected synthetic rubber as an input for rubber goods.

For each industry, separate consideration has been given to all inputs that contribute at least 4 per cent of the value of output. The number of inputs distinguished in the case of individual industries has been between one and six, with automobiles at the upper end of the range. Other material inputs and non-material inputs (transportation, trade, etc.) have been included in separate categories. Within the group of other material inputs, fuels, paper, non-metallic minerals, and metal manufactures predominate; hence we have used a weighted average of tariffs on these products in the calculations. There are no duties on non-material inputs.

In regard to tariffs, we have used the BTN which is employed by the EEC, the United Kingdom, Sweden, and Japan. For the United States, tariff categories have been reclassified according to the BTN in *Comparative Tariffs and Trade*;[26] we have relied on this compilation while adjusting the results for reductions in duties accomplished in the Dillon round of tariff negotiations. Further, the specific duties applied chiefly in Britain have been expressed in *ad valorem* equivalents, whereas the common external tariff has been used in the case of the EEC.

Tariffs shown for the four-digit BTN headings have been expressed in terms of the four-digit items of the Standard International Trade Classification (SITC) that is employed in reporting trade statistics by all the countries under consideration.[27] Since the industrial classification applied is less detailed than the four-digit SITC, it has been necessary to average the tariff figures relating to the latter.[28] In averaging tariffs, we have used the combined imports of the five industrial areas as weights.[29]

---

[26] Committee for Economic Development, *Comparative Tariffs and Trade* (Washington, 1964). U.S. tariffs have further been adjusted to express them on a c.i.f. basis.

[27] The BTN headings by and large correspond to the four- and five-digit items of the SITC. Whenever necessary, averages have been calculated by using import values for individual countries as weights. This solution has been chosen by reason of the incomparability of the national classifications and the small number of observations within each four-digit item.

[28] The correspondence has been established by the use of the *Classification Statistique et Tarifaire* (Luxembourg, Office Statistique des Communautés Européennes, April, 1963).

[29] In view of our previous discussion, this solution appears to be superior to weighting with own imports, or using unweighted tariff averages, while data on world trade are not available in the appropriate breakdown. At the same time, it has been judged permissible to average nominal rates of duties pertaining to individual

Subsequently, effective rates of duties have been calculated by utilizing the formula given in the previous section.

IV

Nominal and effective rates of duties for the thirty-six industries of the five countries (country groupings) under consideration are shown in Table 1. In turn, Table 2 provides the country ranking of tariffs for each industry, the industry ranking of tariffs for each country, and unweighted averages of the latter rankings for the five countries (country groupings) under consideration. In the same table, the thirty-six industries are also ranked according to the labor intensiveness of the manufacturing process, expressed in terms of labor-input coefficients.[30]

With few exceptions, we find effective duties to be higher than nominal rates. This result is explained, in part, by the relatively low duties on materials as compared to semimanufactures and finished goods and, in part, by the absence of tariffs on non-material inputs that do not enter international trade. The differences are especially pronounced—and effective rates are more than double nominal rates—in the case of textile fabrics and hosiery, leather, chemical materials, steel ingots, and nonferrous metals. Being semifinished products that require little technological sophistication for their manufacture, these commodities are actual or potential exports of the less-developed countries; hence, the results provide evidence for the validity of complaints recently voiced by these countries regarding the protective effect of "graduated" tariffs in industrial areas.[31]

In turn, effective duties are lower than nominal tariffs in the case of printed matter and ships, and, in some of the countries, the protective effect of the low duties levied on these goods is more than offset by duties on their inputs, so that the effective rate of tariff is negative.[32] Further instances of negative effective duty are agricultural machinery in the United States, pig iron in the EEC and Sweden, and paper in Sweden. Finally, a comparison of the ranking of individual commodity categories according to nominal and effective rates of duties indicates that high tariffs on semimanufactures reduce the *relative* degree of protection in the case of most consumer goods (clothing and textile articles, shoes and other leather goods, sport goods, toys, and jewelry) and investment

---

commodities, since the commodity categories of the industrial classification employed generally include goods on the same level of fabrication.

[30] The share of wages plus employer-financed social security payments in the value of output, derived from the input-output tables cited above.

[31] See my *Trade Prospects for Developing Countries*, p. 116; and United Nations, *World Economic Survey. 1962, Part I* (New York, 1963), p. 79.

[32] As noted below, however, the case of ships is hardly more than a *curiosum*, since most industrial countries subsidize their shipbuilding industries in one form or another.

goods (electrical and non-electrical machinery, railway vehicles, and airplanes).

The calculation of effective duties also influences the country ranking of tariffs in regard to individual industries. In terms of effective tariffs, the United States and Sweden appear to be more protective than nominal duties would indicate, while the opposite conclusion holds for the United Kingdom, the EEC, and especially Japan. Thus, if comparisons are made by using effective rather than nominal rates of tariffs, the United States has a higher "rank" in regard to eight commodities and a lower rank with respect to three products, and Sweden has a higher rank in thirteen cases and a lower rank in none. In turn, in the case of the United Kingdom, upward adjustments are made in three instances, and downward adjustments in nine, while the relevant figures for the Common Market are five and ten, and for Japan two and eleven. These changes in rankings find their origin in the relatively low duties on materials in the United States and Sweden that raise the protective effect of a given nominal duty in these countries.

V

So far the discussion has proceeded in terms of changes in the relative position of countries and commodities as we calculate effective instead of nominal rates of duties. To make intercommodity comparisons of effective tariff *levels,* some further clarification of the assumptions underlying the analysis is called for. In this connection, separate consideration should be given to homogeneous (standardized) and heterogeneous (differentiated) products.

In theoretical models of international trade, it is generally assumed that traded goods are homogeneous, and a distinction is made between export- and import-competing industries. The same commodity may be imported and produced domestically in this case, and tariffs will have no protective effect on a commodity exported by the tariff-imposing country.[33] Only a few manufactures (gray cloth, paper, steel ingots, unwrought metals) qualify as standardized products, however, while product differentiation characterizes consumer goods, machinery, and transport equipment, as well as intermediate products at a higher level of fabrication (e.g., rolled-steel products, worked metal, and textile fabrics). At the same time, heterogeneous commodities can be exported *and* protected, and hence the distinction between export- and import-competing industries becomes blurred.

Correspondingly, tariffs levied on differentiated products can have a

---

[33] Product differentiation is implicitly assumed when calculating subsitution elasticities between commodities sold on the world market, however. Cf., e.g., G. D. A. MacDougall, "British and American Exports: A Study Suggested by the Theory of Comparative Costs," *Economic Journal* (December, 1951; September, 1952), pp. 697–726 and 487–521, respectively.

TABLE 1

Nominal and Effective Tariff Rates, 1962

	United States		United Kingdom		Common Market		Sweden		Japan	
	Nominal	Effective	Nominal	Effective	Nominal	Effective	Nominal	Effective	Nominal	Effective
(21) Thread and yarn	11.7	31.8	10.5	27.9	2.9	3.6	2.2	4.3	2.7	1.4
(22) Textile fabrics	24.1	50.6	20.7	42.2	17.6	44.4	12.7	33.4	19.7	48.8
(23) Hosiery	25.6	48.7	25.4	49.7	18.6	41.3	17.6	42.4	26.0	60.8
(24) Clothing	25.1	35.9	25.5	40.5	18.5	25.1	14.0	21.1	25.2	42.4
(25) Other textile articles	19.0	22.7	24.5	42.4	22.0	38.8	13.0	21.2	14.8	13.0
(26) Shoes	16.6	25.3	24.0	36.2	19.9	33.0	14.0	22.8	29.5	45.1
(29) Wood products including furniture	12.8	26.4	14.8	25.5	15.1	28.6	6.8	14.5	19.5	33.9
(32) Paper and paper products	3.1	0.7	6.6	8.1	10.3	13.3	2.0	0.7	10.5	12.9
(33) Printed matter	2.5	2.2	2.7	0.2	3.3	— 0.7	0.7	0.0	1.6	— 4.2
(35) Leather	9.6	25.7	14.9	34.3	7.3	18.3	7.0	21.7	19.9	59.0
(36) Leather goods other than shoes	15.5	24.5	18.7	26.4	14.7	24.3	12.2	20.7	23.6	33.6
(37) Rubber goods	9.3	16.1	20.2	43.9	15.1	33.6	10.8	26.1	12.9	23.6
(38) Plastic articles	21.0	27.0	17.9	30.1	20.6	30.0	15.0	25.5	24.9	35.5
(39) Synthetic materials	18.6	33.5	12.7	17.1	12.0	17.6	7.2	12.9	19.1	32.1
(40) Other chemical material	12.3	26.6	19.4	39.2	11.3	20.5	4.5	9.7	12.2	22.6
(42) Cleaning agents and perfumes	11.2	18.8	11.1	11.2	13.8	26.7	10.9	27.9	26.2	61.5
(43) Miscellaneous chemical products	12.6	15.6	15.4	16.7	11.6	13.1	2.5	0.0	16.8	22.9
(45) Non-metallic mineral products	18.2	30.4	13.6	20.9	13.3	19.8	6.0	10.0	13.5	20.8
(46) Glass and glass products	18.8	29.3	18.5	26.2	14.4	20.0	13.8	22.6	19.5	27.4
(48) Pig iron and ferromanganese	1.8	9.3	3.3	17.9	4.0	—13.8	0.0	0.7	10.0	54.3
(49) Ingots and other primary steel forms	10.6	106.7	11.1	98.9	6.4	28.9	3.8	40.0	13.0	58.9
(50) Rolling-mill products	7.1	— 2.2	9.5	7.4	7.2	10.5	5.2	13.2	15.4	29.5
(51) Other steel products	5.1	0.5	17.0	46.8	9.9	20.9	5.4	9.5	13.4	14.1
(54) Non-ferrous metals	5.0	10.6	6.6	19.4	2.4	5.0	0.4	0.6	9.3	27.5
(55) Metal castings	6.6	10.0	16.0	26.9	12.4	21.0	8.0	34.7	20.0	32.5
(56) Metal manufactures	14.4	28.5	19.0	35.9	14.0	25.6	8.4	16.2	18.1	27.7
(57) Agricultural machinery	0.4	— 6.9	15.4	21.3	13.4	19.6	10.0	16.0	20.0	29.2
(58) Non-electrical machinery	11.0	16.1	16.1	21.2	10.3	12.2	8.8	11.6	16.8	21.4
(59) Electrical machinery	12.2	18.1	19.7	30.0	14.5	21.5	10.7	17.7	18.1	25.3
(60) Ships	5.5	2.1	2.9	—10.2	0.4	—13.2	0.9	— 5.8	13.1	12.1
(61) Railway vehicles	7.0	7.3	21.1	33.3	11.1	0.2	8.7	13.8	15.0	18.5
(62) Automobiles	6.8	5.1	23.1	41.4	19.5	36.8	14.7	30.5	35.9	75.7
(64) Bicycles and motorcycles	14.4	26.1	22.4	39.2	20.9	39.7	17.1	35.8	25.0	45.0
(65) Airplanes	9.2	8.8	15.6	16.7	10.5	10.8	3.7	3.0	15.0	15.9
(66) Precision instruments	21.4	32.2	25.7	44.2	13.5	24.2	6.6	14.9	23.2	38.5
(67) Sport goods, toys, jewelry, etc.	25.0	41.8	22.3	35.6	17.9	26.6	10.6	16.6	21.6	31.2

Source: Tariffs: National tariff schedules. Trade: National and international trade statistics. Input-output coefficients: Office Statistique des Communautés Euro- péennes, *Tableaux "Entrées-Sorties" pour les pays de la Communauté Européenne Economique*, October, 1964.

TABLE 2

Rankings of Labor-Input Coefficients, Nominal and Effective Tariff Rates, 1962

	Standardized Input Coefficients*	United States Nom. A†	United States Nom. B‡	United States Eff. A	United States Eff. B	United Kingdom Nom. A	United Kingdom Nom. B	United Kingdom Eff. A	United Kingdom Eff. B	Common Market Nom. A	Common Market Nom. B	Common Market Eff. A	Common Market Eff. B	Sweden Nom. A	Sweden Nom. B	Sweden Eff. A	Sweden Eff. B	Japan Nom. A	Japan Nom. B	Japan Eff. A	Japan Eff. B	Five Areas Nom. C§	Five Areas Eff. C
(21) Thread and yarn	29	1	19	1	8	2	30	2	19	3	34	4	32	5	31	3	29	4	35	5	35	32	27
(22) Textile fabrics	27	1	4	1	2	2	10	4	7	4	9	3	1	5	9	5	5	3	14	2	7	9	3
(23) Hosiery	17	2	1	3	3	3	3	2	7	4	6	5	2	5	1	4	1	1	4	1	3	1	1
(24) Clothing	26	3	2	3	5	1	2	2	9	4	7	1	14	5	5	5	14	2	5	1	10	2	7
(25) Other textile articles	24	3	7	3	19	1	4	1	6	4	7	1	14	5	8	5	13	4	25	5	32	8	14
(26) Shoes	22	4	11	4	17	2	5	1	12	3	4	3	7	5	6	5	10	5	16	5	8	4	8
(29) Wood products and furniture	23	4	15	3	14	3	25	3	23	2	10	2	10	5	22	5	21	1	32	1	13	17	16
(32) Paper and paper products	18	4	33	4	33	3	32	3	33	2	27	1	26	5	32	5	35	2	36	2	33	33	34
(33) Printed matter	7	3	34	1	31	2	36	2	35	2	33	5	34	5	34	3	32	4	13	5	36	36	35
(35) Leather	32	3	23	3	16	2	24	2	15	1	29	4	24	5	21	4	12	1	8	1	4	24	12
(36) Leather goods other than shoes	13	3	12	3	18	2	15	2	21	4	12	4	15	5	10	5	15	1	30	1	14	11	17
(37) Rubber goods	16	5	24	5	22	1	11	1	5	4	11	3	6	4	12	3	8	3	7	4	24	16	11
(38) Plastic articles	21	2	6	4	12	1	17	1	17	3	17	3	8	5	3	5	9	1	17	1	12	3	4
(39) Synthetic materials	28	2	9	1	6	3	27	4	29	4	21	3	25	5	20	5	24	1	31	3	16	18	22
(40) Other chemical materials	25	2	17	2	13	1	13	1	10	4	23	4	20	5	27	5	27	3	3	3	26	25	21
(42) Cleansing agents and perfumes	30	3	20	4	20	4	29	5	32	2	16	3	11	5	11	2	7	1	3	1	2	15	13
(43) Miscellaneous chemical products	12	3	16	3	24	2	23	2	31	4	22	4	27	5	30	5	33	1	21	1	25	26	25
(45) Non-metallic mineral products	11	1	10	1	9	2	26	2	26	4	19	4	22	5	24	5	26	3	26	3	28	23	23
(46) Glass and glass products	5	2	8	1	10	3	16	3	22	4	14	5	21	5	7	4	11	1	15	2	22	12	19
(48) Pig iron and ferro-manganese	35	3	35	3	27	3	34	2	28	2	32	5	36	5	36	4	34	1	33	1	6	35	30

(49) Ingots and other primary steel	36	3	22	1	1	28	2	1	4	31	5	9	5	28	4	2	1	1	29	3	5	30	2
(50) Rolling-mill products	33	4	26	5	35	31	4	34	3	30	3	30	5	26	2	23	1	1	22	1	18	29	32
(51) Other steel products	31	5	31	5	34	18	1	3	3	28	2	19	4	25	4	28	3	3	27	3	31	28	24
(54) Non-ferrous metals	34	3	32	3	25	33	2	27	3	35	4	31	5	35	5	31	1	1	34	1	21	34	31
(55) Metal castings	3	5	29	5	26	20	3	20	3	20	4	18	4	19	1	4	1	2	12	2	15	19	18
(56) Metal manufactures	10	3	13	2	11	14	1	13	4	15	3	13	5	18	5	18	5	3	19	3	20	14	15
(57) Agricultural machinery	15	5	36	5	36	22	2	24	3	18	3	23	5	15	4	19	1	1	1	1	19	22	26
(58) Non-electrical machinery	8	3	21	3	23	19	2	25	3	26	4	28	5	16	5	25	1	1	20	2	27	21	28
(59) Electrical machinery	4	4	18	4	21	12	1	18	3	13	3	17	5	13	5	16	2	1	18	2	23	13	20
(60) Ships	9	2	30	2	32	35	4	36	5	36	5	35	4	33	3	36	1	3	28	1	34	31	36
(61) Railway vehicles	6	5	27	4	29	9	1	16	3	24	5	33	4	17	3	22	2	2	24	2	29	20	29
(62) Automobiles	19	5	28	5	30	6	2	8	3	5	5	3	4	4	4	6	1	1	1	1	1	7	6
(64) Bicycles and motorcycles	20	5	14	5	15	7	3	11	3	2	2	3	5	4	3	3	1	5	5	5	9	5	5
(65) Airplanes	1	4	25	4	28	21	1	30	3	25	3	29	5	29	5	30	2	2	23	2	30	27	33
(66) Precision instruments	2	3	5	3	7	1	1	4	4	17	4	16	5	23	5	20	2	2	9	2	11	10	9
(67) Sport goods, toys, jewelry, etc.	14	1	3	1	4	8	2	14	4	8	4	12	5	14	5	17	3	3	10	3	17	6	10

* Ranking of countries (country groupings) according to the share of wages plus employer-financed social security payments in the value of output, derived from the input-output tables previously cited.

† Ranking of countries (country groupings) according to the rate of duty for individual industries.

‡ Ranking of industries according to the rate of duty for individual countries (country groupings).

§ Unweighted average of the ranking of industries according to the rate of duty in the five areas.

protective effect in every country and lead to the substitution of domestic for foreign merchandise in everyone's consumption. A multilateral reduction of duties will, then, give rise to an increase exchange of consumer goods without necessarily affecting produced quantities in the participating countries. In turn, tariff reductions on investment goods and intermediate products at higher levels of fabrication may result in intensified intra-industry specialization and longer production runs through a decrease of product variety in the individual firms.

Among the developed countries under consideration, a broad similarity exists with respect to the ranking of industries according to their effective duties. Effective tariff rates are generally high on textile fabrics and hosiery, clothing and shoes, steel ingots, and, with a few exceptions, on other textile articles (chiefly sacks, bags, and linen goods), sport goods, toys, and jewelry, as well as on automobiles, motorcycles, and bicycles. In turn, relatively low effective duties are shown for paper and printed matter, ships and airplanes, pig iron, rolling-mill products, and non-ferrous metals, and also for machinery and railway equipment.

The observed similarities in the ranking of commodities by effective tariffs provide an indication of the possibilities for increased intra-industry exchange among the countries in question. In order to derive more definite conclusions in regard to individual industries, however, account should be taken of substitution elasticities between domestic and foreign products, and one should also consider the implications of tariffs for trade with outsiders—most of which are developing countries.

The general tendency among developed countries is to protect the domestic production of textile fabrics. The textile industry has long been the "sick man" of the manufacturing sector in many of these countries, and it has often been compared to agriculture by the proponents and the opponents of its protection alike. At the same time, its "footloose" character, the relative simplicity of the technological process, and the labor intensiveness of its manufacture make the textile industry a candidate for becoming the first manufacturing export industry in many developing countries. Correspondingly, the main effect of the all-round protection of textile fabrics in developed economies is likely to be a retardation of the expansion of exports from less-developed areas. Similar considerations apply to sacks and bags, toys and sport goods, and, among mechanical goods, to bicycles.

In most of the developed countries, effective duties are also high on consumer goods, including clothing and shoes, as well as automobiles. As a possible explanation, it may be suggested that in the case of these commodities cost differences are relatively small among the industrial countries, while the possibilities of substituting foreign commodities for domestic merchandise are considerable and protectionist pressures are also strong. The strength of protectionist pressures is partly explained by the fact that, whereas the opposing economic interest will influence—

and moderate—tariffs on intermediate products and investment goods, the consumers rarely have a say in tariff setting.

Effective duties are low on intermediate products that utilize specific —and bulky—inputs in their manufacture, such as paper, non-ferrous metals, and, with the exception of Japan, pig iron.[34] Moderate levels of protection are shown in the case of machinery and railway equipment, too. These products are generally highly differentiated in their international exchange contributes to lower manufacturing costs in all industrial countries. On the other hand, the low degree of protection of ships is largely illusory, since industrial countries generally provide subsidies to domestic shipbuilding, whereas "buy-national" provisions assist the domestic airplane manufacturers in some of the producing countries.

But can these admittedly "partial" explanations of the structure of tariffs in the industrial countries be replaced or supplemented by the application of some general principle? One such classifying principle is the labor intensiveness of the manufacturing process in individual industries. It has often been suggested that industrial countries, and especially the United States, tend to protect labor-intensive manufactures.[35] Our results do not reveal such a tendency, however, and no definite relationship is shown between labor intensiveness and effective rates of duties. Thus, the rank correlation coefficient between labor-input coefficients and effective duties is between $-.08$ and $-.14$ in European countries and the United States, and $-.41$ in Japan. With the exception of the Japanese case, these estimates are not significantly different from zero at the 5 per cent level of confidence, and the results are little affected if—following Basevi—we calculate effective rates of protection for labor under the assumption that capital is freely mobile between countries.[36]

It is suggested here that the explanation lies in the inadequacy of Heckscher-Ohlin–type theories that rely on a single classifying principle —factor proportions—in attempting to explain international specialization and consider protection in its effect on the income of the scarce factor. In appraising the structure of protection in the industrial countries, we can hardly neglect technological factors, however. It would appear that these countries find it expedient to heavily protect industries where developing economies can easily compete because labor-intensive production methods can be used and the technological process is rather

[34] Still, as we have noted above, duties on nonferrous metals provide a disincentive to the transformation of ores into metals in the less-developed countries. In turn, considerations of fuel economy may limit trade in the case of pig iron.

[35] Cf., e.g., Beatrice N. Vaccara, *Employment and Output in Protected Industries* (Washington: Brookings Institution, 1960); and William P. Travis, *The Theory of Trade and Protection* (Cambridge, Mass.: Harvard University Press, 1964), pp. 191–93.

[36] For the United States, similar conclusions have been reached by Basevi, who compared various measures of labor intensiveness, on the one hand, and effective duties on value added and on labor costs, on the other (*op. cit.*).

U

simple. In turn, relatively low tariffs are levied on machinery whose manufacture is relatively labor intensive but requires advanced technology and organizational know-how that are not available in less-developed countries.

Interest attaches also to intercountry differences in the protection of individual industries. Rank correlation coefficients calculated in regard to effective tariffs for pairs of countries indicate considerable similarities within western Europe. On the other hand—aside from the United Kingdom–Japanese comparison—the discrepancies in the structure of tariffs are the most pronounced between the United States and Japan, which are at the opposite end of the spectrum in terms of industrial development. Thus, while in intra-European comparisons the rank correlation coefficients are in the .65–.85 range, in the U.S.–Japan comparison the relevant coefficient is .395 (Table 3).

It stands to reason, then, that the United States and Japan show the largest deviations from the ranking of duties in the five importing areas, taken together. Among the European countries, discrepancies are the most pronounced in the case of the United Kingdom, where selected industries are heavily protected. In turn—possibly as a result of the averaging of national tariffs undertaken in connection with the EEC's establishment—the European Common Market fits the general pattern rather well, and neither do we observe large deviations in the case of Sweden. Thus, the rank correlation coefficient between effective tariffs in the various countries and country groupings, on the one hand, and an unweighted average of these rankings, on the other, is .732 in the case of Japan, .737 for the United States, .770 for the United Kingdom, .867 for Sweden, and .907 for the EEC.

Among individual commodities and commodity groups, synthetic and other chemical materials, as well as glass and non-metallic mineral products, are high on the U.S. list. In the case of synthetic and chemical materials, the effective rate of duty is raised by reason of the use of the

TABLE 3

Rank Correlation Coefficients for Effective Tariffs
in Thirty-six Industries, 1962*

	United States	Kingdom United	Common Market	Sweden	Japan	Five Areas Together
United States	....	.481	.512	.506	.395	.737
United Kingdom	.481	....	.746	.650	.362	.770
Common Market	.512	.746	....	.827	.565	.907
Sweden	.506	.650	.827	....	.689	.867
Japan	.395	.362	.565	.689	....	.732
Five areas together	.737	.770	.907	.867	.732	....

* Spearman rank correlation coefficient. All coefficients except those relating the United States and Japan, and the United Kingdom and Japan, are statistically significant at the 1 per cent level; the latter are significant at the 5 per cent level.

American selling price as a basis for determining duties on several of these products,[37] while U.S. tariffs are notoriously high on glass and its manufactures. In turn, in the case of agricultural machinery, airplanes, and automobiles, the degree of protection appears to be substantially lower in the United States than in the other countries under consideration. Agricultural machinery and airplanes are leading U.S. exports, whereas the observed disparities in tariffs on automobiles may be related to differences in the degree of substitutability between domestic and foreign cars in the United States as against European countries and Japan. Despite the inroads made by European producers in the American market, the possibilities for substitution between the large American and the small European cars appear to be rather limited. On the other hand, car manufacturers in European countries and Japan have to contend with the competing products of each other's industries, and governments use high tariffs to insure safe outlets for domestic production in the home market. The consequences of a reduction in the degree of protection are evident in France and Italy, where the decrease in tariffs following the establishment of the Common Market has led to an influx of foreign cars.

Mention can be made of the relatively high degree of protection of steel products and railway vehicles in England, miscellaneous textile articles (chiefly sacks and bags) and paper in the Common Market, metal castings in Sweden, and pig iron and rolling-mill products in Japan. Finally, in terms of effective tariffs, the ranking of plastic and synthetic materials is lower than the average in the United Kingdom; the same conclusion pertains to precision instruments in the Common Market and in Sweden, and to sacks and bags, as well as to rubber products, in Japan.

VI

We come now to the question raised in the introductory sections of this paper regarding the "height" of national tariff levels.[38] The reader will recall that estimates of the height of tariff levels are designed to indicate the restrictive effect of duties on trade flows, defined as the difference between potential and actual imports. To insure international comparability, the decrease in imports due to the imposition of tariffs (dM) may, in turn, be expressed as a proportion of potential imports (M).

Under the assumption that cross-elasticities of demand and supply can be neglected and that the primary resources used in industries producing import substitutes are available at constant costs, the restrictive

---

[37] To achieve international comparability, we have estimated the rates of duties with respect to import values in cases where the American selling price is used as a basis for the determination of tariffs. The commodities in question include coal-tar-based chemical materials and products and rubber footwear.

[38] I am indebted to Harry G. Johnson for improvements in the mathematical formulation of the argument.

effects of tariffs on the imports of a given commodity will consist of three components: (1) the restriction of domestic consumption, (2) the increase in domestic production, and (3) the increase in the demand for this commodity as an input in the production of other protected goods. Let C_i denote the domestic consumption, P_i the domestic production, and M_i the imports of commodity i in a free-trade situation, while η_i stands for the elasticity of domestic demand and ϵ_i for the elasticity of supply of value added.[39] The effect of duties on the imports of commodity i can now be written as

$$dM_i = - \eta_i C_i t_i - \epsilon_i P_i z_i + \sum_i a_{ij} \epsilon_j P_j z_j. \tag{2}$$

And, for all importables, taken together, we have

$$dM = - \sum_i \eta_i C_i t_i - \sum_i \epsilon_i P_i z_i + \sum_i \sum_j a_{ij} \epsilon_j P_j z_j;$$

$$= - \sum_i \left[\eta_i C_i t_i + \epsilon_i P_i z_i \times \left(1 - \sum_j a_{ji} \right) \right] \tag{3}$$

$$= - \sum_i (\eta_i C_i t_i + \epsilon_i v_i P_i z_i);$$

$$\frac{dM}{M} = - \sum_i \left(\eta_i \frac{C_i}{M_i} t_i + \epsilon_i v_i \frac{P_i}{M_i} z_i \right) \frac{M_i}{M}. \tag{4}$$

Let us first assume that identical nominal tariffs (t_o) are levied on every commodity. By transforming equation (4) into (4a), the restrictive effects of tariffs on imports can be shown to vary in proportion

$$\frac{dM}{M} = - \sum_i \left[\eta_i \frac{C_i}{M_i} t_o + \epsilon_i \frac{P_i}{M_i} \left(t_o - \sum_j a_{ji} t_o \right) \right] \frac{M_i}{M}$$

$$= - t_o \sum_i \left(\eta_i \frac{C_i}{M_i} + \epsilon_i \frac{P_i}{M_i} v_i \right) \frac{M_i}{M}. \tag{4a}$$

with the common tariff, t_o. Further, under the assumption that for individual commodities the share of imports in domestic production and consumption, the proportion of value added to output, as well as domestic demand and supply elasticities and the structure of imports, are identical internationally, the restrictive effect of tariffs would be proportional to the values taken by t_o in the particular countries.

Assume, instead, that C_i/M_i, P_i/M_i, v_i, η_i, and ϵ_i are identical for every commodity in all the countries but allow tariff rates to vary. Utilizing the relationships indicated in (5) to transform equation (4) into (4b), it will be apparent that the restrictiveness of national tariffs will

---

[39] Under the assumption of constant input-output coefficients, ϵ_i is also the elasticity of domestic supply.

depend on intercountry differences in regard to the averages of nominal *and* effective duties, calculated by weighting with potential imports.

TABLE 4

Over-all Tariff Averages° and Standard Deviations, 1962

	Nominal Tariffs			Effective Tariffs			Uniform Tariff Equiva- lents
	Weighted Average	Standard Devi- ation	Coefficient of Vari- ation	Weighted Average	Standard Devi- ation	Coefficient of Vari- ation	
United States	11.6	6.9	.59	20.0	16.6	.83	16.7
United Kingdom	15.5	6.2	.40	27.8	12.1	.44	23.8
Common Market	11.9	3.6	.30	18.6	11.5	.62	17.3
Sweden	6.8	4.6	.67	12.5	10.6	.85	12.2
Japan	16.2	7.6	.47	29.5	15.6	.53	26.4

° Tariff averages calculated by weighting with the combined imports of the five areas.
Source: Table 1 and United Nations, *Commodity Trade Statistics, 1962* (New York, 1964).

$$\frac{dM}{M} = - \left(\eta_i \frac{C_i}{M_i} \bar{t} + \epsilon_i v_i \frac{P_i}{M_i} \bar{z} \right) ; \tag{4b}$$

$$\bar{t} = \frac{\sum_i t_i M_i}{\sum_i M_i} ; \qquad \bar{z} = \frac{\sum_i z_i M_i}{\sum_i M_i} . \tag{5}$$

Correspondingly, under these assumptions, an unambiguous conclusion regarding the restrictiveness of national tariffs could be given as long as both nominal and effective tariff averages pointed in the same direction.

A comparison of tariff averages indicates that, among the countries under consideration, the over-all average of nominal as well as that of effective duties is the highest in Japan, with the United Kingdom as a close second and Sweden at the opposite end of the scale. The United States and the EEC occupy the middle ground: the over-all average of nominal duties is slightly higher in the Common Market than in the United States, while the opposite conclusion holds with regard to averages of effective tariffs (Table 4).[40]

Aside from comparisons of tariff averages, much attention has been given to the dispersion of tariffs, and it has been alleged that a greater dispersion of the tariff distribution in the United States, as compared to the Common Market, increases the restrictiveness of U.S. duties.[41] The

---

[40] Tariff averages have been calculated by using the combined imports of the countries in question as weights. For reasons mentioned above, the combined imports of these countries have been taken as a "proxy" for the structure of their potential imports.

[41] The existence of a positive correlation between tariff dispersion and the restrictiveness of duties has been claimed by R. Bertrand and M. Mesnage (for reference see nn. 4 and 5), while their argument has been criticized by R. N. Cooper, *op. cit.* Note, however, that Cooper considers nominal tariffs only.

data of Table 4, indeed, show greater tariff dispersion for the United States than for the Common Market, although the differences are reduced if the dispersion of effective, rather than nominal, duties is calculated. But, a perusal of equation (4b) suggests that the restrictive effect of duties is unrelated to their dispersion. This result can be understood if we consider that, in the absence of "excess protection," there is no presumption that a 20 per cent duty on refrigerators and a 10 per cent tariff on washing machines would restrict imports more than a 15 per cent tariff on both.[42] At the same time, it may be argued that, after the successive tariff reductions undertaken over the past fifteen years, much of the "fat" of protection has been sliced off.

Next, we remove the assumption that the ratios of imports to consumption and to production are identical in the countries under consideration. In fact, these shares differ considerably from country to country, thereby affecting the restrictiveness of tariffs in the individual areas. The proportion of the imports of industrial goods to value added in manufacturing is the lowest in the United States (4.7 per cent in 1961) and the highest in Sweden (44.9 per cent). In turn, the relevant ratio is 16.4 per cent for the United Kingdom, 12.1 per cent for Japan, and, if trade among the member countries is excluded, it is 10.5 per cent in the European Common Market.[43] Thus, it would appear that the tariff figures overestimate the relative degree of protection in Sweden and, to a lesser extent, in the United Kingdom, and underestimate it in the case of the United States, while the EEC and Japan occupy a middle position.

The restrictiveness of tariffs is further affected by intercountry differences in domestic demand and supply elasticities. The paucity of comparable estimates does not permit us to derive definite conclusions in regard to the former, but we may assume that, among the industrial countries, differences are relatively small. On the other hand, information on the rate of unemployment and capacity utilization indicates that domestic supply elasticities may be higher in the United States than elsewhere. High supply elasticities, then, would increase the restrictive effect of a given tariff on U.S. imports.

---

[42] However, if eq. (2) is transformed so as to indicate the expansion of imports following the elimination of duties, changes in import prices will be denoted by $t_i/1 + t_i$ rather than $t_i/1$, and, under *ceteris paribus* assumptions, the country with the greater dispersion of tariffs will experience a smaller increase in imports (for proof, see Harry G. Johnson, *The World Economy at the Crossroads* [Oxford: Clarendon Press, 1965]). This result follows from the properties of the harmonic mean, but, under present day conditions, its practical significance is negligible. Thus, in the example cited above, the elimination of tariffs would lead to an increase of imports by 39.7 per cent in the former case, and 39.1 per cent in the latter if imports of refrigerators and washing machinery were of equal value and had an import demand elasticity of −3.0.

[43] Organization for Economic Cooperation and Development, *Statistics of National Accounts, 1955–1962* (suppl.; Paris, 1964); and United Nations, *Commodity Trade Statistics, 1962* (New York, 1964).

Nothing has been said so far of intercommodity differences in regard to the variables determining the effects of tariffs on imports. It will be apparent that, in the presence of such differences, overall tariff averages will not appropriately indicate the restrictiveness of duties. Nevertheless, if information on all the relevant variables is available, we can calculate a "uniform-tariff equivalent"—defined as the common rate of duty levied on all imported commodities that has the same restrictive effect on imports as the actual tariffs.[44] The formula for the uniform-tariff equivalent is

$$t_o = \frac{\sum_i \left[\eta_i C_i t_i + \epsilon_i P_i \left(t_i - \sum_j a_{ji} t_j \right) \right]}{\sum_i \left[\eta_i C_i + \epsilon_i P_i \left(1 - \sum_j a_{ji} \right) \right]} \; ;$$

$$(6)$$

$$= \frac{\sum_i (\eta_i C_i t_i + \epsilon_i v_i P_i z_i)}{\sum_i (\eta_i C_i + \epsilon_i v_i P_i)}.$$

VII

In the previous section, we have assumed that the primary resources utilized in producing import substitutes are available at constant costs. This assumption is indeed appropriate if unemployment prevails in the tariff-imposing country, since, in this case, an expansion in the output of import-competing industries does not necessitate drawing resources from other sectors of the economy. But, under full-employment conditions, resources will move into the import-competing sector from other industries, and, if all countries impose tariffs, production for export will decline. The shift in primary resources will, then, be accompanied by a fall in demand for material inputs in the export sector, and equation (2) has to be amended by adding a term for the reduction in the demand for imported inputs used in the contracting industries.

Let us now consider the effects of multilateral tariff reductions on trade in manufactured products among the industrial countries. Correspondingly, in equation (2), C'_i, P'_i, and M'_i will replace C_i, P_i, and M_i, when the former refer to actual ("tariff-ridden") rather than potential consumption, production, and imports, while $t'_i = t_i/1 + t_i$ will replace t_i. Tariff reductions will be associated with an expansion of exports and imports in every country, and the demand for imported inputs used in producing exports and import-competing goods will change in opposite directions.

But, as we have noted in Section V, with respect to differentiated com-

---

[44] This concept is due to W. M. Corden; its application has been suggested to me by Professor Johnson. For simplicity's sake, I have assumed that no inputs are exported.

modities produced in industrial countries of similar economic structure, a clear distinction between exports and import-competing products cannot be made. Thus, following a reduction of tariffs, the British will buy more Italian cars and vice versa, and similar developments are expected in regard to other consumer goods. In turn, in the case of machinery and intermediate products at higher level of fabrication, increased intra-industry specialization is foreseen. The import content of exports and of import-competing goods may, then, differ little, and if—as a first approximation—we assume that every country will experience a balanced expansion of its exports and imports, the effects of tariff reductions on imported inputs can be neglected. Accordingly, equation (2) would take the form[45]

$$ dM'_i = \eta_i C'_i t'_i + \epsilon_i P'_i z'_i . $$

Assume further that, while the variables determining the restrictiveness of tariffs may differ from commodity to commodity, these are identical for commodities at the same level of fabrication that serve similar needs. Under this assumption, we can use averages of nominal and effective tariffs calculated for individual commodity categories to provide an indication of the expansion of imports following the elimination of tariffs. Such a calculation will have added interest, since intercountry differences in the tariff averages pertaining to individual commodity categories will also indicate the relative advantages and disadvantages bestowed on large sectors of the economy through tariff protection.

Averages of nominal and effective duties have been estimated for consumer goods,[46] investment goods,[47] and two categories of intermediate products. Semi-manufactures whose main inputs are natural raw materials have been classified as intermediate products I,[48] while all intermediate goods at higher levels of fabrication have been included in intermediate products II.[49] Finally, industries that produce intermediate as well as final goods have been classified according to the main uses of their products as determined from the input-output tables.[50]

The results of the calculations shown in Table 5 support our previous

[45] We have assumed that the values of the domestic demand and supply elasticities are not affected by the move from C to C' and from P to P'.

[46] Hosiery, clothing, other textile articles, shoes, other leather goods, cleansing agents and perfumes, automobiles, bicycles and motorcycles, precision instruments, toys, sport goods, and jewelry.

[47] Agricultural machinery, electrical and nonelectrical machinery, railway vehicles, and airplanes.

[48] Thread and yarn, wood products, paper and paper products, leather, synthetics, other chemical materials, non-metallic mineral products, glass, pig iron, and non-ferrous metals.

[49] Textile fabrics, rubber goods, plastic articles, miscellaneous chemical products, ingots and other primary forms of steel, rolling-mill products, other steel products, metal castings, metal manufactures.

[50] We have not included printed matter and ships in any of these categories; the former has been omitted because of the special character of its trade, the latter because of the prevalence of subsidies.

TABLE 5

Average of Nominal and Effective Rates of Duties
for Four Commodity Categories, 1962*

	United States		United Kingdom		Common Market		Sweden		Japan	
	Nominal	Effective	Nominal	Effective	Nominal	Effective	Nominal	Effective	Nominal	Effective
Intermediate products I	8.8	17.6	11.1	23.1	7.6	12.0	3.0	5.3	11.4	23.8
Intermediate products II	15.2	28.6	17.2	34.3	13.3	28.3	8.5	20.8	16.6	34.5
Consumer goods ..	17.5	25.9	23.8	40.4	17.8	30.9	12.4	23.9	27.5	50.5
Investment goods..	10.3	13.9	17.0	23.0	11.7	15.0	8.5	12.1	17.1	22.0
All commodities ..	11.6	20.0	15.5	27.8	11.9	18.6	6.8	12.5	16.2	29.5

* Tariff averages have been obtained by weighting with the combined imports of the five areas.
Source: Table 1 and United Nations, *op. cit.*

conclusions regarding the disparities between nominal and effective duties and the general similarity of tariff structures in the main industrial countries.[51] As regards effective duties, we find that the large share of products requiring specific and bulky resource inputs for their manufacture tends to reduce the average of duties for the first group, while tariff averages are uniformly higher for intermediate products at higher levels of fabrication, and generally increase again in the case of consumer goods. Still, an intercountry comparison of tariff averages indicates a higher-than-average degree of discrimination in favor of consumer goods in Japan, and a lower-than-average one in the United States, whereas the Common Market and the Swedish tariff structures appear to favor intermediate products at the lowest levels of fabrication. Finally, with the exception of the latter two countries, the lowest duties are levied on investment goods.

We have also utilized the information provided in Table 5 to prepare illustrative estimates of the probable effects of the elimination of duties on imports into the individual countries for assumed values of the relevant variables. In the first place, we have assumed that, in the countries under consideration, the following demand and supply elasticities apply to the four commodity categories: intermediate products I, −0.2 and 0.1; intermediate products II, −0.3 and 0.2; consumer goods, −1.0 and 0.8; and investment goods, −0.3 and 0.3.[52]

[51] To insure comparability with the preceding tables, the averages of t_i rather than $t_i/1 + t_i$ have been calculated.

[52] By comparison, Robert M. Stern assumed demand and supply elasticities of −0.25 and zero for crude materials, −0.4 and 0.2 for semimanufactures, −0.5 and 0.25 for non-durable finished manufactures, and −1.0 and 0.5 for durable finished manufactures ("The U.S. Tariff and the Efficiency of the U.S. Economy," *American Economic Review*, Papers and Proceedings [May, 1964], pp. 459–79), while J. E.

The next question concerns the ratio of domestic production and consumption to imports in the various countries. For several reasons, information on the proportion of imports to value added cannot be directly utilized for this purpose. To begin with, while the latter involves calculating the ratio of the value of trade to value added in manufacturing, the relevant comparison is between the value of trade and the value of industrial output—or apparent consumption—that also includes non-industrial inputs as well as imports used as inputs. Accordingly, the figures previously cited should be adjusted downward. At the same time, as I have elsewhere shown, the required adjustment will depend on the size of the country, because the proportion of imported inputs to the value of output (consumption) tends to decline as the size of the country increases.[53] Thus, while in the case of Belgium and the Netherlands the adjustment factor is 2.5, it is 2.1 for Italy, 1.8 for France and Germany, and approximately 1.6 for the United States.[54]

Allowance should further be made for product differentiation, transportation costs, and intercountry differences in tastes. All these factors tend to reduce the amount of domestic output that is competing with imports, thereby necessitating an upward adjustment in the calculated shares of imports and a further narrowing in intercountry differences in these shares. This conclusion can be readily understood if we consider that in larger countries a wider assortment of domestic goods is available that are designed to serve particular needs, and transportation costs from the frontier to the place of consumption are also generally higher.

The latter factors are of special importance in the United States, and we have followed J. E. Floyd in assuming a ratio of consumption to imports of 4 in this country.[55] In turn, we have assigned a value of 2 to Sweden, under the assumption that the factors necessitating downward and upward adjustments with regard to the share of imports in value added approximately balance in this case. Finally, we have calculated with consumption-import ratios of 3 for the European Common Market and Japan and 2.5 for the United Kingdom. In all instances, we have taken consumption-import and production-import ratios to be identical, given

---

Floyd calculated with a demand elasticity of −0.3 and a supply elasticity of 0.5 for all commodities, taken together ("The Overvaluation of the Dollar: A Note on the International Price Mechanism," *American Economic Review* [March, 1965]). In contrast with these authors, we have assumed that the relationship between demand and supply elasticities differs as between commodity categories.

[53] For the Common Market countries I have calculated the proportion of industrial imports to value added in manufacturing and to apparent consumption from the input-output tables. The relevant magnitudes are 90.2 and 36.4 for Belgium, 35.6 and 19.9 for France, 48.1 and 27.4 for Germany, 31.2 and 14.5 for Italy, and 82.9 and 34.3 for the Netherlands ("Planning in an Open Economy," to be published).

[54] U.S. Bureau of the Census, *U.S. Commodity Exports and Imports as Related to Output* (Washington, 1965), and n. 53.

[55] The same ratio has been applied to every commodity category

the fact that the countries in question export *and* import the commodities included in our four commodity categories.[56]

Substituting the assumed values into equation (7),[57]

$$\frac{dM}{M} = \sum_k \left(\eta_k \frac{C'_k}{M_k} \bar{t}'_k + \epsilon_k \frac{P'_k}{M'_k} \bar{z}'_k \right) \frac{M'_k}{M'}, \qquad (7)$$

we find that the elimination of duties on manufactured goods would lead to the largest relative increases in imports in Japan (39.9 per cent), followed by the United States (38.2 per cent), the United Kingdom (30.9 per cent), the European Common Market (28.2 per cent), and Sweden (14.0 per cent). At the same time, we can indicate the influence of assumed differences in consumption-import ratios on the results by comparing the latter with estimates of uniform-tariff equivalents; under the assumption of identical consumption-import and production-import ratios for all countries, increases in imports would conform to inter-country differences in regard to t_o. The estimated uniform-tariff equivalents are 26.4 for Japan, 23.8 for the United Kingdom, 17.3 for the Common Market, 16.7 for the United States, and 12.2 for Sweden.

It appears, then, that the relatively small share of imports in domestic consumption (production) increases the restrictiveness of the American tariff to a considerable extent, while the opposite conclusion applies to Britain and Sweden. Should we also consider that domestic-supply elasticities may possibly be higher in the United States than elsewhere—or assume larger differences in consumption-import ratios—the U.S. tariff may appear to be the most restrictive among the countries in question. Thus, if supply elasticities in the United States were one-half higher than in other industrial countries, American imports of manufactured products would rise by 54.1 per cent following the elimination of duties. On the other hand, the increase in imports would be 67.8 per cent if consumption-import and production-import ratios were assumed to be 5 rather than 4 in this country.

These conclusions provide some indication of the possibilities of increases in imports of manufactures in the countries under consideration following an all-around reduction of duties, and they can be useful in evaluating the possible consequences of the Kennedy round of tariff negotiations on trade flows. In regard to the latter, however, consideration should also be given to export-supply elasticities, since the expansion of exports associated with tariff reductions will be attenuated if exported commodities are supplied at increasing costs.

Intercountry differences in export-supply elasticities are determined, to a considerable extent, by the share of exports in manufacturing production and the availability of excess capacity. Both these factors point to

---

[56] The relationship utilized by Floyd, $P/M = C/M - 1$, would apply only if we dealt with standardized commodities.

[57] Subscript k refers to the individual commodity categories.

higher export-supply elasticities in the United States than elsewhere.
Thus, the degree of capacity utilization is generally lower in the United
States than abroad, and proportion of industrial exports to value added
in manufacturing is also the lowest in the United States.[58] Relatively
high export-supply elasticities in the United States, as compared to the
other main industrial countries, would, then, contribute to the expansion
of U.S. exports following an all-around reduction of tariffs.[59]

Finally, in attempting to use these results in appraising the possible
consequences of the Kennedy round, it would be necessary to take account of the fact that our conclusions pertain to relative changes in exports and imports rather than to absolute increments; the latter will also
depend on the balance of trade of these countries and the share of
manufactured goods in their exports and imports.[60] At the same time,
notwithstanding the export orientation of the industrial countries, ~~the export orientation of the industrial countries~~, the expansion of exports does
not provide a measure of welfare gains. The relative magnitudes of welfare gains will be determined by the reduction in the cost of protection
and changes in the terms of trade, when the need for a realignment of
exchange rates in case of an unbalanced expansion of trade further complicates the picture.

---

[58] The relevant figures are 9.0 per cent for the United States, 20.0 per cent for the
European Common Market, 33.3 per cent for Japan, 36.3 per cent for the United
Kingdom, and 45.1 per cent for Sweden.

[59] These essentially short-run considerations assume relevance in the long run if
wage and price adjustments are not fully reversible.

[60] In turn, an improvement (deterioration) in the trade balance will be mitigated
through an increase (decline) in imports of material inputs.